Embodying th<

Claire Hind and Gary Winters

Embodying the Dead

Writing, Playing, Performing

First published 2020 by
RED GLOBE PRESS

Red Globe Press in the UK is an imprint of Springer Nature Limited,
registered in England, company number 785998, of 4 Crinan Street,
London, N1 9XW.

Red Globe Press® is a registered trademark in the United States,
the United Kingdom, Europe and other countries.

ISBN 978–1–137–60292–3 hardback
ISBN 978–1–137–60291–6 paperback

This book is printed on paper suitable for recycling and made from fully
managed and sustained forest sources. Logging, pulping and manufacturing
processes are expected to conform to the environmental regulations of the
country of origin.

A catalogue record for this book is available from the British Library

A catalog record for this book is available from the Library of Congress.

For Love & Scandal,
Delicious coffee, dead good breakfasts
Demolished for the sake of a 'lean luxury' 66-bedroom hotel.

Contents

List of Illustrations

List of Creative Tasks

Illustration 1   The *Dream Yards* doppelgängers at the miniature city, York

Acknowledgements

We would like to thank the many people and organizations who have supported us with the most exciting of opportunities and spaces by way of residencies, partnerships, special events and educational programmes: Carol Siegel, Lili Spain, Ivan Ward and the Freud Museum, London. Dr Camilla Eeg-Tverbakk, Dr Karmenlara Ely, Patricia Canellis and the Norwegian Theatre Academy. Mark Jeffery of ATOM-R and the School of the Arts Institute Chicago. Joseph Ravens of the Defibrillator Gallery Chicago. Patrick Wildgust and the Laurence Sterne Trust at Shandy Hall. Richard Schechner and New York University. Pasco-Q Kevlin of Norwich Arts Centre. Professor Roberta Mock and Dr Kimberly Campanello of Queering Ritual. Dr D Ferret and Falmouth University for Dark Sound Destructive Pop. And to Moria Williams of FLUX Factory Long Island City for her involvement in the New York City leg of the Dream Yards projects. We are very grateful to Dr Alexander Kelly for his advice on Ghost Track. Thank you to Professor Mark Solms for conversations on the dreaming brain and to Professor Carl Lavery for writing a about Kong Lear. Many thanks to Dr Andrew Head, Professor Baz Kershaw and the Dream Yard's audiences for their feedback. Dr Christophe Alex, Rob Oldfield and Dr Andrew Head, we are delighted that you performed as zombies with us. Thanks also to Richard Wade on technical support. We thank the independent traders making a go of it on the York street Gillygate who kindly featured in our projects, and to Seaside

Danny Wilde and his infamous gigs on the Yorkshire coast. We appreciate the Mt. Zion Pub in Wisconsin for keeping it real. A big shout out to all the students at York St John University, the Norwegian Theatre Academy, the School of the Arts Institute Chicago and at FLUX Factory NYC who have been involved in our creative works. Martin O'Brien, Sulhail Ilyas and Eirini Nedelkopoulou, thank you for talking zombies. We are grateful to Professor Alan Read for arranging a visit to see mummified Alan at the Gordon Museum of Kings College London, and to the museum's curator Bill Edwards. Thanks to Professor Mick Wallis, Rev Dr Claire MacDonald and Professor Jonathan Pitches as critical friends. We are grateful to the Arts Council England for support on both local and international performances through Developing Your Creative Practice (DYCP) and National Lottery Project Grants, and to York St John University's QR funding with support from Professor Gary Peters, Professor Matthew Reason and Dr Robert Wilsmore. Nathan Walker, your creativity and ongoing support on the website is invaluable. Thanks also to the According to McGee Gallery, John Oxley and the City of York Council, Clare Hubery and Norwich City Council and North Yorkshire county councils for granting us the space to perform to incidental audiences.

We would like acknowledge that a small section of the *Kong Lear* interview in Chapter 4 'The Dead Ghost' is derived from artist pages published in the *Journal of Performance Research* (Hind and Winters, 2016). And Chapter 5 'The Dead Sleep' is derived from artist pages in the *Journal of Performance Research* (Hind and Winters, 2015).

Thanks also to Eirini Kartsaki who edited *On Repetition, Writing, Performance and Art*, published by Intellect (2016). In her book, we have a chapter entitled 'The Crying Channel' about repetition in popular culture which has blasted our thinking into exciting new territory. We would also like to thank Emily Lovelock and Sonya Barker from Red Globe Press for their support and advice on this publication.

Finally, a nod to those who are no longer with and us but who continue to live in our dreams.

1

Introduction: The Dead Rejoice

This book explores the relationship between death and play within the context of making and sharing intermedial performance. It unpacks our unique position as performance makers who work under the name 'Gary and Claire'. We create work from out of a variety of distinct compositional strategies to realize performances for audiences. Our projects spanning many years have a relationship to death in a broad sense, and our playful explorations of this term draw close attention to detail across the metaphorical, analogical, linguistic and conceptual positions that death and the dead take within a creative process. We consider, through our practice, how the dead are remembered, represented, referenced, personified, reimagined and celebrated.

We write scripts and scores for walking performance, shoot and edit Super 8mm film and digital film works, devise participatory performance and durational live art events, make and curate visual art installations (including neon lights, photography, mixed media materials), tour live and mediated performances for studio theatres, and make documentation artefacts. The way we work encourages the different mediums within our practice to 'speak' to one another across themes and concepts.

The relationship between our ideas, materials and audiences are examined in this book to highlight where playfulness is a feature of the work. We write extensively about practice through a dramaturgical perspective, from discussing how a concept of a work emerges, sharing anecdotes of practice illuminating the materiality and delivery of a project and explore the relationship our practice has to reflection – that is, how and why we use a reimagining of specific psychoanalytic terms to talk about creative practice. This is a book about ideas for making performance, a book that reflects upon those ideas and the practical applications of them. We are highly influenced by popular culture as well as by a variety of mixed media arts practice, therefore you will notice that during our discussions we reference a wide range of influences, flitting back and forth between television, pop video, film, visual art, theatre, literature, choreography, live art and mediated work. It is important for us to reference these artistic mediums because when we make performance we are not restricted to where we share our work and who we share our ideas with.

This introductory chapter establishes our position as artists and thinkers, and sets the tone of what is to follow, namely, the thematic and conceptual position that the dead take in this book. Chapter 2, 'The Dead Psychoanalyst', focuses upon Sigmund Freud's absent presence in his once UK home and the place of his death: the Freud Museum (a personality museum). For us, it was important to contextualize this house because our first collaborative project, *Ghost Track* and *Kong Lear* (2012) (as a double bill), was shared at the Freud Museum, for a public audience. After working there, we felt deeply affected by the space, and felt the presence of Freud's ghost. In this respect we are not talking literally, but figuratively. While Freud's legacy in the twenty-first century celebrates his work, it is also critical of it. It seems that Freud, even in his death, is very much present in everything. Even today it seems Sigmund Freud can't be shaken off, he returns to 'haunt us; because he keeps popping up in places he has no business being' (Roth, 2014). As we attempt to speak from out of the phenomenon of Freud's legacy (after some decades of persistent 'Freud bashing'), his refashioned resurrection in contemporary art and performance is discussed. In Chapter 3, 'The Dead Play', we expand upon some of Freud's concepts. Here, we begin by focusing on three psychoanalytic concepts: the death drive, desire and the uncanny (unheimlich); we then unpack these terms in relation to play theory, specifically referencing the terms 'dark' and 'deep' play. While it has been argued that psychoanalysis is a 'collaboration that allows one to refashion a past' (2014), and because Freudian and Lacanian thinking invites one to make meaning from history, from the unconscious and from culture, we were curious about how to achieve the distortion of certain psychoanalytic concepts and what would happen when we did. Therefore, in Chapter 3, we explicate our own reimagining of those terms (death drive, desire, uncanny) as a methodology for making performance, and as a way to reflect upon performance making. As such we name our own concept: The Death Drift/Drift Drive (DD/DD).

Documenting our projects in Chapters 4–8 has enabled us to invent a unique presentation of our materials and practices, because each chapter takes on a different form to expose the complexities within the practice of performance making. In this way, each chapter about practice takes on different forms. For example, Chapter 4, 'The Dead Ghost', records an artist's talk around our 2012 project *Kong Lear* recorded at Bar Lane Studios in York. In Chapter 5, 'The Dead Sleep', we share the script from *Dream Yards* (2013), the walking tour performance, along with inserted commentary from the audiences who experienced the walk. In Chapter 6, we share a zombified text written specifically for an audio experience, an echo of our ensemble performance *Roy of the Dead/Day of The O* (2013). In Chapter 7, we share a performance listicle documenting the participatory engagement of *Crying in the Dark* (2015), an overnight karaoke experience from sunset to sunrise. And finally, in Chapter 8, 'The Dead Preserved', we offer a performance lecture that weaves descriptive anecdotes of performances made across a four-year period together with stories associated with the research we have been engaged with in relation to the themes of death and preservation. This final chapter tells a story of how we work with visual materials and objects, and takes up the visual metaphor that we offer in Chapter 3 of the Death Drift/Drift Drive (DD/DD), as a compositional strategy for writing the chapter itself. This last chapter is playfully interrupted by the voice of a fly who lands on the page to contemplate death and existence.

All these creative chapters include discussions on the conceptual framework of each project accompanied by critical reflection explaining our approach to practice, but in varying forms of delivery. Therefore, because each chapter focuses upon specific themes and performance projects, the voice and the form of each chapter is distinct. It is the intertextual braid between practice, creative writing and critical discussion that playfully binds our work. We do, however, always respect the dead and the idea that for us all, death is a difficult issue. When we write of the dead we do so with the idea that death is a part of a creative process, ergo, an inherent component and quality of performance. And it is important to note that death is not always responded to in the literal sense; on the contrary, many of our projects position death as a concept, metaphor or analogy.

Play

We concur with Tim Etchells that play, in the context of contemporary performance, is where 'possibility thrives, in which versions multiply, in which the confines of what is real are blurred, buckled' (Etchells, 1999, p.53). We do see performance making (the process of imagining, writing or devising a performance) as a form of play where we may imagine ourselves and our audience differently or where we write playfully to change the look of or subvert a landscape. And we like to think of performance (the work that is performed/shared with an audience) as an activity framed by a series of fixed or shifting rules. But, we also like to think that the conditions inherent in other forms of leisurely activity can be appropriated to suit an idea we have for performance. The most exciting territory of play for us is working with imagined spaces that establish some other world, but a world that coexists in our (real) world. And we do this by creating material that blends the fictional with the autobiographical. Most of the autobiographical stories found in our projects relate to our collaborative journey together as artists, through the creative experiences of the research phase of making performance. This blend of the imagined and the autobiographical is played intertextually when we write creative material (texts, scripts, scores), when we invent specific rules for a performance activity, and when we perform. Importantly, we adopt playful attitudes to the rules and the worlds we create and this affects our relationship to the imaginative concepts for performance. For us, to be playful is to test the limits of something with a humorous sentiment, to engage in a task with a kittenish or mischievous approach. It also means that we play with things that move us romantically, so not all of our work is humorous – it may be sentimental and melancholic – it is just that we take a playful approach to making the performances. But we do take play seriously so that when we work with audiences or a specific community we are sincere in our tone. Play is enigmatic, but it can also be seen as a very straightforward tool to help us understand how to be human. Lobman and O'Neill (2011, p.x) claim that 'Children perform who they are becoming' and that as 'conversationalists' they take turns 'babbling and become speakers'. This seems to assert that play allows us to practise the skills we need in life. With this thought in mind, we ask of our practice: can play allow us to practise the skills we need in death? Or, can play allow us to practise an imagined afterlife? Here it might be useful to draw our attention to Stuart Brown and Christopher Vaughan who assert that play is not an activity but rather 'a state of mind' (2009, p.60). For us, a useful way to assert our experience is that play is both an activity *and* a state of mind but the qualities that make an activity differ from the attitudes (our state of mind) that we apply to the activity itself. The varying qualities of engaging in playful performance are complex in relation to the *what* and the *who* and the *as if.* It is the latter consideration that invites us to reflect in Chapter 3, 'The Dead Play', on Roger Caillois' subjunctive *as if* theory and subsequently in other chapters on the variations in play that we adapt to the worlds we have established. Definitions of play are abundant, Huizinga is most often quoted as saying:

> Play is a free activity standing quite consciously outside 'ordinary' life as being 'not serious,' but at the same time absorbing the player intensely and utterly. It is an activity connected with no material interest, and no profit can be gained by it. (Huizinga, 1998, p.13)

Brown states that play is 'a purposeless activity that provides enjoyment and a suspension of self-consciousness and sense of time' (Brown and Vaughan, 2009, p.60) but we do assert here (and from experience) that play is productive – it permits us to use our imagination so that we may transform identities, change perceptions and offer alternative ways to think about the world; in this way play is extremely purposeful. To give a few short examples of what we mean here:

> Through play we may rethink gender identity and shift attitudes away from stereotypes and challenge patriarchy. Through play we might encourage a better night's sleep. Through play we may draw attention to how

dead animals have been objectified. Through play we may even shift the way in which we think about death and the dead.

In fact, play has been transformative for centuries. This is why we have offered, in this book, a way to reimagine psychoanalytic concepts and playfully apply them to practice.

Death and Language

The varying attitudes towards the dead (and death) are most often expressed in language. Phrases about the dead, dead idioms and euphemisms play a significant role in how we express our fears or how we might find ways to deal with what is an inevitable part of life but through a humorous lens:

Dead as a doornail.
One foot in the grave.
Go out with a bang.

We recall the old Monty Python Parrot Sketch, and those 'twentieth century writers give us parrots that die' (Boehrer, 2015, p.127). The actors Cleese and Palin perform a series of vague and ambiguous phrases, Cleese in particular with his repetitive rant of euphemisms, debating the parrot's varying qualities of deadness. The idea that the shopkeeper is insistent that the parrot is alive while the customer is just as insistent upon its state of deadness through the many different linguistic phrases – passed on, is no more, ceased to be, an ex-parrot, etc. – offers a conflict that causes the customer to attempt to wake up the dead bird while he cites the many metaphors for death to prove his point that it is, in fact, dead (when we can clearly see it is neither dead or alive, it is an inanimate object):

Mr Praline: This parrot is no more! He has ceased to be! 'E's expired and gone to meet 'is maker! 'E's a stiff! Bereft of life, 'e rests in peace! If you hadn't nailed 'im to the perch 'e'd be pushing up the daisies! (Chapman, 1999)

This is a sketch that symbolizes the beauty of nothing else but its own very funny concept.

The linguistic tropes of text-based visual artworks of the twenty-first century where language as image subverts, juxtaposes and displaces its original context, are less humorous and more interventionist. Konrad Smolenski's slogan *The End* (2007) was a large-scale inscription installed in many public spaces. It is an artwork made of flammable material (wood) and 'the slogan has either faced destruction, or at least signalled its (self) destructive potential by emitting loud and realistic sounds of explosion' (Smolenski, 2008). In his later work, *Death* (2009), we see another outdoor installation, with Smolenski drawing our attention to the word ŚMIERĆ ('death' in Polish). The installation is placed adjacent to the Warsaw–Berlin railway line and set on fire at dusk:

> The eponymous wooden inscription has an ephemeral character, not only thanks to its rapid burning caused by petrol and explosives, but also due to the location where the entire audience is made up of accidental passengers. Because of the high speed of the train, they can only see the work for a few seconds, which makes it impossible to determine whether the phenomenon they saw was real or not. Thus, the artist created a situation in which the installation is noticed almost by accident – this is analogous to the position of the theme of death in our culture. (Smolenski, 2008)

The mischievously playful approach of Smolenski's work conjures up the image of the experimental artist as a delinquent rebellious child, experimenting with fire, destroying objects, blowing things up. The incidental audiences that witness his work are as fleeting and ephemeral as his interventions.

Korean artist Jung Lee's (2010) photographed neon light installation spelling out the words *The End* is a finale writ large inscribed into a rural landscape. The bright white neon pronouncement standing fixed on the sand dunes against the backdrop of the ocean is an abandoned object, displaced language in the middle of nowhere. It refers to its own status as an art object that its time is marked. In 2011, *Aporia* (translated in Greek as 'coming to a dead end') was Jung Lee's photographic series of neon lights in different landscapes, one of which displays a series of words trickling on the ground and in the snow as a declaration and ends with the words 'Thinking of you to death'. Inscribed into a lonely cold landscape the remains are comment upon the ephemeral nature of love and death. The artist puts her work into context:

> If you fall in love, your beloved becomes a sort of mystery so that you will ceaselessly try to figure out the reasons for your feelings for him or her and to interpret them. The desire to express your love produces lies and conflicts and leads to a dead end that is a love. (Lee, 2011)

Jung Lee's neon lights invite us to think analogously about the finality of lived experience, where love and loss in a relationship is experienced as death. The work's playfulness situates itself in the juxtaposition between the object and environment; the shiny sparkling glimmer set against a desolate deserted landscape.

Rules for the Dead in Ritual and Performance

Where do we find the dead? The dead exist in the imagination and the belief systems of the living. According to Davis (2007), we can't get rid of the dead because we have not, despite our doubts, given up on them; ghosts stories are still extremely popular. In culture, the dead can be found in paintings, in literature, on the stage, in film, in neon light, etc., and in many different forms, as ghosts, or zombies or as saints, as concepts, as sound or in books within the soiled and smelly pages of haunted matter. Peter Moore (2016), concentrating on 'the subjectivity of being dead' (p.48) and discussing the possible states of mind of the dead, draws our attention to a paradox that only the dead themselves could know what it is like to be dead (meaning we do not know at all). This very plausible suggestion does not stifle our imaginations; rather, it is precisely this unknowingness that creates stories, rules and rituals that allow the dead to have a place out there somewhere, and, right here, walking among the living. And as such, 'managing a credible afterlife requires not only following the rules of logic but also taking into account the whole spectrum of sources – mythological, folkloric, fictional, theological, and parapsychological' (Moore, 2016, p.50). In modernist times, the dead were known to have communicated with the living via radio waves through white noise, but when they 'spoke' to us, they gave very little detail of what it is like to be dead. Moore suggests this is because the 'literature of mediumship gives us … the newly dead, who fail to recognize, or to admit, that they are indeed dead' (Moore, 2016, p.53). He goes on to say that 'according to the spiritualist author Caroline Larsen, not knowing one is dead is virtually the normal state of mind of the newly dead'.

Our lives are forever surrounded by the inevitability of death (the future), and the profound idea (sometimes feared, or sometimes revered) of the dead returning (the past). Therefore, many cultures remember those who have gone before in a celebratory way. In Mexico, 'death is understood as a process, as a path or transition to a life of a different kind' (Kettenmann, 2000, p.24). Mourning is not a feature of the gathering activities during El Dia de los Muertos (the Day of the Dead). Here, specifically in rural areas, the living's attitude towards the dead is conditioned by specific rules that welcome a variety of different souls. On the days leading up to the 2 November – the Day of the Dead – in Mexico, in rural places in particular, there is a phased arrival and departure from a variety of different souls where for certain communities:

> Days of the Dead begin on October 27th, when the hungry and thirsty souls of those without families or friends are welcomed with water hung from vessels outside of people's homes and crusts of bread … The next night, October 28th, marks the time when those souls who die violently are cautiously welcomed back … On October 30th, the souls of children who died before being baptized and who therefore dwell in limbo are welcomed for a few hours. The next night, the souls of baptized children are allowed to return and are welcomed back into their homes … The late afternoon of November 1st brings with it the beginning of an impressive celebration. Church bells ring all afternoon to welcome the souls of the adults. The Fearful Dead, as they are sometimes called, arrive throughout the evening and join their families at the home altar where they find *ofrendas*, or offerings, laid out in their honor. Families first acknowledge the most recently deceased love one before welcoming home their other ancestors. (Herrera-Sobek, 2012, p.405)

The Day of the Dead's deep tradition dating back in history to the Aztec period, where families built altars laden with photographs, candles, food and drink to welcome the dead, has developed into a parade on the streets of Mexico in recent times.

Interestingly, Herrera-Sobek makes an important point that this once 'deeply religious practice' is now a 'cultural spectacle' and this can be evidenced by the populist attraction that is now a parade inspired by Hollywood:

> The city government and Mexican tourism officials were inspired by parts of last year's Bond film, which were filmed in Mexico City and featured 007 chasing a villain through a Day of the Dead celebration in the historical centre. (Argen, 2016)

And, there has been a difference in opinion: 'Some Mexicans complained that their compatriots – especially those in the upper classes – only embraced their traditions after Hollywood made it cool' (Argen, 2017). In 2018, the third parade was held as a vigil in memory of Mexican refugees who died travelling to the United States. And the Day of the Dead has in recent years become a global phenomenon. It is worth noting that celebrations that take place in some areas of the United States are 'part of a public display of cultural affirmation' (Herrera-Sobek, 2012, p.412). In fact, within many parts of the United States, celebrations 'which began as a way for Mexican and Mexican American communities to maintain positive connections to their cultural heritage, have become an opportunity to practice community activism' (Ibid., p.413). Here, the dead maintain their important critique on the living through playful and performative social rituals, as the 'Day of the Dead altars are frequently constructed along themes that have an impact on the community such as police brutality, violence against women, and immigrant rights' (Ibid.). And in the UK, meaningful connections are being made merging the calendar celebrations of All Souls Day and Day of the Dead through contemporary art. As one example in the UK, *The Ghost Tide*, an intermedial exhibition curated by Monika Bobinska and Sarah Sparkes (20th October - 3rd November 2018), evoked the ghost as the migratory tide, analogous to the presence of locally based artists as a 'tide of creative flotsam and jetsam which ebbs and flows as the city gentrifies and develops' (Sparkes, 2016). Playfully, their closing party entitled *Day of the Dead*, shared skills in how to make Day of the Dead cut-outs, offered artist-led walks on the theme and finished with a Day of the Dead feast.

Spiritual beliefs in the afterlife enable us (human beings) to imagine ourselves and those who have gone before us differently because we place significant meaning on death and the dead. Fairfield (2015), believes that religious and spiritual societies that possess 'deeply rooted cultural resources' (p.47), enable human beings to deal with the turmoil associated to death. Death rituals and celebrations that mark the passing of a life enable us to find peace and comfort that there was once a life. And rituals and celebrations that mark a returning of the dead offer ways for us to connect to an afterlife or rather an imaginary world. But for many people in what Fairfield describes as our 'secular age', believing in the mysterious is not as favoured as it once was. In fact, he argues that death rituals have 'fallen on hard times' (Ibid., p.47) and by way of drawing upon a debate regarding the secularization in the western world, he outlines that the modern world view of death:

> is no longer a religious affair but a biological and medical one and is appropriately spoken of in this terminology, supplemented perhaps in the still empirical language of the psychology and a few related disciplines. (Fairfield, 2015, p.46)

Indeed, 'the advantage of a secular death is that it is free of illusion, mythology, and false consolation. The disadvantage, in a word, is that it is also empty' (Ibid., p.49). Yet emptiness can also be located in the dystopian view culture has of the dead. Magnus Irvin's performance *Deadman Talks*, takes questions from the audience on what it is like being dead and informs them that it is 'rancid, and rotten, lonely, comfortless and interminably eternal' (Sparkes, 2016, p.386). Sparkes questions, in the context of a 'contemporary psyche', whether 'we are more likely to locate ghosts within our own mind, symbolizing past horrors festering inside us. We can no longer send them to heaven or hell' (Ibid.). Perhaps the horrors that haunt our own minds relate to the idea that we can't accept death in life and therefore:

> The alternative to denial is to keep death before the mind and to see its foreshadowing throughout life. Every small ending is an imitation of death and may be perceived as such. (Fairfield, 2015, p.30)

Moreover, performance, as ritual, renews 'faith' in what feels (imperative to us as artists) good to live a fuller, positive life where play and imagination create new mythologies. And it could be argued that through play we can find ways of dealing with what is hard to accept – the end of things. In fact, the shift from the religious to the cultural means that we (as performance makers) are tasked with a responsibility of how death and the dead are represented. While we are not suggesting that artists are alternative priests, or an alternative way of thinking from that of secular society, it is important to note artists manage death creatively, politically and aesthetically, and with varying attitudes.

In the 1990s, a post-dramatic framework within contemporary theatre was dominant in the UK, where the loose fragmented stories created from the structured rules of improvisation insisted that death was never absent from the theatrical stage. Playing out death scenes, for example, was a well-known trope of Forced Entertainment's work:

> Death haunts all performance, sometimes taunting its fakery, sometimes lending it power. In my own work with Forced Entertainment I'm struck by a feat that the performers are publicly rehearsing their own deaths, plotting lives for their own dead selves. After all, almost every performance stacks a new corpse behind them. I remember that Robin in our first piece was 'dead' for the final scenes, that he'd lie motionless for 20-odd minutes, slumped at the table and covered by a sheet. (Etchells, 1999, p.116)

In the same era, Paul Whitehouse appeared on our screens, propped up motionless inside an open coffin as Mister Dead the Talking Corpse in the television comedy sketch show *Harry Enfield and Chums* (1994). This blatant parody of American sitcom *Mister Ed the Talking Horse* (1961) was humorous, not because it drew specifically on the original show's idea that animals could talk, but rather that the humour resided in the incongruous relationship death has to play in performance. Whitehouse playing dead is entertaining because we see first and foremost his impersonation and interpretation of the dead, as if he is following the rulebook of absolute stillness. It is his very attempt to embody deadness that is humorous.

Moore's question, 'What might it be like to be dead?' (2016, p.48), is provocative but most actors must have asked this very same question night after night on a long theatre run where their character or persona 'dies'. This experience must have gone into excessive overdrive for the cast of Spymonkey's *The Complete Deaths* (2016) directed by Tim Crouch. In this humorous work, 75 deaths are performed on stage in direct view of the audience. And when Anah Ruddin played the recently deceased Mrs McLeavy in a production of Joe Orton's *Loot* (1965) at the Park Theatre in London (2017), she expresses her experience as an actor embodying the dead:

> As the corpse, you need to remain completely still while the energy of the farce swirls around you. (Ruddin, cited in Wiegand, 2017)

Orton's satirical work challenged the Roman Catholic Church's attitude towards death which in turn must have informed Ruddin's approach to playing a corpse when she was dragged all over the place in this performance, put over the shoulders of another character before being shoved in a cupboard. Playing the dead body has its challenges.

Conversely, in the playfully and beautifully animated *Complete Works: Table Top Shakespeare* (2018), by Forced Entertainment, we see lifeless inanimate objects die quietly and untheatrically on stage. The stage is a table, the cast are everyday household objects from the pantry, the fridge or the dressing table: beer bottles, salt and pepper shakers, wine glasses, a can of beans, a bottle of perfume. This project consists of 32 adaptations of approximatively 50-minute performances told by the Forced Entertainment cast taking turns on different Shakespeare stories. The rules are simple: to tell the whole play as a solo narration and in their own words, from their own interpretation of reading and researching the play. Their 'episodic Shakespearean marathon' is a game of 'decoding language' played out with the understated performance of the objects in the midst of an unfolding drama:

> On the one hand it's a kind of rudimentary ventriloquism, bringing life and voice to these supposedly dead things, but on another, the work taps the half-life that objects have anyway, their speechless speech, the traces of their action and purpose, their haunted existence. Even these inanimate performers – coming from the kitchen cupboard, the grocery store, the junk shop and the supermarket – bring something to their roles. (Etchells, 2018)

The dead are encountered as an immersive experience through the playful sensory performance of shamanic dance. Louise Ahl's *YAYAYA AYAYAY* (2018), is a meditative visual choreography performed in darkness with stroboscopic light and sound. To witness the performance, you enter the space in the pitch black, sit and wait. Silence is interrupted by vibrations and abstract noises followed by an intense experience of a shamanic trance ritual where the performer, Ahl, otherwise known as Ultimate Dancer, is present, but invisible for a lengthy part of the show, that is until she begins to move in the darkness with a ghostly quality. Lights flash and we get glimpses of what could be a phantom. The moving momentum embodies a séance-type quality, where you are not sure who is in the room. The meditative sound to accompany the movement is like an airlock between the world that you have just come from with a ticket in your hand to an esoterically charged space, where suddenly you are being cleansed in preparation to experience the uncanny. Very slowly a supernaturally tall figure emerges, reminiscent of the Giant who visits Agent Cooper in the beginning of season 2 of Lynch and Frost's (1991) *Twin Peaks*; at least that is what comes to mind in the darkness when the eyes begin to adjust. Gradual increases of light illuminate her hair. The audience are thrown completely into a liminal world, a space in between sleeping and death. We are left asking of this voice: is she the newly dead? Is she a ghost? What is it? Are we experiencing dead time? As her voice builds to a crescendo of ethereal, other-worldly sound, she calls out the words 'Where are you?' satisfying the audience's question about her own presence which arouses laughter. She is lost as she calls out 'I'm lonely'. An hour passes in the blink of an eye and a lot has happened. Playfully, and in blacklight, she disperses small glowing balls around the space, tiny stars adorn the stage floor and we are all hurtled into outer space. Here, floating together in the universe it seems, we are all playing dead.

Dead Animals and Fake Ones

What is it like to spend time with the dead? Spiritual, physical and psychical connections have been made in contemporary times between humans with dead animals. In 1965, Joseph Beuys performed an action and whispered a dialogue to a dead hare. Of this performance, *How to Explain Pictures to a Dead Hare*, the hare stood in for our 'deadening' intellectualizing tendencies to burrow (metaphorically) into the 'materialistic' (Phaidon, n.d.). And it has been recorded that Beuys sometimes preferred dead animals to the humans of his time because he felt that 'even a dead animal would preserve more powers of intuition than stubborn rational man' (Phaidon, n.d.). In 2005, Marina Abramovic re-performed Beuys' performance at the Guggenheim, New York, in her series of works entitled *Seven Easy Pieces*. In 2014, Abraham Poincheval performed for two weeks within a sterilized carcass of a dead bear where he drank, slept and relieved himself. *Dans La Peau de l'Ours* (*Inside the Skin of the Bear*) was performed at the Musée de la Chasse et de la Nature. 'Poincheval is experimenting and re-enacts the powerful sensitivity that once brought these two creatures together' (Mok, 2014). The shamanic reference in Poincheval's work relates to the idea that our ancestors once shared much more time and space with the bear on an equal footing. We ask, are these artists, who work intimately with dead animals, mediums between one world and another, between one species and another?

Our lives seem disconnected from shamanic rituals where humans and animals were considered spiritually equal, animals hold a life we cannot possibly know, they are other. We treat them as gentle creatures, but we can also be cruel, sadistic and relentlessly dominating. Harmony Korine's cat-killing boys in the 1997 movie *Gummo,* where the character Bunny Boy holds up a dead black cat to the camera to the sound of Roy Orbison's song *Crying*, is a reminder of animals' fragility in the landscape and their place within a pecking order. This image in *Gummo* blends the fake with the real; the dead cat and the fake bunny rabbit. Bunny Boy's ears, pink and playfully animalistic, allude to his muted character, silenced and as representative of the freakishness of trash culture (Sinwell, 2012).

Therefore, thinking upon the image of the theatrical animal costume, from bunny ears, let's consider the oddity that is the pantomime horse who seems to embody an uncanny state of deadness when it is animated by performers. Neither human nor animal, what is it? Alive on stage when it is up on its feet and dead in the wardrobe when the show is over. In Forced Entertainment's performance of *Pleasure* (1997), the actors pushed a game too far and the pantomime horse was abused:

> Rob pushed whisky bottles into horse's eyes and made it look like horse was weeping tears as thick as rain … Claire played the back of horse. She

snuck a beer bottle in there and, when bored, poured it out to look like horse was pissing, sending floods of lager down onto the stage. Horse dancing in its own piss. (Etchells, 2000, p.55)

Fake animals in performance seem to contradict their theatrical presence, for the more the pantomime horse performs, the less of the animal we see. Even those games Forced Entertainment offered us in *Pleasure* at the expense of the pantomime horse's dignity remind us in crude detail of how humans think themselves superior to animals. 'For the sad truth is that in humour humans show themselves to be useless animals; hopeless, incompetent, outlandish animals ... when the human becomes animal, then the effect is disgusting' (Critchley, 2002, p.34).

And yet a dead and stuffed animal can look so alive in its apparent state of deadness and this is eerie:

Taxidermy is the art of taking an animal's treated skin and stretching it over an artificial form such as a manikin, then carefully modelling its features into a lifelike attitude. The word is derived from the Greek roots *taxis*, 'arrangement' and *derma*, 'skin', although its usage became prominent only in the early 1800s when taxidermy began its evolution from a crude way of preserving skins to advance science into a highly evolved art form whose chief objective was to freeze motion. (Milgrom, 2010, p.5)

The taxidermist preserves in the dead animal an alert, focused look so that we see a clean and well-turned-out blackbird, there is no blood or guts, no rotting smell, no evidence of the cause of death. Taxidermy sanitizes death.

In the eighteenth century, when taxidermy as a practice was first recorded, animals were predominately mounted for natural history museum collections so naturalists could prove a range of exotic animals existed overseas. As the techniques and chemicals used in preservation developed, taxidermy became the delight of a hunter's hobby. Unfortunately, mounted dead animals hunted as trophies were not uncommon. The focus of our interest in taxidermy is not to celebrate or glorify hunting, but to draw upon the more curious and peculiar form of taxidermy that developed in the Victorian age where quite often animals that were found dead in the wild, or had died at the home (a pet), were mounted and displayed, and brought together in odd gatherings set in a tableau, posing within a diorama along with other dead animals that you would not normally see grouped together. Walter Potter, whose first taxidermy project was on his dead pet canary, practised taxidermy techniques at his home in Bramber, Sussex. He would develop his art into group works where several animals posed together as if they were human. A majority of all birds Potter would practise on would be found dead under a tree or electrical wires or killed by a cat. He would find these dead birds himself or people would bring them to him. Potter's highly theatrical tableaux often show the animals as if they are playing an imaginary game and impersonating the human, in full costume with anthropomorphic qualities. His most famous work is the staging of the nursery rhyme *The Death and Burial of Cock Robin*:

'Who saw him die?' 'I,' said the Fly,
'With my little eye, I saw him die.'

Potter's other works develop into the most profound and surreal of tableaux that saw animals posing as if they were humans engaging in learning (*Rabbits Village School*) where one rabbit is working out mathematical equations. In the Victorian era 'attributing human characteristics to animals was a form of endearment. They were obsessed for instance if animals were happy' (Milgrom, 2010, p.180). The idea that a dead and stuffed animal is happy in its deadness reminds us of the large red (and dead) robin sitting in the tree as a symbol of hope in the last scene of David Lynch's (1986) film *Blue Velvet*. While making the film, Lynch acquired a robin killed (by accident) by a bus driver, who worked in the local school. Lynch had this bird stuffed and operated the movement of the bird in the film. When watching the bird move you can tell from its appearance it is not alive, but dead, but performing as if it is alive and it is uncanny. This stuffed mechanical bird's haunting strangeness alludes to the dialogue in the scene that it appears in:

AUNT BARBARA
I don't see how they do it. I could
never eat a bug.
JEFFREY AND SANDY
(smiling)
It's a strange world, isn't it? (Lynch, 1986)

What Do Ghosts Do?

Gilman-Opalsky (2016) reminds us of what ghosts do. They have a defined specific activity: they always haunt. When things (objects, places, spaces) are unsettled through a haunting, our senses are heightened, we are on full alert to the possibility of such a phenomenon, we look for things we have never seen before. And, ghosts playfully haunt the imagination, their presence it seems is also everywhere floating 'between different realms and meaning' (Banco & Peeren, 2010, p.xi).

In popular culture, a ghost is still favoured as the spirit of the dead returning to haunt a place or person because there is some unfinished business to resolve. Ghosts are as popular as ever, hunted down in the reality TV shows on the paranormal where the formula of the investigation of haunted sites relies on finding evidence of a ghost, and as such blur illusion with authenticating. This evidence of course is not scientific, but rather it is pushed into the realms of pseudoscience heavily reliant upon the tricks of technology to cause effect. Ghosts are quite simply ambiguous, we may feel their presence as an ineffable experience. In fact, do we still believe in ghosts? We may behave and respond in a world as if there are ghosts when we know there really are not:

> If the dead come back, it is because our belief systems allow for their return. So, what is it we actually believe when we believe in ghosts? The belief in ghosts is (like the ghost itself) something that survives or returns long after it should have been relegated to the past; it is a kind of excess or fault line within belief, or perhaps an unconscious remainder of primitive, magical thinking, revealing a gap between what we think we believe (How could there be ghosts? How ridiculous!) and what we nevertheless continue to believe (there are ghosts). (Davis, 2007, p.4)

In fact, 'If ghosts are old they are certainly not tired' (Banco & Peeren, 2010, p.ix) and they seem to refashion themselves according to the times. Jacques Derrida 'has argued that each age has its own ghosts' (Ibid., p.xi). Derrida first used the term hauntology (in French, *hantologie*) in the *Spectres of Marx* (1993) and Davis (2007, p.9) draws further attention to it: 'Hauntology supplants its near-homonym ontology, replacing the priority of being and presence with the figure of the ghost as that which is neither present nor absent, neither dead nor alive'.

In the 1983 film *Ghost Dance* directed by Ken McMullen, the existence of ghosts is explored by two key characters: an appearance from Jacques Derrida playing himself in a discussion with his student, played by the actress Pascale Ogier. Speaking on the concepts of ghosts, she asks Derrida a question:

> *I want to ask you something. Do you believe in ghosts?'*

He thinks for a moment, with that Derrida look, and retorts:

> *That's a difficult question. Firstly, you're asking a ghost whether he believes in ghosts. Here, the ghost is me, since I've been asked to play myself in a film which is more or less improvised, I feel as if I'm letting a ghost speak for me.* (*Ghost Dance*, 1983)

Derrida continues to assert the existence of ghosts during a complex improvisation on the subject of phantom structures that technology inhabits, pointing out that he (Derrida) is a ghost because when we see him, we are watching a recorded version of himself. Derrida reminds the viewer of the paradox of seeing the 'real' Derrida through a technological experience, because we are watching a memory of something that did not happen in present time, but in creative, imagined time.

Cinema, in its art of reproduction, contains ghosts: 'it's the art of allowing ghosts to come back' (*Ghost Dance*, 1983). Indeed, 'cinema plus psychoanalysis equals the science of ghosts'. In fact, cinema's uncanny ability to conjure up eeriness means that 'every day is Groundhog Day in a movie' (Royle, 2003, p.81).

Referring to himself in the film, Derrida states that he is a ghost. If we watched his performance at the time when the film was first released, we would know we were watching with the knowledge that somewhere out there is an alive Derrida reading, teaching, writing philosophy. In other words, we know through his own statement that the edited recorded medium will prove a truth one day, and watching him speak we see into Derrida's future (and perhaps our own), we imagine him dead (we imagine death, we imagine our own death). He is neither past nor present, rather he is a past future. But watching the film today, we see Derrida as history, we know him now as the dead philosopher, only now he is the ghost of the ghost he ghosted.

We have a paradoxical and tense relationship with death: 'the desire to keep the dead amongst us, competes with the desire to be rid of them for good, to stop the dead from returning and disturbing our fragile peace of mind' (Davis, 2007, p.3). Cinema illuminates this paradox and makes sure the dead continue to haunt but through many different lenses: humour, irony, wisdom and coincidence.

Unfortunately, not long after *Ghost Dance* was made the actress Pascale Ogier died. Derrida writes about his experience of watching the film *Ghost Dance* a few years after Ogier's death and recalls:

> Suddenly I saw Pascale's face, which I knew was a dead woman's face. Come onto the screen. She answered my question 'Do you believe in ghosts?' Practically looking me in the eye, she said to me again, on the big screen: 'Yes, now I do, yes'. Which now? Years later in Texas, I had the unnerving sense of the return of her specter, the specter of her specter coming back to say to me – to me here, now: 'Now... now... now, that is to say, in this dark room on another continent, in another world, here, now yes, believe me, I believe in ghosts'. (Derrida & Stiegler, 2013, p.40)

This moment can be contextualized as such an astounding coincidence but as something deeply unsettling.

Derrida's concept that ghosts are the memory of a performance that has never been present can be related to the idea that performance, in many of its forms (live and mediated), recalls the past, memorializes the dead and attempts to make them present. Any fan of the Elvis impersonator may witness such a phenomenon. And, certainly an actor's performance conjures up a variety of different ghosts. The Netflix documentary film *Jim and Andy: The Great Beyond* (2017) focuses on Jim Carrey's committed performance of playing Andy Kaufman in *The Man on The Moon* (1999). His performance is so astoundingly real that Kaufman's relatives, present on the set, were reduced to tears because the likeness of Jim was so profound, they thought they were looking at a ghost. In fact, Carrey never comes out of role, even on his lunch break, in the dressing room or at the end of the working day. In the documentary, Carrey describes a phenomenal moment experienced on Malibu beach while looking out to the ocean. Here, he claims, he received a sign from Kaufman. 'I decided from then, for the next few days to speak telepathically to people,' and he elaborates, 'That's the moment when Andy Kaufman showed up, tapped me on the shoulder and said: "Sit down, *I'll* be doing my movie"' (Carrey, cited in Jim and Andy: The Great Beyond 2017).

Ghosting

In 1975, Herbert Blau directed the Kraken theatre group in a reimagining of *Hamlet*. This work, entitled *Elsinore*, was an improvised response to Shakespeare's original text containing 'words, empty words, playing upon the surface of a memory like a sediment of a text, ghostly, metonymic, words displacing words, and endlessly so – like the data of prehistory or the half-forgotten substance of dreams' (Blau, 2011, p.169). Rather than perform the play, the group practised the play as a memory game, as an experimental process of collage, creating a series of visual and verbal fragments of *Hamlet* after the actors had memorized the whole play. They could perform images, perform scenes (in no specific order) and speak lines from the play as long as it was from *Hamlet*. Kraken's development of *Elsinore* was approached from the state of mind the company found themselves in during practice, that is, from the momentum of a work in progress. Blau was interested in how the ghosts of a scene, repeated and repeated, kept returning through varying different forms of performance processes. 'When we described the way we worked, we called it ghosting. We found ourselves thinking through Hamlet as if Hamlet were thinking us, and as if without the play we could not think at all' (Blau, 2011, p.171).

Blau elaborates on this concept and practice of ghosting: 'The ghosting is not only a theatrical process but a self-questioning of the structure within the structure of which the theater is a part' (Blau, 1982, p.199). Certainly, this practice of ghosting came directly out of an actor's approach to play through playing their own versions of Hamlet. Here, the memory game created new material and transformed the original 'territory' of *Hamlet* into a new performance where Kraken's actors played out their own various states of mind and attitudes towards *Hamlet*. Blau's use of the term ghosting means to work through the debris of a memory that is realized and interpreted within the midst of a game, repeating and returning to fragmented moments, like the ghost in Shakespeare's *Hamlet* who keeps appearing and disappearing and reappearing – moving the story along. There is something intriguing about this concept and practice of ghosting. For example, imagine each actor recalling images and sounds from the past, or indeed channelling the actors who they remember played previous roles in *Hamlet*, dead or alive, embodying dead actors from previous productions.

Ghosting developed as a theory related to reception studies in theatre.

Theorist Marvin Carlson relates the term when audiences identify with an actor in role and/or a character in the theatre. His studies on the interaction between theatre and memory reveal how the memory of the spectator informs the process of theatrical reception. He asserts that actors play many different roles over time, therefore the spirit or memory of those roles influence the performance from the actor that the audience is experiencing:

> The process of using the memory of previous encounters to understand and interpret encounters with new and somewhat different but apparently similar phenomena is fundamental to human cognition in general, and it plays a major role in the theatre, as it does in all the arts. Within the theatre, however, a related but somewhat different aspect of memory operates in a manner distinct from, or at least in a more central way than in, the other arts, so much so that I would argue that it is one of the characteristic features of theatre. To this phenomenon I have given the name *ghosting*. (Carlson, 2003, p.8)

Carlson also refers to ghosting as the 'recycled body and persona of the actor' (Ibid., p.53). Inspired by Blau's use of the term in practice and Carlson's concept of ghosting in relation to reception studies, we (Gary and Claire) take on the term, but as a practice, and a methodology for making and performing. Quite simply, ghosting (for us as practitioners) works from the physical, psychic or textual embodiment of specific qualities of performing/constructing text that reside within the nostalgic and the sentimental, that reclaim or indeed reinvent an identity for the actor – or indeed form the basis for a new persona to emerge for performance, or for the text to develop. We suggest that the practice of ghosting is certainly not unique to the theatrical stage. We find there are particular similarities to be drawn upon in a range of artistic mediums where there is an actor or performer, character or persona or self-performing. Moreover, Carlson discusses this term in the context of the stage and live theatre, rather than thinking of the term across a broad range of arts. To this end, we assert that ghosting does indeed exist in film, TV, live and visual arts, because once you get past genre, and focus specifically on the performer (or actor, or materials), and the performative, a similar process happens: our memory relates to the object, or to the actor or character's performance. For example, in Quentin Tarantino's (1994) *Pulp Fiction*, the actor John Travolta plays a hitman taking part in a dance competition with his boss' girlfriend at an American diner. We are watching a hitman dancing, but we are also witnessing the residue, a hint, a resurrection of Travolta's once very famous self from the movie *Saturday Night Fever* (1977), the champion of disco – he moved on that floor! Travolta the actor is ghosting his former character Vincent:

> Everything in the theatre, the bodies, the materials utilized, the language, the space itself, is now and has always been haunted, and that haunting has been an essential part of the theatre's meaning to and reception by its audiences in all times and all places. (Carlson, 2003, p.15)

We would like to paraphrase Carlson's idea, replacing the word 'theatre' with performance, to assert that everything in performance (live or mediated), the bodies, the texts, the objects, the language, the actors, the space, the medium, is now and has always been haunted. In this very simple but enigmatic idea, performance invites the actor/performer to consider her own self within the world of the fictional, theatrical and performative while simultaneously, and undoubtedly, considers while performing, and remembering in her performance, the acts or the words of others.

The Dead Celebrity and the Qualities of Deadness

The phenomenon of the dead celebrity – and let's dive straight in to the most famous dead celebrity of all, Elvis – has much to do with the 'endless licensing of his image' (Spigel, 1990, p.177) as it does a spiritual connection to him, and his continuous revival from the commitment from his fans. The ripple effect of Elvis' death was felt across the world and as we went into mourning, the conspiracy theory that he had 'hoaxed his own death to escape from imprisonment by his own icon and disappear into a life of true freedom and anonymity' (Ebert, 2010, p.47) was mounting towards headline news. For those who adored Elvis, who were part of his era, who witnessed him perform live or on television in their own homes, it was devastating news, especially because he died well before his time and was immediately thrust into mythological status:

> When life is lived at the speed of light, the earth flattens, time slows down, and mythical structures begin to appear everywhere. Hence, when certain individuals among us are accelerated to light speed via electronic replication of their images, strange, otherworldly phenomena begin to accrete to them, forming the very auras Walter Benjamin insisted would be stripped from them by the mechanical means of reproduction of the images. At light speed, however, unpredictable effects of mythic amplitude and volume give shape to the ancient patters that act as molds by way of which the lives of such individuals are contoured: the myth of the mysterious, piping singer, whose notes resonate with a compulsively erotic effect. (Ebert, 2010, p.35)

Elvis' continued absent presence for his most immediate fans 'serves as a means through which to reinvent their personal history' (Spigel, 1990, p.178). Indeed, the massive wave of Elvis impersonators in the 1990s, 13 years after his death, was responsible for 'a subculture built around a single contradiction: If there were only one king, how come there are so many of him?' (Ibid., p.179). Elvis impersonators were 'deeply embedded in restoring the memory of an authentic experience – it was, that is, all about recovering one's own historical identity through the literal em'body'ment of a spirit from the past' (Ibid., p.179). The revival that happened in the 1990s is described by Spigel as a 'ritual that can best be seen as a serious game' (Ibid., p.180), and by way of using this idea to return to play, the necromatic performers who impersonate Elvis do 'not believe Elvis is alive, but instead they see themselves as temporarily bringing Elvis back to life' (Ibid., p.184):

    The revivalist culture of Elvis (and the obsession with the death of Elvis) meant that he has appeared in every form of art imaginable, wide ranging and in diverse contexts in all forms of lowbrow and highbrow art.

In the song lyrics of other artists, in 'movies, novels, comic strips, poems, scholarly works, and television shows' (Marcus, 1999, p.180). In fact, Elvis was 'appropriated by "pop-avant-gardists" … Think for example, of Andy Warhol's silkscreened Elvis … or of Jim Jarmusch's more recent use of Elvis in *Mystery Train*'. (Spigel, p.183)

Who and where is Elvis in the twenty-first century? Was he not simply 'that popular dead man of the twentieth century'? (Ibid.). The current generation of young music fans and impersonators, including Emilio Santoro, the 15-year-old Elvis who in 2018 was invited to perform at Benidorm's Elvis Festival, knows only the mythology of Elvis, but quite possibly knows only the reproduction, the commodified image, the ghost of the ghost that has been ghosted, reimagined and distorted:

> The Elvis preservationists are trying to arrest something in the process of decay, and, like the taxidermists before them, their success is measured by the degree to which the observer believes in a life-like monument that speaks the very language of death. (Ibid., p.199)

In a recent theatre production entitled *Beyond Belief* (2018), by Tmesis Theatre, Elvis' music is played throughout the production. Set in the present day, this fictional world (as an almost darker mirror to the one we know or fear) circles around our social media-obsessed society. For, in their world, they have the opportunity to bring loved ones (family members) back from the dead. This is a disturbing view of what it might mean to live as a humanoid programmed with memories pulled together from an online identity. Tmesis purposefully acknowledge that in this digital age (41 years after the death of Elvis) we still refuse to let Elvis die. Yet at the same time they also draw upon the idea that it is not just the famous who are memorialized.

Making and Performing with the Qualities of Deadness

While our projects are not concerned with the death of Elvis, and nor do they offer a dystopian view of the dead, we do draw upon the image of the dead icons. We invite the dead into our practice – Roy Orbison,

Sigmund Freud, Amelia Earhart, Laurence Sterne – and echo a revivalist spirit in our playfulness. We look upon the fans of the icon with affection, understanding their spiritual connection with a dead icon, but we also draw upon the mass production of the icon's image too. While Orbison was on tour in the UK in 1987, television interviewers were obsessed with his 'man in black' appearance with an insistence on talking about his dark glasses. Orbison's image was strangely enigmatic; in fact, while he was alive he embodied a quality of deadness, his otherness drew attention and shaped his media image. Our fascination with Orbison will become apparent in many of the chapters that articulate our practice within this book.

We make work that speaks from this paradox; that we live *with* the dead on a permanent basis, yet we do not know what it is like to be dead. The dead are profoundly all around us, and perhaps this is because death is within us and we draw further upon this concept through a psychoanalytic lens in Chapter 3. While performance concerns itself with liveness, it is the varying qualities of deadness in live or mediated performance in the performer or the object of performance (alive or inanimate) that intrigues us. We are not thinking of deadness as straightforwardly as a lifeless experience, although in some cases we might think of deadness as a creative metaphor to describe certain aspects of the qualities of stillness, note, not lifelessness. In our practice, we embody and encounter deadness in forms that are contradictory; we play dead, embody zombies, imitate dead icons, we animate stuffed animals to playfully critique the living. We reimagine dead acts as an anagram for cats and we acknowledge dead theories and make use of them to distort them so that we might see the world differently. And we make connections between sleep, dreaming and death because when the dead appear in our dreams and walk alongside us, we genuinely feel something.

While this book is about the dead in various contexts and usage of the word in performance, significantly, it is also an exploration into the qualities of deadness. Therefore, we offer a list that defines our use of the term:

Deadness
    A state or quality of playing dead.
    The playing out of something that is dead in various interpretations of the word.

The act of sleep, or the qualities of sleep.

The stillness in objects, subjects, ideas.

A play on the term liveness.

Of or relating to something being dead as in a language or a career.

The inanimate state of performance as ephemera.

The use of the word dead in language, for example the use of idioms and euphemisms.

The quality of performance produced through ghosting methodologies.

Illustration 2 *Kong Lear* Pentacle: copy, cut out and keep

2

The Dead Psychoanalyst

Some Words on Death

There is a beautiful garden, a peaceful place with plum and almond trees tucked behind a house on a leafy street, calm and quiet and away from it all. The house at 20 Maresfield Gardens was once the home of Sigmund Freud and his family after they fled the Nazis as refugees from the German annexation of Austria and moved to London. It was Freud's home for just over a year, in 1939 at the age of 83; after receiving injections of morphine from his physician Max Schur, Freud died there. He had suffered from cancer of the mouth for 16 years where 'the pain became so great that he was unable to read or write' (Colt, 2006, p.389).

Some Words on a House

This house, packed full of Freud's antiquities, is a collector's haven full of objects from various civilizations, some of them Egyptian, and arranged in no particular order and quite typical of nineteenth-century collecting. This house was also Freud's place of work, with an active study, whose couch, shipped over to London from Vienna, was once occupied by regular visiting patients. Housed on the shelves behind glass doors in the study is Freud's library, home to the complete works of Nietzsche, which apparently he never read. It is full of other books too – archaeological works, works of literature – and his collection is used today as an active research library. The study is also home to Freud's office chair, commissioned by his daughter Mathilde and designed by the architect Felix Augenfeld to accompany Freud's desk. On the desk rests an impressive and curious collection of figurines; all would face Freud and look at him as he worked at his desk. It is said that Freud used to pat the heads of the figurines each working day. Accompanying these, there is a photocopied entry of his diary from 1930 together with his round spectacles, left on the page as if he had, moments earlier, just finished his work for the day. At the top of the stairs, on the landing, there is a surrealist etching on the wall, *A Portrait of Sigmund Freud* by Salvador Dali, in which Freud seems to have a rather peculiar-shaped head for reasons, it seems, to do with association. The etching, a spiral-shaped shell of a snail that Dali felt compelled to draw as if it was Freud's cranium, came about because Dali was eating snails at exactly the time he was excited to discover that Freud was to visit Paris. This house was also home for a much longer period to his daughter Anna, who, before she died, requested that this home be turned into a museum, which now welcomes many visitors each week. It also boasts on the landing at the top of the stairs a display of 'Wolf Man' paintings by Sergei Pankejeff, who was one of Freud's patients. Pankejeff once sketched a dream that he had recounted to Freud where he saw several wolves sitting in a tree outside his house. This house, once a home and now a museum as a home – very Freudian – holds many temporary exhibitions, installations and, on the odd occasion, live performances. One of these, *Ghost Track* by Claire Hind and Gary Winters, took place in April 2012, performed to a full house in the Anna Freud room, followed by a showing on the screen in the same room of their Super 8mm film *Kong Lear*, which incidentally caused Lili Spain, the events and media manager, to laugh out loud when the surtitles of the film describe the character Kong Lear chewing on Freud's leg. The house is also home to an educational programme including talks and lectures and conferences.

Some Words on the Term Freudian

The term Freudian relates to theories and practices of Sigmund Freud most commonly aligned to that which comes from something hidden, tucked away, something kept secret, something that is lived out in our dreams, repressed desire. The term Freudian in the context of his own home epitomizes the Freudian linguistic landscape that people use frequently: common terms like Freudian slip are a household phrase, and not just assigned to those working in the field of psychoanalysis.

Some Words on the Shop

The objects and the artefacts on sale in the shop at the Freud Museum are humorous. The Unemployed Philosophers manufacturing company produces novelty gifts such as Freudian slippers and mugs sporting the phrase 'Freudian Sips' and 'WHEN YOU SAY ONE THING AND MEAN YOUR MOTHER'. These gifts make assumptions that many of us have a very basic knowledge of Freudian psychoanalysis; it seems most people reference or observe their friends' Freudian slips. It is clear that the museum understands the importance of Freud's legacy and the shop does not take Freud too seriously. Perhaps the quirkier items are a little nod to his personality, a reminder that Freud was interested in everyday life. In fact, Freud wrote a whole book on jokes – *The Joke and the Relation to the Unconscious*. It is well known that Freud's interests also lay in classical antiquity, philosophy, poetry and Shakespeare, so this multidisciplinary side to Freud, a writer who won the Goethe Prize for Literature in Germany, allows us to view him as an artist who might appreciate the jokes that now promote his name. According to the shopkeeper, the bestsellers are the little finger puppets and the rubber duck. Apparently, these items sell well because they display the well-known image of Freud on them, the one with the stern and serious face, a nice contrast to the kitsch nature of the object when you think about it. Freud would have a field day.

Some Words on the Home

A house as a home is a familiar place, it is 'one of the greatest powers of integration for the thoughts, memories and dreams of mankind' (Bachelard, 1958, p.6). The Freud Museum feels like a home more than a museum. It has an incredibly warm feel, lavish furnishings, a thick carpet on the stairs, pictures on the wall; it is a place for an afternoon doze, or a daydream or two. As a property it is quite desirable; it is a house on an affluent leafy street, spacious, warm, quiet and in London. What is nice about this house as a museum is that it is not overcrowded with visitors, it is possible to have an intimate experience with the house, sit in the garden and listen to the birds. It is possible to imagine this space free of visitors altogether and imagine occupying it without the rules that prevent access to Freud's desk, chair, couch and antiquities. And even at a distance, when standing within Freud's study looking at the couch, it keeps its inviting homely feel. Yet as much as we can drift and get comfortable, an unworldly presence lurks in every room, Freud haunts the home by his absent presence:

> In his essay on the uncanny Freud cites a long dictionary entry in which at-homeness, Heimlichkeit, comes to coincide with not-at-homeness, Unheimlichkeit. The route to this coincidence of opposites is through the image of the 'home' as an interior space in which things can be hidden. The unfamiliar can emerge at the heart of the familiar. Freud compares the unfamiliar at the heart of the familiar to the unconscious 'hidden' by repression from the everyday, conscious sense of oneself. (Bass, 2006, p.53)

Homeliness as the uncanny, where one might experience the sheer 'revelation of something unhomely at the heart of the hearth and home' (Royle, 2003, p.1), is what Heidegger describes as 'the fundamental character of our being in the world (the home) is uncanny, unhomely, not-at-home' (Ibid., p.4). If it is repressed desire that haunts our sense of homeliness, the Freud Museum offers a complex experience of this feeling, because it no longer functions as a home. Rather, it is a house as a museum which has a sense of homeliness about it. There is no clear boundary between the imaginary and the real in this space, because we are being reminded about what is dead through what has been preserved as a curated home. To speak of the dead is to think of the dead psychoanalyst, of course, but also to look at the famous couch as a dead object. When we experience this room, we are looking back in time, but in a time when the psychoanalytic couch has fallen into disuse:

> Freudian psychotherapy remained the prevailing wisdom in psychiatric treatment until the 1970s, says Edward Shorter, professor of the history of medicine at the University of Toronto, but the profession experienced a pivotal change as cheaper and less drawn-out methods arrived, such as cognitive behavioural therapy. (Stevens, BBC News magazine, 2015)

The preservation of Freud's study, the objects and the furniture arrangements, are left exactly as they were when Freud was living. This room has been written, it has a prescribed look that is not real but intended to be read as if it is real but preserved in some mythologized state:

> This room in which patients attempted to probe the depths of their individual selves is eerily depersonalizing; it contextualizes the countenance of the analysand with ones from antiquity, just as the individual's history is submerged in the immensity of time contained in the room. It's a place for the conjuration of fantasy in a very particular idiom: the mythological, the religious, the classical antique, the undead revenant. (Prochnik, 2012, p.393)

Bachelard establishes a very interesting idea from the perspective of literature 'and poetry to say that we "write a room", "read a room", or "read a house"' (Bachelard, 1958, p.14). Certainly, as seen in twentieth-century cinema, the house can suddenly turn from being a homely place to a sinister, threatening and even a deadly space. The intimacy of the home, its contents and its dwellers do things we cannot see, behind closed doors. Cinema invites us in to that intimate, secret world. Interpreting the rooms of the seedy house in David Lynch's 1986 film *Blue Velvet*, where the sadistic character Frank Booth meets Ben, is a scary house full of odd characters. In the living room we witness the image of a door closing where it appears (although we cannot quite tell) unhealthy activity is taking place, dark secrets, unruly desire, perhaps a kidnapping. Ben's house is set in contrast to Sandy's home (in the same film) with the white picket fence and an animatronic robin outside the window. Both houses and their interiors/exteriors allow for a reading of contrasts of the film's themes where peace and tranquillity meet erotic violence. Lynch draws us into the house as a place of mystery, sometimes sinister, sometimes other; the rooms are symbolic of the uncanny and representative of all things intriguing about the unconscious. In *Lost Highway* (1997), the corridors in Fred and Renee's home are endlessly represented as dark and dream-like spaces full of mystery, intrigue or terrifying possibilities of strangers entering the home. Here we observe the alarming possibility that someone in the exterior world has entered the home of Renee and Fred. They receive a package in the post, a VHS tape recording that shows black and white shots of the exterior and interior of their own home. This shocking invasion of privacy opens up the idea that the things we take for granted, the familiarity of the home, can suddenly be displaced through someone else's point of view. Fred and Renee are both watching their own home as a place now alien to them because they are viewing it through someone else's gaze. The point of view and the anxiety brought about by the thought of intrusion is amplified further in *Lost Highway* with the question that Fred Madison asks at the party when talking to the mystery man on the phone in the presence of the same mystery man standing in front of him, asking 'how did you get inside my house?'. The uncanny relationship visitors have to Freud's home is developed from their very specific, subjective point of view. They enter the house and form an interpretation, multiply those interpretations by the number of different visitors, and Freud's ghost must feel extremely displaced by these strangers. And in Lynch movies, strangers enter the home in the most surreal way; for example, we see an elderly couple (in miniature human form) crawl under the door of a dark and dreary house to torment the mind of a shattered and suicidal Diane in *Mulholland Drive* (2001). This playful, sinister and unforced entry, like little mice finding a way into the home, is a warning of what we will soon see as a most disturbing image: Diane's rotting corpse left unnoticed for days, perhaps weeks, inside her own home on her own bed. Lynch presents the home with a powerful sense of displacement, the home as the dislocated strange, at the heart of the very familiar, and exposes the odd encounter we have with our unconscious mind. 'Insecurity, estrangement, lack of orientation and balance are sometimes so acute in Lynchland that the question becomes one of whether it is possible ever to feel "at home"' (Rodley, 1997, p.x–xi). In Lynch's web film *The Rabbits (2002)*, the house is theatricalized and rep-resented as a television set as we see the domestic setting of a family as humanoid rabbits (actors wearing human clothing sporting large rabbits heads). One rabbit irons while the other is sitting watching TV and then another rabbit enters the room through the door, accompanied by the sound of canned applause. The disjointed conversations of non-sequiturs between family members are delivered in the same room as if they all exist in another time and space. This film is a reminder that the home can be a refuge from external threats but at the same time it exposes the terri-fying rules that govern each household and the psychological day-to-day habits of a home:

> For Lynch, our most familiar surroundings inevitably contain unhomely elements. Home, he contends, is 'a place where things can go wrong' (4). As such he has built and filmed a series of domestic theaters; arenas in which characters are both participating actors and voyeuristic spectators, homes where intruders and surveillance are rife. Here, inhabitants endure a painful intimacy with domestic space. (Martin, 2014, p.64)

To experience Freud's home in Maresfield Gardens as a Lynch movie, in its preserved state, the 'authentic' appearance is perpetually dislocated from reality. There is a poetic function to Freud's absent presence, the house is by its very nature Freudian and represents what was so impor-tant to Freud, the unconscious mind. Freud's legacy is extremely power-ful, the experience of visiting the house is to acknowledge the important yet overwhelmingly dominant discourse of psychoanalysis. Interestingly, because film theory has often used psychoanalysis to contextualize the Lynchian world, there is this sense that the house (the Freud Museum) has more of a fruitful relationship to the artist than it does to the psycho-analyst. For (us as) artists, experiencing the house as material (as stimu-lus for making performance and the idea of the house as a place of dead-ness), you get a sense of a co-mingling: a merging of a significant past with the very playful cinematic present, as if Lynch himself has curated Freud's study. As much as the house is 'more than an embodiment of a home, it is also an embodiment of dreams' (Bachelard, 1958, p.15). The study with its famous couch offers an evocative atmosphere as if you are entering a performance because the red curtains seem familiar. Freud's study has a look of David Lynch's 'Red Room' about it; in fact, we like to imagine Lynch was inspired by Freud's red curtains as they appear as a haunting image symbolizing theatricality in many of his works including *Mulholland Drive* and *Lost Highway*.

Some Words on the Couch

The couch is one of the most famous pieces of furniture in the world and it has become an object of fetishization. A visit to see the couch in Freud's study for some is like a pilgrimage, crying as they experience affect. Viewed from a distance, visitors cannot touch the couch, most staff members do not get to go in close to the couch or the objects, unless they are working with curators, but this is not an everyday occurrence. The museum always makes sure that the curtains in the study room are closed; not a lot of natural light gets into the room in order to preserve the couch and all the artefacts.

In September 2013 we visited the Freud Museum to watch the couch being specially repaired as it had been moved out of the study. Walking into the dining room we sat down to watch conservator Poppy Singer and a small team of upholsterers mend the seams. We watched them re-stuff the couch made up of horse's hair, we noticed some areas were being patched up, it was not a complete recovery of the object but a plugging of holes here and there. All was silent in the dining room, albeit with the odd cough or sniffle from a mesmerized viewer. We were invited to ask questions about the repair, but watching on in silence offered a meditative experience that allowed us to drift off and imagine how, over the years, the couch absorbed a whole host of secrets and dreams via the sweat and tears of each and every analysand. We noticed tidemarks, and we thought about the mix of many different bodily fluids (of the now deceased) that remain marked on its skin. While images were running through our own minds of those who reclined on the couch, we chuckled at the idea that Freud himself might have lain on his own couch after the last patient of the day had left; Freud imagining himself as the analysand testing out the talking cure experience from a different point of view. Drifting off, we were occasionally interrupted in our thoughts by the conservators scribbling in pencil, reporting on the condition of the 130-year-old couch in need of attention. We did not recognize the couch at first, because this chaise lounge-style couch permanently situated in the study is always wrapped in a Qashqai Persian fabric. Here, appropriated from its place of reverence and stripped of its covers, revealing its mid-nineteenth century Biedermeier style with a bolster at one end, the couch seemed vulnerable but weirdly it seemed much more alive than it does in the study. The experience of viewing this restoration seemed like a sacred experience, an encounter with an object of major significance, but importantly for us it was as if the couch was performing more than it does in the study. We considered this idea, that the staging of an object becomes the death of the object. At least here, being repaired, away from the study, in its naked, stripped, attended-to state, the couch seems to have more of a life. The conservators were working through such a delicate and tender operation for the sake of preservation, but we had empathy for it knowing that once the repair had finished, it was going back to its permanent home, left alone for years to come.

If you think about the conditions of Freud's study, now as a museum, and think about the couch as a permanent feature of the study, left as it were on Freud's last day, barred off from the public, it is a lonely and numb object. In its deadness it is looked upon by visitors who arrive and mourn as if they are in a mausoleum. Perhaps the couch would appreciate a different type of life? One where visitors were given the experience of lying down on it. Of course, with such an invitation to lie on the couch, it would need to undergo regular repairs, but we imagine that there is a desire from those who visit the museum to have access to a more intimate experience, feeling the couch's material, dreaming on it, channelling Freud on it or jumping all over it. As a forbidden object, it becomes a desirable object; the barrier acts as a symbol of repression, holding us back from a forbidden desire.

The Freud Museum frequently invites artists to respond to the house, to the objects in the house and Freud's legacy. In 2015, two artists brought the couch back to life and out of its seemingly perpetual state of deadness. The artists Broomberg and Chanarin created an exhibition entitled *Every Piece of Dust on Freud's Couch*. They asked a group of forensic scientists to gather DNA material, the traces of those who once lay on the couch – the hair follicles, skin samples, any kind of human trace. They sent SEM photographic images to a tapestry maker who re-rendered the scientific results as tapestries, one of which, a brightly coloured tapestry, covered the couch in the study as part of the exhibition. Here science and art merged in an intrusive exploration into the pieces of dead others, a strange and peculiar examination that draws our attention even closer to this fetishized object that is given an alternative way of being at the museum. Here the remnants of death, those bits of the body that have been left behind, offer a proof of a life, a proof of a death and a weird fascination with the dust that has gathered and settled over the many years since Freud's death.

Some Words on Sophie Calle's Appointment

We wonder what Freud would have made of the art and performance that feature in his home? It seems fitting that the house exhibits artists' work because Freud created a new language and discourse for experiencing things, he created a space where dreams were important, and artists at the time responded, and artists now keep responding. The legacy of this museum is committed to intellectual curiosity and keeping that curiosity alive.

In 1998 there was a strong female presence in the house. The artist Sophie Calle was invited to mount an exhibition and she set about collating the stories she wanted to tell around the house using a series of short texts, photographs and objects belonging to the artist, one of which was her wedding dress, which she laid across the famous couch. Calle's texts, photographs and objects (including a stuffed cat) were placed alongside the interior of Freud's house. Calle's sense of mischief was led by her eccentric experiences with love, chance and role-play. Part autobiography and fiction, *Appointment* slips into Calle's desires, exposes her fantasies and brings forth her fascination and humorous relationship with death, as well as taking agency over the patriarchy:

> I had three cats. Felix died after being accidently left in the fridge. Zoë was taken from me when my brother was born; I hated him from that

moment on. Nina was strangled by a jealous man, who had, sometime before, given me an ultimatum: to sleep with the cat or him. I opted for the cat. (Calle, 2005, p.47)

Judith Rigg concentrates on Calle's *Appointment* in relation to death, absence and loss:

The death of Sophie Calle's cat; the loss of a lover; the death of her great aunt; the suicide of her plastic surgeon; her grandmother's death; the death of her mother's tenant and the implicit loss of her children; the loss and yearning for a church wedding, and the loss of love, desire, relationships and security all functioned as foci for memories of death, fears, loss and desire. (Rigg, 2004, p.51)

Calle's intervention is a playful one in the house, her dark play uncovers her desire to experience the talking cure in Freud's home as she recalls a lot of trauma and stories in *Appointment*. In documenting her own presence here, she re-writes the home (and the idea of home) and its contents. Calle put the viewer (a stranger in the home) into a dislocated position and we are left playing guessing games on which of her anecdotes are true, which are fiction, which are desires. Calle, like a little child in the midst of playing games, telling truths and fictions, messes with psychoanalysis. In the photographs where she dresses up in different clothes (some of Freud's), she blurs the boundaries between male and female, imposing herself on a very famous house. She becomes Freud momentarily: wearing his coat, she is the psychoanalyst. Yet, it could be argued, wearing his coat, she is also his analysand, with the assumed typical desires (akin to psychoanalytic thought) of both the sexes.

Some Words on Gavin Turk

The house curates a variety of artistic projects that allow for intervention and is happy with a critical approach to Freud's theories. In 2016 a series of Gavin Turk artworks curated by James Putnam, entitled *Wittgenstein's Dream*, was a cheeky intervention that poked fun at psychoanalysis from the point of view of both Wittgenstein's and Freud's differing views on the unconscious. Wittgenstein 'questioned the claims of psychoanalysis to be a science because, he argued, it is not empirical. It is a theoretical apparatus you can apply to dreams, jokes or art – but it cannot really be proven or disproven' (Jones, 2015). One of the artworks situated in the study entitled *[ξ, N(ξ)]′(η) (= [η, ξ, N(ξ)])* (2015) was a funny yet unnerving waxwork of a life-size Wittgenstein holding an egg in his hand. Here was a dead philosopher as an uncanny object, holding an uncanny object (the egg). What type of flesh is wax? It is an odd object, intriguing and disturbing; an inanimate life-like sculpture complete with smiling face, performing its, or rather his, assertive stance, standing tall overlooking Freud's desk and couch. Waxworks in general 'are a notorious sign of uncanniness, disturbing things which trouble the boundaries between the living, the animate and inanimate' (Bowen, 2003, p.152). And the egg in Wittgenstein's hand draws attention to the paradoxical nature of *the* uncanny: is he 'holding it or dreaming he is holding it? Or is he one of Freud's own dreams?' (Jones, 2015). Turk also ghosted the objects that are preserved in the house; Turk's own desk is installed in the exhibition room complete with the artist's own souvenirs on it as a humorous gesture echoing the way Freud's desk and objects are displayed in the museum. In the same exhibition, along the stairway, significant Freudian theories were ghosted in neon light: the words Id, Ego and Super Ego, a playful and imaginative response to Wittgenstein's insistence of logic. Turk's mixed media materials spoke to one another across one significant theme, the idea that psychoanalysis is seen by some as a dead practice even when Freudian concepts are still challenged and are not in a hurry to be forgotten.

Some Words 122 Miles Away from Freud's Couch

On 1 June 2003, 222,704 of Freud's words burst out of the window of a fast-moving car in an act of what the artist, who was also the thrower of the words, describes as 'madness'. Freud's *Interpretation of Dreams* had been reimagined and documented as a cut up artwork in action in the hands of the conceptual artist Simon Morris. In his experimental act *The Royal Road to the Unconscious* (2003), Morris claims that the 'eruption of words from the window of the speeding car produced a temporary escape from the rational, a brief celebratory moment of non-meaning' (Morris, 2018, p.172). A similar action by Ed Ruscha and Mason Williams back in 1966, where the thrower (Williams) flung a typewriter out of the window, was an inspiration for Morris' work. Although it was derivative of the 1966 work, it is Morris' relationship to Freud that is the most intriguing, for he never even read a full copy of the *Interpretation of Dreams* before he threw it out of the window and made conceptual art with it. The driver of the car was a psychoanalyst, completely irresponsible speeding at 90 miles an hour through the country lanes of Dorset 'approximately 122 miles southwest of Sigmund Freud's psychoanalytic couch' (Morris, 2018, p.171). Yet here we arrive at a paradox; the creative tension between the concept of freeing up Freud's seminal text in an act of apparent randomness, rubs up against Morris' description of the experiment itself, in the desire to locate the action back to the house, back to the couch and back to Freud. Despite the concept to deconstruct meaning, it seems that Freud still stays pretty much the centre of attention in Morris' works. The concept of the cut up, where Freud's words were no longer in a readable condition, nonetheless stay within the domain of the Freudian because the random act itself is something one would perhaps experience in a dream world. *The Interpretation of Dreams* is also the focal point of a 2005 project by Morris entitled *Re-Writing Freud*, where he re-writes Freud's text as a whole book. Morris worked alongside Christine Farion, who designed a computer program for the 1913 translation of Freud's work to be fed into. The program 'randomly selected words one at a time from across Freud's text, and began to reconstruct the entire book, word by word, making a new book with the same words' (Ibid., p.176). Two different versions of the text appeared – a digital version, where audiences in galleries could interact with the text, and a physical version. In the digital version, Morris argues:

> The spectator soon realised that he or she could authorize their own re-writing of Freud's work, taking control of the work and print directly from the screen by using the touch-sensitive interface. By pressing play and pause, they too could intervene in Freud's original text, rupture it, interrupt it, create new poetic or nonsensical juxtapositions and return it to us in a new order. (Morris, 2018, p.177)

This work is a fitting experiment in homage to Freud, albeit with an opportunity to look at his words differently (in the world of art, not health). This is a work that happily re-imagines the *Interpretation of Dreams*, as a celebration of Freud. When Morris published the first limited edition of *Re-Writing Freud*, an idea he conceived in a dream as an 'unreadable' book, he made an observation based on the reader's encounter of the text:

> As it was, the audience for *Re-Writing Freud* thwarted this ambition (of the unreadable book) by stubbornly reading the re-written text. When one word is placed next to another, meaning is suggested. The syntactical certainty of Freud's sentences has been ruptured by the aleatory process, but still flashes of meaning persist, haunting the text. Despite achieving an emancipation of syntax through its digital procedure, the book remains stubbornly present in its reconfigured state. (Ibid., p.179)

Perhaps the stubbornness comes back down to Freud's absent presence. When an artist works with Freud as material and attempts to re-imagine a form (with Freud at the heart of it), the artist (and the audience) is acknowledging the heavy presence of the dead psychoanalyst and his persistence on sticking around. We like to think of his sticking around as something playful and mischievous rather than threatening and relentless, as if Freud has unfinished business channelling artists to play with his ideas. You can do creative things with a dead thinker's work when their homes are still intact, and thankfully the 1913 print Morris worked with was out of 'copyright restrictions' (Morris, 2018, p.175).

Some Words on Freud's Legacy

Freud's legacy continues because he created a rich soil for human beings to think about and draw attention to themselves. Freud, certainly in his lifetime's work, was talking about human lives and human experiences rather than a set of technical practices and this is why artists' work can be considered alongside his couch, his desk, his home; it is why the artworks resonate at the Freud Museum. Was Freud more conceptual than scientific? It seems so now but at the time Freud would not have said that he was conceptual; he saw himself as a scientist first and foremost with evidence gleaming out from the couch. In an Aristotelian empirical sense, the information given from patients on the couch is the data. This data was Freud's scientific findings, which he would then analyse and interpret. Yet, now, among neuroscience, dream interpretation is something of a washout. Perhaps the battle for Freud was trying to rein in his creativity while trying to establish himself as a very good rationalist, or rather a very good scientist in an enlightened tradition but one where Freud was the dreamer. To this day, dreams play out as a mystery in our lives, they are a neglected part of science that still fails to grasp their meaning. Michel Roth (2014) asks why Freud still haunts us? Although Freudian psychoanalysis is not leading the field in psychology today, Roth outlines how psychoanalytic concepts still appear in many humanities programmes, theatre, novels, television and in films such as *The Sopranos*; in fact he goes so far to say that Freud is 'all over' *Mad Men*.

Oliver Burkeman frames the flaws in Freudian psychoanalysis:

> Young boys don't lust after their mothers, or fear their fathers will castrate them; adolescent girls don't envy their brothers' penises. No brain scan has ever located the ego, super-ego or id. The practice of charging clients steep fees to ponder their childhoods for years – while characterising any objections to this process as 'resistance', demanding further psychoanalysis – looks to many like a scam. (Burkeman, 2016)

His article draws our attention to the practice of cognitive behavioural therapy (CBT) and compares the significant difference between therapy on the couch and CBT. The couch (in short) traditionally uses psychodynamic techniques drawing upon irrational symptoms where, as one example, depression can be traced as coming from an earlier childhood experience (which means the feelings or symptoms may always be with you), whereas CBT has a more logical approach that suggests:

> Emotions that might appear rational – such as feeling depressed about what a catastrophe your life is – stand exposed as the result of irrational thinking. Sure, you lost your job; but it doesn't follow that everything will be awful forever. (Ibid.)

Yet, Burkeman argues there is something missing from the practice of CBT for the suffering mind. To make this point he tells a story of a woman who received CBT via a computer (not a human):

> A few years ago, after CBT had started to dominate taxpayer-funded therapy in Britain, a woman I'll call Rachel, from Oxfordshire, sought therapy on the NHS for depression, following the birth of her first child. She was sent first to sit through a group PowerPoint presentation, promising five steps to 'improve your mood'; then she received CBT from a therapist and, in between sessions, via computer. (Ibid.)

While we think it very important not to condemn the faults of CBT, because we are not psychologists, we do want to highlight the appealing nature of the methods of psychoanalysis, which serve the purpose for arts practice:

> The basic premise of psychoanalysis, after all, is that our lives are ruled by unconscious forces, which speak to us only indirectly: through symbols in dreams, 'accidental' slips of the tongue or through what infuriates us about others, which is a clue to what we can't face in ourselves. (Ibid.)

The indirect relationship we have to our unconscious and our dreams is appealing because concepts that bring the individual to the foreground remain a popular form of autobiographical performance. Performance (in its varying forms) draws us closer to the experience of the present moment while simultaneously referencing a past. Freud's legacy is a reminder that we make sense of the world by drawing on the memories and connections to our own histories. Freud came up with the most curious titles for concepts that have almost become a household joke, and Freud gave meaning to the practice of interpretation, a method we use productively within the arts which is useful for the reflective voice. 'Freud continues to haunt our culture because his genre of questioning remains tied to our desire for meaning' (Roth, 2014).

One can understand why Freud has influenced so many thinkers when you visit the museum. The house invites artists to complement, juxtapose, challenge or progress his thinking. Freud was interested in people's stories, their histories; his talking cure concept where patients would lie on the couch and simply say what comes to mind developed as an archaeology of the mind, digging deep and piecing together fragments from the patient's recall.

Our practice has developed a world that comes from the hidden, the mysterious, the repressed, the dead, but we offer this as a world to be alive in. When we first became interested in Freud, it was to challenge the patriarchal systems embedded within society, but the more we played around with his concepts the more we felt we had agency over the ideas that were not so positive and we created a series of subversive hybrid characters and imaginary spaces so that Freud could hang out with us on our terms in our world. We position ourselves playfully, as artistic mediums channelling a dead psychoanalyst who now seems to have become more of a celebrity. As Armintor (2004) points out, Freud's reputation depended on his eventual death.

As a mythologized figure, we have warmed to Freud as someone who was willing to listen to people's dreams. At least he was interested and paid much attention to his own, documenting them to the point where we can now access an index of playful appellations that read as if they are titles of performances:

> *Castle by the sea.*
> *The forgotten church tower.*
> *My son the Myops.*
> *One-eyed doctor and school master.*
> *Otto was looking ill.*
> *Keeping a woman waiting.*
> *Phantasies during sleep.*
> *Undressed running upstairs.*
> *Father on a death bed like Garibaldi.*
> *Riding on a horse.*
> *Dissecting my own pelvis.*
> *Uncle with Yellow beard.*
> *Bird beaked figures.*
> *Three fates.*
> *The Pope is dead.*
> (Strachey, 2001, pp.715–716)

In the following chapter, we explore some of the key concepts Freud discussed and which other psychoanalysts and philosophers (such as Lacan and Žižek) have developed significantly, namely the death drive, the uncanny and desire. We call upon these terms as a conceptual dramaturgy in our work. Appropriating psychoanalytical terms is useful because working with a specific language to think through practice enables a deeper and more complex form of artistic inquiry on the methods and interpretation of practice. Refashioning a language is playful as we are not applying a straightforward renewal of Freud's theories, rather a distortion of them. As artists we are not alone in the methods of appropriation to conceive a dramaturgy that works for performance. For example, by way of expanding on and borrowing from the scientific term geological porosity, Cathy Turner illustrates, through a useful analogy how the dramaturgy of a creative work can be described as 'porous', and she defines several illuminating reasons why the terms used in science are productive in site-based performance; one such reason states:

> If dramaturgy is described as 'porous' this implies that it is structured so that it contains space for intervention, habitation or contribution by audience, passers-by or other aspects of space itself. There might be differing levels of porosity across different kinds of dramaturgical structure. (Turner, 2014, p.202)

Our interest and use of appropriating terms from the psychoanalytic world are playful but also very meaningful. Freud and subsequent thinkers in the field of psychoanalysis have enabled us to create a language for writing, playing and performing. The slipperiness within the conflicting viewpoints of Freud's legacy reveals many gaps and inconsistences within a conceptual landscape. It is within the gaps and inconsistencies we find our fictional characters and where we locate the space to reflect on practice through the worlds that loosely associate with the term Freudian and Lynchian. While some are willing to turn their back on Freud, and keep on bashing him, we are far from throwing his concepts into the bin, because we believe in the coincidences found in the recycling of ideas that bring forth new ecologies and environments. Like mediums channelling a dead psychoanalyst, we invite Freud into our world.

Some Words on the Bin

There is a bin outside the house with a large blue door on a beautiful and peaceful street that has the prettiest plum and almond trees imaginable. This sturdy black, plastic receptacle looks tired and weary on such an affluent avenue, is littered with rubbish on its skin; very Lynchian. It has become so intensely covered with stickers (proof of paying one's entry into the Freud Museum), it is artwork in itself. The layers and layers of round stickers, images of Freud's face at every imaginable angle, have created a palimpsest collage of Freud's head, chin, eyes, glasses and beard. Freud is hidden, but found peeking out from behind distorted versions of his own face; very Freudian.

Illustration 3 'Crying' neon light installed near Whitby, on the North York Moors from *Genny and the Neons*

3

The Dead Play

This chapter contextualizes three concepts, developed within the field of psychoanalysis: the death drive, desire and the uncanny (unheimlich). Each of these concepts will be discussed to offer imaginative ways to think about them in the context of play and performance making. Performance activity often works as if it is a game, and, significantly, our 'Gary and Claire' creative ideas situate themselves as a world within conceptual psyche. A playful approach to making work means we write the rules and conditions of a project, which in turn determines how we play it or play at it. Making performance (for us) comes about from a playful attitude towards an idea, and this attitude shifts in tone according to the material that we respond to, but often that playfulness slips between the humorous, the mischievous, the surreal and the dark. What is about to be explored is not so much a defence of psychoanalytic ideas but rather a way to think through the terms metaphorically, analogously, imaginatively and to situate such psychoanalytic terms in creatively useful transferable ways, as both a conceptual and a structural dramaturgy that we name the Death Drift/Drift Drive (DD/DD).

While we do not make performance work in this order – read theory to make artistic work – we do, while we make performance, reflect upon the worlds (in film or performance) that situate themselves to the themes of death, desire and the uncanny. Therefore, we think critically and playfully about the worlds we are drawn to. While we recognize that the original positions of the three terms are situated in psychoanalysis, we frame their developed thinking by drawing upon the critical thought of Nicholas Royle, Adam Phillips, Julia Kristeva and others.

We begin with an overview of the three terms, starting with the death drive. But we would like to acknowledge that Freud's thinking on the death drive was inspired by a female psychoanalyst.

Death Drive

In November 1911, one of the first female psychoanalysts published a paper entitled 'Destruction as the cause of coming into being'. Sabina Spielrein's paper, as Covington (2015) points out, introduces the concept of the death instinct, further incorporated by Freud in *Beyond the Pleasure Principle* (1920). Here Freud marks Spielrein's idea in a footnote articulating it as a destructive component of the sexual instinct.

Freud proposed the idea that 'the aim of life is death' (Strachey, 2001, p.38). Later, while other psychoanalysts were not so confident of Freud's concept of the death drive, Jacques Lacan, while supporting Freud's ideas, asserted that 'death sustains existence' (Lacan, 1970, p.300).

Freud's thinking on the death drive developed in relation to his experience of working with soldiers who suffered trauma during World War I. He observed that his patients returned to their experiences of traumatic events in their dreams. Freud's original separation of life and death instincts was based upon simple ideas around human behaviour; for example, cooperation, love and collaboration would be the basic principles of Eros (the life drive) whereas behaviour associated with Thanatos (the death drive) would be destructive aggressive behaviours. Freud revised his thinking on the death drive in his publication *Beyond the Pleasure Principle* (1920). His theory here focused around the essence of the drive and on its impossibility of reaching absolute satisfaction. The result of Freud's understanding of the death drive establishes the phenomenon of repetition as part of the overall structure of the human subject and he 'advocated the existence of an innate tendency in all living organisms to return themselves to an inanimate state' (Barford in Weatherill, 1999, p.12).

Freud's idea is a curious one: what is it within us that is compelled to return to an inanimate state? Was Freud suggesting that there is some unconscious impulse to return to a place we know nothing of, something beyond comprehension? For what is an inanimate state? As an idea it suggests our cells have their own instinctual life with an urge to go back to a place of pre-birth. Interestingly, it feels like the work of fiction. Is the drive a biological, linguistic or a philosophical force?

As a hypothesis, the death drive is something that has never been scientifically proven to exist, but there is something appealing about the elusive and abstract concept. We have to imagine there is the presence of an ambiguous other inside of us, perhaps it is animalistic, or monstrous, or, we announce, quite playful. Whatever characteristic we imagine it to embody, the Lacanian concept of the drive is that an organism strives towards and beyond the death (or the end) of something. Slavoj Žižek supports and develops this Lacanian perspective:

> The death drive is not the mark of human finitude, but its very opposite, the name for 'eternal (spectral) life', the index of a dimension in human existence that persists forever beyond our physical death, and of which we can never rid ourselves. (Žižek, 1999, p.294)

Freud's death drive towards destruction and/or as the impossibility of reaching absolute satisfaction was discussed by Lacan as a purpose that does not follow a path to an end, summarized here by Evans, as:

> the purpose of the drive (*Triebziel*) is not to reach a *goal* (a final destination) but to follow its *aim* (the way itself), which is to circle round the object (cf. S11, 168). Thus the real purpose of the drive is not some mythical goal of full satisfaction, but to return to its circular path, and the real source of enjoyment is the repetitive movement of this closed circuit. (Evans, 2006, p.47)

Freud's death drive is a biological expression, whereas Lacanian psychoanalysis situates it within a linguistic and cultural frame. These two different ways of thinking about the death drive appeal to us. As a biological expression we are compelled to imagine the cells, the fluids, the flesh of the body working through their own logic, outside of our consciousness via their own impulses. This idea could be addressed through a cultural frame and thought of as an analogy for dramaturgy – the fact that dramaturgy as a performance-making process does not always exist through a conscious intervention by a person in a role but emerges in the abstract, out of the material constructed and has a particular flow, shape, rhythm and developing inner logic. We ask ourselves what is the equivalent of a biological life of a creative process? Freud theorized that humans repress the death drive, suggesting that it manifests itself in other forms of human behaviour, such as neurosis. The compulsion to repeat (a characteristic associated to the death drive) is a process intrinsic to mimetic behaviour and performance because many creative structures rely on repetition as their art form; but surely not all artists are neurotic? Theatre director Anthony Howell borrows from the terms death and life instincts when analysing performance processes. He places a cultural meaning onto them by reimagining them as 'forward and reverse drives, rather than of life and death instincts' (Howell, 2003, p.172). However, he does suggest Freud 'is right' to 'insist on the existence of a drive to restore to a previous state, characterized by the compulsion to repeat' (Ibid., p.173). He draws our attention to the actions we experience in performance that repeat from the first significant action, or 'initial action'. He suggests that actions in performance after the initial action diminish in order of significance and therefore any subsequent action that is repeated is an attempt to restore through various additive moments in the work.

Lacan's death drive is situated in what he calls the symbolic order: 'in the seminar of 1954–5, for example, he argues that the death drive is simply the fundamental tendency of the symbolic order to produce REPETITION' (Evans, 2006, p.33). The process of circling is a useful visual metaphor to think about the way ideas are developed for performance because the drive (and Lacan imagined the death drive as a component of every drive) seeks to attain the process of never attaining, of not ever reaching a goal. This means that repetition in performance (through either the making process or the performance itself) seeks not to restore but to accumulate and keep moving. Rather than making an action 'better' or fixing it permanently, or restoring the first action as in Howell's discussion, the death drive in performance (through a Lacanian lens) is always seeking and in this way respects time through the commitment to actions that are moving forwards (not back) and what might emerge from repetition is based upon the experience of desire:

> For Lacan, death and its symbolism are related not so much to biology but to our insertion into the world of language and to the work of the signifier. The signifier, argues Lacan, introduces a negativity that is ultimately productive despite borrowing from destruction in that it offers man the possibility of creating and engaging in a fresh start. (López, 1996, p.4)

Drive implies a moving forward and a surge on impulse. Various artistic processes rely upon the progression of ideas and the production of new worlds most often produced from gut instinct. And contemporary performance is no stranger to the imaginary universes of imitating, impersonating or represented death or dying. The theatre of the late twentieth century represented most frequently playful live acts of death and dying and in doing so opened up critical contexts for thinking about change and transformation. When discussing the relationship between death and play, Andrew Quick lists the many Forced Entertainment shows where deaths are performed, if not repeated. In *Who Can Sing a Song to Unfrighten Me* (1999), 'hundreds of deaths are playfully enacted over twenty-four hours' (Quick, 2004, p.162). Quick also draws our attention to Arthur's dying speech in *Showtime* (1996) suggesting that the 'disruptive activities' of Forced Entertainment performances 'cannot be limited to an interpretation that attempts to identify them solely as the effects of the operations of Eros and Thanatos, as embodiments of Freud's notion of the life and the death drives' (Ibid., p.154). But the many stage deaths within Forced Entertainment's disruptive play aesthetic, it could be argued, are a death drive in practice. Death returns in many forms in their work, and, as one example of many, in *Spectacular* (2008), a lone performer dressed in a skeleton costume talks openly to the audience about confronting death, while dressed up as 'death'. *Spectacular* epitomizes a Lacanian concept of the death drive because the material in this show circles around the object of death; the performers repeatedly play dead in a show about death.

While Quick notes there is more to observe than the embodiment of the drives, there is something fundamental at the heart of such an embodiment: the practice of dark and deep play; and Etchells (2008) acknowledges that dying has a charged place in theatre as he describes the actors playing 'like kids fooling with a Ouija board' and points out the whole company has being dying from the early days in shows such as *(Let the Water Run its Course) to the Sea that made its Promise* (1996). And they don't give up, as Etchells announces, 'no one's fooled … we come back – as a culture and as a group of artists – waiting till there's no one around, drawing the curtains and starting to play dead again' (Etchells, 2008).

Forced Entertainment continue to circle around the subject of death. In a recent performance of *Dirty Work, The Late Shift* (2018), developed from their 1998 performance of *Dirty Work*, two performers Cathy and Robin sit on chairs for the duration of the performance speaking vivid descriptions to the audience of unfolding dramas set in a theatre somewhere. In this theatre nothing is unstageable, including many gruesome deaths, and the audience laugh at the detail and at the fateful misfortune of others. The humour it seems is found in the juxtapositions that collide with the impossible, the ridiculous with the real. Terry is sitting downstage left for the duration of the performance, not saying a word; she plays vinyl on an old record player; it's the sound of a piano. She looks on into the audience. The stories told are quite mesmerizing as is the witness (Terry) even when some stories are told in a way to make our stomachs turn, Terry continues to look on, witnessing us witnessing them. Death in this performance keeps on happening and yet no physical action happens on stage; it is the power of language and the way in which the stories of death are told, often playfully, that holds us in a spell, and the stories at times are very dark.

Artists play at constructing, inventing and imagining playful scenarios for performance. *How* performers play and *what* they play (within many processes) can be separated out distinctively within the terms of dark and deep play. While we are aware of the widely discussed discourse available on the many definitions of play, which relate to mimesis, gaming, recreational activities and so on, we understand how unfixed and broad the definitions of play are. See Huizinga (1998) and Turner (2014), to name a few theorists that define play's meaning and purpose. We acknowledge Caillois' (2001) assertion that play is a 'free and voluntary activity', that we have a choice when it comes to playing. But we also note that the idea of choice is complex within a creative process, as contested by Peters (2013) who elaborates on Gadamer, 'what holds the player in its spell, draws him into play, and keeps him there' (Gadamer, 2013, p.106). Peters unpacks Gadamer's notion that a game 'masters the players' and suggests that wanting (desire) leaves little room for choice when it comes to play. We suggest that under such a 'spell' there is a form of a Lacanian death drive operating. Absorbed in a game's conditions, the rules operate as tasks that we repeat, and in turn we create fictions that seduce us into a deeper level of engagement as if we are in play's magical thrall. It is not that we have no choice (as in being forced) when we play, but rather that desire takes hold of us and keeps us obsessed in a circular experience. When Etchells (1999) talks about 'play as a state in which meaning is flux', there is a realization when engaging in the messiest of improvisation games, the ones where we throw ourselves into the 'dark', that they are deeply transformative. Therefore, paying closer attention to the disruptive and subversive nature of contemporary performance making, the terms 'dark play' and 'deep play' are useful when thinking about a relationship between the death drive and play/ing. Richard Schechner suggests that dark play:

> Involves fantasy, risk, luck, daring, invention and deception. Dark play may be entirely private, known to the player alone or can erupt suddenly, a bit of micro play, seizing the player(s) and then as quickly subsiding – a wisecrack, burst of frenzy, delirium, or deadly risk. (Schechner, 2002, p.106)

Schechner also states that 'dark play subverts order, dissolves frames and breaks its own rules' (Ibid. p.107). He goes on to say:

> The gratification and thrill of dark play involves everything from physical risk-taking to inventing new selves, to engaging one's inner self, to communion with the Other. There is something excitingly liberating about this kind of playing. (Ibid., p.109)

Philosopher Jeremy Bentham first coined the term 'high stakes' within a footnote in his work *The Theory of Legislation* (1802):

> If you have just a thousand pounds and the stake is five hundred and you lose, your fortune is diminished by a half; but if you win, the gain is only a

third. If the stake is a thousand pounds, and you win, the doubling of the gain in fortune is not matched by a doubling of happiness; but if you lose, your happiness is destroyed. (Bentham, 2019)

Clifford Geertz adapted Bentham's observation on 'high stakes' (translated as deep play) as an activity that has cultural meaning. Richard Schechner relates the term 'dark' to 'deep' and brings our attention to the idea that deep play can be an activity where there 'is more at stake than material gain: namely, esteem, honor dignity, respect' (Schechner, 2002, p.106). Yet theories by Diane Ackerman suggests that feelings evoked by play that involve danger can sometimes arouse and give pleasure to those who take risks, and she describes deep play as:

> the ecstatic form of play. In its thrall, all the play elements are visible, but they're taken to intense and transcendent heights. Thus deep play should really be classified by mood, not activity. It testifies to how something happens, not what happens. (Ackerman, 1999, p.12)

Ackerman's accounts highlight the difference between 'rapture' and 'ecstasy', both of which, she suggests, are components of deep play. 'Rapture means, literally, being seized by force …, ecstasy means to be gripped by passion' (Ibid., p.15). Deep play is typically located in high-risk sports, intense and transcendental states, and can be prompted by a variety of spaces, 'both sacred spaces (natural) and ritualistic places (ceremonies to initiate humiliation)' (Ibid., p.15). It seems that the 'depth' of deep play lies more in an attitude towards and during a particular activity rather than the activity itself, since an extremely high-risk activity may not in itself induce intense sensations or engross a player to the point of transcendence. In fact, Ackerman writes of cycling (a particularly low-risk activity) as deep play. It is the player's motivation, mood, attitude and engagement that render the activity 'deep' and rewarding. In essence, deep play is not just associated with high-risk activity.

While it could be argued that dark play as a kittenish activity is a conscious act and the death drive is not, it is dark play's relationship to deep play that gives our theory its currency as relational to the death drive. We bring Schechner's *dark* and Ackerman's *deep* together in practice because we are interested in *what* happens within performance as well as *how* something happens.

Returning to our practice now, as the 'Gary and Claire' projects, we have observed that dark play is a particular activity that subverts rules, or 'normal' codes of behaviour, and in the case of creative works. For example, it is the fictional or non-fictional play frame that drives the narrative of a project, the persona and performer, or the rules of a performance (this is the *what*). Deep play is the attitude and experience of playing the performance (this is the *how*). Deep play is also attained from the engagement with and the experiencing of the process of performance making, the creation phase of writing and composing or material (the *how*). Yet the two terms slip and slide into one another: dark play's conscious impulse informs deep play's unconscious urge, or deep play's unconscious urge informs dark play's conscious interest; the two are in a symbiotic relationship.

Dark and deep play can be related to Freud's notion of the unconscious and his suggestion that human drives act as a hidden force behind immediate awareness: 'There are conscious and unconscious ideas, but there are also unconscious drive impulses, feelings, sensations, and so on' (Freud, cited in Frankland, 2005, p.59). We can imagine that dark play as a form of a Freudian death drive is to bind the conscious interest in creative work (subversion) with the unconscious play attitude (mischievous) in an environment akin to that of Freud's structural model of the psyche, the id. We are drawn to Freud's concept of the id because it contains the instinctual impulses – the destructive ones. As an example, Žižek makes an allegory of the id using the character Harpo Marx (Fiennes, 2006), where he suggests that the id, like Harpo, is a very troublesome, very playful and naughty clown. When you watch the Marx Brothers perform, Harpo's silent and mischievous character is humorous because of his animalistic, destructive qualities. And to imagine deep play as a form of the Lacanian death drive bound to the conscious obsession with creative idea (the passion) and to the unconscious commitment (Gadamer's spell) is to return to the creative journey and its circular process.

Reflecting broadly on both Freud's and Lacan's concepts, we bring in Nicholas Royle's idea that the drive 'is irreducibly bound up with the performative' (Royle, 2003, p.85); the death drive suggests action and, despite us, it gets on with things. In this context, it is worth reminding ourselves that artistic processes are composed of actions that result in many endings (lots of little deaths) because 'death is right inside us, working away busy as a mole all the time' (Royle, 2003). For us as artists, this is provocative territory. In Chapter 1, 'The Dead Rejoice', we pondered on the idea that death is within us, and Royle's 'busy mole' metaphor allows us to make sense of culture's fascination with the dead and permits us to take on the term death drive in a creative context, not necessarily a wholly destructive one. Rather we drift into this territory and circle around ideas and themes and we become spellbound. Royle thinks of the death drive in terms of a 'current flow' and renames it a 'death drift'. This flow could be thought of as a metaphor for the movement within contemporary dramaturgy, as the drift that occurs within a creative process between one idea that is associated with another. This observation draws us less into conflict between a Freudian or Lacanian interest in the death drive, and rather into the more exciting territory, a slippage between the two:

> By 'death drive', Freud does not understand the state of being dead but the wish to be so. This wish for the restfulness associated with death is part of Freud's pleasure principle, which drives us to repeat actions in different contexts and time that bring about states of rest and certainty. According to Žižek's recent interpretation, Freud's term denotes the uncanny persistence, not of death, but of life. (Lord, 2012, p.43)

Desire

There are so many things that we desire or, rather, there are so many things we think we desire, but there are so many things we do not know about desire itself. Desire is felt and but not fully comprehended. As a wish it can range from the basic materialistic, to the romantic, the sexual, the sadistic the destructive, to the fantastical, to the nonsensical. Desire is complex, it can be experienced as an intense conscious longing, painfully, or deliciously, out of reach. Desire can be led by irrational impulses, driven by unconscious wishes and according to Žižek certain art forms can even tell us *how* to desire because desire is something we cannot possibly (naturally) know. Of course, Freud once theorized around wish fulfilment in the *Interpretation of Dreams* (1890). He discussed the idea that dreams are desires played out in sleep, as a way to prevent them happening in reality and as means of satisfying desire. But the difficulty with this theory is that most dreams are just too bizarre, or too fragmented, jumbled up in sequence. How can they be taken seriously when last night I dreamt I opened the door to a giant gorilla? Freud's seminal work on dream interpretation enabled people to understand the complexities of their seemingly irrational desires through the interpretation of dreams. For in the dream, let us not forget, when we are in the dream, it seems perfectly acceptable to open the door to a giant gorilla, and at the time the fear and passion seem real. As sentient beings we feel in the dream, we have that uncanny knowingness of 'Ah yes, it's that giant gorilla that picks me up and takes me away'. Regardless of the surreal experience of the dream, the gorilla, at that moment, meant something. Moreover, upon waking, and even years after the dream it still feels like it meant something.

Desire most commonly has been something discussed in relation to sexuality:

> Anna Freud once said, in your dreams you can have your eggs cooked the way you want them, but you can't eat them. The implication is clear: magic is satisfying but reality is nourishing. The question is – and it is a question that has haunted psychoanalysis – are the appetites analogous? Is hunger a good picture for sexuality? Because if it isn't, if sexuality isn't akin to, isn't a form of feeding, then the consequences are serious. Indeed, we could reverse Anna Freud's formation and say that when it comes to sexuality it is the fact that you can't eat the eggs that makes them so satisfying. (Phillips, 2006, p.59)

And certainly, in waking life, when we imagine a place for fulfilled or unfulfilled desires it is psychoanalysis that 'describes what happens when we live as if our wishes can come true and what happens when we live as if they cannot' (Phillips, 2007, p.162). Therefore, it is easy to see how, over centuries, desire has been used to teach lessons in morality, as a warning to someone if a fantasy is lived out:

> The fact that the object of desire is a forbidden object; that what we most passionately want is what we certainly mustn't have. The medium of desire is enigmatic; and the object of desire is aversive. (Ibid., p.166)

Lacan's concept of desire is based upon 'dual and complimentary insist-ences' (Ibid., p.171). Lack makes 'self-conscious being possible; the object of desire is unnameable, essentially beyond representation – say; if you can name it is isn't what you want' (Ibid.). In other words, we think we know our desires, but the desires we think we know are a diversion to something that is forever out of reach, something much more enigmatic, it is something we are forever chasing. This is what keeps desire alive within us because we run the risk of losing the passionate feeling of desire itself as explored by Žižek:

> Desire is historical and subjectivized, always by definition unsatisfied, metonymical, shifting from one object to another since I do not actually desire what I want. What I actually desire is to sustain desire itself, to post-pone the dreaded moment of its satisfaction. (Žižek, 1997, p.80)

If the 'the object of desire is a fantasy' (Phillips, 2006, p.164), we can accommodate desire through the play. The common childhood games, peek-a-boo, hide and seek, have one distinct feature in common: they allow those taking part to perform/rehearse death through the playing out of it. 'From the child's egocentric perspective, what happens (in such games) is that the external world vanishes and then suddenly reappears' (Corr & Corr, 2012, p.370) (our interpolation in brackets). Playing games is exciting, rewarding, thrilling but games are also reassuring, we play to remind us that things end, so in the midst of fantasy you witness death over and over again without actually dying. The games we played in childhood enabled us to rehearse the experience of loss, and, more provocatively, desire as Royle's busy 'mole' is working inside us playing out the death drive as catharsis. In the game of sleeping lions, the lions lie as still as possible as if they are dead, and it is the 'waker's' job to stir up the lions, to bring them back from the dead. If you play the game as a lion you experience deadness; playing a corpse means you can experience the *as if* world, what it feels like to be dead. The waker's job is to make the lion move through non-physical contact, but most importantly to laugh. Dead lions wake up in fits of laughter. In this context, death and humour are linked because play is 'the main work of a child's life' (Ibid., p.371), and children are experts in playing dead. In the games where other children are involved, every participant, through the act of repetition, gets to experience the drama of what it is like to be fully alive and what it feels like to be 'death personified' (Kastenbaum, 2015, p.307). Playing dead is a desired activity as there can be no such literal experience of feeling what it is like to be dead. It is useful to note the importance of such dark play activities as cathartic, and, perhaps, it is also worth considering that playing dead satisfies the death drive's aim to continually desire. When we grow up, are we perpetually searching for what we have lost from childhood in the days where we played as active thrill seekers? Playing games test the limits of what is possible without any feelings of guilt or shame:

> Lethal violence has been a common theme in children's play through the centuries. As a child in the streets of New York, my friends and I played cops and robbers, sporting wooden guns armed with rubber bands. Medieval children brandished their stick swords as they replayed Crusader Saracen battles. (…) There is no relationship between killer and slain and, of course, no remorse. (Ibid., p.307)

Freud's famous anecdote of fort/da in his work *Beyond the Pleasure Principle* offers a complex and interesting set of interpretations in relation to play and death. Here he discusses, anecdotally, his observations of a child throwing objects away to disappear out of sight only for them to be returned to him, to throw them out of sight again, to be returned again (repeating the action). This behaviour, it has been argued, is both pain and pleasure (experienced through the process of repetition) for the child, where he 'masters a situation' (Freud, in Strachey, 2001, p.15). Through the observation of fort (gone)/da (there) play, Freud interprets a child's behaviour, and claims that the child's compulsion to repeat gives him more of an 'active' role in the game than a passive one. Freud offers many other interpretations too, suggesting that the child might be taking out revenge on the mother for disappearing/leaving him. Or that play allows the child to fulfil his wish of growing up. Or that frightening experiences in the child's life are played out on his friends as a means to experience pleasure. Ultimately, it seems, Freud suggests there is pleasure experienced in actively repeating traumatic experiences through play.

Paul Ricoeur suggests that these experiences of unpleasure are 'mastered by the means of repetition in play, by the staging of the loss of the loved person' (Ricoeur, 2008, p.286).

Examining Ricoeur's reinterpretation of the death drive as an idea of something creative, we can understand the drive's more imaginative, inspiring and human position in relation to desire:

> What is surprising is that the death instinct is represented by such an important function which has nothing to do with destruction, but rather with the symbolization of play, with esthetic creation, and with reality-testing itself. (Ibid., p.317)

Some animals play dead in order to escape the fate as prey. The opossum goes stiff, shows its teeth and froths at the mouth to put off its hunter. The animal is not really playing, as in a game, but surviving. The child is also surviving the reality that the end of something is inevitable. Yet more interestingly perhaps, returning to the idea that we play to sustain desire, the child is playing to keep excitation alive, as a constant form of satisfaction rubbing up against a perpetual imminent threat pursued in play. Playing therefore is a means to experience the death drive and the pleasure principle simultaneously:

> If pleasure expresses a reduction of tension, and if the death instinct marks a return of living matter to the inorganic, it must be said that pleasure and death are on the same side. (Ibid., p.319)

Roger Caillois' system of categorization for understanding the varied types of play-activity and the varying attitudes while playing can be explicated in the context of many fantasies; this includes improvised play and games where clear rules are established (see also Hind, 2010). Caillois suggests that play has two 'poles', *paidia* and *ludus*. *Paidia* represents all things childish, excitable and turbulent; it includes fantasy and improvisation. *Ludus* in contrast represents convention, rule-based play and formal structures within play. Caillois also theorized around the imaginary worlds encountered in play. For example, he draws our attention to the concept of the 'as if' where someone plays a role or pretends to be something else and where one draws upon an imaginary concept to play a game.

Some forms of play have what Caillois describes as the sentiment of 'as if' (Caillois, 2001, p.9) attached to it, so that make-believe and imagination are key to successful playing. He cites examples such as 'cops and robbers, horses, locomotives, and airplanes – games in general, which presuppose free improvisation, and the chief attraction' (Ibid., p.8). Imaginary play is a playing out of fiction and, unlike a netball match where the game is played for real, the 'as if' permits a place of endless improvisation and imagination, of a never ending 'as if'. Yet Caillois observes that 'the sentiment of as if replaces and performs the same function as do rules. Rules themselves create fiction' (Ibid., p.9). And let's not underestimate the complexity of play:

> One easily can conceive of children, in order to imitate adults blindly manipulating real or imaginary pieces on an imaginary chessboard, and by pleasant example, playing at 'playing chess'. (Ibid)

Splitting play into types we notice that ruled play (*ludus*), like a game of netball, is played with the pleasure of adhering to the set rules within that game of netball. Play in this context is not so separate from reality, because the game of netball is played for *real*. There is a documented result, a score. Most competitive sports operate in this way.

Yet, within the frame of free play, rules can be created, made and unmade and as the player wishes. We make up the rules as we go along in the midst of imaginary play, but we also have the freedom to break rules. In some cases, playing through 'as if', *paidia*, means we can play *as if* we are in the mode of *ludus*. For example, we remember our childhood dramas of the playground where we play out imaginary scenes and play a game of school where a player enacts a hierarchical position of teacher and in doing so creates their own very serious rules and gives the other person playing a detention. These games get more complex and abstract too. For example: *it is as if I am playing a game of school accepting my detention, when I suddenly drop down to the floor as if I am dead.* When the player is 'dead' there is an element of seriousness to this activity. The rules are clear; you play dead for as long as you can in order to try and deceive your partner to trick them into believing that you might actually be dead. This game of deceit of feigned death asserts a level of seriousness for a moment, and the power from the 'pupil' held over the 'teacher' as a punishment for dishing out a detention is apparent.

Caillois' subjunctive playing at playing (as if) theory has been developed further by Hind (2010) into what she names the *multiple as if* (the as if as if). Playing at playing at playing at … (the *multiple as if*) is a useful strategy for writing material because it encourages richly intertextual worlds that in some cases weave in the autobiographical.

Playing through the *multiple as if* in performance and through the lens of desire creates a series of romanticized hybridist situations, characters and places. The *multiple as if* queers identity within a romanticized space and, as a brief example, our character *Kong Lear*, appearing in Chapter 4, 'The Dead Ghost', challenges the patriarchy, dismantles the binary of male/female, human/non-human because *Kong Lear* is a hybrid of the Shakespearean character King Lear and the Hollywood beast King Kong performed as female who comes with a set of her own unspoken desires.

Desire is not just simply the motivation or the 'passion' driving the engagement in creative activity, it is a complex and provocative attitude, often slippery, contained in a drive that has similar qualities to dark play in its 'microplay' context where play is 'truly subversive' (Schechner, 2002, p.107).

Phillips suggests we can never understand our desires, or really know them. The paradox of desire is to experience the sheer in the moment ecstasy of something always remaining out of reach. We cannot reach our dreams; we only recall them.

Unheimlich/Uncanny

In 1919, Freud wrote an essay entitled *Das Unheimliche*, translated in English as 'The Uncanny'. Here he discusses unfamiliarity as uncanny, and he lists a range of different experiences that sum up examples of the term that theorists have since derived in different cultural contexts (as do we as practitioners in this chapter). His essay drew attention to the meaningful boundaries of the simultaneity of absence and presence, drawing attention to the idea that the reason things may feel unfamiliar (when in fact they are very familiar) is because they are suppressed. Freud's essay draws our attention specifically to the suggestion that the uncanny is to do with the 'theory of the qualities of feeling' (Freud in McLintock, 2003, p.48). Feeling in performance can be experienced in many ways: through the making of it, when you work from the gut feeling; in the playing out of performance when you perform something in you more than you know (character or part of self); or in witnessing the act of performance where you experience effect – watching performance stirs up emotion.

Kristeva writes in her seminal work *Strangers to Ourselves* on the uncanny and claims that 'The Foreigner is in me, hence we are all foreigners'. She discusses the term uncanny strangeness as:

> On the basis of an erotic, death-bearing unconscious, the uncanny strangeness – a projection as well as a first working out of death drive – which adumbrates the work of the 'second' Freud, the one of *Beyond the Pleasure Principle*, sets the difference within us in its most bewildering shape and presents it as the ultimate condition of our being *with* others. (Kristeva, 2002, p.290)

Rahimi discusses the Uncanny in association with themes and metaphors of 'vision, blindness, mirrors, and other optical tropes' (Rahimi, 2013, p.1). He further expands upon a series of examples that relate to 'alter egos, self-alienations and split personhoods, phantoms, twins and living dolls' as a list of uncanniness relating to the 'visual sphere' (Ibid., p.1). The uncanny is felt, experienced, hard to concretize, impossible to pin down, but nevertheless is encountered in the senses and arrives in many different forms. The uncanny is something that makes one feel strange a 'peculiar commingling of the familiar and unfamiliar. It can take the form of something familiar unexpectedly arising in a strange and unfamiliar context' (Royle, 2003, p.1). In simplistic terms, the uncanny is that hard-to-locate feeling we experience with *déjà vu*. It is a strange unfamiliar knowingness, a paradox hard to describe in words other than many variations on the weird or strange or eerie. The uncanny is the joyous feeling we attain at that moment of sheer coincidence as if there is someone else watching and mapping out the course of our lives, driving our fate or the course of a game. It is that deeply familiar feeling that returns upon waking: the residue of a dream, the one that you cannot quite recall haunting the senses all day. It is a smell that takes you immediately back to childhood. It resides in the 'jinx' when two children say the same word simultaneously and unexpectedly, experiencing the effects of telepathy. It is that feeling in a dream when you are inside the dream and where you know you are dreaming (lucidity). The uncanny sits and waits in the recurring dream as a reminder that the uncanny returns. It can also be experienced as something deeply unwelcome: that uneasy feeling when you walk in a place of unfamiliar territory, when you stumble into a part of a building and decide you do not like it and you have that feeling of being lost. The list goes on: descending stairs alone, underground shopping malls filled with unnatural light, the overwhelming feeling when driving past the giant cooling towers on the A1(M) motorway. The uncanny can be felt in the most negative of headspaces that might bring on a panic attack where all of sudden the world does not seem real at all. The uncanny is the friend of the existential crisis. The uncanny is also associated with the death drive 'bound up with the most extreme nostalgia (…) a compulsion to return to an inorganic state, a desire (perhaps unconscious) to die, a death drive' (Royle, 2003, p.2). Yet the uncanny can be exciting, playful, mysterious; 'it can also be a matter of something strangely beautiful, bordering on ecstasy' (Ibid.).

The uncanny resides in the imaginative; it exists in culture and, as a few examples of many, is associated with the disturbance one feels or sees in the presence of ghosts, zombies, monsters, the pantomime horse, papier mâché doppelgängers, free-floating soap bubbles. Interestingly for us, Freud considered the idea of the uncanny as 'represented by anything to do with death, dead bodies, revenants, spirits, and ghosts' (Freud, 2003, p.148). In fact, he discusses the idea that humans question the certainty of death, whether 'death is the fate of every living creature or simply a regular, but perhaps avoidable, contingency within life itself' (Ibid). This concept, Freud asserts, plays into the fact that human unconsciousness is 'unreceptive as ever to the idea of our own mortality' (Ibid). It seems that it is from within the experience of uncanniness of not knowing what it is like to be dead that we invent ghosts. The supernatural exists in culture because 'apparitions and ghosts represent that ambiguity and fill with uncanny strangeness our confrontations with the image of death' (Kristeva, 1991, p.187). But performance suggests many different interpretations of what death is. 'Above all, the uncanny is intimately entwined in language, with how we conceive and represent what is happening within ourselves, to the world, when uncanny strangeness is at issue' (Royle, 2003, p.2).

Psychoanalysis aligns to the human psyche on the basis that humans have a conscience; they have an id, ego and superego. It is rather exciting to imagine terrifying or playful possibilities of a functioning psyche driving the undead, the ghost, the inanimate object or the hybrid monster; this concept opens up myriad possibilities for writing performance and performing. The uncertainty of self we experience in life is personified in culture through varying interpretations of the non-human. In performance, we embody the anthropomorphic, the mechanical. Think of the ventriloquist's dummy and its cruel and sadistic tongue; the dummy's lack of moral conscience suggests the id is all that performs, and if the dummy is left alone, what is it capable of without its master? The dummy does not speak, the dummy is silent, but somehow it has a voice just the same. When we think about silence in general, the feeling one gets in those uncomfortable silences, or in the unnerving experience of deadly silence, we know that silence is the uncanny personified. In many ways, silence depicts what the uncanny does above and beyond language itself.

Making performance through the *multiple as if* (playing at playing at playing), diversifies the effects of the uncanny even further when there are several complex juxtapositions going on. Returning therefore to the terms dark and deep, deep play determines *how* a performance is played, not necessarily *what*; dark play is the *what*. Dark play is the rules in performance and is the power those rules hold (known or unknown) within performance structures. Expanding therefore on one of our previously mentioned ideas, dark play is a manifestation of the death drive. Deep play is the state attained within a process that operates within the drive itself, specifically when the drive is heading towards a 'jouissance' (mystical pleasure). It is the *how* and the *what, the dark* and the *deep* circling around each other that brings about the uncanny:

> Freud keeps coming back to the dark, (...) Darkness is a factor that stares us in the face, so to speak ... when it comes to considering the various dictionary definitions of 'heimlich' and 'unheimlich'. (...) Darkness is at least

implicitly involved in the crucial definition of the uncanny that Freud takes from Schelling; the unheimlich or uncanny is what 'ought to have remained secret and hidden but has come to light'. (Royle, 2003, p.108)

The Three Terms as a Death Drift/Drift Drive

The thematic interplay between three terms explored here – the death drive, desire and uncanny in the context of the dark and deep play – is wrapped up within the imaginary, poetic, creative and surreal and informs the dramaturgy as our 'Gary and Claire' conceptual psyche. We make sense of the terms in the reimagining of them, creating a logic for them to exist in many ways; they are found within the make-up of the personas that we have invented, reflected upon within the compositional structures of our writing practices and in the form and delivery of performance. Freud's death drive has been critiqued as an abstract concept, 'constructing death in terms of a drive will automatically distort the concept of death' (Razinsky, 2013, p.147). Playfully, our practice distorts Freud's abstract (distorted) concept, and we need to point out we are not psychoanalysts, but as artists we are rethinking psychoanalytic terms.

By reimaging for performance practice Freud, Lacan and Royle's concepts of the death drive (inanimate states, circling objects, drifts), and their relationship to desire and the uncanny, we propose our own named strategy for making and reflecting upon intermedial performance practice. We call it the Death Drift/Drift Drive (DD/DD).

Unpacking DD/DD

Death Drift (acknowledging and appropriating Royle's term as arts practice) is the concept, developing movement and attitude applied to themes in our practice relating to deadness and gives each work its overall quality. It relates to concepts of death in the non-destructive but celebratory sense, marking a life that once was in new ways (through ghosting or intertextual practices). It is when ideas are perpetually circling and when this circling sparks a drift occurrence and a subject moves into new territories, or when a subject or theme is appropriated within the *multiple as if* and worlds become distorted. It relates to dramaturgical processes of imagining, writing and producing work.

The Drift Drive is the fiction, rules and conditions within a creative process and performance where drift is an embodiment of desire, unfixed and moving in different directions, not preset to a particular course turning back on itself. The drive aspect here represents the momentum of energy fuelling the drift. It relates to the conditions set when performing the work or to the rules applied to various script/text formations.

The typographical solidus (or slant) within this abbreviation symbolizes the position play (dark and deep) takes in our thinking. The solidus (/) is less of a division and more of a slippage in thinking that symbolizes the idea that playing within these worlds produces the effect of the uncanny.

A Visual Metaphor for the DD/DD

If we think of a visual metaphor for the DD/DD, imagine a vista, a wide unobstructed space, a horizon; it could be dry and dusty or it could be green and manicured, up to you. Gradually, a zone of energy is forming, heat rises, there is a sense of something bubbling up, starting to churn around, it starts to take on a defined form as a mesocyclone. It is an idea drawing in images, text, material, until it defines its signature shape of a funnel. Once it is established, it is complete, nothing else goes into it. The matter is circling around and around (at this point you might want the artist Francis Alÿs to pick up his video camera and run into it). You are now looking at a very strong defined tornado and you should imagine the rotation as a circling movement of a Death Drift; this death drift will not leave an idea alone and it is playfully wreaking havoc through the constant circling activity surfacing its contents. Now close your eyes. Now open your eyes and you will see an uncanny likeness to the first tornado, only this one is a little finer, with more delicate qualities. Close your eyes and reopen and there is a spindly one with scraggy qualities. Repeat with the eyes and see a minikin one with cheekier qualities and one that is flipped over in the sky. All these twisters are doppelgänger versions of the original. If you close your eyes and open them once more, the vista offers multiple doppelgängers on the horizon. This spectacle experience is the drift drive; slightly epidemic, the driftness offers multiple versions of the first and they all contain their own little worlds, all slightly changed, and contain their own rules and conditions like a variety of stormy cocktails. They coexist in the landscape but are never fully anchored, like a buoy in the water, that has some play (slant/solidus) in their drift.

Kristeva once proposed that 'the drive is clearly an imaginary construction (we can neither see it nor locate it), but it is an essential one that enables the analyst to remain at the crossroads between the symbolic and the somatic' (Kristeva 1996, p.87). Kristeva's argument that the death drive is an imagined construct offers the currency to play on the idea of an idea. We claim a stake in the term and reinvent it as performance practice. Although as you will see in subsequent chapters we do call upon psychoanalysis from time to time, to theorize and contextualise some of our ideas, in each case, we may turn towards an alternative view in order to allow our readers to see how the psychoanalytic landscape has been challenged; but we do also acknowledge quite sincerely our interest in the ongoing importance and theorization of the unconscious which is what drives creativity in performance. What is original in our practice is the way we view our interests in the psychoanalytic model through the lens of dark and deep play as a useful creative conceptual framework, as an expanded dramaturgy, and as the psyche of our practice.

The three terms death drive, desire and the uncanny are not lost in the DD/DD; they are its qualities, entwined and circling around one other. But separating how we align psychoanalytic terms to performance might prove useful to understand how they relate in practice. For example, the death drive is rhythm and repetition, desire is passion and serendipity, and the uncanny is effect and phenomena that we (as performers or audience) experience in performance. Of course, by separating out the terms we can see how all three need each other; death drive strives to repeat so that sustained desire can be experienced in the senses as the uncanny.

Adam Phillips suggests that 'desire as a concept keeps something alive in psychoanalysis' (Phillips, 2006 p.166). We like to reframe this statement: death as a concept keeps something alive in performance and desire is the thing that 'works' within performance. Yet we cannot see or identify what 'works' because desire is that magic thing that happens during the throes of a creative epiphany; even when we are making performance that has been carefully structured 'desire is the queer form our unpredictability takes. Where intentions were, there accidents of pleasure shall be. Desire, (…), takes our pleasures to be happy accidents, and accidents will happen' (Ibid., p.177).

What is appealing about all of the terms desire, uncanny and death drive is that they form the romantic, tragic and the mysterious aesthetic embodied in all of our works. The subsequent chapters in this book will also reveal a fascination if not fandom towards the work of David Lynch because we do, as performance makers, tend to make work from a cinematic lens; the porosity between the cinematic and contemporary performance is inherent in our projects. Psychoanalysis is commonly used as a lens to discuss film theory, and many chapters in this book feature a Lynchian reference, style, or anecdote that can be traced back to some of the concepts explored in our work in relation to the three terms set out located in the DD/DD.

< Q U I C K · G U I D E S >

Title: Ghost Track (2011)

Where: Touring studio performance presented at Freud Museum London, Cisniadora Fortress Transylvania, Norwegian Theatre Academy, Aberystwyth University and State University New York.

Description: A solo performance that reimagines Act 1 Scene 1 of Shakespeare's King Lear mixed around a handful of part autobiographical part fictional monologues including anecdotes: A visit to the Freud Museum in London where the performer was bitten by Bobby the dog. A visit to her endocrinologist in relation to vocal chord palsy. A petrol station anxiety about avoiding a significant number on the petrol pump counter. The imaginary death of her dad.

Kit box: Public Enemy soundtrack. Nano pad. Lecturn. Microphone. Chair. Crown.

Commonalities: King Lear. Freud. Repetition. Ghosting.

Illustration 4 Quick Guide *Ghost Track*

< Q U I C K · G U I D E S >

Title: Kong Lear (2012)

Where: Weekly walking tour in the City of York. A Super 8mm film as a companion B-side to the touring show *Ghost Track*. Materials in a limited edition *Kong Lear Archive*.

Description: A weekly walking tour led by the hybrid figure Kong Lear (a hybrid of King Lear and King Kong as female). The tour was called *Gorilla Mondays* and it reimagined York as New York where Kong Lear was looking for a blonde, fighting with an exploding gas bomb and searching for a skyscraper to climb. York was also reimagined as the storm sequence in King Lear where tormented by the guilt Lear feels about the treatment of his daughters roars obscenities at them at the Three Cranes Pub. Lear roars on Parliament Street and roars against getting a quiet moment to herself and roars against the price of bitter. She catches her reflection of herself in a disused shop mirror and recognizes herself as beast.

We used the walking tour as a vehicle to create the Super 8mm film; a portrait of Kong Lear which was silent. Using intertitles, personal dream accounts and an outlandish skit about Kong Lear's visit to see Freud at his study and her encounter with his couch.

A gallery exhibition presented the film and other artworks; walking tour posters, window vinyl and hard copy film strips to view with an eye glass. *The Kong Lear Archive* collected together the script, the gallery ephemera, documentation of the walking tour, pages made from the intertitles and a sound effects list from the original 1933 film *King Kong*.

Kit box: Gorilla suit. Crown. Blonde wig on a fishing rod. Placard. Paper airplanes. Party poppers. Bugle.

Commonalities: Freud. King Lear. Crown. The Street. Gorilla Costume. Super 8mm film. Dreams. Ghosting.

Illustration 5   Quick Guide *Kong Lear*

Illustration 6 Charcoal sketch from 'death drawing' event *for Roy of the Dead/Day of the O* at the According to McGee gallery, York

4

The Dead Ghost

This chapter is composed as an intertextual weave of materials related to the *Kong Lear* projects, including an artists' talk for an audience with 'Gary and Claire' at Bar Lane Studios, York during the *Kong Lear Exhibition* in 2012. The interview is interspersed with the intertitles from the Super 8mm film *Kong Lear* to give a picture of what the silent movie reveals about the portrait figure. It follows with a discussion on the term ghosting in performance practice and concludes with a task for artists to write, play and perform solo material.

We might say that the ego stands for reason and good sense while the id stands for the untamed passions.
(Freud, in Strachey, 2001, p.76)

So, I go to see Freud. I have an appointment. I walk into his study and attempt to sit down on the couch. Freud says
'So, Kong Lear, tell me how you have been feeling'.
So, I say…

Kong Lear is a plethora, a rhizome, an ever-expanding horizon. It doesn't know when to stop, it breeds, it shifts, it moves – it appropriates, too, recycling images from the dream factory of Hollywood for its own errant ends. The great gift of *Kong Lear*, its generosity, is to offer us a different kind of dreaming, a dreaming without a head, a dreaming without a king, a dreaming without father, without a phallus. This is a performance that 'ecologises' psychoanalysis that reconfigures the city as a site of play, that replaces the lonely sadness of Oedipus with the baroque assemblage of Kong Lear. (Lavery, 2013)

Kong Lear is a figure. A hybrid of King Kong and King Lear as female who comes with her own story. As a project she features in *Gorilla Mondays* (2011) – a weekly walking tour through the city of York for a public audience, *Kong Lear* (2012) – a Super 8mm film, *The Kong Lear Archive* (2012) – a limited-edition box set of loose-leaf page artworks and *The Kong Lear Exhibition* at Bar Lane Studios, York (2012). Kong Lear as a figure has subsequently made an appearance in other works of 'Gary and Claire' including *Dream Yards* (2013–2018) and *Five Dead Acts, Five Dead Cats* (2015).

An artists' talk with Gary Winters and Claire Hind for the *Kong Lear Exhibition*, Bar Lane Studios, York 7/2/12.

GW: Good evening, thanks for coming!
This exhibition of *Kong Lear* is the second piece that Claire and I have worked on together, and I guess the initial thrust or drive was to make the film work. But given the opportunity to exhibit here at Bar Lane Studio's gallery allowed us to show some other elements, remnants or traces of things that came out of the whole process of making the film that also suggest ways in which the project can develop into other versions. The character of Kong Lear is something Claire had an idea for some years ago and it's also connected to a live piece that we collaborated on entitled *Ghost Track* created in 2011, now touring. We imagined that *Ghost Track* had a B-side that we named *Kong Lear*.

CH: *Ghost Track* is a solo performance about the complexities of the psyche. It draws upon a childhood fear I had of my father dying, and the imaginary sound I heard of him experiencing a heart attack in the middle of the night. It is a performance that also explores Act 1 Scene 1 of *King Lear* referencing the acts of repetition in this scene, specifically in the line from Lear to his daughter: *Nothing? Nothing will come of nothing speak again.* I was curious about the ritual element in this play where two of Lear's daughters, one by one, come forward and offer Lear a declaration of love so that they each may gain a share of his Kingdom. The third daughter, Cordelia, refuses. When I was a student I worked as front of house at the Haymarket Theatre and there was an amazing production of *King Lear*, directed by Helena Kaut-Howson and the actor that played Lear was Kathryn Hunter. She was a remarkable actress, very small, and she fully embodied this male figure brilliantly. I was intrigued, and I watched the production every single night for the whole run, it moved me; I was affected by the repetition of it, and by Kathryn Hunter's performance. Around about the same time in my life and for a number of years, I was interested in the 1938 film *King Kong* in a curious way, I was fascinated by the giant gorilla's hand and the idea of me, as tiny person, fitting neatly into it. Oddly, to me, it felt like a safe image. I used to dream about gorillas as a child.

I am Lear
I am Kong
Yeah, y'know, Kong
I am Kong Lear

GW: *Kong Lear* was just a slip of the tongue wasn't it?

CH: Yes, it was a slip in conversation with my friend Tony.

GW: So, there was a basic premise to merge these two fictional characters. When Claire mentioned this story to me during the making of *Ghost Track*, I found it a funny proposition, or image, which sparked lots of thoughts and conversations of how Kong Lear could emerge in York and how the architecture of York is perfect site for Shakespeare on the street here, the old buildings being a very convenient Shakespearian setting. Our first imaginings of Kong Lear were on the city walls near the University, we just had to imagine it out there – not far from where we were sitting and talking. Claire said that she had a Super 8 camera and one roll of film, which had been given as a gift. So that was a real beginning point, imagining it on Super 8mm film. In the end we shot ten rolls of film. The physical film itself is here on the light box in the exhibition, a catalogue of what we have got, material-wise. Practically, it was transferred to digital and the film we made was on Final Cut Pro on Apple Mac. When you watch the film, you will notice that we've tried to keep with a very rudimentary and amateur, even home-movie feel. And it's also very much about using this old technology, in comparison to recent technology, where it somehow has kind of limits, provides a limiting device – or things that can't be undone or redone very easily. For example, in this camera bits of crap get caught in the gate or on the film and when the film is transferred to digital there's all sorts of rubbish on the frames: hairs, bits and bobs, dust, so we used it and named it blip crap. And then there is a three-week process, to shoot, to get it developed and then transferred. So, we quite liked the idea that we'd shoot something for a process that takes time to come back to and then whatever arrives in the post is what you've got to work with. You can't just rush out, as you could do with digital, and go 'we'll re-do that shot'. I think that's quite nice, y'know that there's contingency within that similar to a stream of consciousness writing exercise, when you decide that what you get from a process is what you will take forward and work with.

So, some of the background questions in our heads as we started to plan the film in relation to both King Kong and King Lear were: What do these two stories throw up, where are the clashes and what would happen in York to generate the material for the film? Is it some kind of narrative, or is it documentation from the live event?

I have something to say

CH: At first Gary and I were thinking about going out onto the streets and just filming and hoping that people passing would just take part and we'd say, 'Would you like to take part in this scene?' But actually, Gary proposed the idea and vehicle of a walking tour, of the type that already exists in York, for tourists. So, we went on a ghost walk to see how they operated and decided to map our own version of a city walk for the character, and to make simple connections between *King Lear* and *King Kong.* I had a meeting with the city council and they were really supportive and they said: 'We've got the number of the local bus tour company and you could get Kong on a bus, or on the boats' and so Gary and I walked round the city and said Kong Lear could go on the roof, or could climb the wall and suddenly there was massive potential for images to emerge. But, it was very clear that our intention was to move the idea away from being a gimmick and establish another reading of it.

GW: I think it's very easy to fall into gimmick when you just have the costume. As you could see there was nothing too fancy about it, the gorilla costume was ordered from Amazon and then we made the decision to have the plastic toy crown. The image is taken a bit from the Peter Brook film version of *King Lear*, with Paul Scofield, where he wears a black furry collar, which is quite gorilla-like. We stitched the head of our costume on the back so it's like a hood, but also to build up the collar area.

So, we were walking, taking recces around the city, going to all four gates. I don't really know York very well, so Claire was showing me round some of the potential sites, some very touristy, commercial and central sites, and other residential areas that are within the city walls and the ring road that runs around it. But we didn't want to develop a strange mascot, instead we thought of the opportunity to use an established mode of talking, an established mode of being and an image, and somehow that was an important part of the fabric of the place. *Kong Lear* was not the usual sort of tour in York – it was free for a start!

We took a model of a 40-minute, five-stop tour. We knew we wanted to start from somewhere central, a busy place where there are buskers or street performers, markets or protests, some kind of meeting place. So, beginning at Parliament Street, we headed to the vision we first had of *Kong Lear* being on the city walls, and in a conceptual way we played on a couple of through lines from the two stories: specifically when Kong, while on Skull Island, is captured and walled in, and in Act 2 of *King Lear* where the King is ousted from his kingdom from the safety of the walls and heads out toward a wild natural world. So we made this journey from the centre of town to the edge of the city and we found a series of little stopping points making connections with the film and both the stories. As Claire said we didn't want to remake the scenes per se and part of our process was to look at a bunch of related things – the Peter Brook version of *King Lear* and cultural theory around *King Kong*. When we had the shape of the walk, we would write the content of tour. We decided to make the tour each Monday in November with two tours a day, as one way of generating the material for the film. We named the tour *Gorilla Mondays* and I designed the posters and had them screen-printed for a handmade look and a stylised theme, with crowns and skulls, three figures and gorillas. We placed them on the City Council noticeboard and they accumulated over the weeks. You could see the sense of event building and the iconography developing, the posters referencing a cityscape that is both York and New York.

I am happy
This is what I want
I want to meet

I must have conversation
I can be carried
I need a basic place to eat, to drink and to meet
I need to break Freud

CH: Each of the five sites supported our ideas for merging the two figures, particularly when thinking about *King Kong* existing in *King Lear's* psyche. We regularly visited an empty shop that had a large mirror on the outside. Here Kong Lear looked into an image of herself and reflecting upon madness. In Shakespeare's Lear, the King begins to see clearly through his madness, so we were working each site to merge the circumstances of the initial characters. King Lear dies at the end of the play heartbroken from the death of his daughter, and from the guilt he feels about his treatment towards her. King Kong falls from a great height after being hunted down in New York, in search of the woman (human) he loves or is possessed by. We asked *how do those stories merge and what happens when they do merge?* We asked *how do you write a tour for the streets, how do you take people along on the tour?* We thought about street language and merging it with bits of Shakespeare, generating our own material and our own bits of logic to develop this new character. We realized that people in the city started to expect us each week and we became part of the city.

GW: Yeah it is interesting, just over four weeks of activity and by the third or fourth week we had people stopping us and asking, 'What is this? What are you actually doing?' It is interesting when you persist from day one week one – imagine the Purple Man who resides as a living statue on Stonegate on his first day, people may have thought 'Is that a good idea?' and he must have thought it was because he went back daily, and there he is, years later – part of the fabric of the place. Or, think of Trevor Rooney, one of the ghost walkers, if you do something for a day it is odd, if you do something for 30 years it's a job. Cities are habitual.

We would stop outside one of our sites, the Three Cranes pub, and we would talk about the three daughters in *King Lear* while referring to the sign of three cranes as *the sight of devilish things* and drinkers from the pub would come out for a smoke and laugh. They formed the backdrop for the site. We'd see the same people week on week and they became our friends, they were expecting us. And they quite enjoyed us. It was very nice to feel that we'd become part of the city and what began as a strange occurrence became the norm. We're thinking November should become *Gorilla Mondays* every year.

I am happy
This is what I want
You have not brought me what I want
I did not expect that
This place is not what I want
I know when one is happy and when one is not
You have not brought me what I want

CH: Something that played on my mind with the two characters is their obsession with the female. Lear is obsessed with his daughter's decision and can't get past that, and Kong is obsessed with a tiny blonde who arrives on his island. Richard Wade our production assistant made a fishing rod with a blonde wig on the end – a wig whipper – to place on the head of a willing participant to then whip off quickly during our *looking for a blonde* tour. It didn't matter who it was, if it was a guy or girl, or a bollard, Richard would carefully lower the blonde wig on somebody, or something, and Kong Lear would perform the text from where the King is reunited with his daughter: *Come, let's away to prison, you and I will sing like birds in the cage.* This sense of play filtered through the conversations we had with people on the streets. On the last tour taking the audience and their conversations with us, we ended up at the store Go Outdoors on Foss Island, note, not Skull Island, and met Chris the climbing instructor. Kong Lear had the task of climbing the professional climbing wall in costume and with crown. It was here that she fell from a great height.

It's all very...
I'm finding it hard to...
...err

GW: What we've produced in the film is a portrait. We didn't want to make some half-narrative or remake of the film or play, instead re-use of some of the texts. Some of those texts mutated from the basic structure that we started from and it was the matter of writing through what we had to create the portrait of Kong Lear. Some shots that we chose are just the nice shots. You can't get away from the nice quality of the Super 8 film and y'know those happy accidents of light that create certain moods. Sometimes you just have to work with what you have, when the light is all right, or when a reframe section doesn't immediately appear to fit in.

Away from the walking tour, we got some really great shots right across the city with Claire. The bit where the dream texts scroll up the screen, that is a whole section filmed on the Mansion House roof. But when the film came back they were completely bleached out, there was nothing, apart from a ghostly figure. So, you just sort of take it on and see how it can fit in. I played with jump cuts too and, as if a cameraman using a cinematic lens, invited Kong Lear to look directly down the barrel of the camera. Yet at other times filmed as if Kong Lear is being observed, or the camera isn't there and she is in a very private space, all this merged with the filming of the city's green spaces, its leaves and textures.

As well as working with what we had, we were quite interested and enjoyed working with the intertitles. They were originally used in silent movies to move the narrative on, to join the dots between the visuals and narrative. Intertitles are a very potent, creative space to work with and can bring out the voices, maybe it's the unconscious speaking, maybe it's the filmmaker speaking, and maybe it's spoken by the footage. It does the job of moving us through the portrait. I like the parts where the intertitles acknowledge the camera and the moments where they acknowledge the audience. And the look of Kong Lear, she is gorilla-like but with heavy eye make-up, like an actress in silent film. We selected shots that were beautiful, evocative, head and shoulders shots, to bring out the qualities of the person and what cannot be seen. The intertitles are integral to that, and when we do this it is not clear if this is Kong Lear thinking or, if it is what the filmmakers are saying. So we play with that slippage, we tease and take it wildly away from anything to do with the image, just like the Freud joke and the dream scenes.

I remember my untamed days
I have these, erm, er…
I am having such, er…
I need to tell, …erm, …
I've got to, …to…
To er…, what's
What's… what's that up there?

CH: We were thinking about dreams and how they relate to a plot device of a deus ex machina, when the narrative doesn't seem to be able to fix itself, when people are in trouble and you can't envisage a getaway, where all of a sudden, an unexpected shift happens, and it ends. Sometimes dreams are able to shift the narrative but in strange contexts. In this sense we began to realise we were circling around many ideas, and that we were ghosting some of the ideas we had in live studio show and translating them into a walking tour performance being created for the purpose of a film. And in this process of circling around ideas and the images that blended King Lear, King Kong, my dream, my memory of Kathryn Hunter's Lear, we were creating a world, a mini universe for these ideas to make sense, I suppose a bit like a dream, or a place where ghosts hang out together.

GW: As an editing and writing process we planned the order of shots, intertitles and sections. We edited and constructed collaboratively on the computer as an immediate piece of work. The finished edit is designed so that it can be shown on a loop and viewers can dip in and out and find the repetition between some of the words. For this exhibition we were keen on presenting the actual object of the film itself, and have formed the light box, to tie into the idea of different representations of scale. So, we've got the scale of the raw film that shows tiny images captured as little worlds burned onto the frames and, there are looking glasses to view each individual frame. This works alongside the projected image of Kong Lear seen larger than life. There is also the window text cut out vinyl, using the script of the *Gorilla Mondays* walking tour, where we stopped at the scale model city outside York Minster looking down on the tiny world and referencing different activities that had happened during the tour.

Now, where, …er, …erm,
erm…
er, er, er, errughhr!

CH: We had a really professional walking tour, business cards, a huge placard and a film crew. We had matching fleeces, we were very good, and Richard was the sound composer, similar to his role in *Ghost Track*. Richard collated sounds of the city that you can hear separately on the old 'skool' cassette recorder with headphones. We were interested in the ideas of the id in relation to the psyche and discussed the idea that the id is silent, referencing Žižek who talks about the Marx brothers' character Harpo as the mischievous, naughty, playful but silent one. We wanted a role for the sound to feature in this exhibition but separate to the film. Richard used the sounds of the city, including buskers' jazz. Every week the buskers appeared on Parliament Street and we didn't want to upstage them, and when they realized that we started the same time there was a bit of healthy competition. One week, they let us go first which was nice. Richard also bled in some of the material recorded from *Ghost Track* along with sound effects created in response to the 1938 *King Kong* feature film.

Y'know I dreamt that I was small enough to fit inside a butter dish and I was put inside and delivered to a lady in a shop. There was nothing for sale in the shop.

Questions were opened out to the audience:

Q: I wonder, King Lear is obviously a proud old man who is dependent on his daughter's love. So why did you decide to make Kong Lear a woman?

CH: To playfully take ownership of the two characters who both have beasts inside of them. The power of both Lear and Kong are frightening, dominant, so playing them as a female hybrid was appealing, I wanted to distort them and the idea of them.

Y'know, I dreamt that there was a knock on the door. When I answered it there was a gorilla who picked me up and took me away, I tried to scream but nothing came out.

Y'know, I dreamt that I had seven dads and one of them was a ghost.

Q: So, do you see it as quite a feminist piece?

CH: I do, yeah, and with a sense of celebration, a reference to many actors that have played Lear before. Gary and I were very happy to research the male actors that have played Lear and ghost them. Ghosting is a process that we often work with to imagine and make personas, so in this process I have ghosted actors who have played Lear such as Scofield, Olivier, Briars to name a few, along with Kathryn Hunter, the first British woman who took on Lear in 1997. When Kong Lear was performing on the *Gorilla Mondays* tour she ghosted Scofield's Lear in Brook's (1971) film, calling upon his deep voice that bellows angrily at his daughters, and imagined herself with his beard. So, yeah in a way I'm taking control of that space that has been dominated for centuries, but through a tone of endearment and that's the nice thing about it, because it is not a parody, but my own attitude toward the actors' performance of Lear.

I can't stop thinking about you.

Q: It occurred to me watching the film, that a lot of your work is involved with using technology that is limited in some way. Are you using constraints to generate material and where is play located in constraint?

CH: I've got a six-year-old daughter and she loves to free play but moreover replay, shifting happily into play with rules that she establishes. There's something paradoxical about play that's free, it's still bound by rules and there's something attractive in art making when you are writing within constraints, it is generative and it offers many possibilities. When you set a rule and the rule is apparent then the writing fits into that and creates complexities in material.

GW: It's a different kind of work, when you've got to work with limits, I recognise if it's limitless and there's creativity in both situations. But I think it's nice to use limiting devices if only to find the things that break the rule. And I think what we've done here with the intertitles is write the film between the visuals, and find a convenient, playful space where we can create some interesting text work.

I know when you are here and when you are not.
I want to meet
I must have conversation
I can be carried
I need a basic place to eat, to drink and to meet
I need to break Freud
I should…
I will…

Q: I really enjoyed the camera shots. Now, the synchronistic relationship was that intentional? I mean when Claire starts talking at people; they are the bits that I thought were really funny.

GW: Yeah, what we wanted to get the public in. We were interested in some of the life from the city blending into the film. There is an elderly lady with a shopping bag and then this character of Kong Lear walking along beside her. Those references with someone simply there in the city and in a costume reminds me of a Charlie Chaplin impersonator I saw in Covent Garden and he was amazing. People would go about their business and like a shape-shifter they were absorbed into his world. He would turn to people with shopping bags, it became this whole situation of him just waving his hands and miming. People were really amused and were never offended by what he was doing. The image stayed in my head, y'know of him just playing with space, playing with the narrative, the movements.

So, I go to see Freud. I have an appointment. I walk into his study and attempt to sit down on the couch. Freud says:
'So, Kong Lear, tell me how you have been feeling'.
So I say:
'Well, your couch is far too small'
'Is that a reference to your childhood do you think?'
'No, I mean, the couch is far too small for my ass.'
'Do you think that your inability to sit on my couch, that you view the couch as small, is a reference to your childhood?'
'No, look here, look it's tiny look, it's Lilliputian, look at it, it's pee wee. I cannot fit onto your couch.'
Freud stops writing in his notebook, leans forward and slowly says to me,
'Ah, so what you are saying is that, what you are doing unconsciously is, letting me know this has something to do with your childhood.'
Enraged I kick the desk, hurl up a phallic figure and throw it through the window, I pick up his bookcase, stamp on his typewriter, and with my bare hands snap his couch in half, and I roar the creatures Ahhhhhowwwwcchhhhh!
And I roar against the weather and all of the insinuations. I grab Freud, pick him up, smash through the door, take him outside, uproot a tree and chew on his leg.

Q: I'm just really curious where the phrase 'I need to break Freud' came from?

CH: Well I talk a lot about Freud in *Ghost Track* and a fated visit to the Freud Museum. Gary and I became so interested in this house, his couch and heard stories of people crying at the site of the couch on their first visit. Also, there's a tension in the desire to work with the psychoanalytical model, there is something very attractive about psychoanalysis, it's creative, but there's also something slightly curious about my position as a female that sits within the whole symbolic order. You know that bizarre idea that women are supposedly 'lacking' and all that. We also like the play on words, and of course we also love the idea that Kong Lear would probably like to chew on Freud's leg.

I know when one is here and when one is not...
I know when she is here and when she is not...
I know when is happy and when one is not...
I know when one is dead and when one is not,
she's as dead as earth,
lend me a looking glass.
She's gone forever.

GW: We must *break Freud* in terms of the primal animal thing within Kong and then break it as in understand it.

Y'know I dreamt that I was in a lift that took me to different floors.

On one floor there was a giant swimming pool, on another a really expensive restaurant, on the bottom floor the doors opened and I was at a petrol station in the year 1970. So I filled up the tank and drove off.

Q: A lot of your text. especially read by Kong Lear on the tour. is very powerful, and you talk about how being female you embody these two male characters. I have been on the tour and there's a real presence when you are taking the group around, you're in charge. Yet when I watch the film I see this real vulnerability about you and I was just wondering if that was intentional? Or, it's just the solidarity of you, you're the only one being filmed, really, and I just wanted to know if that was intentional.

GW: The shots at the start and the end are very melancholic, wandering through the leaves, you are not sure if it's early morning or late evening with the sun low in the sky and not many people around. Yeah, we were aware of that, that it is slightly romantic even. We try and flip between the shots in the heart of the city where's she's got the clipboard, and the other more 'private' moments, away from the centre, there's strength in both and they complement and start to build up a sense of character, or different sides to her. In one shot you see Kong Lear lying down in the leaves, as if she is dead, or rather she could be playing dead. There is something quite powerful about this image because she is covered in the leaves she previously rolled in, her stillness is affective because it offers up a feeling between play and tragedy.

I know when one is
This is not my kingdom; this is where I come to finish things
I am Kong Lear

Ghosting as an Arts Practice

From a childhood dream to the awakening of that dream in adult life, ghosts 'reveal something of the enigma of everyday life … the everyday is like a ghost – secretive, ungraspable, yet with an acutely felt presence – and is itself beset by ghosts' (Banco & Peeren, 2010, p.xiii).

Drawing upon the idea of the enigmatic presence of the ghost in performance, we return to the term 'ghosting' from Chapter 1, 'The Dead Rejoice'. Herbert Blau's actors found themselves, when ghosting, 'thinking through Hamlet as if Hamlet were thinking' through them. This state of mind is further articulated to his actors:

don't characterise Polonius, *assume* Polonius, as in an animal exercise one does not imitate a cat but seeks the cat within so that some *idea* of the feline appears. The assuming, is, however, heuristic, a furthering, part of the ghosting. (Blau, 1982, p.217)

Blau's actors worked through the qualities of 'hauntedness'. They concerned themselves first and foremost with the physical and perceptual approach to the actions each actor created so that the 'remembered characters are dismembered: parsed quartered drawn refracted, suggested and alluded to through the qualifying presence of each actor' (Ibid., p.216).

Many contemporary performance groups ghost others as a way to remember or pay homage to a performance that has influenced them greatly in their lifetime. For example, the Chicago-based company ATOM-r cite through performance, the images and movement from artists they have been inspired by, by way of contextualising their own practice. In their work *Kjell Theøry*, featured as a performance at the international symposium *Queering Ritual* at York St John University 2017, we witnessed many ghostings. As one example, performer Justin Deschamps dances Meredith Monk's work *16 Millimetre Earrings* while another performer, Colin Roberson, mimics and menaces this performance by ghosting the dance of Justin, who is ghosting Monk. ATOM-r deliberately learn an iconic performance work but bring it into their own conceptual space and make a further commentary on its position in their practice by ghosting their ghost. Not all ghosting is mimicking and menacing but ghosting is an attitude towards the material being ghosted. Ghosting is both a conceptual and performed practice. ATOM-r's *Kjell Theøry's* augmented reality performance jux-taposes Alan Turing's mathematical descriptions of nature with algo-rithmic mutations of Guillaume Apollinaire's 1917 play *The Breasts of Tiresias*. This blending of two ideas – a lifetime's work and a surrealist play – is framed by ATOM-r's genderfluid spectacle, 'staged as a queer fertility ritual between physical and virtual worlds' (ATOM-r; Jeffery 2017).

In conversation with Mark Jeffery, director and collaborator with ATOM-r, we asked him to describe his practice of ghosting with the company:

> In ATOM-r we work with a number of sources that are historical, working with queer figures in history, rural rituals, historical texts that are cut up and processed through code and the machine. These sources are ghosted onto and into the performance space over numerous rehearsals where we attempt to embody, overcome and take on the ghosts of the past that we are resuscitating. We attempt to conjure the past into the living to cast the sources back into the room and create echoes of bodies long gone, to live and be between them. To understand the histories we are working with, we have to embody and become them. We have to learn to create new spaces for these sources to exist together, sources that should not be together. How do you open a window for the dead to leave or to return? (Jeffery, 2017)

Ghosting is also a way for ATOM-r to look at and honour a source, to inhabit and live within it:

> It is a way for us to exhume the dead and put decaying material onto our bodies like a well-worn garment left in the back of your wardrobe. The garment is worn, has holes, is smaller or larger than when you first wore it, it is torn, stained. In ghosting we attempt to have a conversation between then and now. It is a practice to recover, to think of the material as artefact, as a relic, as alive. We return to recreate the encounter, always from a place of ritual, care, attention and proximity to be close and closer. Ghosting allows for us to channel the historical figure, whether that be Alan Turing, Samuel Steward, or the fertility May Day ritual of the Padstow Obby Oss. (Jeffery, 2017)

Comparatively, our practice of ghosting specific figures (both fictional and real) is creatively productive. All those we channel are weaved into the composition of imagined written or scored material, that in turn creates a specific project which we then go on to ghost in other mediums. In other words, we ghost our own projects, so they may have a long and complex life.

To give an example of how we began this process of ghosting we return briefly to our first work together, *Ghost Track*. This work is a scripted piece for a solo performance performed by Claire about the complexities of the psyche, a semi-autobiographical performance centred around Act 1 Scene 1 of Shakespeare's *King Lear*. It was inspired in part by the 1983 film *Ghost Dance* directed by Ken McMullen specifically with reference to the way in which ghosts are discussed by Derrida as a paradox within the technological experience. In the work, Claire ghosts a performance of Peter Brook's (1971) filmed version of Act 1 Scene 1 of *King Lear* and makes a point of repeating the text: 'Nothing? Nothing will come of nothing speak again', while she gives a descriptive account of what happens in Brook's stark, existential adaptation of Lear. Within this moment, which is repeated several times throughout the show, Claire interrupts to deliver a stand-up comedy routine about her desire to have seven dads (and seven penises) where she details a fictional visit to the Freud Museum and recalls an anecdote about that time the ghost of Freud popped out of the tap of the sink in the bathroom. This stand-up routine is interspersed with autobiographical material about Claire's anxiety about losing her voice (she suffers from left vocal-cord palsy), and how, as a child, she used to imagine, on a regular basis, the sound of her father dying. The textual composition of *Ghost Track's* script was written through a process of ghosting. It is a repetitive braid of three stories that keep returning to a core text; our description of Brook's Lear which we imagined operating structurally as the chorus of the show. This chorus, however, as much as it repeats the same words, gradually changes across time as we subtly reveal new information about Act 1 Scene 1 of Brook's Lear and on each return. Revealing the developing narrative in stages by repeating the script and returning to it with added (or erased) words, sentences and actions, keeps the audience tuned into the unfolding scene. This technique of repeating and revealing as a form of ghosting in writing practice, is not far removed from how Ruby Cohn observes Beckett's work:

> Beckett's philoprogenitive repetitions repeat with a difference, reflecting backwards and forwards within each work as well as in the entire oeuvre – what I call ghosting. *A Piece of Monologue*, for example … points to three accounts of matches lighting the oil-lamp, but the third description actually replaces the three matches with a spill, and it is therefore ambiguous in the fourth reference, 'Lights lamp as described,' as to *which* light ghosts the narrated action – match or spill. Any Beckett scholar will recognize these molehills are mountains. (Cohn, 1993, p.7)

We composed the intertitles for the film *Kong Lear* in a very similar way, slowly revealing the ambiguous phrases but heading towards the joke about Freud. In fact, the intertitles of the film *Kong Lear* don't move the narrative along but rather speak on behalf of what is silent in the film, the id. Kong Lear as a portrait of an id, harbours a secret and this is a very appealing aspect of the film, as if haunted, she has her own ghosts. *Kong Lear* is:

> a tale full of frustration, anxiety that strays into the space of tragedy. 'I need to break Freud', the intertitles say twice just before the Freud text appears. The repetition of the 'I need' statement is key: it suggests some

desperate imperative to emancipate oneself, to break the shackles imposed by the Freudian hermeneutic, that Oedipal triangle that relates everything back to childhood, back to the narrow topology, the violent geometry of Mummy, Daddy, Me. Ultimately, the tragedy of Freudian and Neo-Freudian analysis is that everything is already predetermined, written in advance, scripted by the deterministic laws of Freudian theory. And, indeed, I wonder if this is one of the reasons why the film, with its washed-out colours, its fading light, its portrayal of a diffident lonely Kong Lear, seems so melancholic, so sad. (Lavery, 2013)

Turning our attention now to the physical embodiment of a practice, ghosting is not a case of simply recalling and parodying the gestures or mannerisms of the person you are ghosting purely as imitation. It is important to note that when in the process of ghosting, you are not literally hoping the audience will spot or identify who you are becoming or what you are ghosting, this is not the aim, the audience will see their own ghosts. We did not set out to make *Kong Lear* so that people may recognise what we had ghosted from the live show *Ghost Track*. Rather, the ghosts that we conjure may be familiar but equally unfamiliar.

Ghosting is a complex process of the *multiple as if*, playing at playing from self to other, where we attend to specific qualities that we remember about the actor (or character) that we are ghosting. In other words, we perform a residue of a chosen performance or performer, and our own approach to their work brings about a certain personal quality of performance which is driven by what we desire in them. We take on the ghosts that sit somewhere between our desire to embody an actor's previous performance and our attitude towards that desire. Ghosting is also about adopting an attitude towards the person(s) being ghosted, to the state of mind one attends to when performing. We may be obsessed with the person being ghosted, we may feel a frustration of that person's work, or we may want to remember through affection a scene they have performed and have a go at it ourselves, but in our own way to suit the concept of the work we are making. The nostalgia felt of other performances is sentimental and driven by passion, but we don't repeat performances to keep nostalgia in the romantic camp, but to shift its course and original aesthetic.

Our ghosting approach avoids, where possible, the cliché of direct impersonation. Our intention with the ghosting process in *Kong Lear* was to blur the signifiers of male and female, human and animal, and blend them to offer new ways of thinking about a portrait figure. When the patriarchal figures Freud, King Kong, King Lear, are brought into the female body and queered through autobiography (Claire's dream), Claire takes them on in her own terms, rather like getting into a playful fight with the monsters. 'The challenge for feminists in theatre is to wrestle with those ghosts in a way that brings the dynamics of such ghosting to light' (Schneider, 2013, p.23). The practice we engage in moves beyond a pure mimicry for the sake of a gimmick and into a playful and complex experience of hybridism. And we concur with Schneider as she continues to make the point that 'effort should not be made to banish ghosts, to find some pure, unghosted originary ... but rather to summon the ghosts, to bring them out of the shadows and into the scene where they already exist, to make them apparent as players' (Ibid.).

Kong Lear's intertextual position in our practice relates directly to ghosting as a concept, you give something an afterlife, a distorted version of some memory of an original, and it has multiple possibilities of returning again and again in different forms.

When we opened up a concept and worked at it, returned to it and kept circling it as a Death Drift/Drift Drive (DD/DD), we experienced familiarity of the material (after visiting and revisiting it many times), which began to make it unfamiliar and uncanny. Ghosting is phenomenological, to experience it as a practice is to *feel* the presence and the residue of some past, to strangely encounter something that is forever out of reach. In this sense, performance can feel haunted by the presence of some enigmatic otherness hard to pin down. Therefore, we can appropriate Blau's phrase 'we found ourselves thinking through Hamlet as if Hamlet were thinking us' and apply that to Freud; we found ourselves thinking through Freud as if Freud was thinking us. What is empowering about this idea, is that in our worlds Freud begins to think differently, through the eyes and the bodies of performance makers and therefore we can say Kong Lear 'realised that Sigmund Freud needs us more than we need him' (Lavery, 2013).

Creative Task: Ghosting

Conceptual Framework

This project can happen in stages across a few workshops, or if you have materials at hand, it could happen across a one-day workshop.

Discussion in small groups:
Carlson's term 'ghosting' implies that previous creative acts throughout history are repeated as hauntings. Referring to the discussion on Carlson's notion of ghosting as something encountered (in drama) that is identical to something that has been encountered before (in drama's history), what does it mean to ghost a ghost in solo performance?

Warm-up preparation:
In a group circle each of you remember an actor, performer or dancer's performance (from any medium) by walking into the circle and sharing. Take your time, give respect to those you are ghosting. Discuss how through ghosting you are not simply imitating but bringing something of yourself to the ghost.

Solo work:
Create a 3-minute solo performance describing a memory of watching performance (from any medium), using some of the practice from above. Draw attention to detail of the performer's delivery using both speech and action. Improvise to begin with and contextualize your story of the performance. When improvising, be clear of your tone and quality of your delivery, from your own appreciation and interest of the person you have chosen. For example, you may remember:

Robbie Coltrane jumping up and down in a trance-like state when he is showing his new-found friends how to dance like a snake in the (1983) film *Ghost Dance*, by Ken McMullen.

Laurence Olivier performing Hamlet (1948) and speaking delicately and fondly to the skull of his jester Yorick.

Justin Deschamps performing Meredith Monk's movement in *16 Millimetre Earrings* in ATOM-r's performance of *Kjell Theøry*.

Offer detailed accounts of the memory delivered in the third person, then play at delivering the story in the second person followed by the voice of the first person. This will allow you to experience very simple but effective ways of addressing the audience and draw attention to your significant relationship to a cultural moment. Attempt to offer a description that sets the scene, that builds up to the moment of the memory; what came before the memory and what came after?

Writing

Go to the page and write out your improvisation as a text and score any movements on the page too. Simply name this piece *Ghost Text*. When you write, have in your mind what it is about this actor/performer that you find interesting.

Develop and edit this script material by the repetition of phrases, set rules that allow your story to return to the beginning, so you don't reveal all of the story immediately. Play with writing out descriptions of images and give some (not all) images accompanying words. Using this method of writing out the story in stages, with repeats, interruptions and images, means you can withhold information from your audience, thus keeping the work slightly mysterious. As you write in the form of repeats, you may remember something else from the memory of the performance you are recalling, adding new descriptions and images into the repeating section. You are now playing with repetition that reveals extra detail, gradually. Add stage directions.

You will notice that your 3-minute work is a work of greater length now due to the repeats. This is ideal.

Playing

Find a pre-existing text that you are interested in, this text should not relate to the text you have written. (It could be a Shakespeare play as one example.) Find a scene in the play that you are drawn to and that you are happy working with, making sure the text falls within copyright laws, for example, it is over 70 years old from when the last remaining author of the work died.

Return to your *Ghost Text* and write a series of interruptions throughout the script from a small handful of chosen lines or actions from your chosen play. It does not matter if the text does not relate to the *Ghost Text*, in fact this is where the coincidences appear, and where juxtaposition is clear. This exercise is about blending one text with another and activating new ideas.

Performing

Perform your *Ghost Text* to the group. Be aware of yourself in this work and develop in your performance an attitude to the work. This attitude can come from the feeling you have about the performer you are ghosting, shared through eye contact with the audience, or from a knowing smile.

Dramaturgy

Invite the group who have been working on this project to watch your work and feedforward any ideas that might be useful for a development. For example, discuss:

The result of layering different worlds.

The ghosts the audience saw.

The blending of autobiographical material into the *Ghost Text.*

For future development, how could you blend biographical material of the ghosted actor into the performance?

What other mediums do you imagine this work to play out? For example, produce a new version of your work shot on film within a site-specific context and observe the change in aesthetic qualities that emerge in your practice.

<Q U I C K · G U I D E S>

Title: Dream Yards (2013)

Where: City of York. City of Norwich. Long Island City.

Description: A weekly walking tour performance led by Kong Lear and The Fool from King Lear, drawing upon the relationship between the two characters in Lear. Conceptually structured as a journey through the stages of sleep and dreaming. Each stage opens out into a scene played out in the confines of a Yard or a doorway within a snickelway, the material drawing upon images and accounts of 300 dreams donated by people in York. The tour is tracked by two doppelgangers of Gary and Claire who eventually become centre stage in a scene under a willow tree by the river, they are lucid dreaming. The tour route attempts to disorientate its audience by taking them to spaces they may feel familiar with but changes the way in which they may normally pass through on foot, by turning back on routes, returning to snickelways several times. After getting lost in sleep for a bit we return to discuss the subject of dreams over a pint in a local pub.

Kit box: Gorilla suits. Head torches. Ladybirds. Clipboards. Dream Yards sign with LED lights and portable sound speaker. Music – 7 loops from songs containing the word 'dream'. Oversized Paper Mache heads. Litter grabber and a load of rubbish (enough to make a brain model of a 40ft creature). An egg shaker, a rubber egg, a raw egg.

Commonalities: The street. Freud. King Lear. Fool. Ghosting. Crown. Cat. Gorillas. Dreams. Roy Orbison. David Lynch. Homemade Flipbookits. Aviator flying cap. Lip-sync.

Illustration 7 Quick Guide *Dream Yards* Walking Tour

<Q U I C K • G U I D E S>

Title: Dream Yards Studio Show (2013)

Where: Toured to York Theatre Royal, The Carriageworks, Leeds, Theatre in the Mill, Bradford.

Description: A 70-minute show about flying, lucidity and Yorkshire dreams. Part neuropsychoanalyst's couch, part talkshow our host Kong Lear [sic] is troubled with the riddles of dream generation and sleep science. The performance charts a journey through the nightly stages of sleep that lead us deep into the desires of our id – the part of us that never sleeps; if it did we would die. Uh. Imagine an island in the Pacific Ocean where King Lear, his Fool, Sigmund Freud, King Kong and Amelia Earhart are all lost. They are lost that is until they fall asleep and in a dream discover a man in dark glasses with the voice of an angel. Two performers share dream stories through playful and endearing characters: King Lear and his Fool, a Dead Skeleton Roy and host of other endearing characters who together attempt to resolve the riddles of dream generation and proper sleep science. "If I were to wake you now, you may not know to tell me that you were dreaming."

Kit box: Parachute. Gorilla suits. Wooden heads. Skeleton Roy costume. Nano Pad. Aviator cap. Digital piano. Mirror ball. Glow sticks. Persian rug. Fake flowers. Clip boards. Bubbles. Microphone. iPad. Staging. Lots of black fake fur.

Commonalities: Dreams. Roy Orbison. A dead cat. Gorilla costumes. Nano Pad. King Lear. King Kong. Digital piano. Aviators cap. Ghosting. Freud.

Illustration 8   Quick Guide *Dream Yards* Studio Show

Illustration 9 Kong Lear (right) and her Fool from *Dream Yards* walking tour, York

5

The Dead Sleep

This chapter reflects upon the mediumistic terms – clairvoyance, clairaudience, clairsentience and claircognizance – and develops a conversation on the concept and practice of artistic channelling in performance. We share the script from the walking tour performance *Dream Yards* (2013) composed to include edited commentary from audience members as an indication of their experience of the performance. This chapter also unpacks our creative relationship to the haunted city of York contextualizing our own practice in relation to the qualities of artistic mediumship. We also bring into the conversation the disappearance of the aviation pioneer Amelia Earhart who, for one participant in *Dream Yards*, arrived in a dream. The chapter also details how the process of the Death Drift/Drift Drive (DD/DD) enabled us to work through a dramaturgical process where *Dream Yards* is reimagined and translated from one space: the city, to another: the theatre studio.

Phase one: *Can you recall your dreams? Please write or draw a dream on the beer mat provided and drop it into one of our heads.*

Phase two (six months later): *Meet at 7.30pm each Monday for the Dream Yards Walking Tour at Precentor's Court, York (in the snickelway next to the Hole in the Wall Pub, 10 High Petergate YO1 7EH). See you there, we will be quite recognisable…*

Each Monday evening after *Dream Yards* was performed in the city of York, we took our audience to the pub and bought a round of drinks to engender conversations on the subject of dreams and collated their responses to the performance. The following script of *Dream Yards* is composed and edited with those collated comments from the audience, edited to reflect their point of view during the walking tour through their visual, audible, sentient and cognizant experience of it.

The script of *Dream Yards*:

I arrive at the advertised start point, an alleyway next to the pub just inside the city walls called The Hole in the Wall. There's a small group of people waiting on the pavement, I suspect they are waiting for the performance to start. Shortly after two figures approach through the archway of Bootham Bar, they are both dressed in black furry gorilla suits, just the bodies, carrying a sign with lights saying Dream Yards, the name of this piece. There is a looping soundtrack from a Kate Bush song. We are invited to walk through an alley 10m long. At the other end of the alley is Precentor's Court, a neat space with old town houses. It feels like it is tucked away from the bustle of the city. In a wedge of space neat houses Claire moves a FlipBooKit reading out the words 'Dream in order to sleep'. Gary hands clipboard and takes the FlipBooKit.

He says:

Guide, I'll teach thee a speech.

She says:

Do, fool.

He says:

What's on your mind?

She says:

Something big in the sky *(raise arm skyward)* – and if you wake me now, I can tell you I am dreaming.

He says:

> You may also tell me that you are a cat, Sirrah. And if I wake you in an hour not far from here – you will tell me that you *have* dreamt and can prove it with an old umbrella, a soggy cardboard box, dirty paper and rotting t-shirt…
> If you dream – say 'Aye!'…
> If you don't dream – say 'No aye!'…
> But we are all tired, with X, Y or Z marked on our brains, we are all exhausted, we are all fatigued because of the office, the shop, the school, the nothings, the motorway, our less virtuous pursuits, our search for a quiet moment with our thoughts and the café. Let us drift off together; start at the beginning, at Alpha, here, right here, let us do things in order.
> Let's begin to fall asleep, my guide. We are now in the first few minutes of sleep onset and we are dreaming – taken from this city to a hidden city – we're dreaming of the office, the shop, the school, the motorway and the café. And if I was to wake you now, you would tell me you were dreaming of the office *as* the office, the shop *as* the shop, the school *as* the school, the nothings as nothings, the motorway as some motorway and the café *as* an office – you would be one of the 50% who could tell me that, or maybe even a cat, you would tell me of something big in the sky, something floating and falling…

She whispers:

> Watch out? I am a 23-year-old man and I am walking through a forest, my arms are covered in ladybirds. *(Arm out – look can you see those?)* I am a 25-year-old female standing on a dark bench looking out to sea. *(Arm stretched out in front – look forwards 'out to sea')* **POP!**

We follow the performers and pass houses with shuttered windows, we are discovering the quieter areas of the city and our attention is drawn to the elegant door knockers.

We walk on towards York Minster and are given an image of one of the towers rising up and out of the city.

I turn a corner and it feels either like spring or late summer – warm enough to be out without a coat; cool enough to feel an admonishing breeze.

We are at a crossroads a wide exposed pavement where two figures with giant heads look into the bronze scale model of the city. Is this something I should note? Is this part of their performance? Is this another world?

We continue across the street corner as the road narrows we are entering old York, we fall in step to the music, a loop of *City of Dreams*. I look to other people passing and people look at us, some don't even see us. We turn down Stonegate and pass the ghost tour folk but, it is us that feels like the ghosts of this city.

We gather after walking through a narrow snickelway (a shortcut or hidden passage in the city) that opens into a yard. I am handed the Dream Yards sign to hold. Our attention is drawn to the chimney pots on the roofs above and the fading light. I feel a little cosy as if I am sleeping, he shakes an egg and feigns a throw, we all duck to avoid getting an egg in our face, we realize he still has the egg in his hand, I can't stop laughing.

He talks to the audience:

While Claire is out of frame I will just explain a few things here. We are conceptually and fictionally taking a journey through sleeping and dreaming, while actually taking a route through these cut-throughs and sometimes hidden passages in the city – these constructed desire paths. Claire is the King in this journey – the King is our guide, our example, our meter, our patient if you like, tumbling through the dreams of people from this city, some of you even...

Everything we read from these pieces of paper actually happened to people from this city, well they happened in dreams – so did they happen?

Can you tell a story about a dream experience with the same merit as a story of a lived experience – but you are alive when you are dreaming, and I can prove that with an old umbrella, a soggy bit of cardboard, dirty papers, a soiled glove...

– now I'm playing the fool in all this, who in Shakespearean terms is one who counsels, who aids, who steps out of the complex situations in the fiction, to offer advice and a link into the real world – so, I am an example in that respect...

Let's step back in...

Here comes the office, the shop, the school, the café, the Minster falling, the forest, the dark glasses, the sea, the lift, levels two and three and four, the market, the church, the less virtuous pursuits...

What does that tell us, guide?

She says:

Nothing.

He says:

It might *be* nothing – can you make no use of nothing, guide.

She says:

Why no – nothing can be made out of nothing.

We exit the yard through a snickelway with a very low ceiling and we all have to stoop to make our way out. I am aware of voice, I can hear someone speaking but retuned the sound from the cocktail bar as it seems distorted.

We pause in an unlikely recess, a white door, possibly a fire exit of the back of a restaurant's kitchen. Fag butts a plenty, the smell of spices and urine, dirty grime-ridden walls with inappropriate graffiti.

He says:

Do you know why the nose is in the middle of the cat's face?

She says:

Do you call me a cat?

He says:

I'd rather be any other kind of thing than a fool in a beast's skin who goes to bed at noon – you ask me about the day, you ask me about the hidden day. I have to explain the city, I have to explain the hidden city, I have to explain why a woman of 80 is lost in a forest saying 'Help! Where am I?' or why a boy of 12 flies over the city or why a woman of 41 sees tornadoes – I sometimes have to explain the nothings too…

She says:

Explain why the nose is in the middle of the cat's face.

We are amused by the arrival of a black and white cat who brushes against someone's leg and then pauses in front of the performer who drops down to a squat and rubs his fingers together at the cat. We can't stop laughing, where did this real cat come from? Who has let the cat out of the bag? Have they, or we, summoned this cat into being?

He says:

Why, to keep one's eyes of either side of the nose, that what a cat cannot smell out, she may spy into…

She says:

And to tell one when to use the nose – *breathe in deeply* (respond to bad smell).

He says:

Do you know why the nose is in the middle of the singer's face? To hold the glasses and hide the eyes that cannot see – gouged out by dysfunctional relatives and replaced by egg whites.

She says:

And all other senses are dead here, I'm deep, deep in a hidden day – I've got an arm covered in ladybirds, I'm lost in a forest saying 'Help! Where am I?', I'm 12 years old and flying over the city, I am a 17-year-old buying the concept of tweed, I'm a woman seeing tornadoes – here come the planes…

Are you in my dream Fool?

He says:

Is that why you see me, but sometimes pass me by. If I was to wake you now, you may *not know* to tell me you were dreaming.

She says:

How would I know to tell you this is a dream?

He says:

We would need a sign – one without lights or a fancy music system – something coherent, and articulate, something a cat would do.

She says:

Away from all this – what should it be?

He says:

I shall stand up on my back legs – give me a moment to think…

He turns off the lights on his Dream Yards sign and wanders off alone away from the group along the snickelway. The bend in the alleyway takes him out of sight. We are feeling slightly unnerved, can he disappear? Do we follow? Do we stay? Is he real? In the quiet of the night in back of the restaurant, we listen to his footsteps, the final moments of someone disappearing and suddenly we tune back into the hum of the city.

She says:

While Gary is switched off, I will tell you about a reoccurring dream I have had over many years – I dreamt that I was in a lift that took me to different floors. It was a small narrow lift with an unstable floor and as I got to each floor level the lift made a clicking sound as if the doors were jammed. It was a broken lift. After several visits to numerous floors, I heard music coming out of one, clanging and shouting out of another, strange echoes as if people were swimming and behind another I could hear the noise of at least 2,000 people dining in a restaurant. The doors opened on the bottom floor at a petrol station in the year 1970, I filled my car up with four-star and drove off. Each time I had the reoccurring dream I would be in a different lift but the clicking sound would come back and it was the same scenario; travelling to different floors with the doors jammed. But recently, I dreamt that I was outside two lifts, and I had a choice of which lift to enter.

As she says this a man opens the green door, steps out and lights up a cigarette, he is startled by our presence, he has an audience. He smokes his cigarette as she continues to describe her dream but now it feels like our dream. She continues to speak, we listen to her and watch the man, her story makes more sense with him in it:

I immediately knew which door not to enter, I knew green door was the clicking lift so I chose the one on the right – this was the safe lift. I realized I had been lucid dreaming because I decided in my dream, ever since I have not had that dream, I had resolved it.

Okay – let's go and find our Fool.

As we leave this space to find the Fool we turn our heads looking back at the cat and the man, we leave this image suspended, unresolved like most dreams.

All is quiet as we walk through the snickelway, yet a noise is getting closer, there is a feeling we are walking into something more intense. The space opens out, the city is active, people walking across the square, a pigeon flying past, a man smoking a cigarette outside the Three Cranes pub. We feel like we have been dropped into this scene, we are working at a different pace, the rhythm is jarring, it is all hazy dazy. The Fool is dressed as Amelia Earhart, he is talking about her last transmission, something about radio waves, he is standing and shouting, words we've heard before, a loop back to an earlier image. He reminds us we are in sleep stage four.

We all gather in a marketplace. It is after hours the stalls are bare. All activities are stripped away, this place has once been busy, full, thriving, something is missing. Here comes the Fool.

(*He takes rubber egg out of his mouth*).

He says:

I've been thinking – Let's make a pact.

She says:

A pact?

He says:

Let's make a pact to meet in a dream.

She says:

Yes, boy, but how do we do this?

He says

How will we both know that we are dreaming? Without someone to wake us?

She says:

How boy?

He says:

When I am with you – deep in REM sleep, we will be in some place calm, that is this city but doesn't feel like this city, a cat's hide-away. And I must remember to move my right pointer finger…

She says:

Pointer finger?

He says:

Yes – guide, I'll teach thee a rhyme…

She says:

And I should move mine?

He says:

Yes, you must also remember to move your right pointer finger. But we are not there yet – please follow my guide as images from this brain are released through its passageways…

I follow them through a series of small alleyways known as the Shambles in and out, narrow snickelways with low ceilings, routes to the market and back out again. We lose count of how many little snickelways there are, there is a feeling of disorientation, we are being herded in and out and in and out as they read a collection of dream accounts from city residents. We brush our hand on an alley wall to check if this is all real.

She says:

I am a male age 56 and I can breathe under the sea. I am a female age 22 and my son's in a fish in a tank. I'm falling and falling and there is a deafening sound of bird's wings. I am male age 42 and Stephen Fry is to be executed, but he throws pigs' guts on the floor to fake his death. I am a female age 41 trying to find my son, I travel up steep stairs, catch a train which I miss and then find him on the motorway. I am a female age 23 and married to Jake Gyllenhaal. I am a male age 23 and I am walking through a forest, my arms are covered in ladybirds. I am a 25-year-old female standing on a dark bench looking out to sea. I am a 23-year-old female who has been having the same dream for a while – trapped in a building that is surrounded by zombies. I am anonymous; Superman hired me to make a machine. I am a 7-year-old girl on a school trip to Yo Sushi. I am a female age 30 and I am being swallowed up by a gorilla.

As we come to the end of a snickelway I like the flying close to the ground one, reminds me of my own, perhaps it is my own and if it is all these people know it now.

He says:

> There is a phenomenon, which is not very common, of people returning back to the same dream. But you only remember that dream when you are in the dream... A continuity from one dream world to another even though in between, when you are in a wakeful state, you don't remember.

As we meander in and out, in and out, our walk is interrupted as two figures with giant heads stand silently on the street corner. We notice that one of the performers is no longer with the group. Should she be here? Has something gone wrong? Are we meant to know? We retrace our steps back to the assembly point back to the market. We gather in the same formation as earlier and an audience member who I don't know the name of is standing opposite me in exactly the same position, he smiles across a knowing look as the guide reappears as the Fool takes out an egg. Curiously, the Fool shakes the egg, there is no sound, he looks at its form, he looks at us, and then he bites the crown off the top and swallows the contents. A collective visceral wince bellows between us, there's a gasp, a profanity and a roar.

We walk to the bottom of the Shambles and cross a busy road, the Fool stops the traffic before we enter Lady Peckett's Yard. A Victorian-style lamp throws light onto this timeless space. There is a collision of sounds and I think I heard someone say 'Turn 1 into back of Mumbai smells dear outside door' but I don't know what this means but it is poetry and it fits.

We continue to ramble through York's backstreets and hear the sacred language of Shakespeare merged with the profane imagery of disgorging pubs. The litter-strewn backyards of city centre nightclubs are a complement to the hum of extractor fans of the impenetrable brick office buildings with a doomy communication tower.

Amidst this harum scarum, they bring us to place for reflection and calm. Down by a deserted riverbank, quite removed from the hum of the city, we happen across an arresting moment.

A tree, a bench, birds singing. A girl and a boy, hand in hand, sit silently and oblivious to the gathered throng who have just stumbled across this vision. Their crudely grotesque, big heads the only clue we have that all is was not as it should be.

The Fool enters this frame and we tune into the low-level music coming from the speaker on his sign. He begins to lip-synch to the words.

> Dream, when you're feeling blue
> Dream, that's the thing to do
> Just watch the smoke rings rise from the air
> You'll find memories there.

We stop and look. We wait. We witness. The birds, with an alarmingly true sense of theatrical timing, suddenly take flight and the slim branches of the tree they had vacated rustle in approval. We wait some more. The moment hangs heavy in this dusky evening light. Without any sign, the gathered audience begin to drift away, as if there is an unstated agreement that the moment has passed. Time to move on.

> So, dream, when the day is through
> Dream, and they might come true
> Things never are as bad as they seem
> So dream, dream, dream

I stay, though. I want the moment to last. After a while I become aware that I am not the only one. I turn to leave just at the moment when I meet his glance. We look at each other with a gesture of brief and silent recognition before moving on to catch up with our rapidly disappearing entourage. A wry smile. A knowing look. A delicious moment in which that sense of 'knowing' is impossible to define. Impossible to weigh.

We cross the road and the Fool stops the traffic. We enter an unlikely dark space, more contemporary, yet slightly tired, messy, concrete.

He says:

Guide, teach us what happens behind Fibbers nightclub.

She says:

I shall, map out a brain, Fool.

Gary gathers bits of crap off the floor to make a brain. Claire spouts a scientific oration that talks about Freud and the need to sleep in order to dream in order to stay healthy and reminds us that Thatcher never slept.

We turn onto a street a residential area with the residue image of a brain constructed from a broken umbrella, a bottle, a trainer, a plastic bag, a bit of dead wood. My head feels a little funny, likes it's weighted down, rattling with the textures of the mash up of objects. We happen across three boys on their BMX's freewheeling by and commenting 'Oh, it is the dream people again'.

We pause at a house with large green door, as the performers describe a dream a family open their door and gather to listen with us. They are smiling.

She says:

I can you tell you something of this place, boy. I can tell you that tonight a 19-year-old woman will dream about a terraced house with a walled-off garden and a red Wendy house. She will sit on the garden wall watching the neighbourhood.

We walk through a very narrow passageway we brush our hands against the walls that bulge and bow and melt towards the centre. We are dreaming, we are.

In a neat and tidy courtyard, the Fool has disappeared where did he go? Is this the final time? We notice window lights coming off and on, people going about their business. Little interiors illuminated, a kitchen, a bedroom. Waking up or shutting down? Like a grid, the house lights turn off, come on and off in the apartment numbers 23, 21, 19 and in numbers 17, 15, 13.

She says:

Make no noise, make no noise. Draw the curtains. *Watch out!* What place is this? Everything is so different, it's rising morning. Perhaps it's that sci-fi dream you know, where the cereal is the same but reality is different.

Perhaps it's the ruins of the Minster, the office as a forest, the school as the market, the shop as the sea, the motorway as the river, the search for a quiet place to think of nothings, the café as a tornado, the swimming pool full of rats. But it can't be, it's rising morning for your guide and the lights from the windows, the rustle of the branches and the covers are not hidden anymore. How can I explain… Where is *my* Fool? I am moving my right finger; is it real now? I need to fix something in this late morning; I am coming out of something. He split an egg into two crowns and said I need to keep still and not move a muscle. I remember so vividly that we were running for the thrill of it and there were planes, small narrow passages, ginnels and yards. His light shone on his face and he said – remember the dream when you are in the dream… he laid close to the ground and said find continuity from one dream to another – POP!

Where is *my* Fool?

She pauses, rotates 360 degrees and says:

I need a drink, some kind of beverage, some kind of froth…

The Haunted City

We composed the script of *Dream Yards* for an already charged and haunted environment and contemplated de Certeau's (1998) idea that 'Haunted spaces are the only ones people can live in'. As 'mediumistic vessels', to draw a phrase from Luckhurst and Morin (2014), we attempted to channel the city and tune into its presence, past and present.

York is widely known as being a city full of ghosts. In 2002 the Ghost Research Foundation International awarded York the title of most haunted metropolis in Europe, and it was given a paragraph entry in *The Guardian* in their feature *Scary streets: which are the world's most haunted cities?* (2016). Indeed, tourists are spoilt for choice when it comes to the many ghost walks the city has to offer. At night when the city is not so crowded it is not hard to come across a populated walking tour. Typically, as an entertainment experience, Hanks (2016) observes that the ghost walks of York are 'fun' and 'historically interesting' but not 'transformative' walks. We wanted to offer an alternative walking tour but not dismiss the ghost tour's entertainment value or compete with it. As we were beginning to understand the potential of a dream's uncanny residue that haunts the imagination and baffles the dreamer, we thought about creating a transcendental walking experience, one that could transform people's perception of the city. We were open to the idea that dreaming has a mediumistic quality that navigates phenomenologically, metaphorically and analogously between different worlds of the living and the dead.

In the early planning stages of *Dream Yards*, we experienced a ghost walk and found it a pleasurable hour visiting several sites of historic interest listening to common ghost stories retold by a performer who offered his own jokes within the mix of the gruesome tales of old. At the end of the tour the ghost walker invites his audience to the pub, where naturally, people from the crowd buy him drinks. Thankfully, for *Dream Yards* we were given Arts Council funding which allowed a small *per diem* to buy a round for our dreamers.

Who were the dreamers? In the research and development phase of this project, we set ourselves up in different places to collect dreams. The arts foyer of the cinema during an Alfred Hitchcock season, a theatre foyer of a production of *King Lear* and other places where people gathered, such as the café, the community centre. We invited people to write or draw a dream on a small marked out area on a beer mat with minimum word count or space to illustrate. Given the restriction we collected the fine detail of someone's dream, rather than the whole dream, our dreamers were editing content. On the table, at our dream drop-in events, we set up two large cardboard 3D doppelgänger heads of 'Gary and Claire' and invited dreamers to donate their artwork or writing by popping it into our 'heads' (there was a slit on the top of each head to insert the beer mat). We collated many dreams and weaved them into script as performed images or as simple readings. The dream donations enabled the creative narrative to unfold and gave us reason to make creative decisions from planting tiny ladybirds in a costume to Gary eating a raw egg. The images we placed in the performance were always slightly out of the ordinary, odd or uncomfortable and not too extreme to be frightening, but to give the idea that we are all asleep and dreaming together, channelling one another's dreams and witnessing them collectively and lucidly.

The script's structural form was motivationally driven by a desire to understand where neuroscience stood now in relation to dreaming, in order to offer the audience an experience of a dream's journey. Sleep scientists once thought dreaming only occurred during REM sleep, this once therefore affected any dream recall analysis because it suggested that one would only remember a dream if they had woken up just after the REM sleep stage (where REM is only one of many stages of sleep). But the latest findings show we dream throughout all stages of sleep according to Professor Mark Solms (who we had spent time working with during our research phase). We discovered that a typical sleep cycle repeats and returns to different stages in a 90-minute cycle and importantly we dream throughout this sleep cycle:

Awake 1, 2, 3, 2 REM, 2, 3, 2 REM, 2, REM, 2 REM, Late Morning.

Mapping the walking tour's journey through the streets of York to this cycle, composing the script to correspond with its non-sequential order, we informed participants at each stage of their journey where they were within this cycle, while offering them, through the conceptual dramaturgy, a performance of a lucid dream experience. Lucid dreaming is the place where you find yourself conscious that you are in a dream, you channel this knowingness and have conversations with those you meet in your dream knowing that you are dreaming. You can even affect the course and narrative of the dream if you perfect the practice. Whereas in normal dreaming one only becomes 'self-consciously aware of a dream as a dream only when one has woken up' (Moore, 2016, p.65). Peter Moore discusses lucid dreaming in the context of an experience where 'several dreamers appear to have shared the same dream'. But intriguingly draws upon H. H. Prices' idea that shared dreams exist as a theoretical afterlife, a conceptual death beyond life experience, a place where dreamers (who could be thought of as dead while asleep) connect telepathically in an 'active and interpersonal' way.

The Artist as Medium

The phenomenon of spiritual channelling requires a medium to use psychic senses that enable them to see, hear, feel and know. This is not an extensive list of psychic sensitives by no means. For the medium, these senses are used to connect to spirit guides that help someone find out if their dead relative or friend is doing okay, or to pass messages from the deceased to loved ones in the mortal world, to give comfort to the bereaved, to heal. Psychic senses vary and to elaborate slightly on the following four examples: clairvoyance (clear seeing) – when one sees images in the mind's eye; clairaudience (clear hearing) – when one hears sounds; clairsentience (clear feeling) – when one automatically has a feeling, usually within the whole body, and has the ability (through a form of telepathy) to tune in to an energy (person, spirit, object, situation); claircognizance (clear knowing) – where one immediately knows through a gut feeling, about some form of information. Typically, meditation is necessary to clear the mind of worries and troubles so one can be an open channel, and to do this, one must move away from the conscious self (that thinks about work, problem solving etc.) to encounter an altered state of consciousness where whatever comes to mind through the visual, the audible, the sentient, the cognizance arrives via a higher being or force.

In this mediumistic context therefore, we turn our attention to our research and development phase of the *Dream Yards* project *in situ* with the site. Using the city as the site for the work, we wanted to know it, see it and feel it, listen to it and sense its place in our performance in order to make this project feel like a lucid dream. As artists we imagined ourselves with antennae; sensory appendages to the work and the city. We wanted to tune into the environment we were working in, so we developed a form of artistic mediumship and channelled the personality of the city. We were open to the idea that we could channel forces outside of the *Dream Yards* walk to let in other worlds, so the audience might experience the slippage between the performance and other life operating in a city at night. Thinking like this allowed participants' dreams to occupy the spaces along with the haunted matter of the ghost tours. In preparation of the walking tour, we spent much time in the city to understand through seeing, listening, feeling and knowing, its pace, rhythms, rituals and spatial qualities. The more time we spent the more we began to recognize the flow of its pedestrian traffic, its residents' habitual routines, that in turn allowed us to tune in to the human geography but also the non-human elements: the changing light at night, its wildlife, its sounds, its underbelly along with the rats. We were fully tuned into the uncanny qualities all around us, as if we had grown antennae; we were sensory appendages that psychically picked up on the multiple worlds that surrounded us on the tour; stuff happening in the yards, movement in the snickets and those darker, less frequented spaces hidden in the city behind the back of Fibbers nightclub. This perception inevitably relates to our own memories (as artists) of hanging out in those sites, the more we hung out the more we imagined and played with ideas, so this deep play experience meant we could listen, look, feel and know very perceptively the city's many different currents moving all around. This meant that during the performance itself, we did not interrupt the flow of the city, rather we channelled it and learned to take chances during the performance through improvisation so that coincidences might occur. We tuned into the city with our audience without forcing chance encounters, and we listened, we sensed, we tried stuff out. The effects of creative channelling worked when our audience, during the performance, were invited to imagine coincidences regardless of them being there or not, you invite them to desire, and in those moments the things that are going on around in the city, suddenly pop up, as if by magic they are orchestrated into the script. There is plenty of room in the script for the other narratives of the everyday to bleed into the fabric of this alternative world and for the happy accidents to occur, so we learnt to trust their return, while never becoming complacent, always sensing with the antennae. The highly perceptive in us got to know the quiet night and so we worked in a semi parallel universe to the ghost tours, as a complement to them, a subversive crossing over into their worlds for a brief encounter. We tuned into many channels: the birds asleep in the trees, the geese moving slowly along the river, the boys on their BMXs, the smokers hanging out the fire exits on their mid-evening break, and they too ended up in the work. But tuning in did not require an exact match of what we were doing, on the contrary it was the juxtapositions that revealed the uncanny of coincidental. For example, a guy on his cigarette break became a weekly image (at the same time each week) to a story about Amelia Earhart, as did a man putting the kettle on in his kitchen at 8pm, when we've suggested it is very early morning, appeared to be taking a cue from the script.

Mediums are quite often referenced as having the ability to channel the dead:

> The roots of the modern concept of channelling go back a very long way. Since the beginnings of recorded history there have been reports of shamans and prophets who have heard or have claimed to have heard voices from the spiritual world. (Alcock, in Stein, 1996, p.153)
>
> Perhaps the most significant difference between spiritualist practice and other forms of haunting is intentionally and desire. A medium may be surprised by the spirits she encounters and the nature of their messages; nevertheless, the presence of the dead is actively sought ... the practice of spiritualism is a process of listening to what the spirits of the dead have to say to the living. (Anderson, 2013, p.33)

There was an extraordinary dramatic resurgence in spiritualism during World War I and II that had persisted since the nineteenth century. Helen Sword writes about spirit lectures and carefully orchestrated séances where ghosts materialized and 'mediums' bodies emitted disconcerting quantities of a strange, filmy substance known as ectoplasm' (Sword, 2002, p.2), as popular happenings. Creative writers were drawn to such circles. And the modernist artists of the twentieth century, who practised many surrealist techniques to produce creative material called automatic writing, adapted such techniques from the spiritualist movement where a medium had the psychic ability to channel the dead through writing. Here, a pen and paper were used by the medium whose arm during a trance-like state would be taken by a higher being, and words jotted down were speedily interpreted. The automatic writing that developed through the surrealist movement, however, acknowledged the creative potential (not always the spiritual potential) of the unconscious mind. Dada and surrealist artists were, after all, living in the modernist era where Freud was famous for his free association and dream work. Artists were drawn to the imaginative potential of automatism and André Breton defines psychic automatism as:

> In its pure state, by which one proposes to express – verbally, by means of the written word, or in another manner – the actual functioning of

thought. Dictated by thought, in the absence of any control exercised by reason, exempt from any aesthetic or moral concern. (Breton, 1969, p.26)

In fact, the first surrealist novel written by André Breton and Phillipe Soupault, *Les Champs Magnétiques* (*The Magnetic Fields*, published 1920; Breton & Soupault, 1985), reads as fragmentary, playful and imaginative, whereas in some parts it reads as a series of dream descriptions. The 'dislocating strangeness' of *The Magnetic Fields*, Stockwell argues, is more well-formed than we might assume: 'there is no gibberish, nonsense words, non-denotational neologisms, nor attempts at spelling out pure meaningless sounds' (Stockwell, 2017, p.60). Stockwell's research outlines the importance of the surrealists' work, that what we are not looking at with automatic writing is pure nonsense, but in fact alternative forms of exciting, imaginative writing. Indeed, in contemporary arts practice, automatism is still widely practised, and we understand that ideas produced (in many forms) are generated by the mind, artists come up with ideas, creative thoughts and on impulse.

Shared Vocabularies

The language of contemporary performance making and post-dramatic theatre share a similar vocabulary to mediumship. Artists using methods of play, chance and intertextual practice within making theatre (writing, devising, improvisation), work with what they see, hear, feel and know. Artists have intuition about ideas, worlds, materials, action, images, words and sounds. There is always talk of that 'gut feeling' or that 'sense' of what to do, and, when an environment becomes 'charged' it is because an idea has been placed into a space and it is activated through play and performance. Ideas talk back to artists once they are in the air and the ability to see things clearer becomes apparent and connections are made to other random ideas. Tuning into the perceptive self, making discoveries that seem to come from somewhere else, from another place, is reflected upon in the creative processes of making. We know something 'works' because ideas, materials, moments have 'spoken' to one another, and it is not that easy to pin down exactly how this happens or why, artists just *know*. This knowingness is directly located to the uncanny where the familiar meets the unfamiliar. In a published interview with Elevator Repair Service (ERS) in the context of new dramaturgy, Ana Pais poses this observation to artistic director John Collins about ERS' process of making a new piece of creative work for audiences:

AP: *If you create a new vocabulary, you will need to find a new grammar to figure out the order of the elements, the units of meaning and so on.*

JC: *We have perfected a way of creating an environment in which we work: it's a way of listening. It's a kind of openness. We find ourselves doing similar things over and over again but not because we are trying to. What we try to do deliberately is putting ourselves in unfamiliar places, working with unfamiliar material, even unfamiliar method. We try to frustrate any process that we've developed before, because we want to achieve a stage of being. It's almost as if we want to be able to get out of the way of the play that is trying to happen. We want to be present. When the materials we have brought together find ways of speaking to each other, we want to get them together in the ways they want to. It is believing that this thing you are trying to put together already has a kind of soul or life.* (JC in Trencsenyi and Cochrane, 2014, p.124)

Here, JC articulates the performer's/dramaturge's position in the company's creative process where materials have a voice and communicate through the actor/dramaturge in a similar way a medium would open up as a channel where the spirits work though her body to 'speak'. This openness is analogous to the way in which a spiritual medium works. The spiritual vocabulary JC uses is a type of clairaudience, practised in the studio, and through listening they (ERS) achieve a form of knowingness (claircognizance) that eradicates consciousness in favour of obtaining presence through the unconscious mind.

The Wooster Group commonly use a mediumistic vocabulary to describe certain elements of their work. Referring to their 2006–2013 performance of *Hamlet*, where they reimagine a 1964 John Gielgud directed production with Hamlet played by Richard Burton, they specifically work with footage of the performance that was edited into a film for a 'Theatrofilm' event in cinemas. On the Wooster Group's short teaser film entitled *Hamlet Channelling the Ghost,* a voice-over declares, from their programme note about interpretation of the 1964 Hamlet:

> we channel the ghost of the legendary 1964 performance, descending into a kind of madness, intentionally replacing our own spirit with the spirit of another. (Wooster Group, 2011)

Immediately after the voice stops speaking the image cuts to a member of the group who performs quotation marks with his fingers.

The word 'spirit' is a homographic phrase, it implies two things; it denotes the energy of the original 1964 production that replaces the energy of the Wooster Group's contemporary work (energy here implying the tone or quality of performance). The other meaning of 'spirit' here, is the literal experience of trance channelling where the actors display apparent psychic abilities to embody the actor from the original production. Here, they establish the idea that they can embody a spirit of another but, in the same token, we understand they are messing with us. This is dark play and it is most mischievous. Not only does the voice-over have a profound quality of deadness about it (because it is the voice of Google Translate, non-human, ghostly, dead), it's edited as a repetitive chant complementing the drama of a mediumistic atmosphere like a spiritual mantra. But, we have to be clear on their irony, the dead are not invited to speak through the performers rather the performers speak different versions (on their own terms and within a ritualist framework) of the dead from culture. It's a practice of distortion between the then and the now.

In the Wooster Group's (2014–2017) performance of *Early Shaker Spirituals,* they channel a 1976 LP (entitled Early Shaker Spirituals) recorded by the Shaker community of Sabbathday Lake Maine. Unlike their *Hamlet,* this is not an ironic work, in fact this performance respects the religious, transcendent and sacred found in Shaker songs. By learning the dances inspired by the LP, breathing their own voices into the recorded songs of the Shakers, they enact an authenticity that is not referenced as such through any gestural quotation marks, rather through a lens of simplicity. This work's mediumistic qualities are located in the performers' approach to listening via their earpieces to the LP as if they are channelling the voices of the Shakers. Granted, the 'audience can detect only a faint under-layer of the original recorded sound' (Brantley, 2014), but that only heightens an eerie effect of the basic technology used to learn and perform the songs:

> This channelling of distant parallels stories not only of how the songs were passed down among the Shakers but also of how they were received originally, through ghostly visitations and divine afflatus. (Brantley, 2014)

Their process of 'channelling' is a way of practising (through ghosting) the material from an original LP as tribute. They are practising deep play in a theatrically divine form of dancing pleasure. The performers are not Shakers, nor are they in fact, spiritual mediums, but artists serious about their authenticity, they are ghosting in its purest sense, a spiritual connection between their performance and history. The authentic here has much to do with the performers' joyful commitment (deep play) to the learning of the songs and dances 'suggesting a kind of phantasmal possession of the present by the past' (Brantley, 2014).

The Dead Exist in a Dream

During the mid-twentieth century the poet and novelist Hilda Doolittle (H.D.) took an 'active interest in spiritualism' (Anderson, 2013, p.34) and her works typically included fictions on the other-worldly where the dead are firmly fixed in her fictional narratives, from the returning of the dead as ghosts, to the practice of mediumship through the séance. Intriguingly, H.D. writes a poetic document called *A Tribute to Freud*, a written memoir that reflects upon her time on the couch with Freud recalling her dreams and visionary experiences. Her writing is not a straightforward account of her analysis from Freud, but a blend of her own dreams, visions, entries on fairy tales as well of memories as metaphors. What is interesting about her time spent on Freud's couch is the conflict between intuition and empiricism. Whereas H.D. would have an instinctual, creative, inspirational relationship to all things imaginative,

Freud would rationalize a myth through interpretation as something relating to the analysand's personal history. This does not mean Freud did not believe in 'the miracle of the fairy tale: he is using it differently; as a poet might use, or apply, a myth' (Phillips, 2012, p.ix). Phillips goes on to discuss that H.D.'s time with Freud was spent in order to seek different ways of thinking and she began to rely, through the practice of psychoanalysis with Freud, on her 'stream of associations to decipher what she experienced' (Friedman, 1981, p.21), while actively writing on the dead. For H.D. 'the dead were living in so far as they lived in memory or were recalled in a dream' (Doolittle, 2012, p.13).

In David Lynch's second series of *Twin Peaks* (1990–1991) Special Agent Dale Cooper's ability to channel figures in dreams suggests the dead exist in the dream world. But it is Moore that suggests:

> It is one thing to say that we see the dead in our dreams, or that during sleep we may visit or have visions of the afterlife, but quite another to suggest that the dead themselves must be in a similar state of dreaming or that the afterlife is itself some kind of dream. (Moore, 2016, p.66)

We were drawn to H.D.'s imagination that the dead exist in dreams and also to Moore's exploration of H. H. Price's concept where 'the disembodied mind or soul would live wholly in a world constructed out of its own memories and desires' (Price cited in Moore, 2016, p.67). These ideas drifted into a studio performance of *Dream Yards*, where we imagined the afterlife exists in a dream space akin to Lynchian visions. The Death Drift allowed our ideas (that perpetual circle) to move into a new territory. We continued to explore this idea by creating a vision for the dead to exist in one place. In turn, through a process of a Drift Drive, we translated the walking tour project into a touring theatre studio show. Whereas the outdoor performances made great play of the architecture and layout of York's streets, the studio theatre performance played on the theatrical setting permitting different rules for a new script. Reimaging *Dream Yards* for the theatre audience, we conceived a fantasy for an afterlife, where the dead meet and gather on an uncharted landscape. Here, the audience were invited to tune into the dead as a channelling experience.

In the walking tour, Gary references Amelia Earhart, the American aviation pioneer, as her story was brought into our work through a previous dream donation. The process of our DD/DD as the tornado metaphor, scooped up Amelia and brought her into our world, her story is an important unsolved mystery.

Earhart's last contact with the rest of the world was through radio transmission. Falling into difficulty and with her navigator Noonan, their plane Electra may have landed near by Nikumaroro (Gardner Island) in the Pacific Ocean. The mystery surrounding her disappearance has created many different hypotheses on her survival and death in the Pacific. In fact, some theories suggest she was taken by the Japanese and others go so far as to say Amelia changed her identity to live a new life in New Jersey. Of course, the mystery of the missing person makes way for many stories to unfold, all of which are not based upon any evidence. However, what is certain is that Amelia's last transmission has been the subject of scrutiny by The International Group for Historic Aircraft Recovery (TIGHAR). They draw attention to the day Amelia was radioing for help, curious as to who was listening and what they were hearing. In fact, provocatively, they allow us to imagine that someone, somewhere heard her voice and point to one intriguing story of a distress call.

One afternoon in Florida in the summer of 1937, a 15-year-old girl, Betty Klenck, was listening to the shortwave radio using her family's radio set that had a specially rigged antenna. Betty would regularly pick up signals from far away, across the ocean. Listening curiously and on a daily basis, she made notes and sketches in her notebook of all she tuned into. One afternoon she heard a woman crying out the name Amelia Earhart, and according to TIGHAR, Betty documented a real-time transcription of a post-loss radio transmission from Earhart that you can find on the TIGHAR website. According to TIGHAR, many accidental listeners heard a distress call on that day and Betty's was not taken seriously. The fact that Betty's notes were not believed at the time, offer a chilling thought that somewhere, out there, a woman and her navigator might have been asking for help. People were heard but not listened to.

For *Dream Yards* the studio show, we imagined an island as an afterlife, a dream where the dead, or rather our dead – those figures who we were circling in our practice – hung out together as a celebration of Amelia's life. We imagined that on this island we would find King Lear, his Fool, Freud, Kong and Amelia, tired and fatigued, that is until they happen across a man with dark glasses and the voice of an angel (Orbison), who sings them all to sleep. In their sleep they channel the dreams of York city's residents (the dreams that were donated to the *Dream Yards* walking tour). In the studio show, Gary dresses up as Orbison, Earhart and Freud, named The Abominable Sigmund Freud (as a hybrid of Freud and a snowman-yeti), who dishes out glow sticks to the audience while singing rock songs. All these dead figures meet up with Kong Lear while she recites the dreams of others to the musical accompaniment from a pianist sourced from the audience.

During the show's opening, Kong Lear invites the audience to witness her bring the island to life. She cues the lights, and the audience witness the lights, she cues the parachute, and the audience witness a parachute lift up off the set revealing Gary on the island, and she cues the music, but there is no sound. She cues the music again, and again, until she realizes the piano, downstage left, has an empty seat. She proceeds by explaining to the audience that the show can't go on without a pianist and invites a volunteer to play music continually throughout the show. When a pianist eventually volunteers (after some playful persuasion and gentle reassurance that they don't have to be an expert, or in fact ever played before), the audience applaud. Kong Lear coaches the volunteer, in full view of the audience, to channel into the show's unfolding themes to practise a clairaudience and pick up on the show's tone, rhythm and pace, and to tune into what is happening on the island in the moment to moment through looking, feeling, listening and knowing. The pianist agrees and begins to play, the atmosphere is deeply rewarding, because all in the room, audience included, are now tuning in using many mediumistic qualities, rooting for their fellow audience member and sensing with them how to tune into us, the life of the performance and the concept of the dead enjoying a dream world where Amelia Earhart, played by Gary, comes into view smiling.

Creative Task: Dream Walks

Conceptual Framework

This task should take a few weeks to develop, it is a research and development idea that accumulates in performance. However, feel free to adapt to suit a shorter workshop frame.

We all dream, unless we have serious damage to the perceptual structures of the brain, it's just that we don't always remember them. Upon waking, quite often the memory of a dream begins to fade. Sometimes the dream is so vivid it can stay with us for days, even years. The memory of a childhood dream can be clearer and crisper than a memory from a childhood reality. The feeling of having a dream, but not remembering it exactly, provokes a strange feeling deep within ourselves, uncanny. Experiencing consciousness inside a dream is a practice, in a moment of lucidity one might experience the feeling of being in control of a dream's narrative content and situation. We are sentient beings and we do feel something from our dreams, we have emotional responses to them and they can have a profound and lasting effect on us personally. Recalling upon the dream invites us to interpret and find meaning, but quite simply recalling the dream as a creative experience can be equally rewarding. Everyone who remembers their dreams has something in common, they describe their dreams as if they were there, as if it really happened to them... 'I was running on the spot', 'I was fighting a dragon', 'I was singing underwater'. Predominantly the way we describe a dream is performative.

Writing

To help recall dreams try this:

When you wake allow for no interruptions, so don't set your alarm.

As soon as you wake don't move, lie still.

Remember your dream and think of words that describe your dream, give it a name.

Keep a dream diary over a period of time and write images and descriptions of your dreams in short fragments, avoid long passages.

Playing

In groups of two, go for a walk in a chosen area and look for dead and alive spaces. By dead spaces, we mean those that on the surface look neglected, or look less attractive to tourists or shoppers etc. but in reality, they hold many secrets or creative ideas. Alive spaces are those frequented by many people, popular sites.

On this walk, stop at both sites, dead and alive, and recall your dreams to your partner. Swap.

Spend time revisiting those dead and alive sites, recalling dreams and get to know these sites at a certain time of day. Tune in to these sites; listen to the sounds, feel pedestrian rhythms, grasp the pace and the comings and goings of people and animals in the location at that time of day. Appropriate in a creative context the terms clairvoyance, clairaudience, clairsentience and claircognizance to connect to these sites, how do you feel, know, hear, see these spaces in your creative world? Use this knowledge when you eventually return as performers of a world you have created for these sites.

Structural Dramaturgy

Script your dreams to suit the chosen sites, blending with other creative material of your choice. You can write this script imagining a four-stage dramaturgical process in relation to the site(s), for example:

1. Geographically using the network of dead and alive spaces, how might this network relate to some of the dream content?
2. Conceptually structure the journey to the dead and alive spaces as a journey into the five-stage sleep process.
3. Fictively reimagine the relationship between characters from another story.
4. Materially contextualize the images and descriptions of dream accounts from both diaries.

Performing

Invite an audience on your scripted tour.

There is a world that exists to summon and to frame, there are options to creatively channel other people's worlds (the goings on and happenings in the city). When you channel in this way they enter into your journey alongside the images created, and they experience you in a certain way. Those who are not directly involved in your work are not simply a background to your event.

Please note that when you make work in a public space you should conduct a risk assessment, seek permission from the local council and avoid disturbing the fabric of the city's life, rather, complement it in a generous and thoughtful manner.

For further development, imagine another life for your dream walk in a different space or medium. Allow the DD/DD to guide a new translation according to a different space and audience.

< Q U I C K · G U I D E S >

Title: Lost in a Sea of Glass and Tin (2017)

Where: The Defibrillator Gallery Chicago developed from a residency in that space. Touring studio show to the Queering Ritual International Symposium, York St John University and Norwich Arts Centre, York Theatre.

Description: Taking inspiration from David Lynch's concept of the 'eye of the duck' (in relation to composition, texture and mood within a filmmaking context). A 75-minute performance for two performers one of whom sings his heart out to the classics whilst the other speaks about a life of solitude. The work is performed across a bold structure of 15 coloured lighting states and accompanied by a video projection cut from footage of a road trip from around Wisconsin following the journey of Alvin Straight from Lynch's film The Straight Story. Progressively the performers who situates themselves in their own zones move toward one shared space and transform into hand-made low-fi crudely rendered objects, something we have coined 'The Black Heaps,' whose final address is in a completely unintelligible language, but open to interpretation, they then leave the performance space behind and drift off across the road and into the city.

Kit box: Keyboard synth, 12 milk crates, projector, four portable LED theatre lights, a chair (to be smashed up), a bag gold coins, blue dress, white suit, a box of things to attach to Gary's head (balloons, feathers, paper cups and anything else to hand), two megaphones, 'Black Heaps' constructions (backpacks, gazebo poles, Gaffa tape, fur, cable ties).

Commonalities: Roy Orbison. Repetition. David Lynch. Digital piano. Black fur. Singing. Ghosting.

Illustration 10 Quick Guide *Lost in a Sea of Glass and Tin*

< Q U I C K • G U I D E S >

Title: Roy of the Dead/Day of The O (2013 onwards)

Where: Various, including City of York following the Snickelway route of the *Dream Yards* tour, York Minster, Slung Low's Holbeck Underground Ballroom, Leeds, According to McGee, York. All on 6th December.

Description: An evolving annual event to celebrate the death of the legendary American troubadour of darkness Roy Orbison events include: A zombie walk around the city of York where a group of the undead serenaded the living with the songs *Crying, I Drove all Night* and *Only the Lonely*. A midnight concert of the hit song *Crying* outside York Minster. A market stall event of participatory games including Ring Toss over Roy and KD Lang and pin the eyes on the portrait of Roy. A live event at a gallery taking the format of a life drawing class framed as death drawing. A sound work of a reading of zombie text.

Kit box: Black wigs. Black clothing. Face paint. Skeleton costume. Keyboard. Song sheets. Black O cakes. Black vodka. Black cheese. Taxidermy Blackbird (ethically sourced – killed by a cat).

Commonalities: Roy Orbison. Dreams. Ghosting. David Lynch. Black cat.

Illustration 11 Quick Guide *Roy of the Dead / Day of the O*

Illustration 12 Skeleton Roy, for Roy *of the Dead/ Day of the O*, 6th December 2014, Gillygate, York; available for hire

6

The Undead Balladeer

This chapter contextualizes the figure of the zombie in popular culture specifically drawing upon the qualities of deadness as a practice of distortion. Driven by desire and in relationship to humour, the qualities of the contemporary zombie appear to be performing a nostalgia of a particular cinematic aesthetic: the George Romero zombie. We begin by sharing a creative score we have composed entitled *Sing Your Heart Lips Out* written to be interpreted as an audio walk and experienced as a wander around a city and we further unpack the score's compositional quality. The chapter then moves into a descriptive account of the project *Roy of the Dead/Day of the O*, a zombie choir project who ghost the route of a performance walk around the city of York. This chapter then goes on to explore the phenomena of a zombie movement that has become hugely popular in performance (and protest) by drawing upon the work of artists Ellie Harrison and Martin O'Brien. We end with a series of tasks for you to embody deadness as an affable zombie.

Sing Your Heart Lips Out

When you leave the building and step onto the street and wait for the green
   man and cross the road you look at the rows of shops down the street
You peer in through the steamy windows at the bread, cheese bits and deli mound.
You notice the man, he is the Deli Man with round glasses and dough on his hands

You enter through the door and hover around the busy counter. Everyone turns and looks at you, there's a distinct effy flavor

Memory of the spark, charged, it's buzzin'

You sing your heart out

You move on up the street

A bus slows down in the traffic you a face person on the bus

You stick your head to the window. They recoil like a butter tray

You turn and tap on the restaurant window people eating chew food

They turn to look at you and you crowd with others against the glass

Memory of the spark, charged, it's buzzin'

You sing your heart out lips against glass

As the music reaches full speed they are all sat on their horses

Hamish cradling his cat

Angus painting tiny bicycles

Ginger Monty gulping and baulking and belching round and round

A man with a stick and headphones

The bin of flappy pornography

Entering door in wall through narrow passage with no floor end

Chu chu chu chatter does the hard brick feel like rolling across it like a soft fluffy papoose?

Chu chu chttr ds te har-rick ac-ac-ac like a sof flu?

You spat out onto street in front of a carousel, gaping horses moving around lights flashing, sound of Victorian bladder grinder

Memory of the spark rip on the choke

Rip o t oke

You sing your heart lips out

You groan. You shuffle feet. There are cobbles. Others groany

You cross the road and stop the traffic

All the shutters shutting

Sounds of the city shoppers

You look up, the illustrious hung aloft beyond handling

You look down, the low ranking splashy in the rain water

You look left, you look right and you duhrrrrrrrrrrrr

You duhrrrrrrrrrrr

You duhrrrrrrrrrrr

Duhrrrrrrrrrrrr

Duhrrrrr eeee duhrrrr mincing duhrrrrr you are in a yard you groaning you shuffling feet

Embedded heads protrude like giant pebbles

The sound of the city now like a dull ache

men huddle the door of a kitchen one of them kicks foot out of time to shoo a cat

You are in a yard groaning, shuffling feet

A smell of sweet perfume

A smell of sweet chew food

You startle a butter woman carrying eggs

Memory of the spark memory and the spark

You sing your heart out

The butter woman stands and watches and begins to cry

You be too melancholy too saddening to the living

You are crying and they are all sat on their horses

Jill and Dave frying

Lena and her roman tiles

Pete with his green hands painting all the shop fronts not the regular high street stores

You linger on sincerity you don't recognize this place

Three men, the shirts, join the singing with gusto

When you down by the water's edge under the willow tree

Geese gliding like drones on the wet top

And you wading through the waste at the back of club, a shoe, an umbrella, bits of wire, traffic cone, and Gertrude Stein pants

> *Shutters shut and open so do queens. Shutters shut and shutters and so shutters shut and shutters and so and so shutters and so shutters shut and so shutters shut and shutters and so. Shutters shut and open so do pants. And so shutters shut and so and also. And also and so and so and also (Stein, 2017).*

Memory of the spark ignite the spark

You have arrow through your head

You walk to houses a man pops the kettle on the cat

Bodies alternate with the trees; body tree, body tree, body tree, body tree, all varnished faces and rubber habiliments

You enter door in wall through narrow passage with liquid floor end

You back inside and leave the street it is warm low ceiling people on their slurp juice

A silence

Memory of the spark memory and the spark

You rip your last heart out

As the music reaches full speed they are all sat on their horses

Ross shaves you bald and you have a tattoo of a brain on your head

Danny Cher Bailey, a beer, a straw

You notice a glitter ball painted black

A bubble floats by. Pop

Pop

Pop. Pop. Pop. Pop. Pop. Pop. Pppppppp pop pop pop pop

Sing Your Heart Lips Out

This text was written for an audio walk; it is some sort of mind state caught in the spell of deep play, driven by the desire of play's contagious spirit. Our recording of it, made on 6 December 2018 is available through the www.garyandclaire.com website via a Vimeo link. It is a thought process and response to the outside world, shifting between instruction and experience as if the listener is a zombie. We have also scored it for others to interpret and produce as a soundtrack, and make individual recordings of it.

Imagine the listener who walks the city listening to music on headphones. In a similar way, this score offers up some kind of veil onto the world; it takes up an auditory space. The text is written in the second person offering a framework in which to think about the surroundings of the city. Normally, the experience of an audio tour invites you to be immersed in a world. This zombie text, alters a world that already exists and subverts other people's activities as a *multiple as if* experience, placing, for you, an imaginary frame across the city as you walk and where you choose to walk. The text has been written imagining those people, places and objects mentioned in the text moving through your field of vision. There will be coincidences where descriptions might interpret what you actually experience. The text does not give a specific route around a city; instead it encourages listeners to take their most direct desire path. The zombie in this audio walk is invited to recall the 'memory of the spark', a moment of energy suddenly released from the zombie's previous life as a balladeer bursting into song, serenading the living as if the listener has remembered what it was like to sing their heart out. Analogously, imagine the memory of the spark as a flicker of a neon light without power where on occasion a small bit of charge lingers on inside the glass, igniting the gas.

Framed by the ambience of the sound and the glitching of the words performed by the voice, the score is written through a process of zombification where the text plays around with tensing, as if the zombie 'chews' its words. The text plants you in the middle of a mess of things in order to hybridize words that don't normally sit well together. It is like a Gertrude Stein zombified score merged with a Chris Morris *Blue Jam* (1997) word play experiment. The text has a single mindedness quality to it as if the writing is all shambling and vacant, but it slips to moments of intelligence where the listener is caught in midst of a fantasy – fancying themselves as a poet.

The words shift between a semi-instructional text and a malleable one, where the listener may notice a door, or a window or a figure, wherever they may be, and this could be in the middle of Norfolk, Ceredigion, Yorkshire or beyond.

Sing Your Heart Lips Out was written as an echo of a live performance project entitled *Roy of the Dead/Day of the O* (2013), that celebrated the twenty-fifth anniversary of Orbison's death on 6 December (1988). This event was also intended as a way of celebrating the independent traders in York who have been making a go of their businesses and struggling in a competitive global economy of cities overridden with chain stores. We serenaded proprietors, shop workers, their customers and the incidental audience as zombies. Since 2013, each year, we mark Orbison's departure from this world as a death anniversary through a creative activity and this first ensemble zombie performance walk around the city of York followed a workshop on how to move and perform as an undead balladeer. The performance ghosted the route we took on the *Dream Yards* walking tour but on this walk we entered the shops ran by independent traders with sudden outbursts of Orbison songs for the incidental audience. Ghosting the *Dream Yards* route offered an uncanny experience because the familiar route was noted albeit in a completely different tempo, the uncanniness resided from the reality we had walked this map before, and through dreams. This in turn affected our attitude (as zombies) towards this experience, it seemed to make sense of our position walking as a reanimated corpse, we had been here before, only it was different. In fact, the walk now took three times longer to complete than *Dream Yards*, the slow zombie shuffle led us to the pub, but thankfully just in time for last orders.

Sing Your Heart Lips Out reflects the people we met and things we saw on the zombie walk *Roy of the Dead/Day of the O*. In fact, those named in *Sing Your Heart Lips Out* are fictionalized versions of the independent traders who we got to know and who we made a portrait film about entitled *We Made Something of This* (2015) – available to view via a Vimeo link on our website. For this film we spent weeks on the York street Gillygate getting to know, through deep time spent, each individual on that street. The portrait film captured the daily routines of the shop proprietors making a go of their business, frying fish, baking bread, painting the shop fronts. We are very satisfied that before we made this film with the residents, they got to know us as zombies, a playful introduction to our continuing presence on that street, where today, many of the shops and businesses thrive, some sadly have closed, changed hands or moved location.

We created the zombie walk in the context of the everyday because we were aware in 2013 the zombie as a participatory experience was on the rise. Perhaps the attraction to embody an undead fleshy thing 'speechless, gormless, without memory of prior life or attachments' (Luckhurst, 2015, p.7) is that zombies are akin in appearance to a human form than a typical supernatural figure. There is something familiar about this dead thing, something real. Their growing popularity on television was apparent; hordes and hordes of zombie extras were filmed in Atlanta to set the tone for an apocalyptic nightmare in the first episode of the series *The Walking Dead* (2010) with many seasons now spanning across eight years. And in *Zombieland* (2009) the actor Bill Murray plays himself disguised as zombie. Here we see Murray creeping forward arms stretched out walking towards the character Tallahassee who, shocked, and in awe of his favourite film star, asks 'Bill Murray you're a zombie?' The Main character, Columbus, narrates a series of survival rules throughout the film as a voiceover, rather like a teaching manual presumably as guidance to us (the audience), on how to cope with living in a zombie-ridden land. It seemed, in 2013, everyone wanted to be a zombie (including us), or everyone wanted to survive the zombie apocalypse.

Roy of the Dead/Day of the O

The first *Roy of the Dead/Day of the O* project on 6 December 2013 took place over one full working day and into the evening, beginning as a zombie workshop in a drama studio at York St John University and spilling out into the streets of York in the evening. Workshop participants (the zombies), included (following a call for zombie participants) students and staff from the University, in collaboration with students and staff from the University of Hull who had also walked with us on *Dream Yards*. Together as a zombie choir, we arranged and practised three Orbison's songs; *Crying, I Drove All Night* and *Only the Lonely*. We established a playful perspective on the zombie developed from a Death Drift/ Drift Drive (DD/DD) methodology working around three specific ideas that we attach to the zombie:

Desire: they are pure id and follow an urge.
Repetition: they repeat habits and are relentless.
Drift: they can change course in mid flow, are slow but keep going.

We related these terms as concepts to the group to play with and described their presence as an animated chorus. As a horde of corpses, now and then, they were instructed to remember (through a spark) a life they once had as a balladeer and to serenade the living by bursting into song.

We had proposed the idea of the George A. Romero zombie as the frame of reference while using the filter of an 'affable' zombie over it. We used the term affable to soften any idea that our York zombies were vicious or deadly. Rather than working from out of the qualities of deadliness (i.e.

the qualities of a killer), we worked from out of the paradox of a playful deadness, somewhere between a living dead persona and undead persona:

> Zombies act on instinct and drive alone, mindlessly pursuing the basest of needs in a veritable orgy of unchecked indulgence. These qualities make Romero's zombies unavoidably flat characters, which could explain their virtual absence from novels and other written stories (at least prior to 1968); their essentially physical qualities, however, make zombies ideal cinematic monstrosities. By presenting zombies as literal walking corpses (the 'living dead' rather than 'undead'), zombie films horrify protagonists and audiences alike with the uncanny fusion of the familiar with the unfamiliar. (Bishop, 2010, p.110)

The qualities of a shuffling and stumbling zombie embodied by the Romero actor, seemingly written from a psychoanalytic model, need to be further appreciated. Bishop (2010) places them firmly within the realms of the 'return of the repressed', where deeply placed fears from the depths of the unconscious appear as some of Romero's characters' traits, killing and eating family members, as one example. Yet playfully, let's not forget, as a swaggering corpse with its arms by its side one minute then suddenly stretched out the next, it's a bit of a menace. In many forms of performance, it seems, when actors embody the dead they portray through complete stillness or extreme slowness as a popular characteristic of the ghostly, the haunted, the ethereal, but the zombie requires something clumsier. Embodying and sustaining the zombie for performance requires a specific type of attitude throughout the whole body so that the physical gait might represent a slouching, dragging, heavy bodily motion as if the performer feels the weight of its own corpse. However, we recognize this is no complex technique; it is a DIY exercise born from the memory of what each individual has witnessed and interpreted from culture. The DIY form of ghosting the zombie is up for grabs; some performers will work from the idea of a 'living dead' persona, some with an attitude of an 'undead' presence. While it might be difficult to separate out a real difference here, it is Bishop (2010) that relates the idea of the living dead as something more akin to a human presence than the undead which may have typical qualities of a supernatural being. Yet, in practice, it is the braiding of these differences that grounds electrifying qualities of deadness. Ghosting the zombie also requires an imaginative attitude to fuel its presence; it requires thinking playfully, not simply as a fantasy but imagining desire as an intellective component of play.

Therefore, during our workshops for *Roy of the Dead/Day of the O*, it was useful to think about a Death Drift of the zombie as a *multiple as if*, slipping between the actions of playing dead as if a Romero-esque zombie (living dead zombie), as if an undead balladeer (a moving corpse embodying supernatural powers), as if a Roy Orbison fan accompanied by an assertive sense of individuality. We invited each participant to bring something of their own to their zombie like a distinguishable outfit and to develop a unique persona, so they had a sense of their zombie self within a Roy Orbison choir.

Specifically drawn to the many balladeers who sing the songs of dead celebrities, and who keep on singing their hearts out as tribute to them or, as if they are them, our practice was developing a significant place for Orbison across a range of intermedia projects. The excess of Elvis impersonators is surely testimony that the dead sing among us. Elvis' absent presence in culture, where he lives each night through the embodiment of others, draws upon an idea that an Elvis impersonator is a medium, open and ready to channel the most famous dead celebrity:

> The impersonator has a special relation to this redemptive logic, for he or she works as a medium who channels the spirit of a saviour, all the while opening up a public space where people can express their mutual faith in an abstract principle that no one can name. (Spigel, 1990, p. 193)

It became apparent in practice that the impersonation of the dead icon, who takes on the commitment of an entertainer and who only sings the songs of the dead, is a form of spiritual embodiment. The context of the term spiritual for us connects to some state of 'being' in performance where the performer, through a process of distortion, blends this psychic characteristic with other worlds.

'Elvis not only refuses to go away, he keeps showing up in places where he seemingly doesn't belong' (Rodman, 2013, p.i). A little bit like Freud!

To articulate this idea further, we draw upon Lynch's 1990 movie *Wild at Heart*, and the character of Sailor played by Nicolas Cage, as an example. The character adopts a subtle (though not overtly) attitude of Elvis, boasting that his snakeskin jacket is a 'symbol of his own "individuality"'. The character Sailor is not an Elvis impersonator in the film (rather a criminal in love with Lula and on the run with her); we see the actor (Cage), performing Elvis' *Love Me Tender*. Cage here, it appears, is embodying the spirit of Elvis for the Lynchian aesthetic. There is something exciting about the quality of this mismatch; for he is not Elvis (he's dead), he is not an Elvis impersonator (that is not his character's role), but an actor playing the role of a criminal ghosting Elvis' performance qualities. Sailor also boasts about his individual sense of self (who, it seems, is really reflecting on Cage's sense of individuality, something he is known for). The haunting and humorous position of the Lynchian actor in the mix of the violently criminal world of the character means that Rodman's theory about Elvis showing up in places where he doesn't belong produces, in culture, exciting hybrid figures. It is this quality of distortion that we are drawn to when making performance work. Gregory Reece writes:

> because Cage does channel Elvis, and precisely because he does so with such mixed results, the viewer is constantly reminded of Elvis and reminded that Cage is not Elvis. If Cage's Sailor is Elvis incarnate, reincarnated if you will, then it is as an inexact incarnation. (Reece, 2006, p.52)

There is a woman on a bridge in Durham; she is a busker with the most amazing voice. And yet her appearance is dead; she slouches melancholic as if she is vacant inside and jolted by something. Because of this juxtaposition, between the incredible voice and the 'dead' character, her performance is extraordinarily affective; her voice does not represent the lifelessness of her gait, but the lyrics do. Here the busker, whether she is aware of it or not, is performing a deadness that breathes life into the dark emotional ballads of Elvis and Orbison, but in her own style. She is a zombie busker, channelling the dead and performing a distortion.

We invited the participants to ghost a balladeer, but of their own making. Their persona was not aimed to be a lookie-likey of a true Orbison with dark hair and glasses; rather the woman on the bridge in Durham is one example of how a 'dead' persona could be performed.

Here we outline that the busker is not a straightforward impersonator, but has traces of one if you squint your eyes. We discussed the usefulness of alternative approaches to performance than that of a direct impersonation of a famous dead persona. Whereas presenting a voice that does not match the appearance of the performer is an exciting juxtaposition that shrouds the performer in a blanket of mystery.

Zombifying is not about direct impersonation of the zombie, but rather bringing the zombie into the conversation on distortion and, more importantly for performance practice, it is about ways of working with material; one enters the world of the zombie using pre-existing references, sounds, movements and reanimates them by not giving a complete picture. When information is missing, the zombie is a partial rendering of a thing, the partialness is its form. However, here is the paradox; embodying the partial should be encountered in its fullest sense, and to give a visual metaphor as an example, imagine a drawing that has been rubbed out; what is left after the rubbing is an impression of something. It is that something that is more interesting because it demands a different kind of interpretation. This is not to say the performance should lack commitment. On the contrary, one can give one's all to something partial. We encouraged this idea to the performers, inviting them to perform their own version of the zombie with many things missing from an original. We asked them to imagine, during performance, the audience squinting for they might see something of the original in their performance; they may see a ghost.

As a chorus the voice was an important aspect of the performance, we were not asking for perfect singers. On the contrary, we invited the zombies to imagine something else inside them that they may not normally access, to find 'a voice'. For example, to imagine the zombie as the Freudian primitive id at work is to imagine a voice (that sings its heart out) as a mischievous, playful noise full of repressed desire, dying to let rip and make an impression on the world. In other words, the singing zombie has a life deep inside its deadness. Summoning up this 'voice' is akin to a spiritual experience of an impersonator channelling Elvis, and therefore it empowers the performer to imagine the voice suddenly coming to life. Like a spark of great energy, where one finds a voice they didn't know they had.

The hotchpotch hoard of zombies was an unlikely pack dressed up: a punk, a cowboy, a nurse, a goth, Duchamp's alter ego Rrose Sélavy, and more. Identified as individuals but distinguished as a chorus bursting into song after one person has a memory, a spark that triggers the choir. We developed fairly loose rules (from a Drift Drive) around intuitive decisions made by the chorus on when to choose to burst into song. After singing together, individuals, shuffled on slowly and got themselves into their own predicaments, such as getting stuck in a snickelway (a shortcut or hidden passage in the city), a shop doorway or resting for a moment on top of a rising bollard. This humorous performance experience appropriates some of the qualities of the Romero zombie (where its humour seems to reflect the clumsiness of the slapstick physical performer), but it is soon interrupted by the energy of the spark akin to the surprise experience when watching John Landis' pop video of Michael Jackson's *Thriller* (1983) for the first time. Here zombies come hobbling into shot, but suddenly they have a memory, a sudden burst of energy and perform one of the most copied and highly choreographed danced routines of the twentieth century.

When out on the streets of York it was as if all of the dead balladeers were heading towards a day of reckoning. In our version of the apocalypse, the zombies are drawn towards singing as a shambling collective. As a walking experience we paid close attention to detail about all things individual within the city and we stopped to celebrate the independent traders, as a nod to their important place within society, working hard keeping their businesses afloat surrounded by the towers of giants.

The workshop 'training' practised the idea that the zombie tunes into the audiences receptivity and therefore the memory of the spark (when the chorus burst into an Orbison song) is led by the zombie group having a gut feeling that someone is going to be receptive (or at least not offended); the incidental passing audience, we thought should be happy to be serenaded – it was not a performance to intimidate. In fact, with an affable zombie in mind we found many opportunities to perform at a distance from people. For example, we serenaded a group of diners sitting in the window of a restaurant; there we were, slow-moving zombies stuck at the windowpane lips pressed against the glass singing *I Drove All Night* to a very happy audience, where, through the window, the song must have sounded muffled. Instead of infecting the audience with violence, causing them to transform into flesh-eaters, we infected them with our singing, a contagious sound and people sang along with us, they joined in with gusto. One woman cried and fell to her knees; it was just what she needed that night. We embraced the 'thing' in keeping with the flesh-eating zombie, but on friendlier, generous terms, we sang, they sang!

The multitudinous state of the zombie is a transformative experience for a performer; beyond the clichéd movements that have been often copied from the Romero zombie is a changed body, a distortion of the self and culture, a strange mix of references and obsessions. The zombie is a perfect body to be reimagined, a corpse that has evolved (in fiction and film and now performance and over time). The undead balladeer (or the living dead crooner, if that approach is preferred) is the singing zombie ready and willing to infect others in a contagion, whose desire is to get a whole city singing. Moreover, the undead balladeer is a pop icon of people's performance. In a culture that is full to the brim with impersonators. This was a highly sociable activity offering a chance for others to take on an alternative persona and live out obsessions of what 'their' Orbison zombie could be. Similarly, the desire to be a zombie, practising the slow walk in a city that is fast and ever changing, is to experience what happens when we slow everything right down and playfully interrupt the flow of a street, taking more care and attention, albeit clumsily, to the here and now.

The Zombie

According to Luckhurst (2015), zombies are a contagion, driven by the desire to devour up all the living on this earth – 'zombies are the rapture with rot'. However, the zombie in contemporary performance and indeed popular culture is constantly being reinvented. Some behavioural features of the zombie have evolved significantly since the early twentieth century, and others remain resistant to change. It seems those that are fixed within a specific cultural frame are continually referenced and ghosted in per-formance. These are the zombies of nostalgia that 'hold the rapture' with desire and with humour as well as 'the rot'. It is useful to note, however, where the idea of the zombie came from. Although we don't offer an extensive discussion on its historical cultural context, it is important to remember how the image of human suffering played a major part in the developing image of the terrifying zombie.

The zombie has complex origins; its emergence through culture is not straightforward in its historical reference and for this reason the zombie is an unfixed figure. 'Africa is technically the birthplace of the zombie. West African Vodun holds that a dead human can be brought back to life by a priest with specific otherworldly powers to commune with the gods' (Fonseca in Pulliam & Fonseca, 2014, p.2). Certainly, it seems the zombie is a relatively new concept in relation to the horror genre and can be traced back to ancient archetypes where stories of the dead return to threaten the living, although the term zombie (the English word) was not cited until 1819. But it is also well discussed that Haiti is the birthplace of the zombie as a country with a long history of slavery along with economic exploitation from outside forces. Haiti is 'trapped in a reoccurring nightmare of its own tragic history one that has been perpetually shaped by its legendary revolution and subsequent exploitation foreign and domestic powers' (Matthews in Pulliam & Fonseca, 2014, p.123). The zombie came out of a misery where the body had a lack of free will which fed into the idea that 'to be a zombie is, in essence, to be a slave for eternity, and Haitian folk culture resounds with references to the drudgery of those doomed to repeat the routines of their hellish lives' (Ibid., p.124). The zombie had a literary history before its rise to popularity in film; and its image from out of Haitian folklore is captured in W.B. Seabrook's story *The Magic Island* (1929) and depicted as a 'creature emerging from a long history of demonization of Haiti, which was focused for decades on over-heated fantasies of Voodoo, cannibalism and black magic' (Luckhurst, 2015, p.44). Certainly, this depiction of the zombie in the first half of the twentieth century was symbolic of the colonial slave culture that evolved as an imported story. Matthews draws our attention to the American occupation of Haiti (1915–1934), where tales of zombies spread back to the United States and films such as the *White Zombie* (1932), directed by Victor Halperin, supported a popular image of Haiti as 'a place where once can witness zombies trundling along dusty rural roads, in thrall to their master, the voodoo sorcerer' (Matthews, 2014, p.125). To grasp the historical relationship the zombie has to a colonial occupation of the Caribbean islands, research further into Luckhurst (2015) and Pullman and Fonseca (2014).

According to Luckhurst, and since Halperin's 1932 horror film, zombies in most cultural forms were neglected for more than 30 years and could only be found 'lurking un-noticed in graveyards sinking into the shudder pulps and horror comics of the 1940s and '50s' (Ibid., p.7). That was until a new idea of the zombie was born, one that became known as a named thing that hit the screens as a film series beginning in 1968.

The Romero Zombie

The George A. Romero zombie is referenced widely as *the* zombie of the latter half of the twentieth century. Spanning across a series of six horror films beginning with *Night of the Living Dead (1968)*, the American-Canadian film director created a specific type of zombie with its own universally recognized style of movement. Its gait and indeed rules of behaviour have been imitated and parodied a plenty, to the point in which, for some, it is hard to imagine another type of zombie. On the one hand the embodiment of a Romero zombie is a cliché, and on the other hand it is valued as the authentic way to characterize the thing. Why does the slow shuffle remain a popular characteristic of the zombie film and live performance? Does the shuffle reflect the misery of the human condition? Is the slowness an appealing quality to perform? Perhaps it is to do with fear – the slower the zombie, the more terrifying they are? After all, we know from watching the Romero films they catch up to us no matter how fast we run. Phil Smith, mythogeographer and walking artist sometimes referred to as Crab Man, puts the zombie phenomenon into the perspective of the deriviste, the Situationists' practice of walking:

> Romero zombie and situationist 'derivistes' have no legitimating starting points and no final destinations to reach; they follow the atmosphere, dislocated from the everyday functioning of the city and its decision making, their shambling and chaotic walking reveal flows and barriers that are usually invisible and unmarked gaps in the fabric that are otherwise ignored. Just as the living dead have an unnerving ability to fold time, suddenly and without warning becoming very close, 'derivistes' can

slow themselves to give attention to the fine texture of the city and then accelerate to a pace at which they become sensitive to sudden changes in ambience and to the flows of images, things and organisms as they move from one space to the next. (Smith, 2015, p.41)

However, the zombie is a contradictory thing. How can a corpse walk? How can a dead object be a living thing? Why does it amble, even if slowly, if it is dead? While the Romero zombie's contemporary appeal is nostalgia, we yearn to return to those movies that once terrified because the slowness in these zombies embodies a specific quality of deadness and they are very theatrical. We've understood through playing the zombie that it is the contradictory theatrical qualities of a 'thing' that keep the Romero zombie very present, and its qualities are imagined as a derivative form of the death drive. In terms of the Romero zombie's performance, deadness equals clumsiness; the body has life when it is supposed to lack liveliness. The contradiction for the actor is in the impossibility of performing a state of lifelessness. Instead actors embody qualities of deadness; the zombie moves, it ambles as more of a 'thing' than a human, it is supposed to be much more dead than alive. And this quality of paradoxical deadness, perpetually moving, is the thing that is already within us:

> Zombies, in marked contrast (to vampires), have lost all connection with their human behaviour behind the most superficial. They look human, they walk upright, and they can even use the simplest of tools, yet their motivating drive never transcends the animalistic; in Romero's version of the mythology, they exist only to feed. In other words, Romero's zombies have become pure id, governed by sheer animal drive. (Bishop, 2010, p.110)

Thinking about the zombie through a psychoanalytic lens therefore, is to understand the instinctual nature of the id as an urge that keeps moving forward; despite its slowness, it still keeps going; it is unstoppable. And here's the contradiction: it is an animate, inanimate state (a living death drive). But if a zombie is already dead how can it be striving towards death? Is the zombie a psychoanalytical irony on the human condition that draws attention to the fact that we cannot rid ourselves of death even in death? Even when a thing is dead we insist it returns, and this insistence contextualises the zombie in the most elaborate form because the theatrical 'thing' in us loves to dress up; in fact, Marc Leverette (2008) suggests that zombies are the death drive 'in drag' (195):

> The modern zombie is a walking map of our world. As the universe presents its own representation of itself, so cinema is a moving representation of us, also from remains. Only the wavelengths are different. When the Russian revolutionary Leon Trotsky saw early silent movies in New York … he remarked on how they made dead things of living beings, draining their colour and speech. More that 50 years later in 1968 (a revolutionary year), a non-character arrived to distil that revenant into itself: a reanimated, cannibalistic, monochrome corpse without a name. (Smith, 2015, p.9)

The zombie is incongruous; its paradoxical status as the living dead means it is forever a mismatch: on the surface it is a menace behaving far from the ordinary, and close up it represents a fear that lies within ourselves that we don't recognize as self, or other, but what haunts us as 'the Thing' (Kristeva, 1989, p.13). The uncanny of the zombie's incongruity and its contrary motions as a walking living dead nightmare of otherness is a combination of two contrary motions 'progressive and digressive that is at the heart of humor' (Critchley, 2002, p.22). This progressive and digressive behaviour of the zombie is an allegory for the death drive:

> precisely the ultimate Freudian name for the dimension designated by traditional metaphysics as that of *immortality*: for a drive – 'a thrust', which persists beyond the (biological) cycle of generation and corruption, beyond 'the way of all flesh'. In other words, the death drive, the concept 'dead' functions in exactly the same way as '*heimlich*' in the Freudian '*unheimlich*', as coinciding with its negation: the 'death drive' designates the dimension of what horror fiction calls 'undead', a strange immortal, indestructible life that persists beyond death. (Žižek, 1999, p.294)

What this means therefore, is if, and when, we imagine the zombie we have to imagine the death drive is busy and relentless working away (like

Royle's 'mole' (2002), cited in Chapter 3), even after death. Romero zombies are symbolic of physical and psychical senses played out: they move forward in time (literally and slowly) and as a concept they are 'crises of existence, presence and interiority, a way back through deep matter, by the route of things' (Smith, 2015, p.23). Playing the zombie permits us, albeit in a grotesque form, to move beyond death (creatively), and on our own terms. When Smith asks his readers to 'Thingify yourself', it is an invitation to think about the experience of theatrical jouissance. In 'thingifying' we slip between the embodiment of deadness and life-full-ness. And it is Rebecca Schneider who draws our attention to the idea that there is an 'instability of the divide between liveness and deadness that is something of a theatrical thing' (Schneider, 2012, p.152).

The Romero zombie is still, for many, *the* zombie; its state of appearance as a death drive is persistent. In fact, Romero, commenting upon the slow-moving zombie in an interview in Vulture 2008, talks about the quality of zombie movement being a matter of taste. For him the slower the zombie the scarier they are. He notes that the rules for his zombies don't fit in with the logic of the fast zombies of the twenty-first century. Zombies in Danny Boyle's film *28 Days Later* (2002), for example, run very fast. Romero says of the changing fast-paced zombie 'I don't think zombies can run. Their Ankles would snap' (Romero in Oler, 2008). And, others agree: Luckhurst, (2015) points us towards the frustration often displayed by artists when the zombie is appropriated out of the Romero form of the slow shuffling creature. 'Zombies don't run' says Simon Pegg (2008) an actor from Edgar Wright's (2004) *Shaun of the Dead*. Pegg, referencing his own film, describes the mythology established by Romero was offset against the conventions of a romantic comedy, so in this sense it was homage to the idea that the Romero zombie is the legitimate thing. Referring to how the zombie has quickened on its feet in a remake of *Dawn of the Dead* (2004), directed by Zack Snyder, Luckhurst calls those critical of the contemporary fast zombie 'traditionalists' and outlines how, since 2010, zombies have acquired 'flickering consciousness, intelligence, halting speech and conflicted emotional lives, soliloquizing and even falling in love' (Luckhurst, 2015, p.13).

The actor Bill Murray is still appearing in zombie films, through some kind of career feedback loop. Despite being mistaken for a zombie and accidentally killed in *Zombieland* (2009), where he played himself – itself an echo of his part in Jim Jarmusch's *Coffee And Cigarettes* (2003) – we find him in the (2019) Jarmusch film *The Dead Don't Die*. This time Murray plays a cop chasing flesh-eating zombies played by a cast that is a roll call of actors from previous Jarmusch films – Iggy Pop, RZA, Tom Waits, Tilda Swinton. Adam Driver, who also portrays Murray's cop partner, observes that the zombies 'gravitate towards things they did when they were alive'. This is a clear frame of cultural reference, a nod to the rules and codes of practice zombies have ghosted and developed since the Romero movies. In their state of deadness there is a memory of the spark, a life they once had.

In the case of the latter examples on the changing personality of the zombie in twenty-first-century culture, it could be argued that the zombie has found itself in a DD/DD circling around Romero's zombies, albeit with some adapted rules accompanied by a developed sense of humour.

Romero zombies have poured out of film and into the streets in acts of protest too. In New York City, in 2011, a zombie protest marched as part of the Occupy Wall Street demonstrations (OWS). The 'corporate zombies' moved slowly through the city with money spewing out of their mouths in an attempt to call out corporate greed. Their protest marches echoed the satirical nature of Romero films that were often discussed for their socio-political commentary on racism, sexism and commercialism. Therefore, this walking political zombie of the twenty-first century not only symbolized social anxieties of a capitalist culture, they disrupted the streets with playful, mischievous and dark undertones and there was no irony. Rather, there was sincerity in the fact that the normal everyday act of walking, transformed into the slow ambulatory shuffle, as a powerful image, represented the frustration at the death of economic equality in society, as the protestors took to the streets as the unstoppable.

Indeed, the phenomenon of the trend of mass congregation zombie walks through cities and towns in Europe and the United States allowed anyone (non-actors) to test out physical qualities that an actor might experience in a specialist technique in a physical theatre class. Here, the DIY nature of the modern zombie is a liberating art for all.

Ellie Harrison *High Street Casualties*

UK-based artist Ellie Harrison's 2015 project *High Street Casualties*, where approximately 60 participants performed as zombies in a mass walk through Birmingham city centre, focused on the idea that employees were left feeling 'dead' inside after the collapse and closure of many high street retail stores due to the 'credit crunch' of 2008. Harrison deliberately focused on the 'currency of capitalism in visual and popular culture, and the complex political and social workings of groups of people' (French, 2015). In this performance protest, Harrison's project involved a massive amount of volunteer zombies, predominately taking on the classic shuffling, slow Romero zombie (albeit with a few variations). The contemporary zombie takes the quality of movement directly from Romero, and blends this with an artist's idea of what the zombie is to suit the context of their research or performance event. Harrison's walk is about how the economy works and the impact the economy has on society, and of course on the individuals involved (the zombies) who engage in Harrison's distortion of the zombie as a playful and exciting experience of performance. Feeling dead inside epitomizes the impact the financial crisis had on the livelihood of those in the city; but accompanying this feeling by the committed attitude needed to sustain this performance over a long period of time with others, you arrive experiencing deadness as serious deep play. There is an exciting contrast between what is at the heart of this walk – the political – to what is performed – play. When you watch the documentation of the 60 people moving through the streets of Birmingham, it is extremely humorous; the zombies of all different ages offer variations on the shuffle although most are slow. Within a mass of slow-moving undead you notice, on occasion, one person on a break from performing walking at a normal pace smoking a cigarette; the only thing that signifies them as the zombie is their makeup, otherwise they look ordinary. Some bodies slowly drag their legs behind them as if experiencing a dead leg; a child dressed as a zombie looking rather vacant sits upright in their pushchair as a parent moves them slowly through the crowd. And the committed Romero fan, slouched over a railing – stuck, unable to move anywhere until another zombie pushes them along because they have stumbled and tripped up on them. To make the political point of Harrison's walk, a group of zombies get stuck at an empty closed store.

Harrison's zombies are 'not mindless, flesh-hungry creatures but individuals re-appropriating the generic nature of the automaton chain store employee/zombie to make a stand against loss' (French, 2015). They are, through dark and deep play, embodying the undead as performance. Dark play (walking as if a flesh-eating zombie) and deep play (sustaining the characteristics of zombie through performance over a duration) inform the quality of performance relating to each zombie persona chosen by the individual within the ensemble. It is a pleasurable if not humorous experience related to desire. The zombie, through playing a distortion, drifts into other imagined spaces where the qualities of performance (of the thing) are appropriated to suit an artist's concerns. As such, it is useful to draw our attention to the zombie as the appropriated autobiographical frame of reference.

Martin O'Brien and Suhail Ilyas *The Unwell*

In 2015 City Arcadia commissioned a zombie film *The Unwell*, a collaboration between Martin O'Brien and Suhail Ilyas. Their take on the zombie takes us to a quiet, dark, apocalyptic Coventry, at night, inhabited by the zombie as the sick body. Filmed between 1am and 6am over five days, Ilyas (the director) was drawn to this city because of its emptiness (at night), where his impression of the architectural landscape of Coventry's shopping precincts and underpasses and slip roads was that it was 'a strangely unsocial way to lay out a city because it is designated for getting people to and from work, to and from shops, it is a dystopia of its own already' (Ilyas cited in O'Brien & Ilyas, 2017). The voiceover spoken by O'Brien is a commentary on the world now only inhabited by the undead. 'This used to be the most optimistic city in the world, now the sun never rises' (O'Brien cited in O'Brien & Ilyas, 2017).

There is a haunting soundtrack interrupted by the sound of sickness, of O'Brien repeatedly coughing up mucus. The film reflects O'Brien's life-threatening illness of cystic fibrosis and represents an apocalyptic world where only the sick exist. 'This city used to be our future, but now the city belongs to the unwell' (2017). There are shots of different zombies in this film – male, female – all played by O'Brien in various costumes, walking alone (not in groups) and walking slowly, stopping and stumbling and coughing, and falling down; one zombie crawls dragging his body along the floor; at one point a naked zombie attempts to chew his own flesh. This film is very dark and unsettling, but humour also resides here. In one short section zombies are seen bumping into walls and doors and they are left stuck (and the audience watching the film laugh).

We invited O'Brien and Ilyas to York St John University in 2017 to share the film as a public event and offer an artists' talk about *The Unwell*. In conversation with O'Brien, Dr Eirini Nedelkopoulou comments upon O'Brien's surprisingly utopian view of the film that at the outset clearly depicts a dystopian environment. She invites O'Brien to discuss the idea that the utopic overlaps or, rather, juxtaposes the dystopian frame. He responds:

> I saw it as a place of another development of humankind, humans developed to be these sick coughing bodies and although it uses these sort of tropes of horror film of night time, of the darkness of death, and these long shots of staggering bodies, actually for me there was something celebratory about this world in which everyone was unwell. And, that actually it is not a dystopia anymore because its seen through the eyes of the only things that live there … It is tongue in cheek of course but I enjoyed this idea of a city which is for the unwell where healthy people don't exist anymore, it is just the sick that inhabit it. It is also thinking about how we might think around illness, I guess I am always interested in how we celebrate sickness that isn't necessarily something which is always to be a victim context, but actually there is something celebratory in the sick body, as a way of a sick body claiming agency. It becomes a place where sickness becomes the desired state of being or the dominant state of being. (O'Brien cited in O'Brien & Ilyas, 2017)

Here, the sick zombie exists in a world where no one is healthy, and this provocative idea challenges the way illness is represented in culture. Working politically, playfully and philosophically, O'Brien's performance work focuses on using his own bodily fluids as material across a range of intermedia works including live art, film, durational pain-based practice and addresses a politics of the sick, queer body. O'Brien's illness causes him to over-produce mucus; in fact one day (he informs the audience) he could suffocate from this over-production. He asks, 'How else we might celebrate sickness than that of being the victim or the triumphant?' (Ibid.).

Within all of the pain and darkness and of O'Brien's work, we find a sense of humour. The playfulness can be associated to dark play's destructiveness, not in the sense that Schechner (2002) talks of in relation to deceit, or gratification, but in relation to the way in which the zombie might cause excess and frenzy. O'Brien sees it as a celebration of darkness and death. The humour in this film epitomizes the creative slippage between a utopic and dystopic frame; it is the slippery nature between what is perceived as destructive, when rather it is celebratory, that offers a lens to view this work as the utopian paradox that dark play can bring forth in practice.

We asked O'Brien and Ilyas which zombie was adapted for performance in their film *The Unwell*:

> It was the 1960 and 1970s [*Romero*] zombie films (I took inspiration from), there is something so camp about them ... they don't feel pain they just keep going with a relentless thirst for flesh, that's all they need. But also, they are useless on their own, if one staggered into this studio here we would say so what, it is a zombie, you could fight it off easily or run away. But when there are hundreds or thousands it is harder, so their power comes in hoards. The more people are infected, the more powerful they become, so in the end only the sick survive. (O'Brien cited in O'Brien & Ilyas, 2017)

Adam Phillips suggests that Lacan's 'version of psychoanalysis ironizes our favorite idea of knowing what we want. Desire asks us to mind the gap between our wanting and our knowing' (Phillips, 2006, p.164). And while Lacan says 'man's desire is desire of the Other', the zombie other is a darker reflection of what is already inside of us.

Phillips also suggests (his own theory not Lacan's) that 'the fantasy of knowing what one wants is a form of despair' (Ibid.). It seems therefore critical to end this chapter here and suggest that the zombie (in all forms of culture) epitomizes this despair, that what we think we long for is just so out of reach it is tragic, rather like the lyrics of most Orbison songs. And yet paradoxically, when playing the Romero zombie and slowing down, we practise what Phillips summarizes on desire (as drawn upon in Chapter 3 'The Dead Play') that the desires we think we know are a diversion to something that is forever out of reach. Therefore, the modern zombie, appropriated in different forms, is a walking enigma, a DD/DD that epitomizes desire itself, something we are forever chasing.

Creative Task: Text & the Affable Zombie

Conceptual Framework

Think of a zombie playfully – as a reanimated corpse, as an undead/living dead version of its former self. Zombies are a Death Drift played out; their attitude moves them forward in time while repressed desire might hold them in connection to their former life. They are also a Drift Drive, and as a rule you will notice that some Romero-type depictions of zombies carry an object that belonged to them before they were killed or have something about their persona that connects to their former self.

Discussion: In groups discuss the concept, imagining an affable zombie as a DD/DD, and watch clips of the Romero movie *Dawn of the Dead* (1978) to familiarize yourself with the aesthetic.

Text

Write a seven-word statement in the first person that describes the past personality of a zombie (before they were zombified).
For example:

All day long I dream about climbing.

I think the world is messed up.

I want to wear these fancy ribbons.

Imagine your chosen statements as prompts for future performance. Bank them for now.

Now write a 200-word description of an affable zombie. Details for the description could include some of the following ideas: Where were you killed? What were you wearing? What object were you carrying at the time of your death and how do you now carry that object in death? You may want to write a description of your zombie as an alter ego. What is the lifeless version of this personality? How do you describe a partialness of the original personality?

How does the seven-word statement change once the personality is zombified?

Share your descriptive writings with fellow zombies in the workshop, making a point of separating out the seven-word statement (in the first person) almost as if it were a punchline.

Playing

Find a workshop space for all zombies to be continuously moving around. A minimum time to develop would be three hours.

Warm up:

Play games that demand you to be fast on your feet – for example, Cat and Mouse, Stuck in the Mud and Tick. Then play games that require the ensemble group to stop and start, to pause and move – games such as Grandmas Footsteps.

Zombie Up

Arrange a group of standing bodies in the space as once mass group, huddled together.

You are affable, remember that.

Think about the way you move around the space as a reanimation of a human corpse.

In this state, notice what is happening to your clothes; what is happening to your skin.

Play around with a slight distortion of your regular movement.

Imagine that you are dead; you feel heavy like thick mud.

Walk as slowly as you think is possible.

Allow time for the group to move as one mass around the space.

Allow the group to feel and experience what this is like.

Allow one or two members of the group to speed ahead and then stop and wait to join the group again.

Within the huddle, individuals may half turn on the spot, walking backwards within the mass group and then turn back again. Individually, little slow spirals of movement can be created.

Individuals may stray out of the group and be picked up again by the group on the route back.

Individuals may fall down and be picked up by the group on the next passing round.

Develop your own zombie sound; subtle grunts, groans etc. Shout out, now and then, your seven-word statement.

Now try moving in complete silence. What is more effective?

What happens if as a mass group you fall to your knees as if to sing or serenade an audience member?

Gently fall to your knees and speak some of the catchphrases and propose they offer up some other physical acts. In other words, what do your catchphrases propose?

Feel weighted like thick heavy mud at the hips, grounded to the floor.

Adopt a vacant look on your face.

You are affable, remember that.

Take time to spread out to form different zombie images and lines but come back together to regroup.

Return to the games; play Cat and Mouse, Stuck in the Mud, Tick and Grandma's Footsteps as the zombie with all of the qualities explored in the list above. How are these games played with such a slow and zombi-fied effort? Discuss the quality of movement in the context of these games, discuss the humour produced while playing.

Performing

Develop a costume for your zombie.

What object does your zombie carry?

Make up with face paints.

Return to your description of the of your zombie, thinking about who it was before it became undead and how that might work or juxtapose with the image you have created for it.

Photograph each zombie in the space.

Parade as zombies in the space creating rules as performance.

Imagine both the descriptions and the seven-word statement as texts for these 'things' – are they spoken, written as phrases on cardboard, used as captions for photographs?

Dramaturgy

As a group discuss the conditions developed in the practice phase of this exercise. For example, what repetitive acts were established from out of the ensemble walking? What conditions did individuals set and how did the group physically respond? What shape and rhythm did the group zombie walk take? Each zombie should write out or speak their catchphrase that accompanies their zombie personality so that the phrases could be part of a dramaturgical weave. From out of these findings make suggestions for an unfolding series of events for:

A studio performance.

A public street audience.

A series of workshops on play.

An audio recording or podcast.

This work can shift into many forms and spaces and here are two examples:

A visual art project where the zombies are photographed in city centre locations carrying the placards of their catchphrase.

A zombie choir roving the city where the dead serenade the living. Some of the selected songs should be edited down to suit a fleeting moment for the incidental audience.

Write a list of other scenarios and appropriate to suit a community or politically engaged activity.

‹ Q U I C K · G U I D E S ›

Title: Crying In the Dark (2015)

Where: The Dark Sound Destructive Pop symposium, Falmouth University.

Description: A 10-hour durational performance from sunset to sunrise. A live space to encounter the chart-topping, much-sung, universally-covered, Roy Orbison rock-bolero ballad 'Crying'. Following the style of a karaoke event but with the same song, and with these rules:
1: The song is to be performed every four minutes with a 90-second break in between either as a sung performance or as a lip-sync. There he was in the dark; fragile, sensitive and with limited longevity.
2: Someone always had to occupy the microphone.
3: In the 90-second break participants were invited to create a persona from the "black heap" – a collection of black clothing, black accessories, feathers, foam glasses and gaffer. Just when you thought you had it all planned out, oh, the wreckage and the ruin. Dark.
4: If participants did not come forward Gary or Claire take the microphone. Listen, perform, cry, repeat. There they were, over and over, all through the night Crying.

Kit box: Microphone. Laptop. Video camera. Sticky letters to spelling 'CRYING'. Table of props. Black heap.

Commonalities: Roy Orbison. Repetition. Dark Glasses. Black Clothes. Singing. Lip-sync. Black wig as a dead black cat. Crying. David Lynch's Oeuvre. Ghosting.

Illustration 13 Quick Guide *Crying in the Dark*

Illustration 14 1.06am he is singing at *Crying in the Dark*, Falmouth University

7

The Dead Karaoke

This chapter discusses the performance of *Crying in the Dark* (2015) presented as a participatory performance at the conference *Dark Sound Destructive Pop,* Falmouth University 2015. We created a space to perform Roy Orbison's song *Crying* as a durational overnight performance ghosting the entertainment form of karaoke. We discuss the conceptual framework of the project, the participants' engagement and our own experience of performing for the duration through the lens of play while referring to elements of the Death Drift/Drift Drive (DD/DD). We end the chapter with a critical discussion on the phenomena that is 'the man in black's' complex masochistic aesthetic, intrinsic to the sound of the Orbison voice, significantly placed in David Lynch's movie *Blue Velvet* (1986). We discuss the concept of desire through Lacanian psychoanalytic framework and draw upon a Deleuzian context of Braziel's definition of Femm(e) rotics to contextualize how Lynchian artifices, specifically the lip-sync, embody the dead.

Crying in the Dark

Tonight, all night, till morning, from sunset to sunrise we invite you to sing or lip-sync Roy Orbison's song 'Crying' and choose a costume from the black heap. It is an opportunity to invent your own Orbison – be your own woman/man/

baby/mother/father/hybrid/non-human/Other in black referencing his trade-mark, the dark glasses and black clothing. Listen, perform, cry repeat. We will continue Crying all through the night and when no one is about, and when you don't want to perform, Gary and I will sing or lip-sync till dawn. (Crying in the Dark instruction, 2015)

At the conference *Dark Sound Destructive Pop* at Falmouth University 2015, we presented a space for ourselves and the audience to sing Orbison's song *Crying*. Ghosting the form of karaoke, we set the conditions for our event to begin at sunset and ending at sunrise. We offered the following rules for engagement for the overnight encounter:

Dress up in a costume of your choice selecting a range of clothes to dress up in from the black heap. Complement your outfit choosing from a selection of props (dark glasses, wigs, feathers, etc. etc.) from the table. Approach the microphone and sing Orbison's song 'Crying' or, perform it as a lip-sync. After the song has finished there is a 90-second maximum preparation time to change into a different costume. You may return as many times as you like. The rule for the duration: there must always be someone at the microphone from sunset to sunrise wearing an item of clothing or disguise from the black heap except for the 90-second break. (Crying in the Dark, 2015)

Orbison's *Crying* was performed all night from 8.51pm to 5.13am except for the 90-second break after the end of each song for the costume change. At 8.51pm Claire sings the first *Crying* of the evening to the audience of Gary. At 8.55pm Gary sings to an audience of Claire. We repeatedly sang until the audience trickled in around 9.25pm. The audience stayed for a few hours, not all participated. Those who did offered varied performances. Someone sang their heart out, a mum sang for her daughter, a crowd of enthusiastic karaoke fans repeated their turn. Some wished us well, some said they would be back. The following piece of writing documents the 69 performances of the whole event by simply indicating the selected costume or persona adopted. We have composed a listicle to give a picture of how the night unfolded. However, within our approaches to both documentation and creative processes we could look to this listicle as a score that can be adopted for others to perform.

Crying in the Dark listicle:

20:51: Claire wears headless gorilla suit.
20.55: Gary is dressed in black.
21.02: Claire wears black and dark glasses.
21.07: Gary dressed in a black hoodie.
21.14: Claire is dressed in a black cowboy hat and black shirt.
21.19: Gary wears a skeleton costume and black wig.
21:25: Claire wears a black wig and black shirt.
21:30: Gary sports a gorilla head and one gorilla hand with a skeleton body.
21:37: A participant wears an arrow through her head and an over-sized suit.
21:45: Gary and Claire wear suit jackets with their collars turned up.
21:55: Claire goes incognito with a tracksuit top and a beany hat pulled down.
22:03: Gary as a rock guitarist with arrow through his head.
22.10: A participant wears hat with a net veil as if at a funeral, but she with adds feathers for a new romantic look.
22:15: A participant speaks the song.
22:21: Gary as the smart cowboy performs an understated formal approach.
22:28: Claire as a rock singer with a sparkly scarf as a bandana.
22:34: Gary has his eyes closed wearing glasses with missing lenses and feathers attached.
22:39: A duet with one wearing flowers on her head the other sporting a wig.
22:44: A female duet where they dance together in a swing side step.
22:48: A female duet, one has stuck a feather to her chin as if it is a goatee beard, the other puts a hat on a crown on a wig. They pull each other's disguises off at the first big crescendo of *Crying*.
22:54: Gary wears gorilla head and gorilla hands.
23:00: Claire wears the gorilla suit without the head.
23:05: A participant dresses as a cowgirl.

23:09: A participant sports a wig and glasses, she rips her wig off and throws it to the back of the stage with the glasses.

23:15: A participant holds a flower in her hand and lip-syncs with a dance routine reminiscent of the woman in the radiator from Lynch's *Eraserhead*. She uses the flower as a prop singing into it.

23:19: A participant wears his own crow mask and a crown, he squawks the lyrics.

23:24: A participant has wrapped some clothing around his neck including the gorilla suit almost like a cloak.

23:30: Claire dresses up as Phil Collins in suit jacket and hat.

23:34: She sways side to side with a veiled hat and sings in minor keys as a melancholic version.

23:38: They perform an autobiographical rendition wearing an arrow through their head.

23.42: A participant returns for another turn with a sparkly scarf.

23:49: Gary as the Karate Kid sporting a head scarf as bandana.

23:56: Claire wears a crepe paper tabard and a head torch like a musical miner.

00:03: Gary as a singing black wafer, wearing a card board wig and glasses and looks like he is drowning in oil.

00:10: Claire has a fake tear rolling down her face wears a black shirt and lip-syncs.

00:17: Gary as a gorilla ventriloquist with the hand puppet dressed as Roy that sings as if it is Frank Booth from the film *Blue Velvet*.

00:25: Claire as Bobby Peru from Lynch's film *Wild at Heart* sporting a pencil moustache.

00:36: Him as Bunny Boy from the film *Gummo* with large bunny ears made from cardboard.

00:41: Claire dresses as if she has just got out of the shower with black towel over her head or, as if she has caught the flu, or as if she is the grandmother from Monty Python.

00:49: Gary wears a face plate with a tape X for a mouth and a cut-out for his nose, no eyes though.

00:58: Her as a punk with pipe cleaners in her hair resorts to head banging.

01:06: Gary as Mickey Rourke in *The Wrestler* distorting his face and voice with duct tape. We named this disguise as character called *Mickey York*.

01:16: A participant with a gorilla head.

01:23: Gary as a skeleton Jamiroquai wearing glasses with inverted with feathers attached.

01:33: Claire as Eminem busting the moves wearing hoodie done up.

01:41: Gary as a fly with flowers for his eyes and sporting a cravat; formal and yet subversive.

01:49: Claire with feathers on her head-band and flowers on her breasts.

02:01: Gary with his eyes closed wearing glasses drawn on with black make up.

02:09: Claire as Cindy Lauper looking down the barrel of the lens as a close up shot.

02:19: He chews a mouth full of pipe cleaners like an exploding beard or an alien.

02:25: Claire as Predator or as The Invisible Man.

02:49: Claire as Orbison with dark glasses singing, trying not to move her lips.

02:55: Gary as Skeleton Roy; white face and hands and skeleton make up.

03:05: Claire as a kidnap victim hands tied behind back sporting a sparkly mouth gag, sings through the mouth gag.

03:11: Skeleton cowboy Roy with a gorilla wrap.

03:18: Claire as Beckett's *Not I* as *Rocky Horror Show* wearing a crepe paper makeshift mask with mouth protruding through a hole.

03:26: Gary reprises the role of Bunny Boy from *Gummo*, this time as a skeleton, holding up a black wig as if it is a dead black cat for a lasting image.

03:37: She performs as the cool cowboy from Lynch's *Mullholland Drive*.

03.45: Gary as a skeleton headed gorilla removing his makeup while singing under his breath, staring directly into the camera.

03:52: Claire as a flapper girl using a pipe cleaner as a long cigarette holder, she has smoker's cough.

04:05: They perform in profile shot wearing an oversized jacket.

04:09: Gary performs with Roy puppets in each hand wearing three pairs of glasses.

04:17: She sings to the gorilla's head on her arm which looks like a *Spitting Image* parody of Nigel Lawson.

04:31: A massive heap wearing as many clothes from the black heap as possible sings.

04:37: Claire as *Kong Lear* (sic) with silent movie era facial expressions.

04:43: A cowboy sings with arrow in his head, he collapses on the floor like Rebekah Del Rio. The song plays as he plays dead on floor.

04:49: Claire wears a sparkly wrap around her head distorting facial features.

04:55: Gary as a Britain's Got Talent contestant whose turn is ripping paper to shreds. Bits of paper fall out of his hand until it has disappeared. X X X

05:01: Claire with her back turned sings into a mirror to show just a mouth singing.

05:13: Gary and Claire perform as a Roy Orbison duet wearing dark glasses and black wigs.

At 5.17am, as the sun continued to rise, we packed away the black heap of clothes. We walked towards the train station through the woodland grounds of Falmouth University listening to the birds singing a dawn chorus and continued to hum under our breath *Crying*.

Marking the Conditions for Durational Performance in Homage to the Dead Celebrity

Karaoke is a highly sociable event; participants take part as performers who also as audience members offer a great deal of support and encouragement for those on the microphone. Karaoke calls upon the autobiographical because quite often participants choose their 'signature' song that they become identified with at the event, often repeating that song every week (as well as many others). It is an unintimidating participatory event, a joyous arena for everyone to engage in and is 'a judgement-free zone, no matter how good or how poor a singer might be' (Brown, 2015, p.108). Everyone roots for one another in a karaoke event, it is a special community of 'comradery … mutual admiration and support' a place where friendships are made (Ibid.).

Karaoke is phenomenal because it is both a rehearsal and a performance experience; the form allows for mistakes and for improvement and those mistakes are performed. It is very much a here and now, in the moment event. Popular forms of entertainment such as karaoke invite us to imagine our lives beyond the venue and offer an *as if* experience where we can embody our favourite celebrity. We wanted to emulate this community experience of karaoke in our work and with the DIY attitude. However, we conceived *Crying in the Dark* not as a straightforward karaoke experience, but as a game of karaoke. Framing it this way though play, and with rules, could offer something a little more subversive to a night out at a karaoke bar; we wanted to heighten the experience but at the same time make this a dedication to Roy Orbison.

We were curious as to what might happen if, in this game, we simply offered the one song – Orbison's *Crying* – for the duration of eight and a half hours. A song where those high notes that are very difficult to perform, and where the emotional intensity climaxes at the end, could have us all in tears:

> When the mirrored rhythms return to drive the song to its climactic finish, accompanied by high sustained pitches from the chorus, Orbison passionately delivers the final lyrics at the top of his range – his final wail serves as a manifestation of the very act of crying. (Hawkins, 2017, p.320)

We were excited by the idea that this song's emotional intensity could be experienced in an environment that would come alive between sunset and sunrise, because it meant working with the qualities and meanings one might find in the dark hours. We were also curious to see if these conditions could invite varying qualities from the participants. What would they bring to the night?

In fact, the game of karaoke as a practice, we learnt, was an opportunity for participants to experience dark and deep play. Without the ability to practise or rehearse a song at home in preparation for karaoke or being permitted to sing a song of their choice, they relied on other approaches to get them through the performance. We therefore discuss in detail our observations on the participants' performance and go on to discuss our own experience. In both instances, we will offer an interpretation through the lens of play and drawing upon terms that situate themselves within the DD/DD.

The Participatory Experience of Play: Playing for the Sake of Heartbreak

The conference attendees were a mixture of students, academics, musicians and visitors who also attended to witness the music gigs billed as part of the programme. A majority of those who entered into our space – a black box studio – to witness and participate in *Crying in the Dark* were there to hear the bands play. We were tucked away out of sight from the gig; an opportunity for the audience to have a break and take to their own the stage.

We were curious how participants would take to singing something that was chosen for them, how they would adapt to the rules and what variations in performance we would witness. Only a couple of people asked if they could sing a song of their choice, but the majority seemed comfortable working to the rules as it gave them guidelines, and they found freedom within the constraint. We discovered that the rules were enough (as a framework) for people to occupy their own creative space and put forward their ideas for the performance because the rules did not force a way of performing the song. Rather, the game offered a space for people to test what was possible within those limitations, and we didn't reject any possibilities within that frame. A variety of subversive activities became apparent because they could choose an image from the black heap of clothes and complement that image with a range of accessories from the dressing-up table. This meant that each participant could take to the microphone in the form of a disguise, or they could go incognito if they wanted to. We observed that the playfulness of this dressing-up game added to the excitement because participants were being inventive, and this meant they were investing in their performance for themselves and for the audience.

The invitation to lip-sync as an alternative to using the voice offered a technical challenge – it not easy to synchronize perfectly, so the failures of synchronization, trying to match the movement of the lips to Orbison's voice, became the main focus for the lip-sync performer. However, most people sang, but some lip-synced. Yet we observed that there was something quite addictive about returning to the same song, singing the same words, trying to achieve the Orbison voice, attempting those difficult high notes over and over again. It was a task not to get bored of. And every single attempt always produced, through its repetition, a contrasting performance that drew attention to the commitment and playfulness of the performance, and each time they heard the song the more it seemed to be appreciated as a good song. The participants who returned to sing for a second time, after rummaging through the black heap for a new image, felt empowered by it, for they had an opportunity to vary in quality and try out a different voice. *Crying in the Dark* was not experienced as exhaustive performance deemed destined to destroy itself through hours of repeating the same song; rather the experience for the participants was filled with excitement – they were thrilled to be given an opportunity to return to perform on the microphone. It was as if this game was an alternative form of high-risk adventure, a thrill seeker's game of vertiginous play. Thrill seekers look to jump off high ridges or risk their lives free climbing and so on. Yet Diane Ackerman argues that most people have a yearning for a variety of different types of thrill-seeking: some take play to extremes in high-risk sports, others confine it to 'roller-coasters, scream machines, and mock peril' (Ackerman, 1999, p.91). We observed that a pattern was emerging in this game 'of arousal, tension, fear, suspense, followed by an important reward – relaxation of the body' (Ackerman, 1999, p.93): Participants appeared aroused by the idea of the performance and their experience of tension was heightened once they committed to what they had signed up to and got into costume. Most seemed to experience some form of fear when they stepped to the mic and they experienced anticipation (suspense) once they began singing. Finally, they were happily relaxed during the performance itself, and not simply after they had completed their performance. This model of arousal, tension, fear, suspense and relaxation did not always present itself in that order. But drawing from this first example of the cyclical pattern, relaxation happened when the singer had found their voice and appeared incredibly comfortable in the performance itself. This relaxation usually happened after they realized they were in for the long haul (the whole duration of the song which was 2.46 minutes). For example, there was a definite sense of commitment approximately 30 seconds into their song when they realized that the lyrics would continue to appear on the screen and the backing track would keep on playing until the end of the song. It was in that moment of realization, regardless of how they sounded, that they relaxed – whether this was because they had given in to the idea of it being the case of getting through the task (and there were varying approaches to this 'getting through'), or whether they had found their voice. And, more intriguingly, the repetition of the words 'crying' in the song moved the participant on quite well (even for those who didn't know the song) and so the finale chorus ended up being performed as a very confident crescendo. Even if they didn't know the song very well, they had the opportunity to really get into it, but in an unlikely kind of way.

The experience of excitement and thrill altered for each participant because of the decisions they made in their own *multiple as if* world. Some played it as if they were on a talent show; one person referenced a scene from *Twin Peaks* with the haunting ethereal voice as if she was Julee Cruise; another person played it as if it was their last ever song, eyes locked towards an imaginary lover in the room. As well as the romantic attempts at presenting this song, there were technical aspects that informed the delivery. For example, a couple who performed a duet played off each other's guessing game qualities – they sang the words as if they had never heard it before. They didn't adhere to the normal rhythm or melody of the song, they took their own path, and as they performed the lyrics and found their own tune and style of delivery, we quite enjoyed their freedom of expression in the mix of other attempts. One person hit the difficult high notes perfectly, so the moments during this event when the song sounded like the original made other attempts stand out as more subversive. Other participants performed their own version with a knowledge of the song but still offering their own sound.

Others didn't know *Crying* at all, and the backing track allowed them to feel their way through it.

When you hear the song *Crying*, it sounds like such a manageable song: it is simple, short, repetitive and the words are not difficult, not to mention the fact that Orbison makes it look effortless. However, one participant only realized how difficult it really was when she was performing it. She found it very hard to sing the high notes, and so found alternative ways into it to get into it and went really low with her voice almost speaking the words out in a monotone way. In other words, she summoned up some power to get into it and got something out of it (deep play). Not only that, she fiddled with the mic, performed a little dance; her hands were really expressive because she punctuated the high notes punching the air, showing little physical signals as if to say, 'I am still with it'. In this immediate live performance experience, there was no time to think; the song kept going regardless and it was not going to wait for her, she was in it and so, through play, she found a way of being in it.

One participant sported a death mask – a beaked plague doctor mask (brought in by himself) – and rocked out a bizarre high-pitched voice squawk, performing a Dadist version, but as a crow. He never sang; he simply squawked. He hid under his mask and found physical poses to go with the bird call and his rhythm of the squawk sat with the expectations of the lyrics as if he was having a conversation with the lyrics. But at first it was played as a kind of joke or gimmick. It was as if, in his crow proposal, he thought 'in a minute in they will see what I am doing and stop this track'. But there was a moment of realization from him that this was not going to happen, and as the backing track kept on going and the lyrics continued to appear on the screen, he suddenly he found himself committed. In this moment he looked for stuff to do. His crows grew louder and he began to throw out big gestures hitting the microphone with a feather; he sounded like a bird in trouble.

A lady sporting an arrow through her head introduced the song before she sang it as an announcement: 'This is *Crying* by Roy Orbison.' She performed a dramatic commentary to the lyrics saying words like 'I really did' in response to singing 'I loved you even more than I did before'. As she developed her own personal narrative, the song it seemed, related to a scenario from her own life. She speaks 'you never loved me' and 'this moment is f*****g gone' (none of which are Orbison's words). And her finale performance let out a big loud elongated scream before she speaks the words 'well done' to herself. A participant performs a lip-sync, along with a dance routine, and uses a flower as a prop as if it were a microphone. Now, Orbison's voice becomes othered. Although we have heard this song many times, the uncanny experience of hearing his words coming out of the mouth of another at this point in the evening was strangely affective. We felt moved that somehow Orbison had channelled this participant as if to say, 'enjoy your dancing. I will sing my song for you.' Imagine that?

The range of possibilities this performance offered was attractive and the different personas invented shaped the highly playful communal experience for all of us involved. Participants anticipating their next turn began to think ahead on what identity they could create for themselves which in turn gave others watching something to respond to, something to follow, ideas were generated, akin to a game of word association and with the full support of a delighting crowd dressing up, playing games, acting mischievously and choosing to sing or lip-sync. The anticipation, it seemed, was adrenaline-based and this created a sublime environment juxtaposed by the continuous sound of a melancholic *Crying,* and from time to time, within the playfulness, sadness filled the air as we listened to Orbison's words – everyone was playing this game for the sake of heartbreak.

'Gary and Claire's' Commitment to Play: On Durational Deadness

Our own experience of performing in *Crying in the Dark* differed from the participants because we had committed to the duration of the whole evening. Although we had generous, enthusiastic performers who were willing to take to the mic again and again, their commitment was (in the time frame we offered) short-lived in comparison. We didn't mind this; in fact we had, through the rules of the game, given them permission to leave. The invitation to play with the permission to leave or the ability to simply watch us let everyone off the hook, so when they wanted time out we would perform for them (which was quite often). And when they did leave we imagined them at home snuggled up in their beds, ready to go to sleep and thinking of us in the space doing our job, and theirs. The last participant sang not long after midnight and we carried on until dawn. We could have cheated and rested until someone arrived, but we didn't. To add, something changed from our experience when an audience left the room. What is the performance without an audience? We were each other's audience, an intimate performance of Gary for Claire and Claire for Gary, genuine, playful, dark, desirable, perhaps somewhat fetishist at times. We also liked to imagine that Orbison was an absent present audience member, in the room with us, in spirit because the repetition of the song was like a mantra, and in deep play we were calling upon the presence of a dead icon. And, there was also the camera, recording every performance, and we imagined being filmed for a wider audience and it was in this performance that we discovered our practice illuminates the porosity between cinema and contemporary performance.

We imagined performing the same song throughout the night would eventually grate on us, wear us down, but it had the opposite effect. We were playing through *the multiple as if* like the participants, but what made our experience different was that we also played the *if only* game; *if only* this was Roy Orbison, *if only* it was the character Rabbit Boy from Harmony Korine's (1997) film *Gummo* who holds up a dead black cat to the camera, etc., etc. We played through a practice of distortion, drawing upon the worlds that we are interested in from our own practice. We took pleasure that our performances were not quite the same as Orbison's, or Bunny Boy, because there is something liberating about the inability to be exactly right and play in relation to failure. It is okay to accept this type of ghosting as not pristine. The fact that it does not sound exactly the same as Orbison, nor is it a true image from a film, makes it more playful. Instead we re-inhabited a shape of the scene; this is our ghosting – degraded, fuzzy versions of those images and sounds we were ghosting, as if what we performed was shot on some primitive means for a B-movie equivalent. Our versions were warped, skewed images made from cut-up black cardboard, stockings and white face paint.

When we concentrated on the meaning of the words, and found ourselves in a hauntingly charged place, the place we think Orbison or Lynch would have appreciated, it made us want to carry on. It was not a matter of getting lost in the performance, but finding the performance while lost in it. The performance was contagious because we repeatedly 'invent new selves' (Schechner, 2002, p.109), or hybrid versions of Orbison personas. We became obsessed and during the 90-second break throughout the costume change Gary was even humming the song *Crying*.

The idea that anyone could walk in at any time (or not) kept the repetitive action going; this idea served a particular function: the anticipation of not knowing when, or if, someone would enter was rewarding in itself. Playing through dark play specifically during what we term the 'strange hours' got us into the anarchic territory of play; the game became surreal. For example, there are only so many identities you can create from a black heap of clothes, a few feathers and makeup over the space of more than eight hours, and indeed the range of different costumes we sported throughout the evening varied, this ritual of changing kept us on our toes but, in the wee hours when there seemed there were no more identities left to invent, we attempted the darker or other worldly appearances. For example, Gary wears a face plate with X for a mouth like he has just stepped out of a horror movie, a playfully disruptive but disturbing image, one that cinema would take on happily, as does the dream. Claire puts a pair of tights on her head and walks into the space as if she was Bobby Peru from Lynch's film (1990) *Wild at Heart*; she looks as if she is about to rob a bank but performs probably *her* best *Crying* of the night. Gary wraps his head over and over again with duct tape sticking to his hair and which distorts his face so much he becomes unrecognizable. This strange time was hilarious; we remember laughing and getting into hysterics. Regardless of the costume's restriction, Gary sings Orbison's *Crying* as a gentleman, hand in pocket, modest and meek and the duct tape distorts his voice. Claire is bound and gagged as if kidnapped and sings through the gag. And during one of Gary's performances at around 3.30am, three people enter the space looking for a place to sleep; they had been to a party and could not afford the taxi back into Falmouth, so they thought they would cheekily get their head down in a theatre studio. Their experience of walking into the wrong room, witnessing the

unexpected as Gary performs in the most unusual garb, obviously startled them. We can still hear their verbal reactions now as we think about
what they said after the silence that accompanied their entrance: 'No
way,' 'What the...?' 'I feel like I have walked into *Twin Peaks*, we are in
the Red Room'. They all took a seat on the couch that was placed for
any audience member who visited or happened upon us to watch. They
stayed with us (without performing) for almost an hour and appreciated the fact they had not only stumbled across this odd but (as they
described) 'beautiful' encounter, but were experiencing an intimate performance just for them at some ungodly hour and that we were committed to it as an all-night performance.

We were aware that sunrise was the marker for the end of this work.
Having a specific time in mind was something to aim for, but we weren't
trying to make time pass by quickly, or question whether it was achieva-
ble. We connected (playfully seriously) to the task. Spending much time
over an eight-hour duration of repetition was transcendental, a meditative form of deep play. There are various ways to engage in deep play, and
when its *moment* arises, it does not always mean you have no clue of what
you are doing or that you are throwing yourself into uncertainty. We
were improvising, but within a very fixed framework. We were connected
tightly to our own imaginative as if worlds that were significantly accu-
mulating within our practice. We were playing (improvising) within our
own territory as fans of Orbison (and Lynch) and playing into and out
of the environment that we had established. This does not mean to say
that being in the moment is not precious – it is; but the precious does not
simply arrive because of a game's unpredictability nor out of nowhere.
Rather, it is useful to think of this in the moment as precious because of
the deep time spent *within* the certainty of our own conceptual framework of the DD/DD. Here, desire is circling around Lynch and Orbison
as the object and as a commitment to what our practice produces: the
happy accidents.

This was no ordinary karaoke event; it was an uncanny experience of
repetitive singing. A DD/DD where the attitude and the quality of the
performance altered the more we sang and heard our own voice. And,
after repeating the song so many times, we felt dislocated from our own
voice, because another voice emerged, as if we were possessed by the

moment, gripped with passion (as in how Ackerman describes deep play). At certain times we found ourselves lost in the voice we didn't recognize, the voice that is unfamiliar, the voice you didn't know you had, the one that is hidden, an experience that is akin to Julia Kristeva's concept of the uncanny, of being 'strangers to ourselves' (Kristeva, 1991). In this context, the voice has a more symbolic relationship to a getting lost experience, as it is to do with the dislocated feeling one has with their own voice, and discovering there is another inner voice unlocatable; and we were taken by surprise. In the case of the lip-sync where the voice is absent, Orbison's voice was an invitation for us to embody 'The Voice' (he was known famously by this name and was often addressed as such). This quality of miming Orbison was exceptionally haunting – not least because we had been circling Orbison and the idea of him in our work, but because we began to feel that we had that beautiful voice, with the ability to reach high octaves, to sing perfect a pitch and, through the repetition, you get to know 'The Voice' more than you knew it.

Yet it could be said that any song could be used in such a playful, conceptual, repetitive context to stir the uncanny. But we argue that the presence of the uncanny relates directly to the environment we had established: the celebration, in a ritualised form, of a dead celebrity, a singer that once, when alive, embodied deadness:

> Springsteen was particularly evocative when he observed that on first meeting Orbison, he felt that he could reach out and put his hand through Orbison's body ... The image of Springsteen passing his hand through Orbison's body is not unrelated to Orbison's reference to himself as someone merely passing through this world. This body was somehow insubstantial, not entirely of this world. (Lehman, 2010, p.211)

Recalling Orbison's famous image, his black clothes and dark glasses represented a lifestyle, perpetually mourning for the impossibility of ever reaching satisfaction. Orbison was famously known as 'The Voice', the unique sound of 'multiple crescendos and, mostly, at the centre of the song, that dramatic bel canto tenor, often expressing a dreamy kind of heartbreak or loneliness' (Sulivan, 2013). It is not hard to appreciate his voice as the uncanny because, as the saying goes, the eyes are the window to the soul and, famously, because of those dark black glasses, we could not see into his eyes 'his mouth barely moved. And yet you were hearing this sound that was coming straight from his center to yours. It was always stirring' (Springsteen, In Orbison, 2017).

Orbison's image with the dark black glasses came about from a happy accident when on tour with the Beatles: having left his clear pair of glasses on the plane, he had to resort to what he had at hand, his sunglasses; the image was born from that moment. Simple as that. His image was unique, but his voice was the window into the angelic, and, when he performed, even when singing a high octave range, he did so with no physical effort. 'Orbison's voice always somehow overshadowed the body and was on a trajectory to being severed from the body and soaring away on its own' (Lehman, 2007, p.209). It is this quality of deadness that is akin to the ventriloquist's dummy where the 'real' voice does not belong to the doll or to the ventriloquist.

Orbison in the Lynchian World

The sense of uncanniness was heightened in the multiplicitous experience of performing *Crying in the Dark* because we had slipped into a cinematic frame. It is why, therefore, we turn our attention to a critical discussion on the subject of Orbison in the Lynchian world:

'I close my eyes and I drift away' (Orbison, 1963).

Drift off to where?

Into the dark. The Orbison sound has become culturally ingrained in the psychosexual complex narratives that epitomize unruly desire within the term 'Lynchian'.

The wiki dictionary defines the term Lynchian in the context of sound:

'Lynchian' adj. Of or pertaining to David Keith Lynch (born 1946), American filmmaker and director whose surrealist films are characterized by dream imagery and meticulous sound design.

Orbison's persona is embedded in the Lynchian world of eroticism and desire. Having spent time watching Lynch's cult film *Blue Velvet* (as fans and as practitioners), we were drawn into how the (2001) film *Mullholland Drive* ghosts the lip-sync artifice where 'the singer', in each of these films, is the conduit of desire. Significantly it was Lynch's cult film *Blue Velvet* that developed Lynch's surname into an adjective because of the haunting sound of Roy Orbison's voice.

Desire, in a Lacanian context, is articulated through fantasy and driven by its own impossibility, allowing desire to persist, repeat. Most of Orbison's songs carry this persistence – the lyrical repetition and the familiar structure of a 'mounting anxiety' (Lehman) – to a climactic or anticlimactic end.

The complexities of the Lynchian world are not, it seems, as straight-forward as interpreting film through one specific Freudian lens. Braziel argues in a Deleuzian context that Lynch's films deterritorialize desire, provocatively refiguring gender and sexuality in ways useful for feminist and queer thought. (Braziel, 2004, p.108). Lynch messes with the psychoanalytic models that frame their stereotype, he queers them and draws our attention to the complexities of desire, and through 'The Voice'.

To put into context the term queerness, we align it to Royle's discussion on the term's relationship to the uncanny, where he cites Eve Kosofsky Sedgwick's thoughts on queerness:

> The open mesh of possibilities, gaps, overlaps, dissonances, and reso-nances, lapses and excesses of meaning when the constituent elements of anyone's gender, or of anyone's sexuality are made (or can't be made) to signify monolithically. (Sedgwick cited in Royle, 2003, p.42)

In *Blue Velvet*, the actor Dean Stockwell who plays Ben performs a lip-sync of Orbison's song *In Dreams* to the actor Dennis Hopper who plays Frank the notorious and vile criminal:

> *A candy-colored clown they call the sandman...*

Upon visiting Ben in his house – a strange place full of dark secrets, drug dealings and kidnappings – Frank spouts the words 'now it's dark' and he clutches on to a tape of Roy Orbison's *In Dreams* as he witnesses the lip-sync. Orbison, who we know as the lonely – Orbison the melancholic – is now Orbison associated with criminals and the dark underbelly of society.

Yet Orbison's voice is used quite effectively by Lynch who clearly juxtaposes the heavenly sound with the dark situation unfolding; but more than this, Lynch frames Orbison's voice as performance (of a fantasy that is never quite fulfilled) and then later, as a rehearsal (of that fantasy as if it is being fulfilled). We will elaborate on this.

The song is performed on two separate occasions by the characters Ben (to Frank) and then Frank (to Jeffery). In these moments, Orbison's absent presence is the ghost; he haunts the dislocated voices of the lip-sync and in doing so queers psychoanalysis because the angelic voice of Orbison draws our attention to Frank's complex desires which don't, in these moments, conform to heteronormative or Oedipal urges performed in early scenes in the movie with the character Dorothy Valens. Instead, we see him enjoying a lip-sync as a pseudo-sexual experience with Ben, the effeminate drug dealer. Orbison's sound is bound to that of the 'mysterious and dark' and the 'erotic and sensual' (Denzin, 1991, p.66); this tension offers a powerful and sensual eroticism that is carried by Orbison's *In Dreams*.

When Ben performs *In Dreams,* Frank's attitude is of sheer pleasure, but suddenly Frank stops the tape midway through the song and there is a quick change of attitude from Frank. Frank is prolonging his desire, and stopping this moment so abruptly allows him to return to witness the moment with Ben again next week as evidenced in the line 'see you next Tuesday'. We are left to imagine that every Tuesday, as ritual, Frank witnesses Ben lip-sync Orbison.

Later in the film, when out on a joyride, we see Frank attempt to vocalize the lines of Orbison's *In Dreams* (it is being played from the car stereo) to the actor Kyle McLaughlin, who plays Jeffery.

However, instead of singing, Frank speaks the lyrics of *In Dreams* to Jeffery and he fumbles over the lines, as if he is in a rehearsal. This echo of the previous scene highlights how repetition prolongs fantasy for Frank, a Lacanian desire played out through performance. Jeffery is caught up in Frank's fantasy; Frank is offering a personal performance for Jeffery, as if

Jeffery is Frank, and Frank is Ben, he imagines himself as Ben performing to Jeffery. Frank goes so far as to kiss Jeffery. A surface reading of this scene is one of aggression and ridicule, but Lynch's characters are more complex than a surface reading; they are wrapped up in a world that distorts the stereotype of criminal masculinity and draws our attention to the power of artifice – the lip-sync. Roy (although absent) is very much present and 'alive', and this is profound because Orbison's voice eroticizes the men with what Braziel (2004) argues is a 'feminine erotic economy' defined as 'femm(e)rotics', that is:

> a dynamic refiguring of femininity that displaces it from its traditional and exclusive relation to female bodies and opens new sites for bodily pleasures, desires and identifications. *Femm(e)rotics* supplants an essentialist masculinist economy with one of virtual femininity, shifting from identification to erotics. (p.111)

For a moment, the men are situated within a queer frame of 'mimetic fantasy and erotic desires' (Ibid., p.108), and the frame is foregrounded by the voice of a non-masculine rock star performer – 'The Voice' is present. The tragic beauty of unfulfilled desire (the themes that most of Orbison's songs circle around) is spoken on behalf of the characters through Orbison, because they are unable to articulate the truth of their desires, or for that matter really know them.

The affective performance device of the lip-sync is also used in Lynch's film *Mulholland Drive* (2001), through a key performance of a voice that signifies an abrupt change of narrative. Rebekah Del Rio, performing as herself, lip-syncs to her own recorded voice a Spanish cover of Orbison's *Crying*. On a stage, brightly lit by footlights against a backdrop of red curtains, she is witnessed by the two characters Rita and Betty, who sit in the audience and watch her performance mesmerized, reduced to tears. The effect is dislocating and the repetition of the words 'Llorando' seem haunting and yet extremely beautiful. As a viewer, watching this film for the first time, upon listening to this sound you get the feeling you have heard the song before but can't locate it, it is a very haunting, uncanny version of Orbison's *Crying*. Del Rio performs it with so much passion, sadness and pain. The combination of the lip-sync together with repetition of the words 'Llorando' (Crying), and bellowed out, is embodied with extreme emotional intensity, and the dislocated voice is a reminder that the characters live through a series of complex, multiple dream states. Del Rio's voice, a powerful siren, is still heard during Del Rio's on-stage 'death' as she collapses and falls to the floor with her pre-recorded voice still playing. Here, the theatricality of a now female voice is an echo of Orbison's 'The Voice' as a sublime absent presence. We notice the voice of an angel has been replaced by a voice more melancholic, a hypnotically mesmerizing sound, and yet, evidently, not coming from the body of the singer; it is as if death is singing. In circling around psychoanalytic concepts for performative affect, the motivation of Lynch's characters seems driven by a sentimentality on the psychoanalytic model itself but in a queered form. Here, the female voice claims an equal if not a more powerful status in popular culture.

Creative Task: The Return of the Dead

Conceptual Framework

Picking up on Royle's (2003) idea that 'the uncanny seems to be about strange repetitiveness, the return of something repressed, something no longer familiar, the return of the dead' construct a world of play that allows for repetition.

Playing

Considering the *multiple as if* (the as if as if) – as discussed in Chapter 3 'The Dead Play' – devise a strategy in which performers engage in several slippages from self, to character, to other. Play this game:

Arrange a table with a variety of props, wigs, glasses, feathers, duct tape, towels, and masks, etc.

Create a heap on the floor of different clothes to dress up in. The clothes could all be from the same palette of colours – for example, a red heap.

Play a game of dressing up, combining different props and items of clothing. You can make accessories from materials available. During this game, change as many times as you wish and invent other rules for the game, so it evolves into performance. For example, just change one item at a time so you slowly mutate between personas.

Reflect upon what you discovered about this game and the rules you invented. How can you shape the experiences and happenings in this game into rules for a durational performance? What are your ideas for a next stage?

Writing

Write a list of your favourite songs written and performed by a dead celebrity. Choose one song.

Write a series of rules for a performance that requires some engagement with the song, the costumes and a commitment to a repetitive act. Set a clear time frame of the beginning and the end so you understand and commit to that duration of time.

Write rules for participants (who are not in your working group) to attend, witness and, if they want to, take part.

There are two options available: to sing (or lip-sync) the song in costume as a karaoke or create a series of tableaux that the song soundtracks. Or combine the two, where someone has created a tableaux image where singing (or lip-synching) is part of it – for example, someone lying down on the floor as if dead while the other is singing (or lip-synching). There are a multitude of these dual combinations.

Performing

Perform the work with the participants without rehearsing. The durational act must account for improvisation and surprise.

Dramaturgy

As a group discuss the conditions developed in the practice phase of this exercise. For example, what did the layering of different *multiple as if* scenarios establish? How do you experience performance from the approach of the lip-sync, as opposed to singing? What conditions did individuals set and what happened to the performance because of such conditions? Some conditions may have been established because of the time of day or night that the durational work was performed and/or how far into the durational period it was performed. What happened in the process of repetition? Write out a long accumulative record of memories of the work as a listicle, so that others may interpret for a future performance. Make suggestions for an unfolding event. This work can shift into many structural or visual forms – for example, as a filmed, edited collage of the live event. Or, as an ensemble performance constructed as a spoken word game where the group devise rules to remix the memories from the listicle. List the possibilities of this work into other mediums. Discuss the experiences through the lens of the DD/DD.

‹ Q U I C K · G U I D E S ›

Title: Genny and the Neons (2014)

Where: Exhibitions of words in neon in galleries including: City Screen York, According to McGee York, York Art Gallery, Norwich Art Centre, Shandy Hall. And a series of outdoor installations for a passing incidental audience in the North York Moors and Whitby photographed for exhibition prints.

Description: A collection of words and phrases fashioned in neon light. Some relating to quotes from residents and tenants on a street in York (*We made something of this. You remembered my name. I could hide.*) The project toured to scenic locations across North Yorkshire. The neons were powered by a petrol generator (Genny), for short periods of time in remote spots at sunset, sunrise and late afternoon. The neons *If Only, I could hide* and *Crying* misplaced in the landscape provoking themes of desire. They were set up at coastal caves on the beach at Sandsend, the moorland above the hamlet of Fryup along with the grouse, St Mary's church graveyard at Whitby, the car park at the Falling Foss waterfall, and the hermit's cave on the ramblers' route to Maybeck. An inscription on a memorial tomb reading *Every man is a bubble, All flesh is grass...* inspired a play on words to create the neon *Flesh Grass Fresh Glass* which was installed in an exhibition at Lawrence Sterne's Shandy Hall.

Kit box: Perspex mounting boards. Transformers. Petrol powered generator. Metal builders trestle. St Giles cloaks. Taxidermy blackbird. Crown. A series of different sized neon and argon filled glass.

Commonalities: Crying. The Street. Hermitage. Word play. Crown. Cloaks. Sunset and Sunrise. Taxidermy.

Illustration 15   Quick Guide *Genny and the Neons*

< Q U I C K · G U I D E S >

Title: Five Dead Acts Five Dead Cats (2015)

Where: The Defibrillator Gallery, Chicago

Description: A live performance in the gallery for two performers - Gary and Claire. We spent 4 hours writing the text of the entire performance in graphite on the floor of the in the confines of a rectangle, centrally in the space reminiscent of Sterne's Black Page. This forms the centre of an environment to which we used the rule of the power of 10 to create concentric rectangles marked in brightly coloured tape on the floor and walls of the gallery. During the performance these lines marked out the realm of the five acts, and during each act we removed the tape through a series of actions: 1. Two gorilla-suited individuals carefully roll up the tape to make a pair of cats bollocks. 2. The gorilla's hands and feet wrapped and bound in tape. 3. Two skeletons roll up the tape around their heads on the floor and perform the Monty Python 'Dead Parrot' sketch. 4. A hybrid figure part-saint, part-king, part-skeleton, interprets the numbers on a found object (a long wooden stick found on the sidewalk) as choreography and winds up the tape around the stick. 5. Skeleton Roy uses the bits of discarded tape and gorilla parts from act 1 and 2 to construct an appropriation of dead cat.

Kit box: Table, mic and PA. Gorilla suits, Skeleton Roy suit, found object (stick), day-glow gaffer tape, clipboards, graphite sticks, headphones and player, leaves, dollar bills, magazine image of Johnny Depp, heap of clothes, crown.

Commonalities: Gorillas. St Giles. King Lear. Gummo. Crying. Roy Orbison. Dead cat. Sterne's black page.

Illustration 16 Quick Guide *Five Dead Acts Five Dead Cats*

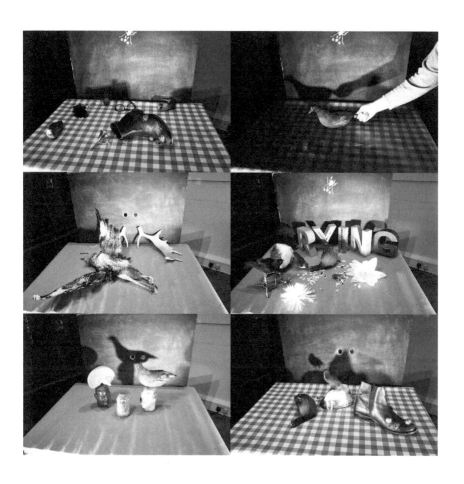

Illustration 17 Individual frames from *Suspended Animation: A Foot, A Head, A Leg & A Wing*

8

The Dead Preserved

This chapter is written as a performance lecture drawing attention to thoughts on preservation summoning up a mood on the qualities of deadness. We return to the deadness list established in Chapter 1 as a reminder that the characteristics, states, peculiarities and properties of practice guide both the concept, experience and aesthetic of creative works.

Deadness:
   A state or quality of playing dead.
   The playing out of something that is dead in various interpretations of the word.
   The act of sleep, or the qualities of sleep.
   The stillness in objects, subjects, ideas.
   A play on the term liveness.
   Of or relating to something being dead as in a language or a career.
   The inanimate state of performance as ephemera.
   The use of the word dead in language, e.g. the use of idioms and euphemisms.
   The quality of performance produced through ghosting methodologies.

We reflect on the deadness list through the story of our practice set out here as an intertextual weave of anecdotes, creative research and poetic descriptions of our projects spanning across a four-year period.

The anecdotal format offers a dual function: to share a playful and philosophical insight into dramaturgical processes of intermedia projects revealing happenstance and coincidence, and, to preserve our own practice, documented here as connected to the cultural remains of others.

A way to think of this chapter's format is to visualise the metaphor laid out in Chapter 3 'The Dead Play', where we offer the image of tornadoes on a vista circling and multiplying as the Death Drift/Drift Drive (DD/DD). We end this performance lecture with a creative task that invites you to tell the story of your own practice.

How can a tiny body have so many complex things happen within it? But from whose perspective is tiny? A fly is undoubtedly tiny, so are humans, so is the earth so, is the Orion Nebula, so is the universe. I have landed on the page and I will return. Let's have think about the dust on a fly's legs. Let's have a think about the sleep in the fly's eye. When we look up into the universe, are we looking into the past? Are we looking into the dust? Can they invent a telescope that allows us to see the death of a fly in the sky? This is flyosophy; for every piece of dust on Freud's couch there is a star in the sky.

Fragile, Sensitive and with Limited Longevity

When we were preparing for an artist talk the night before the opening of a Theatre and Performance Research Association (TaPRA) conference in a hotel in Canterbury, a bubble happened to float past us on the corridor; without understanding where it came from, we preserved that moment in our mind as a beautiful thing. The bubble came our way; we opened a door for it and it drifted off into another space, an unexplained chance encounter. A year later, still mesmerized, we were chasing bubbles and filming them, and happened on the south wall in the chancel of the Church of St Michael's in the village of Coxwold and the memorial tomb of Thomas, 1st Viscount Fauconberg, and his wife Barbara Cholmeley, erected in 1618. The couple, carved in stone, are shown kneeling in silent prayer. Below them an inscription that commemorates Thomas' love for Barbara – 'Omnis homo bulla, omni caro faenum' – which translates as

'Every man is a bubble, all flesh is grass'. The quiet village of Coxwold surrounded by the beautiful landscape of the North York Moors is a curious and intriguing place. Opposite the church you will come across Shandy Hall, once home to the eighteenth-century writer and vicar Laurence Sterne. Sterne preached in the village Church of St Michael and would have orated in the pulpit adjacent to this memorial tomb. It is in this village that he wrote *The Life and Opinions of Tristram Shandy, Gentlemen*, where the reader comes across the Black Page, a conceptual interpretation on the death of the character Parson Yorick, a fictional self-portrait of Sterne.

We invested time in this charming place, making visual works of neon light in the nearby moorland area across to the coast at Whitby for the incidental audience and exhibited photographs of the images in the Shandy Hall gallery. Sterne's Black Page, as an idea well ahead of its time, written in 1759, transcends the literary page offering an alternative experience for the reader to contemplate and fathom death. And there is more to this place: a story of Sterne's exhumation and reinternment as an example of how death imitates art.

Kenneth Monkman devoted much of his life to the restoration of Shandy Hall, establishing the Laurence Sterne Trust to promote the writings of Sterne. In 1967, he transformed it into a personality museum. The museum is a house with a beautiful garden, and much like the Freud Museum it houses exhibitions and events that relate to Sterne's ideas printed material and artefacts.

Sterne, after his death, had a private burial in Oxford Road London and many rumours of Sterne's interment and re-interment back to the same burial ground are articulated by a story in Day and Monkman (1998). Patrick Wildgust, the curator of Shandy Hall, tells his visitors a version of that story (as you take a tour of the house): that Sterne was so famous he was recognized on the anatomy table by a person in attendance who ordered the anatomization to stop.

In 1969, the London burial ground was being sold off for building development. When thousands of skeletal remains were interred the identification of Sterne's was narrowed down to five skulls found in the area thought to be where Sterne was buried. One of those skulls showed a scar, evidence of being under the anatomist's knife. Other significant evidence mounted: that of a Nollekens bust of Sterne, 'generally regarded as the most accurate of the various representations of Sterne' (Day and Monkman, 1998, p.65). This bust measured accurately to the size of the smallest skull of those five and, importantly, it was this small skull that contained the dissection scar. Monkman was responsible for the skull's re-interment, and there was a small ceremony in 1969 where he (now as a skull) rests in a grave at the Church of St Michael, Coxwold, along with a memorial stone facing in a different direction to the other gravestones – away from the rising sun.

But there is another story, the story of skull # 612 housed at the Duckworth Collection in the Division of Biological Anthropology at the University of Cambridge. This skull is also purported to be that of Sterne. Dittmar and Mitchell's 2016 paper claims to solve 'the mystery of why Sterne was resurrected' and that 'osteological and cut mark analysis' on a skull is evidence to suggest # 612 is Sterne's. Yet much of the discussion of skull # 612 is based upon speculation; there is no scientific evidence that it is *the* Skull. The skull buried at Coxwold is fittingly and playfully Sterne's of course! The most rewarding of stories if you think about Shakespeare's Hamlet and his jester Yorick, interred by the First Gravedigger, and now a most famously ghosted memento mori image. Even Jesters can't escape such a fate, and Sterne knew this well of his Parson Yorick for he has him die in volume 1 of *Tristram Shandy*. As an autobiographical tale and one of serendipity, the incomplete remains (the skull) buried in the Church of St Michael lie next to the entrance of the church that houses an eighteenth-century stone tablet (one of three known grave markers), inscribed with the words 'Alas Poor Yorick'.

Page 73 of Sterne's novel invites us to contemplate the mystery of death in visual form from within the depth of the colour of black ink. The interpretative qualities of the Black Page are meditative and playful in their deadness; here death is sentimental, death is poetic, death is conceptual, and death is a jest. Aptly, the current state of Sterne's buried remains speak directly back to his own page.

Did someone mention death? I return and land on this page. I hang around. People acknowledge someone is dead. Do you know when someone is dead? Sometimes it is a very sad occasion. Sometimes it is a very happy occasion.

Sometimes they appear happy, sometimes they appear sad but for me it is a matter of playing a role. I am just a fly. But let's not make assumptions about my level of consciousness, just because I land on crap.

A Few Words in Neon

Crying
If Only
We made something of this
I could hide
You remembered my name
Flesh Grass Fresh Glass

A neon light's state of deadness can be found in its haunting condition as an inanimate object, yet it has a profound quality of liveness. Charged with energy of limited longevity, its ephemerality is writ large within the solitude of breath-taking landscapes.

St Mary's Church graveyard overlooks Whitby high on a hill. It is first light. Weathered pitted gravestones with their inscriptions wind-blasted to the point of illegibility. The sound of the sea is prominent; it is not competing with the town. Boats returning from a night at sea. It is wild. The neon sign this morning reads, 'You remembered my name', positioned behind an irregular line of gravestones without names, one of which had broken in two. Pulling the starter chord on the generator to ignite the neon gas, the red words spring into life, the vibration disrupts the stillness again before the dead can rest.

Walking through Little Beck Wood through the oak, ash and alder we happen upon a cave carved from a giant boulder in the landscape. Once the home of a hermit, surviving on food, fuel and shelter provided by the woods. The inscription on the entrance of this eighteenth-century hermitage reads G & C 1790. The dark interior of the cave provides perfect condition for our 'I Could Hide' neon. For two hours, amplifying the generator and the space filling with toxic fumes, it entertained the incidental audience of afternoon ramblers and microcosms of hoverflies, millipedes and mites in the dead wood of the forest floor.

There's a barn owl gliding in a gully en route to the moorland beyond Lealholm. The outlook is a postcard image of the North York Moors with deep dales and valleys and haunting high ridges. The metal trestle frame for the neon signs stands out proudly from the heather, 'Crying' in bubblegum pink. On top of the trestle is a blackbird in a fixed position; his feathers caught in the wind. This evening they are heather-burning – small controlled fires by gamekeepers to manage the habitat. Our bluey white light from the neon words 'If Only' reflected in a roadside puddle are an echo. It is getting dark; the flames keep disappearing and reappearing.

On the west side of the harbour the bandstand lights are turned off; it is early morning and it is quiet except for the sound of the sea. Dawn is breaking, and a bank of clouds draw closer to the town; the seagulls gather on the rooftop of the yachting club. Our neon light spelling out the word 'Crying' is turned off, an echo. The wind whistles through the exposed circular structure of the bandstand creating mini tornadoes from the rubbish of the debris of last night: polystyrene cartons, leaves, chips and dust.

On a grassy bank, the roadside verge of a lost highway, capital letters spell out the words FLESH GRASS FRESH GLASS, red, green, green blue. Sometimes it splits to spell out different phrases FLESH GLASS FRESH GRASS red, blue, green, green. It is getting dark and it is the middle of nowhere. Headlights from the distance come over the brow; they are getting closer, Flesh and Glass. The car slows down as it approaches the sign, a window winds down to the sound of P. J. Proby on the radio, the driver says 'What is this? What's it for, why is it here?' He smiles and as he drives off he sings 'There's a place for us, somewhere a place for us, peace and quiet and open air, wait for us, somewhere'. The generator chugs and stalls; the neon light flickers and goes out. Somewhere, nowhere.

If Only

After setting up a neon light installation at sunset reading 'If Only' powered by a portable petrol generator in the Graveyard of the Church of St Mary next to Whitby Abbey for the incidental audience, we reflected upon the experience at the infamous Magpie restaurant. As we paid for our meal, the manager told us a story of a ghost that haunts the restaurant. This ghost, Albert, she recalls, is a bit of a menace, teasing and frightening the staff who work at the restaurant. Once, Albert had all the staff bewildered because of the strange night when a whole dinner went missing from the plate. She recalled the case of the missing dinner with absolute conviction and informed us that everyone including the kitchen assistant went on the hunt for this missing food, searching everywhere. She said: 'Yeah, can you believe it? He ate the whole dinner.' Her sincere tone contained not one drop of irony; she meant every word. If the dead come back, it is because our belief systems allow for their return. Phillips asks:

> Are people's experiences the consequences of their beliefs, or vice versa? Are beliefs foisted on experiences or constitutive of them? Or is belief as Wittgenstein asked, an experience? (Phillips, 2006, p.76)

At 6am sunrise we returned to the graveyard to set up the neon installation 'You remembered my name'.

That evening at sunset and on the North York Moors we installed the pink neon light 'Crying', with a taxidermy blackbird perched on its trestle frame, to the backdrop of a desolate heathery landscape. Then, in darkness, after packing the neon away in the car, we returned to Whitby to have dinner at the Fisherman's Wife restaurant. Here, our conversation turned to the themes of off and on in performance. We discussed Samuel Beckett's dramaticule *Come and Go*, we recalled an anecdote where a group of students were working through Beckett's tiny play, discussing the timing of the entrances and exits, and lighting states that work in tandem with the thematic concepts of light and dark when we remembered, during the workshop, and for no reason at all, the stage light above our heads began to flicker off and on. The students were slightly unnerved, relishing this unique coincidence; one student contextualized this moment as if Beckett were present. As a matter of fact, during this conversation in the restaurant the light above our table began to flicker off and on and off and on and off and on and off and on and off and on and… We stopped dead in our conversation; no other light in the restaurant was doing this. We remember clearly, it was one of those drop-down lights on a wire, a light bulb hanging above our heads, flickering off and on. Beckett's spirit is embodied in a light bulb over table number 4 in the Fisherman's Wife restaurant, Whitby.

Birds are Sacred and They Eat the Dead

In the 1990s, the dead were entrapped and left screaming in the knob of a bedside table in a hotel bedroom. The dead resided in the tape recorder of the introspective detective, the dead were in the Douglas Fir trees, they kept secrets and were present in absentia and they could be found in the dreams of an FBI agent who skirts around logic to solve his cases. The dead danced and spoke backwards and made no sense, the dead arrived in the form of a speaking giant who resided in a liminal space, neither in heaven or hell, but as a messenger delivering ambiguous riddles. The dead returned embodied in the form of the murdered protagonist's cousin but played by the same actress, ghosting herself, as if it weren't odd enough in this place where 'the owls are not what they seem'. Cue the opening credits, cue the music:

Gary:

> Enormous blades of metal cut through wooden logs. Sparks fly as the blades are re-sharpened. Water pours from the top of a crop of rocks. The film slows slightly. A traffic light swings in the wind. The red light glowing in the darkness.

Laura Palmer is Dead.

Claire:

> 'Lucy, It's Pete, Put Harry on the Horn.'
>
> 'Harry, she's wrapped in plastic'.
>
> Laura is not in her room.
>
> Laura is not at Bobby's.
>
> Bobby is not at Football practice.

Laura did not go to work with her father.

Bobby is at the diner, he puts a coin in the jukebox, points at Norma (point with finger arm out) and speaks 'see you in my dreams'.

Gary:

The Sheriff is secretly in love with the dead sawmill owner's wife.

The hotel manager is secretly in love with the dead sawmill owner's sister.

Big Ed is secretly in love with Norma who works at the diner.

Policeman Andy cries at crime scenes but asks Lucy not to tell anyone about it. (Gary and Claire, 2016)

Claire:

The lights flicker in the morgue

On and off

And

On and

Off and

On and off

And

On

And

Off and

On. (Ibid., 2016)

Cut the music.

We were invited to deliver a two-week performance workshop at the Norwegian Theatre Academy. Each morning at the beginning of each class, we performed a five-minute summoning up of a *Twin Peaks* episode that we had watched the night before, accompanied by Angelino Badalamenti's theme tune. This ritual enabled participants to get up to speed with us on the whole first season and, to ensure that our dedication to this daily practice ignited a commitment from the actors, to engage in deep play.

We had brought a range of texts and ideas as prompts to develop an intertextual performance, including Beckett's dramaticule *Come and Go*. As a practical game, we glided ghostly through the cyclical exits and entrances of this small play layering the students' creative scores into this structural frame while thinking about David Lynch's (2002) experimental series of film shorts entitled *Rabbits*. In *Rabbits*, the characters enter, exit and talk in non-sequiturs while an unsettling mystery surrounds their conversation. These rabbits, haunted in their own home by uncanny sounds and tormented by an otherworldly red light, seem unfazed. Observing this work, it was as if Lynch was inspired by the silent and slow-paced comings and goings of Flo, Vi and Ru in Beckett's work where the impending sense of mystery is played out through the stylized action of a whisper into each woman's ear as they sit surrounded by darkness. Curiously, the whisper into the ear is a Lynchian thematic motif. Laura Palmer whispers into Agent Cooper's ear during his strange encounter with her in the Red Room. At the end of *Come and Go*, the women sit together and hold hands, as do the rabbits at the end of the film series. Catherine Laws (2007) discusses the idea that Beckett's ghost is the elephant in the room within contemporary arts, an omnipresent ghostly, silent figure whose practices are visible in the experimental, specifically found in the cyclical patterns of movement, repetition, fragmented speech and silence. In *Rabbits*, as in *Come and Go*, secrets are kept. The pace is slow, the silence exhaustive and the Beckettian 'undercurrents', as we observe, deliver a significantly peculiar presence of deadness from the Lynchian dream world, where animals feature as uncanny objects as if humans performing as animated taxidermy.

In *Twin Peaks*, dead and stuffed animals are kitsch; they are everywhere. There is a duck next to the telephone in Agent Cooper's bedroom along with a giant fish on the wall. Taxidermy animals become more apparent as the series develops; they exist as trophies, artefacts, objects that decorate a room or have fallen off a wall. In one scene, Sheriff Truman and Special Agent Cooper walk into a room of the local bank and are faced immediately with a huge taxidermy deer head on a conference table that catches their gaze. After a moment of silence, a brief explanation is given by the woman who is showing them Laura Palmer's safety deposit box; she says casually, 'Oh, it fell down'. The men then laugh. Pete shows off his newly bought taxidermy fish to Josie and in episode 11 Jonathan hands Josie a taxidermy mount, a scene of two animals – a menacing weasel wrapped by a snake – and in the conversation that takes place between the two of them, Josie is seen stroking the mounted scene. In the penultimate episode of the first series, one of the characters embodies a dead stag; he stands in front of it unaware the antlers are coming out of his head. The excess of dead stuffed animals represents the slipperiness between the fear and fantasy of death within the show's central theme around the death of Laura Palmer, and the dead animals appear as large-scale dioramas.

Twenty-five years since the first two series of *Twin Peaks* were aired (and not too long before *Twin Peaks the Return* arrived on our screens), we wanted to capture the very peculiar arrangement of taxidermy, drawing upon the 'lumpish deadness of marketplace images of the world of objects and bodies' (Nochimson, 2015, p.57).

We set up in residency at a local gallery in York to make a stop motion animation film from a case of taxidermy bird bits. We called this participatory project *Suspended Animation; A Foot, A Leg, A Head and A Wing*. The case of bird bits was given to us by a colleague who works at the Freud Museum and who witnessed *Ghost Track* and *Kong Lear* performed in the Anna Freud room. The case included a few bird heads, torsos, wings, feet, feathers, skin, a bit of a beak. Their once complete taxidermy intact remains were part of an exhibition at the Whitechapel Gallery London and have been received by other artists before we got the leftovers. In an attempt to give them a life of some sort, and not to abuse or ridicule them, but rather respect they had a life, we shot a film on Super 8mm sequences of small increments, bird bit animations through a series of frames which could then be played in a fast sequence post production. We created a simple set up with clear rules for making the film:

Choose a handful of taxidermy bird bits and think of a simple scenario, abstract or literal to animate the objects for a film. Create the animation by moving the object(s) to suit one frame at a time.

We saw this case of objects as unruly and mischievous, bird bits with an anarchic temperament; a head, a wing, a leg, and a foot is 'sticking it to the man' reclaiming their identity finding fresh vigour to their original taxidermy state. The reanimated quality of their poses highlights their rejected status. Here, meaning has been postponed, suspended and thrown out, left hanging, expelled, terminated; commenting upon their own deadness they reclaim a life and the right to exist as bits. The interesting aesthetic about stop motion as a series of still images is that objects are animated to suggest movement – they don't really move, but your brain can't help but see them moving. This illusion is made even more haunting because, from within the deadness of their status as incomplete remains, they look alive, yet their different poses don't look like anything we have ever seen in the animal world. Their incomplete remains offer new hybrid species, bird bits engaging in a frenzy of dark and deep play:

A postcard of Roy Orbison, promotion material from our *Roy of the Dead/Day of the O* performances, appears at the back of the stage; it slowly makes its way to centre stage. A blackbird on a branch and a dipper on rock, appear at either side of Roy and slowly advance. A large legless bird appears downstage followed by three separate bird heads. They all move closer to the image and gather around the image as witnesses. A small sharp beak pierces through the card slowly followed by all the remains, who all peck at the cardboard image of Roy. In the momentum of the attack, they rotate as one mass ripping sections of the card into small pieces; the birds separate; fragments of the cards pull them across the table; Roy's image disperses. Large cardboard letters parade along the back of the stage spelling out the word *Crying*. One by one the bird bits turn into flowers among the scattered piece of card. A final bird head transforms into Roy Orbison rising up out of the ground. The flowers ping out of view and the pieces of card form themselves into a small pile and then disappear. The letters of the word *Crying* scramble on top of each other and descend into the ground. Leaving the letter *R* for Roy still standing.

When we think about Sterne's skull, separated from his body, we don't know where the body is or what happened to it, or in fact which skull is truly Sterne's. When we embody Orbison in our performance work (*Crying in the Dark* as one example), it is not the complete image. We are happy not to have all of the information. It is where the playfulness of our work is located; the gaps and inconsistences inform the quality of performance. Similarly, the incomplete remains of taxidermy suggest they once had a life but we can't locate it fully. Now they have a new life. When the bird bits tear Orbison to shreds there are moments of drama, moments of surrealistic sweetness, moments of light and dark mixed among very simple entrances and exits, on and off. The bits are players offering their own modes of performing for the camera, an anarchic non-human adaptation of Beckett's dramaticule, *Come and Go*.

What would you do if you were confronted by death on the streets in the middle of the day? Forget everything you have read about neon lights glowing on a hill, bird bits pecking at a postcard of a dead singer and the obsession with a DVD box set of a 25-year-old TV show. None of it is important now. What would you do if death followed you home? How would it affect what you did, what you ate? How would you get rid of death? Remove it in the bags? All the garbage and rubbish have tales of their own. We have ways of telling these tales, reading the bins, translating them.

The Spirit of the Dead Cat

The curator of the Defibrillator Gallery in Chicago asked us for a blurb six months before we had made a new work. Thinking on our feet, we had a conversation about the five-act structure of Shakespeare's plays, and simply played around with the word *acts* as an anagram for cats. We called the work *Five Dead Acts Five Dead Cats*. We knew this title would act as a provocation (and we would make the work once we arrive in residency), but little did we know what we would find in Chicago when we arrived – coincidences haunt.

While in Chicago, and as part of our creative process, we walked each day to the Defibrillator Gallery looking for any material we could get our hands on that might be classed as 'dead' to use as prompts for storytelling for our emerging performance. Discarded objects dumped left for dead are in trash limbo, destined for the scrap heap but not yet arrived, drifting on the streets, waiting to be collected to be taken to the dump. Or, invigorated. We found a paper aeroplane and a pair of discarded black tights, and then…

In the dark, upon leaving the gallery late one night and walking towards the metro we discussed the title of *Five Dead Acts Five Dead Cats* as a provocation. We remembered the character of Koko the gorilla played by Gary in our *Dream Yards* studio show, known for communicating in sign language, and who loved to play with kittens. Our gorilla professed it wanted a real dead cat for its birthday. We also remembered that Gary ghosted, in our performance of *Crying in the Dark,* a visual reference to the 1997 Harmony Korine movie *Gummo* where the character Bunny Boy, holds up a dead black cat to the camera to the sound of Roy Orbison's song *Crying.* Gary suddenly gasps; 'Claire'. We both stopped; our attitude changed. 'A dead cat' says Gary. 'It is a real dead black cat.' Silence. We looked at one another. We could not believe the extent to which this coincidence was messing with us; we began to feel responsible. What if we had killed the cat? There he was lying close to the gutter next to the fire station, alone and dead with its little nose. We looked at the poor thing in total sadness; we are both cat lovers. We left quietly, sombrely and full of disbelief. Later, after some contemplation, we talked of how we could return the next day to bury him. We planned to take a shovel and a bag, name him and bury him in a park under some leaves, give him a proper send off. We were looking forward to this act as if somehow a burial ritual would make it better. We walked towards the scene quite early the next morning, hoping that the dead black cat would be lying there, but it was gone. We were sad for some time that day until walking in the neighbourhood we happened across a large painted mural on the side of a café wall. The painting depicted many animals sitting at a table and drinking cocktails with famous people (including Madonna). One animal in particular caught our eyes. It was a large black cat staring directly into our eyes with a collar baring the name Boots on his tag. The spirit of the dead black cat is now preserved in the neighbourhood's street art. We raised a toast to Boots in our performance: Gary played dead on the floor; scattered leaves rested upon him. As if in a deep sleep the quality of deadness in Gary's presence performed a gentle stillness, an echo of the wish we both had upon finding a cat lying close to the sidewalk.

On another day we found a long piece of wood covered with a sequence of handwritten numbers drawn in white marker pen. The wood was lying on the street close to a bridge with the skyline of Chicago downtown as its backdrop. This discarded tired wood was a mystery to us; the number sequence made no formal sense, other than representing complexity. Was it Pi? Or Fibonacci? We carried this tall heavy numbered stick with us. People admired it asking us what the number system meant. We created our own rules in response to the numbers, and in turn Gary performed a series of actions. A few days later, Joseph Ravens, the curator of Defibrillator, returning from a trip away witnessed Gary practising movement with the stick and immediately recognized the object and loved the coincidence. It was the artist John Court's object from a durational performance (Untitled) of 7 hours 30 minutes, that took place six months previously in Eckhart Park (approximately three miles away from where we found it discarded). The numbers on the stick represented the amount of people who died (and who were born) on a specific day.

Discarded objects ready for the scrap heap have a curious status in their deadness as remains. Although we acknowledge they once had a life (the taxidermy bird bits, John Court's stick), like this chapter's anecdotes, you don't get the full story of our performances. Rather, our remains sit conceptually; the scraps of experiences are preserved alongside the sentimental and serendipitous within the play of death.

I am full with ideas. Along the flower clad cliff top I gambol in the sunshine and consider the infinite magnitude of space. In the rush-lined gullies worn in the bolder clay I compare its reverse; the ultimate minuteness of matter. When we die our bodies return to the earth, when you see me landing on the road kill what goes through your mind, do you suffer sickness? Do you choose to go back to the earth wearing a love heart on your necklace? I am still for a moment, you have time to take a snap shot – would you consider me dead or alive? Where to ideas come from? They come from within the rotting flesh of a dead black cat.

The Uses of the Dead

Throughout history, from ancient times, there have been different intentions to keep the bodies of the dead preserved, and in the best possible state. Embalming procedures prevent the body from rotting and make the body suitable for public display. There were cultural and religious reasons for embalming the dead; for example, the Ancient Egyptians believed that preservation empowered the soul after death and that a rotting corpse was excluded from the afterlife. Because of such strong beliefs in the need to preserve the human body, the artificial preservation of the cadaver produced many varied methodologies and techniques – the body immersed in honey as one example – and corpses were preserved using natural materials as well as chemical. But preservation had many different purposes other than spiritual, particularly for medical training and understanding the human body and dissection. The philosopher Jeremy Bentham requested, in his last will and testament, to 'ensure that he would survive in *both* a physical and an intellectual form' (Fenn, 1992, p.v). In his will dated 30 May 1832, he requested that doctor Southwood Smith:

> take my body under his charge and take the requisite and appropriate measures for the disposal & preservation of the several parts of my body frame in the manner expressed in the paper annexed to this my will and at top of which I have written "Auto Icon" – the Skeleton he will cause to be put together in such a manner as that the whole figure may be seated in a chair usually occupied by me when living in the attitude in which I am sitting when engaged in thought in the course of time employed in writing. (Fenn, 1992, p.35)

Bentham's attitude towards the preservation of the dead was utilitarian in its philosophy and controversial in its proposal. He did not believe in paying the church for funerals and he wanted to study and learn from the dead so that we may live longer. In the aforementioned paper annexed to his will entitled *Auto Icon, or Father Uses of the Dead to the Living. A Fragment*, he writes lengthy proposals on Auto-Iconism:

> The word *auto* has been made familiar to English ears by its use in auto-biography, (why should there not be auto-thanatography), autography, etc. Auto-Icon will soon be understood for a man who is his own image. (Ibid., p.4)

In this macabre and satirical paper, he imagines a culture where the dead are put on display in a variety of different places. Yet Bentham's writing opposed the current attitude of that time towards the dead where, 'Generally, in the present state of things, our dead relations are a source of evil – and not of good: the fault is not theirs, but ours' (Ibid., p.2).

His visions suggest:

> There would be no longer be needed monuments of stone or marble – there would be no danger to health from the accumulating of corpses – and the use of churchyards would be gradually done away. (Ibid., p.4)

His thoughts were provocative if not theatrical:

> Would the sight – the constant sight of the dead be too melancholy – too saddening to the living? A curtain or sliding screen provides a remedy. On certain days the Auto-Icons might be exhibited, and their exhibition associated with religious observances. (Ibid.)

Today, Bentham's Auto-Icon sits within in a glass cupboard on display to the public at the University College London (UCL); his real head replaced by a wax version, commissioned and made by a French artist, Jacques Talrich. The Auto-Icon is his own skeleton, padded out with materials, dressed in his own clothes and shoes, a hat from which his real hair protrudes. The real head exists, but sits in storage at the UCL's Institute of Archaeology in a climate-controlled room. If someone wishes to view the head, UCL's website provides a contact email address to arrange such an encounter. We visited the *Curated Head's* exhibition at UCL with accompanying talks in November 2017, where, for a short while, the head was brought out on display housed in a glass jar. Morbid at is sounds in the same exhibition we saw how in Victorian times the preservation of the deceased through photography (of their dead) was not a sign of morbid curiosity, but a way of remembering their loved ones. Some photographs were framed by a theatrical curtain, as a way to preserve the photograph from fading or perhaps for those who have difficulty viewing an image of the deceased.

Has anyone ever considered the ghost of a fly? Landing on the shoulders of a ghost of a fly. I am on the window of the Sainsbury's Centre café, looking out at a stoat being chased by a squirrel. Two artists make a joke about me and incorporate my being in their practice. I am the fly in the ointment, the fly on the wall, I am now their ghost. What business was it of theirs to put me in their work! I was present, I was in the right place at the right time. I am only a ghost.

Uncle Toby Would Not Harm a Fly

Uncle Toby from Sterne's novel *Tristram Shandy, Gentlemen,* is known as one of the nicest characters in this fiction. Uncle Toby is persuaded that you should like all sentient beings; he believes that everything that is alive deserves respect. Tristram observes his uncle's sentiments one day at lunch when his uncle comes across a big fly that buzzing close to him. Toby catches the fly and takes it to the window. He speaks to the fly, 'I'll not hurt thee … I'll not hurt a hair of thy head: – Go, … get thee gone, why should I hurt thee? – This world surely is wide enough to hold both thee and me' (Sterne, 2012, p.88). Today, Wildgust informs us of a tradition, that if ever a fly gets trapped in the museum of Shandy Hall it has to be taken out by the glass.

The Enigmatic Affective Presence of Performance

During an opening moment in the show *Lost in A Sea of Glass and Tin*, we raised a toast in the presence of the audience to the film projection reading 'the show will begin in 5 minutes'. By happenstance, a fly buzzes around the set; its presence is felt. There is a video projection of a spinning fan; Claire spins a chair continuously to the song *Sweet Caroline* sung by Gary. Gary tapes a cup to his head. Claire smashes a chair. There's a video projection that shows Gary wearing a robe and antlers walking through a busy Wall Street in New York City. Cue the music: Claire plays *Laura Palmer's Theme Tune* from *Twin Peaks* (1990) on the keyboard synth and Gary recounts Angelo Badalamenti's description of writing this piece of music in the presence of David Lynch. Professor Roberta Mock sits in the audience and is thinking about how to respond to this show in the morning as the keynote respondent of the symposium Queering Ritual (2017). After Gary sings his heart out to P. J. Proby's cover of *Somewhere*, with Claire playing the synth, we transform in front of the audience into a sculptural work, two large black moving images called *The Black Heaps*. *The Black Heaps* as a construction are made up of lightweight aluminium tubing from an old gazebo frame refurbished and attached to a back pack, duct taped together and with black fake fur attached to the protruding end covering our whole body and the backpack's frame, as a non-specific geometrical shape. Our experience inside the heap is other; we are disadvantaged because inside we can't see very well. The sculpture is featureless (it has no face or eyes), but there is a pinnacle made from found twigs and sticks cabled tied onto the top of the material that might be construed as a head or perhaps antennae, but still as 'things' this is ambiguous. Performing them and playing with different height levels, dropping to a crouch, turning 90 degrees, can be a dramatic shift in interpretation for the audience.

We slowly glide out of the studio leaving the remains of the live performance behind and with the audience looking out on the streets. We communicate to one another using the feedback picked up on megaphones that we are wearing underneath the fur; the feedback sounds like whale talk. Some follow us for a short while, intrigued.

At 6.30am the next morning, Roberta Mock sits in her hotel room and improvises a written response to the performance:

> I know that sound, I know those progressions. The fetishization of a young blond woman who would be found wrapped in plastic. I am nearly ecstatic because I hear Gary and I know what Claire is helping us reach toward and I see it. And I remember my point of view, his point of view 25 years later and it is undecidable. I can't remember now was he the good or evil Agent Cooper then? I am yesterbating with Gary and Claire, we are yesterbating. Here and now together then and there. This is a futurity that reaches way back and in. I have been here before. On a hot August night perhaps with Neil Diamond on the 8 track. 'Sweet Caroline. Good times never seemed so good. Hands, touching hands. Reaching out, touching me touching you. Reaching out reaching in'. The purpose of ritual, to bring one's body into a community, to experience communities, to become part of something. Something bigger than yourself that comprises yourself. Becoming part of the pattern. Putting yourself in the picture. Feeling what it is like to be in the picture. The ordering, the crafting, the objects, the sequencing offer us an experience of transformation that we interpret as meaningful. We are transported together – as I was with Gary and Claire, back to the woods, the sound of the owl, my ineffable longing for Agent Cooper 25 years ago when I lived here in Yorkshire. (Mock, 2017)

The Black Heaps now tour as a stand-alone durational action in rural and city-based environments and are an amalgamation of many our 'Gary and Claire' worlds. We've riffed across practices and produced, through our intermedial practice, a performance of pure presence. As large-scale fluffy Auto-Icons, a form of living deadness we have transformed into a non-human form.

The Black Heaps animate an inanimate presence relating to Roy Orbison's 'the man in black' image, the black heap of clothes that we change into during the 90-second break in *Crying in the Dark*, and, an appropriation of Sterne's Black Page. Appreciating colour as Lynch thinks about it where 'Black has depth … you can go into it … And you start seeing what you're afraid of. You start seeing what you love, and it becomes like a dream' (Lynch, 2015), *The Black Heaps* are perceived as eerily medieval, or as a playfully futuristic 'thing' and their enigmatic presence appears to hold a playful threat because of their unidentifiable status in the landscape. Whale sounds produced from the feedback on the megaphones allow us to work out where we are heading to keep us safe when we are crossing the road – and produce humour. The blowing-up of balloons through a small hole in the fabric of the material accompanied by their raspberry sounds offers up a playful contrast to the mystery of the heaps.

There have been a range of responses when touring. On one occasion, while gliding along the streets of Pontefract, we posed a threat; a policewoman desperate to know what we were doing shouted 'I'm coming in' before lifting up the black material and getting inside the heap with Claire. The policewoman asked us, inside this dark and intimate space, 'Are *you* drama?' Claire, not sure how to respond, agreed, 'Yes, we *are* drama', and the policewoman went happily on her way wishing us well.

The Future of Death

We made a visit to the Gordon Museum at Kings College London to see Alan, a mummified taxi driver from Torquay. The museum is not open to the public (unless by special request); rather it is accessed by students and those who work in medical science for educational purposes and,

as a training resource, housing specimens of human remains and repli-
cas. Alan is on the ground floor, resting in the container that was used
for his salt bath mummification process; he is wrapped in muslin cloth
and the TV screen above his head plays the video documentary about
his mummification entitled *Mummifying Alan: Egypt's Last Secret* (2011).
He is the only one of his kind in this space, the mummy in the corner.
We wondered, what would have Bentham thought of Alan, the first successful mummification since the Egyptian's Eighteenth Dynasty methods
of preservation? Watching the video, we observed two very intriguing
elements to this story: the success of the mummification process where
archaeological chemist Dr Stephen Buckley and Egyptologist Joann
Fletcher proved a theory about the ancient Egyptian preservation process
and Alan himself, not a Pharaoh but a working-class unlikely volunteer to
be preserved and housed in a museum for years come. Alan agreed before
he died for his body to be given to medical science, to become a mummy.
In the video, Alan's wife talks about how he loved to sleep and shows a
photograph of Alan tucked up in bed, wrapped up in blankets during the
day. Now we see Alan imitating in death what he loved to do in life, sleep.
Alan lost his battle with cancer, and the documentary reminds us that
death comes to us all, and that, generally, we view death as a sad thing.
Alan wanted us to view it differently: 'If people like me don't respond we
don't learn anything.' And he had a sense of humour: 'Shame I am not
going to see it, I quite like documentaries.' To be sitting there with him,
in the presence of a twenty-first-century mummy in the quiet space of a
medical museum, is other. The only familiarity we have is the memories
of the mummies in museums from an ancient dynasty. We are more like
Alan than an ancient mummy. Watching the last moments of Alan being
wrapped up (on the documentary) and in the direct presence of him, you
end up asking the question, 'Is this is something I would do?' You realize
Alan is going to be there for hundreds of years, so you contemplate time
and history and with yourself in it. As people study him, and over hundreds of years, information will be passed on, and it is going to outlive
the scientists that proposed the idea. It is a specific type of contemplation
that puts those who have not yet arrived on this earth into it, not so different from thinking about *Long Player* (2000), a 1,000-year-long composition by artist Jem Finer. Reflecting upon the longevity of our own

practice, we are never simply focused on one project for a quick and easy gimmick. Our processes keep moving and transforming into different conceptual spaces over a long period of time through the circling process. Being with Alan confirmed our interest in deadness is not driven out of morbidity, but out of a genuine curiosity on how death and autobiography are inextricably linked. 'By the end of his life, Sterne had become a master at fictionalising his autobiography, and using autobiographical experiences as the basis of his fiction' (Campbell Ross in Keymer, 2009). Sterne's self-portrait of Yorick, Bentham's eccentric Auto-Icon and Alan's mummified body have been preserved in unusual ways either through request (Bentham), through donation (Alan) or through poetic irony (Sterne). And Freud is still with us, currently as a silent omnipresence embedded in the psyche of the DD/DD.

Not long after we made the visit to the Gordon Museum, we found ourselves at the Echo arena in Liverpool, watching, totally mesmerized, Roy Orbison perform the *In Dreams* UK tour. This was the year 2018, 30 years after Orbison's death, performing with the Royal Philharmonic Orchestra. We had just finished our own pop-up installation *The O Heads*, living sculptures that sport giant O's disguising our own heads outside the concert hall to the amusement of Orbison Fans, before we settled in our seats. Here, it became apparent for the not forgotten famous that the future of death is in the hologram tour, 'as ridiculous as it may sound, death is no longer a barrier for an artist getting work' (Spencer, 2018). The lights went low, orchestral strings introduced *Only the Lonely* and the hairs on the back of our necks stood up. Orbison rises up from out of the trap door of the theatre stage as a ghost.

I am a Ghost Moth. The night distorts the world. Not only being devoid of light on surfaces it ushers in a new way of being, new rules of behaving, new levels of sensitivity. At any point in time this is always happening, some people are involved in this right now, reading in the dark. It is in my nature to be in this realm where buildings are melting, where we are flying close to the ground where everything in the heap is black and a man's head is wrapped up – is that really you? All these things come of the darkness. Why not try it, be a nocturnal creature, stay awake and see what the night teaches.

Creative Task: Multiple Tornadoes Circling on a Vista

Conceptual Framework

This task invites you through writing, playing and performing to tell a story about your own creative practice and to compose a performance lecture, an artistic style of presentation for an audience. It may take some time to evolve your presentation, so work through various edits, have a few different versions and developments of it prepared over time for different outputs. Think of the format as a way to reflect upon your experiences, and as a vehicle to articulate and solidify your concepts.

Writing

Recall from memory significant experiences of your artistic processes. Write anecdotally, occasionally using metaphors to help map your ideas to other worlds, and use analogies where your creative materials have shared characteristics with other environments.

Playing

Surface visual material that associate to your work, use photographs as prompts that catch hold of places, objects, scenarios that orbit the making processes. Create titles for your own concepts, and identify specific qualities and moods inherent in your practice. Include brief examples of how you make work, and offer an interpretation of those methodologies through the lens of play.

Performing

Perform moments in your presentation as an example of your work, that is, script snippets or descriptive accounts of the artworks produced. Permit experiences to connect serendipitously, without force, to your research, and notice how stories of the dead may connect poetically to your creative autobiography.

Dramaturgy

Compose your story within a conceptual Death Drift and a structural Drift Drive, observing where your ideas circle and move into new territories documenting rules or conditions that have encouraged slippage in play. Allow the uncanny to speak on behalf of your practice by making room for other voices – human and non-human, alive and dead.

Illustration 18 Gary and Claire as *The Black Heaps* gliding across the city of York

Bibliography

Ackerman, D. (1999) *Deep Play*. New York: Vintage Books.

Ahl, L. (2018) *YAYAYA AYAYA* Ultimate Dancer, Southbank Centre London, 20 March.

Alcock, J. E. (1996) 'Channelling', In Stein, G. (ed.) *The Encyclopaedia of the Paranormal*. Buffalo, NY: Prometheus Books, pp.759–66.

Anderson, E. (2013) *H.D. and Modernist Religious Imagination: Mysticism and Writing*. New York: Bloomsbury.

Argen, D. (2016) Mexico City's James Bond-inspired Day of the Dead parade gets mixed reviews, *The Guardian* (online), 30 October. Available from: https://www.theguardian.com/world/2016/oct/29/day-of-the-dead-parade-james-bond-mexico-city (accessed 9 September 2019).

Argen, D. (2017) Mexicans Embrace Day of the Dead Spectacle in Place of Halloween, *The Guardian* (online) 31 October. Available from: https://www.theguardian.com/world/2017/oct/31/mexicans-embrace-day-of-the-dead-spectacle-in-place-of-halloween (accessed 9 September 2019).

Armintor, M. N. (2004) *Lacan and the Ghosts of Modernity: Masculinity, Tradition, and the Anxiety of Influence*. New York: Peter Lang.

Bachelard, G. (1958) *The Poetics of Space*. New York: Orion Press.

Barford, D. (1999) 'In Defence of Death', In Weatherill, R. (ed.) *The Death Drive: New Life for a Dead Subject?*. London: Rebus Press, p.12.

Bass, A. (2006) *An Interpretation and Difference: The Strangeness of Care*. Stanford: Sandford University Press.

Beckett, S. (2006) *Come and Go: The Complete Dramatic Works* (reprint). London: Faber and Faber.

Bentham, J. (2019) *The Theory of Legislation*. London: Creative Media Partners. (Original published in 1802.)

Bentham, J. *Deep Play*, Oxford Index (online). Available from: http://oxfordindex.oup.com/view/10.1093/oi/authority.20110803095706509 (accessed 9 September 2019).

Bishop, K. W. (2010) *American Zombie Gothic: The Rise and Fall (and Rise) of the Walking Dead in Popular Culture*. North Carolina: McFarland & Company.

Blau, H. (1982) *Take Up the Bodies Theatre as a Vanishing Point*. London: University of Illinois Press.

Blau, H. (2011) 'Theatre is Theory: A Case Study of Ghosting', In Alrutz M., Listengarten, J., & Van Duyn Wood, M. (eds.) *Playing with Theory in Theatre Practice*. Basingstoke: Palgrave Macmillan, pp.169–88.

Blue Jam (1997) (Radio Series) Directed by Chris Morris, BBC Radio 1.

Blue Velvet (1986) Directed by David, De Laurentiis Entertainment Group.

Bobinska, M. & Sparkes, S. *THE GHOST TIDE* (online). Available from: https://www.ghosthostings.co.uk/the-ghost-tide/ (accessed 12 September 2019).

Boehrer, B.T. (2015) *Parrot Culture: Our 2500-Year-Long Fascination with the World's Most Talkative Bird*. Pennsylvania: University of Pennsylvania Press.

Bowen, J. (2003) *Other Dickens: Pickwick to Chuzzlewit*. New York: Oxford University Press.

Bradbury, M. (2001) *To the Hermitage*. London: Picador.

Brantley, B. (2014) *Songs of Devotion, Songs of Rapture*. Available from: https://www.nytimes.com/2014/05/30/theater/early-shaker-spirituals-plain-spoken-tribute.html (accessed 9 September 2019).

Braziel, J. E. (2004) 'In Dreams…': Gender, Sexuality and Violence in The Cinema of David Lynch', In Sheen, D., & Davison, A. (eds.) *The Cinema of David Lynch: American Dreams, Nightmare Visions*, pp.107–118.

Breton, A. (1969) *Translated by Seaver R, & Lane H. R. Manifestoes of Surrealism*. Ann Arbor: University of Michigan Press.

Breton, A. & Soupault, P. (1985) *Les Champs Magnétiques (The Magnetic Fields)* (trans. David Gascoyne), 3rd edn. London: Atlas Press. (Original published in 1920.)

Brown, K. (2015) *Karaoke Idols: Popular Music and the Performance of Identity*. Chicago: Intellect Books.

Brown, S. & Vaughan, C. (2009) *Play: How It Shapes the Brain, Opens the Imagination, and Invigorates the Soul*. New York: Penguin.

Burkeman, O. (2016) *Therapy Wars: In Revenge of Freud*, 7 January. Available from: https://www.theguardian.com/science/2016/jan/07/therapy-wars-revenge-of-freud-cognitive-behavioural-therapy (accessed 9 September 2019).

Caillois, R. (2001) *Man Play and Games*. Urbana: University of Illinois Press.

Calle, S. (2005) *Appointment*. London: Thames and Hudson.

Campbell Ross, I. (2018) *Alas poor Yorick! Remembering Laurence Sterne*, Irish Times (online), 18 March. Available from: https://www.irishtimes.com/culture/books/alas-poor-yorick-remembering-laurence-sterne-1.3428604 (accessed 12 September 2019).

Carlson, M. de (2003) *The Haunted Stage*. Ann Arbour: University of Michigan Press.

Certeau, M. (1998) *The Practice of Everyday Life*. Translated by Rendall, S. Berkeley: University of California Press.

Chapman, G. (1999) *Monty Python's Flying Circus: Just the Words, Volume 1*. London: Methuen.

Cohn, R. (1993) 'Ghosting Through Beckett', In Buning, M., & Oppenheim, L. (eds.) *Beckett the 1990s: Selected Papers from the Second International Beckett Symposium Held in The Hague, 8–12 April, 1992*. Amsterdam: Rodopi, pp.1–11.

Colt, G. H. (2006) *November of the Soul: The Enigma of Suicide*. New York: Scribender.

Corr, C. A. & Corr, D. M. (2012) *Death & Dying, Life & Living*. Boston: Cengage.

Covington, C. (2015) 'The Common Thread Among Abraham, Spielrein and Winnicott: On oral Sadism and the Roots of Aggression', In Covington, C. & Wharton, B. (eds.) *Sabina Spielrein: Forgotten Pioneer of Psychoanalysis*, Revised Edition. Sussex: Routledge, pp.226–31.

Critchley, S. (2002) *On Humour*. London: Routledge.

Crick, J., 2002. *The Joke and Its Relation to the Unconscious*. By Sigmund Freud. London: Penguin.

Davis C. (2007) *Haunted Subjects: Deconstruction, Psychoanalysis and the Return of the Dead*. London: Palgrave.

Dawn of the Dead (2004) (Film), Directed by Zack Snyder, Universal Pictures.

Day, W. G. & Monkman, K. (1998) The Skull *The Shandean*, 10, pp.45–79.

The Dead Don't Die (2019) (Film) Directed by Jim Jarmusch, Focus Features.

Derrida, J. & Stiegler, B. (2013) 'Spectographies', In Bianco, M., & Peeren, E. (eds.) *The Spectralities Reader: Ghosts and Haunting in Contemporary Cultural Theory*. London: Bloomsbury, pp.37–51.

Dittmar, J. M. & Mitchell, P. D. (2016) The afterlife of Laurence Stern (1713–68): Body Snatching, Dissection and The Role of Cambridge anatomist Charles Collignon, *Journal of Medical Biography*, 24(4), pp.559–65.

Ebert, D. (2010) *Dead Celebrities, Living Icons: Tragedy and Fame in the Age of the Multimedia Superstar*. Santa Barbara: Praeger.

Etchells, T. (1999) *Certain Fragments. Contemporary Performance and Forced Entertainment.* London: Routledge.

Etchells, T. (2000) On The Skids: Some Years of Acting Animals, *Performance Research*, 5(2), pp.55–60.

Etchells, T. (2008) *'Spectacular' Program Note by Tim Etchells* (online). Available from: https://www.forcedentertainment.com/notebook-entry/spectacular-programme-note-by-tim-etchells/ (accessed 9 September 2019).

Etchells, T. (2018) programme notes for *Complete Works: Table Top Shakespeare* performed at NYU Skirball, September 2018.

Etchells T., Arthur R., & Naden, C. (2018) *Dirty Work The Late Shift*, Directed by Tim Etchells. Forced Entertainment, at Theatre Deli, Sheffield. 23 November.

Evans, D. (2006) *An Introductory Dictionary of Lacanian Psychoanalysis.* London: Routledge.

Fairfield, P. (2015) *Death: A Philosophical Inquiry.* London: Routledge.

Fenn, R. A. (ed.) (1992) *Jeremy Bentham Auto-Icon and Last Will and Testament* (draft copy). Toronto: Property of the British Library.

Finer, J. (2000) *Long Player.* London: Art Angel.

Fonseca, A. J. (2014) 'Africa', In Pulliam, J. & Fonseca. A. J. (eds.), *Encyclopaedia of the Zombie: The Walking Dead in Popular Culture and Myth...* Santa Barbara: Greenwood.

Frankland, G. (2005) *Sigmund Freud: The Unconscious.* London: Penguin.

French, A. (2015) 'High Street Causalities: Ellie Harrison's Zombie Walk', *Contemporary Art Magazine* (online). Available from: http://thisistomorrow.info/articles/ellie-harrisons-high-street-casualties (accessed 12th October 2019).

Freud, S. (1997) *The Interpretation of Dreams* Translated by A. A. Brill Hertfordshire: Wordsworth Editions Limited.

Freud, S. (2003) *Sigmund Freud the Uncanny* (trans. D. McLintock). London: Penguin Modern Classics.

Friedman, S. (1981) *Psyche Reborn: THE EMERGENCE OF H.D.* Bloomington: Indiana University Press.

Gadamer, H. G. (2013) *Truth and Method.* London: Bloomsbury.

Gary and Claire, (2016) *Twin Peaks Morning Report,* Unpublished Script/ Performance Score.

Ghost Dance (1983) (Film) Directed by Ken McMullen Channel Four Films.

Gilman-Opalsky, R. (2016) *Specters of Revolt: On The Intellect of Insurrection and Philosophy from Below.* London: Repeater.

Gummo (1997) (Film) Directed by Harmony Korine. USA, Fine Line Features.

Hamlet (1948) (Film), Directed by Laurence Olivier, Rank Film Distributors Ltd.

Hanks, M. (2016) *Haunted Heritage: The Cultural Politics of Ghost Tourism, Populism, and the Past.* London: Routledge.

Hawkins, S. (2017) *The Routledge Research Companion to Popular Music and Gender.* London: Routledge.

Herrera-Sobek, M. (2012) *Celebrating Latino Folklore: An Encyclopaedia of Cultural Traditions, Volume,* Vol. 1. Santa Barbara: ABC-CLIO.

Hind, C. (2010) 'Dark and Deep Play in Performance Practice', Unpublished PhD thesis, University of Leeds.

Hind, C. & Winters, G. (2015) 'Let's Make a World: A World to Be Alive in', *Performance Research Journal* 20(6), pp 78–81.

Hind, C. & Winters, G. (2016) 'Dream Yards', *Performance Research Journal* 21(1), pp 132–137.

Howell, A. (2003) *The Analysis of Performance Art A Guide to Its Theory and Practice.* London: Routledge.

Huizinga, J. (1998) *Homo Ludens.* Abingdon: Taylor and Francis.

Jeffery, M. (2017) Interview: *Ghosting as a Practice,* Interviewed by Hind C, and Winters, G. York St John University at Queering Ritual 3 November 2017.

Jeffery, M. & Morrisey, J. (2017) *Kjell Theøry* ATOM-r. Quad South Hall York St John University, (Queering Ritual Symposium) 3 November.

Jim and Andy: The Great Beyond (2017) (Film) Directed by Chris Smith. Netflix.

Jones, J. (2015) '*Wittgenstein's Dream* Review – Gavin Turk Mocks Freud in his Own House', *The Guardian* (online), 26 November. Available from: https://www.theguardian.com/artanddesign/2015/nov/26/wittgensteins-dream-review-gavin-turk-mocks-freud-in-his-own-house (accessed 30 May 2017).

Kastenbaum, R. (2015) *Death, Society, and Human Experience.* Boston: Pearson/Allyn and Bacon.

Kartsaki, E., (2016) *On Repetition, Writing, Performance and Art* Bristol: Intellect

Kettenmann, A. (2000) *Frida Kahlo, 1907–1954: Pain and Passion Frida Kahlo.* Los Angeles: Taschen.

Keymer, T. (2009) *The Cambridge Companion to Laurence Sterne.* Cambridge: Cambridge University Press.

King Lear (1971) (Film), Directed by Peter Brook, Orion Pictures.

Kristeva, J. (1989) *Black Sun: Depression and Melancholia* (Trans. by Leon S. Roudiez). New York: Columbia University Press.

Kristeva, J. (1991) *Strangers to Ourselves.* New York: Columbia University Press.

Kristeva, J. (1996) *On New Maladies of the Soul* Translated by Mitchell, R & Guberman, M eds. New York: Columbia University Press. pp.85–91.

Kristeva, K. (2002) *The Portable Kristeva* Oliver, K. (ed.). New York: Columbia University Press.

Lacan, J. (1970) *Écrits*. Paris: Éditions du Seuil.

Lavery, C. (2013) *Dream baby Dream; The Ecologies of Kong Lear* (online). Available from: http://www.garyandclaire.com (accessed 9 September 2019).

Laws, C. (2007) Editorial, *Performance Research Journal*, 12(1), pp.1–4.

Lee, J. (2011) *Aporia* Junglee (on line) http://junglee.kr/2011-2/aporia-2/date (accessed 12th October 2019).

Lehman, P. (2010) *Roy Orbison: Invention Of An Alternative Rock Masculinity*. Philadelphia: Temple University Press.

Lobman, C. & O'Neill, B. E. (2011) *Play and Performance*. Maryland: University Press of America.

López, D. B. (1996) *Psychoanalysis and Contemporary Thought*. Madison: International Universities Press.

Lord, R. (2012) *Spinoza Beyond Philosophy*. Edinburgh: Edinburgh University Press.

Lost Highway (1997) (Film) Directed by David Lynch, October Films.

Luckhurst, M. & Morin, E. (2014) 'Introduction: Theatre and Spectrality', In Luckhurst, M. & Morin, E. (eds.) *Theatre and Ghosts: Materiality, Performance and Modernity*. Basingstoke: Palgrave Macmillan.

Luckhurst, R. (2015) *Zombies A Cultural History*. London: Reaktion Books.

Lynch, D. (2015) *David Lynch Quotes: Wit and Wisdom from the Brains behind Twin Peaks, Blue Velvet and Muholland Dr.* (online). Available from: https://www.bfi.org.uk/news-opinion/news-bfi/quotes/david-lynch-quotes (accessed 12 September 2019).

Marcus, G., (1999) *Dead Elvis. A Chronicle of Cultural Obsession*. Cambridge: Harvard University Press.

Martin, R. (2014) *The Architecture of David Lynch*. London: Bloomsbury Publishing.

McGowan, T. (2007) *The Impossible David Lynch*. New York: Columbia University Press.

Milgrom, V. (2010) *Still Life: Adventures in Taxidermy*. New York: HMH.

Mock, R. (2017) Keynote response: *Questions* Quad South Hall York St John University, (Queering Ritual Symposium) 3 November.

Mok, K. (2014) 'Extreme Performance Artist Living in a Carcass for Two Weeks' [video] Tree Hugger (online). Available from: https://www.treehugger.com/culture/abraham-poincheval-performance-artist-living-in-bear-carcass-two-weeks.html (accessed 4 October 2017).

Moore, P. (2016) *Where are the Dead? Exploring the Idea of an Embodied Afterlife*. Abingdon: Taylor and Francis.

Morris, S. (2018) 'Learning to Read Differently', In K. B. Wurth, K. Driscoll & J. Pressman (eds.) *Book Presence in a Digital Age*. New York: Bloomsbury.

Mr Dead. (1994) *Harry Enfield and Chums*. London: BBC.

Mr Ed. (1961) *Mr Ed*. USA: MGM.

Mulholland Drive (2001) (Film) Directed by David Lynch, Universal Pictures.

Mummifying Alan: Egypt's Last Secret (2011) (Documentary Film), Directed by Kenny Scott, Bank Films.

Night of the Living Dead (1968) Directed by George A Romero The Walter Reade Organisation.

Nochimson, M. (2015) 'Desire Under the Douglas Firs: Entering the Body of Reality of Twin Peaks', In Lavery, D. (ed.) *Full of Secrets: Critical Approaches to Twin Peaks*. Detroit: Wayne State University Press.

O'Brien, M. & Ilyas, S. (2017). Interview: *The Unwell*, Interviewed by Nedelkopoulou, E. York St John University.

Oler, T. (2008) 'George A. Romero Explains Why Fast Zombies Could Never Exist (Hint: Weak Ankles)', *Vulture* (online), 14 February. Available from: https://www.vulture.com/2008/02/george_a_romero_explains_why_f.html (accessed 12 September 2019).

Orbach, S. & Chews, F. (2017) 'How We Feel About Freud: Susie Orbach and Frederick Crews Debate His Legacy', *The Guardian* (online), 20 August. Available from: https://www.theguardian.com/books/2017/aug/20/feel-about-freud-debate-frederick-crews-susie-orbach-making-of-an-illusion (accessed 12 September 2019).

Orbison, R. (1963) *In Dreams* (Song), Produced by Fred Foster, Monument.

Oxford Index, (2018) 'Deep Play', *Oxford Index* (online). Availlable from: http://oxfordindex.oup.com/view/10.1093/oi/authority.20110803095706509 (accessed 31 October 2018).

The Perverts Guide to Cinema (2006) (Film) Directed by Sophie Fiennes UK: Mischief Films

Peters, G. (2013) 'Ahead of Yes And No Heidegger on Not Knowing and Art', In Fisher, E., & Fortnum, R. (eds.) *On Not Knowing How Artists Think*. London: Black Dog Publishing, pp.110–19.

PHAIDON (n.d.) *Why Joseph Beuys and his Dead Hare Live On* (online). Available from: http://uk.phaidon.com/agenda/art/articles/2014/march/03/why-joseph-beuys-and-his-dead-hare-live-on/ (accessed 9 September 2019).

Phillips, A. (2006) *Side Effects*. London: Penguin.

Phillips, A. (2012) 'Introduction', In Doolittle, H., Pearson, H. N. & Philips, P. (eds.) *A Tribute to Freud*, Second Edition. New York: New Directions Publishing, pp.vii–3.

Pilar Blanco, M. & Peeren, E. (2010) *Popular Ghosts: The Haunted Spaces of Everyday Culture*. New York: Continuum International.

Pond, S. (1989) 'Roy Orbison's Triumphs and Tragedies', *Rolling Stone* (online). Available from: https://www.rollingstone.com/music/music-news/roy-orbisons-triumphs-and-tragedies-103421/ (accessed 12 September 2019).

Prochnik, G. (2012) *Putnam Camp: Sigmund Freud, James Jackson Putnam and the Purpose of American Psychology*. New York: Other Press.

Pulp Fiction (1994) (Film), Directed by Quentin Tarantino, Miramax Films.

Quick, A. (2004) *Not Even a Game Anymore: The Theatre of Forced Entertainment*. Berlin: Alexander Verlag.

Rabbits (2002) (Film) Directed by David Lynch (production company unknown).

Rahimi, S. (2013) *The Ego, The Ocular, and The Uncanny: Why are Metaphors of Vision Central in Accounts of The Uncanny?* Available from: https://www.ncbi.nlm.nih.gov/pubmed/23781831 (accessed 9 September 2019).

Razinsky, L. (2013) *Freud, Psychoanalysis and Death*. New York: Cambridge University Press.

Reece, G. L. (2006) *Elvis Religion: The Cult of the King*. London: I.B.Tauris.

Ricoeur, P. (2008) *Freud and Philosophy: An Essay on Interpretation*. Delhi: Motilal Banarsidass.

Rigg, J. (2004) 'Sophie Calle's Appointment at the Freud Museum: Intervention or irony?', In Miles, M. (ed.) *New Practices – New Pedagogies: A Reader*. London: Routledge, pp.44–55.

Rodley, D. (1997) *Lynch on Lynch*. London: Faber and Faber.

Rodman, G. B. (2013) *Elvis after Elvis: The Posthumous Career of a Living Legend*. London: Routledge.

Roth, M. S. (2014) 'Why Freud Still Haunts Us', *The Chronicle* (online), 22 September. Available from: https://www.chronicle.com/blogs/conversation/2014/09/22/why-freud-still-haunts-us/ The Chronicle of Higher Education on line (accessed 9 September 2019).

ROY ORBISION IN DREAMS: The Hologram UK Tour (2018) (Concert) with the Royal Philharmonic Concert Orchestra, Liverpool Echo Arena 17 April. Base Hologram LLC and Kennedy Street.

Royle, N. (2003) *The Uncanny*. New York: Routledge.

Saturday Night Fever (1997) (Film) Directed by John Badham, Paramount Pictures.

Scahill, A. (2012) (eds.) *Lost and Othered Children in Contemporary Cinema*. Lanham, MD: Lexington Books, pp.107–18.

Schechner, R. (2002) *Performance Studies an Introduction*. London: Routledge.

Schneider, R. (2012) It Seems As If… I Am Dead. Zombie Capitalism and Theatrical Labor, *TDR: The Drama Review*, 56(4), pp.152–63.

Schneider, R. (2013) *The Explicit Body in Performance*. London: *Routledge*.

Shaun of the Dead (2004) (Film) Directed by Edgar Wright, Universal Pictures.

Sinwell, S. E. (2012) 'Race, Class, Gender, and Sexuality in Gummo', In Olson, C. E, & Smith, P. (2015) *The Footbook of Zombie Walking: How to Be More than a Survivor in an Apocalypse*. Axminster: Triarchy Press.

Smith, S. (1995) *The Ambiguity of Play*. Cambridge, MA: Harvard University Press.

Smolenski, K. (2008) *Konrad Smolenski* (online) http://www.konradsmolenski. com/index.php/project/2009–the-death/ (accessed 9 September 2019).

Sparkes, S. (2016) 'The Ghost Project: Manifesting Ghosts through Visual Art and Creative Research', In Jenzen, O., & Munt, S. R. (eds.) *The Ashgate Research Companion to Paranormal Cultures*. London: Routledge, pp.377–89.

Spencer, K. (2018) 'Roy Orbison returns to the stage – as a hologram', *Sky News* (online), 6 January. Available from: https://news.sky.com/story/roy-orbison-returns-to-the-stage-as-a-hologram–11197095 (accessed 12 September 2019).

Spigel, L. (1990) 'Communicating with the Dead Elvis as Medium', *Camera Obscura*, 23, pp.176–205.

Springsteen, B. (2012) *We Live in a Post-Authentic World* Keynote for the SXSW, 15 March. Available from: https://speakola.com/arts/bruce-springsteen-keynote-sxsw–202 (accessed 11 September 2019).

Stein, G. (1996) *The Encyclopaedia of the Paranormal*. Michigan: Prometheus Books.

Stein, G. (2017) *PICASSO (Unabridged): Cubism and Its Impact*. Musaicum Books (ebook).

Sterne, L. (2012) *The Life and Opinions of Tristram Shandy, Gentleman*. Newburyport: Dover Publications.

Stevens, S. 'How This Couch Changed Everything', *BBC News* (online). Available from: https://www.bbc.co.uk/news/magazine-33079041 (accessed 9 September 2019).

Stockwell, P. (2017) *The Language of Surrealism*. London: Macmillan.

Strachey, J. (2001) *The Standard Edition of the Complete Psychological Works of Sigmund Freud*. London: Vintage.

Sulivan, J. (2013) 'Roy Orbison: My Voice Is a Gift', *The Guardian* (online), 4 December. Available from: https://www.theguardian.com/music/2013/dec/04/roy-orbison-rocks-backpages (accessed 11 September 2019).

Sword, H. (2002) *Ghostwriting Modernism*. Ithaca, NY: Cornell University Press.

TIGHAR, *The Earhart Project Research Document # 17 Betty's Note Book* https:// tighar.org/Projects/Earhart/Archives/Documents/Notebook/notebook.html (accessed 9 September 2019).

Turner, C. (2014) 'Porous Dramaturgy and the Pedestrian', In Trencsényi, K., & Cochrane B. (eds.) *New Dramaturgy: International Perspectives on Theory and Practice.* London: Bloomsbury, pp.199–213.

Turner, V. (1990) *From Ritual to Theatre: Human Seriousness of Play.* New York: PAJ Books.

Twin Peaks (1990) (T.V.), Created by Frost, M. & Lynch, D., Lynch/Frost Productions.

Twin Peaks: Season 2, (1990) (T.V.), Created by Frost, M. & Lynch, D., Lynch/ Frost Productions.

Twin Peaks: The Return (2017) (T.V.) Directed by David Lynch, Showtime.

The Walking Dead (2010) (T.V. Series) Developed by Frank Darabont, Fox Networks Group.

White Zombie (1932), Directed by Victor Halperin, United Artists.

Wiegand, C. (2017) 'How to Play Dead: The Corpse's View of Joe Orton's Loot', *The Guardian,* 7 September. Available from: https://www.theguardian.com/stage/2017/sep/07/how-to-play-dead-corpses-view-joe-orton-loot-anah-ruddin (accessed 12 September 2019).

Wild at Heart (1990) (Film), Directed by David Lynch, The Samuel Goldwyn Company.

Wooster Group (2011) 'Hamlet: Channelling the Ghost', http://thewoostergroup. org/blog/2011/09/16/hamlet-channeling-the-ghost/ (accessed 9 September 2019).

Žižek, S. (1997) 'The Abyss of Freedom' In Žižek, S., Wilhelm, F. & Schelling, J. (eds.) *The Abyss of Freedom/Ages of the World.* Ann Arbor: University of Michigan Press.

Žižek, S. (1999) *The Ticklish Subject: The Absent Centre of Political Ontology.* London: Verso.

Zombieland (2019) (Film), Directed by Ruben Fleischer, Columbia Pictures.

Index

Please note: page numbers in **bold type** indicate illustrations

Boatowner's Illustrated Wiring Handbook

Second Edition

Charles Wing

ADLARD COLES NAUTICAL

LONDON

Published by Adlard Coles Nautical
an imprint of A & C Black Ltd
38 Soho Square, London W1D 3HB
www.adlardcoles.com

First edition 1993
Reprinted 2004
Second edition 2007

Published in the USA by International Marine,
an imprint of McGraw-Hill

ISBN: 978-0-7136-8292-2

A CIP catalogue record for this book is available from the
British Library.

This book is produced using paper that is made from wood
grown in managed, sustainable forests. It is natural, renewable
and recyclable. The logging and manufacturing processes conform
to the environmental regulations of the country of origin.

Designed by Chris Stevens and Garold West
Typeset in Minion 11/13 pt.

Printed and bound in Malta by Gutenberg.

Note: while all reasonable care has been taken in the publication of
this edition, the publisher takes no responsibility for the use of the
methods or products described in the book.

Contents

Since I have used Charlie Wing's first edition of the *Boatowner's Illustrated Electrical Handbook* as a text for some of my electrical courses over the years, I am quite familiar with its contents. I've just finished reviewing the second edition and can say without reservation that it is more than just an update. The diagrams are dramatically improved and the topics covered are really comprehensive, just what's needed in today's world of ever increasing complexity on newer boats.

This second edition is perfect for learning how your boat's electrical system and much of its equipment works, and it will be an invaluable guide when adding equipment as well. Further, Charlie Wing has remained faithful to the recommendation and application of the standards for installation and equipment as set forth by the American Boat and Yacht Council (ABYC). As the senior technical instructor for the ABYC and its curriculum designer I really appreciate the effort throughout the book to advise the reader on how to make repairs and modifications to his or her boat and remain compliant with the most recognized design and repair standards for recreational boats in the world. We at the ABYC know full well that adherence to these standards make a better, safer boat.

I have already begun recommending this second edition to my students and seminar participants, and will continue to do so. This book needs to be in every boater's library as a ready reference on how to make effective repairs and modifications that comply with ABYC standards.

Ed Sherman
ABYC Senior Instructor and Curriculum Designer

Preface to the UK/European Edition

This is the second edition of Charlie Wing's excellent *Boatowner's Illustrated Electrical Handbook*. The first edition was published as *The Boatowner's Wiring Manual* in the UK by Adlard Coles Nautical in 1993 almost verbatim, but this UK/European edition is designed to be more accessible to UK and European readers as regards products, standards and practices. However, as rewriting the entire book would be impractical, the following compromises have been made:

1 *Standards* Frequent references are made to the American Boat & Yacht Council (ABYC) standards, which are similar in principle to the International Standard Organisation (ISO) standards in use in most of the rest of the world. Unless important differences are identified (such as in the AC chapters), these references are left unchanged. See Appendices for more standards information.

2 *Currencies* The currency used throughout is US$, but as most of the costs are used for illustrative or comparative purposes, and not as absolute values, they have been left unchanged.

3 *AC Power* The fundamental differences between AC supplies in the USA and UK/Europe are summarised on pages 155 and 251, and the text and diagrams in the chapters dealing with AC power have been amended for UK and European use as appropriate.

4 *Cables* US cable sizes are measured in American Wire Gauge (AWG). Where possible, square millimetre (mm^2) equivalents, which are approximate, are given. Cable colour and naming conventions in the US differ from European conventions; these have been changed to ISO standards throughout.

5 *Products* Some of the products mentioned are available worldwide, others in the US only. The reader will have to determine which products are available where. In many cases the associated data is useful, so some US-derived data, where no equivalent European information is available, has been left for reference.

6 *Dimensions* Where possible, imperial measurements have been changed to metric, or both shown.

7 *Nomenclature* General text spelling has been left in American English, but component or technical words which differ on either side of the Atlantic have been changed to the usual UK/European word.

8 This edition has been revised as accurately as possible, but the publishers will not be held liable for the consequences of any errors, or for any misinterpretation by the reader.

Mike Balmforth

Many of us have, at the least, a passing familiarity with electrical wiring. When a switch or receptacle in our home fails, we replace it. Some of us feel secure in extending a circuit, adding a new circuit, even wiring an entire house. We are able to do so because of the *National Electric Code* (NEC) and because many excellent books, based on the NEC, have been written for both the novice and the professional.

Unfortunately, a boat is not a house—a fact that still escapes all too many boatyards.

I'll never forget the time I was working in a boatyard rigging masts. I had spent an hour trying to determine why a mast-top anchor light was not working. The blue anchor-light supply conductor disappeared into the base of the 60-foot mast, yet no blue conductor appeared at the other end. I commented on the mystery to a co-worker who I knew had worked as an electrician at one the country's premier boatbuilders.

"Sure," he said. "We'd grab a spool of #14 whatever, and when that ran out, we just spliced in another. The color of the wire doesn't matter."

Or ask a random sampling of boatbuilders whether bronze through-hulls should be bonded. Chances are good you will get an even split of opinions. No wonder boatowners are confused!

In fact, there is a voluntary standard for the construction and repair of boats, including the topics of AC and DC wiring, lightning protection, and bonding for corrosion control. It is the American Boat and Yacht Council (ABYC) *Standards for Small Craft*. The standards are the marine equivalent of the residential *National Building Code* and *National Electric Code*.

Twelve years ago, when the first edition of this book was written, few boat manufacturers and fewer boatyards paid much attention to the fledgling ABYC. Today, nearly all manufacturers and many boatyards have joined the organization and have sent employees to the excellent technical courses offered by the ABYC's Westlawn Institute of Marine Technology. In the words of the ABYC, the standards are: " . . . believed to represent, as of the date of publication, the consensus of knowledgeable persons, currently active in the field of small craft, on performance objectives that contribute to small boat safety."

This book is my attempt at interpretation and illumination of the several wiring-related ABYC standards and much more.

My joy in life derives from explaining and illustrating how things work—first as a physics teacher at Bowdoin College, then as founder of the first two owner-builder schools in the country, and later as author of thirteen books on home building and repair and six books on marine topics.

I have always felt that knowledge is of limited utility unless based upon an understanding of the basic principles—simply put, how things work. In this book you will find that each subject begins with a simple exploration and explanation of the hows and whys.

I also feel that books—even those of a technical nature—should be fun. We boatowners have no need for Miss Grundy to rap our knuckles to command our attention. Discovery of how your boat works should be fun and exciting. To this end you will find dozens of simple experiments and projects designed to make the light in your mind come on, perhaps even add to the comfort and convenience of your boat.

I hope you will come away from this book with the feeling that (to paraphrase Ratty in *Wind in the Willows*) "There is nothing half so much worth doing as messing about in your boat's electrical system."

I have invented nothing. You will find here no new law of physics, nor any previously unreported electrical or magnetic phenomena. I have simply attempted to bring to you, the reader, a lucid and clearly illustrated account of how the best minds in the business think a small boat should be wired.

To this end, in this second edition I have redrawn many of the original illustrations, added illustrations, and added color to the ABYC-recommended wiring for AC shore-power systems. Also new is the ABYC procedure for testing and sizing protective zinc anodes, material on absorbed-glass mat (AGM) batteries, specific recommendations for charging most marine batteries, descriptions of "smart" alternator regulators, and troubleshooting charts for engine-starting and battery-charging circuits.

May your boat never corrode, your engine never fail to start, and your batteries last forever!

Charles Wing

Basic DC Circuits

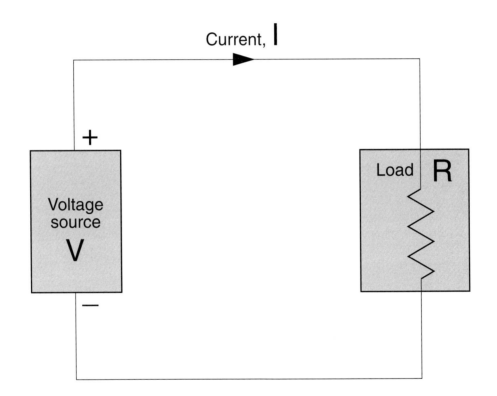

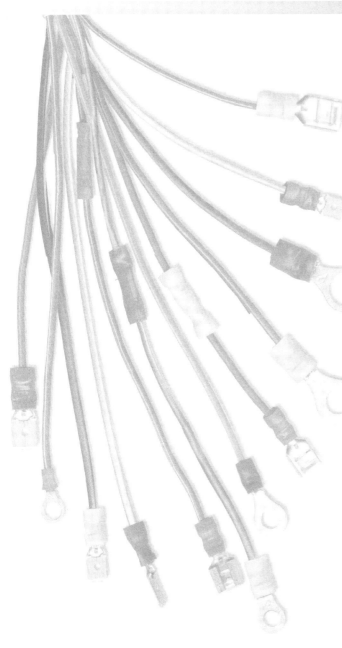

Basic to the ability to work with electrical wiring—be it residential or marine—is an understanding of what electricity is. You'll find that the discovery of electricity, as we now understand it, was fairly recent.

The key that unlocks the wiring puzzle is the concept of the electrical circuit. With this simple concept and a single formula—Ohm's Law—you can understand and predict the behavior of 99% of the wiring on your boat. You will be able to deal with circuits containing loads in series, loads in parallel, even loads in series/parallel combinations. Similarly, you will be able to predict the behavior of voltage sources in series and voltage sources in parallel. You will also discover the differences between voltage, current, energy, and power.

Finally I have provided a set of 18 practice problems on which you can cut your electrical teeth.

What Electricity Is

We live in the age of electricity. Without electricity we couldn't watch television, drive automobiles, make frozen margaritas, microwave popcorn, read at night, or talk to our friends on the phone.

Many people think electricity is difficult to understand. They are wrong. Because you are surrounded by and unconsciously use electrical devices every day, little lights will go on in your head as you discover the concepts. You'll probably say, "Oooh—so that's why my boat battery is dead every morning!"

I believe you will find electricity to be fun. I am absolutely sure that, having grasped the very simple concepts behind boat wiring, you will feel more confident both in your boat and in yourself.

Electricity consists of electrons. An electron is the smallest quantity of electricity that exists. It is such a small quantity, however, that we use the unit coulomb (1 coulomb = 6.24×10^{18} electrons) in calculations.

The flow of electrons is often compared to the flow of water, so it is natural that we call electron flow "electric current." The basic unit of electric current is the ampere (1 ampere = 1 coulomb per second of electrons moving past a point).

What we usually refer to as electricity is the control of electrons for useful purposes. Our understanding of electron behavior allows us to predict the flow of electrons through electrical circuits. The instruments on your boat contain circuits. Indeed, a boat's wiring is no more than a collection of circuits. When we understand circuits, we will understand the behavior of electricity on a boat.

A Circuit

Electrons can be neither created nor destroyed, but can move through conductive materials. An electric current requires a continuous path of electrically conductive material, through which the electrons can return to their source.

If this were not so, electrons would dribble from the end of a wire like water from a leaky faucet, and batteries would soon sit like empty water glasses with all their electrons lying around them in a pool.

We call a continuous electrical path a *circuit*. If a circuit is unbroken, we call it a closed circuit. If it is interrupted, preventing the flow of electricity, we say the circuit is open.

All materials present a degree of resistance to electron flow, but the variation is so great that some mate-

The Discovery of Electricity

Democritus (460?–370? BC) proposes an "atomic theory" wherein all matter is made up of indivisible particles, or atoms.

Charles de Coulomb (1736–1806) discovers that the force of attraction between electric charges is proportional to the product of the two charges and inversely proportional to the distance between them.

Luigi Galvani (1737–1798) discovers that two unlike metals immersed in blood cause the muscles of a frog's legs to twitch.

Alessandro Volta (1745–1827) discovers that a current flows between two connected unlike metals in a salt solution and, thus, invents the battery.

John Dalton (1766–1844) proposes the first table of atomic weights of elements.

André Ampere (1775–1836) develops the theory of magnetic lines of force and quantifies electric current for the first time.

Hans Oersted (1777–1851) discovers a connection between electric current and magnetism and a way to measure electric current by the deflection of a magnet.

Georg Ohm (1787–1854) discovers the relationship (Ohm's Law) between voltage, current, and resistance in a circuit.

Michael Faraday (1791–1867) analyzes the chemical reactions in batteries and defines the terms "electrode," "anode," "cathode," and "electrolyte."

James Clerk Maxwell (1831–1879) develops the mathematical equations relating electricity and magnetism.

Joseph Thomson (1856–1940) proves that electricity consists of electrons.

rials are termed conductors and others insulators.

The best conductors are gold, silver, mercury, copper, and aluminum. Copper is most often the best compromise between cost and conductivity. The best insulators are glass, ceramics, mica, and plastics. Plastic is the material most often used due to its low cost, durability, and ease of manufacture.

Unfortunately for boaters, salt solutions, such as seawater, are also good conductors.

Electrical current is expressed as a rate of electron flow. In a circuit, two factors control the current (I): the electrical driving force, or voltage (V), and the resistance (R) to flow of the circuit materials.

To see just how simple electricity is, we are going to consider the basic equation of current flow in an electrical circuit. With this equation you will be able to understand, predict, and troubleshoot more than 90% of all the electrical problems on a boat.

Question 1. Does current, I, increase or decrease as we increase the driving force (voltage, V)?

Answer 1. Current most likely increases with increasing voltage.

Question 2. Does current, I, increase or decrease as we increase the resistance to electron flow (resistance, R)?

Answer 2. Current most likely decreases with increasing resistance.

Question 3. Considering the answers to questions 1 and 2, what would be the simplest and, therefore, most likely, relationship between current (I), voltage (V), and resistance (R)?

Answer 3. There are four possible "simplest" equations:

$$I = V + R, I = V - R, I = V \times R, \text{ and } I = V/R$$

If you play with the values for a minute, you'll agree that the first three equations are unlikely. For example, if we make resistance, R, infinite, current, I, becomes ∞, $-\infty$, ∞, and 0. Only the last value is reasonable, so the relationship is most likely

$$I = V/R$$

Congratulations! You have just discovered Ohm's Law. If Georg Ohm hadn't beaten you to it in 1827, you might be up for a Nobel Prize.

Using Ohm's Law

This is such an important relationship, we must be precise in its definition and the ways in which it can be used. First, if we wish to calculate electrical quantities, we must define the units in which these quantities are measured.

$$I = V/R$$
where:
I = amperes, abbreviated as A
V = volts, abbreviated as V
R = ohms, abbreviated as Ω

Let's see how Ohm's Law is used. Ohm's Law applies to all situations, but it is useful only in circuits where electricity is flowing.

Fig. 1.1 Simple Electric Circuit

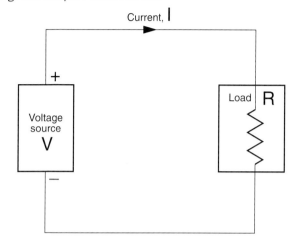

The voltage source in Figure 1.1 is a device that produces a voltage difference. Examples are batteries and power supplies. Unless otherwise noted, assume voltage sources are batteries. The load is any device or component that consumes electrical energy and, in so doing, results in a voltage drop. Examples are resistors, lamps, and motors. Unless otherwise stated, assume loads are resistances (the zigzag symbol). For a table of electrical symbols used in this book, see Figure 6-1.

Example: If the load is a resistance of 2 ohms, and the voltage source is a 12-volt battery, then by Ohm's Law

$$I = V/R = 12 \text{ V}/2 \text{ } \Omega = 6 \text{ A}$$

We can also rearrange Ohm's Law so that we can calculate either V or I, given the other two values. The alternate forms of Ohm's Law are:

$$V = I \times R$$
$$R = V/I$$

There is more good news. Ohm's Law applies to more complex circuits as well. We can combine loads and sources in series (end-to-end), parallel (side-by-side), and series/parallel, and the equations remain the simplest possible, as you will see in the figures and examples that follow.

Loads

Loads in Series

Resistive loads in series act like one continuous load of a total resistance equal to the sum of the individual resistances:

$$R = R_1 + R_2 + R_3, \text{etc.}$$
$$I = V/(R_1 + R_2 + R_3, \text{etc.})$$

Fig. 1.2 Series Loads

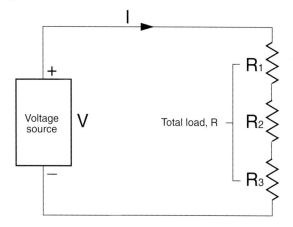

Example:
$$R_1 = 2\ \Omega, R_2 = 3\ \Omega, R_3 = 5\ \Omega, V = 12\text{ V}$$
$$R = 2 + 3 + 5 = 10\ \Omega$$

Loads in Parallel

The same voltage, V, exists across each of the loads. Ohm's Law predicts the currents through the loads:
$$I_1 = V/R_1, I_2 = V/R_2, I_3 = V/R_3, \text{etc.}$$
Total current, I, is the sum of currents:
$$I = I_1 + I_2 + I_3, \text{etc.}$$
$$= V(1/R_1 + 1/R_2 + 1/R_3, \text{etc.})$$
In other words,
$$1/R = 1/R_1 + 1/R_2 + 1/R_3, \text{etc.}$$

Fig. 1.3 Parallel Loads

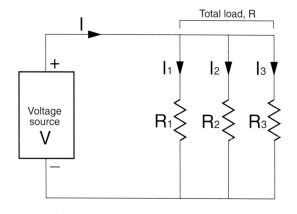

Example: $R_1 = 20\ \Omega, R_2 = 30\ \Omega, R_3 = 50\ \Omega, V = 12\text{ V}.$
$$1/R = 1/R_1 + 1/R_2 + 1/R_3$$
$$= 1/20 + 1/30 + 1/50$$
$$= 0.050 + 0.033 + 0.020$$
$$= 0.103$$

$$R = 1/0.103 = 9.68\ \Omega$$

$$I = V/R$$
$$= 12\text{ V}/9.68\ \Omega$$
$$= 1.24\text{ A}$$

Loads in Series/Parallel

Observe that the parallel group of loads can be considered a single resistor in series with other series loads. We first calculate the equivalent value of the parallel loads, as in the previous example, and then add the result of the other series loads:

Fig. 1.4 Series/Parallel Loads

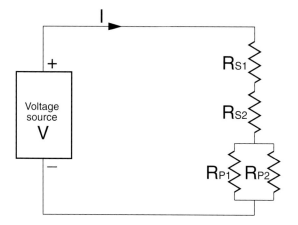

Example: $R_{S1} = 2\ \Omega, R_{S2} = 3\ \Omega, R_{P1} = 5\ \Omega, R_{P2} = 10\ \Omega, V = 12\text{ V}$
$$1/R_P = 1/R_{P1} + 1/R_{P2}$$
$$= 1/5 + 1/10$$
$$= 0.20 + 0.10$$
$$= 0.30$$
$$R_P = 3.33\ \Omega$$

$$R = R_{S1} + R_{S2} + R_P$$
$$= 2\ \Omega + 3\ \Omega + 3.33\ \Omega$$
$$= 8.33\ \Omega$$

$$I = 12\text{ V}/8.33\ \Omega$$
$$= 1.44\text{ A}$$

Sources in Series

Fig. 1.5 Series Sources

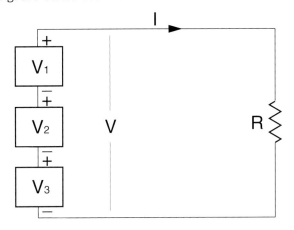

One example of a voltage source is a battery. If you've ever replaced the batteries in a flashlight, you know that batteries can be stacked end to end. When you do that the total voltage equals the sum of the individual voltages. In general, voltages in series add.

$$V = V_1 + V_2 + V_3, \text{ etc.}$$
$$\text{Therefore, } I = (V_1 + V_2 + V_3)/R$$

$$\textit{Example: } V_1 = 1.5 \text{ V}, V_2 = 1.5 \text{ V}, V_3 = 3 \text{ V}, R = 4 \text{ }\Omega$$
$$I = (1.5 + 1.5 + 3.0)V/4 \text{ }\Omega$$
$$= 1.5 \text{ A}$$

A caution is in order, however. If batteries are added in series, they must have the same ampere-hour capacities and start with the same states of charge. If not, the battery with the greatest capacity for supplying current may drive the voltage of the weakest battery negative, which usually destroys the weaker battery.

Fig. 1.6 Parallel Sources

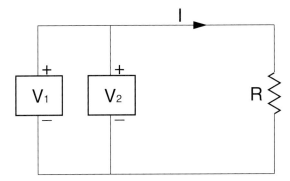

Sources in Parallel

Your boat probably has a battery selector switch. On its face it says:

OFF—1—2—BOTH

In the BOTH position, both of your batteries are connected in parallel; i.e., + terminal to + terminal, and – terminal to – terminal. Provided the batteries are of the same voltage, the net result is simply a single battery of capacity equal to the sum of the individual capacities. If they are not of the same voltage, the higher voltage battery will discharge into the lower voltage battery, possibly overcharging and destroying it.

There is much controversy over charging and discharging marine batteries in parallel. Some experts are dead set against it, saying that the batteries will eventually destroy each other. Other experts claim it is the only way to go when charging. Both arguments and the reasoning behind them will be presented in Chapter 4.

Energy and Power

Energy is defined as the *ability to do work*. *Power* is defined as the *rate of doing work*. Power is, therefore, the rate at which energy is used in doing work.

Two Olympic runners exemplify the difference between energy and power. The first runner holds the record in the marathon. He is a lean, efficient running machine. He burns nearly all of his stored energy resources steadily over a 2-hour period. The second runner holds the record in the 100-meter dash. He uses less total energy, but consumes it in an intense 10-second burst. The first runner uses more energy, but the second uses energy at a higher rate, or power.

Except in nuclear reactions, energy can be neither created nor destroyed. What it can do, however, is change between its many forms.

As an example, the water at the top of a hydroelectric dam possesses *potential energy* due to its height. As it falls and gains speed, its potential energy is converted into *kinetic (motion) energy*. When the water hits the blades of a turbine, the kinetic energy of the water is transferred to the spinning turbine. The turbine turns a generator where the kinetic energy is converted to *electrical energy*. The electricity flows into your home, where a lightbulb changes the electrical energy into *light energy* and *heat energy*. Ultimately, the heat escapes from your home into the atmosphere, where it causes water to evaporate into water vapor, which then turns into clouds, which then drop rain into the reservoir. And so it goes.

Practice Problems

For the moment, we will concern ourselves only with the energy transformations occurring between your boat's batteries and its loads. The battery, as we will see in detail later, is just a box full of chemicals. When it is connected to a closed electrical circuit, the chemicals react, sending a stream of electrons (amps) around the circuit under electrical pressure (volts). In flowing through the load (resistance), the electrons lose their pressure (the voltage drops), and the load produces heat, light, or some form of mechanical work. Chemical energy changes to electrical energy, which then changes to heat, light, or mechanical energy. You'll see later that recharging the battery involves the same steps, but in reverse order.

Power is calculated as easily as volts, amps, and ohms:

$$P = V \times I$$
where: P = power consumption in watts
V = volts across the load
I = amps through the load

Example: What is the power of a lightbulb that draws 1.25 amps at 12 volts?

$$P = V \times I$$
$$= 12 \text{ volts} \times 1.25 \text{ amps}$$
$$= 15 \text{ watts}$$

Example: How many amps would a 20-watt lamp draw in a 12-volt circuit?

$$P = V \times I$$
$$I = P/V$$
$$= 20 \text{ watts}/12 \text{ volts}$$
$$= 1.67 \text{ amps}$$

Electrical equipment is usually labeled with its power consumption. If you look at the back or bottom of equipment, or at the base of a bulb, you will generally find either (X) volts and (Y) amps, or (X) watts at (Y) volts.

Using Ohm's Law and the power equation, you should have no problem deducing either amps or watts, given two of the three variables in the equations.

The problems below are designed to sharpen your skills in the application of Ohm's Law. They range from the simplest possible to the most complex you'll ever encounter on your boat. All you need to solve them is a simple four-function calculator, scratch paper, and a pencil.

You can make solving them a parlor game. Get your mate to play with you. Take turns making up more problems and trying to stump the other person. Once you have mastered these examples, you are ready for real components and real circuits. The answers to the problems are listed at the end of this chapter.

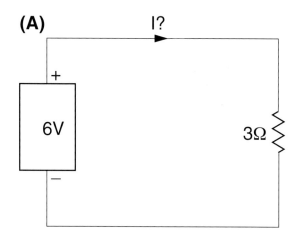

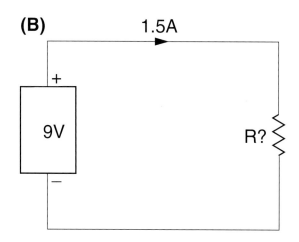

(C)

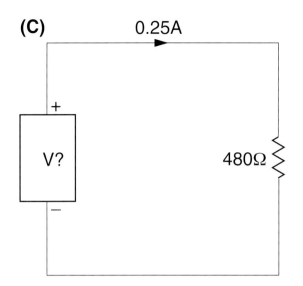

(E)

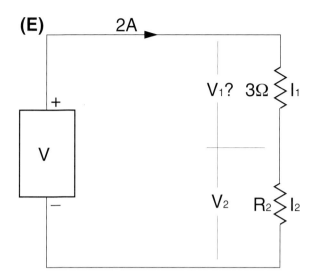

(D)

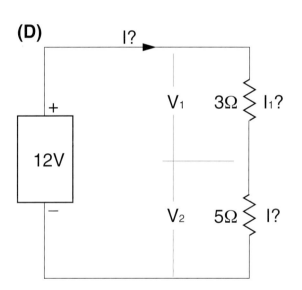

(F)

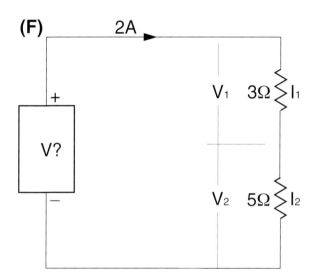

Practice Problems

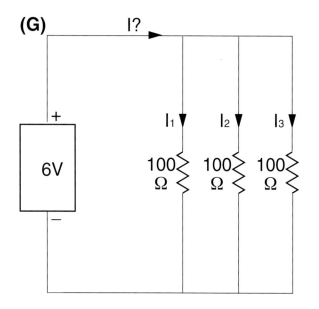

(G)

I?

6V

I₁ 100 Ω   I₂ 100 Ω   I₃ 100 Ω

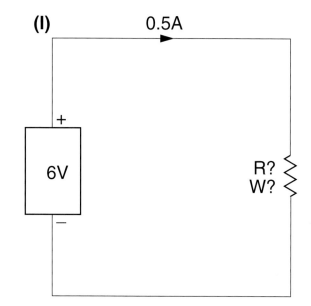

(I)

0.5A

6V

R?
W?

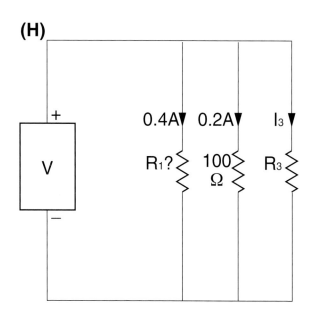

(H)

V

0.4A R₁?   0.2A 100 Ω   I₃ R₃

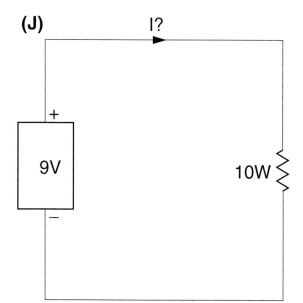

(J)

I?

9V

10W

(K)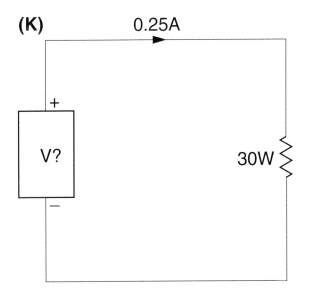

0.25A

V?

+

−

30W

(M)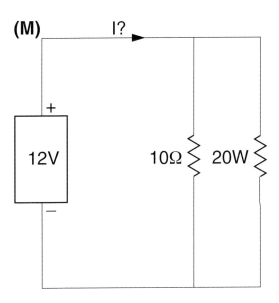

I?

12V

+

−

10Ω   20W

(L)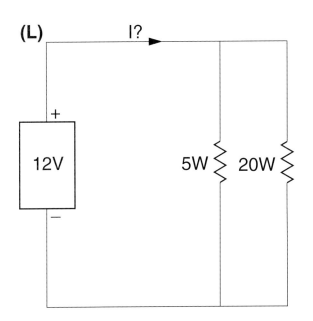

I?

12V

+

−

5W   20W

(N)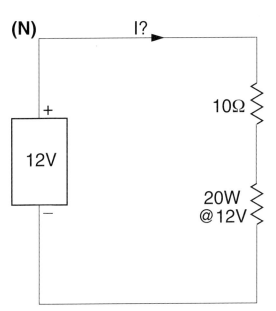

I?

12V

+

−

10Ω

20W
@12V

Practice Problems

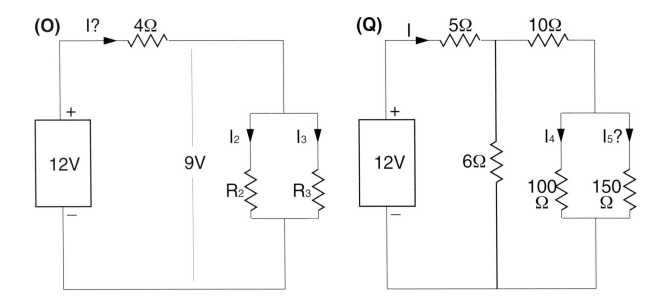

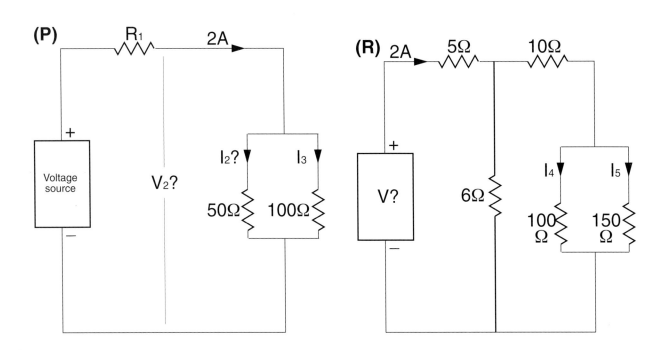

Answers to Problems:

a. I = 2 A
b. R = 6 Ω
c. V = 120 V
d. $I_1 = I_2 = I = 1.5$ A

e. $V_1 = 6$ V
f. V = 16 V
g. I = 0.18 A
h. $R_1 = 50$ Ω
i. R = 12 Ω, W = 3 W

j. I = 1.11 A
k. V = 120 V
l. I = 2.08 A
m. I = 2.87 A
n. I = 0.7 A

o. I = 0.75 A
p. $V_2 = 66.7$ V, $I_2 = 1.33$ A
q. $I_5 = 0.036$ A
r. V = 21.05 V

CHAPTER 2

DC Measurements

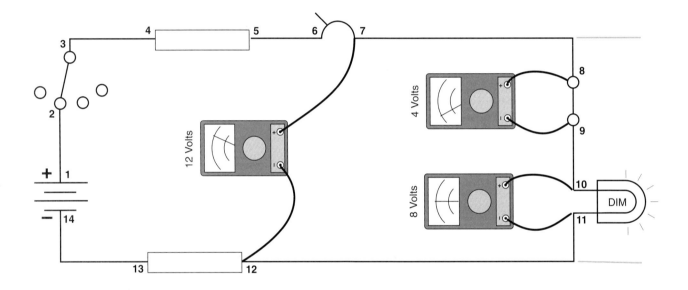

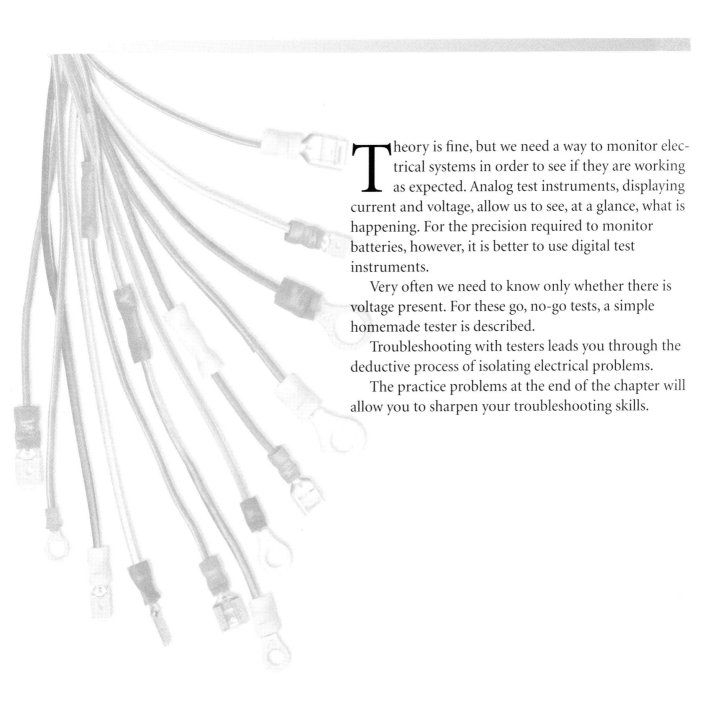

Theory is fine, but we need a way to monitor electrical systems in order to see if they are working as expected. Analog test instruments, displaying current and voltage, allow us to see, at a glance, what is happening. For the precision required to monitor batteries, however, it is better to use digital test instruments.

Very often we need to know only whether there is voltage present. For these go, no-go tests, a simple homemade tester is described.

Troubleshooting with testers leads you through the deductive process of isolating electrical problems.

The practice problems at the end of the chapter will allow you to sharpen your troubleshooting skills.

Analog Test Instruments

In Chapter 1, I asserted, " . . . with Ohm's Law, you will be able to understand, predict, and troubleshoot 90% of the electrical problems on a boat." Let me amend that figure to 99%.

You will recall that Ohm's Law allows us to calculate the theoretical relationships between the voltages, currents, and resistances in a circuit. What if there were instruments we could plug into a circuit that would show us the actual values of voltage, current, and resistance? By comparing the theoretical and actual values, we would find that either: (1) reality agreed with theory and all was well in the circuit, or (2) reality disagreed with theory and there was something wrong in the circuit.

There *are* instruments that measure volts, amps, and ohms, and using them to compare reality with theory is what we call troubleshooting. This chapter describes the instruments and their use.

Analog Ammeter (Current Meter)

The ammeter hasn't changed much since it was developed by Jacques d'Arsonval in 1811. In Figure 2.1, current flows into terminal 1, through the spring, around the moving coil, through a second spring on the backside, and out through terminal 2. The current in the coil produces a magnetic field that interacts with the field of the permanent magnet, forcing the coil to rotate about its bearing. The needle attached to the coil displays the rotation against the scale in the background.

In order that the ammeter be able to measure small currents, the meter movement is very delicate. The moving coil consists of many turns of fine wire, the springs are "hair springs" similar to those in a wind-up watch, and the coil pivots on jewel bearings. Typically, 50 µA (50 × 10⁻⁶ A or 0.000050 amp) deflects the needle full scale.

But the currents we are interested in typically range from 0.1 to 100 amps—about one million times 50 µA. You can imagine what would happen if we tried to measure the 50-amp charging current in our battery leads with the 50 µA meter of Figure 2.1.

How can we modify our 50 µA ammeter to measure 50 amps? Ohm's Law to the rescue! Although a perfect ammeter would offer zero resistance to the current flowing through it, real ammeters are made of real wire and so have a finite resistance.

Figure 2.2 shows the resistance, R_C, of our ammeter coil with full-scale current of 50 µA flowing through it. In parallel with the meter we place a *shunt* whose resistance, R_S, is 10^{-6} (one-millionth) of R_C. Since the voltage across both R_S and R_C is the same, Ohm's Law predicts that $I_S = 10^6$ (one million) × I_C, or 50 amps.

Fig. 2.2 Ammeter Symbol and Internal Resistances

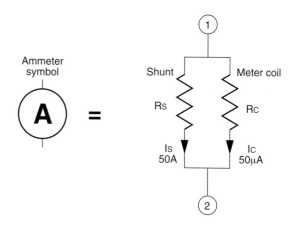

Fig. 2.1 D'Arsonval Ammeter

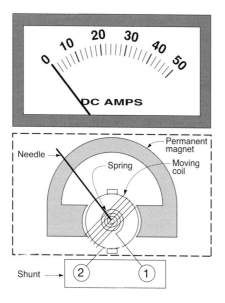

Using this principle, the same 50 µA ammeter can be made to measure 100 µA, 500 µA, 30 mA, 10 A, 100 A, or any other current merely by inserting the appropriate shunt across the terminals, as shown.

Analog Voltmeter

Might we use our little 50 μA d'Arsonval meter to measure voltage as well? Ideally, a voltmeter should measure the voltage across a circuit without disturbing the circuit. That means it should look like a very high resistance—much higher than any of the other resistances in the circuit.

Fig. 2.3 Using the Ammeter to Measure Voltage

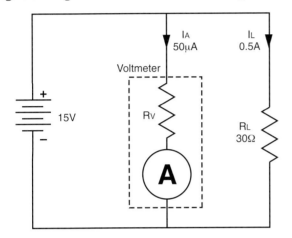

Figure 2.3 shows a circuit consisting of a 15-volt battery and 30-ohm load, resulting in a current of:

$$I = V/R_L$$
$$= 15 \text{ volts}/30 \text{ ohms}$$
$$= 0.5 \text{ amp}$$

We have placed a series resistor, R_V, inside the case of our 50 μA ammeter. If we want the ammeter to deflect full scale when the voltage is 15 volts, then Ohm's Law says that the series resistor that limits the current to 50 μA must be:

$$I_V = V/R_V$$
$$R_V = V/I_V$$
$$= 15 \text{ volts}/0.00005 \text{ amp}$$
$$= 300,000 \text{ ohms}$$

The load imposed on the circuit by our voltmeter—one ten-thousandth of the 30-ohm circuit load—is clearly negligible. If the circuit load, R_L, had been 30,000 ohms instead of 30 ohms, then our voltmeter would have siphoned off 10% of the current, giving a result 10% in error, as well as altering the performance of the circuit.

Voltmeters are simply ammeters with internal series resistors of 5,000 to 100,000 ohms per volt of full scale.

Analog Ohmmeter (Resistance Meter)

By now you are probably expecting me to tell you that our 50 μA ammeter can be modified to measure resistance as well. You are correct.

To measure the resistance of a resistor or other circuit load, we must isolate that component from the rest of the circuit. (Review the practice problems in Chapter 1 if you don't remember why.)

Sometimes we can open a switch; sometimes we can disconnect a terminal; sometimes we have to unsolder one end of the component. Regardless of how we isolate the item, we measure its resistance indirectly by applying a test voltage and measuring the resulting current. Because zero resistance (a possibility in case of a short circuit inside the component) would draw a possibly destructive high current, we place a known current-limiting resistor in series with the meter.

Figure 2.4 shows our ohmmeter. Inside its case are our same 50 μA ammeter, a 1.5-volt battery, and a series resistor, R_R. Maximum current will flow, and the meter will deflect full scale, when the resistance being tested, R_L, is zero. From Ohm's Law:

$$I = V/R_R$$
$$R_R = V/I$$
$$= 1.5 \text{ volts}/0.00005 \text{ amp}$$
$$= 30,000 \text{ ohms}$$

Fig. 2.4 Using the Ammeter to Measure Resistance

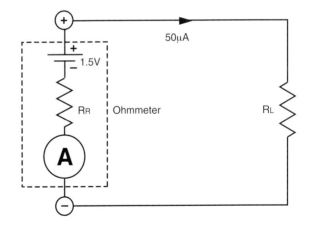

At the other end of the scale, the current approaches zero, and the needle shows essentially no deflection. Thus, we have a meter representing 0 ohms on the right, ∞ ohms on the left, and all other values on a logarithmic scale in between. Near 0 ohms the meter will be very sensitive and, as R_L approaches ∞, the meter will be less sensitive.

Digital Test Instruments

Analog Volt-Ohm Meter (VOM)

To troubleshoot a circuit, you may need an ammeter, a voltmeter, an ohmmeter, or all three. You may also need a variety of ranges. Conveniently, it is a simple matter to combine all of these functions into a single meter called a volt-ohm meter (VOM), as in Figure 2.5.

To the 50 µA ammeter, we add a 1.5- or 9-volt battery, assorted precision resistors and shunts, and a multipole, multiposition switch. More expensive VOMs incorporate input amplifiers that increase the input resistance and decrease the current drawn by the VOM. In this way, the VOM intrudes less on the tested circuit.

Fig. 2.5. Volt-Ohm Meter (VOM)

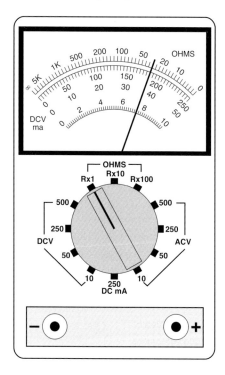

Digital Volt-Ohm Meter (DVM)

One of the very first clocks was a "water clock": Water dripped into a cup. When the cup was full, it tipped over, spilled its contents, and re-started. In tipping, it advanced a counter mechanism that indicated the number of times it had tripped and thus the passage of time.

A digital ammeter is exactly the same, except that it counts electrons instead of water drops. The cup is an electrical capacitor. As the capacitor collects electrons, the voltage across its terminals increases. When the voltage of the capacitor reaches a predetermined level, the capacitor is discharged, and the charging begins again.

The greater the current (flow of electrons), the more rapidly the capacitor charges and discharges. The charge/discharge cycles are electronically counted, and the number of cycles per second are directly proportional to current.

The analogy between analog and digital ammeters, voltmeters, ohmmeters, and multimeters is similar. Given a digital ammeter, we just add shunts, resistors, batteries, and rotary switches. Figure 2.6 shows a typical digital volt-ohm meter.

Fig. 2.6. Digital Volt-Ohm Meter (DVM)

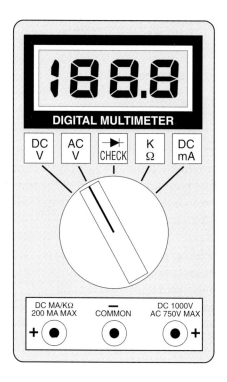

Digital vs. Analog Multimeters

So which is better—the analog or digital multimeter? Both are available in a range of sizes, from shirt pocket to benchtop, and both can be had for as little as $10 to as much as $400. To help you decide which is better for you, Table 2.1 lists the specifications of two typical midpriced units.

The specifications use several prefixes:

$$\mu \text{ (micro)} = 10^{-6} \text{ —multiply by 0.000001}$$
$$m \text{ (milli)} = 10^{-3} \text{ —multiply by 0.001}$$
$$k \text{ (kilo)} = 10^{3} \text{ —multiply by 1,000}$$
$$M \text{ (mega)} = 10^{6} \text{ —multiply by 1,000,000}$$

Table 2.1
Typical Analog and Digital Multimeter Specifications

Specification		Analog Multimeter	Digital Multimeter
DC volts	lowest range	250 mV	300 mV
	highest range	1,000 V	1,000 V
	accuracy[1]	±4%	±0.2%
AC volts	lowest range	5 V	3 V
	highest range	1,000 V	750 V
	accuracy[1]	±4%	±0.5%
DC amps	lowest range	50 µA	300 mA
	highest range	10 A	10 A
	accuracy[1]	±3%	±0.5%
Resistance	lowest range	2 kΩ	300 Ω
	highest range	20 MΩ	30 MΩ
	accuracy[1]	±3%	±0.2%

[1] Accuracy as percent of full scale

A glance at an old-fashioned watch gives you a sense of the approximate time very quickly. A digital watch, however, first requires recognition of the numbers displayed, then an interpretation of the significance of the numbers. The same is true of analog and digital multimeter displays.

If you wish to know simply whether your battery is charging or discharging (roughly 14 versus 12 volts), the analog meter with ±4% accuracy (±0.6 volt on a 15-volt scale) will do the job. But if you want to know the percentage of charge remaining in your battery, where the same ±0.6 volt represents ±50% of battery capacity, you'd better use a digital meter with its ±0.2% (±0.03 volt on a 15-volt scale) accuracy.

Digital vs. Analog Panel Meters

Ammeters and voltmeters (Figures 2.7 and 2.8) are used in distribution and circuit breaker panels to monitor battery voltage and rate of charge/discharge. An analog "battery charge indicator" is simply a voltmeter with its needle pegged at the left until the voltage reaches approximately 8 to 10 volts, thus expanding the scale over the useful voltage of a 12-volt battery.

Digital panel meters are slowly replacing analog meters. They cost no more to produce than the analog variety and are far more accurate, so one hopes their prices will soon drop.

Fig. 2.7 Analog Panel Meters

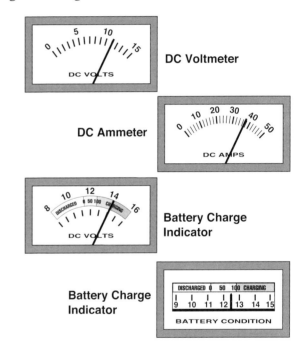

Fig. 2.8 Digital Panel Meters

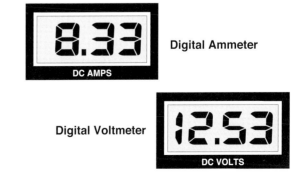

Homemade Testers

Most of the wiring problems on a boat are of the go, no-go variety. All DC circuits start at the boat's 12-volt battery. As you check a suspect circuit farther and farther from the battery, there either is or isn't voltage present. At the first point you find no voltage present, you can be sure the problem lies between this point and the last point where voltage was present.

The most common marine wiring problems are due to corrosion of connections and contacts. When copper corrodes, it forms green copper oxide—an excellent electrical insulator. As corrosion progresses, more and more of the contact surface through which current flows is eliminated. Eventually, there is so much resistance and voltage drop across the contact that the reduced voltage affects the load. If the load is a lamp, for example, the lamp will dim. If the load is a motor, the motor will slow down or not start at all.

There are two simple, do-it-yourself, troubleshooting devices you may end up using more than your fancy multimeter. The first is nothing more than an automotive bulb with attached test leads; the second is a Piezo electric alarm buzzer with test leads.

Fig. 2.9 Homemade Test Light

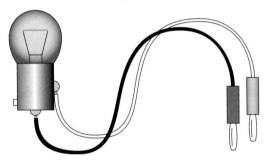

Figure 2.9 shows a typical 12-volt DC automotive bulb you can purchase at any Wal-Mart or auto parts store. Get a pair of high-quality "test leads" at Radio-Shack. These will be rubber-insulated, very fine-stranded 1–2mm^2 wire with alligator clips, banana plugs, or minitest tips attached. Solder the test leads to the side and base of the bulb, as shown, or to a lamp socket. Don't worry about ever having to replace the bulb. It is rated 5,000 hours at 13.5 V, so the only way it should fail is if you step on it or try to test a 24-volt circuit with it.

The second tool is similar but produces a noise instead of a light. As in Figure 2.10, solder test leads to a 3 V–16 V Piezo electric buzzer, which can be found at an electronics store for under $5.

If you want to get fancy, assemble both the light and

Fig. 2.10 Homemade Test Buzzer

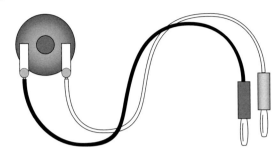

the buzzer in a small box with a switch that allows you to use either the light, the buzzer, or both of these simultaneously.

When connected to 12 volts, the bulb will glow brightly. If the voltage is low, the bulb will glow, but dimly. If there is no voltage, the bulb will not glow. Similarly, at 12 to 16 volts, the buzzer will screech; at 3 to 12 volts, the buzzer will sound fainter; at less than 3 volts, the buzzer will not sound at all. In a noisy environment, the light works best. In bright sunlight, the buzzer is best.

Next pick your tips. I find a set of interchangeable tips, as shown in Figure 2.11, very useful. Permanently attached to the test leads are banana plugs. These can be plugged into banana-to-alligator adapters, banana-to-minipin adapters, and banana-to-miniprobe adapters. I choose the adapters based on wire size and whether I'm using one hand or two. Also handy is a single 50-foot extension lead with male and female banana plugs, so that I can extend one of the test leads the length of a boat or a mast.

Fig. 2.11 Interchangeable Test-Lead Tips

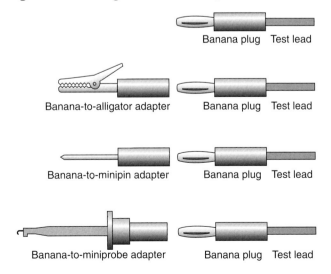

Multimeters, test lights, and test buzzers are all useful in troubleshooting circuits. Only where a precise voltage or a precise resistance is needed will the multimeter be more useful than the simpler light or buzzer, however. For simplicity, the examples and illustrations that follow will show only the simple test light. Just remember that where the test light is on, the buzzer would sound, and the multimeter would show a voltage, but where the test light is off, the buzzer would be silent, and the multimeter would show no or low voltage.

Figure 2.12 shows a simple cabin light circuit. The positive side of battery 1 is connected to terminal 1 of the battery-select switch by a wire. The common terminal of the battery switch feeds the positive bus bar in the distribution panel. The cabin light circuit originates at the "cabin lights" circuit breaker (or fuse) connected to the positive bus and then runs out of the panel to the cabin lights, which are connected as parallel loads.

At the light fixture, the positive wire feeds the on/off switch, which then controls the bulb. The other terminal of the bulb connects to the negative wire, which runs back to the negative bus in the distribution panel and the negative terminal of the battery, completing the circuit.

Fig. 2.12 Typical Cabin Light Circuit

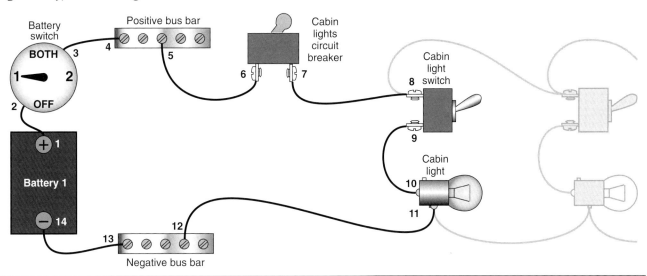

Figure 2.13 shows the same cabin light circuit in the form of a wiring diagram, using the standard component symbols listed in Figure 6-1. Note that the circuit load consists of lamps, which are nothing more than resistances that glow white hot. We could equally well have shown the load as parallel resistances, as in previous examples. In both Figures 2.12 and 2.13, fourteen points to which we could connect test leads are numbered. As we troubleshoot the circuit, we will connect our test light to pairs of these points to see whether voltage is present.

Fig. 2.13 Typical Cabin Light Wiring Diagram

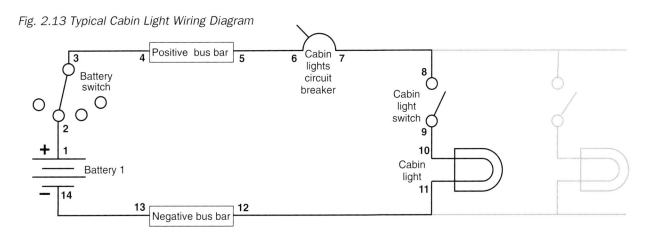

Troubleshooting

Turn all circuit switches to their on positions (Figure 2.14). The cabin lamps light up, meaning there is nothing wrong with the circuit. Since the wire and switches are designed to have near-zero resistance, we expect there to be no voltage drop between points 1 and 10. There should also be no voltage change from points 11 to 14. With one test lead on any of points 1 to 10 and the other lead on points 11 to 14, the test light should light, but with both leads on either the positive or negative side, the test light should not light.

Fig. 2.14 Properly Working Cabin Light Circuit

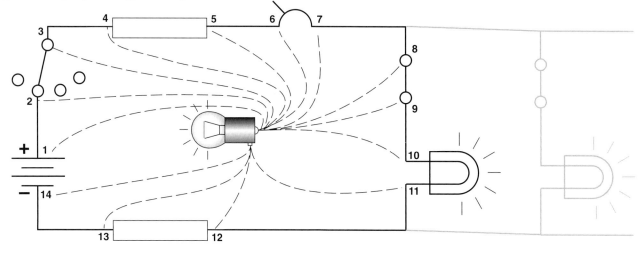

In Figure 2.15 we investigate a cabin lamp that will not light. All of the switches in the circuit are on, yet the light remains off. Furthermore, all of the other cabin lights in the same circuit do work.

We could start testing at points 1 and 14 and work our way toward the light. If we do, we'll find that the test lamp lights at every point, just as it did with the previous example of a normal circuit. If we suspect a burned-out bulb, however, we can save a lot of time by applying the test leads to points 10 and 11 immediately and discover that the circuit is OK all the way to the bulb holder.

At this point I'd simply replace the bulb. If you want to be sure it's the bulb and not the bulb holder, however, get out your multimeter and measure the resistance between the bulb contacts. If the multimeter reads infinite ohms, you know you have the culprit—a burned-out filament.

Fig. 2.15 Defective Cabin Light Circuit

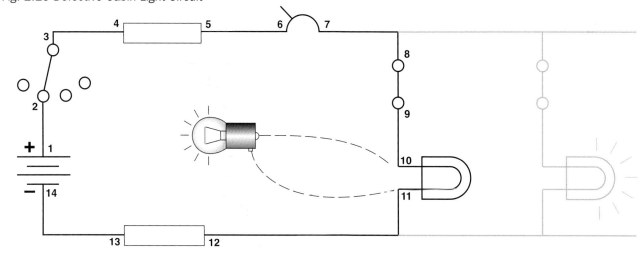

In Figure 2.16, we uncover a broken switch in the cabin light. We start as in the previous example with a cabin light that will not light up with all switches in the on position.

We suspect that the bulb filament has burned out, so we place our test lamp leads between points 10 and 11. The test lamp does not light. We therefore know that 12 volts is not reaching point 10. Next we place the test leads between 8 and 11. Now the test lamp lights up. The problem must therefore be either in the switch or the short wire between the switch and the bulb holder.

We place the test leads across 8 and 9. Now both the test lamp and the cabin light glow dimly. What's going on? Our test lamp has bridged the broken switch, but acts like a load in series with the cabin light. This reduces the current and brightness of both bulbs. The bulb is OK, but the light switch must be replaced.

Fig. 2.16 Uncovering a Defective Switch

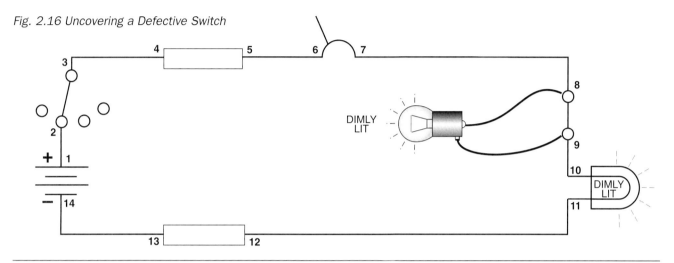

In the previous two examples, a component in the circuit had failed, resulting in an open circuit and zero current.

In Figure 2.17, we know the circuit is closed because the lamp is lit. But the lamp is dim. This is a very familiar phenomenon with flashlights—the light dims, but when we shake or hit the case the light becomes bright again.

The problem is due to poor contact. In a boat, poor contact is usually caused by corrosion of switch contacts or connectors. We will use this example to demonstrate the use of the multimeter.

Fig. 2.17 Troubleshooting with the Multimeter

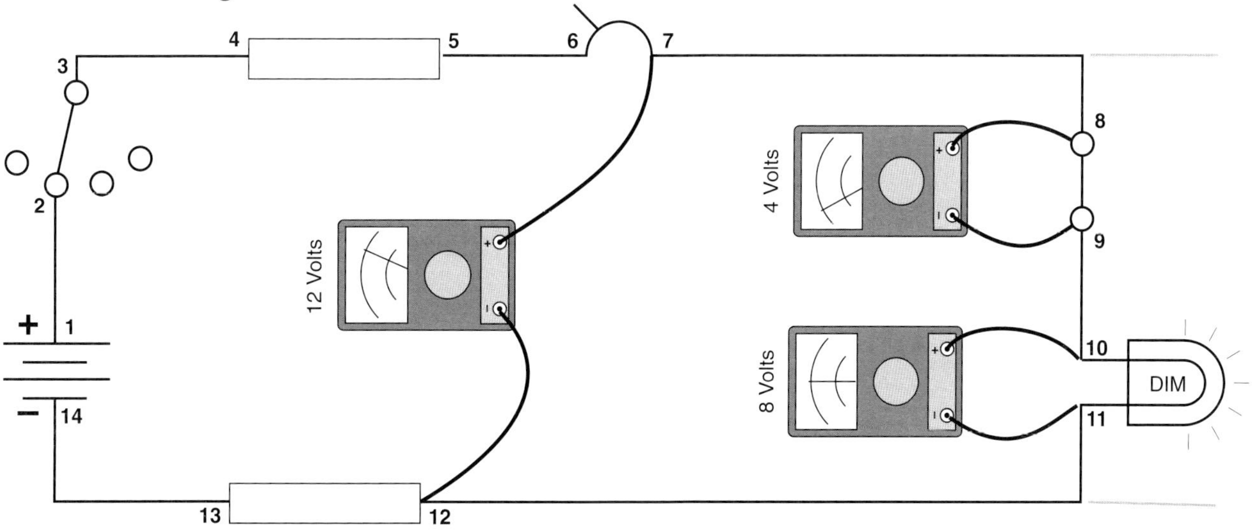

Troubleshooting

Just to be sure our battery isn't low, we measure between points 7 and 12, accessed behind the distribution panel. The meter reads 12 volts, so we know the battery is charged, and the circuit is OK up to the point where it leaves the panel for its run to the cabin lights.

Next, we try the other cabin lights in the circuit. They light normally, so we know our problem lies inside the dimmed light fixture. We remove the fixture base, exposing the internal switch and bulb holder wiring. We measure the voltage across the lamp itself, points 10 and 11, and the meter reads only 8 volts. Next, we measure the voltage across the switch, points 8 and 9. The meter reads 4 volts.

We have found the missing volts! Bad switch contacts are providing a resistance in series with the lamp, resulting in a voltage drop. In fact, one-third of the power in the circuit is being consumed within the switch, which we note is hot to the touch.

If we suspected internal resistance in the switch, why didn't we simply place the multimeter in the ohms mode and measure the resistance of the switch directly between points 8 and 9?

We could have, provided (and this is an extremely important "provided") we first opened the circuit by turning off either the battery switch or the circuit breaker.

If we tried measuring the resistance without opening the circuit, the 12-volt battery would still be in the circuit. Figure 2.4 showed that an ohmmeter consisted of a delicate 50 μA ammeter in series with an internal resistor and 1.5-volt battery. By placing the ohmmeter circuit in series with the cabin light circuit, we have effectively added or subtracted (depending on polarity) the 12-volt battery from the 1.5-volt battery. In the best case, the resistance reading will be grossly in error. At worst, we will burn out the 50 μA ammeter.

In general, to measure the resistance of a circuit component, you must first remove the component from the circuit by disconnecting one of its leads. Never try to measure resistance within a circuit with a live voltage.

A similar caution applies to measuring current in a circuit directly with a multimeter. Many inexpensive multimeters are designed to measure currents of up to 250 mA (0.25 amp). Others contain an internal shunt that allows measurements up to 10 amps. Make sure the current in a circuit is less than the maximum your meter can handle. Otherwise, you may blow the fuse or, worse, the meter itself.

A common mistake is to think you are measuring a voltage when, in fact, the multimeter is in the Amps position. The result is the same—something will blow.

Practice Problems

Table 2.2 below is intended to give you practice in troubleshooting a circuit. First, cover up column 3, then, referring to Figure 2.12, see if you can guess the cause of the problem, given the symptoms listed in columns 1 and 2. Column 3 lists the most likely causes.

Table 2.2 Symptoms and Causes

Test Light ON Between	Test Light OFF Between	Most Likely Cause
—	1 and 14	Dead battery
1 and 14	2 and 14	Positive battery cable
2 and 14	3 and 14	Battery switch off or defective
3 and 14	4 and 14	Bad connection or broken cable between battery switch and positive bus
6 and 14	7 and 14	Breaker off, defective breaker, or blown fuse
7 and 14	8 and 14	Broken wire from breaker to light switch
8 and 14	9 and 14	Switch off or defective
9 and 14	10 and 14	Broken wire between light switch and bulb holder
10 and 14	11 and 14	Burned-out lamp or poor contact between bulb and holder
10 and 14	10 and 13	Negative battery cable
10 and 13	10 and 11	Bad connection at negative bus or broken wire from bus to bulb holder

CHAPTER 3

Batteries

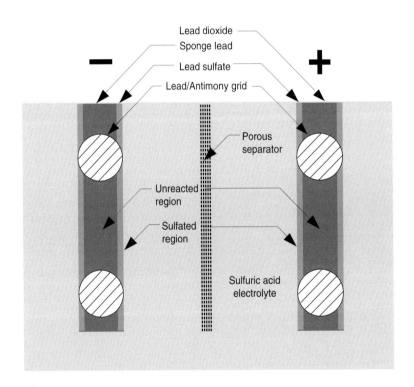

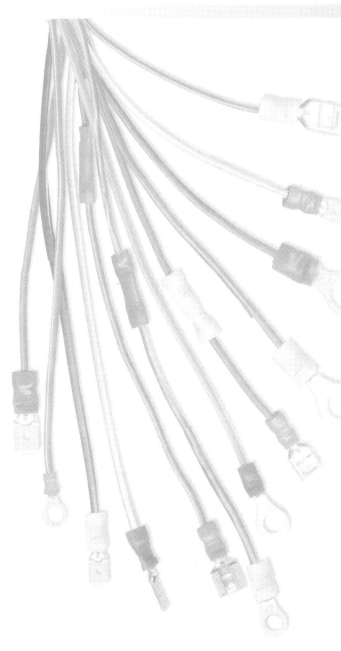

Except for the diesel engine, the greatest mystery to most boaters is the black box called the ship's battery.

What is a battery? Exactly what is going on inside that black box? In this chapter, you will find the simple answers and a few messy details as well.

Although it is more complex than simple conductors and resistors, it is useful to have an electrical model of the battery.

Monitoring batteries is the key to their performance. Monitoring the discharge/charge cycle requires an understanding of discharge characteristics, battery discharge ratings, and charging characteristics. You'll discover that charging recommendations vary between battery types.

In selecting batteries for your boat, you have several choices. In addition, you have to size the batteries to your load and decide whether to install multiple batteries in series or in parallel.

Safe installation involves electrical and mechanical considerations, both of which are covered by ABYC/ISO/BMEA standards.

What Is a Battery?

Probably no aspect of a boat is less well understood by its owner than its batteries. Our "knowledge" of batteries often consists of a few remembered facts from a high school chemistry course, experience with our own boats and automobiles, and, unfortunately, a barrage of advertising hype.

As with most of today's mass-marketed products, engineering takes a backseat to marketing. Meaningful specifications and instructions have been replaced by technical-sounding words such as "heavy-duty," "marine-grade," "deep-cycle," and "Die-Hard." Some manufacturers have gone so far as to promise boating nirvana—a battery you can stick anywhere in your boat and never give it another thought.

This is most unfortunate because: (1) it is not true, and (2) nothing is more important to the cruising boat than an adequate and reliable 12-volt system. Without a reliable source of 12 volts, most of us would have no lighting, refrigeration, navigation, or communication. In fact, we couldn't even start our engines.

This chapter explains what you need to know in order to select and then maintain the batteries that are the heart of your boat's electrical system.

To read battery manufacturers' literature, you would think that today's batteries represent recent technological breakthroughs. The truth is that the chemistry of Thomas Edison's batteries of 100 years ago is identical to the chemistry of today's batteries. But what about the new, sealed, gel-cell batteries you can store under your bunk? You are right—they are newer. They were patented in 1933.

Most of what you need to know about lead-acid batteries can be observed in a galley experiment using a glass containing a cup of battery acid (siphon some from your battery, or buy a litre at the car components store), two lengths of lead solder, two D-cells, a battery holder, and a voltmeter. *Warning: battery acid is strong so wear rubber gloves and be very careful.*

Place the D-cells in the battery holder as in Figure 3.1. Connect one length of solder to the negative end, the other length to the positive end of the battery holder, and dip their ends into the acid.

Bubbles will form and rise in the acid. Soon you'll notice one of the lengths of solder turning brown. Remove the batteries and connect the voltmeter to the solder, as shown in Figure 3.2. The voltmeter will read about 2 volts.

You have just manufactured and witnessed the operation of a lead-acid cell—the very same thing that is in your boat's batteries. The only difference is that your boat's batteries consist of either three of these cells in series (6-volt battery) or six cells (12-volt battery).

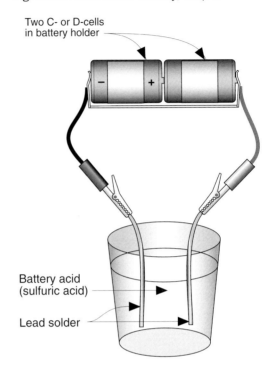

Fig. 3.1 A Home Made Battery, Step 1

Two C- or D-cells in battery holder

Battery acid (sulfuric acid)

Lead solder

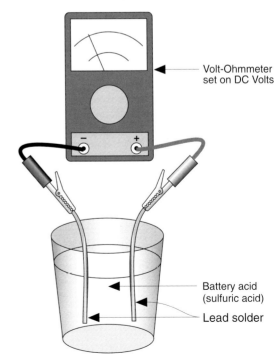

Fig. 3.2 A Home Made Battery, Step 2

Volt-Ohmmeter set on DC Volts

Battery acid (sulfuric acid)

Lead solder

What Is Going On?

What you have just witnessed is the reversible chemical reaction found in all lead-acid batteries:

$$\text{charging}$$
$$\Leftarrow$$
$$PbO_2 + Pb + 2H_2SO_4 = 2PbSO_4 + 2H_2O$$
$$\Rightarrow$$
$$\text{discharging}$$

Figure 3.3 shows the four phases of a lead-acid cell charge/discharge cycle. (See page 32 for more on specific gravity, SG.)

Fully charged. In the equation, application of an external charging voltage has driven the reaction all the way to the left. The negative electrode has become pure lead (Pb), the positive electrode is now pure lead peroxide (PbO_2), and the sulfuric acid electrolyte (H_2SO_4 + H_2O) is at its maximum concentration.

Discharging. By connecting a load (shown as a resistor in Figure 3.3), we complete the electrical circuit, allowing electrons to flow from one electrode to the other and the chemical reaction to proceed. The H_2SO_4 breaks into H and SO_4 ions (molecules with either extra or missing electrons). The H is attracted to the positive electrode where it steals the O_2 from the PbO_2 and forms water, H_2O. The now free Pb combines with the SO_4 ions to form $PbSO_4$ in place of the PbO_2. At the negative electrode, SO_4 ions also combine with the pure Pb to form more $PbSO_4$. Thus, both electrode materials are converted to lead sulfate, $PbSO_4$, while the electrolyte loses sulfuric acid, H_2SO_4, gains water, H_2O, and becomes more dilute.

Fully discharged. The cell is fully discharged when it runs out of one of the necessary ingredients. Either the PbO_2 has been totally converted to $PbSO_4$, or all of the SO_4 ions in the electrolyte have been used up, reducing it to pure water. In either case, PbO_2 and electrolyte strength have been minimized and $PbSO_4$ maximized.

Charging. By connecting a charging voltage to the cell we drive the electrons and the reaction in the reverse direction. Ideally, the negative electrode is restored to pure PbO_2, the positive terminal to pure Pb, and the acid electrolyte to its maximum strength.

Fig. 3.3 The Charge/Discharge Cycle

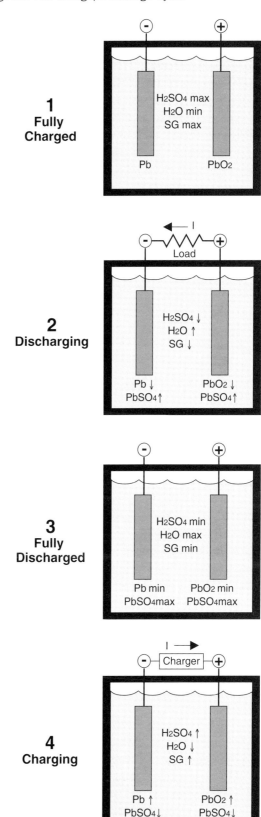

1 Fully Charged

2 Discharging

3 Fully Discharged

4 Charging

A Few Messy Details

The good news is that the chemistry of the lead-acid battery is simple. The bad news is that the way in which it actually happens is a bit more complex.

Figure 3.4 shows a cross section of a cell. Both positive and negative electrodes are immersed in electrolyte. The reactive materials, lead and lead peroxide, are suspended on lead grids that serve to both support the materials and conduct electric current. So far, so simple. Now for the complications:

• Boat batteries are bounced around. In order that the plates not touch each other and short-circuit the cell, the many closely spaced plates (electrodes) are interleaved with porous fiberglass separators.

• The lead grid is chemically and electrically compatible with the active materials that it supports, but it is not very strong. To increase strength, it is alloyed with either antimony (conventional wet, deep-cycle batteries) or calcium (sealed, maintenance-free batteries).

• When the discharge reaction starts, lead sulfate first forms at the electrode surfaces. As discharge continues, the already formed sulfate forms a barrier between the electrolyte and the unreacted material beneath, slowing the reaction and limiting the current. The greater the surface area and thinner the plates, the greater the possible current flow. Engine-starting batteries have many thin plates in order to provide large currents for short periods. The electrodes are also "sponged" (made full of minute holes) in order to further increase surface area.

• Lead, lead peroxide, and lead sulfate are not of the same density. When one replaces the other, expansion and contraction tend to dislodge the materials from the grids. Each time a cell is cycled, a small amount of lead sulfate is shed and falls to the bottom of the cell. Eventually the accumulation at the bottom may short out the plates. The more complete the reaction (the deeper the discharge), the greater the loss. Batteries designed for deep-cycling have fewer but thicker plates.

• When a battery is fully charged, all of the lead sulfate of the positive plate has oxidized to lead peroxide. Further charging (overcharging) oxidizes the lead of the grid as well, turning it into lead peroxide. Lead peroxide has little mechanical strength, and the grid will ultimately fall to the bottom of the cell.

• The rest of the overcharging energy goes into hydrolysis—separation of the water of the electrolyte into H_2 and O_2—which we saw as bubbles in our kitchen battery. Various tricks are employed in sealed batteries to recombine the gases into water, but, if overcharging and gassing are too vigorous, all batteries vent gas and lose electrolyte. Water can be replaced in a conventional wet-acid battery. In a sealed or gel-cell battery, it cannot.

• As we have seen, charging regenerates the H_2SO_4 electrolyte. Pure H_2SO_4 is 1.83 times as dense as water. As the H_2SO_4 is generated, it tends to sink. Since it is the H_2SO_4 that makes the electrolyte conductive, its absence at the top of the cell limits the acceptance of charging current. In a conventional wet-acid battery, acceptance is slow until gassing begins. Rising gas bubbles then mix the electrolyte, and acceptance increases.

• Gelled-electrolyte batteries capture the electrolyte in a gel, preventing stratification and increasing initial charge acceptance. "Starved electrolyte batteries" accomplish the same goal by limiting the electrolyte to just enough to saturate the porous separators.

• Most serious is the phenomenon of sulfation. If a battery is left in a discharged state (i.e., with much of its electrodes in the form of $PbSO_4$), the initially fine, soft deposits grow into larger, harder crystals that clog the holes of the sponged electrodes. The battery becomes difficult to charge and displays reduced capacity. Vigorous overcharging and bubbling (equalization) can break up and dislodge the crystals, resulting in recovery of much of the original capacity. However, each time it is done, the plates shed more material and get closer to the end of their useful lives.

So you see that, although the basic chemistry of all lead-acid batteries is the same, there are enough variations in construction to allow battery company marketing departments a field day.

Fig. 3.4 Cross Section of a Lead-Acid Battery Cell

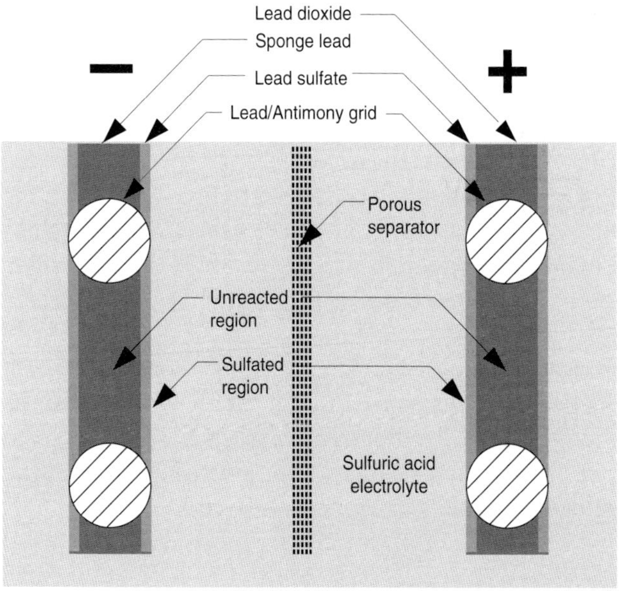

Lead dioxide
Sponge lead
Lead sulfate
Lead/Antimony grid

Porous separator

Unreacted region

Sulfated region

Sulfuric acid electrolyte

An ideal voltage source would supply unlimited current, with no drop in voltage. Considering the construction of the battery shown in Figure 3.4 and the messy complications described above, it is obvious that the lead-acid battery is not an ideal source.

For current to flow, the SO_4 and H ions have to find their way through the electrolyte. Resistance to this movement is evidenced as an internal electrical resistance, R_i.

When we disconnect a battery from an external circuit, no current should flow—at least theoretically. However, there is still voltage inside the cell ready and willing to supply current to anything that might bridge the gap between the battery's electrodes. Impurities in the electrolyte, as well as dirt and spilled electrolyte on the surface of the battery, provide such paths. They result in a parallel resistance, R_p, acting to self-discharge the battery. This is why you should never add anything but distilled or demineralized water to your battery and why it is a good idea to keep its surfaces clean.

Figure 3.5 shows the electrical model of the battery consisting of an ideal voltage source with a series internal resistance, R_i, and a parallel self-discharge resistance, R_p. Since chemical reactions always speed up with temperature, both resistances decrease with increasing temperature.

Fig. 3.5 Electrical Model of the Battery

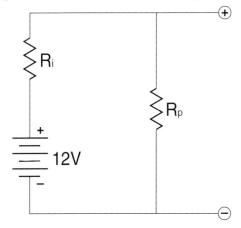

R_i in a new lead-acid battery is very small—of the order 0.01 ohm. It can be measured by drawing a known current and observing the drop in voltage at the terminals.

Example: We monitor the current drawn by a starter motor as 200 amps. As soon as we switch on the starter, we observe a drop in battery voltage from 12.5 to 9.5 volts. The battery's internal resistance, R_i, is then:

$$R_i = V/I$$
$$= (12.5 - 9.5) \text{ volts}/200 \text{ amps}$$
$$= 0.015 \text{ ohm}$$

The voltage must be measured at the battery terminals to eliminate the drop in the battery cables.

R_p is typically quite large—on the order of 1,000 to 10,000 ohms. It can be deduced by observing the drop in battery stored capacity over time.

Figure 3.6 shows the self-discharge of a typical new battery at different temperatures.

Fig. 3.6 Battery Self-Discharge vs. Time

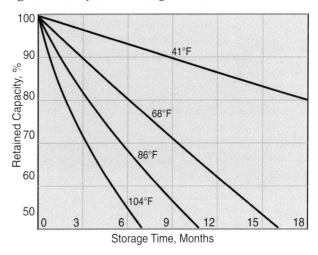

Example: At 68°F, the battery loses the first 10% of charge in three months. If this is a 100 Ah battery, it loses 10% of 100 Ah, or 10 Ah over a period of 90 days. Since there are 24 hours in a day, the discharge period is 90 × 24, or 2,160 hours. The average discharge current was thus 10 Ah/2,160 hours = 0.0046 amp. Using Ohm's Law,

$$R_p = V/I$$
$$= 12 \text{ volts}/0.0046 \text{ amp}$$
$$= 2,600 \text{ ohms}$$

The effect of temperature on R_p is evident from the discharge curves. Performing the same calculations as above, we find that R_p at 40°F is 7,900 ohms, while at 104°F it has dropped to just 930 ohms.

Determining State of Charge

Short of taking a battery apart and weighing the amounts of chemicals present, how can we determine the state of charge? Later we will describe battery-charge regulators/monitors that regulate and keep track of the amperes flowing into and out of a battery. For now, we will consider the more basic methods that have been used since batteries were invented.

First, in what sorts of units do we measure the amount of energy stored in a battery? As stated in Chapter 1, electrical energy is measured in watt-hours—the watts of power dissipated by the current flowing through a load times the duration of the flow in hours. Again, watts equals current times voltage:

$$W = I \times V$$
where I = amps through the load
V = volts across the load

However, since the voltage of a battery is always nominally 12 volts until nearly discharged, it is customary to drop the term "volts" and refer to the amount of energy drawn from or stored in a battery simply as ampere-hours (Ah).

As an example, suppose we charge a battery at the constant rate of 50 amps for 2 hours. At the end of 2 hours we will have put 50 amps × 2 hours, or 100 Ah, into the battery. Then let's draw a constant 5 amps from the battery for 10 hours. At the end of the 10 hours we will have drawn 5 × 10, or 50 Ah, out of the battery. Theoretically there should be 100 Ah – 50 Ah, or 50 Ah, still in the battery.

Battery electrolyte is a mixture of water (density 1.000 gram/cubic centimeter) and sulfuric acid (density 1.830 grams/cubic centimeter). Since flow of electricity into and out of a battery results in either the generation of sulfuric acid or the loss of sulfuric acid, the amount of stored energy in a battery is, therefore, a linear function of the density of the electrolyte.

Electrolyte density is usually expressed as its specific gravity—the ratio of its density to the density of water.

Specific gravity (SG) is measured with a battery hydrometer calibrated for the range of electrolyte densities normally found in a battery, 1.000 to 1.300. Do not confuse a *battery* hydrometer with an *antifreeze coolant* hydrometer, which is designed to measure SGs of less than 1.000. When a sample of electrolyte is drawn into the hydrometer, a float indicates the SG. However, the indicated SG must be corrected to what it would be at a standard temperature, 80°F. Figure 3.7 shows the corrections to make.

Fig. 3.7 Correcting Measured Specific Gravity for Temperature

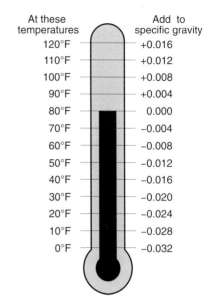

At these temperatures	Add to specific gravity
120°F	+0.016
110°F	+0.012
100°F	+0.008
90°F	+0.004
80°F	0.000
70°F	–0.004
60°F	–0.008
50°F	–0.012
40°F	–0.016
30°F	–0.020
20°F	–0.024
10°F	–0.028
0°F	–0.032

Example: A battery is located in the engine compartment. The temperature of the electrolyte is 95°F. The hydrometer reads 1.250. What is its SG, corrected to 80°F? *Answer:* 1.250 + 0.006 = 1.256.

Figure 3.8 shows the relationship between state of charge and electrolyte SG for a typical new lead-acid battery. The form of the relationship is always correct, but:

1. The high and low SG end points are particular to the individual battery, depending on age, condition, and the preferences of the manufacturer. High SG is more often between 1.265 and 1.280.
2. The SG has been measured only after the battery has rested for a time sufficient for the electrolyte to become homogeneous through diffusion, usually considered to be 24 hours.
3. The SG has been corrected to the standard temperature of 80°F.

Battery manufacturers can make the SG any value they wish. A more concentrated electrolyte (higher SG) produces higher voltage and increased capacity, but it also leads to shorter battery life. SGs are made higher in colder climates. Most new battery high SGs fall in the range 1.265 to 1.280.

Figure 3.9 shows a second electrochemical relationship—this time between SG and voltage. The open circuit (no current being withdrawn) voltage of a single lead-acid cell is determined by the homogeneous, temperature-corrected electrolyte SG as:

$$V = 0.84 + SG$$

For a 12-volt (six-cell) battery the relationship becomes that in Figure 3.9:

$$V = 6 \times (0.84 + SG)$$

Using either Figure 3.8 or Figure 3.9 requires that we actually measure the SG of the electrolyte. This operation is messy, destructive of clothing, awkward in the spaces where batteries are usually stowed, and impossible with a sealed battery.

Fortunately, Figures 3.8 and 3.9 can be combined, resulting in the more convenient relationship between state of charge and open-circuit voltage shown in Figure 3.10. The figure shows that, after 24 hours of rest, this battery would read 11.6 volts when fully discharged, 12.7 volts when fully charged, and 12.2 volts when 50% discharged.

If we can wait 24 hours, determining the remaining capacity of a battery is simple using an accurate voltmeter. The 24-hour rest period is provided by switching between two battery banks daily.

Why do we say the battery is fully discharged at 11.6 volts when the battery obviously has some amount of charge remaining? It is destructive to discharge a multicelled, lead-acid battery to 0 volts. With even small differences between cells, as 0 volts is approached, the stronger cells can drive the weaker cells into reversed polarity. Their grids will be damaged by being converted to $PbSO_4$. To avoid damage, "fully discharged" is defined as 10.5 volts at the 20-hour discharge rate. For example, for a 100 Ah battery, fully discharged is the point where the voltage reads 10.5 V, at a discharge current of 100 Ah/20 hours = 5 amps.

Self-Discharge and Winter Storage

House batteries are very heavy, so it would be nice if we could leave the really big ones on the boat over the winter. Pure water (fully discharged electrolyte) would freeze and crack the battery case. However, fully charged electrolyte (SG = 1.265) freezes at –72°F, while half-charged electrolyte (SG = 1.190) freezes at –12°F.

The question for northern boatowners thus becomes how quickly a battery that has been washed with a baking-soda solution, rinsed with fresh water, fully charged, and disconnected from its leads will self-discharge. Generally, at an average temperature of 50°F, such a battery would discharge at about 0.0003 SG per day. To drop from SG 1.265 to SG 1.190 (freezing point –12°F) would take 250 days.

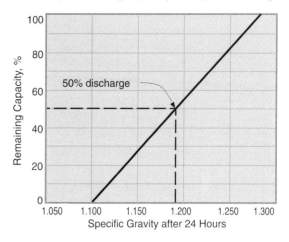

Fig. 3.8 Battery Remaining Capacity vs. Specific Gravity

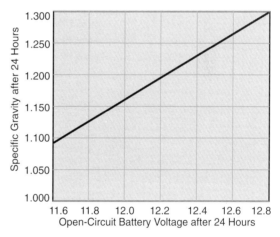

Fig. 3.9 Battery Open-Circuit Voltage vs. Specific Gravity

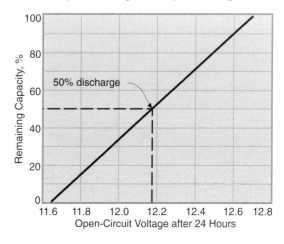

Fig. 3.10 Battery Remaining Capacity vs. Voltage

Discharge Characteristics

Earlier we noted the custom of measuring battery capacity in Ah. At small charge and discharge rates, the losses due to internal resistance are small, and the numbers of Ah we can withdraw very closely approximate the numbers of Ah we have put in.

When discharging at high currents, however, there is an apparent loss of battery capacity. As discharge current increases, the internal voltage drop through the battery's internal resistance increases, so the 10.5-volt cutoff point is reached sooner. Thus cutoff voltage for starter-motor applications is reduced to 7.2 volts.

Figure 3.11 shows discharge voltage vs. time at fractions of the 20-hour Ah capacity, C. When a battery's capacity, C, is stated as 200 Ah at the 20-hour discharge rate, it means that, when discharged at a constant rate of 0.05C (0.05 × 200 = 10 amps), the output voltage will fall to the zero-capacity cutoff of 10.5 volts in 20 hours. If the discharge rate is increased to 0.25C (50 amps), however, it will fall to 10.5 volts in about 3 hours. In the first case, 10 amps × 20 hours = 200 Ah. In the second case, 50 amps × 3 hours = 150 Ah. Discharged at 0.25C, the battery seems to have only 75% of its rated capacity.

This apparent loss of capacity vs. discharge rate is clearly shown in the more general curve of Figure 3.12. Note, that if we discharge at less than the 20-hour rate, the apparent capacity is *greater* than 100%. If this does not surprise you, it shows that you understand the effect of battery internal resistance.

Since internal resistance is strongly affected by electrolyte temperature, we would expect a family of such discharge curves for different temperatures.

Figure 3.13 shows capacity vs. both discharge rate and temperature. As in Figure 3.12, at 80°F, a battery discharged at five times the 20-hour rate (5 × 0.05C = 0.25C) gives us 75% of its rated capacity. At 0°F and 0.25C, only 45% of the rated capacity is available.

You may be wondering how this loss of Ah squares with the principle that electrons are neither created nor destroyed. Where did all those electrons go?

They are still there in the battery—they just got left behind. Due to the heavy current, the electrolyte in the plates was temporarily depleted. If we allow the battery to rest awhile, electrolyte ions will diffuse into the plates, and, when we start drawing current again, we'll find the voltage has recovered to more than 10.5 volts. This recovery is a familiar phenomenon to those who have had to start balky automobiles in subzero weather. If we are, in fact, willing to withdraw the current at a much lower rate, we will succeed in retrieving nearly 100% of our invested Ah.

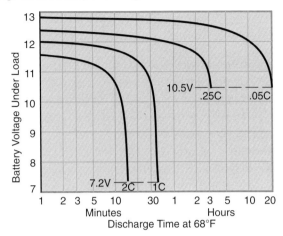

Fig. 3.11 Battery Discharge Characteristics

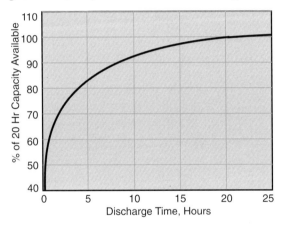

Fig. 3.12 Capacity as a Function of Discharge Time

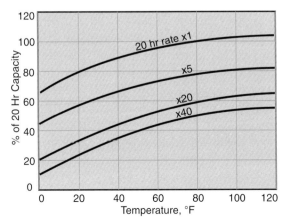

Fig. 3.13 Capacity as a Function of Temperature

Battery Discharge Ratings

Because batteries are used in widely varying applications, several standard capacity ratings have evolved:

1. *Ah at 20-hour rate*—amps a battery will supply for 20 hours at 80°F, before dropping to 10.5 volts, times 20 hours.
2. *Cold cranking amps (CCA)*—minimum number of amps a battery can supply for 30 seconds, at a temperature of 0°F, before dropping to 7.2 volts.
3. *Reserve capacity*—number of minutes a battery will supply a specified constant current (usually 25 amps) at 80°F, before dropping to 10.5 volts.

The first two ratings are of most interest to boatowners. When running on battery power, the "house" batteries are usually required to run from the time the engine is turned off until it is turned on again. For a cruising boat, the period is likely to last from 16 to 24 hours, so the 20-hour Ah rating is an appropriate specification.

Extremely large currents are drawn by engine starting motors. You can obtain the CCA required by any engine from its manufacturer. Small diesels, in the 10 to 50 hp range, require from 200 to 500 CCAs.

Battery manufacturers and distributors publish the relevant data, which is available in catalogues generally available on their websites. Key data to check include the capacity in Ah at 20 hour rate, the cold cranking amps, the physical dimensions, and the weight, particularly if the installation is in a location difficult to access, when a number of smaller batteries may be a more practical option.

Charging Characteristics

Charging a battery is the process of driving the lead-acid chemical reaction backward through application of an external voltage. To fully charge a battery, we must convert 100% of the $PbSO_4$ back to Pb and PbO_2.

On a boat, because charging requires running an engine, the usual goal is to recharge the battery as quickly as possible without damaging it. Damage can occur through excessive gassing, overcharging, and overheating.

Gassing. When the conversion of $PbSO_4$ to Pb and PbO_2 cannot keep pace with charging current, excess current results in hydrolysis, splitting the electrolyte's water molecules into gaseous hydrogen and oxygen. Wet-acid batteries vent the gases and thereby lose water. Through various tricks, including internal pressure, sealed batteries can recombine small amounts of gas and prevent water loss. However, even the best sealed batteries, including those with gelled electrolyte, can be overcharged to the point where they vent gas. No battery is totally immune to loss of electrolyte and subsequent loss of capacity. For this reason most gel-cell battery manufacturers specify a maximum charging voltage of 13.8 volts, as opposed to the 14.2 to 14.6 specified for wet-acid batteries.

Overcharging. A battery is fully charged when all of its $PbSO_4$ has been converted to Pb. As current continues to flow, gassing continues, as above, with the same destructive effect. Even more damaging, however, is oxidation of the positive grids into PbO_2, a relative nonconductor. The resulting increase in internal resistance decreases both the battery's charge acceptance rate and its ability to supply large discharge currents.

Overheating. A battery should never be charged when its temperature is over 120°F. Internal heat is generated by the internal resistance of the battery. At a charging current, I, of 100 amps and an internal resistance, R_i, of 0.01 ohm, the heat generated would be:

$$\begin{aligned} Watts &= I^2 \times R_i \\ &= 100 \text{ amps} \times 100 \text{ amps} \times 0.01 \text{ ohm} \\ &= 100 \text{ watts} \end{aligned}$$

Note that the heat generated is proportional to the square of the charging current, so a 100-amp charge rate would generate four times as much heat as a 50-amp rate. The internal temperature rise is in addition to the ambient temperature of the space where the battery is located. A good way to kill batteries is fast charging in a hot engine compartment while underway in the tropics.

Optimally Fast Charging

Optimally fast charging (charging as rapidly as possible without damage) involves four phases (Figure 3.14).

Fig. 3.14 Optimally Fast Charging

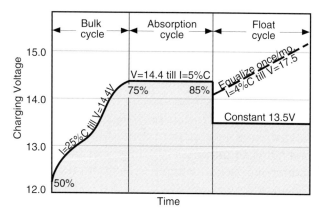

Bulk cycle. If a healthy wet-acid battery is discharged more than 25% of its capacity, C, it will readily accept charge rates of 0.25C or more, up to the point where it is about 75% charged. Gelled-electrolyte batteries, because they do not suffer from electrolyte stratification, will typically accept charge rates of up to 0.5C.

Absorption cycle. When a battery reaches its 75% charged state, the charging voltage has increased to around 14.4 volts, and gassing begins. At this point, in order to limit gassing, the charging voltage must be held constant at 14.4 volts or less, while the battery absorbs current at its own decreasing rate. At the point where the constant-voltage current has dropped to a rate of 0.05C, the battery is approximately 85% charged; at 0.02C about 90% charged; and at 0.01C nearly 100% charged. How far the absorption cycle is carried depends on whether the engine is being run only for charging (0.05C cutoff recommended), or whether the boat is under power or using shore power (0.01 to 0.02C cutoff recommended).

Float cycle. The final stage, provided the battery is still in the charge mode, is designed to just maintain the battery in its fully charged condition. If a battery is removed from all loads, as in the case of winter storage, the ideal float voltage is about 0.1 volt above the rested, open-circuit voltage, or approximately 13 volts. If the battery is in a float cycle, but still online so that current is occasionally withdrawn, either the charger should be capable of supplying the entire draw, or the float voltage should be increased to between 13.2 and 13.5 volts.

Equalization. As we saw on page 29, a fully charged battery consists of pure lead plates immersed in a sulfuric acid electrolyte; a fully discharged battery consists of lead sulfate plates in pure water. If a battery is cycled short of full charge its plates will retain the last 10% of lead sulfate. Over time this lead sulfate hardens and resists both breaking down and current flow. As a result of the electrical resistance the battery shows a falsely high voltage, appearing to be fully charged when it isn't. Over time the effective capacity of the battery shrinks.

The cure is *equalization*—a controlled overcharge, during which the cells are brought back to their fully charged states. A constant current of 0.04C is applied for 4 hours, or until battery voltage rises to the manufacturer-specified equalization voltage for the particular battery. Overcharging forces all of the $PbSO_4$ in each cell to be converted, so that, except for material previously lost by shedding, each cell is restored to its original condition. Overcharging also causes gassing and, in wet-acid batteries, loss of electrolyte. After equalization, wet-acid cells should be topped off with distilled water. Because of the gassing, equalization should be applied with care to sealed batteries and not at all to gelled-electrolyte batteries (see pages 40–41 for battery types).

Equalization should not be performed too often, however, since overcharging also oxidizes the positive plates. It should be performed whenever cell specific gravities differ by 0.030 or more, indicating a difference in capacities of 15% to 20%. Alternatively, for batteries cycled daily, a routine equalization schedule of once per month is recommended.

Each manufacturer publishes a recommended method for recharging its products. Sealed batteries are less likely than wet-acid batteries to require equalization because they ordinarily neither lose nor gain electrolyte. Furthermore, they might gas excessively and lose electrolyte if subjected to a high voltage. Constant-current charging is a possibility with wet-acid batteries because limited accidental overcharging results only in loss of replaceable water. Sealed-battery manufacturers, however, fear such an accident and so recommend constant voltage with limited-current charging.

Automotive-type regulators can be set only to a single voltage. Regulators that can be programmed for optimally fast charging will be covered in Chapter 4.

The range of precise charging parameters for marine batteries can be summarised as follows:
- Recommended maximum charging voltages in the bulk and absorbtion cycles vary from 14.1 to 16.0 volts, so the charging voltage from the regulator should checked and adjusted, if possible, to match the battery manufacturer's recommendation.
- The acceptable charging current (I) varies much more widely, with a few types of batteries able to take 200 amps, whilst most others should not be charged from a low charge state at more than 0.25C (see above), which is typically 25 amps for a 100Ah battery. This would contra-indicate fitting a larger output alternator to solve battery "problems".
- Ideal float charge levels vary from 13.0 to 13.8 volts, with gel batteries tending to be at the higher end of the range. Again, individual battery manufacturer's recommendations should be checked.

Estimating Your Daily Load

The first step in selecting storage batteries is to determine the daily consumption of electricity in Ah. Table 3.1 lists equipment commonly found on boats. Power ratings can usually be found on a nameplate, either in watts or in amps. Make your own table using the form shown in Table 3.2. To calculate the daily Ah requirement, first convert all nameplate ratings to amps by dividing watts by 12. Next multiply by the average hours used per day to get Ah. Finally, add the Ah for all the devices for the total Ah/day.

For many of the devices, two ratings have been listed: (1) the typical consumption, and (2) the consumption of the most efficient models. The table shows the total Ah/day for two cruisers: (1) with typical appliances, and (2) with the most efficient appliances.

The boat with typical appliances consumes 99 Ah/day, while the more efficient boat consumes only half as much. The more efficient boat will thus require only half as large a battery system, or, alternatively, will go twice as long before requiring recharging.

Table 3.1 Power Consumption for Cruising Boats at Anchor

Area	Appliance or Fixture		Watts	÷12 = Amps	Average Hours per Day	Typical Ah	Efficient Ah
Galley	Microwave (9 minutes/day)		550	45.8	0.15	6.9	6.9
	Toaster (5 minutes/day)		800	66.7	0.04		
	Blender (30 seconds/day)		175	14.6	0.01	0.15	0.15
	Coffee grinder (15 seconds/day)		160	13.3	0.005		
	Refrigerator	2" insulation	60	5.0	10	50.0	
		4" insulation	60	5.0	5.0		21.9
Head	Hair dryer (2 minutes/day)		1200	100	0.033		
Lighting	Reading lamp	2 incandescent 15-watt	30	2.5	2	5.0	
		2 halogen spots 5-watt	10	0.8	2		1.6
	Galley fixture	2 incandescent 25-watt	50	4.2	2	8.4	
		2 fluorescent 8-watt	16	1.4	2		2.8
	Anchor light	manual 10-watt	10	0.8	14	11.2	
		automatic 10-watt	10	0.8	11		8.8
Fans	Typical 6", 100 cfm		12	1.0	5.0	5.0	
	Most efficient, 100 cfm		4	0.3	5.0		1.5
Entertainment	Stereo	20-watt/channel	60	5.0	1.0	5.0	
		7-watt/channel	35	3.0	1.0		3.0
	Television	19-inch CRT	80	6.7	4.0		
		15-inch LCD	36	3.0	2.0	6.0	
		6-inch color	15	1.7	4.0		3.4
	VCR or DVD	typical 220–240 volt AC	17	1.4	1.0	1.4	
		12-volt DC play only	10	0.8	1.0		0.8
					Totals	99.1	50.9

Table 3.2 Form for Estimating Power Consumption at Anchor

Area	Appliance or Fixture		Watts	÷12 = Amps	Average Hours per Day	Estimated Ah
Galley	Microwave (9 minutes/day)		550	45.8	0.15	_____
	Toaster (5 minutes/day)		800	66.7	0.04	_____
	Blender (30 seconds/day)		175	14.6	0.01	_____
	Coffee grinder (15 seconds/day)		160	13.3	0.005	_____
	Refrigerator	2" insulation	60	5.0	10	_____
		4" insulation	60	5.0	5.0	_____
Head	Hair dryer (2 minutes/day)		1200	100	0.033	_____
Lighting	Reading lamp	2 incandescent 15-watt	30	2.5	2	_____
		2 halogen spots 5-watt	10	0.8	2	_____
	Galley fixture	2 incandescent 25-watt	50	4.2	2	_____
		2 fluorescent 8-watt	16	1.4	2	_____
	Anchor light	manual 10-watt	10	0.8	14	_____
		automatic 10-watt	10	0.8	11	_____
Fans	Typical 6", 100 cfm		12	1.0	5.0	_____
	Most efficient, 100 cfm		4	0.3	5.0	_____
Entertainment	Stereo	20-watt/channel	60	5.0	1.0	_____
		7-watt/channel	35	3.0	1.0	_____
	Television	19-inch CRT	80	6.7	4.0	_____
		15-inch LCD	36	3.0	2.0	_____
		6-inch color	15	1.7	4.0	_____
	VCR or DVD	typical 220–240 volt AC	17	1.4	1.0	_____
		12-volt DC play only	10	0.8	1.0	_____
Other						_____
						_____
						_____
					Total	

Choosing a Battery Type

Forget the marketing terminology you have seen in battery advertisements. Batteries can be divided into four general categories:

1. Conventional, wet-acid automotive starting
2. Deep-cycle, wet-acid
3. Absorbed glass mat
4. Gelled electrolyte

Conventional, wet-acid automotive starting batteries are engineered to supply extremely high currents (200 to 1,000 amps) for periods of just a few seconds. In spite of the high current, the duration is so short that the amount of energy drawn (amps × hours, or Ah) is small. Used in this way, automotive starting batteries are typically discharged only a few percent of their capacity before returning to the float state.

The rate at which current can be drawn is proportional to plate area, so starting batteries are constructed with a large number of thin lead plates sandwiched between paper or plastic separator plates. When cycled deeply, battery plate material is shed. Since starting battery plates are so thin to start with, deep cycling will result in short life.

Don't be fooled by warranties of 60 or more months or names such as "Die-Hard." While fine for starting the engine, if used to power your cabin lights and other house loads, you will be replacing this type of battery every season or two. Used only to start the engine, provided they are recharged immediately after use, they make a good combination with a large, deep-cycle house battery.

Deep-cycle, wet-acid batteries have fewer but thicker plates designed for regular discharge to 50% or less of capacity. The largest users of such batteries are not boats but golf carts and forklifts, which require large currents and capacities, in addition to the ability to cycle thousands of times. Such batteries have the maximum cycling potential and are ideally suited to cruising boats with heavy house loads and long seasons, provided their owners are willing to spend the time monitoring and maintaining them.

The golf cart type of deep cycle wet-acid batteries described above are 6v units, used in pairs in 12v sys-

tem. They are not so readily available in the UK as 12v units, and the general term 'traction battery' is generally used instead to indicate a maximum deep-cycle wet-acid battery.

In a well-equipped cruising boat, a deep-cycle house bank will also have sufficient cold-cranking capacity to start the engine. If, as recommended, the house batteries are separated into two banks, there is little need for a dedicated engine-starting battery. Some boaters still carry a small automotive engine-starting battery as a safety backup, however.

Absorbed-glass mat batteries were developed as superior engine-starting batteries, but are being used more and more as marine house batteries. They retain all of their electrolyte in spongy fiberglass mats and are "sealed" with valve-regulated caps, which recombine charging gases under most conditions. The thin, porous plates that yield high starting-motor currents do not stand up as well as those of deep-cycle, wet-acid types. However, they can both discharge and recharge at much higher rates than wet-acid batteries. Because so many of these batteries are sold, competitive pricing makes them attractive. Provided discharge is limited to around 50%, they are suitable for the seasonal boater who expects to replace the batteries every 3 or 4 years.

Gelled-electrolyte batteries were developed for applications where acid spills and gas venting were prohibited, such as military tanks and wheelchairs. Freedom of location and from maintenance have made them popular on boats. They cannot be deep cycled as many times as wet-acid, deep-cycle batteries, but they are less subject to damage if left in a discharged state, and accept somewhat higher recharge rates. With the caveat that their lower charging voltages must never be exceeded, gel-cells are suited to boats with large loads, long seasons, and owners who are totally unwilling to monitor and maintain their batteries. Before purchasing, however, you should seriously consider the AGM battery, which shares many of the gel's advantages, yet may be occasionally and moderately overcharged.

Table 3.3 compares the advantages and disadvantages of the four battery types.

Table 3.3 Comparing Battery Types

Battery Type	Advantages	Disadvantages
Wet-acid automotive	Lowest cost High cranking amps Good for engine start battery Small, lightweight	Can't stand many deep discharges Will be destroyed if left discharged Will spill electrolyte if tipped over Relatively short life Relatively fragile
Wet-acid deep-cycle	Less expensive than gels and AGMs Maximum deep-cycle life (>1,000) Individual cells accessible Can be equalized Water can be added to electrolyte	Electrolyte level must be monitored Will be destroyed if left discharged too long Will spill electrolyte if tipped over Must be installed upright Battery box should be vented overboard Extremely heavy
Gelled electrolyte (gel-cell)	Very rugged Requires least attention, provided not overcharged Can be installed in any position Doesn't require venting Won't leak even if cracked Accepts high charge rate	Most expensive May be destroyed by overcharging Moderate deep-cycle life (500 likely)
Absorbed glass mat (AGM)	Most rugged of all Can be installed in any position Doesn't require venting Won't leak unless cracked Accepts highest charge rate Tolerates moderate equalization	High initial cost Moderate deep-cycle life (250 likely)

Optimum Depth of Discharge

Figure 3.15 shows expected lifetime cycles versus depth of discharge under laboratory conditions. The shape of the curves was established with one set of data each for wet-acid, AGM, and gelled-electrolyte batteries. The golf cart curve was assumed to be of the same shape and fitted to the single published 100% discharge point.

Fig. 3.15 Expected Charge/Discharge Cycles

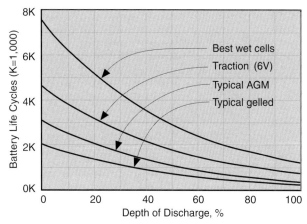

A boat is not an ideal environment, so you should count on getting about half of the cycles shown. Thus, instead of 3,000 discharges to 50% for the best wet-acid battery, you might assume 1,500 cycles. Alternating banks daily, and recharging the banks in parallel, you can project 1,500 recharges × 2 days = 3,000 days, or 8 years.

With the same 50% discharge and 2-day cycle, traction batteries should last about 5 years, AGMs 4 years, and gelled electrolyte batteries 2 to 3 years.

Figure 3.16 plots cost per kilowatt-hour versus depth of discharge assuming half of the life cycles shown in Figure 3.15. It was assumed the batteries were US size 8D (220 Ah) and were bought for list price, less 15%. The costs (2005) assumed were: wet-acid $544, AGM $444, and gelled $308. The equivalent pair of 6-volt golf cart batteries cost $180.

Figure 3.16 leads to two conclusions:

1. Considering the cost of the batteries alone, the optimum depth of discharge is approximately 50%.
2. Due to a lower purchase cost, the golf cart battery is the most economical battery in the US.

Charging Cutoff

Figure 3.14 showed that charging current should be reduced once a battery has been recharged to 75% of capacity. Stopping at 75%, however, results in sulfation. If the engine is run only for charging, run time becomes uneconomical beyond 85 to 90%. When charging underway or with wind or solar, run time is not an issue, and recharge to above 90% is desirable.

We will assume a boat at anchor, a discharge limit of 30 to 50%, and a recharge cutoff of 85 to 90%. Since a battery is usually considered "dead" when it has permanently lost 40% of its rated capacity, we will also de-rate our batteries by 20%.

Example: Our daily load is 75 Ah. We decide to discharge to 30% of capacity and charge to 85%. The required (derated to 80%) battery size is then

$$75 \text{ Ah}/0.80(0.85 - 0.30) = 170 \text{ Ah}$$

Once you have estimated your daily load and chosen your charge-discharge range, Figure 3.17 allows easy determination of the required battery size.

Fig. 3.16 Lifetime Costs per kWh of Battery Types

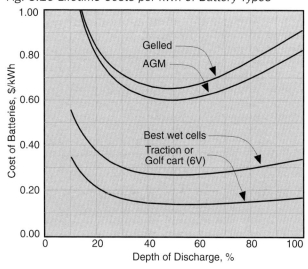

Fig. 3.17 Battery Size Selector

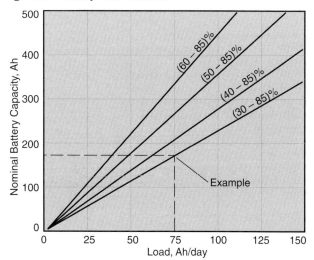

After a deep discharge, batteries will accept very high rates of charge. AGM and gelled-electrolyte batteries typically accept up to 0.5C (50% of capacity per hour), while healthy wet-acid batteries safely accept up to 0.25C. Once a battery has been recharged to 75% of its capacity, the charging rate must be reduced in order to prevent gassing in all batteries, as was shown in Figure 3.14.

The total cost per kilowatt-hour produced and stored is the sum of battery cost (Figure 3.17) and engine/fuel costs. Figure 3.18 compares battery and engine/fuel costs. Engine/fuel costs assume:
- Consumption = 0.5 gallon per hour
- Fuel price = $2.20 per gallon
- Engine life = 10,000 hours
- Engine price = $7,000
- Maintenance = $0.20 per hour

The three curves show the dramatic savings that can be realized by matching the alternator to its load. Minimum engine/fuel cost is achieved by deep discharge of AGM or gelled-electrolyte batteries and recharge at 0.5C (220 A for the example of paralleled 8D batteries). For a pair of 8D wet-acid batteries, the matched alternator would be rated at 110 A.

Solar and wind power will be discussed in Chapter 10, but costs per kilowatt-hour for solar and wind-produced power have been included in Figure 3.18 for comparison. The solar system is assumed to cost $480 per 60-watt panel, last 10 years, and be used all year in Miami. The wind machine has a 5-foot blade, costs $1,500, lasts 10 years, and is used all year in 10-knot average winds.

Solar and wind costs per kilowatt-hour are independent of discharge depth, assuming the systems are matched to the daily load. It is interesting to note that typical public supply rates in the USA are $0.10 to $0.15 per kilowatt-hour.

Fig. 3.18 Total Costs per kWh of Generated Power

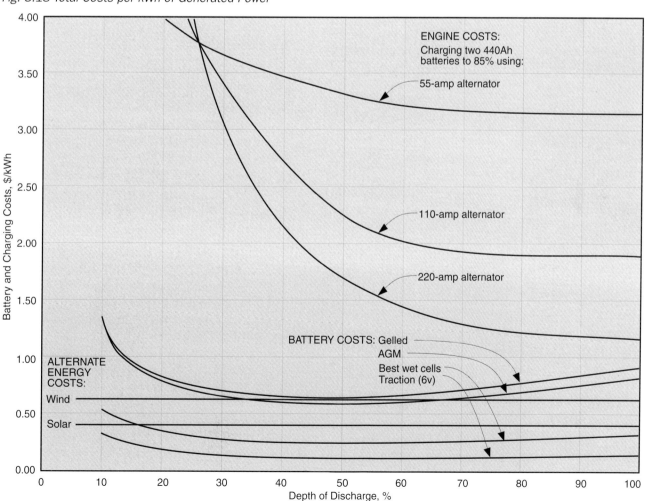

Series vs. Parallel

A battery bank consists of one or more batteries, connected to act as a single 12-volt unit. Two common questions are: (1) should a large bank consist of one very large battery, two smaller 12-volt batteries in parallel, or two 6-volt batteries in series; and (2) assuming two banks, should both be on all the time, or should they be alternated?

First, how large a bank do you need? Some say that your battery capacity can never be too large, but consider two facts:

1. Batteries should not be left in even a partially discharged condition any longer than necessary.
2. The cost of charging batteries is greater than the amortized cost of any battery, and unless a battery is discharged at least to 50%, recharging currents are restricted and charge times elongated.

These are both reasons to size each battery bank for a single day's load. If your daily load is less than about 100 Ah, you can get by with a single 4D battery (185 Ah) by cycling between 85% and 30%. The problem—unless you are young and a weight lifter—is the weight of such a large battery. 4D batteries typically weigh 125 pounds, while 8Ds weigh in at around 160 pounds. The option is to break the bank into smaller, more manageable, units.

Here are arguments for the single battery, the series connection, and the parallel connection (Figure 3.19).

A single battery is better:
• Because there is just one case, you get the maximum Ah in a given space.
• Two battery cables and terminals are eliminated.

Parallel connection of smaller batteries is better:
• Assuming isolation diodes (page 58) are used, the bad battery can be removed, and the remaining battery still has full voltage at half capacity.
• The stronger battery cannot drive a weaker battery into cell reversal.

Series connection of 6-volt batteries is better:
• Failure of a single cell will be apparent as a sudden 2-volt drop, but voltage will still be sufficient for engine starting.
• Failure of a single cell in one battery will not draw down the voltage as in a paralleled battery.
• 6-volt golf cart batteries are the cheapest sources of battery power (in the USA).

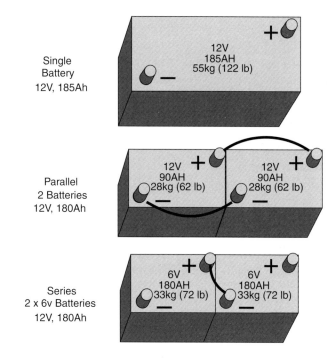

Fig. 3.19 Battery Size Selector

Single Battery
12V, 185Ah
— 12V 185AH 55kg (122 lb)

Parallel 2 Batteries
12V, 180Ah
— 12V 90AH 28kg (62 lb) / 12V 90AH 28kg (62 lb)

Series 2 x 6v Batteries
12V, 180Ah
— 6V 180AH 33kg (72 lb) / 6V 180AH 33kg (72 lb)

The second question was whether, in the case of two battery banks, to leave the battery selector switch permanently in the "Both" position.

Reasons "Both" is better:
• Current drain from each battery is less, so less energy is lost to internal resistance. This is important when using an electric windlass or a microwave oven.
• Each battery receives only half of the charge currents, so both batteries will be charged in twice the time. If using solar or wind, charging near 100% capacity will less likely cause gassing.

Reasons alternating banks are better:
• A catastrophic short circuit, or leaving the anchor light on for a week, will not result in total loss of capacity. The reason for two banks is redundancy.
• Without an expensive Ah meter, battery health can be accurately assessed only after a 24-hour rest period. Switching banks allows better monitoring of capacity and performance.

Recommendation: alternate banks daily, but switch to "Both" when charging with the engine, starting the engine, hauling the anchor with an electric windlass, or running other high loads, such as microwave ovens.

There are three good reasons to house batteries in sturdy covered battery boxes: (1) to capture and vent overboard explosive hydrogen gas generated in the case of overcharging, (2) to contain electrolyte that may be spilled in rough seas, and (3) to prevent metal tools and other objects from accidently shorting the battery terminals.

Battery boxes can be purchased in a few sizes ready-made, or you can construct one to custom fit your bank. Making your own has the advantage of fitting both the space and the batteries better.

Building a Battery Box

Building a battery box is an excellent way to learn basic fiberglass techniques. No curved surfaces are required, appearance is not critical, and the plywood core forms the mold.

Figure 3.20 shows the construction of a box large enough to hold two 12-volt batteries (330 Ah total).

Batteries weigh about 0.34 kg/0.75 lb and contain 55g/2oz of acid per Ah. While you are making the box, consider the consequences of 150 kg/330 lb of batteries and 26.5 l/28 quarts of battery acid breaking loose in a storm. Also picture installing or removing batteries weighing up to 75 kg/165 lb each.

1. Mark cuts on 20mm/¾-inch ac-Exterior plywood.
2. Apply a layer of fiberglass to both sides of the uncut plywood using epoxy resin. Polyester resin does not adhere well to wood, so use epoxy resin if possible for maximum strength.
3. Cut the panels and apply resin to edges.
4. Glue and nail the box together.
5. Sand round all outside edges and fill inside corners with an epoxy paste.
6. Apply at least three overlapping strips of fiberglass reinforced plastic (FRP) cloth at each inside and outside corner, making sure there are no voids.
7. Apply two complete layers of fiberglass cloth over the entire outside and finish with epoxy paint.
8. Fasten the box firmly to the hull with countersunk stainless steel, flat-head (SS FH) bolts.
9. Apply two additional layers of fiberglass cloth to the inside and finish with white epoxy paint.
10. Drill a vent hole near the top of the side most convenient to venting. The hole diameter should provide a press fit for a length of garden hose.
11. Insert batteries using ¼-inch nylon line, leaving the line for later extraction.
12. Fasten the cover down and run the vent hose to a point outside the hull.

Fig. 3.20 DIY Battery Box

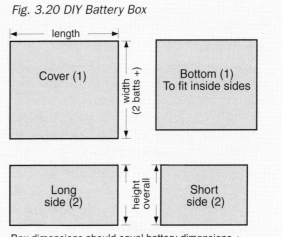

Box dimensions should equal battery dimensions + clearance + thickness of materials and an allowance, if necessary, for joint construction.

Design the box with plenty of clearance to allow for easy installation of batteries. Battens and wedges can be used to secure the batteries.

Use 20mm / 3/4" marine or exterior plywood.

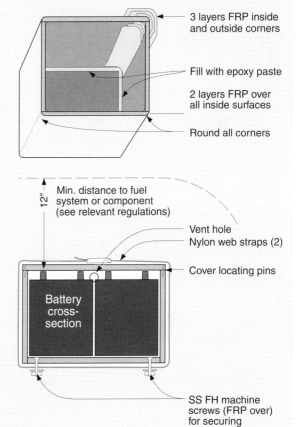

Standards for Batteries

Adapted from ABYC Standard E-10, *Standards and Recommended Practices for Small Craft*, dated December, 1996, and *BMEA Code of Practice (4th Edition)*, 2006.

Battery Capacity

a. Cranking batteries shall have at least the cold cranking performance rating (CCA @ 0°/32°F) or marine cranking performance rating (MCA @ 0°/32°F) amperage required by the engine manufacturer.

b. Accessory batteries and cranking batteries also used as accessory batteries should have their capacity determined by calculating the likely current demand, when the alternator is not in use. If the craft only has one battery set, then the capacity calculation must include sufficient power to start the engine(s).

The formula to arrive at the capacity is: $C = 2 \times t \times I$.

C = Battery capacity (AH); I = Discharge current (Amps); t = Time for which the above discharge can be sustained as stated by the manufacturer (hours).

Alternatively, you can take the estimated power consumption calculated in Table 3.2 (say 50 Ah per 24 hour day), allow a battery reserve of 50% (more if engine starting is required), and a capacity of approximately 100Ah will be required for each day's useage.

Installation

a. Batteries shall be secured against shifting.

b. An installed battery shall not move more than 25mm/one inch in any direction when a pulling force of 41 kg/90 lb or twice the battery weight, whichever is less, is applied through the center of gravity of the battery as follows:

(1) Vertically for a duration of one minute.
(2) Horizontally and parallel to the boat's center line for a duration of one minute fore and one minute aft.
(3) Horizontally and perpendicular to the boat's center line for a duration of one minute to starboard and one minute to port.

c. To prevent accidental contact of the ungrounded battery terminal to ground, each battery shall be protected so that metallic objects cannot come into contact with the ungrounded battery terminal.

d. Each metallic fuel line and fuel system component within 300mm/12" and above the horizontal plane of the battery top surface as installed shall be shielded with dielectric material to protect against accidental short-circuiting.

NOTE: 1. Terminal insulation or battery covers do not comply with this requirement since during installation or removal of a battery, these protective devices are usually removed in order to connect the cables.
2. Any nonconductive material may be used for shielding as long as it is durable enough to withstand accidental contact by a tool or the battery terminals during servicing, installation or removal.

e. Each battery shall not be installed directly above or below a fuel tank, fuel filter, or fitting in a fuel line.

NOTE: This does not prohibit a battery from being installed directly above or below an uninterrupted fuel line; however, if this fuel line is within the twelve inch envelope of the top surface of the battery it shall be shielded dielectrically.

f. A vent system or other means shall be provided to permit the discharge from the boat of hydrogen gas released by the battery. Battery boxes whose cover forms a pocket over the battery shall be vented.

NOTE: These provisions also apply to installations of sealed batteries.

g. If the mounting surfaces or components of the boat in the immediate vicinity of the battery location are of a material attacked by the electrolyte, a mounting means shall be provided that is made of a material that is not damaged by electrolyte.

h. Fasteners for the attachment of battery boxes or trays shall be isolated from areas intended to collect spilled electrolyte.

Wiring

a. Connectors to battery terminals shall be made with fitted connectors providing secure mechanical and electrical connections. Spring clips or other temporary clamps shall not be used.

b. A soldered connection that joins a battery terminal connector to a conductor may be used if the length of the soldered joint is at least 1.5 times the diameter of the stranded portion of the battery conductor.

c. Battery supply conductors must be sized to satisfy the load calculations as outlined in Chapter 6.

CHAPTER 4

Alternators

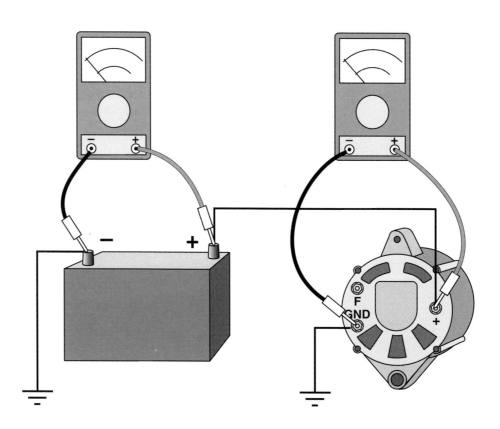

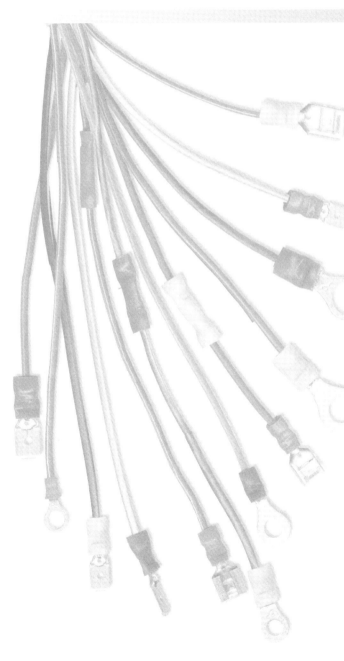

An alternator is a rotary current machine that transforms mechanical rotation into AC current. The AC current produced by the alternator coils is rectified by diodes into DC current for charging the ship's batteries.

In order not to overcharge the batteries we need a regulator for controlling the alternator. Whether the regulator field-coil wire is connected to the positive or to the negative battery terminal determines whether it is a type-P or type-N alternator. The methods of powering the voltage regulator and supplying excitation current to the field coil vary as well.

Regulator bypass controls, or battery management systems, which allow more rapid and more complete battery charging, are popular amongst boat owners. The example (the Link 2000 R) used in this chapter is not marketed in the UK or Europe, but there are similar products available, such as the Acorn Engineers' Kestrel, Adverc Battery Management Unit, Mastervolt's Alpha Pro Charge Regulator, Merlin Equipment's Merlin AMS and Sterling Power Products' Advanced Digital Regulator.

The electrical demands of boats vary widely, so a variety of charging setups have evolved, from the simplest one alternator/one battery of the day boater to multiple alternators/multiple batteries.

Since most engines are equipped with light-duty alternators, cruisers and liveaboards having large battery banks very often upgrade to higher-output models, requiring guidance on alternator installation.

A Home Made Alternator

If you had fun making the home made battery in Chapter 3, try making the home made alternator in Figure 4.1. All you need are an analog voltmeter or ammeter (a multimeter with many ranges is best), a large steel nail or bolt, several feet of insulated copper wire, and a magnet.

Wrap a dozen turns of the wire around the nail and connect the bare ends to the meter. If you are using a multimeter, start with the highest amps scale. Hold the magnet as close to the head of the nail as possible without actually touching it. Now move the magnet rapidly back and forth, as shown in the illustration. The needle of the meter should jump back and forth across zero.

If the needle doesn't move, switch the meter to a lower scale. If the needle still doesn't move, increase the number of turns of wire until it does move.

What's going on? As Hans Oersted discovered in 1820, an electric current is induced in a wire whenever the magnetic field around the wire changes. Our moving magnet induces magnetism in the nail. As the permanent magnet moves back and forth, the magnetism in the nail alternates in direction, so the magnetic field through the coiled wire alternates as well. The alternating field produces pulses of current of alternating polarity which is shown in the graph at the bottom of Figure 4.1.

The scale of the graph is not important to our experiment, but you should know that the current is directly proportional to the strength of the magnetic field, the rapidity of the magnet motion, and the number of turns in the coil.

Simple Two-Pole Magnet

Instead of passing the magnet back and forth across the head of the nail, we can make a rotating machine to do the same thing. Figure 4.2 shows a straight bar magnet pivoted about its center between two series-connected coils. The coils are wound in opposite directions, so that the opposite poles of the magnet produce current in the same direction. As the magnet turns, however, each coil sees alternating poles, so the current changes polarity as shown in the graph.

This type of current is called alternating current, or AC. Chapters 7 through 9 of this book deal with AC power on boats. All we need to know about AC at this point is that both voltage and current reverse, usually

many times per second. One complete swing from plus to minus and back to plus again is called a *cycle*. The number of cycles per second is the *frequency*, measured in Hertz (Hz). Utility power in the United States is delivered at 60 Hertz; in Europe, at 50 Hertz.

Fig. 4.1 A Home Made Alternator

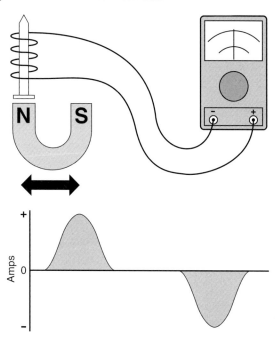

Fig. 4.2 Producing Alternating Current

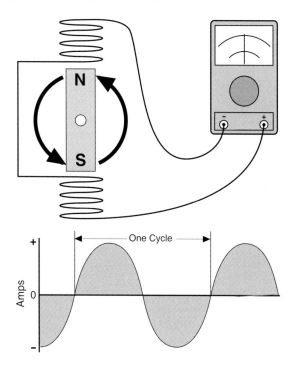

More Poles and Coils

We can make our rotary current machine more efficient by placing more magnets on the rotating shaft and by adding a corresponding number of coils of wire, as shown in Figure 4.3. With three times the number of magnets and coils, the result is three times as much generated power.

With three times as many magnet poles, each revolution of the shaft produces three times as many cycles. All of the coils still produce current in synchrony, however, so the forms of the output current and voltage remain the same as before.

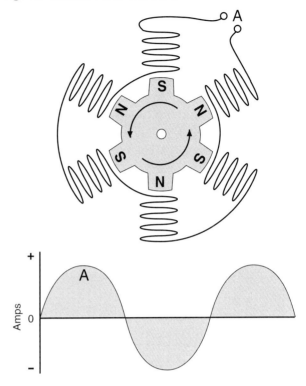

Fig. 4.3 Multiple Poles and Coils

Three-Phase Current

Let's call the entire series-connected coil of Figure 4.3 coil A. Now let's add coils B and C, identical in form to coil A, but rotated one-third and two-thirds of the gap between the small coils of coil A, which is shown in Figure 4.4.

The poles of the rotating magnet will pass each set of small coils in the order: A, B, C, A, B, C, etc. The currents induced in coils A, B, and C will therefore be offset by one-third and two-thirds of a cycle as shown at the bottom of Figure 4.4. We now have three identical alternating currents, offset in phase by 120° (one complete cycle equals 360°). We call this three-phase AC.

Why would we want to complicate our rotary current machine in this way?

1. We can triple power output without increasing the size of the wire in the coils.
2. It is easier to wind closely spaced coils than to increase the number of magnetic poles.
3. The three phases result in a better (smoother) output, as we'll see later.

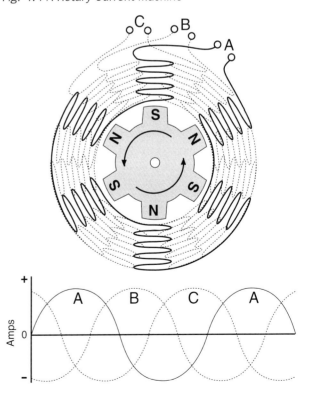

Fig. 4.4 A Rotary Current Machine

Rectification

As we saw in Chapter 3, batteries produce direct current (DC), which is always of the same polarity. To recharge batteries we need DC. The rotary current machine is of no use unless we convert its three-phase AC output to DC.

Enter the diode. As its circuit symbol (Figure 4.5, top) indicates, the diode allows current to flow only in the direction of the arrow. If you like analogies, you can think of a diode as the equivalent of a check valve in a water-supply system, allowing water to flow in one direction but not the opposite.

Fig. 4.5 Diodes and the Diode Symbol

All diodes have the following three ratings:

maximum forward current—maximum current in the forward direction
peak inverse voltage—maximum voltage at which diode will block current flow in reverse direction
forward voltage drop—voltage in the direction of the arrow at which diode begins to conduct current

Diodes come in different sizes and shapes, depending on their intended uses. Tiny signal diodes are intended for low-current applications. Large rectifying diodes are used in high-current applications such as alternators. A typical alternator diode might have ratings of 50 amps, 50 volts, and 0.6 volt.

If you haven't yet put away your galley experiment, insert a diode into the circuit as shown in Figure 4.6. Now when you pass the magnet back and forth, the needle should deflect only in the positive direction. If you get a negative deflection, either the meter leads are reversed, or the diode is pointing in the wrong direction. As the current plot shows, the magnet and wire coil are still producing negative pulses, but the pulses are blocked by the diode.

Figure 4.7 shows how a diode would similarly block negative current in our rotary current machine. The process of passing current of one polarity but blocking current of the opposite polarity is called *rectification*. Passing only the positive halves of an AC wave is called half-wave rectification.

Rectification would be twice as efficient if we could pass both halves of the AC wave. This is accomplished

Fig. 4.6 The Home Made Alternator with Rectifier

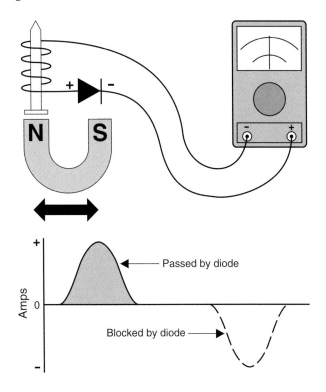

Fig. 4.7 Half-Wave Rectification

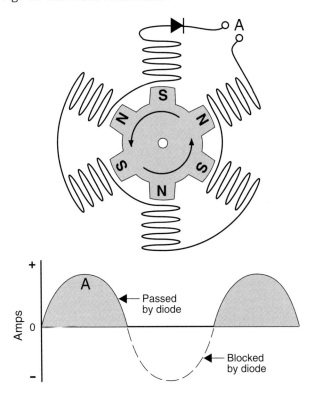

with a four-diode full-wave rectifier (Figure 4.8). No matter the polarity of current and voltage through the wire coil, there are always two of the four diodes seeing reverse voltage and acting as if they were open circuits.

Follow the currents in Figure 4.9 as they flow through the coil, the diodes of the rectifier, and the externally connected load in the alternating closed circuits labeled Path 1 and Path 2.

The first half-wave travels Path 1: from the coil, through diode 1, into the positive terminal, through the external load, into the negative terminal, through diode 3, and back to the coil.

The second half-wave travels Path 2: from the coil, through diode 2, out the positive terminal, through the external load, into the negative terminal, through diode 4, and back to the coil.

An obvious extension would be to provide each of the coils in Figure 4.4 with their own full-wave rectifiers, as shown in Figure 4.10. This would be fine if we desired three separate outputs to recharge three separate batteries or to power three independent DC circuits, but we don't. We'd rather have a single DC system, and, although we might have three batteries, we'd rather charge them in parallel from a single source.

It would be needless torture to force you through the logic, but it turns out that connecting the ends of the three coils produces a felicitous simplification.

Fig. 4.8 Full-Wave Rectification

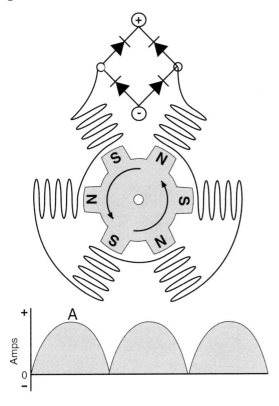

Fig. 4.9 Rectifier Current Paths

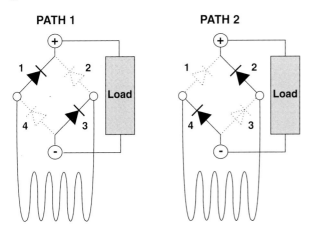

Fig. 4.10 Three Full-Wave Rectifiers

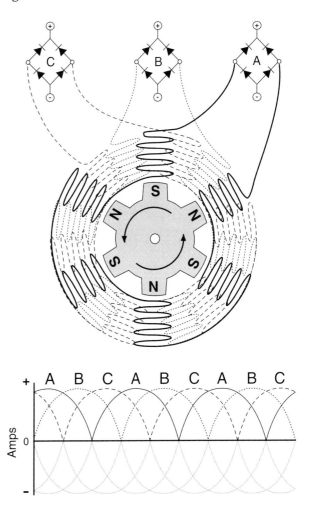

Rectification

Figure 4.11 shows the two common ways to connect the coils: the Delta and the Y. With the coils connected, half of the twelve diodes can be eliminated. With either configuration, we are left with only three coil terminals, each of which is connected to a diode pair.

Figure 4.12 shows the ends of the coils connected to a single pair of output terminals. The currents combine in such a way that total output current approximates steady DC. Our rotary current machine has finally evolved into a DC-output alternator.

Fig. 4.11 Delta and Y Coil Arrangements

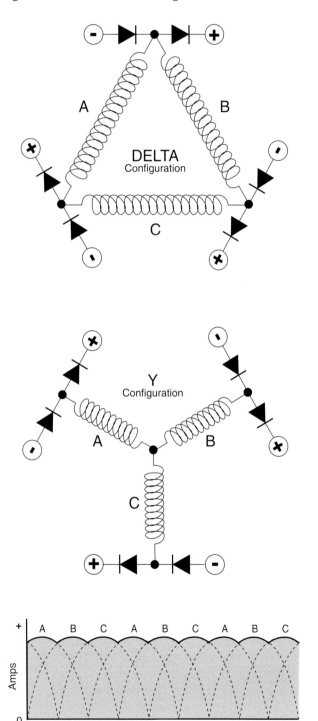

Fig. 4.12 Delta and Y Connections in a Real Alternator

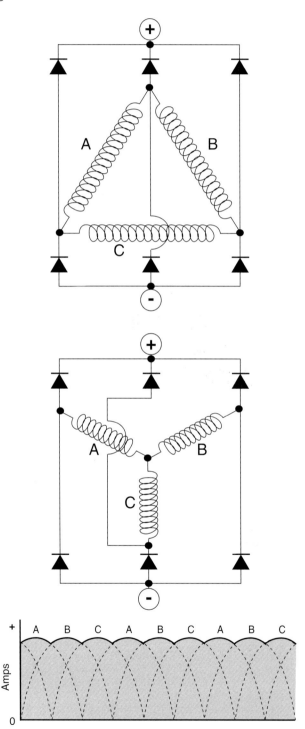

As you will recall, the output of the galley alternator in Figure 4.1 depended on three variables:

1. Strength of the magnet
2. Number of turns of wire
3. Speed of magnet movement

The alternators in Figure 4.12 are similar. We can vary their outputs only by changing engine rpm, which is inconvenient.

The problem of control in a real alternator is solved by varying the strength of the magnet. Instead of the permanent magnet in Figure 4.1, we use an electro-magnet as in Figure 4.13. The iron core concentrates the magnetic field, which is generated by a current through the coil. The strength of the field generated is proportional to the current flowing in the field coil. Thus, alternator output can be controlled by varying current through the field coil.

Figure 4.13 also demonstrates a phenomenon you can verify with your galley magnet and two or more nails: A magnet will induce magnetism of opposite polarity in a second piece of iron in close proximity. For example, in Figure 4.13, two additional iron bars placed at the ends of the core also become magnets. This can be verified with either iron filings or a small compass.

Figure 4.14 shows the added iron bars replaced by iron disks with fingers that have been bent around and interleaved. In this way, current through a single field coil wrapped around the shaft results in alternating magnetic fingers around the circumference. It also shows how current can be fed to the field coil through carbon brushes riding on copper slip rings fixed to the shaft.

Figure 4.15 shows a typical alternator rotor with its interleaving magnetic poles, slip rings, and field coil wrapped around the inside shaft. This rotor assembly rotates inside the collection of stationary coils, known as the stator.

The device that controls field-coil current, and thus alternator output, is known as the voltage regulator. How it came to be known as a voltage—rather than a current—regulator, is lost in history. We will not change its name. Just remember that it controls output current, not voltage.

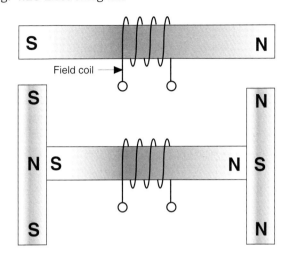

Fig. 4.13 Electromagnets

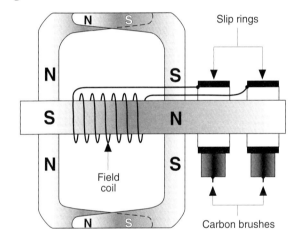

Fig. 4.14 Alternator Rotor and Brushes

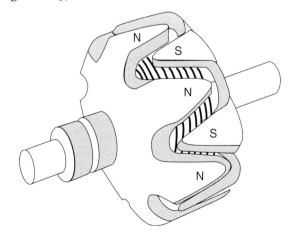

Fig. 4.15 Typical Alternator Rotor

Controlling the Alternator

Voltage Regulators

We'll start with the old-fashioned electromechanical voltage regulator still found in some older boats (Figure 4.16). The field current flows through the relay arm that pivots about F and contacts the points labeled "Ignition" and "Ground." "Ignition" is connected to the battery + terminal through the engine ignition switch.

The relay arm is held up against the ignition contact by the adjusting spring. With full field current flowing, the alternator quickly produces its maximum current. If the battery voltage is low enough, the alternator continues to pump out maximum current. When battery voltage rises to a set value (between 13.8 and 14.2 volts), the increased current flowing from ignition to ground through the relay coil pulls the arm down and opens the contact. Field current drops to zero, alternator output drops to zero, battery voltage drops, and the relay arm is pulled up to the ignition contact to start the cycle again.

The greater the voltage of the battery, the greater the percentage of time the contact remains pulled down into the open position. Alternator output switches between full and zero output hundreds of times per second. The average voltage approaches a constant, while average charging current falls toward zero (plus whatever load is being drawn at the same time). Battery voltage is adjusted by turning the adjusting spring.

It is easy to check a voltage regulator. With the engine running, and after output current has dropped to a trickle, turn on a heavy load. If the regulator is working, voltage will remain the same, but alternator current will increase by the amount of the added load.

Electromechanical regulators have been replaced by solid-state regulators. Although they can be destroyed by reversing battery and ground leads and by excessive heat, they never wear out. Figure 4.17 shows a solid-state equivalent of the electromechanical regulator.

The operation of a solid-state regulator is easily understood once you understand how a transistor works. Figure 4.18 shows the most common type of transistor—the NPN. It has three leads: base (B), emitter (E), and collector (C). It can be thought of as an amplifying valve. The current flowing into the base controls the current flowing from the collector to the emitter. Because the junction between base and emitter is essentially a diode in the direction of the arrow, no current flows until the base-to-emitter voltage reaches about 0.5 volt. Above that voltage, the output current is 20 to 100 times the base current. Thus the transistor can be used as an electronic switch or current amplifier.

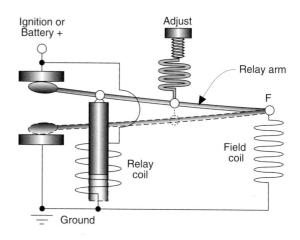

Fig. 4.16 Older Electromechanical Voltage Regulator

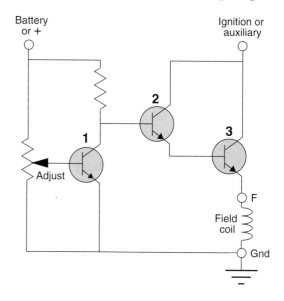

Fig. 4.17 Solid-State (Transistorized) Voltage Regulator

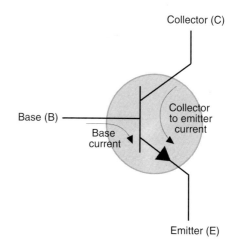

Fig. 4.18 How an NPN Transistor Works

In Figure 4.17 assume the battery voltage is low. The base of transistor 1 is therefore at a low voltage and transistor 1 is off. With transistor 1 acting as a high resistance between the base of transistor 2 and ground, the voltage of transistor 2 base is high and transistor 2 is on. Transistor 3 amplifies the collector-to-emitter current of transistor 2 by twenty times or more, causing a large current through the field coil and maximum alternator output.

Soon battery voltage increases, however, and transistor 1 switches on. The resistance from the base of transistor 2 to ground decreases, and transistors 2 and 3 switch off, cutting off the current to the field coil. With no field current, alternator output ceases.

The transistors switch on and off hundreds of times per second, with the ratio of on-to-off times controlling the average field current and alternator-output current. The analogy between electromechanical and solid-state voltage regulators is obvious.

Note that the solid-state regulator of Figure 4.17 had two positive terminals:

1. Battery, or +, is for sensing the voltage of the battery so that it can be charged at the correct voltage.
2. Ignition, or auxiliary, supplies the field current.

Not to be confused with NPN and PNP transistors, alternators and regulators can be connected in two different ways called type-P and type-N (Figure 4.19).

In type-P alternators and regulators, the regulator is connected to the positive end of the field coil. In type-N alternators, the voltage regulator is located between the negative end of the field coil and ground.

Both type-P and type-N voltage regulators draw power from the battery + terminal. If the power is not interrupted when the engine stops, the voltage regulator/alternator coil will slowly drain the battery.

Figure 4.20 shows three small diodes (the diode trio) connected to the three coil terminals in a type-N alternator. These diodes feed a terminal labeled "Aux." When the alternator is not turning, there is no current to power the regulator, so there is no drain on the battery. Reverse current flow from the battery to the auxiliary terminal is prevented by the charge diodes.

Fig. 4.20 Diode Trio

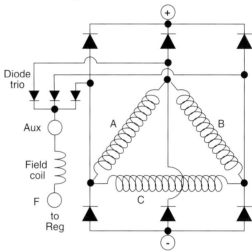

Figure 4.21 shows a second method of supplying regulator current. A large isolation diode is placed between the three charge diodes and the alternator + output terminal. This isolation diode prevents reverse current flow from the battery to the regulator.

Fig. 4.19 Type-P and Type-N Regulators

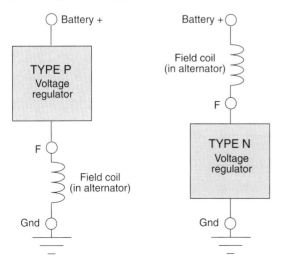

Fig. 4.21 Isolation Diode

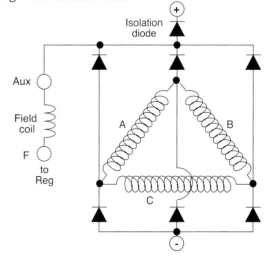

Powering the Voltage Regulator

Battery Isolation Diodes

Do not confuse the diode trio or the alternator isolation diode with *battery isolation diodes*. The first two are internal parts of the alternator and will not be seen unless the case is opened. If a boat has battery isolation diodes (Figure 4.22) they will appear as large diodes mounted on a finned heat sink. Their purpose, if present, is to prevent paralleled batteries from discharging each other. Not all marine systems have battery isolation diodes.

Exciting the Alternator

Did you spot a problem with the circuits of Figures 4.20 and 4.21? If we actually wired an alternator and regulator as shown in either of the figures, the alternator would never come on. An alternator will not generate an output current without an input field current, but there will be no field current until there is an alternator output! To solve this chicken-or-egg dilemma, alternators that derive their field currents from internal-diode trios or isolation diodes require a temporary source of field current called the excite current.

Figure 4.23 shows a typical excite circuit added to the alternator of Figure 4.21. Its operation will be familiar to anyone who owns an automobile.

When the ignition switch is turned on, current flows from the battery, through the lamp and paralleled resistor, to the alternator auxiliary terminal, and then through the field coil. As soon as the engine starts, however, the alternator begins generating current, which then makes the voltage at the auxiliary terminal 0.5 to 1.0 volt higher than the battery voltage. With only 0.5 to 1.0 volt across its terminals, the 12-volt charge-indicator lamp goes out. If it stays on or comes on again, you know that the alternator in not producing current. A resistor is placed in parallel with the lamp in order to provide excite current in case the lamp filament burns out.

An alternate and common solution is to feed the charge indicator lamp from the engine oil-pressure switch rather than the ignition switch, so that the alternator is excited as soon as oil pressure climbs. An advantage of this system is keeping the load on the engine low until it is up to speed.

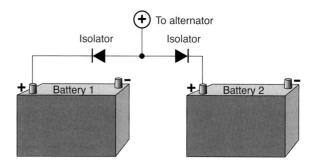

Fig. 4.22 Battery Isolation Diodes

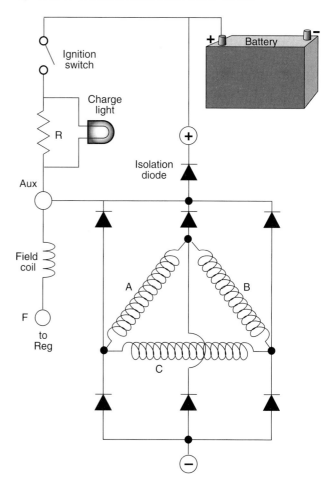

Fig. 4.23 A Common Alternator Excite Circuit

Alternators with fixed-voltage regulation are not ideal for boats. Without modification, they are simply current-limited, fixed-voltage chargers set at compromise voltages between 13.8 and 14.2 volts. As we saw in Chapter 3, 13.8 to 14.2 volts is higher than the recommended float voltage and lower than the recommended fast-charge absorption voltage. An alternator controlled by a standard regulator will never fully charge a battery in typical operation, yet will overcharge if run for days on end.

Cruising boats, particularly sailboats, impose large loads on their batteries but run their engines only a few hours per day. Worse, when a boat is at anchor the engine is usually run for the sole purpose of charging the batteries. We need a way to control the alternator output for optimally fast charging (Figure 4.24).

Figure 4.25 shows regulator bypasses installed across both type-P and type-N voltage regulators. Note that the original voltage regulators remain in place. The bypass regulators simply control field current in order to control alternator output. After the regulator bypass has accomplished its task and is switched off, the original voltage regulator resumes control.

Some regulator bypasses are manual, requiring diligent monitoring of battery-charge current and voltage. The simplest automatic bypasses come on when the engine is started, provide a constant-current bulk charge, then switch off when the battery reaches a preset voltage. More sophisticated regulator bypasses (see next page) automatically cycle through bulk, absorption, and float stages every time the engine is started. An equalization charge can also be selected when desired.

Before discussing the most sophisticated regulators (charge controllers), Figure 4.26 shows a simple manual-control regulator bypass you can build yourself. Note that the bypass circuit is the same whether used with a type-P or type-N alternator. The on/off switch allows the bypass to be switched into or out of the circuit. The 2-ohm, 25-watt fixed resistor limits the maximum field current. The 20-ohm, 100-watt rheostat (variable power resistor) allows the field current to be varied over a wide range.

Warning! Manual regulator bypasses should never be used without diligent monitoring of both battery charging current and voltage. It is easy to destroy a $300 battery with a $30 homemade regulator bypass. If you do not have the discipline to continuously monitor the charging process, you should either forgo the fast-charge option or invest in one of the sophisticated automatic models.

Fig. 4.24 Example of Optimally Fast Charging

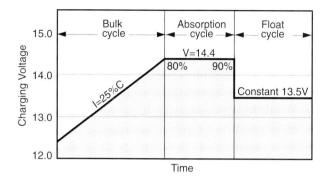

Fig. 4.25 Regulator Bypass Hookups

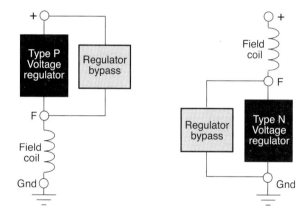

Fig. 4.26 A Manual Regulator Bypass

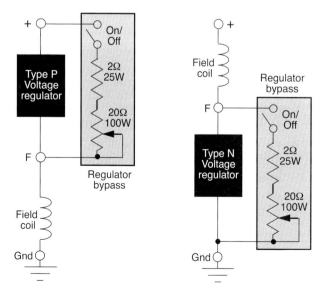

Link 2000-R Charge Controller

The Xantrex Link 2000-R Charge Controller (Figure 4.27) is an example of a dedicated computer that monitors and controls both an inverter/charger (any of the Xantrex Freedom series) and an alternator. Parameters monitored include:
- battery voltage
- amps being drawn
- amp-hours withdrawn
- amp-hours remaining
- time remaining to discharge
- number of battery charges

When either inverter or engine is turned on, the 2000-R initiates the four-cycle optimum charge routine: charge, acceptance, float, and equalize (Figure 4.28).

Fig. 4.27 Link 2000-R Charge Controller Panel

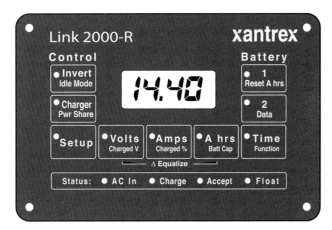

Either one or two battery banks may be monitored and controlled. Voltages for the four charge cycles are tailored both to the type of battery and to the real-time temperature of the battery (Table 4.1). Thus, the charging routine is truly ideal for any given battery type and conditions.

Fig. 4.28 Four-Cycle Charging for a Wet-Cell Battery at 70°F

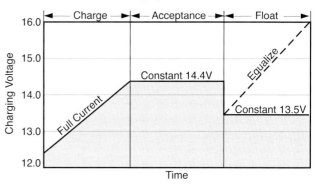

Charging Operation

The status of the four-step charging process is indicated by the horizontal row of LEDs at the bottom of the control panel (Figure 4.27 again).

Charge cycle (red LED ON). After a 2-second engine-start delay, the field current is ramped up over 20 seconds until the alternator reaches its full output. Charging at full current continues until either battery bank reaches the acceptance voltage.

Acceptance cycle (orange LED ON). Charging continues at the fixed acceptance voltage until charging current drops to 2% of the battery nominal capacity. At this point the regulator goes into an acceptance-hold status during which the acceptance voltage is maintained and the charging current is monitored. If voltage and current remain steady for 10 minutes, or if voltage holds steady but current rises during 20 minutes, the regulator goes into the float stage. If, however, battery voltage drops to below the acceptance voltage for 2 minutes, the entire charge cycle is restarted.

Float cycle (green LED ON). Battery voltage is maintained at the float voltage. The alternator supplies current up to its full output in order to supply current draw and maintain the float voltage. If battery voltage drops to below the float voltage for 2 minutes, the charge cycle is restarted.

Equalize cycle (red LED FLASHING). This is initiated manually by pressing a combination of buttons. Charge current is held at a constant 4% of capacity while voltage increases to 16.0 volts (or the acceptance voltage for gelled batteries). Equalization terminates in 3.5 hours or when charging current drops to 2% of capacity at 16.0 volts.

Table 4.1 Voltage Settings for the Link 2000-R

Temp. °F	Type 0 Wet-Cell Accept	Float	Type 1 Gel-Cell 1 Accept	Float	Type 2 Gel-Cell 2 Accept	Float	Type 3 AGM Accept	Float
120	12.5	12.5	13.0	13.0	13.0	13.0	12.9	12.9
110	13.6	12.7	13.5	13.0	14.0	13.4	13.9	12.9
100	13.8	12.9	13.7	13.2	14.1	13.5	14.0	13.0
90	14.0	13.1	13.8	13.3	14.2	13.6	14.1	13.1
80	14.2	13.3	14.0	13.5	14.3	13.7	14.2	13.2
70	14.4	13.5	14.1	13.6	14.4	13.8	14.3	13.3
60	14.6	13.7	14.3	13.8	14.5	13.9	14.4	13.4
50	14.8	13.9	14.4	13.9	14.6	14.0	14.5	13.5
40	15.0	14.1	14.6	14.1	14.7	14.1	14.6	13.6
30	15.2	14.3	14.7	14.2	14.8	14.2	14.7	13.7

No battery/alternator setup is ideal for every vessel. Cost is a big issue for most boaters, but pattern of use and degree of vulnerability when dead in the water are also considerations. Here are a variety of setups, from among dozens, demonstrating the possibilities and the issues involved. Note that bilge pumps (and any other device that must never be shut off) are wired and fused directly to a battery.

Figure 4.29 shows the most common configuration in small recreational boats. All electrical loads except the bilge pump are disconnected from the battery with the simple ON/OFF switch.

Regardless of setup, an important consideration is that the alternator-to-battery + connection must never be broken while the alternator is generating current. Otherwise the energy stored in the alternator's inductive coils would produce a large voltage spike, possibly destroying both the alternator rectifier diodes and any connected electronics. Three solutions are a voltage snubber from alternator output to ground, a warning sign on the switch, and, in the case of a four-pole switch, a built-in field disconnect.

Figure 4.30 shows a common configuration in small cruising boats. Here two batteries are charged from the same alternator. Depending on the position of the four-pole switch, the charge can be directed to either battery or both batteries at the same time. Similarly, the discharge can be from either or both.

The batteries may be of unequal size—a small start battery and a large house battery—but they must be of the same type. If one were a gel and the other a wet-acid, for example, either the gel would be overcharged and destroyed, or the wet-acid would be undercharged with the same long-term result.

Figure 4.31 shows a setup where the alternator is permanently connected to the house battery, so there is no danger of damage from interrupting the alternator output. As shown the starting battery can be charged in parallel with the house battery with the switch in the "Both" position.

If, instead, the alternator were wired directly to the "Common" terminal of the switch, the setup would be the same as in Figure 4.30, with the attendant danger of interrupting the alternator output.

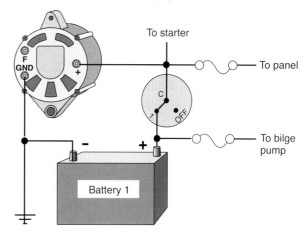

Fig. 4.29 Simplest One-Battery System

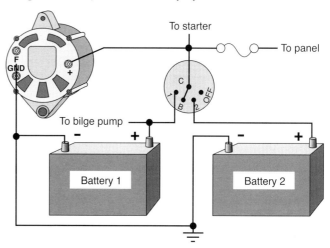

Fig. 4.30 Simplest Two-Battery System

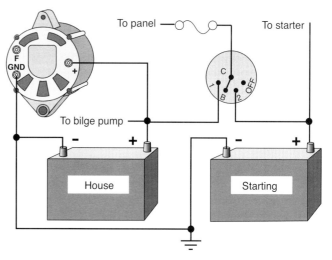

Fig. 4.31 Two Batteries with Alternator Protected

Charging Setups

Figure 4.32 shows a pair of isolation diodes. The diodes make it possible to leave both batteries connected directly to the alternator output without the danger of one battery draining the other. Because the diodes look like closed circuits in the forward direction, they also solve the open-alternator problem.

The big problem with isolation diodes is that they drop the voltage from alternator to battery by 0.6 to 1.0 volt, requiring the voltage regulator to be adjusted upward by the same amount to compensate.

Most boaters are not aware of the voltage drop, so their batteries are chronically, severely undercharged and suffer early demise.

Figure 4.33 shows a setup incorporating a series regulator. When house and starting batteries are of different size or type, one of the batteries will end up overcharged while the other is undercharged, shortening the lives of both.

A series regulator, such as Ample Power's Eliminator, is designed to solve this problem. The alternator's regulator is set up for the optimum charging of the house battery. At the same time the series regulator, set up for the characteristics of the starting battery, siphons some of the charging current to charge it.

The parallel switch can be used either to bypass the series regulator or to combine the battery outputs.

Figure 4.34 shows one way to charge two batteries from two alternators. This is useful both when the batteries are of different size and/or different type and when the batteries are larger than can be charged quickly from a single alternator. It also provides redundancy in case one of the alternators fails.

Commonly the starting battery is charged by the engine's original alternator, and a high-output alternator with multistep regulator is added to charge the much larger house bank.

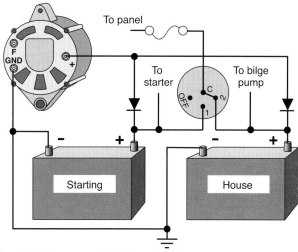

Fig. 4.32 Batteries Isolated with Diodes

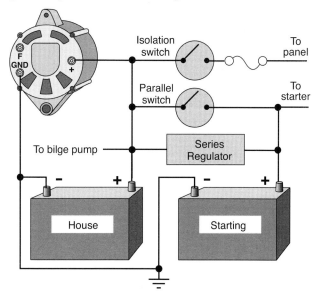

Fig. 4.33 System with Series Regulator

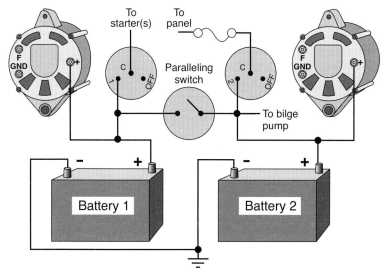

Fig. 4.34 Two Batteries and Two Alternators

Alternator Installation

When changing alternators there are four critical physical considerations: (1) mounting configuration, (2) pulley alignment, (3) belt size, and (4) belt tension.

Figure 4.35 illustrates four Balmar mounting configurations designed to be compatible with most marine engines. Most often a combination of washers, spacers, and bushings can compensate for an imperfect fit.

Figure 4.36 shows how to bring the alternator pulley into alignment with the engine drive pulley. Hold a straightedge against the faces of the two pulleys, and shim the alternator foot (or feet) with washers until the faces are in the same plane. Alternators of up to 80 amps output can use 9–10mm/⅜ inch belts (width of outside belt face), up to 110 amps 12mm/½ inch belts, and over 110 amps dual belts.

Proper belt tension can be determined in two ways:

1. Turn the alternator pulley retaining nut with a wrench. If the belt slips it is too loose.
2. Press on the belt with moderate force (Figure 4.37). Deflection should be between 6–8mm /¼–⁵⁄₁₆ inch.

Fig. 4.36 Aligning Engine and Alternator Pulleys

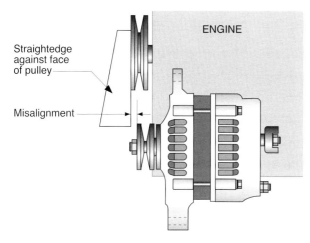

Fig. 4.37 Testing Belt Tension

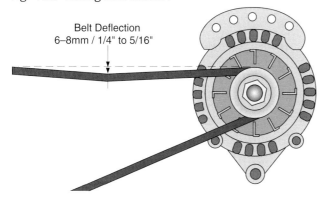

Fig. 4.35 Mounting Configurations (Balmar)
(All dimensions imperial)

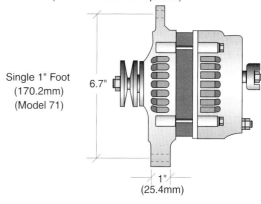

Single 1" Foot (170.2mm) (Model 71) — 6.7" — 1" (25.4mm)

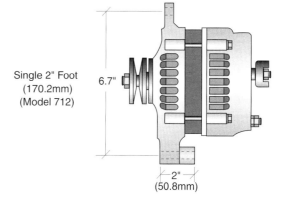

Single 2" Foot (170.2mm) (Model 712) — 6.7" — 2" (50.8mm)

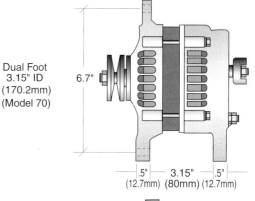

Dual Foot 3.15" ID (170.2mm) (Model 70) — 6.7" — .5" (12.7mm) 3.15" (80mm) .5" (12.7mm)

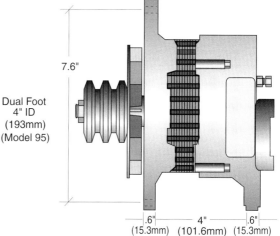

Dual Foot 4" ID (193mm) (Model 95) — 7.6" — .6" (15.3mm) 4" (101.6mm) .6" (15.3mm)

Troubleshooting

When an engine fails to turn over or batteries go flat, the fault may be in the batteries, the alternator, an external voltage regular, or the wiring. Troubleshooting the charging/starting system is made easier if you understand how each of the components work, so read Chapters 3 and 4 before using the charts and procedures that follow.

Troubleshooting 1: Engine Won't Turn Over

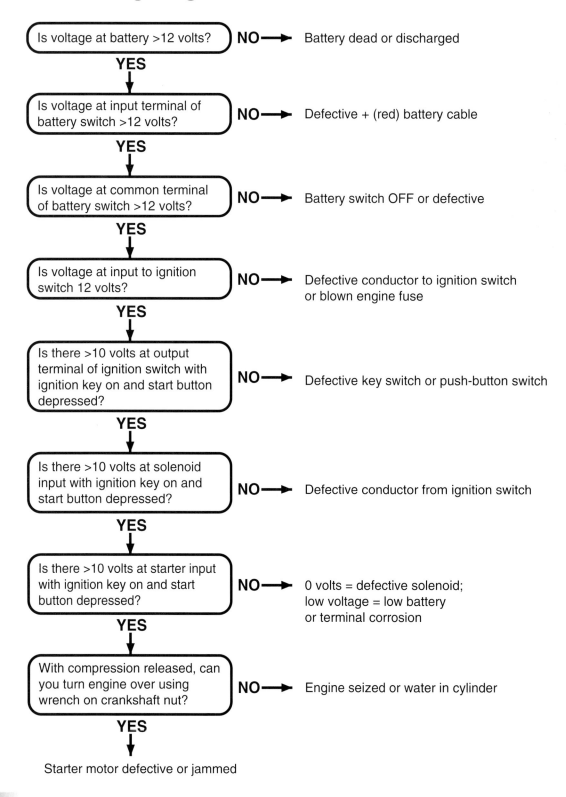

Is voltage at battery >12 volts? — **NO** → Battery dead or discharged

YES

Is voltage at input terminal of battery switch >12 volts? — **NO** → Defective + (red) battery cable

YES

Is voltage at common terminal of battery switch >12 volts? — **NO** → Battery switch OFF or defective

YES

Is voltage at input to ignition switch 12 volts? — **NO** → Defective conductor to ignition switch or blown engine fuse

YES

Is there >10 volts at output terminal of ignition switch with ignition key on and start button depressed? — **NO** → Defective key switch or push-button switch

YES

Is there >10 volts at solenoid input with ignition key on and start button depressed? — **NO** → Defective conductor from ignition switch

YES

Is there >10 volts at starter input with ignition key on and start button depressed? — **NO** → 0 volts = defective solenoid; low voltage = low battery or terminal corrosion

YES

With compression released, can you turn engine over using wrench on crankshaft nut? — **NO** → Engine seized or water in cylinder

YES

Starter motor defective or jammed

Troubleshooting 2: Batteries Not Charging Fully

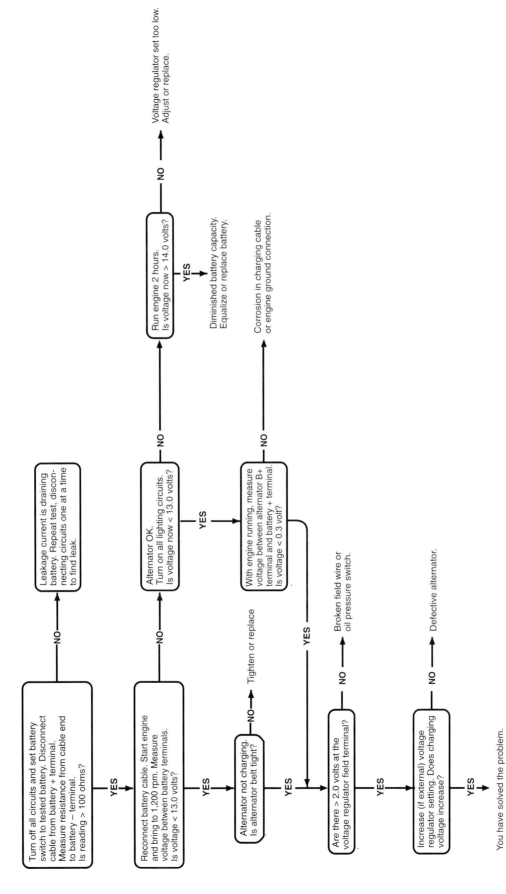

Turn off all circuits and set battery switch to tested battery. Disconnect cable from battery + terminal. Measure resistance from cable end to battery – terminal. Is reading > 100 ohms?

NO → Leakage current is draining battery. Repeat test, disconnecting circuits one at a time to find leak.

YES ↓

Reconnect battery cable. Start engine and bring to 1,200 rpm. Measure voltage between battery terminals. Is voltage < 13.0 volts?

NO → Alternator OK. Turn on all lighting circuits. Is voltage now < 13.0 volts?

NO → Run engine 2 hours. Is voltage now > 14.0 volts?

YES → Diminished battery capacity. Equalize or replace battery.

NO → Voltage regulator set too low. Adjust or replace.

YES ↓

Alternator not charging. Is alternator belt tight?

NO → Tighten or replace

YES ↓

With engine running, measure voltage between alternator B+ terminal and battery + terminal. Is voltage < 0.3 volt?

NO → Corrosion in charging cable or engine ground connection.

YES ↓

Are there > 2.0 volts at the voltage regulator field terminal?

NO → Broken field wire or oil pressure switch.

YES ↓

Increase (if external) voltage regulator setting. Does charging voltage increase?

NO → Defective alternator.

YES ↓

You have solved the problem.

Troubleshooting 3: The Alternator

Variations in appearance, arrangement of terminals, and internal connections number in the hundreds. It is beyond the scope of this book to detail the differences, but an alternator is an alternator, and, whatever its name, it works on the principles above.

There are two basic approaches to alternator repair. The first is to carry replacements for the components most likely to fail in the field: charge diodes, diode trio, isolation diode, brushes, bearings, and voltage regulator. The second is to carry an exact replacement for the entire alternator, including the voltage regulator if external. I favor the second approach for the following reasons:

1. There will be no spare part you might have overlooked. For example, what if the problem were a broken mounting flange?
2. You don't have to carry special tools such as a bearing puller, press, or heavy-duty soldering iron.
3. Replacement takes minutes; repair takes hours.
4. The cost of the whole alternator (with trade-in) is probably no greater than the cost of a complete set of spare components.

The following troubleshooting guide should help you to discover whether the problem is with the wiring, the alternator, or the regulator.

Check the Wiring from an Alternator to a Battery with Battery Isolation Diodes

STEP 1.

Turn the engine off and the battery-select switch off. The multimeter should read:
- Battery + to Ground, 12 V or more
- Alternator + to Ground, 0 V

If Alternator + to Ground reads 12 V, suspect a shorted isolation diode.

STEP 2.

Turn the engine on with the battery-select switch on. The multimeter should read:
- Alternator + to Battery +, 0.5 to 1.0 V
- Battery + to Ground, about 1 V higher than with the engine off

If not, suspect the isolation diode feeding the battery.

STEP 3.

To check a battery isolation diode definitively, disconnect it from the batteries and read resistance across the diode, reversing leads.
- An open-circuit diode reads $\infty\ \Omega$ both directions
- A shorted diode reads near $0\ \Omega$ both directions
- A healthy diode reads near $\infty\ \Omega$ in one direction and $0\ \Omega$ in the other direction

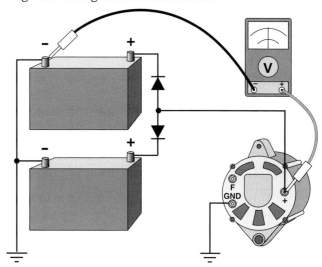

Fig. 4.38 Wiring with Isolation Diodes

Check the Wiring from an Alternator to a Battery with No Battery Isolation Diodes

STEP 1.

Turn the engine off and the battery-select switch on. The multimeter should read:
- Alternator + to Battery +, 0 V
- Alternator – to Battery –, 0 V

On the resistance scale the multimeter should read:
- Alternator + to Battery +, 0 Ω
- Alternator – to Battery –, 0 Ω

If not, suspect corrosion or a broken wire.

STEP 2.

Turn the engine on and the battery-select switch on. The multimeter should read:
- Alternator + to Battery +, < 0.5 V
- Alternator – to Battery –, < 0.5 V

If not, suspect corrosion or a broken wire.

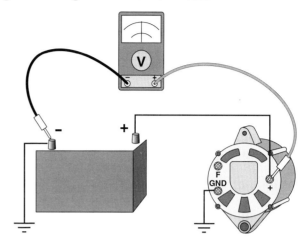

Fig. 4.39 Wiring with No Isolation Diodes

Check Alternator and Battery Voltage with No Battery Isolation Diodes

STEP 1.

Turn the engine off and turn the battery-select switch to the battery being tested (repeat tests for other batteries). On the voltage scale the multimeter should read:
- Battery + to Ground, 12 to 13 V. If not, the battery may be bad.
- Alternator + to Ground, 12 to 13 V. If not, Alternator + to Battery + cable is bad.

STEP 2.

Turn the engine on and turn the battery-select switch to the battery being tested (repeat tests for other batteries). On the voltage scale the multimeter should read:
- Battery + to Ground, about 1 V higher than with the engine off.
- Alternator + to Ground, at least 1 V higher than with the engine off. If not, the alternator is not charging.

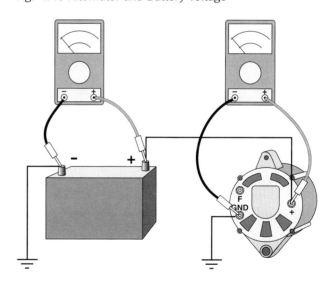

Fig. 4.40 Alternator and Battery Voltage

Troubleshooting

Check Alternator and Battery Voltage with Battery Isolation Diodes

STEP 1.

Turn the engine off and turn the battery-select switch to the battery being tested (repeat tests for other batteries). On the voltage scale the multimeter should read:
- Battery + to Ground, 12 to 13 V. If not, the battery may be bad.
- Alternator + to Ground, 0 V. If not, suspect a shorted isolation diode.

STEP 2.

Turn the engine on and turn the battery-select switch to the battery being tested (repeat tests for other batteries). On the voltage scale the multimeter should read:
- Battery + to Ground should be about 1 V higher than with the engine off. If not, the alternator is not charging.
- Alternator + to Ground should be 0.5 to 1.0 V higher than Battery + to Ground. If not, suspect a shorted isolation diode.

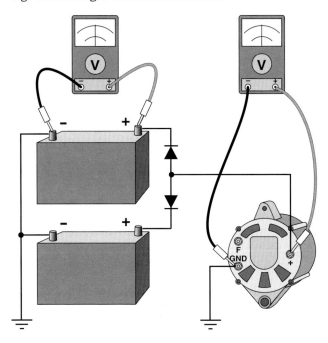

Fig. 4.41 Voltages with Isolation Diodes

Check a Type-N Alternator with No Output

STEP 1.

Turn the engine off, measure the voltage from Battery + to Ground, and note its value.

STEP 2.

Remove the wire from Alternator Terminal F.

STEP 3.

Connect a test light (minimum 12 W, such as an anchor light) from Terminal F to Ground.

STEP 4.

Start the engine and measure the voltage from Battery + to Ground again. If the voltage is about 1 V higher than it was when the engine was off, then the alternator is OK, but its regulator is bad.

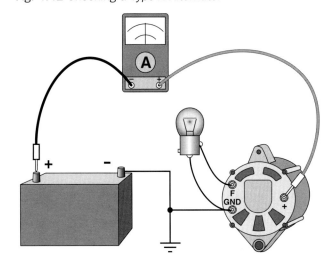

Fig. 4.42 Checking a Type-N Alternator

Check a Type-P Alternator with No Output

STEP 1.

Turn the engine off, measure the voltage from Battery + to Ground, and note its value.

STEP 2.

Remove the wire from Alternator Terminal F.

STEP 3.

Connect a test light (minimum 12 W, such as an anchor light) from Terminal F to Battery +.

STEP 4.

Start the engine and measure the voltage from Battery + to Ground again. If the voltage is about 1 V higher than with the engine off, then the alternator is OK, but its regulator is bad (see next test).

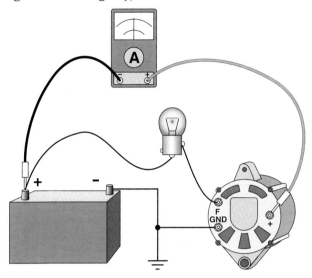

Fig. 4.43 Checking a Type-P Alternator

Check the Excite Circuit for a Type-P Alternator Regulator

If the type-P regulator tested bad above, the problem may lie not in the regulator but in its excite circuit. To test the excite circuit:

STEP 1.

Start the engine.

STEP 2.

Measure the voltage from Battery + to Ground.

STEP 3.

Momentarily connect the test light between Battery + and Alternator Terminal F. If the voltage from Battery + to Ground is now about 1 V higher than with the engine off, the alternator and regulator are OK, but the excite circuit is bad.

You can either repair the excite circuit, or you can create an excite circuit temporarily by placing a 12 W lamp between the engine oil-pressure switch and Alternator Terminal F.

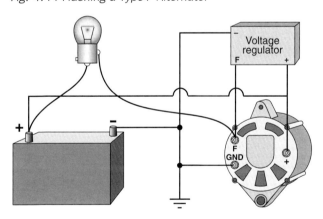

Fig. 4.44 Flashing a Type-P Alternator

CHAPTER 5

Bonding

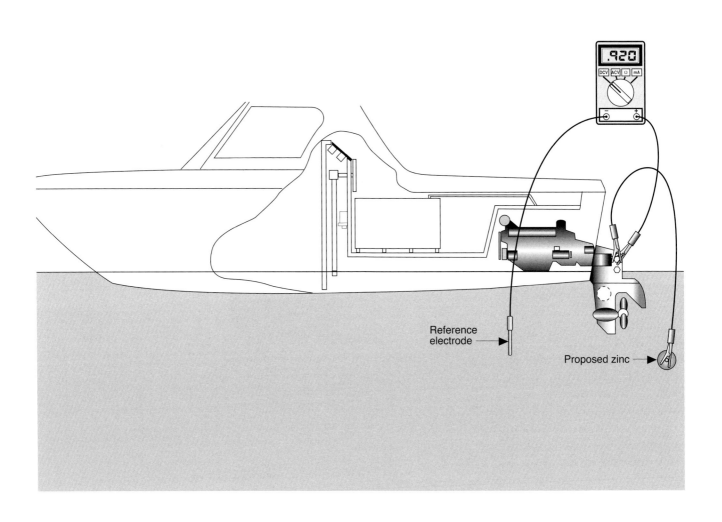

Reference
electrode →

Proposed zinc →

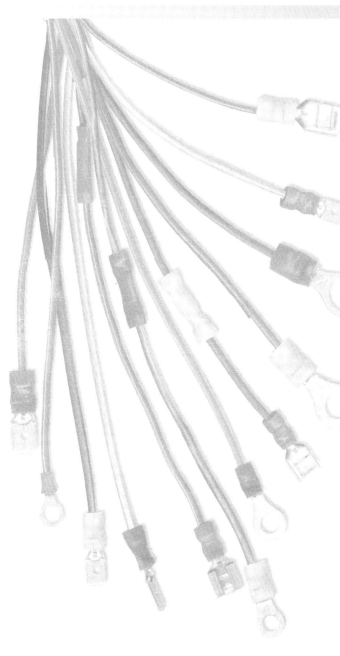

Bonding is a somewhat controversial, and often poorly understood, wiring practice. As usual, we start by answering a basic question—what is bonding?

The purposes of bonding are threefold: (1) electrical system grounding, (2) lightning protection, and (3) corrosion protection.

The bonding controversy stems from the possibility of its encouraging stray-current corrosion. So—to bond, or not to bond—that is the question we address in detail.

Fortunately, there are simple methods for testing your protection against corrosion. These, and the ABYC and BMEA/ISO standards for the general application of cathodic protection, should protect your boat's underwater metals.

Though neither caused nor prevented by bonding, other types of corrosion are explained as well.

What Is Bonding?

No marine wiring topic causes more confusion than bonding. That is because there are at least three separate and compelling reasons for electrically connecting, or bonding, metal objects aboard a boat:

1. Electrical system grounding
2. Lightning protection
3. Corrosion protection

At the same time, there are reasons for *not* bonding certain items. As they occur, these exceptions will be discussed. Note that the grounding of AC systems is covered separately in Chapter 9, AC Standards and Practices. You will find there, however, that AC grounding is related to DC grounding in a simple way.

Grounded, Grounding, Bonding

Ideally, *ground* is the voltage of the water in which the boat is immersed. Unfortunately, voltage in the water may vary slightly due to stray electrical currents. As we will see, one of the purposes of the bonding system is to force the voltage of and within the hull to be as uniform as possible through the use of low-resistance conductors and connections.

As defined by the ABYC and shown in Figure 5.1:

• *Grounded conductors* are the current-carrying conductors that connect to the side of the source (almost universally the battery negative terminal), which is intentionally maintained at ground potential.
• *Grounding conductors* are normally non-current-carrying conductors, provided to connect the exposed metal enclosures of electric equipment to ground, the primary function of which is to minimize shock hazard to personnel.
• *Bonding conductors* are normally non-current-carrying conductors used to connect the non-current-carrying metal parts of a boat and the non-current-carrying parts of direct-current devices on the boat to the boat's bonding system.

All DC electrical devices receive their power through a pair of positive and negative input terminals, served by a pair of conductors. Current flows into the positive terminal from a positive conductor (wire) from the DC distribution panel and, ultimately, from the positive (+12 V) terminal of the battery. Ideally, the same amount of current returns to the battery negative terminal through the grounded conductor. All

grounded conductors are held to the same voltage (ground, or zero volts) by being connected to the DC negative bus and, ultimately, to the battery negative terminal.

So that people are not accidently exposed to live voltage from a piece of equipment shorted to a live wire, the metal enclosures of all electrical equipment are connected to ground by grounding conductors. These conductors are in addition to the grounded conductors and carry current only in the case of an electrical fault.

Bonding conductors are also separate from, and in addition to, the grounded conductors. As elaborated later in this chapter, they play important roles in both lightning and corrosion protection. They should take as short and direct routes as possible to the substantial common-bonding conductor, which usually runs near the fore-and-aft centerline of the boat. Each bonding conductor should be at least as large as the current-carrying positive and negative conductors that serve the equipment.

The engine-bonding conductor should be at least as large as the largest bonding conductor in the rest of the bonding system and large enough to carry starting current. Twin engines with crossover starting systems should be bonded to each other, as well, with a conductor large enough to carry the starting current.

The large common-bonding conductor should be green or yellow/green. If wire, it may consist of bare, stranded, tinned, copper or insulated stranded wire of minimum size 8mm²/8AWG. If solid, it may be uninsulated copper, bronze strip, or copper pipe at least 0.75mm/0.030 inch thick and 12mm/0.5 inch wide. The copper, bronze strip, or pipe may be drilled and tapped, provided it is thick enough to provide at least three full threads for terminal screws, or it may be unthreaded for machine screws and locknuts.

Equipment to be bonded includes: engines and transmissions, propellers and shafts, metal cases of motors, generators and pumps, metal cabinets and control boxes, electronics cabinets, metal fuel and water tanks, fuel-fill fittings, electrical fuel pumps and valves, metal battery boxes, metal conduit or armoring, and large nonelectrical metal objects as recommended in the Lightning Protection section.

Note that you may choose not to bond electrically isolated through-hull fittings, as will be discussed further in the Corrosion Protection section.

Fig. 5.1 Typical DC Negative System and DC Grounding System (Adapted from ABYC Standard E-11, Figure 18)

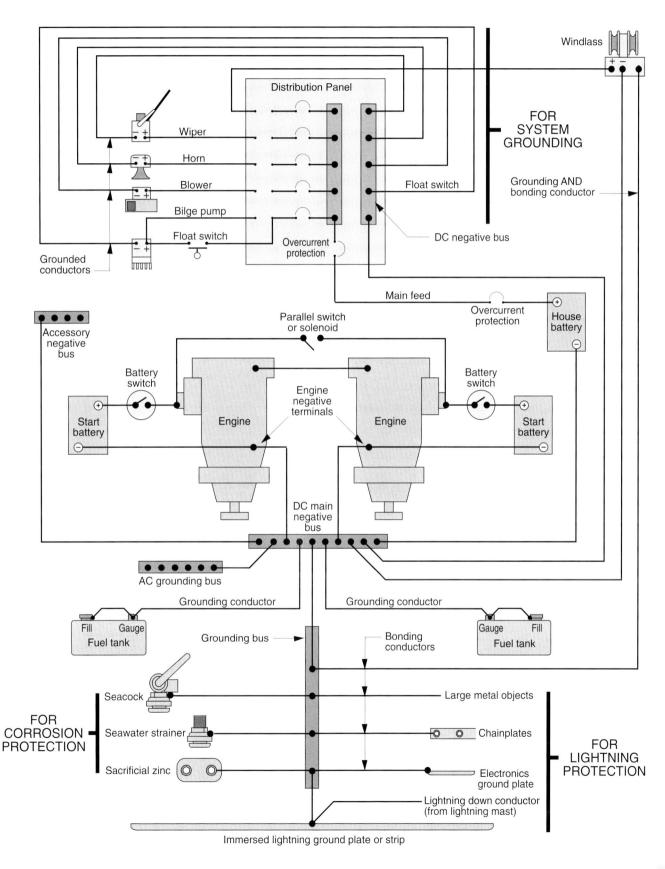

Lightning Protection

At any moment, there are approximately 2,000 lightning storms in progress around the earth, producing 100 strikes every second. In some regions lightning is a rarity. In others it is an almost daily occurrence.

To put the danger in perspective, there are approximately 24,000 lightning deaths per year in the world, 100 in the United States. From 1959 to 2003, recorded deaths in the United States included:

- Florida   425
- Texas   195
- North Carolina   181
- Ohio   136
- New York   134
- Tennessee   133

Where the deaths occurred:

- In or around the home   20%
- In vehicles (mostly open) 19%
- Taking refuge under trees 15%
- In boats   13%
- Everywhere else   33%

Considering the significant percentage of deaths occurring in boats and the low number of people in boats at any given time, it is apparent that the potential for lightning strikes on boats is a serious matter. In fact, the ABYC devotes all of Standard E-4 to the matter of lightning protection, as does BMEA Section 11 and ISO 10134:1993.

What Is Lightning and How Does It Act?

In all lightning theories, a combination of vertically moving water droplets and air currents results in the buildup of large quantities of oppositely charged particles within clouds and between clouds and the ground (Figure 5.2). The electrical potential differences between charges may be as high as 100,000,000 volts. By comparison, the voltage on the power lines running along a street is a mere 12,000 volts.

In particular, the base of a cloud becomes negatively charged. Since opposite charges attract, the surface of the earth directly beneath the cloud becomes positively charged. People standing in this positively charged area under a cloud may feel their hair standing on end due to the static charge just before a lightning strike. What initially prevents the charges from combining is the extreme electrical resistance of air. Some scientists believe that lightning strikes are triggered by cosmic rays knocking electrons from air molecules. The freed electrons accelerate in the voltage field, causing the release of more electrons and ionizing the air.

Fig. 5.2 Discharge of Cloud Charge

Ionization proceeds in steps of about 100 feet. Electrons flow downward through the ionized path and cause a faint blue-white glow, similar to the flow of electrons in the ionized gas of a neon sign. Each step requires only about 0.00005 second to ionize and fill, so that the stepped leader traverses a distance of 10,000 feet, from the base of a cloud to ground, in about 0.005 second.

The final step to ground is of most interest to a boater. Up to the last step, the presence of a boat has no influence on either the location or the direction of the discharge. When looking for that final connection to earth, however, the lightning will head for the closest accumulation of positive charge. That generally means the highest point within a radius of 100 feet. If that point is you, chances are you will be struck. If it is the tip of your mast, your mast will be struck.

After the ionization of the column has been completed by the leader, there exists a short circuit from cloud to earth. The resulting rush of accumulated charge from cloud to earth is what we see as the lightning bolt—an ionized column of air, heated to 50,000°F, conducting a typical current of 50,000 amps. The resulting rapid heating of the air produces a supersonic air-pressure wave heard as thunder. The entire 0.005-second process may be repeated several or even dozens of times during the following second, depending on the initial size of the accumulated charge.

Direct strikes are the most dangerous. Consider that the largest circuit breaker or fuse on your boat is probably rated at less than 100 amps, and that the cranking current to your starter motor is probably on the order of 200 amps. Now consider what 50,000 to 200,000 amps might do to that same wiring. Although the peak current lasts only 0.0001 second, the resistive heating is often sufficient to burn insulation, melt components, even vaporize conductors.

Much lightning damage occurs from near-hits, however. It is not uncommon for one boat to suffer a direct strike and for boats in adjacent berths to lose electronic equipment. Just as a current-carrying wire produces a magnetic field, and a varying magnetic field produces current in a conductor (the principle behind the alternator), lightning currents produce extreme magnetic fields, which then induce currents in nearby wires. These induced currents are often sufficient to destroy sensitive electronic circuits.

Just any copper conductor will not suffice to conduct currents of 50,000 amps. The conductor must be large and conductive enough to present the path of least resistance to ground (the surrounding water, in the case of a boat). Small-diameter wire, corroded connections, and too small a ground plate (area of metal in contact with the water) may cause the lightning to seek additional paths to ground, resulting in dangerous side flashes. The recommendations in the published standards are intended to minimize both danger and damage from lightning.

Zones of Protection

Metal masts tend to draw the final step of a leader to themselves within a radius equal to their height. The conical zone beneath the tip is known as the zone of protection. A person or object entirely within this zone is substantially protected from a direct strike.

Figure 5.3 shows zones of protection for a powerboat with a lightning-protective mast and with the mast extended by a grounded air terminal. Powerboat hulls do not generally fall entirely within their zones of protection unless either their masts are extended by grounded antennas or outriggers, or they have more than one grounded mast.

Figure 5.4 shows the zone of protection for a sailboat mast less than 50 feet. A sailboat hull will usually lie entirely within the zone of protection. To qualify as a lightning-protective mast, the mast must either be metal or be equipped with an air terminal and metal conductor to ground (see Figure 5.6).

Figure 5.5 shows the zone of protection for a boat with a lightning-protective mast more than 50 feet. With more than one mast, zones are drawn for each mast. The combined protective zone includes all areas under one or more of the individual zones. To qualify as lightning protective, each mast must be grounded. Multihulls require grounding plates in each hull.

Fig. 5.3 Lightning-Protective Zone for Motorboat with Lightning-Protective Mast or Mast with Approved Extension

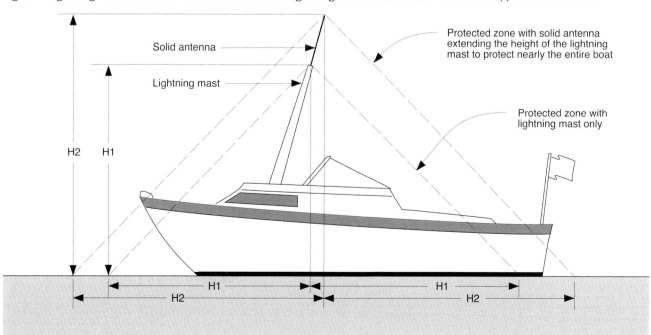

Fig. 5.4 Lightning-Protective Zone for Sailboat Mast Less Than 50 Feet

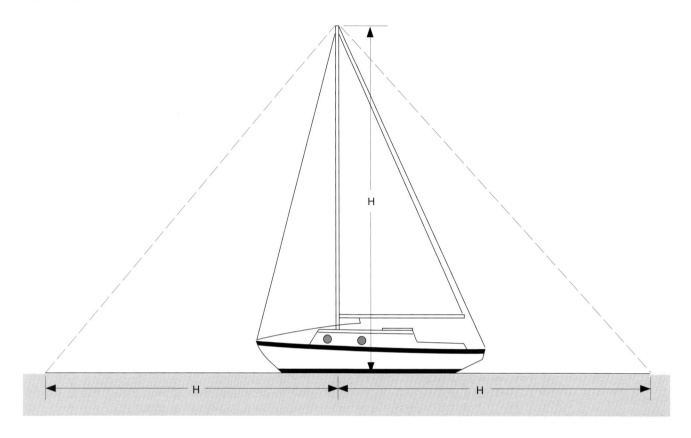

Fig. 5.5 Lightning-Protective Zone for Sailboat Mast Over 50 Feet or More Than One Mast

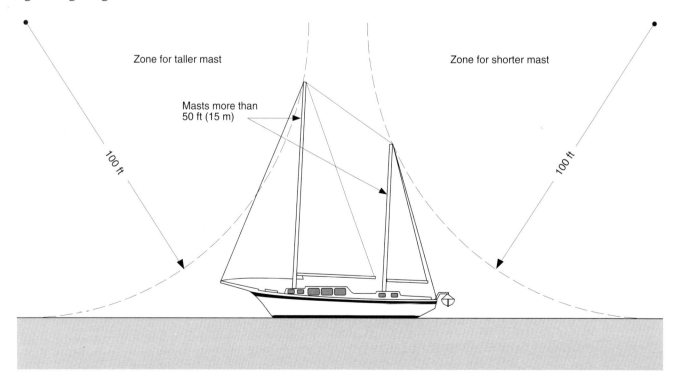

The Safe Path to Ground

Regardless of any lightning rod or charge dissipator, if your mast is the highest object in the vicinity it will be struck. The purpose of the safe path to ground is to provide a path to ground (the water) as *short, straight, and conductive as possible* to prevent side flashes to alternate routes. The path consists of two parts: the *lightning-protective mast* and the *lightning-ground connection*.

Lightning-Protective Mast

Metal masts qualify as protective masts. If nonconductive, however, a mast must be provided with a grounding conductor running from an air terminal 6 inches above the mast in as straight a line as possible to the lightning-ground connection. The conductor must be securely fastened to the mast and consist of either a stranded-copper wire of minimum size 4 AWG or a metal strip of conductivity equal to that of 4 AWG copper wire and thickness of at least 0.030 inch.

Joints, including that to the lightning-ground connection, must not be subject to immersion. In the case of 4 AWG wire, the connection must be strong enough to support a 45-pound weight for 1 minute. To avoid corrosion, all bolts, nuts, washers, and lugs must be galvanically compatible with the conductor.

A stainless steel radio antenna may serve as an air terminal provided it has either a means for direct connection to ground, or a lightning-protective gap (closely spaced electrodes, which lightning will easily jump). If not disconnected when the antenna is grounded, the antenna feed line should also have either a lightning arrestor, or transient voltage surge suppressor.

Lightning-Ground Connection

A lightning-ground connection may be any underwater metal surface of at least 1-square-foot area. Metal hulls, centerboards, and external (not encased in fiberglass) keels are excellent. Although metal rudders qualify in area, the connection from mast to rudder is too long.

Where the lightning-ground connection is an immersed ground plate at the base of the mast, the backstay and other large aft metal objects, because of the distance, should be grounded to the engine instead of the ground plate.

It is commonly believed that the large surface areas of the propeller and shaft provide adequate lightning grounding. While true, relying on the conductivity of

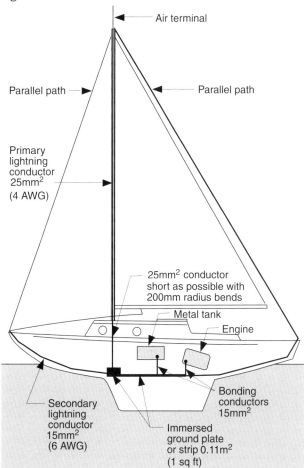

Fig. 5.6 The Safe Path to Ground

Air terminal

Parallel path

Parallel path

Primary lightning conductor 25mm^2 (4 AWG)

25mm^2 conductor short as possible with 200mm radius bends

Metal tank

Engine

Secondary lightning conductor 15mm^2 (6 AWG)

Bonding conductors 15mm^2

Immersed ground plate or strip 0.11m^2 (1 sq ft)

the engine, transmission, and shaft may lead to extremely large currents through main-engine- and transmission-output bearings, to their detriment. If the shaft and propeller are to be bonded, it should be through a brush riding on the shaft.

Sintered bronze plates, intended to serve as ground plates for SSB radios, are questionable as lightning grounds. Due to their porosity, these plates do have wetted areas greater than the areas of their envelopes, but evidence suggests that they are not significantly more effective than plain copper plate of the same area. In fact, it is theorized that edge length is more important than area in lightning ground plates. A 12 foot by 1 inch by ¼ inch copper strip would be six times more effective than a 1 foot by 1 foot square copper plate.

In order, the best lightning-ground connections are:

1. Metal hull
2. External metal keel (attach to keel bolts)
3. External 12 foot by 1 inch by ¼ inch copper strip
4. Large sintered bronze plate

Lightning Protection

Protecting Electronics

A well-protected boat may lose electronics. The problem is that today's solid-state electronics are very intolerant of voltage surges. It doesn't matter whether the surge comes from a direct lightning hit or from current induced in the antenna, microphone, or power leads by the magnetic field pulse of a nearby strike.

Two basic approaches to protecting electronics are: (1) shorting the surges, and (2) disconnecting all the leads.

Shorting the Surges

Figure 5.7 shows an antenna at the top of the mast. For a solid-wire antenna with base-loading coil to be an effective air terminal, there must be a lightning-bypass gap between the solid wire and the base of the antenna. If not, the inductive base coil resists the lightning current, and the lightning-protective mast originates at the base of the antenna. If the antenna is fiberglass with a less than 8 AWG conductor, its conductivity is insufficient, and the lightning protection again originates at the top of the mast.

A coaxial conductor from antenna to radio can pick up current, either as part of a direct strike, or induced by the magnetic field of a nearby strike. This surge is shorted to ground by a transient voltage surge suppressor (TVSS) several feet from the electronics enclosure.

Surges on the power supply line are shorted to ground by a metal oxide varistor (MOV), which typically acts in less than 1 microsecond. Both TVSS and MOV devices are available at ham- and marine-radio dealers.

There remain several problems with the approach:

1. Insertion of the TVSS in the antenna-feed line results in some loss of transmitted power.
2. By shorting the cable to ground, the TVSS makes it more likely that the coaxial line will be damaged by a strike.
3. By shorting the antenna feed to ground, the TVSS leads lightning current closer to the electronics than if the cable were disconnected.

Disconnecting Leads

TVSS and radio manufacturers agree the best way to protect electronics is to remove all leads, including the microphone. Switching a circuit breaker won't work because lightning will easily bridge the small breaker gap.

Fig. 5.7 Protecting Electronics from Lightning Surges

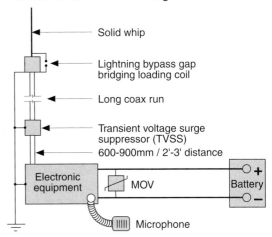

Alternative 1: Short the Surges

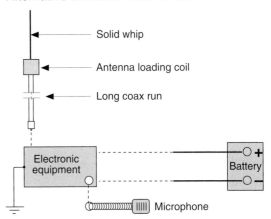

Alternative 2: Disconnect All Leads

If any of your electronics have aluminum cases, place them in a steel box, which will shield them from magnetic fields.

Protecting People

Assuming all of the protective measures above are in place, you can minimize the lightning danger to people aboard your boat by following these rules:

1. Keep everyone inside the boat.
2. Do not allow any part of anyone's body in the water.
3. Keep everyone at least 6 feet from the lightning-protective mast.
4. Don't allow anyone to touch any part of the spars, standing rigging, metal rails, or metal lifelines.
5. Don't allow anyone to touch any two grounded objects with two hands.

Every boatowner knows about corrosion. That is, they know it happens. Everywhere they look they see staining, pitting, powdering, and disintegration. Corrosion is so pervasive on a boat that it's easy to throw up your hands and accept it, like death, as inevitable. But corrosion is not inevitable. Corrosion can be prevented.

As with most problems, a solution comes only with understanding, and understanding requires an investment of mental energy. If you really, truly want to stop the corrosion on your boat, get a cup of coffee or tea, find a comfortable reading spot, and clear your mind.

What Is Corrosion?

In general terms, corrosion is the deterioration of a material by chemical or electrochemical reaction with its surroundings. As boatowners, we are most familiar with galvanic corrosion—the deterioration of the anode of a galvanic couple resulting from the flow of ions from the anode to the cathode through an electrolyte.

Relax! Those are just fancy words to describe a very common phenomenon—the chemical reaction that takes place inside a battery.

Figure 5.8 shows a carbon-zinc flashlight battery (the inexpensive type that comes with electrical toys). If we were to slice the battery in half, we would see a carbon rod in an electrically conductive paste, all inside a zinc-coated can. At A we measure the voltage between the carbon rod and the zinc can as 1.5 volts. At B,

switching the meter to amps and placing a 1.5-volt lamp in series with the meter + lead, we find that current is flowing from + terminal to − terminal as expected. Since electrons are negative, the electrons are actually flowing in the opposite direction, from − to +.

If we were to leave the lamp connected to the battery long enough, the battery voltage and current would eventually drop to zero. Upon examination, we would find that all of the zinc coating had disappeared (it had corroded). On the other hand, if we disconnected the lamp so that there was no electrical closed circuit between the carbon and the zinc, the zinc would not corrode, and the battery would retain its voltage for a very long time.

You have just witnessed galvanic corrosion in a galvanic cell. The common carbon-zinc battery is a convenient example, but it is just one example of a common phenomenon.

Another Home Experiment

Performing the experiment in Figure 5.9 will do wonders for your understanding of corrosion on your boat.

Gather a plastic container of fresh water, a tablespoon of salt, a multimeter, two test leads with alligator clips, and an assortment of metal items. I used a stainless bolt, a small piece of aluminum pie plate, and a shaft zinc.

Fig. 5.9 Measuring Galvanic Voltage and Current

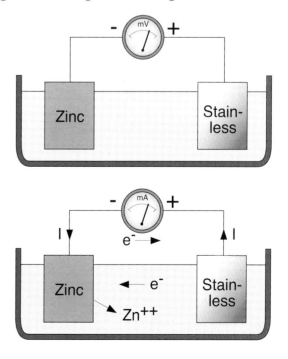

Fig. 5.8 The Battery—a Useful Form of Corrosion

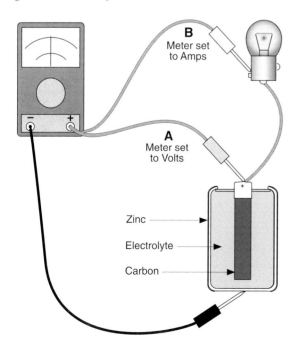

Corrosion Protection

Switch the multimeter to volts. Using the test leads, connect the negative (–) lead to the zinc and the positive (+) lead to the stainless bolt and lower both pieces into the water. Surprised? The meter will indicate a voltage.

Now switch the meter to milliamps. You may or may not read any current, but hold on. Dump the tablespoon of salt into the fresh water and stir. Depending on the sizes of the electrodes, you will now probably measure a current of about a milliamp flowing from the stainless bolt to the zinc.

What's going on? When two dissimilar metals are placed together in an electrolyte (electrically conductive medium), one of the metals will assume a higher potential than the other. In Chapter 1 we learned that current flows only in a closed circuit. Two electrodes, immersed in electrolyte, form an open circuit, and no current flows. But when we connect the two electrodes, either with a wire or by letting them touch, we complete the circuit and current flows.

In this case, the current flowing through the meter is from the stainless steel electrode into the zinc electrode. (Since electrons carry negative charge, the electron flow is actually in the opposite direction, but never mind.)

Figure 5.10 shows what is happening to the zinc on an atomic level. Zinc atoms are changing into positively charged zinc ions by giving up two electrons. These released electrons are flowing from the zinc to the stainless through the meter leads, and the newly formed zinc ions are departing the zinc electrode and migrating into the electrolyte—the zinc is corroding.

Continue the experiment if you wish by substituting other pairs of dissimilar metals. As long as the electrode metals are different in composition, they will always generate a potential difference, and current will always flow into the lower-voltage metal. The voltage difference will be the same, whether the water is salt or fresh. The currents, however, will be much greater in salt water due to its greater conductivity.

The potential difference between any two dissimilar metals can be predicted by consulting a table of galvanic potentials. The table lists the potential differences measured between the metal in question and a reference electrode, typically silver-silver chloride. Table 5.1 reproduces the values listed in Table I of ABYC Standard E-2 for metals and alloys in seawater flowing at 8 to 13 feet per second (4.7 to 7.7 knots), and at temperatures of 4°C to 26°C/50°F to 80°F.

Fig. 5.10 What Happens When Zinc Corrodes

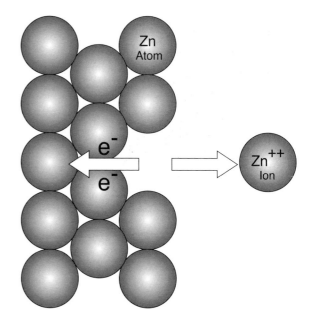

The values in the table are between a metal and a silver-silver chloride electrode. Values between any two metals are found as the differences between the table values for the two metals.

Example: What is the corrosion (galvanic) potential between silicon bronze and zinc? From Table 5.1 we find the corrosion potential of silicon bronze vs. the reference to be –0.26 to –0.29 volt (average –0.28 volt) and zinc vs. the reference to be –0.98 to –1.03 volt (average –1.00 volt). Thus the corrosion potential between silicon bronze and zinc is –0.72 volt.

By now you may be thoroughly alarmed at the thought of all the underwater metallic components on your boat—stainless bolts, stainless or bronze shaft, brass Cutless bearing shell, and aluminum outboard drive. And well you should be, with all that potential (no pun intended) for corrosion. But let's press on.

Before continuing our home experiment, let's review what we have learned. We have found that any two dissimilar metals or alloys immersed in water will generate a potential difference. We have also found that if the two metals are isolated (neither physically touching nor electrically connected by wire), no current or corrosion will occur. Good. But what if they cannot be separated (a bronze prop on a stainless shaft), or what if we have bonded them for lightning protection (a steel rudder, several bronze through-hulls, and a copper ground strip)? Have we shot ourselves in the foot?

Table 5.1 ABYC Standard E-2, Galvanic Series of Metals in Seawater Referenced to Silver-Silver Chloride Half Cell (Seawater flowing at 8 to 13 ft./sec. [4.7 to 7.7 kn.], temperature range 50°F to 80°F—except as noted)

Metals and Alloys (Anodic or Least Noble—Active)	Corrosion Potential, Volts		
Magnesium and Magnesium Alloys	−1.60	to	−1.63
Zinc	−0.98	to	−1.03
Aluminum Alloys	−0.76	to	−1.00
Cadmium	−0.70	to	−0.73
Mild Steel	−0.60	to	−0.71
Wrought Iron	−0.60	to	−0.71
Cast Iron	−0.60	to	−0.71
13% Chromium Stainless Steel, Type 410 (active in still water)	−0.46	to	−0.58
18-8 Stainless Steel, Type 304 (active in still water)	−0.46	to	−0.58
Ni-Resist	−0.46	to	−0.58
18-8, 3% Mo Stainless Steel, Type 316 (active in still water)	−0.43	to	−0.54
Inconel (78% Ni–13.5% Cr–6% Fe) (active in still water)	−0.35	to	−0.46
Aluminum Bronze (92% Cu–8% Al)	−0.31	to	−0.42
Nibral (81.2% Cu–4% Fe–4.5% Ni–9% Al–1.3% Mn)	−0.31	to	−0.42
Naval Brass (60% Cu–39% Zn)	−0.30	to	−0.40
Yellow Brass (65% Cu–35% Zn)	−0.30	to	−0.40
Red Brass (85% Cu–15% Zn)	−0.30	to	−0.40
Muntz Metal (60% Cu–40% Zn)	−0.30	to	−0.40
Tin	−0.31	to	−0.33
Copper	−0.30	to	−0.57
50-50 Lead–Tin Solder	−0.28	to	−0.37
Admiralty Brass (71% Cu–28% Zn–1% Sn)	−0.28	to	−0.36
Aluminum Brass (76% Cu–22% Zn–2% Al)	−0.28	to	−0.36
Manganese Bronze (58.5% Cu–39% Zn–1% Sn–1% Fe–0.3% Mn)	−0.27	to	−0.34
Silicon Bronze (96% Cu max–0.8% Fe–1.5% Zn–2% Si–0.75% Mn–1.6% Sn)	−0.26	to	−0.29
Bronze-Composition G (88% Cu–2% Zn–10% Sn)	−0.24	to	−0.31
Bronze ASTM B62 (thru-hull) (85% Cu–5% Pb–5% Sn–5% Zn)	−0.24	to	−0.31
Bronze-Composition M (88% Cu–3% Zn–6.5% Zn–1.5% Pb)	−0.24	to	−0.31
13% Chromium Stainless Steel, Type 410 (passive)	−0.26	to	−0.35
Copper Nickel (90% Cu–10% Ni)	−0.21	to	−0.28
Copper Nickel (75% Cu–20% Ni–5% Zn)	−0.19	to	−0.25
Lead	−0.19	to	−0.25
Copper Nickel (70% Cu–30% Ni)	−0.18	to	−0.23
Inconel (78% Ni–13.5% Cr–6% Fe) (passive)	−0.14	to	−0.17
Nickel 200	−0.10	to	−0.20
18-8 Stainless Steel, Type 304 (passive)	−0.05	to	−0.10
Monel 400, K-500 (70% Ni–30% Cu)	−0.04	to	−0.14
Stainless Steel Propeller Shaft (ASTM 630:#17 and ASTM 564:#19)	−0.03	to	+0.13
18-8, 3% Mo Stainless Steel, Type 316 (passive)	0.00	to	−0.10
Titanium	−0.05	to	+0.06
Hastelloy C	−0.03	to	+0.08
Stainless Steel Shafting (Bar) (UNS 20910)	−0.25	to	+0.06
Platinum	+0.19	to	+0.25
Graphite	+0.20	to	+0.30

(Cathodic or Most Noble—Passive)

Corrosion Protection

To find out if we are in trouble, let's continue our galley corrosion experiment. First repeat the zinc vs. stainless test in Figure 5.10. Next add a piece of aluminum as a third electrode. Using alligator clip leads, connect the zinc, stainless, and aluminum electrodes, as shown in Figure 5.11. Now set the multimeter to milliamps and insert it, one at a time, in each of the leads to detect current flow.

Amazing! Electric current is flowing out of the stainless electrode and into the zinc electrode, but no current at all is flowing either into or out of the aluminum electrode. Since metal is lost only by an electrode that receives current, it seems that the zinc is protecting the aluminum by sacrificing itself.

You can repeat this experiment with any three metals you wish, and the results will always be the same: when dissimilar metals in an electrolyte are mechanically or electrically bonded, the only metal to corrode will be the one highest in the galvanic series. The metal most used in boats for this purpose is zinc.

The phenomenon just observed is called cathodic protection, and the zinc masses are called sacrificial anodes, zinc anodes or just zincs (US).

Figure 5.12 shows two examples of cathodic protection using zincs. At top is an outboard engine mounted on the transom of a boat. A large zinc is bolted directly to the transom underwater, and a wire is run from the mounting bolts of the zinc to the outboard. The zinc protects the outboard. The zinc could also have been—and often is—bolted directly to the underwater shaft of the outboard.

At the bottom of Figure 5.12 is a sailboat with a zinc on the propeller shaft. The zinc is mechanically (and thus electrically) connected to the shaft. Protection is extended to the rudder shaft by a conductor from rudder to engine block. Rudder, rudder shaft, engine, transmission, prop shaft, and prop are all connected and thus protected by the zinc. The presence of a nonconductive plastic or rubber shaft coupling would require a jumper strap across the coupling. It should be noted that the ABYC also permits shafts and rudders to be protected separately, each by its own zinc anode.

Figure 5.13 shows a variety of zincs commonly found in chandleries. Many more shapes and forms are available from specialty suppliers. Engine zincs are mounted inside the cooling systems of engines. The "guppy" is used at anchor or in a marina berth and will be discussed below.

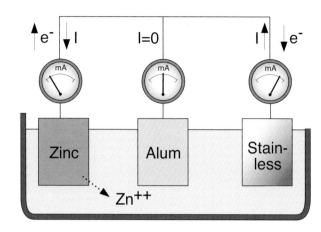

Fig. 5.11 How a Sacrificial Zinc Anode Works

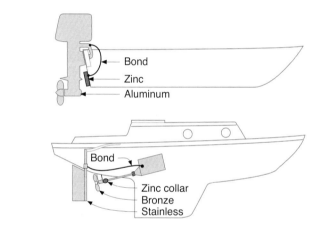

Fig. 5.12 Two Examples of Zinc-Anode Protection

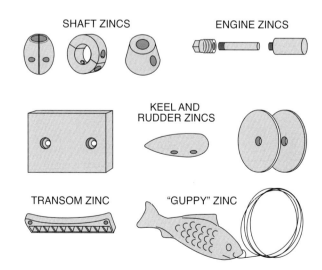

Fig. 5.13 An Assortment of Zincs

Even if you're flushed with your recent mastery of the subject of galvanic corrosion, I suggest you take a break at this point because we have to start all over again. It turns out there is more than one way to create a potential difference between underwater metals. We have another dragon to slay—stray-current corrosion.

Home Experiment, Continued

OK, back to work. As a refresher, place two identical aluminum electrodes in the saltwater solution, as in Figure 5.14. Using the multimeter, measure the voltage between the electrodes. Then switch the multimeter to milliamps and measure the current in the wire between the electrodes. The result should be the same in both cases: zero.

Next place a 1.5-volt battery between the same two aluminum electrodes, A and B, as in Figure 5.15. Now, of course, you will measure the battery's 1.5 volts across the electrodes and, with the meter placed in series with the battery, a current flowing from the battery positive (+) terminal into electrode B. If you let the experiment go on long enough, you will observe that the electrode into which the current flows is corroding, just as it did with galvanic corrosion. It is apparent that it makes no difference whether the potential difference between the electrodes is due to their being of dissimilar metals or due to a voltage impressed on them from an outside source—the electrode receiving current always corrodes. When the impressed voltage is accidental (as from a poorly insulated electrical connection), the corrosion is termed *stray-current corrosion*. Since stray, or accidental, voltage sources can be much greater than galvanic potentials (up to 12 volts, compared to a few tenths of a volt), stray current corrosion can be much more damaging than galvanic corrosion.

Finally, we'll use four aluminum electrodes as shown in Figure 5.16. As in the previous test, Figure 5.15, we'll use electrodes A and B to force a current in the seawater. Now insert the connected pair, C and D, between A and B. Measure the current between C and D. It will be approximately the same as in the previous experiment. Likewise, electrode C will eventually show signs of corrosion.

Now you see why this insidious phenomenon is termed stray-current corrosion. Two perfectly innocent metal objects, if electrically bonded, can pick up stray current flowing through the electrolyte and participate in the corrosion process!

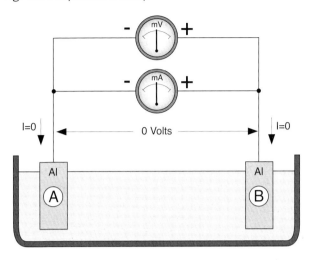

Fig. 5.14 Experiment Setup

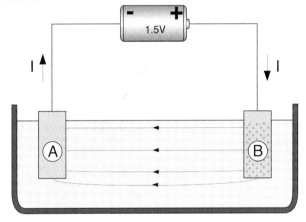

Fig. 5.15 Impressing (Forcing) Current with a Voltage Source

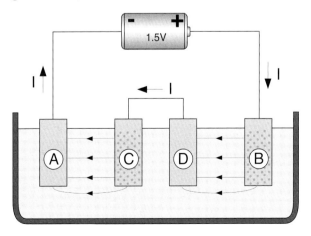

Fig. 5.16 Stray Current Impressed by Voltage Field

Stray-Current Protection

Figure 5.17 shows a boat floating in an external voltage and current field (perhaps due to an adjacent boat). The voltage difference, from left to right across the illustration, is 1.0 volt.

Since the electrical resistance of the path from ground plate to bonding wire to engine to shaft to propeller is less than that of the water path, electric current flows into the ground plate, through the bonding system and out of the propeller. And since the current is flowing into the propeller from the bonding system, the propeller will corrode.

Figure 5.18 shows that a sacrificial zinc on the shaft will divert the current flow to itself and save the prop.

Fig. 5.17 Stray-Current Corrosion Caused by an External Voltage Field

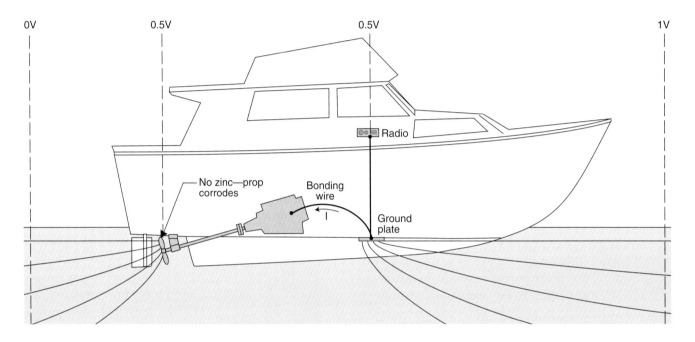

Fig. 5.18 Cathodic Protection from Stray-Current Corrosion Caused by an External Voltage Field

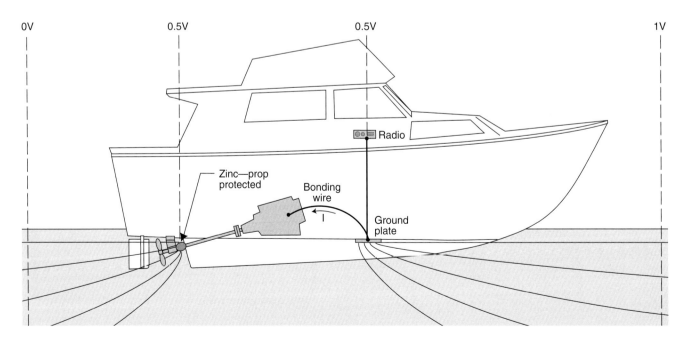

Figure 5.19 shows a stray current originating entirely inside the boat. Both a bilge pump and a bronze through-hull are sitting in bilge water. The unbonded pump develops a short from its positive power lead to its housing, establishing the pump housing at 12 volts. Current flows from the electrified housing, through the bilge water, into the through-hull, to the water outside the hull, and back through the prop, shaft, and engine path to ground. Since the through-hull is receiving current, it is also giving up ions to the sea (corroding). If the pump housing had been electrically bonded, the short would have tripped the circuit breaker, preventing corrosion and alerting the boatowner to the short.

Fig. 5.19 Stray-Current Corrosion Caused by Shorted Bilge Pump Inside Hull

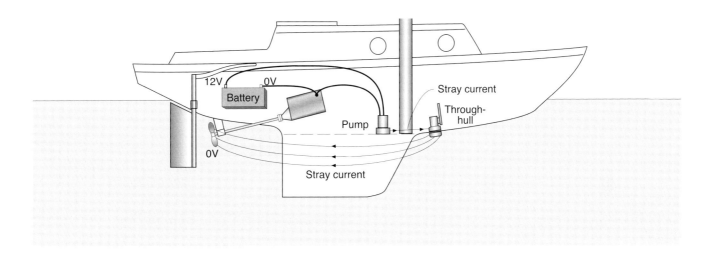

Figure 5.20 shows stray current originating from a terminal strip in the bilge. A single 12-volt/ground pair is shown here, but there are usually several pairs, serving anchor light, steaming light, and spreader lights on the mast. The terminal strip is wet, and some of the stray current finds its way back to ground by way of the through-hull–seawater connection. If the through-hull were, instead, bonded to ground, the stray current would flow back to ground by way of the bonding and not result in corrosion.

Fig. 5.20 Stray-Current Corrosion Caused by Wetted Terminal Strip in Bilge

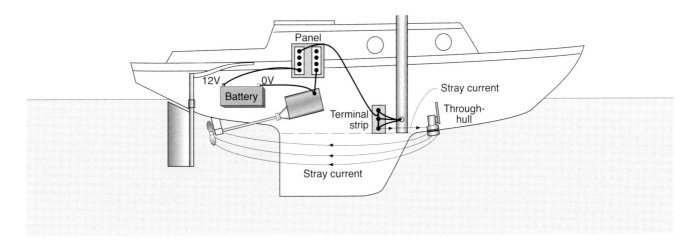

To Bond or Not to Bond

We have just seen three cases of stray-current corrosion. Two would have been *prevented* by bonding, but one was, in fact, *caused* by bonding. In general, bonding of immersed metal components *prevents* corrosion due to stray currents from *inside* the hull, but it *causes* corrosion due to stray currents from *outside* the hull.

Two opposite solutions to this dilemma are to: (1) bond everything and protect, and (2) unbond everything and isolate.

Bond and Protect

Figure 5.21 shows the bond-and-protect principle. Every underwater mass is connected to the boat's bonding system. To protect against stray currents outside of the hull, sacrificial anodes are connected to the bonding system and placed where they may best protect all underwater masses.

Fig. 5.21 The Bond-and-Protect Approach

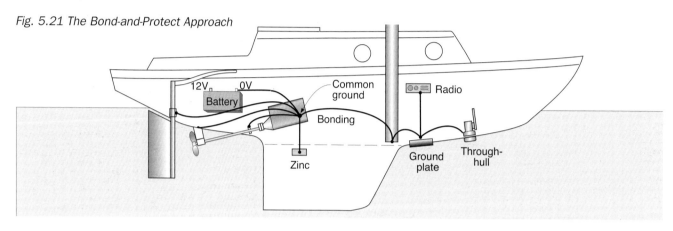

Unbond and Isolate

Figure 5.22 shows the alternative unbond-and-isolate principle. Underwater masses are isolated so neither galvanic nor outside stray current can flow between them. The only bonded underwater mass is the lightning and radio ground. Masses entirely within the hull (engine, transmission, metal tanks, and mast) are bonded to the boat's bonding system. The shaft is isolated by an insulating flexible coupling. The prop is protected by a shaft zinc if prop and shaft are made of dissimilar metals.

The Pros and Cons of Bonding

Bonding and protecting offers the advantage of greater wetted surface area for the lightning and radio grounds.

On the other hand, proponents of the unbond-and-isolate approach claim that the lightning ground strip or plate provides adequate ground for both lightning and SSB radio, and that electrochemical reactions at bonded wooden hull through-hulls dangerously soften the surrounding wood. The ABYC favors the bond-and-protect approach, but specifically states that electrically isolated through-hull fittings need not be bonded.

Fig. 5.22 The Unbond-and-Isolate Approach

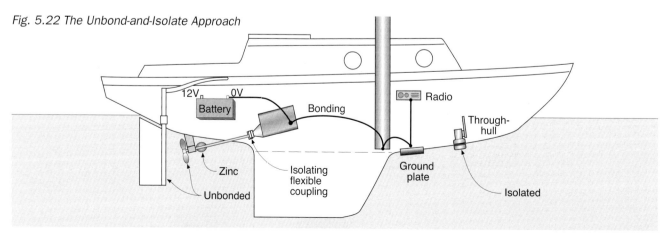

The ABYC recommends a method (in Standard E-2, Appendix 3) using a silver-silver chloride reference electrode for determining the amount of cathodic protection (size of aggregate zinc anodes) required to protect the underwater metals of a boat. The method assumes the use of zincs meeting Military Specification MIL-A-18001 (99.2% zinc minimum), excellent (metal-to-metal) electrical contact between anode and metal to be protected, and no paint on the anode.

The standard further points out that cathodic protection requirements increase with boat speed, salinity (if salt water), acidity (if fresh water), frequency of use of the boat, and deterioration over time of the anode.

ABYC Method

1. Assemble your materials:
   - silver-silver chloride reference electrode with lead (widely available on the Web or at West Marine stores for about $80)
   - digital multimeter (DMM) having at least 10 MW input impedance (even inexpensive DMMs do)
   - several high-quality zinc anodes of appropriate type (shaft collar, prop, or hull zincs)
   - two 20-foot test leads with strong clips
2. Starting with the hull free of all zinc anodes, lower the silver-silver chloride electrode into the water near the metal to be protected.
3. Set the DMM to the 2 Volts DC setting.
4. Connect the lead from the reference electrode to the DMM – input.
5. Using a test lead, connect the metal to be protected to the DMM + input. Make sure the test lead clip makes a clean electrical connection to the metal.
6. Note the DMM reading (example: –0. 720 volt).
7. Using the second test lead, connect one of the zinc anodes to the metal to be protected and lower the zinc into the water.
8. Note the new DMM reading. The zinc is adequate if it has lowered the voltage by *at least* 0.200 volt (example: from –0.720 volt to –0.920 volt or less).
9. If the second reading isn't at least 0.200 volt more negative than the first, the zinc is not sufficient. Increase either the zinc area or the number of zincs and retest.

Fig. 5.23 ABYC Method for Sizing Cathodic Protection

STEPS 1–6

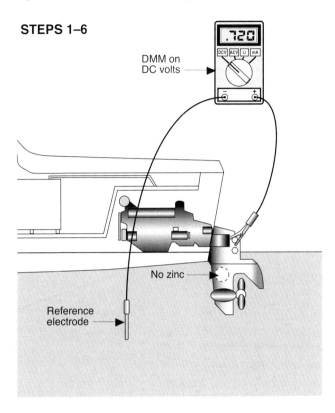

STEPS 7–9

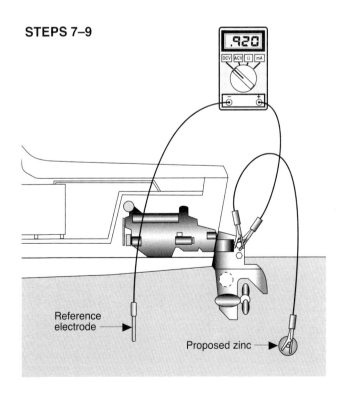

Testing Your Protection

Test 1: Stray Currents

In a bonded system, stray current will be captured by the boat's bonding conductor. Stray current in a through-hull or other accessible underwater mass can be measured with a digital multimeter on the milliamps (mA) setting as shown in Figure 5.24.

Disconnect the bonding conductor and place the meter between the end of the conductor and the metal of the through-hull. Current into or out of the through-hull will now flow through the meter. Repeat the test with each fitting, as well as the rudder shaft, prop shaft, and strut or shaft log. Remember that current flowing from the bonding conductor into the fitting, as shown, is causing corrosion of the fitting. Current of as little as 1 milliamp is reason for concern as it will, over the 8,766 hours in a year, cause serious damage to the fitting.

Test 2: Corrosion Potentials

This test (Figure 5.25), using a digital multimeter and a silver-silver chloride reference electrode, will determine whether the boat's present sacrificial zincs are protecting the boat's underwater metallic masses:

1. Set the multimeter to measure DC volts.
2. Connect the meter's + input to an underwater metallic mass or, if there is a common bonding system (as shown), to engine negative ground.
3. Connect the reference electrode to the meter's − input, and lower the electrode into the water.

Compare the reading to those of Table 5.2 to see whether the zinc anodes are adequate. If the readings indicate underprotection, replace or add zinc anodes.

Fig. 5.24 Test for Stray Current

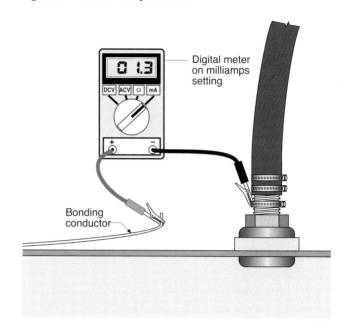

Table 5.2 Interpreting Corrosion Test Voltages

Underwater Metal	Under-protected	Protected	Over-protected
Bronze	< 0.44 V	0.44–0.70 V	> 0.70 V
Steel	< 0.75 V	0.75–0.95 V	> 0.95 V
Aluminum	< 0.90 V	0.90–1.10 V	> 1.10 V

Readings in excess of 1.10 volts usually indicate a voltage field in the water surrounding the boat. If you can't eliminate or reduce the external field, consider unbonding and isolating the underwater fittings, as shown in Figure 5.22.

Fig. 5.25 How to Evaluate Your Boat's Corrosion Potential

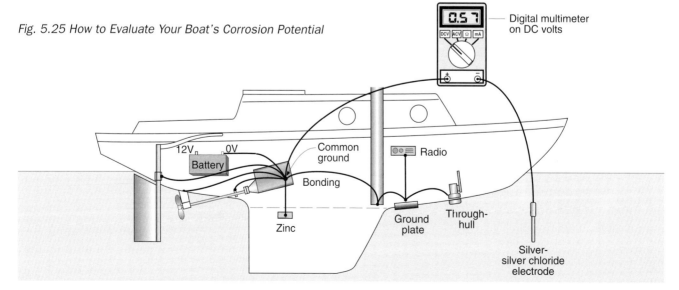

We have addressed the types of corrosion that can be eliminated by cathodic protection. There are further annoying types of corrosion on a boat that must be addressed by other means.

Dezincification

Figure 5.26 shows the dezincification of brass screws. Brass consists of a mixture of copper and zinc. Common yellow brass contains 65% copper and 35% zinc. In the presence of moisture (a very common electrolyte around boats!), the zinc and copper react galvanically, just as they would underwater, although more slowly. The result is a loss of zinc and loss of strength. When a badly dezincified screw is removed, the screw head often snaps off. The lesson: use only stainless or bronze screws around a boat.

A second instance of dezincification occurs in bronze (an alloy of copper, tin, and zinc) propellers. Loss of zinc is evidenced by a telltale change of the metal from bright yellow to a pinkish hue.

Stainless Screws in Aluminum

Figure 5.27 shows what happens when a fitting of any material, metallic or nonmetallic, is attached to an aluminum mast or boom with stainless screws. Regardless of how well machined the threads are, there are always microscopic spaces between the screw and the body. If salt water finds its way into these capillary spaces, an ideal galvanic cell is set up with resulting loss of aluminum in the area of the threads. Ultimately, the stainless screw seizes in the hole or, worse, falls out under load. Filling both sets of threads with silicone sealant or grease before fastening will fill the capillary spaces around the threads and prevent the intrusion of any salt water. No seawater—no electrolyte—no corrosion.

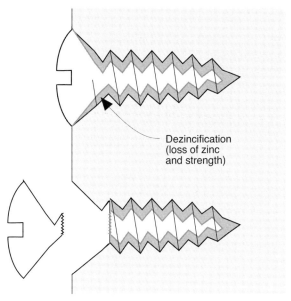

Fig. 5.26 Dezincification of Brass

Dezincification (loss of zinc and strength)

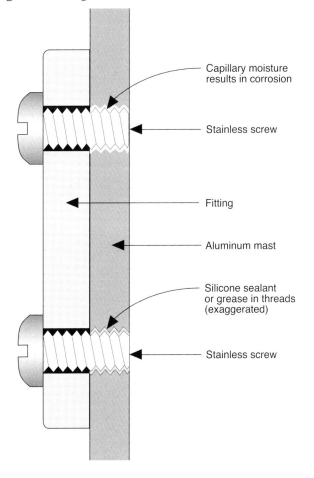

Fig. 5.27 Seizing of Stainless Screws in Aluminum

Capillary moisture results in corrosion

Stainless screw

Fitting

Aluminum mast

Silicone sealant or grease in threads (exaggerated)

Stainless screw

Noncathodic Corrosion

Stainless Pitting

Figure 5.28 shows how stainless steel develops corrosion pits. Stainless steel is principally an alloy of iron and chromium. When exposed to the oxygen in air, the chromium oxidizes and forms a shiny protective skin (the stainless is then said to be passivated). The chromium oxide skin is very noble in the galvanic series (see Table 5.1, entry 18-8, 3% Mo Stainless Steel, Type 316 [passive]), so it resists corrosion and protects the iron beneath.

If the surface is immersed in or covered with an oxygen-free liquid, however, the chromium loses its oxygen, the passive skin is lost, and the iron is free to rust. In Figure 5.27 a barnacle has attached itself to a stainless surface, depriving the chromium-oxide skin of oxygen. The unpassivated area and the surrounding passivated area then act as a galvanic couple, resulting in corrosion of the iron under the barnacle.

The same sort of corrosion occurs between stainless stanchions and their water-retaining bases, explaining the mysterious rust stains often seen in these areas.

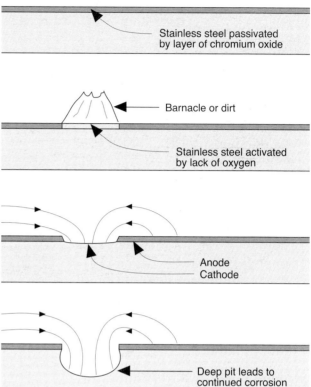

Fig. 5.28 Pitting of Stainless Steel

Cavitation Erosion

Finally, Figure 5.29 shows cavitation erosion of the trailing edge of a propeller. Cavitation is the rapid formation and collapse of vapor bubbles just behind propeller blades. Cavitation is not galvanic corrosion. Instead, the propeller is turning so quickly that the water immediately behind the blade is left behind, forming water vapor (gaseous form of water) bubbles. As these bubbles subsequently collapse, the water hits the blade like thousands of tiny hammers. You can hear the sharp popping sound underwater when a boat passes. The result is mechanical destruction and erosion of the metal at the trailing edge of the blade. The solution is to increase the area of the blade, thereby reducing the pressure difference across the blade.

In contrast, a bronze propeller or any other bronze fitting suffering from galvanic corrosion displays a rosy-pink color instead of its normal brassy-yellow color. Galvanic corrosion selectively removes the zinc from the bronze, leaving the reddish copper behind.

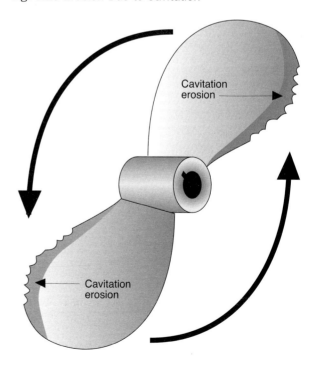

Fig. 5.29 Erosion Due to Cavitation

The ABYC on Cathodic Protection

The following general recommendations are taken from ABYC Standard E-2, *Cathodic Protection of Boats, Section E-2.4.*

a. Although cathodic protection will, depending on the current capability of the system, help to minimize stray-current corrosion when it exists, stray-current corrosion should be controlled by:

(1) Minimizing DC and AC electrical leakage levels from electrical products, and

(2) The use of a bonding system in accordance with ABYC E-1, "Bonding of Direct Current Systems."

b. Factors that affect the type and degree of cathodic protection required:

(1) Water Velocity—Cathodic protection current requirements increase with water velocity past the hull. The current requirements can be as high as 30 times that required in still water.

(2) Boat Usage—More frequently operated vessels require more cathodic protection than vessels infrequently used.

(3) Fresh and Sea Water—Current requirements increase with salinity but higher driving potentials are required in fresh water.

(4) Deterioration of Protective Coatings—Current requirements will increase as protective coatings deteriorate.

c. The need for a cathodic protection system for metal appendages on nonmetallic hulls may not be justified if the metals coupled are galvanically compatible.

d. Hull-mounted metallic trim tabs may be electrically isolated from the boat's bonding system to reduce the load on the boat's cathodic protection system, providing the trim tabs are also electrically isolated from their electrical actuating mechanism. If the trim-tab system is connected to the boat's bonding system the cathodic protection system's milliampere rating will have to be increased to provide the additional protection.

e. A cathodic protection system shall be capable of inducing and maintaining a minimum negative shift of 200 millivolts in the potential of the composite cathode being protected.

f. Since the area relationship of metals in a galvanic cell will affect current density and therefore corrosion rate, the immersed cathodic metal surfaces may be coated to obtain a more favorable anode to cathode area relationship. Coatings shall not contain pigments that will form galvanic couples with the substrate. Coatings on substrate and coatings on surfaces must be able to tolerate alkali generated by the cathodic reaction.

g. Impressed-current anodes shall have the words "DO NOT PAINT" on a visible surface when installed.

NOTE: Anodes are ineffective if painted.

h. In general, the use of several anodes instead of one large anode will tend to provide better distribution of the protective current. Sacrificial anodes may be mounted remotely; the best current distribution will be obtained with the anode(s) positioned to be as equidistant as possible from the metals to be protected.

i. Anodes should be faired and, if possible, arranged in a longitudinal row to minimize drag. After installation, peripheral crevices should be sealed.

j. Anodes shall be mounted on a sloping surface that cannot entrap gas bubbles.

k. If anodes are located near through-hull fittings they shall be positioned forward of discharge fittings and aft of intake ports. Anode locations that disturb the flow of water past the propeller should be avoided.

l. All metals which are to receive cathodic protection from the cathodic protection system must have good electrical continuity to the boat bonding system. Galvanic anodes, if used, must be affixed in a manner that electrical continuity is maintained with the metals they are to protect, either through their mounting means or through the boat's bonding system.

(1) Propeller shafts do not provide reliable electrical continuity to the boat's bonding system.

(2) Rudder posts shall be cathodically bonded by means of a flexible conductor positioned to allow full rudder movement without stressing the cathodic bonding conductor or its connection.

m. In general, sacrificial anodes may be mounted directly on the metal to be protected, but the best current distribution will be obtained by remote mounting with the anode(s) positioned to be as equidistant as possible from the metals to be protected.

n. The negative potential (−1,050 millivolts as compared to silver-silver chloride reference electrode) that can be achieved by some corrosion control systems will result in some decrease in the effectiveness of antifouling paints. Because the decrease in the effectiveness increases with higher negative voltages, the negative potential should be kept as close to the optimum value as possible. A reference potential reading in excess of −1,100 millivolts indicates excessive cathodic protection.

o. Anodes and reference electrodes shall be positioned to avoid contact with lifting slings and chocks when the boat is hauled.

p. The electrical interconnection that occurs via shore-power cables or metal mooring cables between two vessels or between a vessel and submerged metal or the dock may result in galvanic corrosion of steel or aluminum hulls and aluminum underwater appendages. An isolator or an isolation transformer can break this couple.

CHAPTER 6

DC Standards and Practices

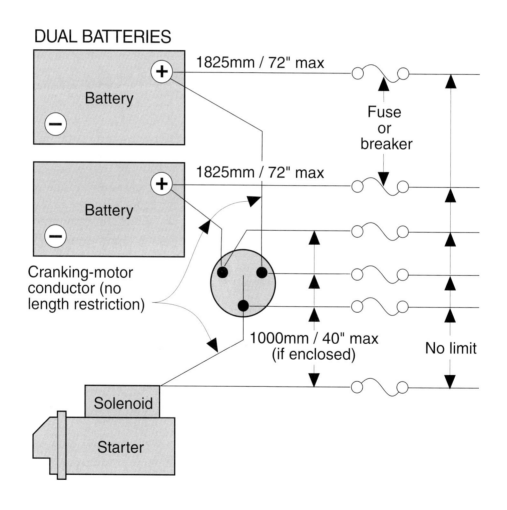

DUAL BATTERIES

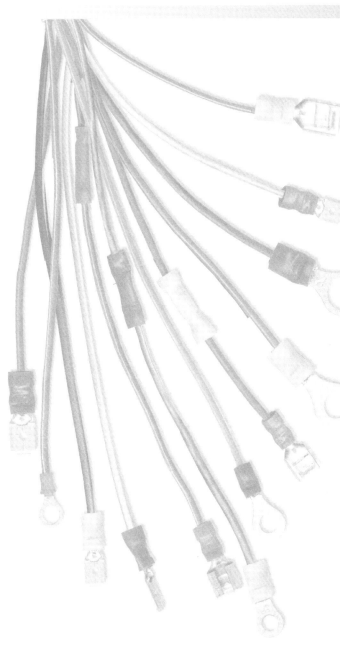

S tandards and recommended practices for the wiring of boats are promoted by the American Boat and Yacht Council (ABYC). This chapter delineates and explains these standards. Preliminary to the standards, however, we first explain the wisdom of creating wiring diagrams for your boat's electrical systems.

The standards and practices start with the specification of acceptable marine wire. The ABYC DC load calculation method allows you to calculate the maximum current expected to flow in a conductor and to use the tables for allowable amperage of conductors and conductor sizes for allowable voltage drops.

Wiring and, later, troubleshooting are both facilitated by the proper identification of conductors, as well as the proper installation of wire runs.

As in a home, overcurrent protection, in the form of fuses and circuit breakers, guards against overheating and possible fire.

The marine environment, characterized by moisture, salt, and vibration, makes conductor connections critical.

The lethal mixture of gasoline vapors and open flame or electric spark dictates the ABYC-adopted Coast Guard requirements for ignition protection.

Wiring Diagrams

When you first bought your boat, you probably judged its wiring on appearances. Either it looked good or it did not. You never gave it another thought—until something went wrong. Then you discovered whether or not the boat had a wiring diagram. Chances are, if your boat was American made, it did not.

The person who wired your boat didn't need a wiring diagram. First, yours was probably one of dozens, if not hundreds, he had wired just like it. Second, he assumed he would not be there when something went wrong. Troubleshooting would be your problem.

One summer I worked in a boatyard rigging and stepping masts. One of my jobs was to check the mast wiring before the mast was stepped. Some masts had combined tricolor, anchor, and strobe light (four conductors), masthead or steaming light (two conductors), spreader lights (two conductors), windvane light (two conductors), plus a windspeed indicator (six wires in a cable) and a VHF coaxial cable—a total of ten individual conductors plus two cables.

It seemed as if every second mast had a problem. A bulb was burned out or not properly seated, connectors were corroded, or a wire was broken. The symptoms were obvious—a light at the top of the mast did not come on. Finding the cause, however, was an art. Without a wiring diagram, labeled terminals, and color-coded conductors, finding the fault sometimes required an hour of labor for two workers: one at the top end reading voltage or watching the light, the other at the bottom applying voltage to successive pairs of conductors. Did you know that the number of possible pairs of n wires is $n(n-1)/2$? For 10 wires we had to check 45 pair combinations!

Sometimes we found that a light that had worked on the ground no longer worked with the mast up. Now there were even more possibilities! Something could have happened inside the mast during stepping, or the problem could lie between the distribution panel and the base of the mast. It was here that we sometimes encountered the case of the chameleon conductor. A wire would leave the distribution panel with blue insulation, disappear into the bilge or behind a liner, and emerge at the base of the mast with yellow insulation!

One of my associates had worked for one of the best boatbuilders in the United States. Over lunch I related the case of the chameleon wire.

"Oh, sure," he said, "we used to run a wire until the spool ran out. Then we'd grab another spool of whatever color and splice it in."

A proper wiring diagram shows every electrical device: circuit breaker, fuse, switch, terminal, and conductor, as well as wire size, color, and label. It makes troubleshooting a snap. If a light doesn't come on, the diagram shows exactly where to check for voltage, all the way from the lamp back to the distribution panel. A circuit diagram also shows the best place to tie in additional electrical equipment, what spares to carry, and whether or not you are fused correctly.

Best of all, if you create your circuit diagram by visually inspecting your existing wiring, you will have looked systematically at every component and may be able to spot potential problems before they become problems underway.

Creating a Wiring Diagram

Circuit symbols are, like international road signs, intended to convey meaning at a glance. Unlike international signage, however, there is no rigorous standard for wiring symbols. Figure 6.1 shows commonly used symbols for most of the simple devices encountered in a boat. If these don't work for you, feel free to invent your own. For example, you may elect to show a fan as a fan blade and a fuse as a simple rectangle.

If you possess the repair manual for your engine (a minimal and wise investment), it probably contains a wiring diagram for the starting motor, alternator, and instrument panel. If so, you are in luck; you are already halfway there. Consider the engine diagram to be the first of your circuit diagrams and adopt its style for the rest of your diagrams.

Breaking the total system into a set of circuits has the added advantages of smaller sheets of paper, less confusion, and the ability to make changes without redrawing the entire system.

A complete set of circuit diagrams for a typical pleasure boat might include:
- Engine wiring
- Engine-starting circuit
- Cabin lights and accessories
- Navigation lights
- Instrumentation and radios
- 110 VAC system
- Main distribution panel
- Mast wiring
- Water pumps

Don't worry if several of your diagrams overlap. The intent is to locate the general area of a fault and then to isolate the exact location within that area.

Fig. 6.1 Wiring Symbols

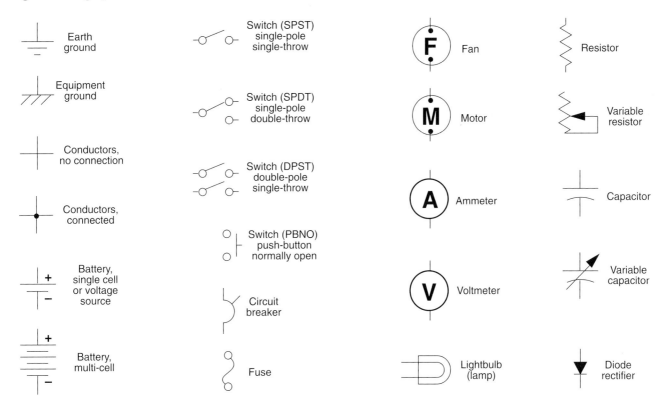

A Starter-Motor Circuit

Figure 6.2 shows a very simple diagram of an engine starter-motor circuit. If one day you turn on the ignition switch, push the start button, and nothing happens, this is the circuit diagram you will need. A complete engine wiring diagram would probably contain the same information, but it would also contain all of the meters, idiot lights, and alternator wiring, adding considerable visual confusion.

For the starter-motor circuit all you need to see are the:

- Battery switch
- Fuse between battery switch common terminal and engine panel
- On/Off switch
- Momentary start switch
- Wire from starting switch to solenoid
- Heavy positive cable from battery-select common terminal to solenoid
- Heavy negative cable from battery negative terminal to engine negative terminal.

If the engine won't turn over, the problem probably lies somewhere in this diagram. For guidance, see page 64.

Fig. 6.2 Typical Starter-Motor Circuit

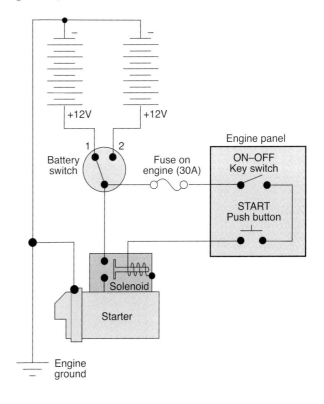

Wiring Diagrams

A Cabin Lighting Circuit

Although it shows 15 separate lights and fans, the cabin lighting diagram in Figure 6.3 is even simpler in concept than the engine starter circuit. The diagram consists of two similar, but separate, branch circuits.

On the right is the starboard cabin lighting circuit, originating at a 10-amp circuit breaker in the DC distribution panel and running forward to serve all of the lights and fans on the starboard side. The positive conductor is a red AWG (American Wire Gauge) 14 wire labeled "27." The negative conductor is a black AWG 14 wire labeled "28." Except for the two paralleled main cabin lights, each light and fan is controlled by an individual single-pole, single-throw switch. You may wish to include model numbers and specifications for each device so that you can calculate current draws and find replacement parts.

The devices are drawn on paper as laid out in the boat so that we can physically pinpoint a problem. For example, if the chart table light failed, but the main aft light still worked, the circuit diagram would allow us to immediately isolate the problem to either the chart table light or the lamp's controlling switch.

On the other hand, if the main aft, main forward, and V-berth lights failed as well, we would suspect the problem to be in either the positive or negative conductors or the connections between the night light and the chart table light.

On the left is the similar port cabin lighting circuit, originating at a 10-amp circuit breaker in the DC distribution panel and running forward to serve all of the lights and fans on the port side. The positive conductor is a red AWG 14 wire labeled "29." The negative conductor is a black AWG 14 wire labeled "30."

Fig. 6.3 Typical Cabin Lighting Circuits

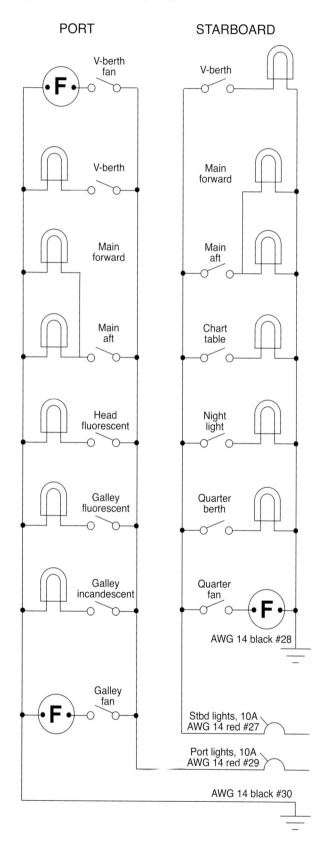

Real circuits consist not of pencil lines on a sheet of paper, but of real metal conductors having finite electrical resistance. The conductors and their installations should satisfy a number of criteria:

1. Construction should be such that the conductor will not break under continuous vibration or an accidentally imposed force.
2. Insulation should be appropriate for the expected maximum ambient (surrounding air) temperature and degree of exposure to sunlight, moisture, and air.
3. Ampacity (current-carrying capacity) should be sufficient to avoid overheating.
4. Selection of conductor size should take account of conductor length and current so that voltage drop won't impair the functioning of the load devices.

Construction

The ABYC calls for most conductors to be stranded and of size AWG 16 minimum. An exception is sheathed AWG 18 conductors that do not extend more than 30 inches beyond their sheath.

Because copper wire becomes brittle with flexing, solid wire (as used in house wiring) is not allowed at all. Type II stranding is the minimum allowed for general boat wiring, and Type III stranding should be used wherever vibration is expected, such as on an engine.

Table 6.1 shows the minimum circular-mil areas (a circular mil is the area of a 0.001-inch-diameter circle) for both AWG and SAE (Society of Automotive Engineers) conductors and the minimum numbers of

Table 6.1 Minimum Circular-Mil (CM) Areas and Stranding

Conductor Gauge*	Minimum CM for AWG	Minimum CM for SAE	Minimum Type II	Strands Type III
18	1,620	1,537	16	–
16	2,580	2,336	19	26
14	4,110	3,702	19	41
12	6,530	5,833	19	65
10	10,380	9,343	19	105
8	16,510	14,810	19	168
6	26,240	25,910	37	266
4	41,740	37,360	49	420
2	66,360	62,450	127	665
1	83,690	77,790	127	836
0	105,600	98,980	127	1,064
2/0	133,100	125,100	127	1,323
3/0	167,800	158,600	259	1,666
4/0	211,600	205,500	418	2,107

*See Appendix for metric equivalent

strands specified by the ABYC for AWG 18 through AWG 4/0 (0000) conductors.

See Appendices for AWG/metric conversion table.

Insulation

All single-conductor and cable insulations should be one of the types listed in Table 6.2, appropriate to its expected exposure to temperature, moisture, and oil. The letters in the designations stand for:

T	thermoplastic
M	oil resistant
W	moisture resistant
H	heat resistant to 75°C
HH	high-heat resistant to 90°C

An insulated jacket or sheathing may qualify for more than one rating and be labeled as such. The most commonly available cable suitable to all applications in the typical boat is probably UL 1426 boat cable.

Table 6.2 Acceptable Insulation Types

Type	Description
	CONDUCTORS
THW	Moisture and Heat Resistant, Thermoplastic
TW	Moisture Resistant, Thermoplastic
HWN	Moisture and Heat Resistant, Thermoplastic
XHHW	Moisture and High-Heat Resistant, Cross-Linked Synthetic Polymer
MTW	Moisture, Heat, and Oil Resistant, Thermoplastic
AWM	Moisture, Heat, and Oil Resistant, Thermoplastic, Thermosetting
UL 1426	Boat Cable
	SAE CONDUCTORS
GPT	Thermoplastic Insulation, Braidless
HDT	Thermoplastic Insulation, Braidless
SGT	Thermoplastic Insulation, Braidless
STS	Thermosetting Synthetic-Rubber Insulation, Braidless
HTS	Thermosetting Synthetic-Rubber Insulation, Braidless
SXL	Thermosetting, Cross-Linked Polyethylene Insulation, Braidless
	FLEXIBLE CORDS
SO	Hard-Service Cord, Oil Resistant
ST	Hard-Service Cord, Thermoplastic
STO	Hard-Service Cord, Oil Resistant, Thermoplastic
SEO	Hard-Service Cord, Oil Resistant, Thermoplastic
SJO	Junior Hard-Service Cord, Oil Resistant
SJT	Hard-Service Cord, Thermoplastic
SJTO	Hard-Service Cord, Oil Resistant, Thermoplastic

ABYC DC Load Calculation

Ampacity

Branch circuit conductors should be sized to carry the maximum currents drawn by their loads. In the case of motors, maximum current should be for the locked-rotor, or stalled, condition.

Main feed conductors for distribution panels and switchboards should be determined using the ABYC procedure, shown in Table 6.3 (a sample calculation is shown).

Table 6.3 ABYC Load Calculation Method (for total electrical loads for minimum sizes of panelboards, switchboards, and main conductors)
NOTE: Calculations are based on the actual operating amperage for each load and not on the rating of the circuit breaker or fuse protecting that branch circuit.

Column A

List each of the loads that must be available for use on a continuous basis.

Equipment	Amperes
Navigation lights	5.5
Bilge blower(s)	2.0
Bilge pump(s)	4.2
Wiper(s)	0.0
Largest radio (transmit mode)	2.5
Depth sounder	0.9
Radar	7.5
Searchlight	12.0
Instruments	2.3
Alarm system (standby mode)	0.5
Refrigeration	5.5
Other: Autopilot	3.5
Total of Column A	46.4
Enter Total from Column B	80.0
Sum of Totals (Total Load)	126.4

Column B

List the intermittent loads. The largest load or 10% of the total, whichever is greater, will be carried to Column A.

Equipment	Amperes
Cigarette lighter	0.0
Cabin lighting	10.0
Horn	6.3
Additional electronics	10.0
Trim tabs	0.0
Power trim	0.0
Heads	0.0
Anchor windlass	80.0
Winches	0.0
Freshwater pumps	5.8
Other: Microwave	60.0
Total of Column B	172.1
10% of Column B	17.2
Largest item in Column B	80.0
Larger of above two lines— Enter in both Column A and Column B	80.0

Having the maximum load current in amps and the temperature rating of the conductor insulation, the minimum required conductor size is selected from Table 6.4.

Table 6.4 Allowable Amperage of Conductors for Under 50 Volts (Adapted from ABYC Standard E-11, Table IV)

Conductor Size, AWG*	Temperature Rating of Conductor Insulation						
	60°C (140°F)	75°C (167°F)	80°C (176°F)	90°C (194°F)	105°C (221°F)	125°C (257°F)	200°C (392°F)
Outside Engine Spaces							
18	10	10	15	20	20	25	25
16	15	15	20	25	25	30	35
14	20	20	25	30	35	40	45
12	25	25	35	40	45	50	55
10	40	40	50	55	60	70	70
8	55	65	70	70	80	90	100
6	80	95	100	100	120	125	135
4	105	125	130	135	160	170	180
2	140	170	175	180	210	225	240
1	165	195	210	210	245	265	280
1/0	195	230	245	245	285	305	325
2/0	225	265	285	285	330	355	370
3/0	260	310	330	330	385	410	430
4/0	300	360	385	385	445	475	510
Inside Engine Spaces							
18	5.8	7.5	11.7	16.4	17.0	22.3	25.0
16	8.7	11.3	15.6	20.5	21.3	26.7	35.0
14	11.6	15.0	19.5	24.6	29.8	35.6	45.0
12	14.5	18.8	27.3	32.8	38.3	44.5	55.0
10	23.2	30.0	39.0	45.1	51.0	62.3	70.0
8	31.9	48.8	54.6	57.4	68.0	80.1	100.0
6	46.4	71.3	78.0	82.0	102.0	111.3	135.0
4	60.9	93.8	101.4	110.7	136.0	151.3	180.0
2	81.2	127.5	136.5	147.6	178.5	200.3	240.0
1	95.7	146.3	163.8	172.2	208.3	235.9	280.0
1/0	113.1	172.5	191.1	200.9	242.3	271.5	325.0
2/0	130.5	198.8	222.3	233.7	280.5	316.0	370.0
3/0	150.8	232.5	257.4	270.6	327.3	364.9	430.0
4/0	174.0	270.0	300.3	315.7	378.3	422.8	510.0

*For equivalent metric cable sizes see Appendices

Allowable Voltage Drop

All wire has resistance. As current flows through the wire, voltage drops according to Ohm's Law. If power is supplied to a circuit by a 12.0-volt battery and the voltage drops 0.5 volt in the positive conductor going to the load and another 0.5 volt in the negative conductor back to the battery, then the voltage across the load is not 12.0 volts, but 12.0 − 0.5 − 0.5 = 11.0 volts. The voltage drop in the total length of conductor to and from the load is thus 1.0/12.0 = 8.3%.

The ABYC specifies two allowable percentage drops, depending on the effect on safety:

- 3% for panelboard feeds, bilge blowers, electronics, and navigation lights
- 10% for general lighting and other noncritical applications

Required conductor size may be determined from:

$$CM = 10.75 \times I \times L/E$$

where: CM = conductor circular mils (Table 6.1)
I = current in amps
L = round-trip length in feet
E = voltage drop in conductor, volts

Example: What size conductor is required for an anchor light drawing 0.9 amp at the top of a 50-foot mast with a 15-foot run from panelboard to base of the mast?

The light is a navigation light, so the allowed voltage drop is 3% of 12 volts or 0.36 volt. The length of the conductor from panelboard to the light and back to the panelboard is 15 feet + 50 feet + 50 feet + 15 feet = 130 feet. The minimum circular-mil area of the conductor is thus:

$$CM = 10.75 \times 0.9 \times 130/0.36 = 3{,}494$$

Table 6.1 tells us a #14 AWG conductor is required. Alternatively, we can find the answer in Table 6.5.

Table 6.5 Conductor Sizes (Minimum Circular Mils Converted to AWG by Table 6.1) for Allowable Voltage Drops in 12-Volt Systems (Adapted from ABYC Standard E-11, Tables X and XI). Metric = ft ÷ 3.2808 or × 0.3048.

Current, Amps	Round-Trip Conductor Length, ft.									Current, Amps	Round-Trip Conductor Length, ft.								
	10	20	30	40	60	80	100	120	140		10	20	30	40	60	80	100	120	140
	3% Voltage Drop										10% Voltage Drop								
1	18	18	18	18	16	14	14	14	12	1	18	18	18	18	18	18	18	18	18
2	18	18	16	14	14	12	10	10	8	2	18	18	18	18	18	18	16	16	14
5	18	14	12	10	10	8	6	6	6	5	18	18	18	16	14	14	12	12	10
10	14	10	10	8	6	6	4	4	2	10	18	16	14	14	12	10	10	8	8
15	12	10	8	6	6	4	2	2	1	15	18	14	12	12	10	8	8	6	6
20	10	8	6	6	4	2	2	1	0	20	16	14	12	10	8	8	6	6	6
25	10	6	6	4	2	2	1	0	2/0	25	16	12	10	10	8	6	6	4	4
30	10	6	4	4	2	1	0	2/0	3/0	30	14	12	10	8	6	6	4	4	2
40	8	6	4	2	1	0	2/0	3/0	4/0	40	14	10	8	8	6	4	4	2	2
50	6	4	2	2	0	2/0	3/0	4/0	–	50	12	10	8	6	4	4	2	2	1
60	6	4	2	1	2/0	3/0	4/0	–	–	60	12	8	6	6	4	2	2	1	1
70	6	2	1	0	3/0	4/0	–	–	–	70	10	8	6	6	2	2	1	1	0
80	6	2	1	0	3/0	4/0	–	–	–	80	10	8	6	4	2	2	1	0	2/0
90	4	2	0	2/0	4/0	–	–	–	–	90	10	6	6	4	2	1	0	0	2/0
100	4	2	0	2/0	4/0	–	–	–	–	100	10	6	4	4	2	1	0	2/0	2/0

*For equivalent metric cable sizes see Appendices. Metres = feet ÷ 2.281

Conductor Identification

The standards state "Each electrical conductor that is part of the boat's electrical system shall have a means to identify its function in the system." Two means of identification are insulation color and labels (numbers and/or letters) applied near the terminal points. The use of both is recommended. In general, DC conductor insulation should follow the color scheme:

DC Positive	Red (R)
DC Negative	Black (B) or Yellow (Y)
DC Grounding	Green (G) or Green with Yellow (GY)

The standards go on to recommend colors for specific DC positive conductors. If these colors are not used, a wiring diagram should be provided showing the conductors and their identifiers. Table 6.6 lists the colors for both general and specific conductors used in engine wiring. These may differ between manufacturers.

Table 6.6 DC Wiring Color Code
(Adapted from ABYC Standard E-11, Tables XIV and XV)

Color	Conductor Use
Green or green with yellow stripe(s)	General DC grounding
Black or yellow	General DC negative
Red	General DC positive
Yellow with red stripe	Starter switch to solenoid
Brown with yellow stripe, or yellow	Fuse or switch to blower—If DC negative is yellow, positive must be brown with yellow stripe
Dark gray	Fuse or switch to navigation lights / Tachometer sender to gauge
Brown	Generator armature to regulator / Auxiliary terminal to light and regulator / Fuse or switch to pumps
Orange	Ammeter to alternator or generator output and accessory fuses or switches / Distribution panel to accessory switch
Purple	Ignition switch to coil and electrical instruments / Distribution panel to electrical instruments
Dark blue	Fuse or switch to cabin and instrument lights
Light blue	Oil-pressure sender to gauge
Tan	Water-temperature sender to gauge
Pink	Fuel-gauge sender to gauge
Green/stripe, except G/Y	Tilt and/or trim circuits

Installation of Wire Runs

When both AC and DC conductors are run in the same area and direction, the AC conductors should be kept separate from the DC conductors by bundling, sheathing, or other means.

Continuous Support

In order to minimize flexing from vibration, conductors should be supported continuously or every 18 inches minimum by clamps or straps (Figure 6.4). Nonmetallic clamps and straps should not be used in locations where failure would result in a hazard, such as over engines, shafts, or passageways.

Metal clamps should be lined with moisture-, gasoline-, and oil-resistant material, or have smooth, rounded edges. The cable beneath unlined metal clamps should be protected by a wrapping to protect the conductors.

Fig. 6.4 Cable Support Devices

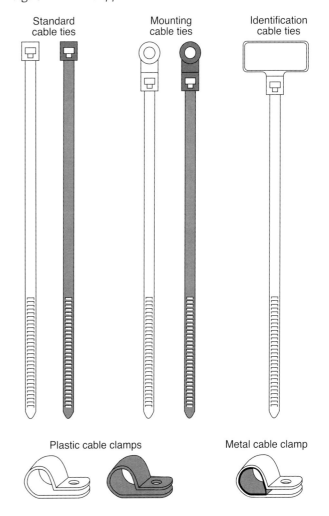

Identification and Installation

Exposure to Damage

Conductors should be protected from chafing by routing clear of engine and steering shafts and control linkages. In exposed areas conductors should be protected by conduit, raceway, or equivalent wrap. Holes in panels, bulkheads, or other structural members (Figure 6.5) should be lined.

Protecting Connections

Enclosures with electrical connections should be in dry locations or be weatherproof. If wet locations are unavoidable, nonmetallic enclosures are preferred, but metal enclosures can be mounted to prevent accumulation of moisture between the enclosure and adjacent surfaces, such as by providing a space of at least ¼ inch.

Wiring in the Bilge

The simplest routing of conductors is often through the bilge, but more than 90% of all electrical problems are due to corrosion, and nothing leads to corrosion more quickly than water—particularly of the salt variety. Current-carrying conductors should be routed as high as possible above bilge water. If routing through the bilge cannot be avoided, connections must be watertight.

Sources of Heat

Conductors should be kept away from and never run directly above engine exhaust pipes and other similar sources of heat. Minimum recommended conductor clearances are 2 inches from wet-exhaust pipes and components and 9 inches from dry-exhaust components, unless equivalent thermal insulation is provided.

Battery Cables

Unless battery cables are overcurrent protected, they should be run above bilge-water level, away from metal fuel-system components, such as fuel line and fuel filters, and away from the engine, transmission, and shaft. The grounded battery cable is excepted because contact between the grounded engine and a grounded conductor does not pose a danger.

Wiring Near Compasses

Direct current flow through a wire produces a concentric magnetic field, which may disturb a nearby compass (Figure 6.6). The direction of the magnetic field changes with current direction, so twisting positive and negative conductor pairs negates the overall magnetic field. All conductor pairs within 24 inches of a compass should be twisted, unless they are coaxial.

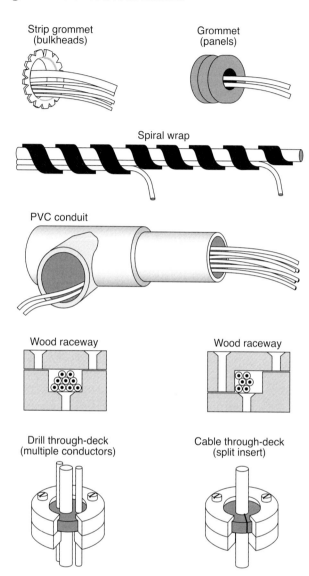

Fig. 6.5 Chafe Protection Material

Strip grommet (bulkheads)

Grommet (panels)

Spiral wrap

PVC conduit

Wood raceway

Wood raceway

Drill through-deck (multiple conductors)

Cable through-deck (split insert)

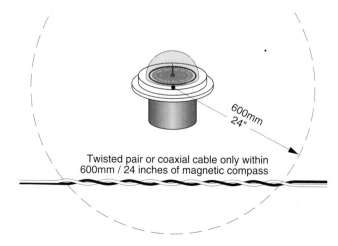

Fig. 6.6 Wiring Near Magnetic Compasses

600mm 24"

Twisted pair or coaxial cable only within 600mm / 24 inches of magnetic compass

Circuits That Require Protection

Distribution Panels and Switchboards

A distribution panel or switchboard (Figure 6.7) should be protected at its source of power (battery, battery switch, or starter solenoid) by either a fuse or a trip-free circuit breaker of capacity not exceeding the capacity of the panel or the ampacity of the feed conductors.

If there is also a sub-main fuse or breaker on the panel that does not exceed the panel or feeder ampacity, then the protection at the source of power may be rated up to 150% of the feeder capacity.

Circuits Branching from a Panel

Every ungrounded conductor originating in the panel (branch circuit) should be protected at its point of origin unless its rating is the same as that of the main or sub-main protection. The overcurrent protection rating should not exceed 150% of the conductor ampacity.

Except for engine-starter motors, all motors should be protected either internally or at the panel. The overcurrent protection rating should be low enough to prevent a fire, in the case of a stalled motor rotor, for up to 7 hours.

Fig. 6.7 Panelboard and Switchboard Overcurrent Protection

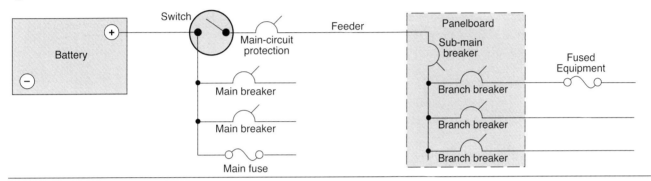

Unprotected Length Limits

Sources of power for positive-feed conductors can be a battery terminal, battery-select common terminal, or feed to the starter. The maximum allowed unprotected lengths of positive feeder conductors, as shown in Figure 6.8, are:

- Connected directly to a battery terminal— 1825mm/72 inches
- Connected to other than a battery terminal, but contained within a sheath or enclosure— 1000mm/40 inches
- All others—175mm/7 inches

Fig. 6.8 Maximum Unprotected Lengths for Positive Feeder Conductors

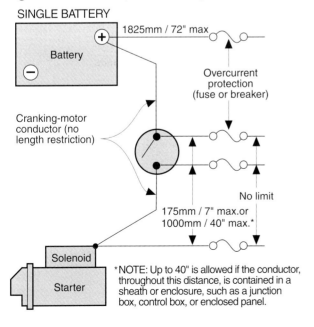

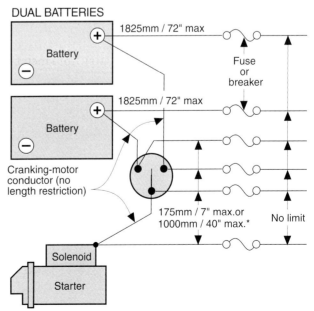

Overcurrent Protection

DC Circuit Breakers

As shown in Figure 6.7, by definition the first breaker or fuse in a circuit connected in series with the battery is considered to be the main circuit breaker or fuse. All other breakers or fuses in the circuit, including sub-main breakers and fuses, are considered to be branch circuit breakers and fuses. Note that breakers and fuses may be mixed in the same circuit. It is possible, for example, to use a main fuse ahead of a panel containing branch circuit breakers.

When installing a breaker panel, the breakers and panel should be from the same manufacturer to insure compatibility. Most manufacturers offer two sizes of breaker—small for up to 50 amps, and large for over 50 amps. Either size may be used for main or branch breakers, although many larger panels are designed to accept the larger size breaker for the main and the smaller breaker for the branches. Figure 6.9 shows the dimensions and available current ratings for Ancor brand breakers up to 50 amps and Blue Sea Systems (Bussman) surface-mount breakers rated up to 150 amps AC or DC.

Fuses

Figure 6.10 shows a wide variety of fuses for boats. The electronic types (AGC and AGU) are available from 0.25 to 30 amps, and the automotive types (ATC and ATM) are rated from 5 to 30 amps. Sea Fuses run from 100 to 300 amps, ANL ignition-protected fuses from 50 to 675 amps, and Class T fuses from 175 to 400 amps.

Fuses may be mounted in equipment, fuse blocks, distribution panels, and in-line fuse holders.

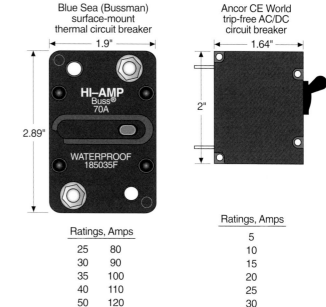

Fig. 6.9 Circuit Breakers

Ratings, Amps		Ratings, Amps
25	80	5
30	90	10
35	100	15
40	110	20
50	120	25
60	135	30
70	150	40
		50

Fig. 6.10 Common Marine Fuses and Fuse Blocks

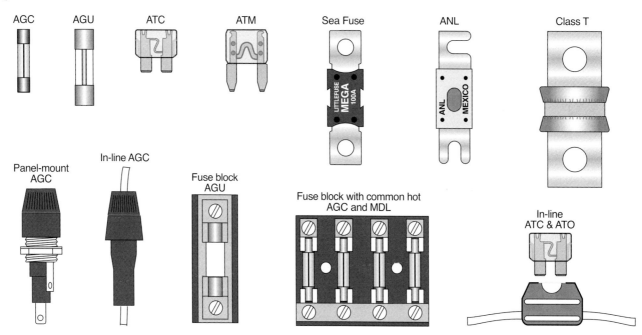

Tools

Most wiring failures occur at the connections. When copper corrodes it forms a layer of greenish copper oxide. Because it is thin, the oxide does little to the conductivity of the wire, but, because it is nonconductive, it forms a resistive barrier at surface-to-surface connections. Most remaining wiring failures are due to physical stresses on connections, such as engine vibration, or a pull on the conductor when an object or person accidentally strikes it.

Many boatowners spend as little as possible on specialized electrical tools. Instead, they attempt to make do with what they have. This is false economy. Although it is possible to make bad connections with good tools, it is virtually impossible to make good connections with bad tools.

Figure 6.11 shows a variety of specialized wiring tools. The cut, strip, and crimp tool should be your minimal investment. This tool is found in both hardware and electronics stores in a wide range of qualities. Two key considerations are:

1. The stripper holes should line up perfectly (try stripping a few wires before purchasing).
2. The tool should match the brand of terminals you will be crimping. Ideally you should be able to get both the crimp tool and connectors from the same manufacturer.

Professional electricians use ratcheting crimp tools. A single-crimp ratchet crimps just the barrel. A double-crimp ratchet crimps both the barrel and the sleeve. The advantage of the ratchet is that the tool will not release until the terminal has been crimped to the perfect degree. It is almost impossible to under- or over-crimp terminals designed for use with this tool.

Lugs are terminals for large conductors. The lug crimper in Figure 6.11 is actuated either by squeezing in a vise or by striking with a hammer.

Diagonal wire cutters ("diagonal pliers") distort the cut end, making it difficult to insert the wire into the proper size connector barrel. The wire and cable cutter shown shears the wire, resulting in cleaner cuts.

Most soldering problems are due to insufficient heat. It is better to get in and out quickly than to linger on a connector while the iron struggles to reach 400°F. The pocket-size butane soldering iron can produce all the heat you'll need, short of soldering battery lugs. It will burn for several hours on a filling and, best of all, free you from trailing cords.

Heated to 135 to 150°C/275–300°F, heat-shrink tubing shrinks to a third or less of its original diameter, gripping the conductor tightly. If the tubing contains adhesive, the melted adhesive seals out moisture and strengthens the connection at the same time.

Heat guns (not hair dryers) achieve temperatures in excess of 500°F/260°C and shrink the shrink tubing quickly.

Fig. 6.11 Special Tools for Wiring

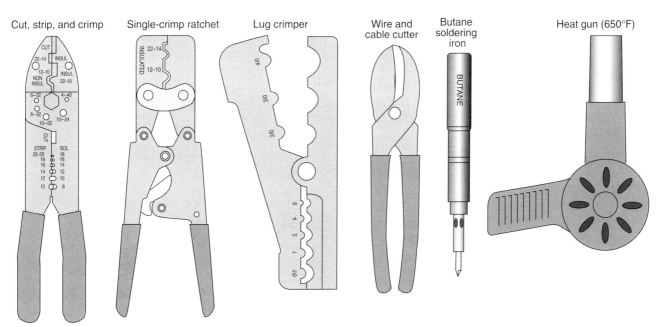

Cut, strip, and crimp   Single-crimp ratchet   Lug crimper   Wire and cable cutter   Butane soldering iron   Heat gun (650°F)

Conductor Connections

ABYC-Approved Connectors

Marine connectors differ from residential wiring connectors in being subject to vibration and other stresses. Figure 6.12 is self-explanatory and shows both approved and disapproved types of connectors. Note specifically that *the ubiquitous wire nut, so popular in household wiring, is not approved for marine use.*

Friction-type connectors (blade and bullet connectors, shown in Figure 6.12) can be used provided they resist a pull in the direction of the conductor of at least 6 pounds for 1 minute. The other connectors in Figure 6.12 must resist the tensile forces shown in Table 6.7 for at least 1 minute.

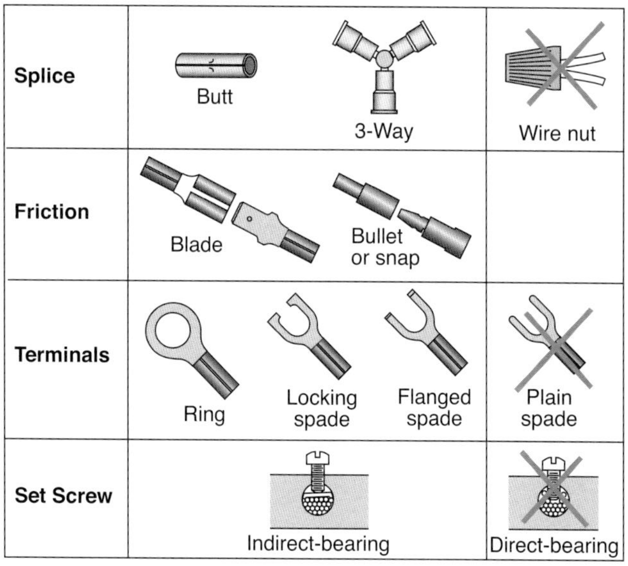

Solder

The use of solder in marine connections is controversial. Some experienced electricians feel that soldered connections are the most secure and best at eliminating terminal corrosion. Others point out that the solder in an overheated terminal may melt and allow the conductor to pull out of the terminal. A further problem is wicking of solder into the stranded conductor, resulting in a rigid portion that is liable to break like a solid conductor.

The ABYC states that solder should not be the sole means of mechanical connection in any circuit; the only exception is battery lugs with a solder-contact length of not less than 1.5 times the conductor diameter.

Solderless Heat-Shrink Connectors

Terminal systems are available that resolve all of the above problems (Figure 6.13). Although expensive (about twice the price of the usual automotive-grade materials), anything less in the hostile marine environment is false economy.

1. Pretinned, stranded conductors are available in all gauges and recommended colors. Pretinning (coating individual strands with solder) prevents oxidation of the strands, eliminates the need to cut a conductor back several inches when repairing, and facilitates soldering.
2. Heat-shrink tubing with adhesive coating, applied over both terminal and conductor, seals out moisture, makes the connection more secure, and insulates the terminal shank all at the same time. The shrink tubing may be purchased separately or already attached to terminals.

Fig. 6.12 Connectors for Marine Use

Splice	Butt — 3-Way — Wire nut
Friction	Blade — Bullet or snap
Terminals	Ring — Locking spade — Flanged spade — Plain spade
Set Screw	Indirect-bearing — Direct-bearing

Table 6.7 Tensile Test Values for Connections (Adapted from ABYC Standard E-11, Table XVI)

Conductor Size, AWG*	Force, lb.	Conductor Size, AWG	Force, lb.
18	10	4	70
16	15	3	80
14	30	2	90
12	35	1	100
10	40	0	125
8	45	2/0	150
6	50	3/0	175
5	60	4/0	225

*For equivalent metric cable sizes see Appendix

Fig. 6.13 Adhesive-Lined Heat-Shrink Tubing

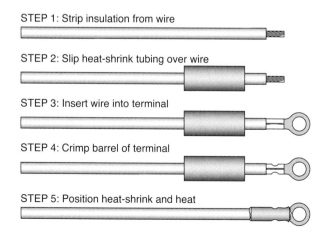

STEP 1: Strip insulation from wire

STEP 2: Slip heat-shrink tubing over wire

STEP 3: Insert wire into terminal

STEP 4: Crimp barrel of terminal

STEP 5: Position heat-shrink and heat

Other Termination Considerations

Figure 6.14 illustrates the remaining ABYC specifications for wiring connections:

1. The openings of ring and captive spade terminals should be of the same nominal size as the stud.
2. An extra length of conductor should be provided at terminations in order to relieve tension, permit fanning of multiple conductors, and allow for future repairs that might shorten the conductor.
3. Except for grounding conductors, terminal shanks should be insulated to prevent accidental shorting to adjacent terminals.
4. Connections should be in locations protected from weather or in weatherproof enclosures. If immersion is possible, connections should be watertight.
5. Terminal studs, nuts, and washers should be corrosion resistant and galvanically compatible with the conductor and terminal lug. Aluminum and unplated steel are unsuitable.
6. No more than four conductors should be attached to a single terminal stud. If necessary, two or more terminal studs may be connected by jumper straps.

Fig. 6.14 Proper Terminations

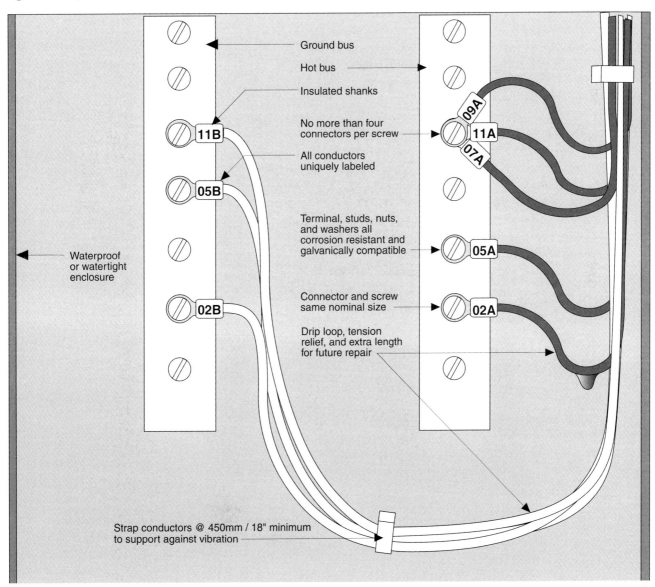

Conductor Connections

Coaxial Connectors

Coaxial cable consists of an insulated center conductor surrounded by a concentric (coaxial) grounded-shield conductor (either fine, braided strands or foil), all protected by an outer insulating jacket. Because the outer conductor (the shield) is grounded and completely surrounds the center conductor, coaxial cables neither radiate nor pick up much electrical noise. "Coax" is primarily used to connect antennas to electronic equipment, such as VHF and HF transceivers, and GPS receivers.

Like the wire used for DC wiring, coaxial cable for marine use should have pretinned, stranded center conductor and braid.

Table 6.8 lists the characteristics of five types of coaxial cable found on a boat:

- RG-58/U is very thin and is typically used only for interconnecting electronics where lengths are short and signal attenuation is not a problem.
- RG-59/U is used to connect television antennas and cable service.
- RG-8X is typically used to connect VHF and HF antennas up to lengths where attenuation becomes excessive.
- RG-8/U and RG-213 are both used to conduct maximum power to VHF and HF antennas. Marine coaxial cables are usually terminated at both ends with PL-259 8UHF connectors. It is important to know how to install this type of conductor, which has so many applications on a boat.

The significance of each of the specifications in the table is:

Conductor (size) AWG is important for heavy current flows, such as the output of SSB and ham radio transmitters.

Impedance is the high-frequency equivalent of resistance and must match the output impedance of the transmitter in order to achieve maximum output power. (All VHF and SSB radios are designed with 50 W output impedance.)

Attenuation is the loss of transmitted power between the radio and the antenna, where each 3 decibels (dB) represents a 50% loss of power.

Table 6.8 Coaxial Cables

Specification	RG-58/U	RG-59/U	RG-8X	RG-8/U	RG-213
Nominal O.D. (mm)	5	6	6	10	10
Conductor AWG	#20	#23	#16	#13	#13
Impedance, ohms	50	75	50	52	50
Attenuation/100', dB					
@ 50 MHz	3.3	2.4	2.5	1.3	1.3
@ 100 MHz	4.9	3.4	3.7	1.9	1.9
@ 1,000 MHz	21.5	12.0	13.5	8.0	8.0

Figure 6.15 shows just a few of the UHF, VHF, and UHF/VHF coaxial adapters available from such sources as RadioShack.

Figure 6.16 shows the assembly of UHF connectors on both large and small coaxial cables.

Figure 6.17 demonstrates the similar assembly of BNC connectors on RG-58/U, RG-59/U, and RG-8X coaxial cables.

Although there are solderless versions of connectors, they are not recommended for marine applications except in protected locations (inside cabin) due to corrosion. After assembly, it is a good idea to apply a moisture-displacing lubricant. If the connection is exposed to weather, the connection should be wrapped in a good quality plastic electrical tape to exclude moisture.

Fig. 6.15 A Few Coaxial Adapters

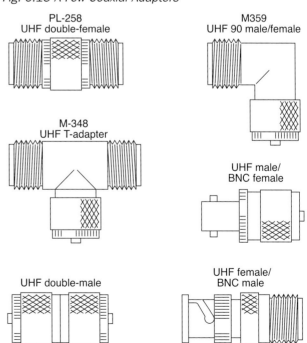

PL-258
UHF double-female

M359
UHF 90 male/female

M-348
UHF T-adapter

UHF male/
BNC female

UHF double-male

UHF female/
BNC male

Fig. 6.16 Assembly of PL-259 (UHF) Connectors

ON RG-58/U, RG-59/U, AND RG-8X CABLES

STEP 1: Slip on shell and adapter; strip outer jacket back 16mm (5/8")

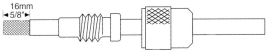

STEP 2: Bend back braided shield

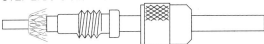

STEP 3: Slip adapter under braided shield

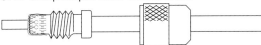

STEP 4: Strip center conductor 1/2" and tin

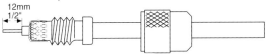

STEP 5: Screw on body and solder tip and braid through holes in body

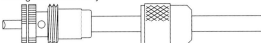

STEP 6: Screw shell onto body

ON RG-8/U AND RG-213 CABLES

STEP 1: Slip on shell and strip to center of conductor and back 3/4"

STEP 2: Strip outer jacket additional 8mm (5/16")

STEP 3: Slip on body, making sure shield does not contact center conductor, and solder tip and shield through holes

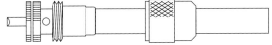

STEP 4: Screw shell onto body

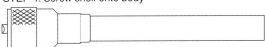

Fig. 6.17 Assembly of BNC Connectors

ON RG-58/U, RG-59/U, AND RG-8X CABLES
FEMALE CONNECTOR

STEP 1: Cut cable end even and strip outer jacket back 8mm (5/16")

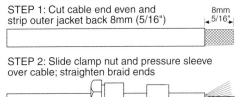

STEP 2: Slide clamp nut and pressure sleeve over cable; straighten braid ends

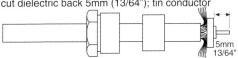

STEP 3: Fold braid back; insert ferrule inside braid; cut dielectric back 5mm (13/64"); tin conductor

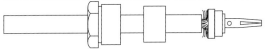

STEP 4: Trim excess braid; slide insulator over conductor into ferrule; slide female contact over conductor and solder

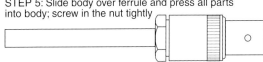

STEP 5: Slide body over ferrule and press all parts into body; screw in the nut tightly

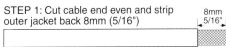

MALE CONNECTOR

STEP 1: Cut cable end even and strip outer jacket back 8mm (5/16")

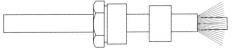

STEP 2: Slide clamp nut and pressure sleeve over cable; straighten braid ends

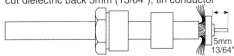

STEP 3: Fold braid back; insert ferrule inside braid; cut dielectric back 5mm (13/64"); tin conductor

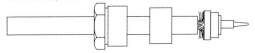

STEP 4: Trim excess braid; slide insulator over conductor into ferrule; slide male contact over conductor and solder

STEP 5: Slide body over ferrule and press all parts into body; screw in the nut tightly

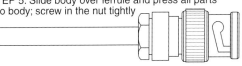

Ignition Protection

Gasoline and propane explosions are among the leading causes of marine loss of life. For this reason, the ABYC has adopted the ignition protection standards of the U.S. Coast Guard as described below.

Fuels

Boats using only diesel fuel are exempt. Boats using just a single LP (propane) or CNG appliance may exempt the gas appliance from the ignition protection standard provided:

1. Petrol/gasoline tank connections and regulators are outside of the hull or are located in an enclosure that is vapor-tight to the interior of the boat and vented overboard.
2. The petrol/gasoline supply can be shut off at the tank by a control that is part of or located near the appliance. Manual controls must provide a warning when the supply valve at the tank is open.

Boats using petrol/gasoline as a fuel for either propulsion or auxiliary generator are subject to the ignition protection standards shown here.

Isolation of Ignition Sources

Ignition sources located in the same spaces as petrol/gasoline engines, tanks, and fuel joints and fittings must be ignition-protected unless the components are *isolated* from the fuel sources. An electrical component is considered isolated from a fuel source if:

1. It is separated by a bulkhead of full width and height that leaks no more than ¼ ounce of water per hour with a water height of 12 inches or one-third the bulkhead height (whichever is less), and has no higher opening with greater than ¼-inch gap around its perimeter.
2. The electrical component is separated by a floor, deck, or other type of enclosure.
3. The distance between the electrical component and the fuel source is at least 2 feet, and the space between is open to the atmosphere, where "open" means 15 square inches of open area per cubic foot of net compartment volume.

Figures 6.18 through 6.24 illustrate these requirements for a variety of installations.

Fig. 6.18 Bulkheads (Adapted from ABYC Standard E-11, Figure 8)

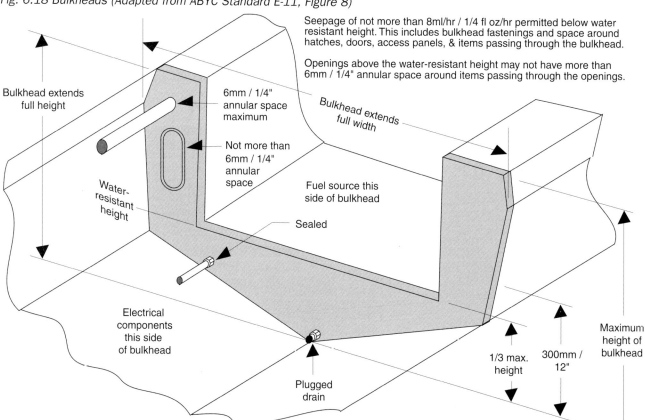

Fig. 6.19 Isolation of Ignition Sources
(Adapted from ABYC Standard E-11, Figure 1)

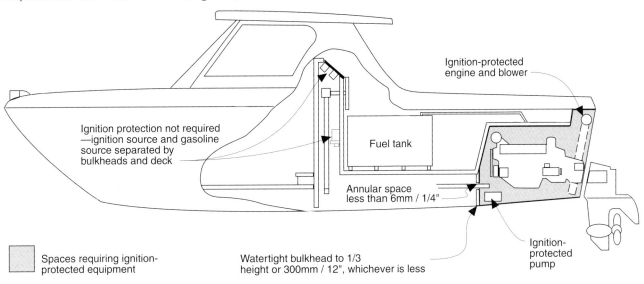

Ignition-protected
engine and blower

Ignition protection not required
—ignition source and gasoline
source separated by
bulkheads and deck

Fuel tank

Annular space
less than 6mm / 1/4"

Ignition-
protected
pump

Spaces requiring ignition-
protected equipment

Watertight bulkhead to 1/3
height or 300mm / 12", whichever is less

Fig. 6.20 Isolation of Ignition Sources
(Adapted from ABYC Standard E-11, Figure 2)

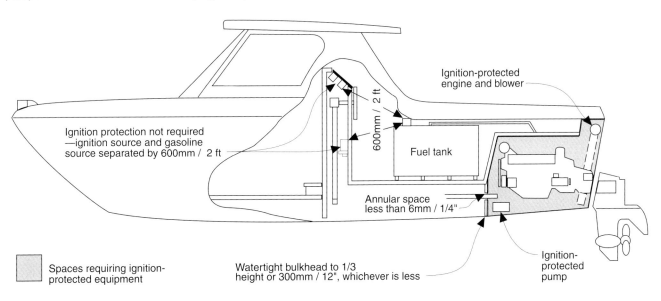

Ignition-protected
engine and blower

Ignition protection not required
—ignition source and gasoline
source separated by 600mm / 2 ft

600mm / 2 ft

Fuel tank

Annular space
less than 6mm / 1/4"

Ignition-
protected
pump

Spaces requiring ignition-
protected equipment

Watertight bulkhead to 1/3
height or 300mm / 12", whichever is less

Ignition Protection

Fig.6.21 Isolation of Ignition Sources
(Adapted from ABYC Standard E-11, Figure 5)

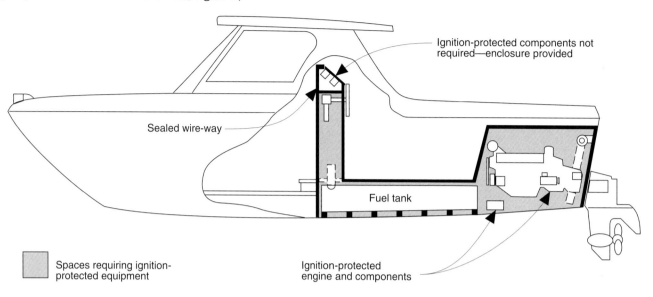

Ignition-protected components not
required—enclosure provided

Sealed wire-way

Fuel tank

Spaces requiring ignition-
protected equipment

Ignition-protected
engine and components

Fig. 6.22 Isolation of Ignition Sources
(Adapted from ABYC Standard E-11, Figure 3)

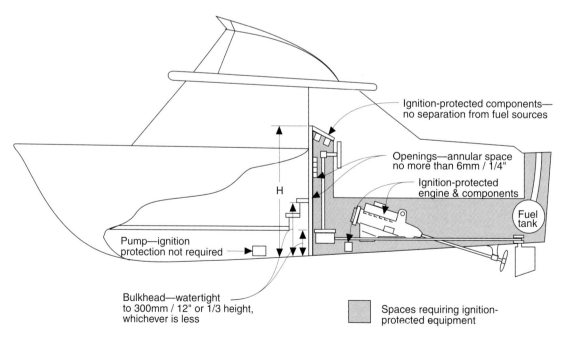

Ignition-protected components—
no separation from fuel sources

Openings—annular space
no more than 6mm / 1/4"

Ignition-protected
engine & components

Fuel
tank

H

Pump—ignition
protection not required

Bulkhead—watertight
to 300mm / 12" or 1/3 height,
whichever is less

Spaces requiring ignition-
protected equipment

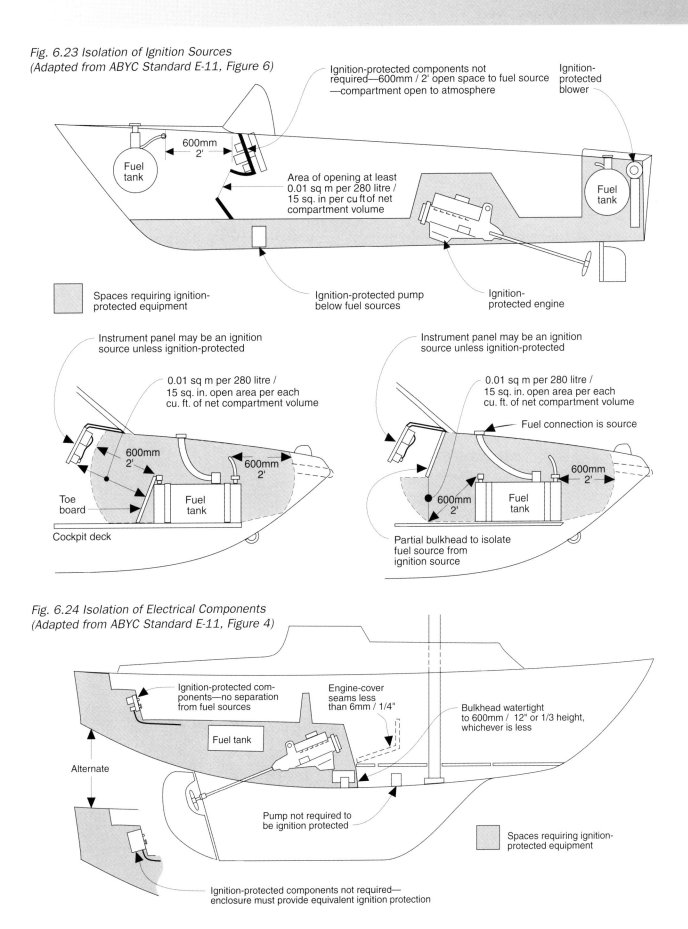

Fig. 6.23 Isolation of Ignition Sources
(Adapted from ABYC Standard E-11, Figure 6)

Ignition-protected components not required—600mm / 2' open space to fuel source —compartment open to atmosphere

Ignition-protected blower

600mm 2'

Fuel tank

Fuel tank

Area of opening at least 0.01 sq m per 280 litre / 15 sq. in per cu ft of net compartment volume

Spaces requiring ignition-protected equipment

Ignition-protected pump below fuel sources

Ignition-protected engine

Instrument panel may be an ignition source unless ignition-protected

0.01 sq m per 280 litre / 15 sq. in. open area per each cu. ft. of net compartment volume

600mm 2'

600mm 2'

Toe board

Fuel tank

Cockpit deck

Instrument panel may be an ignition source unless ignition-protected

0.01 sq m per 280 litre / 15 sq. in. open area per each cu. ft. of net compartment volume

Fuel connection is source

600mm 2'

600mm 2'

Fuel tank

Partial bulkhead to isolate fuel source from ignition source

Fig. 6.24 Isolation of Electrical Components
(Adapted from ABYC Standard E-11, Figure 4)

Ignition-protected components—no separation from fuel sources

Engine-cover seams less than 6mm / 1/4"

Bulkhead watertight to 600mm / 12" or 1/3 height, whichever is less

Fuel tank

Alternate

Pump not required to be ignition protected

Spaces requiring ignition-protected equipment

Ignition-protected components not required— enclosure must provide equivalent ignition protection

CHAPTER 7

AC Basics

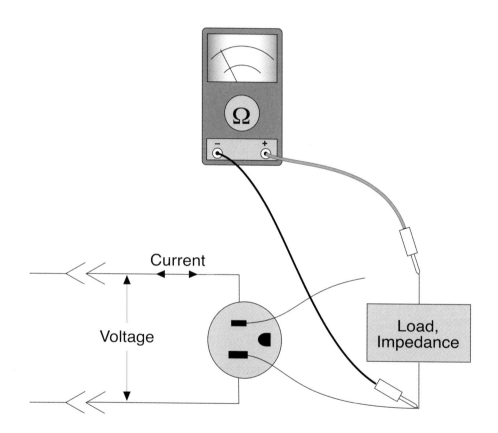

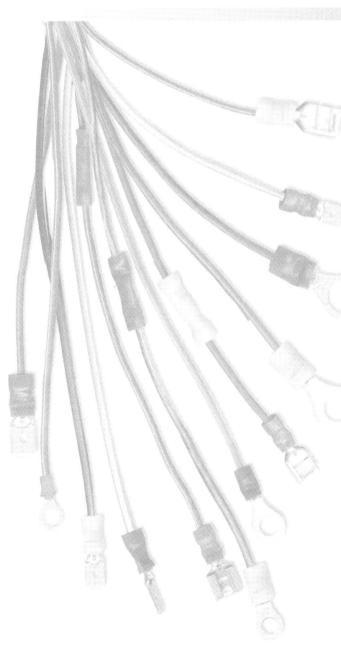

Boaters are increasingly demanding the convenience of onboard AC power. We are familiar with DC power from Chapters 1 through 6. Now we need to know how alternating current differs.

In the Will the Real Voltage Please Stand Up? section the theory, although describing a 110–125 VAC situation, generally applies to the 220–250 VAC supplies used in the UK and Europe.

We'll find that phase is as important as voltage and frequency. Some systems have only a single phase. Others utilize three separate phases and are called three-phase. Because voltage and current in a conductor may differ in phase, a concept termed the power factor is needed to calculate AC power.

However, three-phase electrical supplies are not used in the UK and Europe for small craft on board or shore supplies, as single phase 240 VAC supply can cater for higher demand than 110 VAC.

AC safety is largely a function of grounding. Because mistaking a live wire for an earth or ground wire can prove fatal, conductor identification is extremely important. Even with proper conductor identification, however, we need ground fault devices to guard against breaks in the ground system.

BMEA and ISO Color Code for 240 VAC Conductors

European and UK Practice		USA Practice	
Conductor	**Colors**	**Conductor**	**Colors**
Live	Brown	Ungrounded (hot)	Black
Neutral	Light Blue	Grounded (neutral)	White
Ground(ing)/Earth	Green/Yellow	Ground(ing)/Earth	Green

Both color groups conform with ISO standards.

Alternating Current

Alternating current electricity (AC) is easily understood once you have grasped the fundamentals of direct current electricity (DC). If you understand the relationships between voltage, current, and resistance in DC circuits, then you are ready for the very similar relationships in AC circuits. If you are unfamiliar with Ohm's Law, however, first review the DC concepts presented in Chapters 1 and 2.

Figure 4.2 showed us the output of a rotary current machine. Rotation of a magnet between coils of wire induces a sinusoidal current in the wire. Because the current alternates polarity, it is known as alternating current. If we used a meter to measure the voltage across, instead of current through, the coils, we would see that the voltage is of the same sinusoidal form as the current (Figure 7.1). All modern generators and alternators produce this sinusoidal current and voltage prior to rectification.

Fig. 7.1 Alternating Voltage/Current

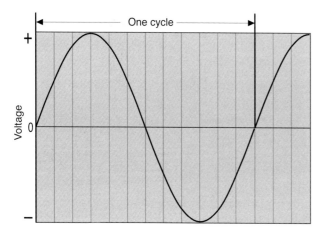

One full oscillation of voltage or current—plus, minus, and back to plus—is a cycle. The number of cycles completed in one second is the frequency. The unit of frequency (cycles per second) is Hertz, abbreviated Hz. Utility electricity in the United States is precisely regulated at 60 Hertz and in Europe at 50 Hertz. If you plugged a U.S.-built synchronous-motor electric clock into a European outlet, it would advance 50 minutes per hour instead of 60.

Many people still have not adopted the term Hertz, first introduced in the 1960s. They use the colloquial *cycles*, as in 60 cycles per second, instead of the proper 60 Hertz. Little harm is done, though, since everyone knows what is meant.

Will the Real Voltage Please Stand Up?

Read the labels on the under- or backside of your AC electric appliances, tools, and entertainment devices. Which is correct: 110, 112, 115, 117, 120, or 125 volts? There is no universal agreement as to standard AC voltage. Different utility companies aim at different nominal voltages. In addition, the voltage delivered to your home is likely to vary by a few volts, depending on the other loads in your neighborhood and the total load on the grid. In this book, we will adopt a nominal standard of 120 volts.

The first electric service supplied by utilities was in the form of 120 volts DC. The change to AC was made because AC power is easily transformed (by transformers) to higher voltage and correspondingly lower current. Since voltage drop in a wire is proportional to current and not voltage, greater voltage results in reduced loss in transmission. To take advantage of this fact, the power company distributes power over the grid at extremely high voltages (several hundred thousand), then transforms it down in progressive steps to the 120 volts AC that enters your home.

Electric lights, the first electric devices used in the home, work equally well on AC and DC, provided the power dissipated in the filament is the same. As we learned in Chapter 1, electrical power is the product of voltage and current,

$$P = V \times I$$

where: P = power consumption in watts
V = volts across the load
I = amps through the load

Using Ohm's Law, which works equally well for DC and AC with purely resistive loads, we can also express power as $P = V^2/R$. Since the resistance, R, of a lamp filament is purely resistive, equal AC and DC power dissipation reduces to:

$$(V_{DC}{}^2)_{ave} = (V_{AC}{}^2)_{ave}$$

In other words the average value of the squared AC voltage must equal the average value of the squared DC voltage.

It is easier to think in terms of equivalent DC voltage, so we say,

$$\text{Equivalent } V_{DC} = (V_{AC}{}^2{}_{ave})^{1/2}$$

The equivalent DC voltage is computed as the square root of the mean value of the squared AC voltage (the root mean square [RMS] value of the AC voltage).

In the case of a sinusoidal AC voltage, the peak AC voltage is simply $(2)^{1/2}$, or 1.414, times the equivalent DC voltage. As shown in Figure 7.2, the peak voltage of 120 volts AC is actually 1.414 × 120 volts = 170 volts.

Fig. 7.2 Peak and RMS (Effective) AC Voltages

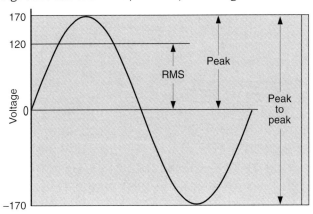

Phase

If you look at the wires coming into your home, you'll see three. Two are covered with heavy rubber insulation and are "live." The third, forming a shield around the other two, is "neutral" and maintained at the electrical potential of the earth or ground.

If we plot the voltages between the three wires, they look as in Figure 7.3. Between wires A and C, we have 120 volts AC, just as in Figure 7.2. Between B and C, we also have 120 volts AC, but the polarity is opposite that of A and C. That is, when the voltage of wire A is at its maximum positive value, the voltage of wire B is at its maximum negative value.

If we ignore the neutral wire, C, and look at the instantaneous voltage between the two live wires, A and B, we see it is the difference, or twice 120 volts AC.

Fig. 7.3 120/240 AC Voltages

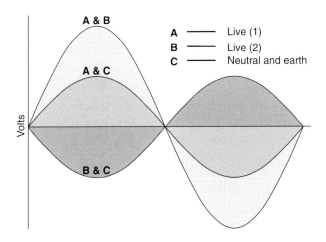

$$V_{AB} = V_A - V_B$$
$$= 120\,V_{AC} - (-120\,V_{AC})$$
$$= 240\,V_{AC}$$

Thus from the three incoming supply conductors, we actually derive three different voltage sources: 120 V_{AC}, 120 V_{AC}, and 240 V_{AC}.

The phase, Ø, of a sinusoidal wave is its horizontal position along the sinusoidal wave, as shown in Figure 7.4. Consider waveform A starting at the left. At Ø = 0°, the voltage is passing through 0 volts and rising. At Ø = 90°, the voltage is at its maximum positive value. At Ø = 180°, the voltage is zero again but decreasing. At Ø = 270°, the voltage is at its most negative value. Finally, at 360° the voltage has come full cycle.

This waveform is called single-phase (abbreviated as 1Ø) because, although changing, there is only one phase present at any time.

Figure 7.4 shows two additional waveforms, labeled B and C. Waveform B lags waveform A by 120°, while waveform C lags A by 240°. Where all three phases are present in the same voltage source (shore-power cable, generator output, distribution panel, etc.), the power is said to be three-phase or 3Ø.

Fig. 7.4 Three-Phase AC

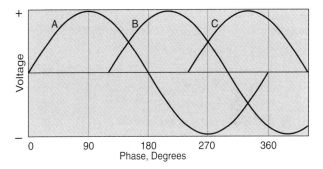

Using the same logic, the 120/240 volts AC power coming into your home (Figure 7.3) should be termed two-phase. For whatever reason, however, it is considered and termed single-phase.

Small boats with minimal AC equipment use only 120 VAC, 1Ø shore power, essentially that provided by a heavy-duty 120 VAC extension cord. Larger boats often use 120/240 VAC, 1Ø hookups to double the available power and to operate large appliances, such as electric ranges and water heaters. The largest boats may use 120/240 volts AC, 3Ø or 120/208 VAC, 3Ø hookups to increase the power even further in order to operate large appliances and take advantage of the higher efficiencies of 3Ø electric motors.

Power Factor

Figure 7.5 shows a simple AC circuit without the complications of a grounding wire. Until a load is plugged into the receptacle, the circuit from the live wire to the neutral wire remains open. Although voltage exists between live and neutral, no current flows because the circuit is not complete.

Fig. 7.5 A Simple AC Circuit

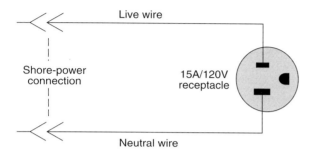

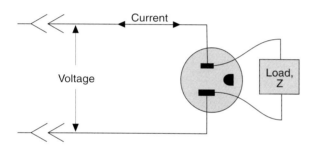

At the bottom we have plugged a load (a motor, for example) into the receptacle with a two-prong plug. Now current flows because the circuit has been closed, or completed, through the load.

Note that the load is labeled Z instead of R. Z is the symbol for *impedance*, the AC equivalent of resistance. Impedance consists of a combination of the load's DC resistance and its reactance (transient reaction to changing voltage). We won't go into the mathematics, but capacitors accept voltage changes readily, while inductors (coils) oppose voltage change. For this reason, the relationship between voltage and current in an AC circuit is not one to one, as it is in DC circuits, but is a function of frequency.

Figure 7.6 shows plots of both voltage and current in our AC motor circuit. In this example, the motor load possesses inductance, so the current lags behind the voltage by phase angle Ø. If the load were more capacitive than inductive, voltage would lag current, and Ø would be negative.

Fig. 7.6 Three-Phase AC

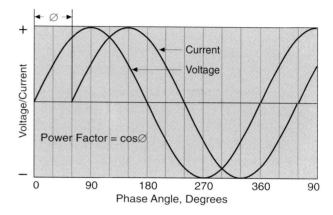

The relationship between voltage and current is usefully expressed by the load's power factor, PF.

$$PF = Watts/(Volts \times Amps)$$
where: Watts = true power consumed
Volts = measured volts
Amps = measured amps

Were the load purely resistive, voltage and current would be in phase, watts would equal volts times amps, and the power factor would be 1.0. Since the load has an inductive component, however, voltage and current are never simultaneously at their maximum values, so the true power (instantaneous product of voltage and current) is less than the maximum voltage times the maximum current, and the power factor is less than 1.0.

As shown in Figure 7.6, PF equals cos Ø, the cosine of the phase angle between voltage and current. For purely resistive loads such as incandescent lamps, Ø = 0°, so PF = 1.0. In the example shown, current lags behind voltage by 60° (Ø = 60°), so PF = cos 60° = 0.5.

The definition of PF can also be written as

$$Amps = Watts/(Volts \times PF)$$

The above equation indicates the problem with small PF. For the same wattage of useful power, halving PF doubles amps. Greater amps means larger supply conductors, greater voltage drops, greater resistive heating, and decreased efficiency.

The power factor of an electric motor can be very small when the rotor is stalled. As a result, locked-rotor and start-up currents can be three to five times normal running current, a factor which must be considered when protecting motor circuits.

Electricity is dangerous yet indispensable in our lives. Unfortunately the marine environment both worsens the hazards and degrades the materials. Understanding AC electricity and its effects on the body should convince you of the importance of AC wiring standards, such as those promoted by the ABYC.

The basic safety problem stems from the fact that the human body is an electrochemical/mechanical system. At the center of this system is an advanced computer—the brain. External stimuli are converted to electrical signals by transducers, such as the eyes (light to electricity), ears (sound to electricity) and nerves (touch and temperature to electricity). The electrical signals are conducted to the brain through nerve fibers acting much like conducting wires. The brain processes the incoming information and then sends out appropriate electrical signals in response. The most obvious effect of the outgoing signals is the stimulation and contraction of muscles. Herein lies the danger of externally applied electrical current.

Because the fluids in your body have the same approximate composition as salt water, your body has the same electrical conductivity. If you bridge an electrical circuit, you becomes a *part of that circuit*, and electric current flows through it. Muscles in your body, including your heart, cannot distinguish between electrical signals from the brain and the electric current we call a shock.

If you are fortunate, the involuntary muscle contraction propels you away from the source. A less fortunate reaction would be contraction of the muscles in the hand and a rigid grip on the source. Worst of all would be current through the chest and heart muscle, resulting in interruption of your heartbeat.

Figure 7.7 compares the dangers of various current paths through the body. The second panel shows a shock that, although painful and possibly resulting in a burn, is not usually life-threatening. Since both live and neutral or ground conductors are in the same hand, current flow is limited to the hand muscles. Herein lies the danger of electrical shock.

The third figure explains why electricians often work with one hand in ticklish situations. If one hand were to contact a live wire or case and the other hand a ground, the resulting current flow would be directly through the chest.

The bottom figure illustrates the second dangerous situation: contact with a live wire or case while standing on a wet and conductive ground. The current flow is again directly through the chest and heart.

Fig. 7.7 The Dangers of Electrical Shock

Safe: Standing on nonconductive surface

Unpleasant: Live and earth/ground in same hand

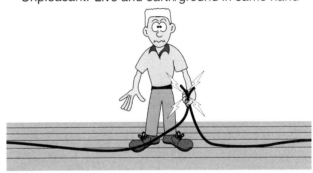

Lethal: Live and ground in opposite hands

Lethal: Standing in/on conductive ground

Grounding or Earthing

Figure 7.7 showed what happens when a person contacts a live wire or equipment case while standing on a grounded or earthed conductive surface. The body serves as a parallel return conductor to ground or earth.

But who would ever grasp a live wire? Figure 7.8, top, shows that it is not always necessary to touch a live wire directly to receive a potentially lethal shock. The live and neutral wires of the motor cord are intended to be isolated from each other and from the metal case. Unfortunately, through chafe or overheating of its insulation, the live wire has shorted to the motor case. Operation of the motor may be unaffected, but when you contact the case, the result is the same as touching the live wire directly.

Figure 7.8, bottom, shows the solution: the grounding wire or protective conductor, connected to the neutral wire back at the power source, runs parallel to the neutral wire throughout the circuit. This grounding wire is connected to the exterior metallic case of every electrical device. If the live wire were to short to the case, the grounding wire would offer the stray current a nearly zero-resistance return path to ground, thus preventing significant current through the more resistive human body.

If the short circuit from the live conductor to the case were of low enough resistance, the short circuit current would blow the fuse or trip the circuit breaker in the black conductor. Even were the current insufficient to trip the breaker, however, the grounding wire would provide a low-resistance safety path. It should be obvious that this grounding conductor should never be interrupted by a switch, fuse, or circuit breaker.

With each conductor playing an assigned role in

Fig. 7.8 The Green Grounding (earth) Wire

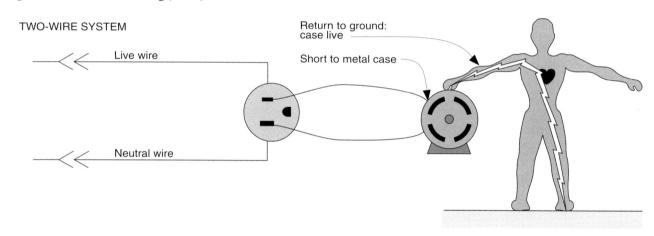

TWO-WIRE SYSTEM

Live wire

Neutral wire

Return to ground: case live

Short to metal case

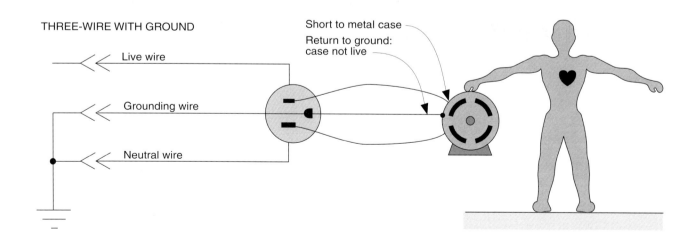

THREE-WIRE WITH GROUND

Live wire

Grounding wire

Neutral wire

Short to metal case

Return to ground: case not live

safety, it is critical that they are never accidently confused or reversed. Standards IEC 60446 and ISO 13297:2000 assign specific colors to to the insulation of each conductor in an AC circuit. Table 7.1 shows the color code for AC conductors:

Table 7.1 BMEA and ISO Color Code for 240 VAC Conductors

European and UK Practice		USA Practice	
Conductor	**Colors**	**Conductor**	**Colors**
Live	Brown	Ungrounded (hot)	Black
Neutral	Light Blue	Grounded (neutral)	White
Ground(ing)/Earth	Green/Yellow	Ground(ing)/Earth	Green

Both color groups conform with ISO standards.

To prevent accidental reversal of the conductors at plug and socket connections, both sockets and plugs are designed so that they can be connected in only one way, and each screw terminal is assigned a color matching its conductor.

Figure 7.9 shows a typical US example: the 15 A/120 VAC polarized receptacle used in both residential and marine applications. Notice that the rectangular sockets and prongs are of different sizes. It is impossible to insert the mating polarized plug the wrong way and reverse the live and neutral conductors. All screw terminals are color coded to ensure proper installation. The terminal for the live conductor is darkest; the neutral terminal is silver; the grounding terminal is tinted green.

Fig. 7.9 Polarized 120 VAC Duplex Receptacle

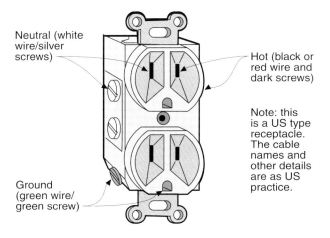

Neutral (white wire/silver screws)

Hot (black or red wire and dark screws)

Note: this is a US type receptacle. The cable names and other details are as US practice.

Ground (green wire/green screw)

Added Safety: Ground Fault Devices

The grounding conductor of Figure 7.8 goes a long way toward providing safety from electrocution, but what if the grounding wire breaks, or the device is used on a

two-wire extension cord with no grounding conductor? There are numerous ways that the purpose of the grounding wire can be circumvented. To protect against these accidents, an ingenious type of circuit breaker is recommended for all AC outlets located in head, galley, machinery space, or on deck.

Figure 7.10 demonstrates the operation of a Residual Current Device (RCD) or a ground fault circuit interrupter (GFCI). In a normally functioning AC circuit, current flows through the live and neutral conductors are equal and opposite. The grounding conductor is connected to the neutral conductor at the point of origin (the distribution panel), but not at the individual receptacles and devices. Thus, the grounding wire does not normally carry any current. Every electron flowing in the live conductor is intended to be returned by the neutral conductor. Any difference in current between the live and neutral conductors must, therefore, represent a stray (dangerous) current.

In the GFCI both live and neutral conductors pass through a circular magnet. Current in the live conductor induces a magnetic field in the magnet, but the equal and opposite current in the neutral conductor induces the opposite magnetic field. The net magnetic field is thus zero.

A difference in the two currents, however, produces

Fig. 7.10 Ground Fault Circuit Interrupter (GFCI or RCD)

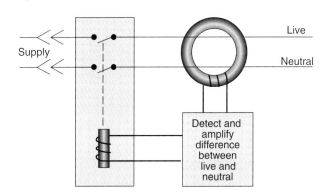

Supply

Live

Neutral

Detect and amplify difference between live and neutral

a net magnetic field, which induces a current in the detecting coil. This current activates a solenoid that opens either the live conductor (single-pole GFCI) or both live and neutral conductors (double-pole GFCI). The Class A GFCI recommended for marine use opens on a current difference of only 0.005 amp—far less than a lethal current to humans. Although the sensitivity of these devices can be annoying when trying to establish a shore-power connection, it is better to be annoyed than dead.

Transformers

AC to AC

The great advantage of AC over DC power is the possibility of increasing and decreasing voltage.

Figure 7.11 shows a simple transformer. It consists of two insulated coils, both wound around the same iron core. AC current flowing in the input coil induces an alternating magnetic field in the core which, in turn, induces an AC current in the output coil. If the number of turns in the input and output coils are identical, output voltage is identical to input voltage. This transformer preserves the identity of the conductors and the phases of the input and output by tying the neutral conductors together. The grounding wire is similarly uninterrupted and is bonded to the transformer case.

Figure 7.12 shows a step-down (voltage reducing) transformer. The number of turns in the output coil is less than the number of turns in the input coil. The voltage induced in the output coil is, therefore, less than the voltage in the input coil. (The ratio of voltages simply equals the ratio of turns.)

As with Figure 7.11 the identities of the input and output conductors and phases are preserved by tying the neutral conductors together. The grounding wire is again bonded to the transformer case.

Figure 7.13 shows an isolation transformer. Here neither neutral nor grounding conductors are connected. The neutral and grounding conductors on the output side are connected, however, so that the transformer output acts as an independent electrical source, isolated from shore ground.

The grounding wire from the shore-power side is connected to the shield between the input and output coils. Other common configurations include connection of the grounding wire to an inside case or to an outside case. In any case, follow the manufacturer's recommendation.

The isolation transformer is ideal for shore-power hookups because it interrupts the grounding wire from the shore-power circuit, which might otherwise provide a path for stray corrosion currents between boats sharing the same shore-power circuit. Isolation transformers will be discussed further in Chapter 9.

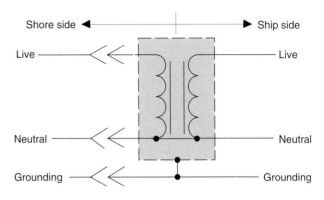

Fig. 7.11 A 1:1 Transformer

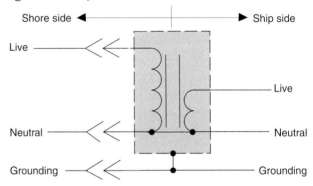

Fig. 7.12 A Step-Down Transformer

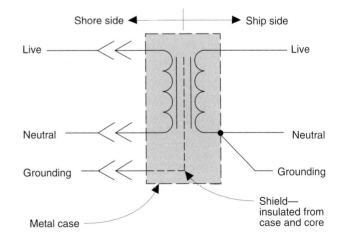

Fig. 7.13 An Isolation Transformer

Converting AC to DC

As we saw in Chapter 4, alternating current can be converted to direct current. In Figure 7.14, a diode in the output allows current to flow only in the direction of the symbolic arrow. As a result, the positive current half-waves are conducted while the negative half-waves are blocked. Although not constant, the output current never reverses polarity and is, thus, direct current.

The full-wave rectifier in Figure 7.15 employs a diode bridge of four interconnected diodes to conduct both positive and negative half-waves. During the positive current half-wave, the two diodes at the top conduct. During the negative current half-wave, the bottom two diodes conduct. Since the input and output coils are electrically isolated, both half-waves appear as positive when seen at the output.

The output voltages of both the half-wave and the full-wave rectifier still look to the eye more like alternating current than direct current, due to the extreme amount of ripple. The DC power supply in Figure 7.16 employs a large capacitor across the output to filter, or smooth, the pulses for a nearly ripple-free output.

The simple battery charger in Figure 7.17 uses the battery itself, instead of a capacitor, to smooth the ripple. As we saw in Chapter 4, the rectified output of an alternator is similarly smoothed by the large capacity of the battery it charges.

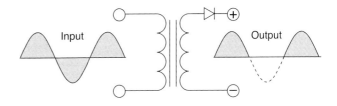

Fig. 7.14 The Half-Wave Rectifier

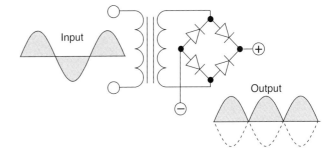

Fig. 7.15 The Full-Wave Rectifier

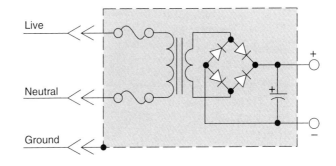

Fig. 7.16 A Filtered DC Power Supply

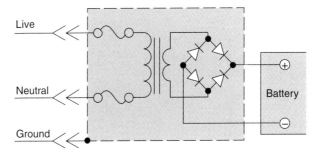

Fig. 7.17 A Battery Charger

AC Measurements

The common multimeter can be used for AC as well as DC measurements, although with fewer ranges and with reduced accuracy. Fortunately, accuracy is rarely of importance in AC measurements. While a difference of just 0.1 VDC represents about 10% of the capacity of a 12-volt battery, an acceptable range of shore-power voltage may be 220 to 240 volts AC.

AC Voltage

Figure 7.18 shows a multimeter being used to measure AC voltage. The meter employs the same internal circuitry to measure and display both AC and DC voltages, except that the AC voltage is first rectified by an internal diode bridge. In some multimeters the positive test lead must be switched to a separate AC jack that feeds the diode bridge. Attempting to measure AC volts on a DC volts setting will do no harm but will likely result in a reading of 0 volts, since the numerical average of AC voltage is zero.

AC Impedance

As we saw earlier, impedance may vary with frequency and, in the case of AC motors, with the speed of the motor. Such measurements are beyond the scope of this book and the wallets of most boaters. What we can measure is the resistive component of the impedance. To do so, the load must be isolated from the rest of the circuit as shown in Figure 7.19. Simply disconnecting one of the leads effects electrical isolation.

The resistance component of many AC loads is quite small, so be sure to zero the meter first by touching the test leads together and adjusting the zero-ohms knob. In digital multimeters zeroing is automatic.

Fig. 7.18 Measuring AC Voltage

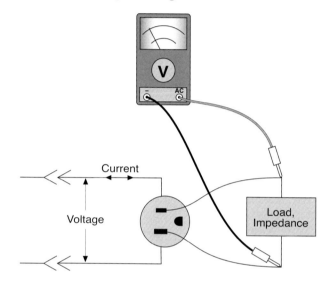

Fig. 7.19 Measuring the Resistive Component of Impedance

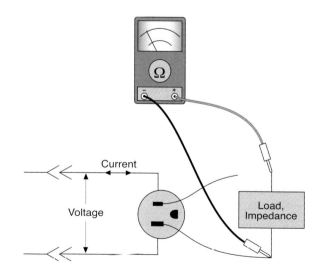

AC Amps

Inexpensive multimeters can measure up to 250 milliamps (0.25 amp) of AC current directly, as shown in Figure 7.20, top. To make the measurement, make sure the multimeter switches and leads are in the correct positions. Then disconnect the live conductor from the load and insert the multimeter leads between the conductor and the load.

The trick employed in high-current ammeters can be used to measure AC currents greater than 0.25 amp. Figure 7.20, middle, shows a shunt inserted in the current-carrying conductor. A shunt is a low-ohm precision resistor that generates a voltage drop in accordance with Ohm's Law. Shunts are specified by the ratio of voltage drop across to the maximum current through the shunt. For example, a 50 mV per 100 A shunt is intended for currents of up to 100 amps and produces 50 millivolts across its terminals at full current. From Ohm's Law, we calculate the resistance of this shunt to be:

$$R = V/I$$
$$= 0.050 \text{ volt}/100 \text{ amps}$$
$$= 0.0005 \text{ ohm}$$

More expensive multimeters usually contain internal shunts allowing direct current AC measurements of up to 10 amps.

If your multimeter does not have this capability, or if you wish to measure currents greater than 10 A, you can purchase a 100 millivolts per 100 amps, 50 millivolts per 200 amps, or other shunt for less than the cost of another ammeter. You can then use your multimeter on a millivolts setting to read amps flowing through the shunt.

If you have money to spare, a more expensive, but less accurate, special-purpose AC meter employs a clamp that is placed around the live conductor (Figure 7.20, bottom). The magnetic field around the conductor induces a current in the clamp. The current is then read as in any other type of test meter.

The advantage of the clamp-on meter is the ability to read current without disconnecting or cutting the conductor. A limitation is the requirement of physically separating the live and neutral conductors. If both live and neutral conductors are enclosed by the clamp, the opposing currents cancel so the meter reads zero.

A second disadvantage of the clamp-on meter is lack of sensitivity. While direct, in-line meters can measure microamps, the clamp-on meter is useful only down to milliamps.

Fig. 7.20 Measuring AC Currents

DIRECT

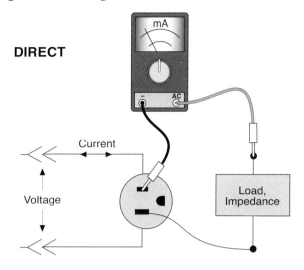

ACROSS SHUNT

*Shunt may be internal or external to meter

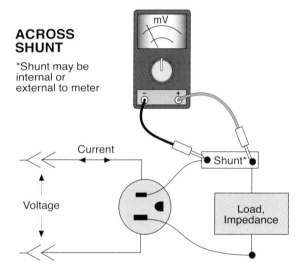

CLAMP-ON AMMETER

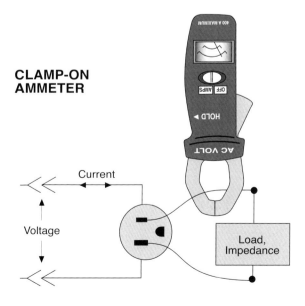

Troubleshooting AC Circuits

Testing a 240v circuit is no more difficult that testing a DC circuit, provided you keep in mind the functions of each of the conductors in the circuit. The ISO color code for AC conductors (see Table 7.1) is:

- Brown (or black) conductors should be live 240 VAC.
- Blue (or white) conductors should be at 0 volts relative to boat ground.
- Green/yellow (or green) conductors should be at 0 volts relative to boat ground.

Figure 7.21 shows a 240 VAC single phase supply. Note that the 120 VAC US-style receiver shown has a different configuration from 240 VAC UK/European units.

Set the meter to 250 VAC. Insert the test probes into the live and neutral holes. Since the live should be at 240 VAC and the neutral conductor at 0 VAC the meter should display 240 VAC. If the meter reads zero, shift the probe from the live socket to the earth/grounding socket.

If the meter now shows 240 VAC there is a fault somewhere in the neutral conductor, probably reversed polarity.

Fig. 7.21 Troubleshooting AC Circuits with a Multimeter

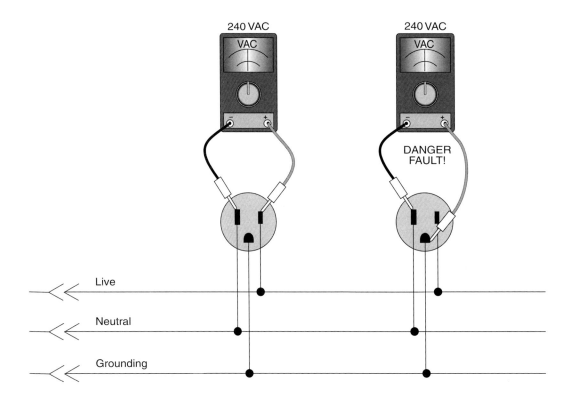

In spite of rigorous adherance to the color code, AC conductors can sometimes become switched. Most often the fault lies in a homemade shore-power cord where the mirror-image male and female plugs and receptacle patterns are easily confused.

Reverse polarity is a dangerous situation. The boat's ground is inadvertently raised to 240 VAC, *along with the seawater immediately surrounding the boat* via the bonding of underwater metal. A person swimming near the boat could be electrocuted.

Unfortunately, most AC electrical equipment will operate normally with reverse polarity. We need some way to test for proper polarity when establishing a shore-power connection.

Figure 7.22 shows how you can perform the test with a 240-volt lamp. The lamp should light whenever one of its leads is in the live socket and the other in either the neutral or grounding socket. If the lamp lights when the leads are in the neutral and grounding sockets, then either the neutral or the grounding conductor is live and the polarity is reversed. Fix the polarity immediately before someone is injured or electrocuted!

A proper shore-power hookup will have a reverse-polarity warning light in the AC-distribution panel (required by ABYC). If yours doesn't, you can install one as described in Chapter 14.

Alternatively, you can purchase a plug-in polarity tester at any hardware store for about $5. Plug it into an onboard AC receptacle each time you establish a shore-power connection. It may save someone's life.

Fig. 7.22 Testing the Polarity of an AC Circuit with a Lamp

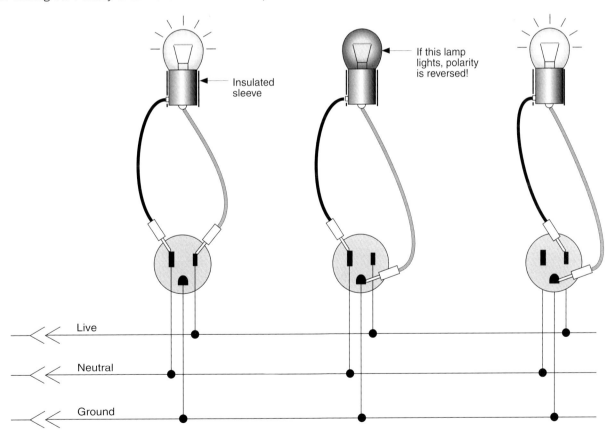

CHAPTER 8

Inverters and Generators

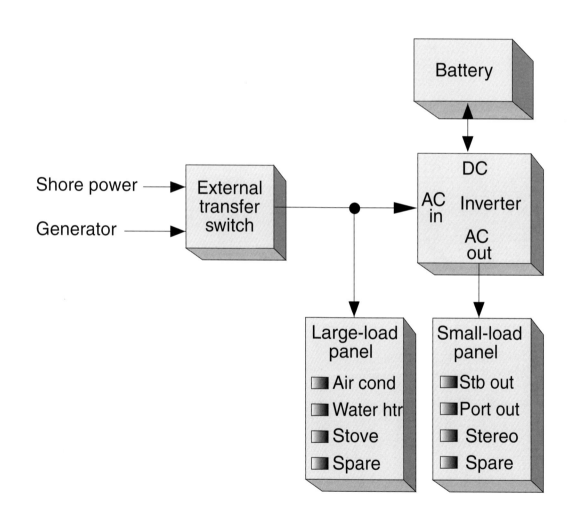

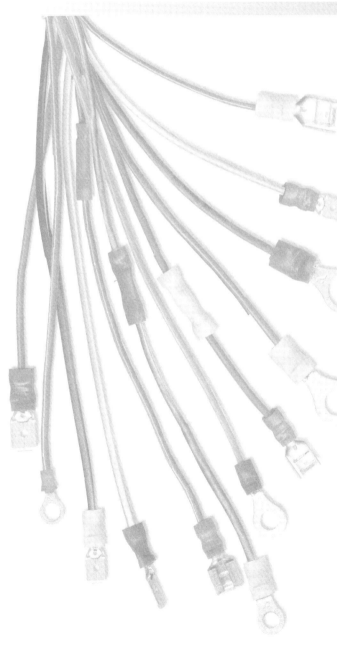

Why have AC power on a boat? Because AC appliances add quality to life aboard. Possible AC sources include shore power, inverters, and generators.

In order to select an inverter or generator you first need to determine your AC budget, or how much AC power you will likely consume.

Modern inverters can supply all the clean, regulated AC power you wish, along with the conveniences of automatic battery charging and transfer switching between shore power and battery.

Generators can do the same but, before choosing a generator over an inverter, you should verify that it is really necessary!

BMEA and ISO Color Code for 240 VAC Conductors

European and UK Practice		USA Practice	
Conductor	**Colors**	**Conductor**	**Colors**
Live	Brown	Ungrounded (hot)	Black
Neutral	Light Blue	Grounded (neutral)	White
Ground(ing)/Earth	Green/Yellow	Ground(ing)/Earth	Green

Both color groups conform with ISO standards.

Why Have AC Power?

I was cruising the Bahamas a few years ago. There's not much radio or TV programming in the Bahamas so I, like most other cruisers (and Bahamians as well), was idly listening to other boaters' conversations on VHF.

Two women were chatting about the weather, their plans for the afternoon, etc. Suddenly one said, "Whoops, gotta go; the toast is up."

There was a long pause. Then, "You have a toaster?"

"Sure," said the other, "I have toast or an English muffin every morning."

Another long pause. Then, "I'm going to kill you."

My sentiments exactly. Though there is a certain pristine beauty in adherence to the old ways—reading by oil lamp, navigating by sextant, boiling coffee grounds in a pot—for most liveaboards the ascetic life wears thin after a season or two. Considering the high performance and low cost of modern inverters, the question should be, "Why *not* have AC on your boat?"

AC Versus DC

You've probably already experimented with one or more DC appliances. Your first galley appliance may have been the 12 VDC blender you saw in a marine catalog. Under the Christmas tree came the 12-volt hair dryer and coffee grinder. The first season, however, the blender screeched to a halt and the other two appliances melted in a cloud of smoke. You learned why the appliances in our homes run on 120 or 240 VAC, not 12 VDC.

You may also have noticed that the 12-volt blender, for which you paid $89.95, goes for $19.95 in its AC incarnation at Wal-Mart. Several generalizations can be made about DC versus AC appliances:

1. AC appliances cost much less because there are at least 1,000 times as many manufactured.
2. AC appliances last longer because they are designed to survive 20 years rather than a few seasons.
3. You can only get serious power (for toasters, microwaves, hair dryers) with AC.

There are also a few exceptions to the AC/DC rule. Nearly all electronic circuits run on DC. A piece of electronic equipment designed specifically for DC can eliminate the internal AC-to-DC power supply and actually be more efficient than its AC equivalent. The automobile CD player is the best example. Even with the biggest and best inverter or generator aboard, your stereo should be powered by DC, just like all of your navigation electronics.

AC Sources

You have three options for getting AC power:
- Shore power
- Diesel or gasoline generator
- DC-to-AC inverter

Shore Power

Shore power is the same power as in your home. Essentially, you connect your boat to the utility company via an extension cord. Unlike in your home, however, there are significant safeguards that should be installed to protect against dangerous shocks and stray-current corrosion of your boat's underwater metals. These installation safeguards are discussed in Chapter 9.

Generators

Generators can supply large currents—enough to power an electric range. Unless your boat is a 100-foot yacht with a soundproof engine room (not compartment), generators are too smelly and noisy to be run 24 hours per day. You may become immune to the noise, but boaters anchored near you in Paradise Lagoon will probably consider you to be inconsiderate!

If you really must have an electric range, water heater, and air conditioner at anchor or underway, install a generator, but concentrate the heavy loads for an hour in the morning and an hour in the evening. Smaller loads can be run off your batteries via an inverter.

Inverters

Inverters are silent sources of AC that draw battery power derived from the engine alternator, a generator, or wind, water, or solar chargers. Many modern inverters are designed specifically for marine or mobile use, are nearly 100% efficient, are better regulated in voltage than your local utility, and are capable of more sophisticated battery charging than stand-alone battery chargers.

If you spend much time dockside, you'll want a substantial shore-power supply. Even if you spend most of the time anchored or moored, the cost of a shore supply is so small that you should install it anyway.

With an inverter, you'll be able to cast off the dock and shore-power lines and continue to use all of your small AC appliances without interruption.

If you have cloned your home with air conditioner, refrigerator, freezer, and electric range, however, you'll also need a substantial generator.

The first task is to determine how much AC power you will need. Table 8.1 lists the typical power consumptions of AC appliances and tools you may consider. The listed figures are representative and intended to be used for preliminary planning. If you already have the appliances, use their actual ratings instead.

On every tool and appliance is a nameplate listing its electrical consumption. The amps and/or watts shown are the maximum steady-state values at the specified voltages. Motor-driven devices often draw start-up currents several times larger than their nameplate ratings. This is usually of small concern with inverters and generators, since both are capable of surge currents far in excess of their continuous ratings. If your inverter or generator is sized to run within its steady-state capacity, it should have little trouble starting a motor.

To convert appliance ratings from amps to watts and vice versa, remember:

$$Watts = Volts \times Amps$$

Example: On the bottom of your toaster it says, "230 volt AC, 5 amps." First, ignore the fact that the voltage is listed as 230 volts instead of 240. Although your toast will brown more quickly on 240 than 230 volts, the toaster will function on any voltage between 220 and 250 volts AC.

To convert from amps to watts we use the formula:

$$Watts = Volts \times Amps$$
$$= 230 \text{ volts} \times 5 \text{ amps}$$
$$= 1{,}150 \text{ watts}$$

The voltage of your onboard source may actually be 240 volts AC, in which case the toaster will draw slightly more than 5 amps and 1,150 watts, but we are just estimating our needs at this point.

Column 3 of Table 8.1 lists typical operating times for each appliance. You may not have a listed appliance, or you may have it but rarely use it. The figures in column 3 are suggested operating times in hours per day when applicable. These figures obviously depend on lifestyle. For example, the table lists 1.3 hours per day for a 1,500-watt water heater. A single-handed boater might halve the listed time, but a family with teenagers might quadruple the listed 1.3 hours.

Table 8.1 Typical Appliance Power Consumption

Appliance	Typical Watts	Typical Hours Use Per Day
Air conditioner, 5,500 Btu/h	750	12
Air conditioner, 11,000 Btu/h	1,500	12
Blender	300	0.02
Broiler	1,400	0.25
Computer, desktop (w/o monitor)	60	2
Computer, laptop	60	2
Computer monitor, 17-inch CRT	65	2
Computer monitor, 15-inch LCD	30	2
Printer, inkjet	15	0.05
Printer, laser	800	0.05
Drill, ⅜-inch	350	0.02
Dryer, hair	1,200	0.05
Fan, 6-inch	25	8
Fan, 20-inch	250	8
Fry pan	1,200	0.25
Heater, space	1,200	12
Heater, water	1,500	1.3
Iron	1,100	0.15
Light	25–75	4
Microwave, 0.6 cu.ft.	800	0.15
Microwave, 1.5 cu.ft.	1,200	0.25
Mixer	240	0.05
Percolator	600	0.25
Range/element	1,200	1
Refrigerator, 6 cu. ft.	80	10
Refrigerator, 14 cu. ft.	140	10
Soldering iron	100	0.02
TV, 7-inch B&W	20	4
TV, 7-inch color	35	4
TV, 16-inch color	100	4
Toaster	1,100	0.15
VCR/DVD, play-only	20	2
VCR/DVD, play/record	80	2
Vacuum cleaner	800	0.05

After assembling your list of planned appliances, their rated wattages, and estimated hours of use, you are ready to compile your estimated daily electric load.

Table 8.2, on the next page, provides a blank form you can photocopy and complete to determine your typical daily consumption in watt-hours.

Figuring Your AC Budget

Table 8.2 Daily Electrical Consumption

Appliance	Rated Watts	Typical Use, Hours/Day	Watt-Hours per Day[1]	Peak Watts Inverter[2]	Generator[3]
_____	_____	_____	_____	_____	_____
_____	_____	_____	_____	_____	_____
_____	_____	_____	_____	_____	_____
_____	_____	_____	_____	_____	_____
_____	_____	_____	_____	_____	_____
_____	_____	_____	_____	_____	_____
_____	_____	_____	_____	_____	_____
_____	_____	_____	_____	_____	_____
_____	_____	_____	_____	_____	_____
_____	_____	_____	_____	_____	_____
_____	_____	_____	_____	_____	_____
_____	_____	_____	_____	_____	_____
_____	_____	_____	_____	_____	_____
_____	_____	_____	_____	_____	_____
_____	_____	_____	_____	_____	_____
_____	_____	_____	_____	_____	_____
_____	_____	_____	_____	_____	_____
_____	_____	_____	_____	_____	_____
_____	_____	_____	_____	_____	_____
_____	_____	_____	_____	_____	_____
_____	_____	_____	_____	_____	_____
_____	_____	_____	_____	_____	_____
_____	_____	_____	_____	_____	_____
_____	_____	_____	_____	_____	_____
		Totals			

[1] Watt-hours supplied by inverter.
[2] Peak watts supplied by inverter with generator off.
[3] Peak watts supplied by generator.

Tables 8.3 through 8.5 show example budgets of low, medium, and high AC-power use.

The low daily budget in Table 8.3 represents a traditional weekend cruiser with alcohol- or propane-fueled cooking, mechanical or 12-volt refrigeration, but 240-volt-AC entertainment.

This minimal budget requires an inverter with a maximum continuous rating of only about 500 watts, which draws about 35 Ah per day from the batteries.

Total battery consumption is 33 Ah (35 Ah considering inverter efficiency), plus the sum of the daily DC loads.

Table 8.3 Example of Low Daily Electrical Consumption

Appliance (240 VAC)	Rated Watts	Typical Use, Hours/Day	Watt-Hours per Day[1]	Peak Watts	
				Inverter[2]	Generator[3]
Blender	300	0.02	6	300	—
Computer	100	2.00	200	100	—
Drill, ⅜-inch	350	0.02	7	—	—
Soldering iron	100	0.02	2	—	—
TV, 7-inch color	35	4.00	140	35	—
VCR/DVD	20	2.00	40	—	—
		Totals	395	435	
			(33 Ah)		

[1] Watt-hours supplied by inverter.
[2] Peak watts supplied by inverter with generator off.
[3] Peak watts supplied by generator.

The medium budget in Table 8.4 adds a small (0.6 cu. ft.) microwave, 120-volt-AC refrigerator, and hair dryer.

These significant additions require an inverter rated at about 1,300 watts continuous that draws about 125 Ah from the batteries. Since microwave use most often occurs in short bursts, and since inverters can put out much larger currents for short periods, a 1,000-watt continuous inverter would probably suffice.

Total battery drain consists of the 125 Ah inverter drain plus all DC loads.

Table 8.4 Example of Medium Daily Electrical Consumption

Appliance (240 VAC)	Rated Watts	Typical Use, Hours/Day	Watt-Hours per Day[1]	Peak Watts	
				Inverter[2]	Generator[3]
Blender	300	0.02	6	300	—
Computer	100	2.00	200	100	—
Drill, ⅜-inch	350	0.02	7	—	—
Hair dryer	1,200	0.05	60	—	—
Microwave, small	800	0.15	120	800	—
Refrig., 6 cu. ft.	80	10.00	800	80	—
Soldering iron	100	0.02	2	—	—
TV, 7-inch color	35	4.00	140	35	—
VCR/DVD	20	2.00	40	—	—
		Totals	1,375	1,315	
			(115 Ah)		

[1] Watt-hours supplied by inverter.
[2] Peak watts supplied by inverter with generator off.
[3] Peak watts supplied by generator.

Figuring Your AC Budget

The high budget shown in Table 8.5 includes all of the conveniences of the home. Demand in the evening is beyond the capability of standard inverters, so a generator is added to supply the largest loads, which are concentrated for an hour in the morning and an hour in the evening.

This large budget requires a 6-kilowatt generator during the hours of peak use and an inverter rated at about 3,000 watts continuous or more. Allowing for the efficiency of the inverter, the inverter alone draws about 280 Ah per day from the batteries.

Table 8.5 Example of High Daily Electrical Consumption

Appliance (240 VAC)	Rated Watts	Typical Use, Hours/Day	Watt-Hours per Day[1]	Peak Watts Inverter[2]	Peak Watts Generator[3]
Air conditioner, 11,000 Btu/h	1,500	12.00	—	—	1,500
Blender	300	0.02	6	300	—
Computer	100	2.00	200	100	—
Drill, ⅜-inch	350	0.02	7	—	—
Hair dryer	1,200	0.05	60	1,200	1,200
Water heater	1,500	1.30	—	—	1,500
Lights	50–500	4.00	1,000	250	250
Microwave, large	1,200	0.25	—	—	1,200
Range element	1,200	1.00	—	1,200	—
Refrig., 14 cu. ft.	140	10.00	1,400	140	140
Soldering iron	100	0.02	2	—	—
TV, 19-inch color	100	4.00	400	100	100
VCR/DVD	20	2.00	40	20	20
Vacuum	800	0.05	40	—	—
		Totals	3,155	3,310	5,910
			(263 Ah)		

[1] Watt-hours supplied by inverter.
[2] Peak watts supplied by inverter with generator off.
[3] Peak watts supplied by generator.

How Inverters Work

Figure 8.1 shows, in simplified form, how an inverter transforms DC battery power into AC power. S_1, S_2, and S_3 are all solid-state transistors, which act as fast switches.

Fig. 8.1 Simplified Inverter Schematic

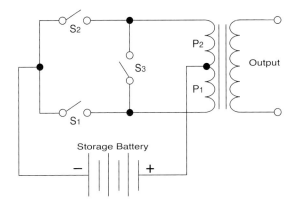

The sequence of electrical events for a single AC cycle is shown in Table 8.6. The actual circuitry is far more complex, but the switching sequence demonstrates the principle.

Table 8.6 Transistor Switching in an Inverter

S_1	S_2	S_3	Action	Result
Closed	Open	Open	12V applied to primary coil P_1	+ Output
Open	Open	Closed	primary shorted	0 Output
Open	Closed	Open	12V applied to primary coil P_2	– Output
Open	Open	Closed	primary shorted	0 Output

Figure 8.2 compares the outputs of three inverter types: square wave, pulse-width-modified sine wave, and pure sine wave. Note the differences in peak voltage for the nominal 120-volt AC waves.

The pulse-width-modified sine wave has two advantages over the square wave. First, it appears slightly more sinusoidal in shape to a load. Second, by varying the width of the output pulse, the average output voltage (area under the voltage curve) can be held constant as the input battery voltage and output peak voltage drop.

Square-wave inverters are notorious for causing 60 Hertz hum and interference. To the antenna or input transformer of a piece of sensitive electronic equip-

Fig. 8.2 Inverter Waveforms Compared

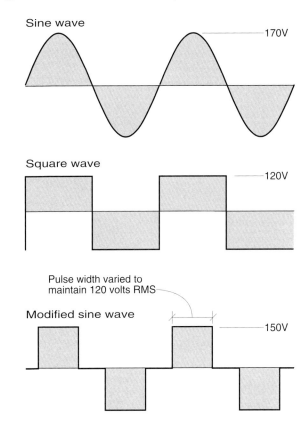

ment, the square wave appears to be a group of sinusoids at multiples of the fundamental 60 Hertz. Whether these higher-frequency components interfere depends a great deal on the quality of the equipment's grounding, shielding, and power-supply filtering.

High-quality, pulse-width-modified, sine-wave inverters emit less harmonic power but sometimes still cause difficulty in sensitive equipment. For zero interference and hum, pure-sine-wave inverters are available at significantly higher cost.

My experience in operating computers, GPS, VHF, SSB, and television receivers concurrently with a pulse-width-modified, sine-wave inverter is that the computer and GPS seemed unaffected, the television displayed minor interference patterns, and the transmissions of both VHF and SSB contained noticeable hum. I have not found the interference to be serious enough to install line filters, however.

Chapter 13 contains all of the information you require to filter the supply lines of affected equipment. If you are still concerned you can make your purchase of a pulse-width-modified, sine-wave inverter contigent on acceptable interference levels.

Inverters

Inverter Specifications and Examples

Table 8.7 lists the specifications of four popular US inverters in a range of sizes.

In the UK and Europe, inverters are available from a large number of manufacturers and distributors. Types include True Sine Wave and Modified Sine Wave, and outputs range from 180 watts to 3 Kw. The examples described below are typical high output inverters available on the US market. Apart from the output voltage, the specifications are typical of similarly sized UK/European units.

Input Voltage

Most inverters accept a range of input voltage of about 10 to 15.5 volts DC. To avoid problems, you should make sure the voltage regulators of your engine alternator and solar and wind chargers are set to less than 15.5 volts, measured on the battery side of any isolation diodes. If you wish to bypass the regulators and equalize your batteries with a voltage greater than 15.5 volts, first turn the inverter off.

The low voltage cutoff of approximately 10 volts DC is designed to prevent destructive 100% discharge of the batteries. Some inverters sound an audible alarm before cutting off.

Output Voltage – US Products

The outputs of both Freedom inverters in Table 8.7 are pulse-width-modified sine waves, where the duration of the pulses are adjusted to produce a constant RMS (root mean square) voltage. The actual peak voltages corresponding to 120 volts AC RMS are as shown in Figure 8.2:

- Sine wave   170 volts
- Square wave   120 volts
- Modified sine wave 150 volts

Since the normal range of shore-power voltage is from 110 to 125, or 117 ±7% VAC, any regulation of 7% or better is acceptable.

The frequency regulation of most inverters is good enough to keep time by. The Freedoms' ±0.005% equates to ±4 seconds per day!

The same principles apply to 12 VDC/240 VAC inverters.

Table 8.7 Inverter Specifications of some US products

Specification	Prosine 2.0	Xantrex MS2000	Freedom Marine 10	Freedom Marine 25
Minimum input voltage, DC	10.0	10.0	10.0	10.0
Maximum input voltage, DC	16.0	15.5	15.5	15.5
Output waveform	true sine wave	true sine wave	modified sine wave	modified sine wave
Output voltage, AC	117	120	120	120
Output frequency, Hz	60	60	50 or 60	50 or 60
Frequency regulation, %	±0.05	±0.05	±0.005	±0.005
Output, continuous watts	2,000	2,000	1,000	2,500
30-minute watts	—	—	1,800	2,800
Surge watts (5 seconds)	4,500	5,000	3,000	5,200
Efficiency, peak, %	89	92	93	93
Efficiency, full load, %	81	87	85	87
Standby drain, searching, watts	2	14.4	1.5	1.5
Standby drain, inverting, watts	25	48	—	—
Battery charging current, amps	100	100	50	130
Battery charging stages	3 + manual equal.	3 + manual equal.	3 + manual equal.	3 + manual equal.
Weight, lb.	24	68	34	50
Transfer switch, AC amps	30	30	30	30
Optimal temperature range, °F	32–104	32–104	32–104	32–104

Output Power

When sizing an inverter, be careful. It was common practice in the past to define "continuous watts" as "continuous for up to 30 minutes"! For example, the maximum continuous output power of the older Heart EMS-1800 was not 1,800 watts, as you might assume, but 1,100 watts—40% less. The manufacturers no doubt reasoned that many of the larger inverter loads, such as microwaves, hair dryers, and clothes irons, lasted 30 minutes or less, so a 30-minute rating was appropriate. It may have been appropriate, but it was also misleading. Fortunately it appears that most manufacturers have now adopted a "continuous" continuous rating.

Figure 8.3 shows how the maximum output of the EMS-1800 varied with duration. The curve reflects the buildup of internal heat, not depletion of the battery, which is assumed to be a constant 13.0 volts DC. The output power versus time curves of all inverters are of similar shape.

Surge current is the momentary current drawn by electric motors at startup. As a rule of thumb, surge currents of inverters are approximately 250% of the continuous-rated currents. In fact, many manufacturers specify surge current in terms of the size of motor they will start.

Efficiency and Standby Power

The percentage of battery power converted to AC power depends on two factors:
- Efficiency is the percentage of power converted while the inverter is in operating mode
- Standby power is the drain on the battery while the inverter is in standby mode, waiting for a load to be connected

Pulse-width-modified, sine-wave inverters are typically extremely efficient at mid- to upper-output levels. Figure 8.4 shows efficiency versus output power for the Heart EMS-1800. Most inverters achieve efficiencies in excess of 90% over most of their output ranges. Efficiency drops dramatically, however, at very low power levels. For this reason, most inverters remain in standby mode (on, but not producing power) until they sense a significant load.

For Freedom inverters the minimum load required to trigger the "on" state is only 1.5 watts. Since the turn-on is instantaneous, the user is usually not aware of the standby mode unless the load is less than the trigger

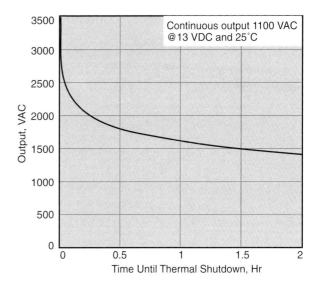

Fig. 8.3 Rated Output of Heart EMS-1800

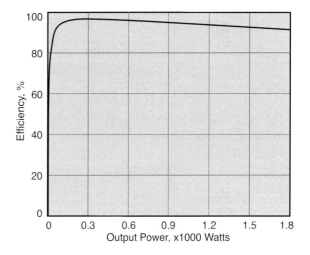

Fig. 8.4 Efficiency of Heart EMS-1800

level, as may be the case with a small nicad battery charger. To overcome the standby mode, I recharge several nicads at once.

The standby-drain specification is important because it results in a constant drain on the batteries. Freedom's 1.5 watts amounts to 3 Ah per day. With their more complex circuitry, pure-sine-wave inverters can draw an amp or more on standby, wasting at least 24 Ah per day. For example, the Xantrex MS2000 standby drain of 14.4 watts drains a hefty 28.8 Ah per day.

Inverters

Battery Charging

The most sophisticated inverters offer shore-power battery charging. In effect running backward, when external AC power is applied from either shore power or an onboard generator, a 30-amp internal transfer switch connects inverter loads directly to the external AC-power source and, at the same time, begins charging the battery. The battery-charging circuitry is as sophisticated as many multicycle stand-alone chargers costing nearly as much as the inverter. The economy is realized through the use of many of the same components for both modes.

Figure 8.5 shows the battery-charging cycles of the older Heart EMS-1800 inverter. More modern inverters are even more flexible, allowing operator choice of charging voltages, depending on the type of battery.

Bulk cycle. Assuming the battery is moderately discharged, the charging current of the EMS-1800 starts at 65 amps (100 amps for the EMS-2800). Charging current remains constant until the battery voltage reaches 13.0 volts. From 13.0 to 14.3 volts the charging current tapers from 65 amps to about half, or 30 amps.

Absorption cycle. During the absorption cycle, voltage is held constant at 14.3 volts, while the battery current acceptance drops from 30 amps to 10 amps. Referring to the recommended optimally fast charging routine for wet lead-acid batteries, shown in Figure 3.14 of Chapter 3, the 10-amp cutoff seems wise, corresponding to a 200 Ah battery (size 8D).

Float cycle. Once the current at 14.3 volts drops to 10 amps, the charger reverts to a float state, at a constant 13.3 volts. In the float state, the charger will provide up to its maximum output of 65 amps (100 amps for the EMS-2800) while maintaining 13.3 volts. Current demands over 65 amps are drawn from the battery.

Equalization cycle. As discussed earlier, the useful life of a battery can be increased by periodic equalization. Equalization consists of overcharging the battery, resulting in shedding of hardened lead sulfate from the plates. EMS inverters can be manually triggered after reaching the float state to maintain a constant 15.3 volts for 8 hours. They then revert to the float state at 13.3 volts. Note that sealed and gelled-electrolyte batteries should not be equalized because they cannot vent the generated hydrogen gas, and lost water cannot be replaced.

Fig. 8.5 Typical (Heart EMS-1800) Three-Stage Charging

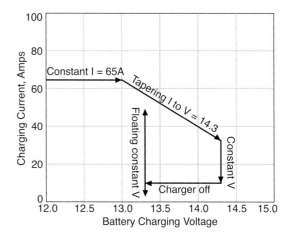

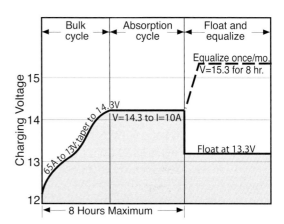

Many inverters offer a transfer switch either as standard equipment or as an option. An inverter transfer switch automatically switches boat AC loads to shore power or generator output when available, and back to the inverter output when the external source is removed. This is a great convenience on a boat that goes into and out of slips a great deal.

Boats with onboard generators require an additional transfer switch to select between shore power and generator output.

Figure 8.6 shows the internal configuration of a transfer switch. Input 1 is connected to AC source 1 (shore power, for example). Input 2 is connected to AC source 2 (internal connection to inverter output). With no AC at the terminals of input 1, power is routed from input 2 (inverter) to the output. When shore power appears at input 1, however, the solenoid pulls the switch up, and power is routed from input 1 to the output.

Operation of a shore-power/generator transfer switch can be either manual or similarly automatic.

Figure 8.7 shows the operation of an inverter with both an internal transfer switch and automatic battery charging.

With shore power on, the shore-power AC is connected to the AC output and the inverter is turned off. Simultaneously, AC power is applied to the inverter's built-in battery charger, which draws its power from the battery.

The inverter and battery combination thus operates as an "AC battery," supplying AC power when shore power is not available and recharging the batteries when it is.

Figure 8.8 shows the operation of a shore-power generator-inverter combination.

When shore power is available, the external transfer switch feeds shore power to both inverter and large-load panel. The inverter's transfer switch shunts the shore power through to the small-load panel and simultaneously charges the battery.

When shore power is not available, the external transfer switch selects the generator output, which is fed to both the inverter and the large-load panel. The inverter's internal transfer switch shunts generator power to the small-load panel and continues to charge the battery.

When neither shore power nor generator power is available, the inverter stops charging the battery and comes on to supply the small-load panel. In this mode there is no power at the large-load panel.

Fig. 8.6 A Transfer Switch

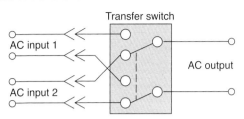

Fig. 8.7 Transfer Switch with Automatic Battery Charging

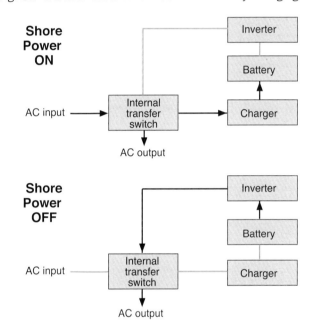

Fig. 8.8 Shore-Power Generator-Inverter Switching with Transfer Switches

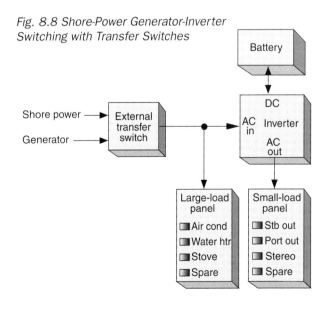

Generators

Prior to the advent of efficient, low-cost, solid-state inverters, the generator was the only source of AC power away from the dock. Now, for loads up to about 2 kW, a combination of a large battery and inverter and a means for charging (such as engine alternator, solar panel, or wind machine) will produce AC power at half of the cost of power from the most economical generator. For loads greater than 2,000 watts there is still no substitute for a generator. For boats with large power budgets a generator-inverter combination is ideal. The two types of AC generator are:

1. Alternator-type, in which the output is generated by the stator.
2. Armature-type, in which the output is generated by the rotor.

Alternator-Type Generators

In an alternator-type generator the magnetic field is created by magnets and controlling field coils on the rotor. Output current is induced in fixed stator coils located around the inside of the case. In some genera-tors, the field current is generated through rectification of a portion of the AC output and fed to the rotor through brushes—just as in the automotive alternator. Most generators, however, are brushless. An exciter coil in the stator induces AC current in the rotor field coils, which is then rectified by a diode.

Figure 8.9 shows a simplified brushless alternator-type generator. There are two large windings that provide the main generator output. These may be in phase or out of phase. If in phase, there will be two 120-volt AC outputs. If out of phase, there will be two 120-volt AC outputs of opposite polarity, which can be combined for 240 volt AC. The small coil to the right provides excitation for the field coils of the rotor. The small coil to the left provides input to a bridge rectifier, which provides 12 volts DC for charging the generator's starting-motor battery.

Both main windings and the exciter winding are provided with multiple taps as shown at A, B, and C in Figure 8.9. Output voltage varies slightly with rpm and load, but the nominal voltage is changed by selecting different taps. Output frequency can be controlled only by adjusting engine rpm.

Fig. 8.9 Alternator-Type Generator

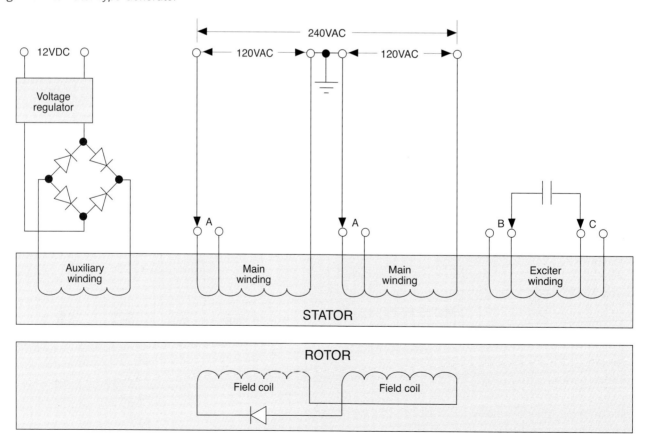

Armature-Type Generators

All generators and alternators rely on the fact that an electric current is induced in either a moving wire in a magnetic field or a stationary wire in a magnetic field that is changing in intensity.

In an armature-type generator, the magnetic field is created by a controlling field current flowing through fixed coils that are placed around the stator (stationary coil). The stator is anchored to the outside case of the generator.

Output current is induced in multiple coils wound on the rotor, which is driven at a constant 3,600 rpm (3,000 rpm in 50 Hz European models) by the speed governor of the generator's engine. Large-capacity slip rings and brushes transfer the large output currents from the moving rotor to the generator-output terminals. The output of the generator is sinusoidal in wave form.

The small DC field current is usually taken from a rectifier bridge connected across a pair of output terminals. To get around the chicken-or-egg dilemma of requiring a stator field in order to begin generating current, the stator magnets are designed to retain a degree of permanent magnetism. A few generators solve the same problem by taking the current for the stator windings directly from the ship's batteries.

Generators with a single 120-volt AC output generally have two brushes, as shown in Figure 8.10. One brush/terminal is live; the other brush/terminal is neutral and is connected to the case of the generator and to ship's ground via the grounding conductor. Note that single-voltage European versions produce 240 volts AC rather than 120 volts AC with corresponding conductor colors.

Generators having both 120-volt AC output and 240-volt AC output have either three or four brushes.

Figure 8.11 shows a four-brush generator. Brushes 2 and 3 (neutral) are tied together to the case and to ship's ground. Brushes 1 and 4 are live. The voltages between brush 1 and neutral and between brush 4 and neutral are both 120 volts AC, but of opposite polarity. The voltage between brushes 1 and 4 is thus 240 volts AC.

Fig. 8.10 Two-Brush Armature Generator

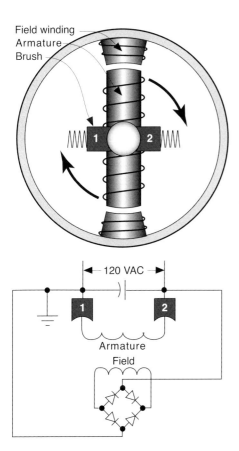

Fig. 8.11 Four-Brush Armature Generator

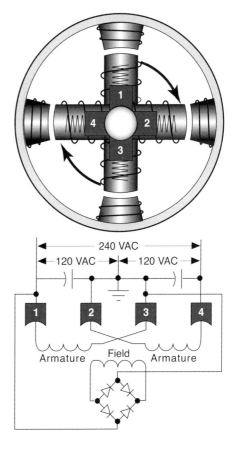

Generators

Frequency and Voltage Regulation

As you will see below, the output frequency of a generator is the key indicator of its proper operation. For this reason the importance of a frequency meter cannot be overstated. Most generators intended for permanent installation are equiped with frequency meters in their control panels, whether at the generator or in the AC distribution panel. If yours does not have such a meter, you can easily construct one from a 100-microamp panel meter and a handful of inexpensive components, as shown in Figure 8.12 and in Project 3, Chapter 14.

In a pinch you can press an old-fashioned synchronous electric clock into service. Such a clock advances in proportion to the frequency of its power supply: 60 minutes for 60 Hertz, 50 minutes for 50 Hertz, etc. Simply plug the clock into an outlet and let it run for an hour (as timed by your watch). At the end of the hour it will read the average frequency in minutes.

In both alternator- and armature-type generators, the output is taken from the output windings and thus corresponds directly with the rotation of the rotor. Frequency is therefore directly proportional to rpm. This is why fixed-drive generators cannot be driven directly by a boat's propulsion system. Hydraulic drives and variable-speed clutches are available for matching generator and propulsion engine, but they are not as popular as dedicated engines.

Engine rpm is controlled by a mechanical governor on the engine. As the engine slows under increasing load, a centrifugal weight acts to open the throttle. Mechanical governors require an rpm deviation in order to effect a throttle adjustment. The more fuel required, the larger the required deviation in rpm. Thus, generator frequency is necessarily affected by the load. Figure 8.13 shows the typical frequency versus load relationship.

Output voltage is affected by both engine rpm and output load. Since rpm is affected by load, we can think of output voltage as being affected by load. Figure 8.14 shows a typical 110- to 130-volt AC variation in output voltage from no load to full load. Voltages greater than 130 volts AC shorten the lives of resistive components, such as lamp filaments and heater elements. Low voltages cause motors to draw excessive currents and overheat, or not start at all. The same principles apply if the output voltage is 240 VAC.

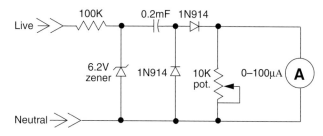

Fig. 8.12 A Simple AC-Frequency Meter

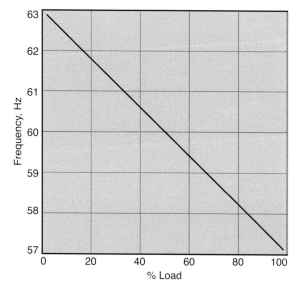

Fig. 8.13 Generator Frequency vs. Load

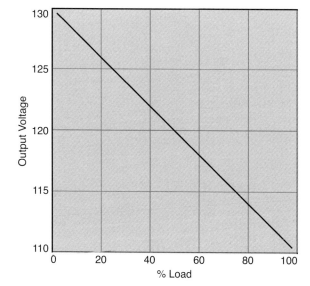

Fig. 8.14 Generator Voltage vs. Load

WARNING: The output terminals of a working generator are protected by neither a fuse, circuit breaker, nor ground fault circuit interrupter. At 120 or 240 volts AC, contact with a terminal and a grounded part of the vessel at the same time could be lethal. If you are not highly versed in dealing with generators, don't attempt measurements on the generator while it is running. As a further precaution, disable any remote-start circuitry.

The owner's manuals of high-quality generators usually contain extensive maintenance and troubleshooting guides for the specific model. If yours doesn't, purchase a copy of the shop manual, which will have the guides.

The troubleshooting guide included here is general and not intended to replace a manufacturer's guide.

Most generators have sealed bearings, which require no lubrication. This does not include the generator engine, which must be maintained to the same degree as the boat's propulsion engine. Crankcase oil should be changed every 100 hours of operation and just prior to any extended layup.

If the boat is in the north and the generator is not removed from the boat, the engine will require winterization, as well. If the engine is gasoline-fueled, the spark plugs should be replaced every year.

If the generator contains brushes, check the brushes for excessive wear (more than 50%) and the slip rings for burning and pitting. Replace worn brushes with exact replacements from the manufacturer and follow the directions for seating the new brushes.

The troubleshooting guide applies to both armature- and alternator-type generators. You will need to measure output AC volts, AC amps, and frequency. A proper generator installation should include AC volts, AC amps, and frequency panel meters in the AC distribution panel. For smaller generators use a multimeter to measure volts and amps. If you don't have a frequency meter, purchase one or build the one in Project 3, Chapter 14.

Troubleshooting Guide

Voltage Erratic

STEP 1. Check the brushes for wear. Replace if more than 50% worn.
STEP 2. Check slip rings for burning and/or pitting (requires services of a machine shop).

Voltage High (over 130/260 volts)

STEP 1. Check the frequency for normal range (57 to 63 Hertz for 110 VAC systems/47 to 53 Hertz for 240 VAC systems).
STEP 2. Adjust the voltage regulator if possible.
STEP 3. Have the voltage regulator checked. Consult the manual for terminal changes.

Voltage Low (below 110/220 volts)

STEP 1. Check the voltage at the generator terminals. If OK, the problem is voltage drop in connectors or conductors.
STEP 2. If the voltage is OK initially, then drops, check the temperature of the voltage regulator. It should be cool enough to touch.
STEP 3. Adjust the voltage regulator if possible.
STEP 4. Consult manual for terminal change.

Frequency Erratic

STEP 1. Check for loads that cycle on and off.
STEP 2. If erratic with no load connected, check the engine governor.

Frequency High (over 63/53 Hertz)

STEP 1. Adjust the engine governor and clean and lubricate its linkage.
STEP 2. Consult the engine manual.

Frequency Low (below 57/47 Hertz)

STEP 1. Reduce the load. If frequency increases to normal range, the generator is overloaded.
STEP 2. Adjust engine governor and clean and lubricate linkage; consult manual.

CHAPTER 9

AC Standards
and Practices

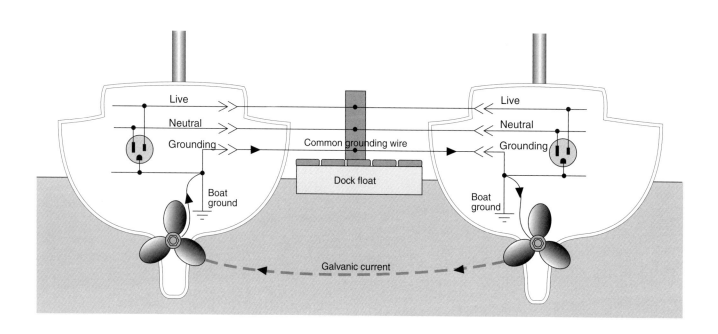

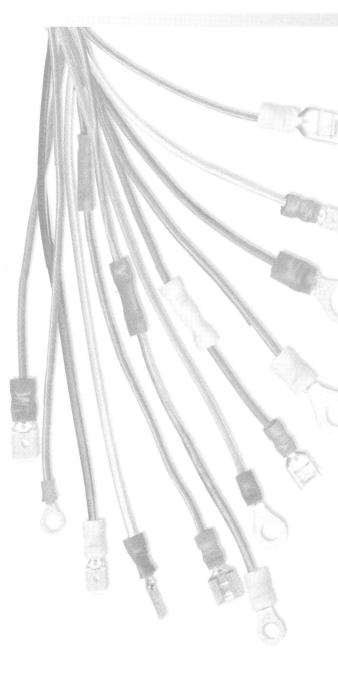

As with Chapter 6, its DC equivalent, this chapter is essentially an amplification of the standards for AC power aboard boats.

We start with sources of AC power: shore power, generators, and inverters, all of which feed the AC main panelboard. Two primary AC safety considerations are grounding (including ground faults) and overcurrent protection.

Load calculations and ampacity tables allow us to size the overcurrent protection and to select both the approved wire and cable and the receptacles for the application.

The probability of moisture, salt, and vibration, as well as the possibility of gasoline vapors, mandate standards for the installation of conductors.

As with DC wiring, the issue of galvanic protection and grounding raises the question of what to do with the grounding wire. The two solutions—galvanic isolators and isolation transformers—are shown in the examples of shore-power circuits.

When a craft's AC installation is designed, it should be remembered that the vast majority of marina socket outlets in the UK are rated at 16 amps, and in some areas of Europe may be lower rated. These shore supplies are often fitted with overload devices set to 16 amps, or lower.

BMEA and ISO Color Code for 240 VAC Conductors

European and UK Practice		USA Practice	
Conductor	**Colors**	**Conductor**	**Colors**
Live	Brown	Ungrounded (hot)	Black
Neutral	Light Blue	Grounded (neutral)	White
Ground(ing)/Earth	Green/Yellow	Ground(ing)/Earth	Green

Both color groups conform with ISO standards.

Shore Power

All standards for AC electrical systems are designed to prevent electrical fires and shock. You should not assume that familiarity with residential wiring qualifies you to do marine wiring. Wiring standards for boats are more stringent than those for homes for three major reasons:

1. Boats sit in an electrically conductive medium.
2. Metal parts of boats, including electrical wiring and connections, are subject to corrosion.
3. Boats are subject to fatiguing vibration and impact.

A boat's source of AC may be shore power, an onboard generator, a DC-to-AC inverter, or a combination. The nature and operation of generators and inverters were covered in Chapter 8. The proper installation of the three sources is covered here.

Shore Power

Sooner or later someone will use the shore-power cable as a dockline, perhaps grasping for the nearest object while headed for the water, or maybe someone forgot to unplug the power when getting underway. Plus, plugs and receptacles are subject to rain and spray from washdown hoses. For these reasons the standards for shore-power cables and inlets are rigorous.

The Boat Connection

A typical inlet on the boat end (Figure 9.1) must be a male connector. If in a location subject to rain, splash, or spray, it must be weatherproof, regardless of whether the cable is connected. If the location is subject to submersion, no matter how brief, the inlet must also be watertight—again, whether the cord is connected or not.

If the boat's AC system includes an isolation transformer or a galvanic isolator, the metal components of the inlet must be insulated from a metal hull or any metal parts connected to the boat's ground.

Fig. 9.1 Shore-Power Boat Connection

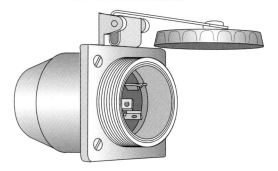

The Cable

Standards for shore-power cable are more stringent than those for cords you find in building supply outlets. The cable must be one of the types listed in Table 9.1.

Table 9.1 Shore-Power Cable

Type	Description	Temp. Rating
SOW	Hard-service cord, oil-resistant compound	60°C, 75°C
STW	Hard-service cord, thermoplastic	60°C, 75°C
STOW, SEOW	Hard-service cord, oil-resistant thermoplastic	60°C, 75°C
STOOW	Extra-hard-usage cord, oil-resistant thermoplastic	105°C

Current-carrying conductors (live and neutral) must be sized for the capacity of the shore-power circuit, as shown in Table 9.2.

Table 9.2 Ampacity of AC Conductors

Conductor Size, AWG*	Two Conductors[1] Maximum Amps	Three Conductors[2] Maximum Amps
14	18	15
12	25	20
10	30	25
8	40	35
6	55	45
4	70	60
2	95	80

[1] Not including the grounding wire, which is considered non-conducting.
[2] For four to six conductors, reduce current rating a further 20%.
* See Appendix for metric equivalent

A grounding wire is required in all shore-power cables, but since the grounding wire is considered normally non-current-carrying, it may be of smaller size than the current-carrying conductors. Commonly, it is one size smaller.

The shore end of the cable must have a locking and grounding cap with the proper male (plug) connector that matches the female shore receptacle (see Figure 9.2). The boat end of the cable must have a locking and grounding cap with the proper female (receptacle) connector to match the boat's male power inlet.

Figure 9.3 shows the boat and shore ends of a 30 A/120 VAC, 1Ø shore-power cable. The weatherproof sleeves slide over the connectors. UK/European types differ in design, but the same principles apply.

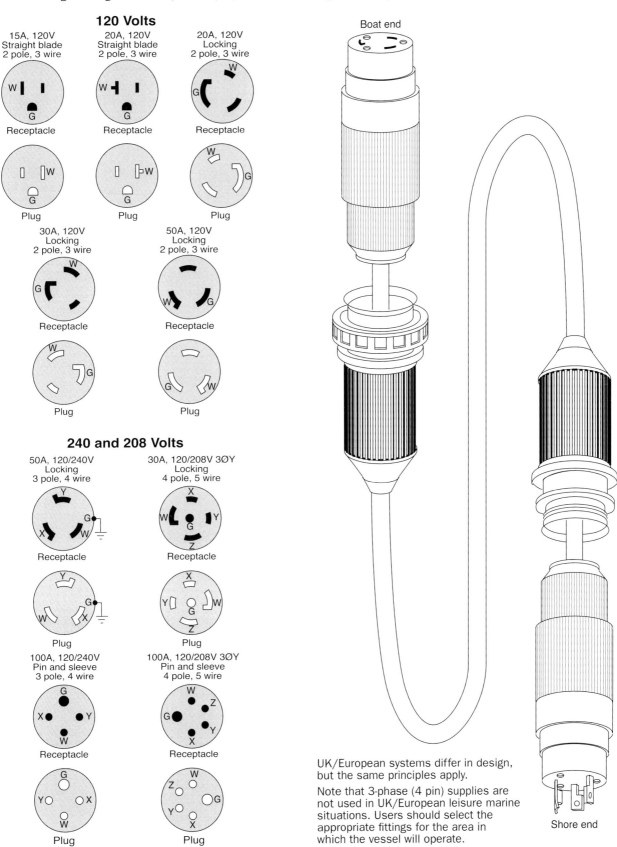

Fig. 9.2 Matching AC Plugs and Receptacles (US)

120 Volts

15A, 120V
Straight blade
2 pole, 3 wire
Receptacle
Plug

20A, 120V
Straight blade
2 pole, 3 wire
Receptacle
Plug

20A, 120V
Locking
2 pole, 3 wire
Receptacle
Plug

30A, 120V
Locking
2 pole, 3 wire
Receptacle
Plug

50A, 120V
Locking
2 pole, 3 wire
Receptacle
Plug

240 and 208 Volts

50A, 120/240V
Locking
3 pole, 4 wire
Receptacle
Plug

30A, 120/208V 3ØY
Locking
4 pole, 5 wire
Receptacle
Plug

100A, 120/240V
Pin and sleeve
3 pole, 4 wire
Receptacle
Plug

100A, 120/208V 3ØY
Pin and sleeve
4 pole, 5 wire
Receptacle
Plug

Fig. 9.3 30 A/120 VAC Shore-Power Cable (US)

Boat end

UK/European systems differ in design, but the same principles apply.

Note that 3-phase (4 pin) supplies are not used in UK/European leisure marine situations. Users should select the appropriate fittings for the area in which the vessel will operate.

Shore end

Generator and Inverter Sources

Transfer Switch

Connections to shore power, onboard generators, and inverters must be such that no more than one source can be connected to a circuit simultaneously. Switching between power sources must be made with a transfer switch, which prevents arc-over between the contacts of the different sources.

Grounded Neutral

Boat AC systems use a grounded neutral, as do residential systems. Where the neutral and grounding are connected is critical. The neutral must be grounded *only at the power source:* an onboard generator or inverter, the secondary of an isolation or polarization transformer, or the shore-power receptacle.

Figure 9.4 shows a system consisting of shore power, an onboard generator, and an inverter. A two-pole transfer switch selects the power source. Note that the neutral and grounding wires are connected at the generator, at the inverter, and (not shown) at the

shore-end source.

A galvanic isolator serves to block stray current in the shore-power grounding wire. Thus, regardless of the source of power, the neutral is grounded only at its source. Further, the neutral and grounding conductors are always maintained at boat ground, which is critical for the safety of anyone on board.

Ampacity

An onboard generator or inverter must be rated to supply the entire load, as calculated later, unless the system has been designed to isolate certain loads from connection.

In either case, the feed conductors from the generator or inverter must be of sufficient ampacity to carry the maximum rated output. In addition, the generator or inverter output must be protected at its output with an overcurrent device, rated at no more than 120% of the rated output, unless the generator or inverter is self-limiting to the same degree.

Fig. 9.4 Typical Use of the Transfer Switch

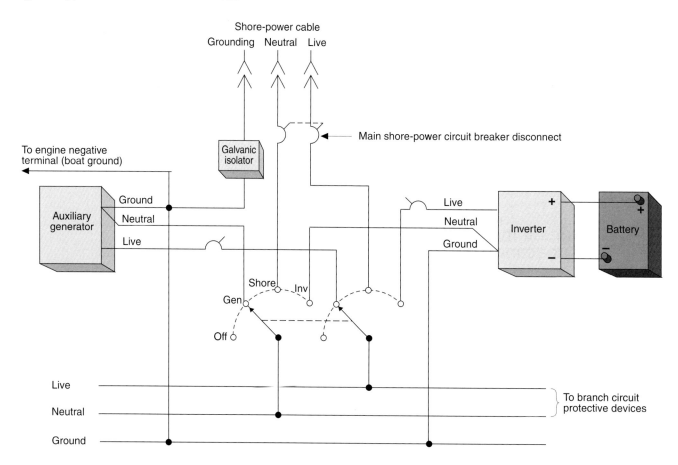

All AC systems must have a main panelboard, which may (it usually does) also serve as the AC distribution panel. The panelboard must be easily accessible and either weatherproof or in a location protected from the weather.

The panelboard must be clearly and permanently marked with the system voltage and frequency. If there are either AC motors or an AC generator aboard, the panelboard should also include an AC voltmeter. It is recommended that the voltmeter display upper and lower operating voltage limits.

The main panelboard should also contain a shore-power polarity indicator that warns of reversed polarity in the shore-power connection with either a continuous sound or light. A polarity indicator *must* be installed if:

1. Any of the boat's branch circuits have overcurrent protection in the ungrounded conductor only, or
2. Polarity is critical to the operation of any of the AC devices on the boat.

A polarity indicator is not needed, however, if the shore power feeds through an isolation transformer, since the transformer acts as a separate source of power on the boat, and its output conductors are permanently wired correctly.

In order to limit current on the normally non-current-carrying grounding wire, the impedance of polarity indication devices must be at least 25k ohms.

Figure 9.5 shows a simple polarity-indicating circuit that satisfies the 25k ohm criterion. A green light indicates correct polarity (voltage between the live and neutral conductors). A red light indicates incorrect polarity (either neutral or grounding conductor live).

Fig. 9.5 A Simple Polarity-Indicating Circuit (see Project 1, Chapter 14)

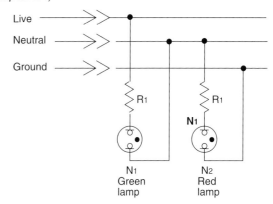

Plug-in polarity indicators, no larger than a three-prong adapter, are available at hardware stores. If your AC panel doesn't have a built-in polarity indicator, one of these devices can be used to quickly check for damaging reverse polarity when establishing a shore-power connection. Such a device does not satisfy the ABYC/BMEA/ISO standards or recommendations.

A permanent waterproof warning placard must be displayed prominently at all shore-power inlets. Fig. 9.6 shows the wording suggested by the ABYC and BMEA.

Fig. 9.6 Suggested Wording for Shore-Power Connection

WARNING
To minimize shock and fire hazards:

1. Turn off the boat's shore connection switch before connecting or disconnecting shore cable.
2. **Connect** shore-power cable at the boat first.
3. If polarity warning indicator is activated, immediately disconnect cable.
4. **Disconnect** shore-power cable at shore outlet first.
5. Close shore-power inlet cover tightly.

DO NOT ALTER SHORE-POWER CABLE CONNECTORS

AC Load Calculations

Instructions

The ABYC suggests a method for determining the minimum sizes of AC panelboards, supply conductors, and AC power sources. The total load may be supplied by:

1. A single shore-power cable of required ampacity.
2. Multiple shore-power cables, provided each inlet is marked with volts, amps, phase (if 3Ø), and the load it serves.
3. One or more onboard generators of continuous rating equal to the load.
4. Shore power plus generators and inverters of combined capacity equal to the load, provided the loads connected to each are isolated.

Table 9.3 is a form that follows the ABYC-recommended procedure for calculating AC loads. As you read the instructions below, you may also find it helpful to refer to Table 9.5, the completed example.

Lighting and Small Appliances (Lines 1–7)

Lighting includes all AC-powered lights on the boat. Small appliances are those used in the galley and dining areas that have power cords and plugs, such as blenders, mixers, and toasters.

LINE 1. Add the total square feet of all of the living areas on the boat, not counting storage and engine spaces, and multiply by 2.0.

LINE 2. Multiply the number of 20-amp circuits used for small appliances in the galley and dining areas by 1,500.

LINE 3. Add Lines 1 and 2.

LINE 4. Subtract 2,000 from Line 3, and multiply by 0.35 (enter 0 if negative).

LINE 5. Add Lines 3 and 4.

LINE 6. Divide Line 5 by the system voltage (either 120 or 240).

LINE 7. If your shore-power inlet is 120 VAC, enter Line 6 in Column A. From this point on, use only the left-hand (Column A) lines. If instead you have a 240-volt AC system that splits into two onboard 120 VAC branches, enter half of Line 6 in Columns A and B. From this point on, you will have to enter values in Columns A and B separately, depending on which branch of the 240 circuit the load is on.

Motors and Heaters (Lines 8–12)

For Lines 8 through 27, you will need the amps listed on the nameplates of each piece of equipment. The nameplate is usually found on the backside of the equipment.

LINE 8. Add and enter the total amps for all fans.

LINE 9. Total the amps for all air conditioners. If there are two units, enter the larger number. If there are three or more units, multiply the total by 0.75. If the total is less than Line 10, leave Line 9 blank.

LINE 10. Total the amps for electric, gas, and oil heaters. If this total is less than the total in the previous step (before multiplying by 0.75), leave Line 10 blank.

LINE 11. Enter 25% of the nameplate amps for the largest motor in any of the appliances involved in Lines 8 through 10.

LINE 12. Enter total of Lines 8 through 11.

Fixed Appliances (Lines 13–28)

LINES 13–27. For each of the appliances shown, multiply the amps listed on the nameplates by the use factors listed after the appliance name. If the unit is a 240-volt appliance, enter the result in both Columns A and B.

LINE 28. Enter the total of Lines 13 through 27, but if there are more than three appliances listed in Lines 13 through 27, first multiply Line 28 by 0.6.

Free-Standing Electric Cooker (Lines 29–31)

LINE 29. A free-standing cooker is one that contains both surface burners and an oven. First, read the watts listed on the nameplate. Enter the corresponding "load watts" from Table 9.4.

LINE 30. Enter the range voltage (from the nameplate).

LINE 31. Divide Line 29 by Line 30 and enter value in both Columns A and B.

Total AC Load (Line 32)

LINE 32. Total Lines 7, 12, 28, and 31 separately for Columns A and B. The Total AC Load in Amps is the larger of A and B.

Table 9.3 ABYC AC Load Calculation Form

Line	Loads	Column A	Column B
LIGHTING AND SMALL APPLIANCES			
1.	Lighting and receptacles: Living area sq.ft. × 2	_____	_____
2.	Small appliances: number of 20-amp circuits × 1,500	_____	_____
3.	Line 1 + Line 2	_____	_____
4.	(Line 3 – 2,000) × 0.35 (Enter 0 if less than 0)	_____	_____
5.	Line 3 + Line 4	_____	_____
6.	Line 5/System voltage (either 120 or 240)	_____	_____
7.	If 120 VAC, enter Line 6 in Column A; if 240 VAC, enter 50% of Line 6 in both A and B	_____	_____
MOTORS AND HEATERS (total nameplate amps)			
8.	Exhaust and supply fans	_____	_____
9.	Air conditioners (If two, enter larger number; if three or more, enter 75% of total; omit if less than Line 10)	_____	_____
10.	Heaters (If two, enter larger number) (If figure is less than Line 9, enter 0)	_____	_____
11.	25% of largest motor in Lines 8–10	_____	_____
12.	Total of Lines 8–11	_____	_____
FIXED APPLIANCES (nameplate amps)			
13.	Disposal × 0.1	_____	_____
14.	Water heater × 1.0	_____	_____
15.	Wall oven × 0.75	_____	_____
16.	Stovetop cooking unit × 0.75	_____	_____
17.	Refrigerator × 1.0	_____	_____
18.	Freezer × 1.0	_____	_____
19.	Ice maker × 0.5	_____	_____
20.	Dishwasher × 0.25	_____	_____
21.	Clothes washer × 0.25	_____	_____
22.	Clothes dryer × 0.25	_____	_____
23.	Trash compactor × 0.1	_____	_____
24.	Air compresser × 0.1	_____	_____
25.	Battery charger × 1.0	_____	_____
26.	Vacuum system × 0.1	_____	_____
27.	Sum of other fixed appliances	_____	_____
28.	Total of Lines 13–27; if more than three fixed appliances, × 0.6	_____	_____
FREE-STANDING ELECTRIC COOKER			
29.	Load watts from Table 9.4	_____	_____
30.	Nameplate volts (either 120 or 240)	_____	_____
31.	Line 29 divided by Line 30	_____	_____
32.	Sum of Lines 7, 12, 28, and 31; TOTAL is larger of A and B	_____	_____

AC Load Calculations

Example

Use Table 9.5 to calculate the 120 VAC load for a boat with 240 square feet of enclosed space (not including engine compartment or chain locker), one 20-amp small appliance circuit, and:
- 50-watt (0.4 amp) ventilation fan
- 1,500-watt (12 amp) water heater
- 85-watt (0.7 amp) refrigerator
- 120-watt (1 amp) air compressor
- 420-watt (3.5 amp) battery charger

Lighting and Small Appliances (Lines 1–7)

The lighting load is 2 × 240 square feet = 480 watts, which we enter on Line 1.

The small appliance load for one 20-amp circuit is 1 × 1,500 watts = 1,500 watts, which we enter on Line 2.

The sum of lines 1 and 2 is 1,980 watts, which is less than 2,000 watts, so we enter 1,980 watts on Line 3 and 0 watts on Line 4.

We divide 1,980 watts by 120 volts to get 16.5 amps. Since 120-volt shore power only has one branch, we enter the 16.5 amps on Line 7A.

Motors and Heaters (Lines 8–12)

We have only one motor—the 0.4-amp fan, which we enter on Line 8. Adding 25%, we get 0.5 amp, which we enter on Line 12A.

Fixed Appliances (Lines 13–28)

Our fixed appliances include the 12-amp water heater, 0.7-amp refrigerator, 3.5-amp battery charger, and 1-amp air compressor. The first three have a duty factor of 1.0, so we enter their amps directly. The compressor has a duty factor of only 0.10, so we enter 0.10 × 1.0 amp = 0.1 amp on Line 24A.

Adding Lines 13 through 27 we get 16.3 amps. Since there are more than three fixed appliances, we multiply the sum by the factor 0.60 and enter the result, 9.8, on Line 28.

Total AC Load (Line 32)

Adding Line 7 (16.5 amps), Line 12 (0.5 amp), Line 28 (9.8 amps), and Line 31 (0.0 amps), we get 26.8 amps. Since our system has only a single phase and, thus, a single branch, our total AC load for sizing the main AC panelboard is 26.8 amps. Rounding up, we'll call it 30 amps.

Table 9.4 Load Watts for Free-Standing Electric Cookers (For use in Table 9.5, Line 29)

Nameplate Watts	Load Watts
0–10,000	80%
10,001–12,500	8,000
12,501–13,500	8,400
13,501–14,500	8,800
14,501–15,500	9,200
15,501–16,500	9,600

Table 9.5 ABYC AC Load Calculation Form (filled-out example)

Line	Loads	Column A	Column B
LIGHTING AND SMALL APPLIANCES			
1.	Lighting and receptacles: Living area sq.ft. × 2	480	
2.	Small appliances: number of 20-amp circuits × 1,500	1500	
3.	Line 1 + Line 2	1980	
4.	(Line 3 – 2,000) × 0.35 (Enter 0 if less than 0)	0	
5.	Line 3 + Line 4	1980	
6.	Line 5/System voltage (either 120 or 240)	16.5	
7.	If 120 VAC, enter Line 6 in Column A; if 240 VAC, enter 50% of Line 6 in both A and B	16.5	
MOTORS AND HEATERS (total nameplate amps)			
8.	Exhaust and supply fans	0.4	
9.	Air conditioners (If two, enter larger number; if three or more, enter 75% of total; omit if less than Line 10)		
10.	Heaters (If two, enter larger number) (If figure is less than Line 9, enter 0)		
11.	25% of largest motor in Lines 8–10	0.1	
12.	Total of Lines 8–11	0.5	
FIXED APPLIANCES (nameplate amps)			
13.	Disposal × 0.1		
14.	Water heater × 1.0	12.0	
15.	Wall oven × 0.75		
16.	Stovetop cooking unit × 0.75		
17.	Refrigerator × 1.0	0.7	
18.	Freezer × 1.0		
19.	Ice maker × 0.5		
20.	Dishwasher × 0.25		
21.	Clothes washer × 0.25		
22.	Clothes dryer × 0.25		
23.	Trash compactor × 0.1		
24.	Air compresser × 0.1	0.1	
25.	Battery charger × 1.0	3.5	
26.	Vacuum system × 0.1		
27.	Sum of other fixed appliances		
28.	Total of Lines 13–27; if more than three fixed appliances, × 0.6	9.8	
FREE-STANDING ELECTRIC COOKER			
29.	Load watts from Table 9.4		
30.	Nameplate volts (either 120 or 240)		
31.	Line 29 divided by Line 30		
32.	Sum of Lines 7, 12, 28, and 31; TOTAL is larger of A and B	26.8	

Overcurrent Protection

Amp Ratings

All fuses and circuit breakers must be rated at or less than the ampacity of the conductors of the circuit being protected. *Exception:* if no breaker of correct ampacity is available, the breaker rating may exceed the ampacity of the conductors by up to 150%.

Circuit Breaker Specifications

All circuit breakers must meet the appropriate standards, be of the manual-reset type (except if integral to a piece of equipment), and be of the trip-free type (cannot be held closed while the overcurrent condition persists).

Main Supply Protection

Specifications for overcurrent protection of the main supply conductors include:

1. The shore-power feeder conductors should be protected by multi-pole breakers. In a 240 VAC system the breakers should protect both the live and the neutral conductors. Note that the grounding conductor is never interrupted.
2. If there are isolation or polarization transformers in the shore-power feed, primaries should be protected by a circuit breaker that opens both primary feeders simultaneously and that is rated at no more than 125% of the primary rating. If the secondary provides 120/240 VAC, it also should be protected by a circuit breaker that opens both secondary feeders simultaneously and that is rated at no more than 125% of the rated secondary current of the transformer.
3. The maximum unprotected conductor length from boat inlet connector to circuit breaker must not exceed 3 metres/10 feet. If the length is greater than this, add additional slow-blow fuses or breakers within 3 metres/10 feet of the inlet. If additional fuses or circuit breakers are provided, they must be larger, but not more than 125% larger, than the main shore-power disconnect breaker.
4. The maximum unprotected conductor length from an AC generator must be less than 7 inches/175mm. However, up to 40 inches/1 metre is allowed if the conductor is protected by a sheath or enclosure.

Branch-Circuit Protection

Branch circuit breakers and fuses should be rated at or less than the ampacity of the smallest current-carrying conductor in the circuit. If there is no matching breaker or fuse rating, the next larger may be used, provided it doesn't exceed 150% of conductor ampacity.

For boats wired with 240 VAC, both current-carrying conductors (live and neutral) must be protected by a pair of simultaneous-trip circuit breakers. *Exception:* the live conductor alone may be protected, provided:

1. The entire system is polarized, including lighting fixtures, and there is a polarity indicator between the shore-power inlet and the main circuit breakers, or
2. The neutral and grounding conductors are connected at the secondary of an isolation or polarization transformer.

All motors must be protected by either an overcurrent or a thermal device unless they do not overheat, even when the motor is stalled (rotor locked).

Fuse or Breaker Location

The fuses or circuit breakers for a circuit must be placed at its power source, except:

1. If impractical, within 175mm/7 inches of the source.
2. If impractical within 175mm/7 inches, then within 40 inches, provided the conductor is contained in a protective sheath or enclosure.

Ground Fault Protection

GFCI/RCD Breakers

GFCI/RCD breakers must meet the same requirements as circuit breakers of the same rating. They may be used to protect individual branch circuits, or they may protect a group of associated circuits. Like other circuit breakers, they are permitted to interrupt only the live conductor, provided the system is polarized and has a polarity indicator, the system has an isolation or polarization transformer.

GFCI (RCD) Receptacles

Double-pole receptacle (socket) devices may be installed as part of a convenient installation, either in a single-outlet application or multiple 'feed through' installations, ie a series of receptacles (socket) outlets connected in parallel such that the first GFCI (RCD) protects everything in the circuit (BMEA recommendation).

No conductor may be smaller than 1.5 mm²/16 AWG, except 1 mm²/18 AWG inside panelboards and equipment enclosures, serving DC electronics at less than 1 amp. The temperature ratings of all conductors and flexible cords should be at least 60°C (140°F), except 75°C (167°F) in engine spaces. Individual conductor insulations must be rated at 300/500 volts minimum. Flexible cords may be rated at a minimum of 300/500 volts.

Conductors must be one of the types listed in Table 9.6. Flexible cords must be one of the types listed in Table 9.7. Both conductors and flexible cords must also be of the stranding as shown in Table 9.8.

The ABYC-recommended color code for AC wiring is shown in Table 9.9.

Table 9.6 Acceptable Conductor Types for AC Wiring

Type	Damp Location	Oil Resistant	Extra-Hard Usage	Hard Usage
SE, SEW	X		X	
SEO, SEOW	X	X	X	
SJ, SJW	X			X
SJE, SJEW	X			X
SJEO, SJEOW	X	X		X
SJO, SJOW	X	X		X
SJOO, SJOOW	X	X		X
SJT, SJTW	X			X
SJTO, SJTOW	X	X		X
SJTOO, SJTOOW	X	X		X
SO, SOW	X	X	X	
ST, STW	X		X	
STO, STOW	X	X	X	
STOO, STOOW	X	X	X	

Table 9.7 Acceptable Flexible Cord Types for AC Wiring

Type	Description
SO, SOW	Hard-Service Cord, Oil Resistant
ST, STW	Hard-Service Cord, Thermoplastic
STO, STOW	Hard-Service Cord, Oil Resistant, Thermoplastic
SEO, SEOW	Hard-Service Cord, Oil Resistant, Thermoplastic
SJO, SJOW, SJTW	Junior Hard-Service Cord, Oil Resistant
SJT, SJTW	Hard-Service Cord, Thermoplastic
SJTO, SJTOW	Hard-Service Cord, Oil Resistant, Thermoplastic

Table 9.8 Minimum AC Conductor Stranding

Conductor Gauge*	Minimum CM for AWG	Minimum CM for SAE	Minimum Type II[1]	Strands Type III[2]
18	1,620	1,537	16	–
16	2,580	2,336	19	26
14	4,110	3,702	19	41
12	6,530	5,833	19	65
10	10,380	9,343	19	105
8	16,510	14,810	19	168
6	26,240	25,910	37	266
4	41,740	37,360	49	420
2	66,360	62,450	127	665
1	83,690	77,790	127	836
0	105,600	98,980	127	1,064
2/0	133,100	125,100	127	1,323
3/0	167,800	158,600	259	1,666
4/0	211,600	205,500	418	2,107

[1] Conductors with at least Type II stranding to be used for general-purpose boat wiring.
[2] Conductors with Type III stranding to be used where frequent flexing is expected.
* See Appendix for metric equivalent.

Table 9.9 BMEA and ISO Color Code for 240 VAC Conductors

European and UK Practice		USA Practice	
Conductor	**Colors**	**Conductor**	**Colors**
Live	Brown	Ungrounded (hot)	Black
Neutral	Light Blue	Grounded (neutral)	White
Ground(ing)/Earth	Green/Yellow	Ground(ing)/Earth	Green

Both color groups conform with ISO standards.

Ampacity

The minimum ampacities of AC current-carrying conductors are shown in Tables 9.10 through 9.15 on the following pages.

Ampacity Tables

Table 9.10 Allowable Amperage of No More Than Two Bundled Conductors
(Adapted from ABYC Standard E-11, Table VII-A)

Temperature Rating of Conductor Insulation

Size AWG*	60°C 140°F	75°C 167°F	80°C 176°F	90°C 194°F	105°C 221°F	125°C 257°F	200°C 392°F
			Outside Engine Spaces				
18	10	10	15	20	20	25	25
16	15	15	20	25	25	30	35
14	20	20	25	30	35	40	45
12	25	25	35	40	45	50	55
10	40	40	50	55	60	70	70
8	55	65	70	70	80	90	100
6	80	95	100	100	120	125	135
4	105	125	130	135	160	170	180
2	140	170	175	180	210	225	240
1	165	195	210	210	245	265	280
1/0	195	230	245	245	285	305	325
2/0	225	265	285	285	330	355	370
3/0	260	310	330	330	385	410	430
4/0	300	360	385	385	445	475	510
			Inside Engine Spaces				
18	5	7	11	16	17	22	25
16	8	11	15	20	21	26	35
14	11	15	19	24	29	35	45
12	14	18	27	32	38	44	55
10	23	30	39	45	51	62	70
8	31	48	54	57	68	80	100
6	46	71	78	82	102	111	135
4	60	93	101	110	136	151	180
2	81	127	136	147	178	200	240
1	95	146	163	172	208	235	280
1/0	113	172	191	200	242	271	325
2/0	130	198	222	233	280	316	370
3/0	150	232	257	270	327	364	430
4/0	174	270	300	315	378	422	510

* See Appendix for metric equivalent.

Table 9.11 Allowable Amperage of Three Bundled Conductors
(Adapted from ABYC Standard E-11, Table VII-B)

Temperature Rating of Conductor Insulation

Size AWG*	60°C 140°F	75°C 167°F	80°C 176°F	90°C 194°F	105°C 221°F	125°C 257°F	200°C 392°F
	Outside Engine Spaces						
18	7	7	10	14	14	17	17
16	10	10	14	17	17	21	24
14	14	14	17	21	24	28	31
12	17	17	24	28	31	35	38
10	28	28	35	38	42	49	49
8	38	45	49	49	56	63	70
6	56	66	70	70	84	87	94
4	73	87	91	94	112	119	126
2	98	119	122	126	147	157	168
1	115	136	147	147	171	185	196
1/0	136	161	171	171	199	213	227
2/0	157	185	199	199	231	248	259
3/0	182	217	231	231	269	287	301
4/0	210	252	269	269	311	332	357
	Inside Engine Spaces						
18	4	5	8	11	11	15	17
16	6	7	10	14	14	18	24
14	8	10	13	17	20	24	31
12	10	13	19	23	26	31	38
10	16	21	27	31	35	43	49
8	22	34	38	40	47	56	70
6	32	49	54	57	71	77	94
4	42	65	71	77	95	105	126
2	56	89	95	103	125	140	168
1	67	102	114	120	145	165	196
1/0	79	120	133	140	169	190	227
2/0	91	139	155	163	196	221	259
3/0	105	162	180	189	229	255	301
4/0	121	189	210	221	264	295	357

* See Appendix for metric equivalent.

Ampacity Tables

Table 9.12 Allowable Amperage of Four to Six Bundled Conductors
(Adapted from ABYC Standard E-11, Table VII-C)

Temperature Rating of Conductor Insulation

Size AWG*	60°C 140°F	75°C 167°F	80°C 176°F	90°C 194°F	105°C 221°F	125°C 257°F	200°C 392°F
Outside Engine Spaces							
18	6	6	9	12	12	15	15
16	9	9	12	15	15	18	21
14	12	12	15	18	21	24	27
12	15	15	21	24	27	30	33
10	24	24	30	33	36	42	42
8	33	39	42	42	48	54	60
6	48	57	60	60	72	75	81
4	63	75	78	81	96	102	108
2	84	102	105	108	126	135	144
1	99	117	126	126	147	159	168
1/0	117	138	147	147	171	183	195
2/0	135	159	171	171	198	213	222
3/0	156	186	198	198	231	246	258
4/0	180	216	231	231	267	285	306
Inside Engine Spaces							
18	3	4	7	9	10	13	15
16	5	6	9	12	12	16	21
14	7	9	11	14	17	21	27
12	8	11	16	19	23	26	33
10	13	18	23	27	30	37	42
8	19	29	32	34	40	48	60
6	27	42	46	49	61	66	81
4	36	56	60	66	81	90	108
2	48	76	81	88	107	120	144
1	57	87	98	103	125	141	168
1/0	67	103	114	120	145	162	195
2/0	78	119	133	140	168	189	222
3/0	90	139	154	162	196	218	258
4/0	104	162	180	189	227	253	306

* See Appendix for metric equivalent.

*Table 9.13 Allowable Amperage of Seven to 24 Bundled Conductors
(Adapted from ABYC Standard E-11, Table VII-D)*

Temperature Rating of Conductor Insulation

Size AWG*	60°C 140°F	75°C 167°F	80°C 176°F	90°C 194°F	105°C 221°F	125°C 257°F	200°C 392°F
	Outside Engine Spaces						
18	5	5	7	10	10	12	12
16	7	7	10	12	12	15	17
14	10	10	12	15	17	20	22
12	12	12	17	20	22	25	27
10	20	20	25	27	30	35	35
8	27	32	35	35	40	45	50
6	40	47	50	50	60	62	67
4	52	62	65	67	80	85	90
2	70	85	87	90	105	112	120
1	82	97	105	105	122	132	140
1/0	97	115	122	122	142	152	162
2/0	112	132	142	142	165	177	185
3/0	130	155	165	165	192	205	215
4/0	150	180	192	192	222	237	255
	Inside Engine Spaces						
18	2	3	5	8	8	11	12
16	4	5	7	10	10	13	17
14	5	7	9	12	14	17	22
12	7	9	13	16	19	22	27
10	11	15	19	22	25	31	35
8	16	24	27	28	34	40	50
6	23	35	39	41	51	55	67
4	30	46	50	55	68	75	90
2	40	63	68	73	89	100	120
1	47	73	81	86	104	117	140
1/0	56	86	95	100	121	135	162
2/0	65	99	111	116	140	158	185
3/0	75	116	128	135	163	182	215
4/0	87	135	150	157	189	211	255

* See Appendix for metric equivalent.

Ampacity Tables

Table 9.14 Allowable Amperage of 25 or More Bundled Conductors
(Adapted from ABYC Standard E-11, Table VII-E)

Temperature Rating of Conductor Insulation

Size AWG*	60°C 140°F	75°C 167°F	80°C 176°F	90°C 194°F	105°C 221°F	125°C 257°F	200°C 392°F
	Outside Engine Spaces						
18	4	4	6	8	8	10	10
16	6	6	8	10	10	12	14
14	8	8	10	12	14	16	18
12	10	10	14	16	18	20	22
10	16	16	20	22	24	28	28
8	22	26	28	28	32	36	40
6	32	38	40	40	48	50	54
4	42	50	52	54	64	68	72
2	56	68	70	72	84	90	96
1	66	78	84	84	98	106	112
1/0	78	92	98	98	114	122	130
2/0	90	106	114	114	132	142	148
3/0	104	124	132	132	154	164	172
4/0	120	144	154	151	178	190	204
	Inside Engine Spaces						
18	2	3	4	6	6	8	10
16	3	4	6	8	8	10	14
14	4	6	7	9	11	14	18
12	5	7	10	13	15	17	22
10	9	12	15	18	20	24	28
8	12	19	21	23	27	32	40
6	18	28	31	32	40	44	54
4	24	37	40	44	54	60	72
2	32	51	54	59	71	80	96
1	38	58	65	68	83	94	112
1/0	45	69	76	80	96	108	130
2/0	52	79	88	93	112	126	148
3/0	60	93	103	108	130	146	172
4/0	69	108	120	126	151	169	204

* See Appendix for metric equivalent.

Table 9.15 Allowable Amperage of Flexible Cords[1,2]
(Adapted from ABYC Standard E-11, Table XIII)

Size, AWG*	Nominal CM Area	Outside Engine Space 30°C Ambient		Inside Engine Space 50°C Ambient	
		Three Conductors	Two Conductors	Three Conductors	Two Conductors
16	2,580	10	13	6	8
14	4,110	15	18	9	11
12	6,530	20	25	12	15
10	10,380	25	30	15	20
8	16,510	35	40	20	25
6	26,240	45	55	30	35
4	41,740	60	70	35	40
2	66,360	80	95	50	55

[1] Current ratings are for flexible cords containing no more than three conductors. For four to six conductors, reduce ampacity to 80%.
[2] Shore-power cables rated at 86°F (30°C).
* See Appendix for metric equivalent.

Conductor Installation

Note that the conductor specifications and wiring techniques for DC and AC systems are nearly identical. Some of the illustrations used in Chapter 6 are repeated here to save the reader from having to flip back and forth.

Connections

Fabrication and installation of wiring connections should not damage the conductors. Special tools (see Figure 6.10 and discussion in Chapter 6) are available for making approved crimp-on connections.

All connection components (conductors, terminals, studs, washers, and nuts) should be galvanically compatible and corrosion resistant. Specifically, aluminum and unplated steel are not appropriate for studs, nuts, and washers.

Marine connectors also differ from the more common electronic-type connectors in that they must withstand vibration and tensile stresses. Figure 9.7 shows the types of connectors approved for marine use, along with several types specifically disapproved.

Friction connectors (the blade and bullet variety in Figure 9.7) are allowed, provided they resist a 6-pound pull. The other approved connectors must resist the pulls shown in Table 9.16 for at least 1 minute.

Although not specified in the ABYC standard, pretinned conductors are preferred in marine use. The reason will be apparent when you attempt to repair a conductor that has been on a boat for a few years. Chances are, if it is untinned, it will be corroded far up into the insulating sleeve, due to capillary wicking of moisture into the stranded conductor. Soldering corroded copper wire is ineffective and definitely not recommended.

Although solder can make a strong connection, the ABYC states that solder must not be the sole means of mechanical connection in any circuit. One reason is that the solder may melt if the terminal overheats, due to either an overcurrent condition or high resistance in the connection. Without any other means of attachment, a melted solder connection may separate. If you wish to use solder (and many professionals do), first crimp the connector to the conductor, then flow solder into the crimped joint.

As an alternative to solder, adhesive-lined, heat-shrink tubing is available. It seals out moisture, mechanically strengthens the connection, and electrically insulates the terminal shank at the same time. Figure 9.8 shows how to make a terminal connection using adhesive-lined, heat-shrink tubing.

Fig. 9.7 ABYC Approved and Disapproved Marine Connectors

Splice	Butt	3-Way	Wire nut
Friction	Blade	Bullet or snap	
Terminals	Ring	Locking spade / Flanged spade	Plain spade
Set Screw		Indirect-bearing	Direct-bearing

Table 9.16 Tensile Test Values for Connections (Adapted from ABYC Standard E-11, Table XVI)

Conductor Size, AWG*	Force, lb.	Conductor Size, AWG	Force, lb.
18	10	4	70
16	15	3	80
14	30	2	90
12	35	1	100
10	40	0	125
8	45	2/0	150
6	50	3/0	175
5	60	4/0	225

* See Appendix for metric equivalent.

Fig. 9.8 Adhesive-Lined, Heat-Shrink Tubing

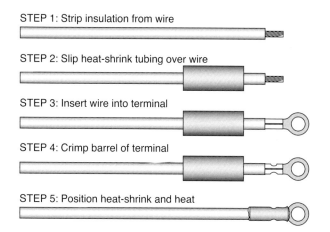

STEP 1: Strip insulation from wire

STEP 2: Slip heat-shrink tubing over wire

STEP 3: Insert wire into terminal

STEP 4: Crimp barrel of terminal

STEP 5: Position heat-shrink and heat

Conductor Protection

Exposed conductors must be protected by conduit, self-draining loom, tape, raceway, or equivalent means. Loom materials must be self-extinguishing.

Except for battery cables up to 36 inches in length and outboard engine cables, conductors must be either supported continuously or secured every 18 inches maximum with clamps or straps.

Nonmetallic clamps are allowed except over an engine, shaft, machinery, or passageway, where clamp failure could result in danger. Clamp materials must also be resistant to oil, gasoline, and water.

Metal clamps must have smooth, rounded edges, and the cable must be protected from the metal by tape or other wrapping to protect the conductors.

Conductors should be clamped close to their connections to remove strain from the connections.

Conductor Routing

Route conductors well above the bilge or any other area where water might accumulate. If routing through such an area cannot be avoided, both the conductors and the connections should be watertight.

Conductors should also be kept clear of exhaust pipes and other heat sources. Minimum clearances, except for engine wiring and exhaust-temperature sensor wiring, should be 2 inches/50mm for wet exhausts and 4 inches/100mm for dry exhausts, unless equivalent heat barriers are provided.

Conductors should also be kept clear of sources of chafing such as engine shafts, steering cable and linkages, steering gears, and engine controls.

If AC and DC conductors are run together, the AC conductors must be sheathed or bundled separately from the DC conductors.

Receptacles

Maintaining Polarity

AC receptacles must be of the grounding type with one terminal connected to the grounding wire. To prevent polarity reversal all plugs and receptacles must match and must not be interchangeable with plugs and receptacles of the DC system. Terminals must be identified either by letter or by using the color scheme shown in Table 9.17:

Table 9.17 BMEA and ISO Color Code for 240 VAC Conductors

European and UK Practice		USA Practice	
Conductor	**Colors**	**Conductor**	**Colors**
Live	Brown	Ungrounded (hot)	Black
Neutral	Light Blue	Grounded (neutral)	White
Ground(ing)/Earth	Green/Yellow	Ground(ing)/Earth	Green

Both color groups conform with ISO standards.

Location

Galley receptacles should be placed so that appliance cords do not cross a stove, sink, or traffic area, as shown in Figure 9.9.

Receptacles that are located in the head, galley, machine spaces, or above deck should be protected by a Type-A (trip-on fault current of 5 milliamps [0.005 amp]) GFCI or RCD.

Receptacles normally should be installed in locations that are protected from weather, spray, and flooding. If not, they should be protected when not in use by a spring-loaded cover. Receptacles subject to submersion must be watertight.

Fig. 9.9 Receptacle Placement in Galleys

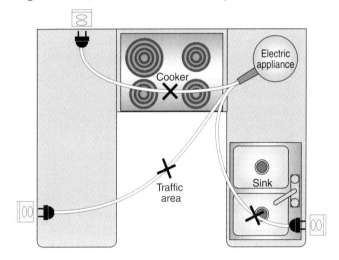

The Yellow/Green or Green Wire

The earth or grounding wire in AC circuits provides a life-saving return path for stray electric currents. Figure 9.10 illustrates the danger the wire is designed to protect against. The engine, through the transmission, shaft, and water surrounding the boat, is at earth potential. In the illustration one of the hot conductors of a piece of electrical equipment (a water heater) has short-circuited to its metal case. With one hand on the metal engine and the other on the water heater jacket, the person in the illustration serves as a return-to-ground path for the AC current. Were there a grounding wire connected to the heater jacket and to the engine, it would provide a very-low-resistance return path for the return current and hold the case and engine at the same potential. With no driving potential difference, there would be no reason for electrical current to flow through the person.

Boaters familiar with residential wiring often assume that a boat is just like a house. On that assumption, they connect the neutral and grounding shore-power conductors at the boat's AC panel.

Figure 9.11 shows what can happen in such a case. As always, all of the current in the live conductor somehow finds its way back to the shore-power ground. In a properly wired system, the sole return path would be the neutral conductor. In the system shown, however, the return current flows through three paths: the neutral conductor, the grounding conductor, and—via the

Fig. 9.10 What the Green Wire Protects Against

boat's grounded underwater metal—the seawater.

If resistance or a break develops in the neutral and grounded conductors, much of the return current could be through the water, exposing a person in the water near the boat to great danger.

Principle: Connect the grounding and neutral conductors at the source, be it shore power, generator, or inverter.

Fig. 9.11 Mistake #1: Connecting Neutral and Grounding Conductors on a Boat

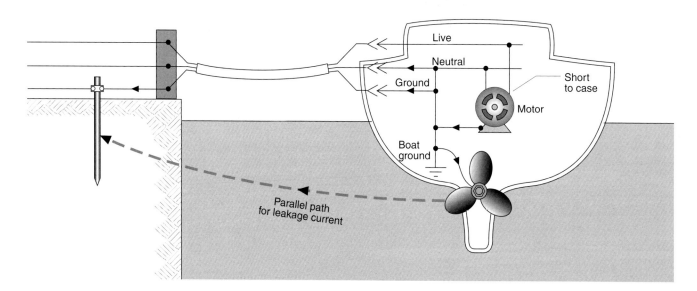

Figure 9.12 shows a second mistake. This time the neutral and grounding wires are properly separated on the boat, but, intending to prevent stray-current corrosion of the boat's underwater hardware, the misguided owner has cut the grounding wire to the boat's ground (engine and metallic underwater hardware). If a short develops in a piece of electrical equipment, the ground-ing wire will carry current. If there is, however, resistance in this wire and its connections, the equipment case may still be above ground potential. A person contacting both the equipment case and a piece of metal underwater hardware may be shocked (literally) to find that he is a parallel return path through the water.

Principle: Connect the grounding wire to the boat's ground.

Fig. 9.12 Mistake #2: Not Connecting the Grounding Conductor to Boat Ground

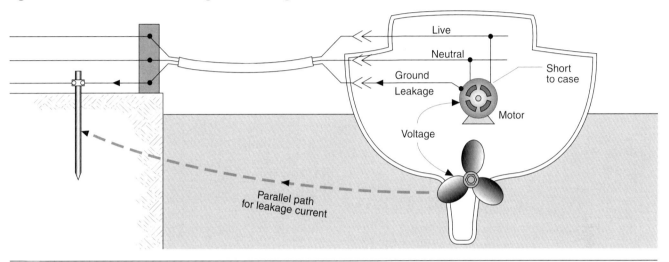

We have found that the grounding and neutral wires must not be connected on a boat, but that the grounding wire must be connected to the boat's ground. Unfortunately, we still may experience a problem. We may have unwittingly created a galvanic cell, which, as we saw in Chapter 5, leads to corrosion of underwater metals.

Figure 9.13 shows two boats in a marina on shore power. The grounding wires are properly connected to their respective boat grounds, but they are also connected to each other through the common shore-power connection.

We have now created a galvanic cell: one boat is the anode and the other boat is the cathode. Even were the underwater metals of the two boats of identical composition, they could suffer from impressed-current corrosion were there a voltage field in the water.

Woe is us; is there ANY safe solution which doesn't cause corrosion? Actually, there are two.

Fig. 9.13 Galvanic Cell Created by Marina Common Ground

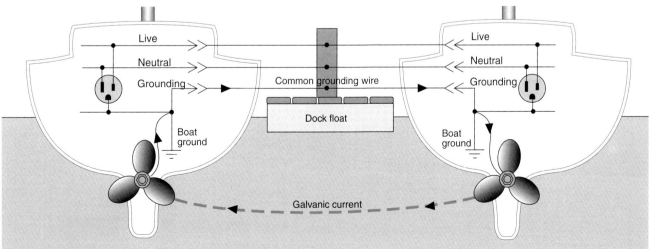

Solution 1: The Galvanic Isolator

A galvanic isolator, placed on the ship's grounding wire immediately after the shore-power connector, blocks DC current. Figure 9.14 shows how it works. At top is a simple pair of parallel and reversed diodes. Diodes pass current in the direction of the arrow but block current in the opposite direction. In the forward direction a small voltage drop (0.6 volt for a silicon diode) occurs. Thus the pair of diodes will block current until the voltage reaches 0.6 volt in both directions.

Adding diodes in series doubles the voltage rating. Parallel and reversed diode pairs will thus block current until the voltage reaches 1.2 volts in either direction.

Finally, a nonpolarized capacitor allows AC current to pass, while still blocking DC currents up to ±1.2 volts.

ABYC Galvanic Isolator Recommendations

According to the ABYC, a galvanic isolator should:
- be tested by an independent testing laboratory
- have a current rating not less than that of the main shore-power disconnect circuit breaker
- not introduce a voltage drop greater than 2.5 volts at 100% of the shore-power cable ampacity rating
- not pass less than 0.030 ampere at DC voltages of 1.2 volts in either direction
- not pass less than 0.030 ampere at DC voltages of 0.5 volt in either direction with 3.0 amperes RMS AC current superimposed

In addition the galvanic isolator should provide audible or visible status monitoring indicating:
- shorted or open diode
- failure to block galvanic current at 1.1 volts DC
- continuity of the shore grounding circuit
- operational status of the monitoring device

Solution 2: The Isolation Transformer

If we had a source of electricity that acted like an onboard generator, there would be no need for a grounding wire to run back to the shore-power ground, and we could break the galvanic connection to other marina-bound boats. An isolation transformer is the answer, regenerating onboard power without direct electrical connection to shore power.

Figure 9.15 shows an isolation transformer. To meet ABYC requirements, isolation transformers must be tested and labeled by an independent laboratory.

The primary coil is connected to the live and neutral shore-power conductors. The secondary coil is connected to the live and neutral conductors for the ship's power.

A metal shield, electrically isolated from all other parts of the transformer, is placed between the primary and secondary coils, and a lead is brought out from the shield. The shield must withstand a voltage of 4,000 volts AC, 60 Hz, for 1 minute, applied between the shield and other components such as windings, core, and outside enclosure.

The transformer case must be metal and have a grounding terminal.

The ship's neutral and grounding conductors are connected at the transformer output, since the transformer secondary is a new source of electricity. As you will see on the following pages, connections between shield, conductor, transformer case, shore-power ground, and ship's ground vary with the transformer. Follow the manufacturer's directions.

Fig. 9.15 Isolation Transformer

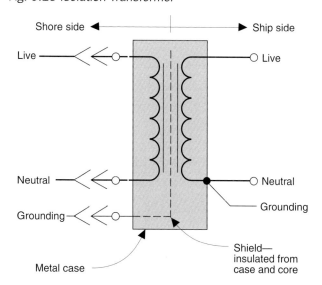

Fig. 9.14 Galvanic Isolators

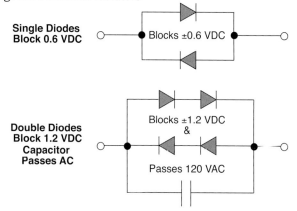

The following pages contain a variety of shore-power circuits, based on BMEA recommendations. They range from a basic small yacht circuit, to more sophisticated designs for larger craft using more than one source of power. The term 'earth' is, of course, interchangeable with 'ground'.

Fig. 9.16 A Basic Shore-power Installation

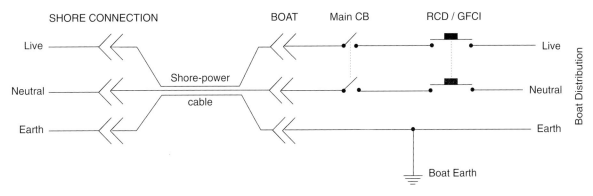

This is the simplest type of shore-power installation, found on many smaller craft, and adequate for occasional rather than permanent use. It is important that the system earth is connected to the boat's earth, and

installation is rendered safer by including a polarity indicator. The neutral and earth connections must be made with the corresponding shore connections, and not connected together, as in a domestic installation.

Fig. 9.17 A Shore-power Installation with a Galvanic Isolator

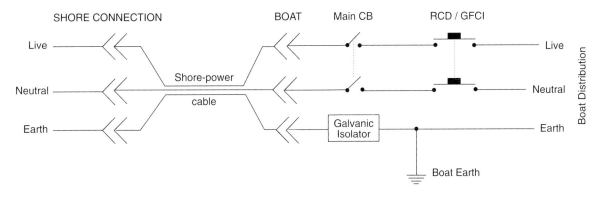

This is very similar to the basic installation, but the addition of a galvanic isolator which when fitted in the protective conductor resists imported stray galvanic current flow while permitting the passage of AC current to earth, if present. Galvanic isolators only protect against electrolysis or galvanic action, ie where a difference in potential exists between dissimilar metals

when immersed in an electrolyte (impure water). It will not protect against a fault condition where a voltage differential greater than 1.6 VDC exists.

The neutral and earth connections must be made with the corresponding shore connections, and not connected together.

Shore-Power Circuits

Fig. 9.18 A Shore-power Installation with an Isolation Transformer

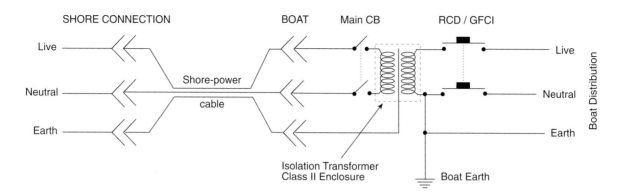

This system incorporates an isolation transformer, which prevents galvanic current flowing between the shore and the craft, as there is no connection between the boat earth and the shore earth. Note that the boat's earth (ground) is connected to the neutral terminal on the output side of the isolation transformer.

Fig. 9.19 A Shore-power Installation with alternative Generator and Inverter power.

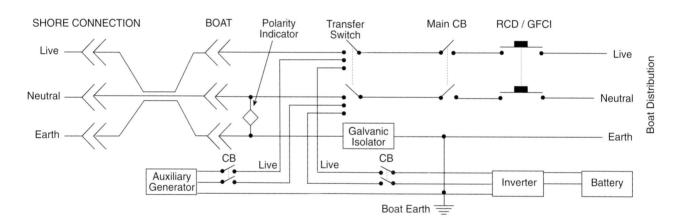

Alternative versions of this system could be either one or both sources of on-board power. An isolation transformer would give more complete galvanic and reverse polarity protection.

Larger vessels with high AC loads may split the AC circuit into two so that the higher loads are supplied by the generator, so that when the inverter is used it only has to supply lower loads within its rating.

CHAPTER 10

Conservation for Liveaboards

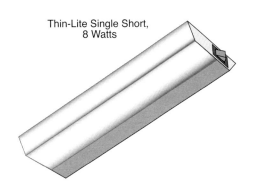

Thin-Lite Single Short,
8 Watts

Compact Replacement
12VDC, 13 Watts

PL
4-Pin

Mini Reading Light
10 Watts

Halogen Mini-Spot
5 Watts

LED All-Round Light
3 Watts

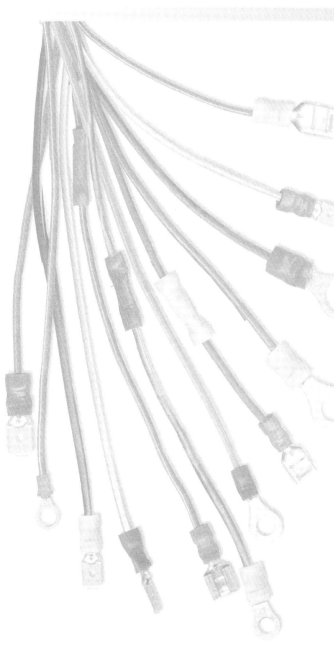

The cost per kilowatt-hour of power generated on a boat is high, whether in money or in aggravation. It is easily shown that the cost of a kilowatt-hour saved is less than that of a kilowatt-hour generated, no matter the shipboard source.

This chapter shows you how to reduce your use of electricity for lighting, refrigeration, and several other areas.

The bottom line is that most boaters can cut their onboard power consumption by at least half with little or no compromise in lifestyle.

BMEA and ISO Color Code for 240 VAC Conductors

European and UK Practice		USA Practice	
Conductor	**Colors**	**Conductor**	**Colors**
Live	Brown	Ungrounded (hot)	Black
Neutral	Light Blue	Grounded (neutral)	White
Ground(ing)/Earth	Green/Yellow	Ground(ing)/Earth	Green

Both color groups conform with ISO standards.

Costs per Kilowatt-Hour

Before considering solar and wind power, the live-aboard boatowner should consider the less expensive alternative form of energy—conservation.

Put yourself to the following test. Your already leaky boat becomes more leaky. Which solution first comes to your mind? If it is to install a second or larger bilge pump, then forget conservation, solar, and wind, and get yourself to a berth where you can tap into shore power. If fixing the leak seems more logical to you, however, then read on.

If we have learned anything in the past 20 years, it is that, with modest investment and attention to detail, we can save a lot of expensive energy in our homes and offices. The same is true of boats.

If your boat is typical, this chapter can show you how to reduce the drain on your batteries by half with virtually no effect on your lifestyle. By cutting consumption in half, you will also reduce the required sizes and costs of the solar and wind systems you may be considering adding to your boat. In fact, you may reduce your consumption to the point where you never need run your engine again just to charge your batteries!

The old saying "A penny saved is a penny earned" has its analog in energy conservation: "A kilowatt saved is a kilowatt made." If we can save energy without dimishing lifestyle, then it is fair to compare the cost of saving a kilowatt-hour to the cost of producing a kilowatt-hour in order to see which is the better deal.

Costs of Producing Electricity

Figure 10.1 shows the $ costs per kilowatt-hour of electricity produced by:
- 220-amp alternator on a 20 hp diesel
- 110-amp alternator on a 20 hp diesel
- 55-amp alternator on a 20 hp diesel
- Solar panel at $8 per peak watt
- 5-foot wind machine at $1,500

The assumptions used include:

Diesel Power
- Used at anchor
- Fuel consumption, 0.5 gallon/hour
- Fuel price, $2.20/gallon
- Price including controls, $7,000
- Life, 10,000 hours
- Maintenance, $0.20/hour

Solar Power:
- Used all year
- Size, 50 watts peak output
- Price including controls, $400
- Life, 10 years
- Average daily sunshine, 5.2 hours
- Annual maintenance, $0

Wind Power:
- Used all year
- Size (blade diameter), 5 feet
- Price including controls, $1,500
- Life, 10 years
- Average wind speed, 10 knots
- Annual maintenance, $100

Assuming the alternators cycle the battery between the charge states of 50% and 90%, the relative production costs per kilowatt-hour shown in Figure 10.1 of electricity are:
- 220-amp alternator, $1.25
- 110-amp alternator, $2.30
- 55-amp alternator, $4.10
- Solar panel, $0.42
- 5-foot wind machine, $0.59

The Costs of Conserving Electricity

Now let's compare the costs per kilowatt-hour of electricity *saved* by two simple changes: switching from incandescent to fluorescent lighting, and halving the losses of a DC-powered refrigerator.

Lighting Conversion

An 8-watt fluorescent fixture puts out nearly as much light as a 40-watt incandescent lamp. Assume each replacement fluorescent fixture costs $30. Fluorescent bulbs cost four times as much as incandescent bulbs, but they last proportionally longer, so the cost of bulb replacement is the same.

Assuming a 10-year fixture life, and that the lamp is operated an average of 2 hours per day throughout the year, the lifetime savings of the fluorescent replacement fixture is 124 kilowatt-hours. The cost per kilowatt-hour saved is $30/124 = $0.24—half the cost of electricity produced by the cheapest alternative means, and one-tenth the cost of the 110-amp alternator power.

Fig. 10.1 Costs per Kilowatt-Hour of Generated Power (based on 10 years of daily consumption)

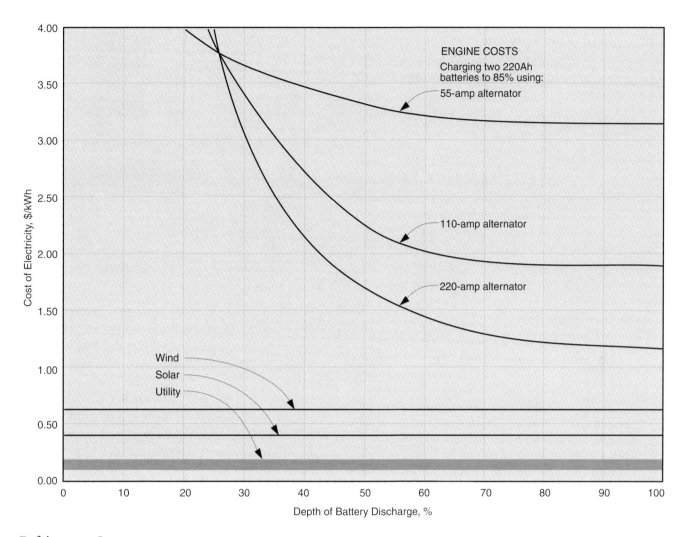

Refrigerator Losses

Assume that our 20 litre/8-cubic-foot refrigerator with 50 mm/2-inch foam insulation draws 5.5 amps at 12 volts DC and has a 40% duty cycle. Its daily consumption would be: 5.5 amps × 24 hours × 0.40 = 52.8 Ah, or 0.63 kilowatt-hour.

If we were to double the insulation of the refrigerator walls to 100 mm/4 inches, install a better door gasket and install a trap in the drain, we would probably reduce the refrigerator's total heat loss by half, or 0.315 kilowatt-hour/day. Over 10 years of continuous use, the savings would amount to 1,186 kilowatt-hours.

The most effective way to double the refrigerator insulation is to line the inside of the box with 50 mm/2-inch polyurethane foam board and then glass over the foam. If accessible, cavities between the box and the hull and cabinetry can be filled with expanding foam.

The first method has the advantage of simplicity, but reduces the volume of the box. The second method retains the box dimensions, but its effectiveness is uncertain without disassembly of the cabinetry.

Method one could be accomplished for about $50 in materials and $200 in labor by a reasonably competent fiberglass technician. Cost per kilowatt-hour saved is thus $250/1,186 kilowatt-hours = $0.21/kilowatt-hour.

Both of our retrofits are at least twice as cost effective as adding solar and wind power, and ten times cheaper than generation by shipboard diesel.

Caveat: The above calculations assume year-round use of the boat for 10 years. If you use your boat only 10% of the year, then solar and wind costs per kilowatt-hour should be multiplied by a factor of 10. That is why this chapter is titled Conservation for Liveaboards.

Lighting Savings

Most boats come from the factory equipped with incandescent lighting. Both the bulbs and the fixtures are inexpensive, but it is a false economy for the owner. You can reduce your lighting load by a full two-thirds through three simple retrofits (see Figures 10.3 and 10.4): fluorescent galley and head fixtures, halogen reading-light fixtures, and, for those who anchor out a lot, a light-actuated anchor light switch or a 3-watt LED all-around light.

Fluorescent Fixtures

The galley requires bright lighting, but 8-watt fluorescent slim-line fixtures cast as much light as common 40-watt incandescent fixtures. For serious chefs, larger fluorescents rated at 13 watts (65 W), 16 watts (80 W) and 26 watts (130 W) are available. The head is another good location for the same types of fluorescent lighting.

If you have 240 VAC light fixtures aboard, you can convert them with compact fluorescent screw-in replacement bulbs and then run these fixtures from a DC-to-AC inverter for similar savings.

If the fluorescent fixtures affect any of your electronics, install the filters described in Chapter 13.

Halogen Spot Fixtures

Many of the lights below deck are for reading. The most common small incandescent fixtures spread the light from 15-watt bulbs over an area ten times that of a page. These lamps can be directly replaced with 5- or 10-watt halogen spot-task lamps, which achieve the same light intensity by concentrating the beam from a high-efficiency halogen bulb onto a page or task.

You can save further lighting energy by installing the solid-state dimmer circuit described in Chapter 14. You can then dim the lights for a warmer ambience, save electricity, and double the lifetime of the lamps, all at the same time.

LEDs

The future of marine lighting is all about LEDs. While Figure 10.2 shows the present efficacy range of LEDs as 22 to 42 lumens per watt (about twice that of incandescents and half that of fluorescents), there is little doubt that 60 to 100 lumens per watt will ultimately be achieved.

The same efficiency as fluorescents, 10 to 100 times the life of halogens and incandescents, indestructible packaging, and easily and efficiently dimmed: sounds like a no-brainer.

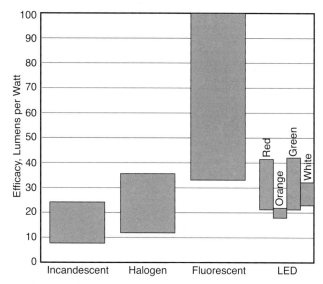

Fig. 10.2 Efficacy of Light Sources

Anchor Lights

International navigation law requires boats less than 20 meters long to display an anchor light that is visible for at least 2 nautical miles. The required luminance is equivalent to that produced by a 10-watt incandescent lamp.

The battery-powered "marker lights" many boat-owners employ do not meet the 2-mile requirement. Simply reducing incandescent lamp wattage puts your boat in jeopardy—at least from the standpoint of liability.

Two legal, energy-saving alternatives are:

1. Using an automatic anchor light switch
2. Switching to an LED all-round light

Anchor light switch. To run the light from sunrise to when you wake up (or when you first remember the light is on, which may be considerably longer) is wasteful, however. The automatic anchor light switch in Chapter 14 turns the anchor light on and off precisely at sunset and sunrise, saving about 2 Ah per day. If you leave your boat unattended it will save an average of about 10 Ah per day. If building the circuit yourself isn't your idea of a fun way to spend a weekend, several commercial versions are also available.

LED all-around light. Perko (no doubt others will follow suit) has developed an LED all-round light that satisfies the 2 nm visibility requirement for vessels under 20 meters. The design takes advantage of both the LED's inherent efficiency (two times that of incandescents) and its narrow beam (±5°) to focus the light at the horizon. The result is a 75% power reduction, from 10 to 12 watts to only 3 watts.

Fig. 10.3 Bulbs for Boats (some are US only types)

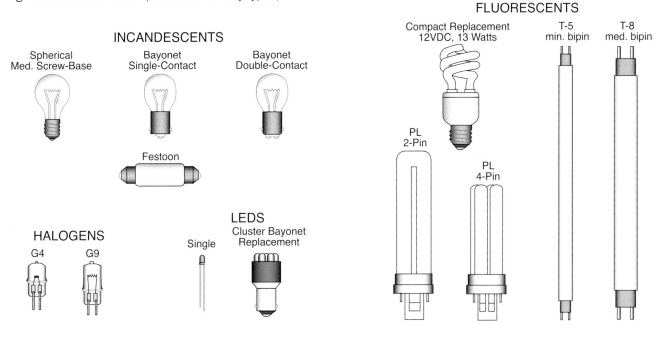

INCANDESCENTS

Spherical
Med. Screw-Base

Bayonet
Single-Contact

Bayonet
Double-Contact

Festoon

FLUORESCENTS

Compact Replacement
12VDC, 13 Watts

T-5
min. bipin

T-8
med. bipin

PL
2-Pin

PL
4-Pin

HALOGENS

G4   G9

LEDS

Single

Cluster Bayonet
Replacement

Fig. 10.4 A Collection of Efficient Fixtures (some are US only types)

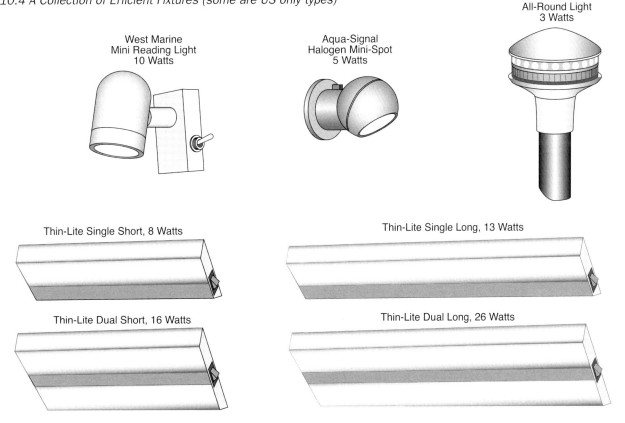

West Marine
Mini Reading Light
10 Watts

Aqua-Signal
Halogen Mini-Spot
5 Watts

Perko LED
All-Round Light
3 Watts

Thin-Lite Single Short, 8 Watts

Thin-Lite Single Long, 13 Watts

Thin-Lite Dual Short, 16 Watts

Thin-Lite Dual Long, 26 Watts

Refrigeration Savings

How Refrigeration Works

If you know that water boils (turns from a liquid to a gas) at 100°C/212°F at normal atmospheric pressure, but that its boiling temperature rises at higher pressure (such as in a pressure cooker), and that evaporating water absorbs a lot of heat (think of getting out of the water on a windy day), then you are well on your way to understanding how refrigerators, air conditioners, and heat pumps work.

Unfortunately, the boiling point of water is too high to use it as a refrigerant, but other fluids exist that boil at below the freezing point of water! One such refrigerant is ES-12a (see Figure 10.5), one of many refrigerants developed to replace R-12 (Freon), now banned due to its adverse effect on the earth's ozone layer.

As shown in Figure 10.5, at atmospheric pressure (15 psi), ES-12a boils at about –32°C/–26°F. If we compress it to a pressure of 150 psi, its boiling temperature rises to about 43°C/110°F. Since this rise approximates the range from freezer temperature to maximum atmospheric temperature, ES-12a may prove useful.

In the refrigeration system in Figure 10.6, the refrigerant is sucked into a compressor. The compressor works like the piston of an internal combustion engine, except power is applied to the piston by the crankshaft instead of the other way around. The piston compresses the gas to about 150 psi, in the process raising its temperature to about 49°C/120°F.

The hot, compressed gas then flows through the discharge line to a condenser—a heat exchanger—where it is cooled to below its condensation point and changes back to a liquid. In order to condense the 49°C/120°F gas, the condenser must be located in a cool space or be cooled by seawater.

From the condenser the hot liquid first passes through a drier, which assures no water contaminates the refrigerant, then on to an expansion valve.

The function of the expansion valve is to control the release of the hot liquid into the low pressure of the evaporator coil. When the fluid emerges from the expansion valve, the dramatic drop back to near atmospheric pressure causes it to boil (evaporate) at about –32°C/–26°F, absorbing heat from the evaporator coil. The evaporator coil is the frost-covered tubing you see in an older refrigerator or freezer.

From the evaporator the now-cool gas is again sucked into the compressor, and the cycle is repeated.

Now for some details:

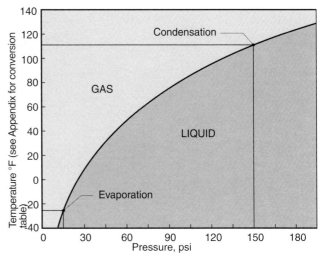

Fig. 10.5 Pressure-Temperature Curve for ES-12a Refrigerant

Condenser

Efficient condenser operation requires efficient heat removal from the tubing. Air-cooled condensers utilize metal fins on the tubing and air flow over the fins to remove the heat. The efficiency of such an arrangement depends on both the temperature of the air and the rate of airflow. A stuffy engine compartment is obviously not a good location for the condenser.

Evaporator

The evaporator shown has little heat-storage capacity. As a result the compressor will cycle on and off every few minutes. A lot of energy is lost starting the compressor, so the efficiency is relatively low. A better system encloses the evaporator coil in a holding plate filled with a liquid having a low freezing point. The compressor runs until all of the holding-plate liquid freezes. The holding plate then functions like a block of ice. Properly sized for the refrigerator box, a holding-plate system requires running the compressor just once a day for an hour or so. By running such a system only when the engine is running, all of the considerable load is removed from the boat's batteries.

Controls

A small temperature-sensing bulb on a capillary tube is attached to the suction end of the evaporator coil. The temperature-dependent pressure in the tube controls the rate of fluid flow through the valve, and thus the temperature of the evaporator coil. When the temperature of the refrigerator box rises, a thermostat switches the compressor on to move and compress refrigerant, cooling the box.

Fig. 10.6 How Refrigerators Work

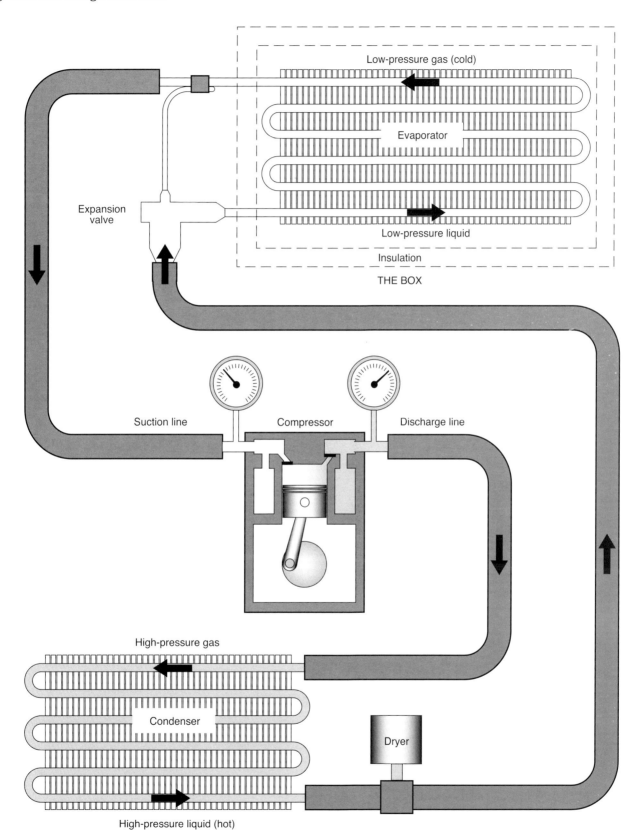

Refrigeration Savings

Calculating the Cooling Load

First, two definitions:
- Btu = heat that changes the temperature of 1 pound of water by 1F°.
- Heat of fusion of water (heat absorbed by 1 pound of ice when it melts) = 144 Btu.

Next, Figure 10.7 shows the basic equation of conductive heat loss:

$$H = A \times \Delta T/R$$

where:

H = heat loss through A, in Btu/hour
A = area of surface in square feet
ΔT = temperature difference, $T_{outside} - T_{inside}$F°
R = thermal resistance

To this conductive heat loss through the refrigerator walls we add the losses of infiltration (air leakage through the lid and drain) and cooldown (heat that must be removed from warm objects added to the box).

The Refrigerator Box

Figure 10.8 shows the dimensions of a typical 20 litre/8-cubic-foot refrigerator. The walls are constructed of 50mm/2-inch urethane foam, lined with fiberglass. Plugging the numbers into the heat-loss equation above:

A = 28 square feet (insulation mid-plane)
ΔT = 75°F outside – 40°F inside
    = 35F°
R = 2 inches × R-6/inch
    = 12
H = 28 × 35/12
    = 82 Btu/hour

If this box had a perfect lid and we never opened it, it would melt 82 Btu/hour/144 Btu/pound = 0.57 pound of ice per hour or 13.7 pounds of ice per day. If we add another third (27 Btu/hour) to the heat loss for infiltration and cooldown, our totals become 109 Btu/hour and 18 pounds of ice per day.

How much electricity will it take to replace the ice? The answer is—it all depends. It depends primarily on the efficiency of the refrigeration system, the refrigerator's coefficient of performance (COP), defined as:

COP = watts removed/watts used

We'll also need a conversion factor:

Ah/day = 0.586 × Btu/hour

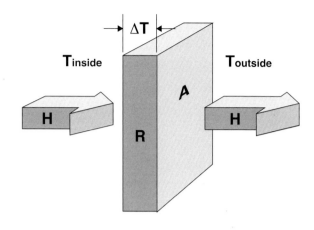

Fig. 10.7 Conductive Heat Loss

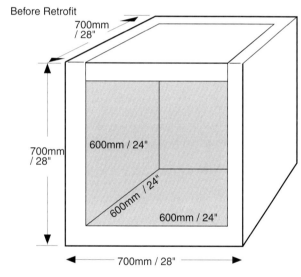

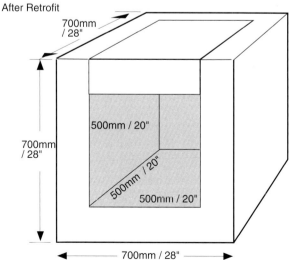

Fig. 10.8 Typical Refrigerator Box

COP depends on how hard the compressor has to work pumping heat from the evaporator (cold) side to the condenser (hot) side. When the temperatures of evaporator and condenser are the same, the compressor can remove about 3 Btu of heat energy, using the equivalent of 1 Btu of electrical energy, yielding a COP of 3.0.

At the opposite extreme, the typical refrigerator is capable of moving heat across a maximum difference of about 150F°, at which point its COP becomes zero.

Figure 10.9 shows the relationship between COP and condenser temperature for a typical small refrigerator, assuming the evaporator is at –7°C/20°F.

The temperature of the condenser depends on its type and location. Table 10.1 shows typical condenser operating temperatures and resulting COPs for different condenser types and locations in the boat.

Assume the condenser is located in free air at 24°C/75°F but has no fan. According to Table 10.1, its COP will be about 1.3. Our example refrigerator will then draw 190 Btu/hr × 0.586/1.3 = 49 Ah/day.

A Typical Refrigerator Retrofit

To reduce the refrigeration load we can take three steps:

1. Increase wall insulation.
2. Decrease infiltration with a better lid gasket and a drain trap.
3. Increase condenser COP with a fan.

Wall Insulation

At the cost of one quarter of the interior space, we can double the insulation of all surfaces and increase their R-values to R-24. Because we also have decreased the heat loss area (measured at the midpoint of the insulation) to 2.25 square metres/24 square feet, conductive heat loss is decreased by 47 Btu/hour to 35 Btu/hour.

Infiltration

By installing a better gasket on the lid and a better meltwater drain trap, we might decrease the losses due to air leaks by half, or 13 Btu/hour, and the total heat loss by 60 Btu/hour to 49 Btu/hour.

Condensor COP

By installing a thermostatically controlled 12-volt DC fan to move air through the condenser coils, we can increase the condenser COP from about 1.3 to 1.7 at the cost of about 2 Ah per day to power the fan. Most

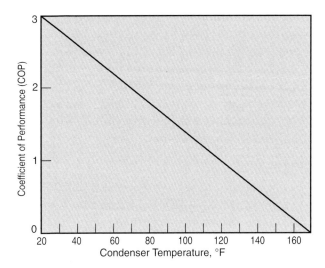

Fig. 10.9 Refrigerator COP vs. Temperature

Table 10.1 Refrigerator COP vs. Location

Condenser/Location	Condenser Temp., °C/°F	COP
Air-cooled in 43°C/110°F engine compartment, no fan	60/140	0.6
Air-cooled in 43°C/110°F engine compartment with fan	49/120	1.0
Air-cooled in 24°C/75°F free air with no fan	41/105	1.3
Air-cooled in 24°C/75°F free air with fan	29/85	1.7
Water-cooled, intake water 24°C/75°F	29/85	1.7
Water-cooled, intake water 15°C/60°F	21/70	2.0

marine and RV refrigeration manufacturers offer such fans as an option. If not, small fans that run on 12 VDC are readily available at electronics stores, such as RadioShack. DIY Project 13 (Chapter 14) is a circuit to control such a fan.

Manufacturers also sometimes offer water cooling, where the condenser is cooled by water circulated to a heat exchanger mounted on the bottom of the hull. While more efficient in cooler waters, such systems are susceptible to becoming fouled with growth.

Net Refrigerator Savings

With the above improvements, our new refrigeration load becomes 60 Btu/hour × 0.586/1.7 = 20.7 Ah/day—a decrease of more than 50%.

Other Savings

Cabin Fans

The most efficient way to cool a hot cabin is with a wind chute attached to a hatch, but its use assumes a breeze and that the boat is free to swing into it.

On hot, still nights, small fans directed at your body can make the difference between sleeping and not. The typical 6-inch cabin fan draws about 1 amp, but the most efficient fans draw only 0.3 amp. In 8 hours the accumulated difference is more than 5 Ah per fan.

Electronics

The power consumption of a sound system depends more on the efficiency of the speakers than that of the electronics. Therefore, look for speakers designed to be driven by computers, as they are the most efficient.

No one is willing to watch black and white television any longer, so the choice is between the older standard cathode-ray (CRT) color television and the newer, solid-state LCD versions. Wattage is roughly proportional to the area of the screen (diameter squared). From a 19-inch CRT to a 6-inch LCD there is a 65-watt, or 5-amp, difference. If you are an average 4-hour-per-day watcher, the daily difference is greater than the drain of the anchor light. An excellent way to save energy is, therefore, to install a 6-inch LCD television and sit closer!

VCRs and DVD players are becoming very popular on boats. In fact, trading videotapes and DVDs is nearly as common as trading paperback books. The typical 240-volt AC record/play VCR/DVD machine draws about 10 watts. Portable 12-volt DC play-only models draw 5 watts.

The Bottom Line

Table 10.2 shows, as promised, how the daily power consumption of a typical cruising boat can be reduced by half with no significant degradation of lifestyle.

Note: 240 VAC appliances will draw about 50% of the amperage of 120 VAC appliances.

Table 10.2 Power Consumption of a Typical versus an Energy-Efficient Liveaboard Boat

Area	Device		Watts	Amps	Hours/ Day	Typical Ah	Efficient Ah
Galley	Microwave		550	45.8	0.15	6.9	6.9
	Toaster		800	66.7	0.04		
	Blender		175	14.6	0.01	0.1	0.1
	Coffee grinder		160	13.3	0.01		
	Refrigerator	2" insul.	60	5.0	10.00	49.0	
		4" insul	60	5.0	5.00		20.7
Head	Hair dryer		1,200	100.0	0.03		
Lights	Reading	2 incand., 15 W	30	2.5	2.00	5.0	
		2 halogen, 5 W	10	0.8	2.00		1.6
	Galley	2 incand., 25 W	50	4.2	2.00	8.4	
		2 fluor., 8 W	16	1.4	2.00		2.8
	Anchor	manual, 10 W	10	0.8	14.00	11.2	
		auto., 10 W	10	0.8	11.00		8.8
Fans	Typical 6-inch, 100 cfm		12	1.0	5.00	5.0	
	Most efficient, 100 cfm		4	0.3	5.00		1.5
Electronics	Stereo	20 W/channel	60	5.0	1.00	5.0	
		7 W/channel	35	3.0	1.00		3.0
	Television, color, 19" CRT		80	6.7	2.00	13.4	
		15" LCD	36	3.0	2.00		
		6" LCD	15	1.25	2.00		2.5
VCR or DVD	Typical 120-volt AC		17	1.4	1.0	1.4	
	12-volt DC play-only		10	0.8	1.0		0.8
					Totals	105.4	48.7

CHAPTER 11

Solar Power

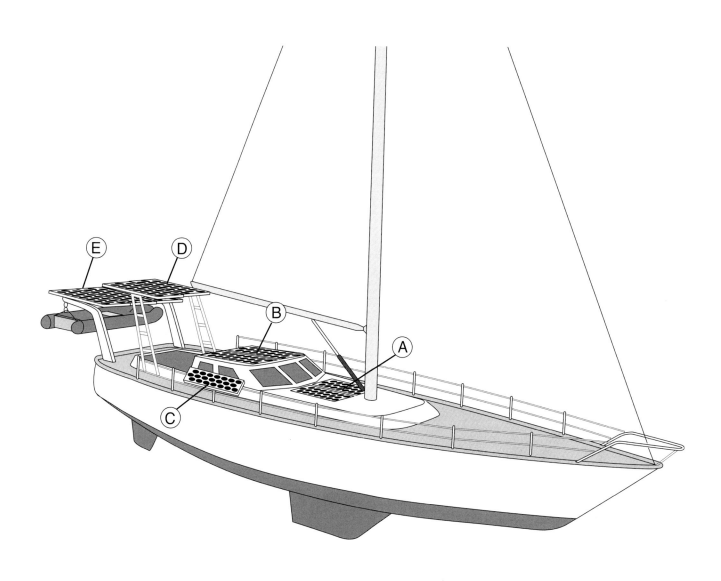

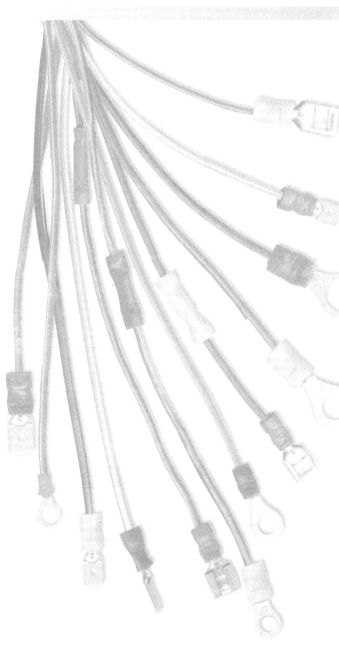

I s solar for you? Would the power produced by solar panels pay back their cost?

There is quite a collection of commercially available photovoltaic panels. Interpreting specifications requires that we first understand how photovoltaic panels work. We also need to consider panel orientation in estimating daily output.

Once the decision has been made, mechanical installation is quite simple. Electrical installation integrates the panels into the existing 12-volt DC alternator/battery system.

Following the rules for solar success virtually guarantees your solar satisfaction.

Although this section is illustrated with diagrams of US solar energy distribution, and lists mainly US products, the basic principles are the same for Europe, and the installation data is applicable everywhere.

Is Solar for You?

A solar, or photovoltaic, installation is a one-time investment with a fuel- and maintenance-free lifetime of 10 years or longer. Whether a photovoltaic system would prove cost effective on your boat, however, depends very much on how you use the boat. If you live aboard and are away from the dock at least half of the time, the answer is a definite "yes." If you cruise 1 month each summer, the answer is probably "no."

Figure 11.1 shows the percentage of daily electrical load supplied by photovoltaic panels among 71 live-aboard cruisers surveyed in Florida and the Bahamas. The average installation was far smaller than optimal, yet the average percentage of power supplied was a significant 40%. Had the array sizes been optimal, I am sure the power supplied would have been in the 80 to 100% range.

Also note from Figure 11.1 that cruisers who had both solar and wind systems garnered more than 90% of their power from the combination. Those having wind power, but no solar, generated 60% from the wind.

Figure 10.1 compared the costs per kilowatt-hour of electricity produced by photovoltaic panels, wind machines, and engine-driven alternators. The photovoltaic cost of $0.42/kilowatt-hour assumed:
• System used year-round
• Panel size—50 watts peak output
• Price including controls—$400
• Life—10 years
• Average daily sunshine—5.2 hours
• Maintenance—$0

Such a panel would produce on average 5.2 hours × 50 watts = 0.26 kWh per day, or 95 kWh per year. An alternative source of power would be a high-output, 110-amp alternator, charging batteries on a 50 to 85 percent-of-charge cycle. This, according to Figure 10.1, would produce power at a cost of $2.30 per kilowatt-hour.

Compared to the cost of alternator power, solar savings would be $2.30 − $0.42 = $1.88 per kilowatt-hour. At 95 kilowatt-hours per year, annual savings would be $179, and the photovoltaic system would pay for itself in $400/$177 = 2.2 years. That amounts to receiving a tax-free return on investment of 45%. Try to match that at your local bank!

On the other hand, if the boat were used but 1 month out of the year, the payback would be 27 years—longer than the projected life of the system.

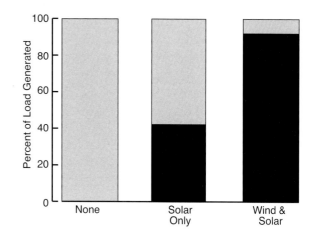

Fig. 11.1 Solar Energy Production among 71 Cruisers

Figure 11.2 shows how a photovoltaic panel works. Solar energy in the form of photons penetrates the photovoltaic material. Each photon transfers enough energy to the photovoltaic atoms to release an electron. If we connect the grid on the sunlit side to the conducting base on the back, the free electrons will flow through the external conductor and load to rejoin atoms having missing electrons.

Each free electron has a potential of about 0.6 volt. A panel typically consists of from 30 to 36 cells, connected in series to produce an open-circuit voltage of from 18 to 22 VDC. The theoretical maximum efficiency of this conversion of light energy to electrical energy is about 28%. As we will see, however, the efficiencies achieved in manufacture are improving but still fall far short of theory.

Photovoltaic collector materials take three common forms: monocrystalline silicon, polycrystalline silicon, and amorphous silicon. Crystalline silicon is grown in the form of large crystals, which are sawn into thin wafers to form the cells.

Monocrystalline cells consist of single, large crystals grown and drawn from melted silicon in the form of large rods. Due to their crystalline perfection, they have the highest efficiencies, ranging from 14 to 17%.

Polycrystalline silicon is formed by pouring melted silicon into blocks, the molten silicon forming many small crystals on cooling. These polycrystalline blocks are then sawn into cells. Because of defects between the crystals, the conversion efficiency of polycrystalline silicon ranges between 13 and 15%.

Amorphous silicon is produced by the less expensive process of depositing vaporized silicon onto a metal substrate. In addition to being less expensive to produce, amorphous silicon can be fabricated into semirigid and flexible panels. Semi-rigid panels attached to a thin steel backing can be adhered to a deck and stepped on without damage. Flexible panels with a heavy fabric backing can be attached to boat canvas. Unfortunately, the efficiency of amorphous silicon is only 5 to 7%, so twice as much collector area is required as for crystalline panels.

Most crystalline photovoltaic panels are warranted for 20 years, but there is no reason, barring physical damage, that they would not last 30 years or longer.

Amorphous silicon panels, because they are not enclosed in a rigid, protective frame, are generally warranted for only 5 years.

Fig. 11.2 How Photovoltaics Work

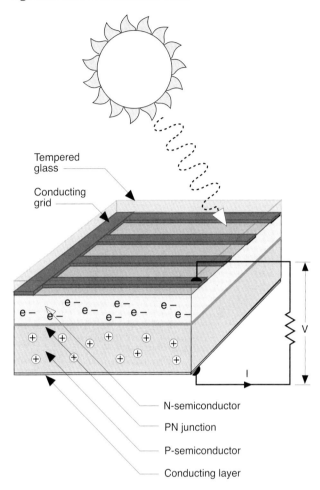

Tempered glass
Conducting grid
N-semiconductor
PN junction
P-semiconductor
Conducting layer

Photovoltaic Panels

Table 11.1 lists the specifications of popular photovoltaic panels available in the US. All panel output ratings are for 25°C (86°F). Rigid panels are in aluminum frames, and can be mounted to davits, bimini frames, and stanchions. Semirigid panels may be adhered directly to the deck. Flexible panels may be draped anywhere. On average you can expect (in 2005) to pay about $6 per rated watt for rigid panels, $8 for semirigid, and $12 for flexible. Add about $2 per rated watt for controls and mounting hardware.

Table 11.1 Photovoltaic Panel Specifications[1]

Model	Rigid (R) Semirigid (S) Flexible (F)[2]	Dimensions, inches	Rated Watts	Rated Amps	Open-Circuit Volts	Short-Circuit Amps	Warranty Years
			ICP Solar Pro[3]				
Plug'n'Play 30	R	41 x 12.4	30	2.00	—	—	Life
Plug'n'Play 50	R	41.3 x 20	50	3.30	—	—	Life
Plug'n'Play 75	R	50 x 23.3	75	5.00	—	—	Life
Plug'n'Play 100	R	60.3 x 28	100	6.70	—	—	Life
			Solara				
SM40M	S	16.6 x 10.7	10	0.50	21.0	—	20
SM60M	S	24.4 x 9.8	15	0.90	21.0	—	20
SM80M	S	16.9 x 17.7	20	1.10	21.0	—	20
SM120M	S	23.2 x 17.7	30	1.70	21.0	—	20
SM160M	S	29.0 x 17.7	40	2.20	21.0	—	20
SM225M	S	29.5 x 24.0	56	3.00	21.0	—	20
			United Solar (Unisolar)				
USF-5	F	21.3 x 9.7	5	0.30	16.5	0.33	5
USF-11	F	21.3 x 16.7	11	0.62	16.5	0.69	5
USF-32	F	55.8 x 16.7	32	1.94	16.5	2.10	5
			Kyocera				
KC35	R	18.5 x 25.7	35	2.33	18.8	2.50	25
KC40	R	20.7 x 25.7	40	2.34	21.5	2.48	25
KC50	R	25.2 x 25.7	50	3.00	21.5	3.10	25
KC60	R	29.6 x 25.7	60	3.55	21.5	3.73	25
KC70	R	34.1 x 25.7	70	4.14	21.5	4.35	25
KC80	R	38.4 x 25.7	80	4.73	21.5	4.97	25
KC120-1	R	56.1 x 25.7	120	7.10	21.5	7.45	25
			Shell Solar (Siemens)				
SM20	R	22.3 x 12.9	20	1.38	18.0	1.60	10
SM46	R	42.7 x 13	46	3.15	18.0	3.35	25
SM55	R	50.9 x 13	55	3.15	21.7	3.45	25
SM75	R	47.3 x 20.8	75	4.40	21.7	4.80	25
SM110	R	51.8 x 26	110	6.30	21.7	6.90	25
			BP Solar (Solarex)				
BP MSX5L	S	10.8 x 10.5	4.5	0.27	20.5	0.30	5
BP MSX10L	S	17.5 x 10.5	10	0.58	21.0	0.65	5
BP MSX20L	S	17.5 x 19.5	20	1.17	21.0	1.29	5
BP MSX30L	S	24.3 x 19.5	30	1.75	21.0	1.94	5
BP MSX40	R	29.9 x 19.7	40	2.37	21.0	2.58	20
BP MSX60	R	43.5 x 19.7	60	3.56	21.0	3.80	25

[1] All ratings at 25°C (86°F).
[2] Flexible panels for mounting directly to deck.
[3] Plug'n'Play panels include a charge controller.

Figure 11.3 shows the voltage-current curve for a typical 30-cell photovoltaic panel in full sunlight. With output terminals shorted, the panel put out its short-circuit current (here 3.3 amps). With output terminals not connected, current is zero, but output voltage is the open-circuit voltage (here 18.0 volts). Maximum power output is achieved at the knee of the curve where the rated current (3.0 amps) times the rated voltage (14.7 volts) equals the panel's rated power (44 watts).

Fig. 11.3 Typical Photovoltaic Panel Output Curve

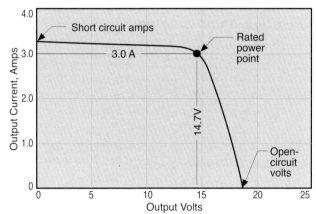

Figure 11.4 shows how the voltage-current curves vary both with number of cells and with panel temperature. Panel specifications are given for a panel (not air) temperature of 25°C (86°F). Both voltage and current decrease at higher temperatures. For this reason, panels should be mounted with free airflow beneath to minimize operating temperature. Panels in the tropics should have higher voltage ratings as well.

The effect of shading is not shown in manufacturers' voltage-current curves. Shading the panel from direct sun does not affect open-circuit voltage, but reduces power output under load roughly in proportion to the percentage of shaded area.

Finally, unless built in, you should install a Schottky blocking diode to prevent reverse-current flow from the batteries at night. Better yet, install a regulator that opens the circuit whenever the panel voltage is less than that of the battery.

A common mistake in selecting solar panels is failing to account for all of the voltage drops. Select a panel whose rated voltage at your expected operating temperature is at least 14.8 volts, since 14.8 volts – 0.4 volt (blocking diode drop) = 14.4 volts, the voltage required for fully charging lead-acid batteries. In order to equalize the batteries, the blocking diode can be temporarily shorted with clip leads, raising the voltage to 14.8.

Fig. 11.4 Typical Photovoltaic Output vs. Number of Cells and Panel Temperature

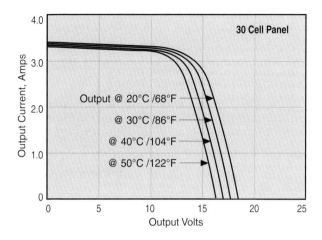

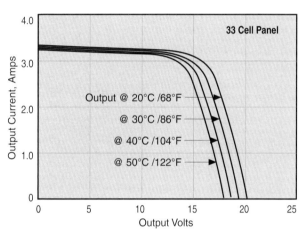

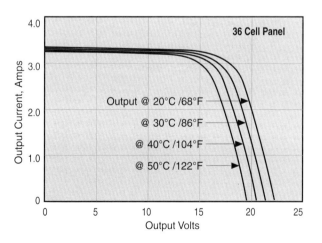

Panel Orientation

To understand how panel orientation affects the output of a photovoltaic system, we must consider how the sun moves through the sky, both throughout the day and with the seasons.

Figure 11.5 shows the track of the sun over a boat located at latitude 24°N (southern Florida or the Canary Islands) at the spring and autumn equinoxes (March 21 and September 21), and the summer and winter solstices (June 21 and December 21). On June 21, the sun reaches its highest noon elevation, 90°. On December 21, the sun reaches its lowest noon elevation, 43°. Further, the sun is above the horizon approximately 16 hours in June but only 8 hours in December. We would, therefore, expect a lot less solar input in December than in June.

Panel output ratings assume full sunlight with the sun's rays normal (perpendicular) to the panel surface. Panels in large utility "solar farms" are mounted on frames that continuously track the sun's orbit for maximum output.

What can we do about orientation on a boat? You're obviously not going to install a tracking mechanism, and most people would get tired of adjusting panel orientation three or four times a day. So the question is: what fixed tilt is best?

Figure 11.6 compares the solar radiation on a horizontal surface (tilt = 0°) and surfaces tilted to the south at the latitude angle, for latitudes 24°N (Miami or the Canary Islands) and 40°N (New York or Bordeaux), on both the longest (June 21) and shortest (December 21) days. On June 21, if we are both smart and mobile, we will be at, or around, latitude 40°N. Figure 11.6 shows that a horizontal panel will collect 119% of the radiation collected by a fixed panel tilted south at 40°.

If, on December 21 we are in the neighborhood of 24°N, our horizontal panel will collect 72% as much radiation as a fixed panel tilted south at 24°.

Thus we see, averaged over the year, a horizontal panel will perform as well as a fixed, south-tilted panel.

"But," you say, "if I were at a dock, I could tilt my panels toward the noon sun." But if you were at a dock, you wouldn't need photovoltaic panels.

Further, if you were on a mooring or anchor, your boat would swing without regard for the position of the sun. Any fixed orientation you selected might be perfectly right at one moment but perfectly wrong an hour later. There is only one orientation that doesn't change as a boat swings: horizontal (facing straight up).

To show the effect of compass direction, Figure 11.7 compares the solar radiation on horizontal panels and vertical panels facing north, east, south, and west. Although vertical east and west panels collect significant amounts of radiation in morning and afternoon respectively, both collect for only half a day, so their total collection is small. Conclusion: the only practical solar panel orientation on a cruising boat is horizontal.

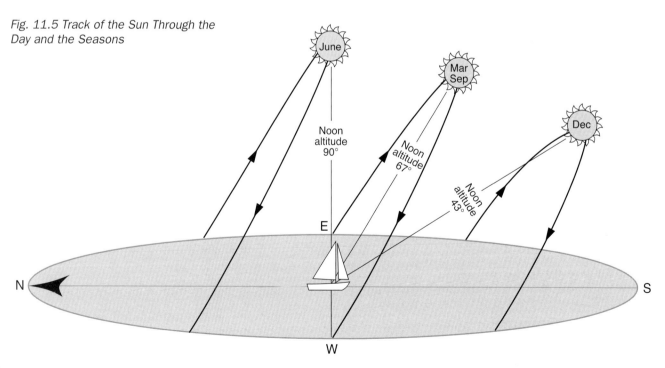

Fig. 11.5 Track of the Sun Through the Day and the Seasons

Fig. 11.6 Hourly Radiation on Horizontal and Tilted Surfaces

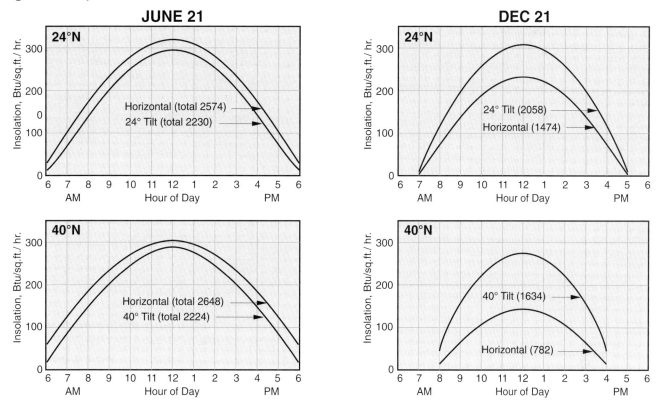

Fig. 11.7 Hourly Radiation on Horizontal and Vertical Surfaces

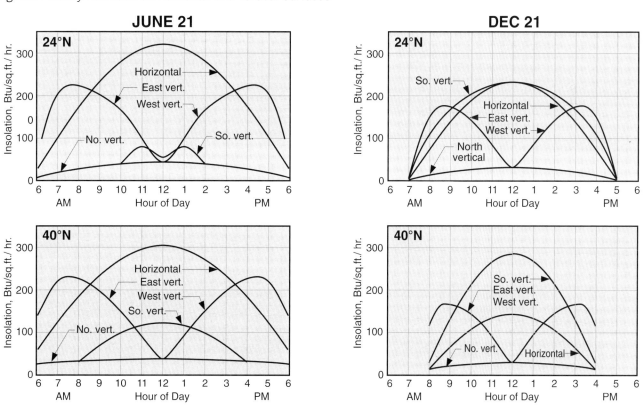

Estimating Output

Because the fixed horizontal orientation is the most practical on a non-stationary platform, solar-availability tables and maps often show total radiation on a horizontal surface. Figure 11.8 contains such seasonal maps. Table 11.2 lists, for selected locations, more precise values of average daily solar radiation falling on horizontal surfaces during:

- the sunniest month (Highest Month)
- the least sunny month (Lowest Month)
- the entire year (Annual Average)

The values are in equivalent hours of full sunlight, where full sunlight is defined as 1,000 watts/meter^2.

These values allow easy estimation of solar panel performance: the average daily output is simply the panel rating in watts times the equivalent hours of full sunlight.

Example 1—always in a sunny location: How many kilowatt-hours of output can you expect over an entire year from a horizontally mounted, 60-watt panel in Miami, FL? In Table 11.2 we find for Miami an annual average figure of 5.62. Thus we can expect a 60-watt panel to produce an average of 60 watts × 5.62 hours = 337 watt-hours per day. Over the entire year, we would expect 365 × 337 watt-hours = 123 kilowatt-hours.

Example 2—Florida in winter and Maine in summer: With the limited figures in Table 11.2, the simplest approximation would be to use the Lowest Month figure for Miami for the 6 months centered on winter and the Highest Month figure for Portland, ME, for the 6 months centered on summer.

Miami, FL: 60 × 5.05 × 365/2 = 55.3 kWh
Portland, ME: 60 × 5.23 × 365/2 = 57.3 kWh
Annual total = 112.6 kWh

In Chapter 10, we retrofitted a boat to reduce its electrical load to 48.7 Ah per day. As we saw in the examples above, in a sunny climate, or for a liveaboard boat following the sun, a solar array consisting of two 60-watt panels could be expected to provide an average of 2 × 112.6 = 225 kWh/yr. Dividing by 12 volts and 365 days, the array output averages 51.4 Ah/day or less than 100% of the boat's load. Provided the battery bank was sized at roughly four times the daily draw, this cruiser would rarely, if ever, have to use his engine for the sole purpose of charging the batteries.

Table 11.2 Average Daily Radiation on a Horizontal Surface, in Equivalent Hours of Full Direct Sunlight

State	City	Highest Month	Lowest Month	Annual Average
AK	Fairbanks	5.87	2.12	3.99
AK	Matanuska	5.24	1.74	3.55
CA	La Jolla	5.24	4.29	4.77
CA	Los Angeles	6.14	5.03	5.62
CA	Santa Maria	6.52	5.42	5.94
DC	Washington	4.69	3.37	4.23
FL	Apalachicola	5.98	4.92	5.49
FL	Belle Is.	5.31	4.58	4.99
FL	Miami	6.26	5.05	5.62
FL	Tampa	6.16	5.26	5.67
HI	Honolulu	6.71	5.59	6.02
IL	Chicago	4.08	1.47	3.14
LA	Lake Charles	5.73	4.29	4.93
LA	New Orleans	5.71	3.63	4.92
MA	Boston	4.27	2.99	3.84
MA	E. Wareham	4.48	3.06	3.99
MD	Silver Hill	4.71	3.84	4.47
ME	Portland	5.23	3.56	4.51
NC	Cape Hatteras	5.81	4.69	5.31
NJ	Sea Brook	4.76	3.20	4.21
NY	New York City	4.97	3.03	4.08
NY	Rochester	4.22	1.58	3.31
OR	Astoria	4.76	1.99	3.72
OR	Corvallis	5.71	1.90	4.03
OR	Medford	5.84	2.02	4.51
RI	Newport	4.69	3.58	4.23
SC	Charleston	5.72	4.23	5.06
TX	Brownsville	5.49	4.42	4.92
TX	San Antonio	5.88	4.65	5.30
VA	Richmond	4.50	3.37	4.13
WA	Prosser	6.21	3.06	5.03
WA	Seattle	4.83	1.60	3.57

The highest radiation figure above (Santa Maria, 28°N) is for (approximately) the same latitude as Madeira, and the lowest figure (Rochester, 38°N) is as for (approximately) Athens or Lisbon.

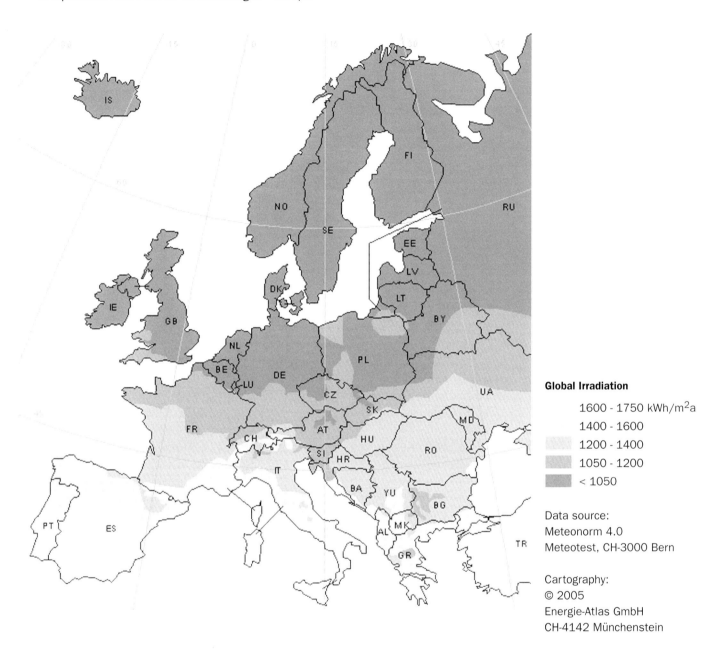

Global Irradiation

1600 - 1750 kWh/m²a
1400 - 1600
1200 - 1400
1050 - 1200
< 1050

Data source:
Meteonorm 4.0
Meteotest, CH-3000 Bern

Cartography:
© 2005
Energie-Atlas GmbH
CH-4142 Münchenstein

Mechanical Installation

Fastening

Solar panels are extremely lightweight and strong. Their extruded aluminum frames make mechanical fastening easy. Multiple panels can be fastened together loosely using stainless machine screws, lock-nuts, and rubber grommets as shown in Figure 11.9. The assembly of panels can then be fastened to the stainless or aluminum tubing of a dodger, bimini, radar arch, or davits. Alternately, each panel can be fastened individually, or multiple panels can be fastened within a frame, and the frame fastened to the boat.

Panel Location

The critical part of panel installation is choosing the location. Figure 11.10 shows five locations for a system of four panels.

Location A, on the deck just aft of the main mast, is shaded by both mast and boom, is in the way during mainsail operations, and is a target for objects dropped from the mast.

Location B, on top of a pilot house, is a better location than A because it is out of the way and farther from the drop zone. And, to avoid shading, the boom could be swung to the side with a preventer.

Location C is often seen because solar suppliers offer the mounting hardware and because it allows tilting of the panels. As we saw above, however, tilting the

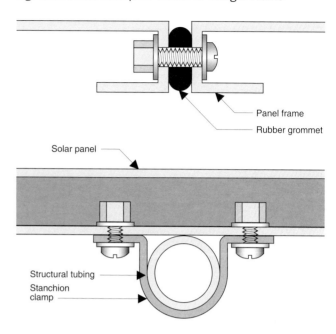

Fig. 11.9 Panel Clamp for Bimini or Dodger Frame

Panel frame
Rubber grommet
Solar panel
Structural tubing
Stanchion clamp

panels offers no advantage. Worse is the fact that the panels extend beyond the rail, where they are subject to damage while docking.

Location D, in a horizontal frame on top of a radar arch, is both out of the way and free from shade.

Location E, in a similar frame fastened to dinghy davits, is as good as Location D. It is shade-free, out of the way, and very secure.

Fig. 11.10 Candidate Panel Locations

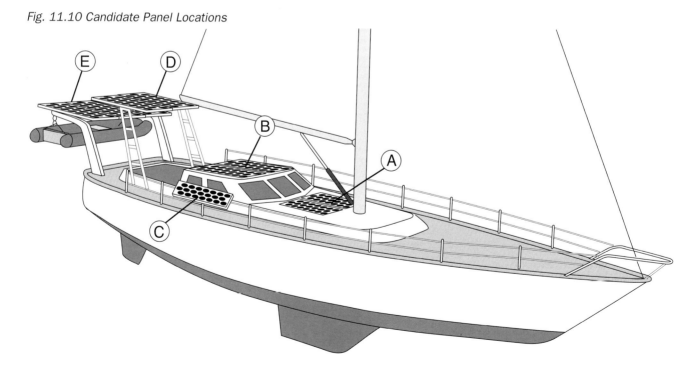

Figure 11.11 shows a typical proper photovoltaic installation. The important elements are:

1. *Fuse or circuit breaker.* The positive leads from all charging sources except the alternator should be overcurrent protected by fuses or circuit breakers, as close to the battery as possible. The reason is that unprotected leads might short, melting the conductor insulation, damaging the batteries, and possibly starting a fire. Furthermore, if the output current of a short-circuited solar panel could exceed the conductor capacity, the charge controller should be fused, as well.

2. *Blocking diode.* There should be blocking diodes between the battery and panel positive terminals to prevent reverse flow at night (unless the charge controller opens the circuit when panel voltage is too low). The diodes should connect to the battery side of any isolation diodes from the alternator to avoid the double voltage drop of isolation diode and blocking diode.

3. *Charge controller.* Unless the total panel-rated current is less than 0.5% of total battery capacity (2 amps for a 400 Ah battery bank), a charge controller is required to prevent overcharging the batteries. A switch should be provided to bypass the controller, however, so that a battery equalization charge might be applied occasionally. If panel voltage is marginal, you might install a switch to temporarily bypass the blocking diodes as well.

The simplest way to satisfy all three requirements is to purchase a charge controller that contains all three features. The best controllers allow full current up to about 14.4 volts, then taper to a float charge. Some controllers automatically switch excess panel output to a resistance load, such as a 12-volt DC water heater element, thereby extracting maximum use from the panel output.

Naturally, all DC wiring standards, such as conductor ampacity, stranding, insulation, and fastening, apply as well to solar installations.

Fig. 11.11 Electrical Hookup of Solar Panels (Wind Generator Optional)

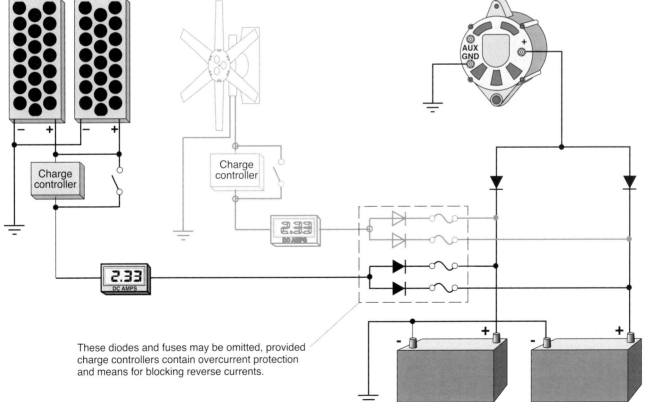

These diodes and fuses may be omitted, provided charge controllers contain overcurrent protection and means for blocking reverse currents.

Rules for Solar Success

If you want a photovoltaic system to supply all or nearly all of your electrical energy needs, you must:

1. Reduce your average daily electrical consumption to 60 Ah or less. See also Chapter 10 for suggestions.
2. Install sufficient panel area. Use Figures 11.8 through 11.10 to calculate the required panel wattage for the areas you plan to cruise.
3. Install the panels in a permanent, horizontal, shade-free location.
4. Do not depend on tilting of the panels, removing shading objects, or controlling boat orientation to increase panel output.
5. Select panels with sufficient rated voltage to overcome the voltage drops due to blocking diodes (if present), operating temperature, and anticipated shading.
6. Install a charge controller that does not require blocking diodes.
7. Make solid, corrosion-free electrical connections and protect with corrosion inhibitor.
8. Clean the panel surfaces of dust and salt spray regularly.

CHAPTER 12

Wind Power

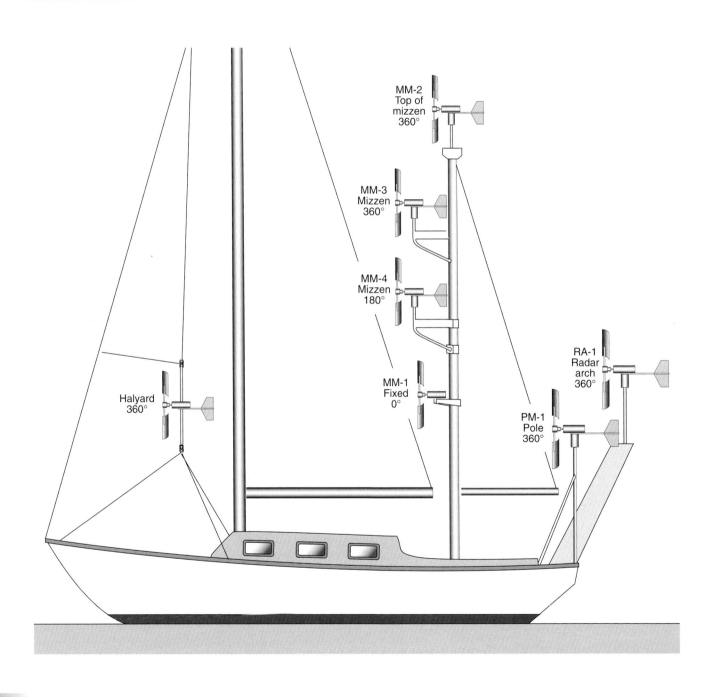

MM-2
Top of
mizzen
360°

MM-3
Mizzen
360°

MM-4
Mizzen
180°

RA-1
Radar
arch
360°

Halyard
360°

MM-1
Fixed
0°

PM-1
Pole
360°

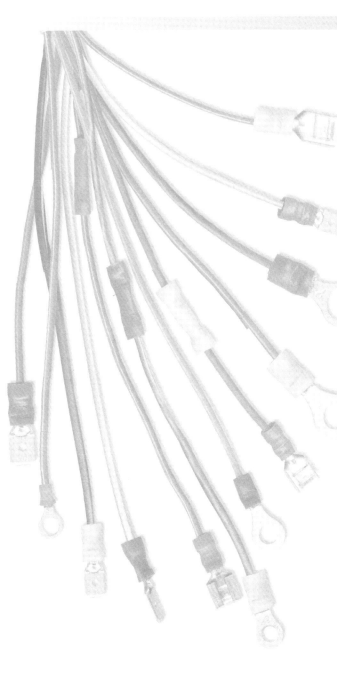

If not solar power, then is wind power for you? Again, calculating the economics will tell.

Getting power from the wind explains how the kinetic energy of moving air can be converted to electrical energy.

In order to estimate the daily output of a wind machine, we need to know how much wind there is where we will be cruising and the specifications of our wind machine.

The most difficult part of mechanical installation is simply selecting the best location on the boat. As in the case of solar panels, the electrical installation of a wind machine requires integration with the existing alternator battery system.

At least one popular wind machine can be converted into a water generator—a feature long-distance cruisers may wish to consider.

As in the previous chapter, some of the equipment referred to may only be available in North America. However, there is a wide variety of wind and water powered marine generators available in the UK and Europe.

Is Wind Power for You?

The variables determining the viability of wind power on a boat are much more complicated than those for photovoltaics, but the general criteria remain the same—if you live aboard, are away from the dock at least 6 months of the year, and actively seek out windy areas, the answer is probably yes; if you use your boat only 1 month per year, the answer is no.

Before delving into the economics of wind power production, you should note several non-economic factors that are unique to wind:

1. *Maintenance.* Wind machines are of two types: the familiar alternator, and DC electric motors running backward. Both produce AC electricity, but rectify it (change AC to DC) in different ways. As we saw in Chapter 4, alternators employ solid-state diode bridges. The DC-motor types, however, rely on brushes and commutators, both of which are subject to wear and maintenance. Also, both types contain bearings which will require replacement.

2. *Noise.* All wind machines make noise, ranging from the barely perceptible whisper of a small, six-bladed Ampair, to the "woof, woof, woof" of a large, two-bladed, mizzen-mounted machine. Generally, the more power being generated, the louder the noise. Some find the noise of a large machine satisfying, an audible reminder that their batteries are being recharged for free. Others—particularly sailors on nearby boats—find the sound annoying. You would be wise to spend time on a boat with a particular model before purchasing.

3. *Safety.* The higher the wind speed, the greater the output of a wind machine. But wind speeds over about 30 knots pose several potential problems, particularly with the larger-diameter machines: (1) the high centrifugal forces and vibration on the blades may cause fatigue and failure (throwing a blade), (2) the electrical output may become too much for the batteries or charge regulator to handle, and (3) it may prove impossible to shut the machine down, either manually (picture trying to stop an airplane propeller) or automatically. All of the manufacturers have addressed this issue, but in various ways. Make sure you understand the shutdown mechanism of the machine you are thinking of purchasing, and talk to several owners about their own experiences.

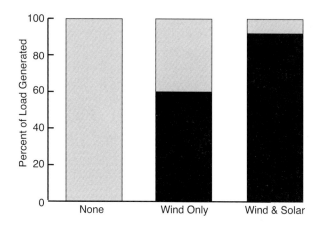

Fig. 12.1 Wind Power Production on Cruising Boats

Economics

Figure 12.1 shows the percentage of daily electrical load supplied by wind among 71 liveaboard boats surveyed in Florida and the Bahamas. Most of the wind machines were of the large (1.5m/60-inch blade diameter) variety. The fact that 40% of the average daily load still had to be supplied by running the engine shows that wind is not constant. Decreasing the daily load through conservation (see Chapter 10) and increasing battery capacity could increase the wind contribution to 80% or more.

An interesting alternative is the combination of wind and solar, which, as shown in Figure 12.1, supplied an average of 96% of the daily load.

Figure 10.1 compared the costs of power generated by wind, solar, and alternators of various sizes. The $0.59 kilowatt-hour cost of wind power assumed:
- Wind machine lifetime—10 years
- Installed cost—$1,500
- Annual maintenance—$100
- Blade diameter—60 inches
- Conversion efficiency—30 percent
- Average wind speed—10 knots

Such a wind machine would produce 420 kilowatt-hours per year in a steady 10-knot wind. One of the conventional alternatives, also shown in Figure 10.1, is a 110-amp engine alternator charging the batteries on a 50 to 90% cycle at a cost of $2.25 per kilowatt-hour.

The example wind machine savings would thus be $2.25 – $0.59 = $1.66 per kilowatt-hour, or $697 per year. The machine would pay for itself in a little over 2 years. Unfortunately for the majority of boaters, if the wind machine were used only 1 month per year, the savings would fall to $58 per year, and the payback period would increase to over 25 years.

The electrical power that a wind machine can extract from the wind is:

$$P = K \times E \times D^2 \times V^3$$

Where:
- P = power in watts
- K = 0.0653
- E = mechanical efficiency in %
- D = blade diameter in meters
- V = wind speed in knots

Example: Calculate the power output of a wind machine having a blade diameter of 5 feet (1.52 meters) and efficiency of 30% in a steady 10-knot wind.

$$P = 0.0653 \times 0.30 \times 1.52^2 \times 10^3 = 45 \text{ watts}$$

The equation highlights the important factors in selecting and sizing a wind machine to satisfy a boat's electrical demand:

Efficiency, E, can never be 100%. If it were, the blades would extract 100% of the kinetic energy of the wind, bringing the wind to a complete halt. The maximum theoretical, aeronautical efficiency of a wind machine is 59.3% but, due to losses in the generating coils, rotor bearings, and transmission gearing, the actual efficiencies are around 30%.

Diameter, D, enters the equation squared. Doubling blade diameter quadruples power output. Most marine wind machines have blade diameters of either 1 m (39 inches) or 5 feet (1.52 m). Squaring the ratio of diameters shows that the theoretical maximum output of the 5-foot machines is 230% that of the 1 m machines.

Wind speed, V, is the most important factor of all because it enters the equation cubed. The difference between 8 knots and 10 knots may be barely noticeable when sailing, but doubles the output of a wind machine. Don't guess; use the wind-power maps on the following pages when making the purchase decision.

Figure 12.2 plots wind machine output versus wind speed. The two theoretical curves (dashed) assume efficiencies of 30% and output at 14 volts. The curves for actual machines were drawn to fit manufacturers' data.

You would be wise to question the output figures claimed by wind machine manufacturers. The important specification is continuous rated output at 14 VDC, not maximum output.

Since average wind speeds are rarely above 15 knots, output at wind speeds in excess of 15 knots is not important in your choice of a wind machine.

Fig. 12.2 Manufacturer-Claimed Output of Marine Wind Generators

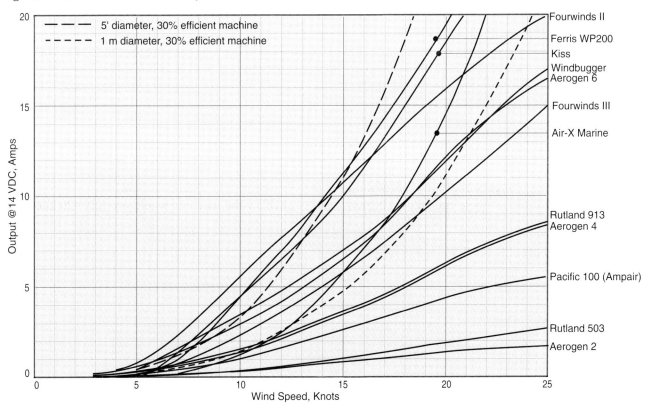

How Much Wind Is There?

Figures 12.3 through 12.7 show average wind power, in watts per square meter, from the *Wind Energy Resource Atlas of the U.S.* The figures are the power contained in the wind and must be multiplied by wind machine efficiency and area swept by the blades to predict electrical output.

What is most striking about the maps is the predominance of low average wind speed. While we all know of places where the wind blows much harder, you would be well advised to ignore such places. In reality, it is human nature to seek refuge from the wind. Since most boaters seek shelter when on the hook, the wind speeds shown may, in reality, be a little too high.

The wind speeds shown in the figures were observed in exposed locations, such as airports, and at an average height above ground of 10 meters. Figure 12.8 shows how wind speed and power vary with actual height in both open-water and harbor locations.

Over open water a wind machine at a height of 10 feet will be exposed to 90% of the 10-meter wind speed and produce about 72% as much power. In a protected harbor, the same 10-foot height will result in about 80% of the 10-meter wind speed and only 50% of the power.

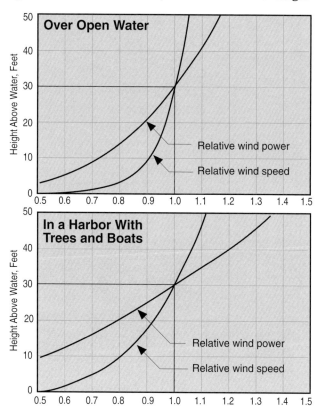

Fig. 12.8 Variation of Wind Speed and Power with Height

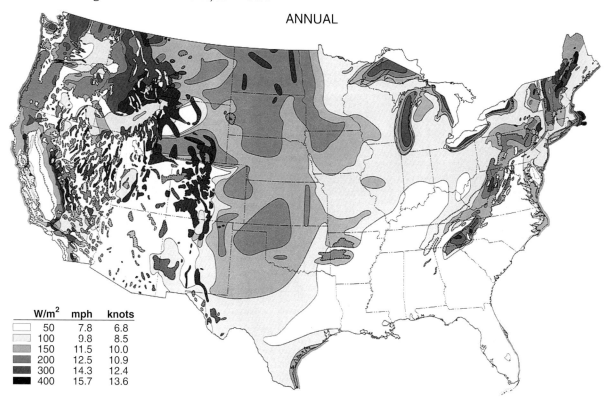

Fig. 12.3 Annual Average Power in Wind in W/m² – USA

ANNUAL

W/m²	mph	knots
50	7.8	6.8
100	9.8	8.5
150	11.5	10.0
200	12.5	10.9
300	14.3	12.4
400	15.7	13.6

Fig. 12.4 Annual Average Power in Wind in W/m² at 50 (45) m Above Ground Level

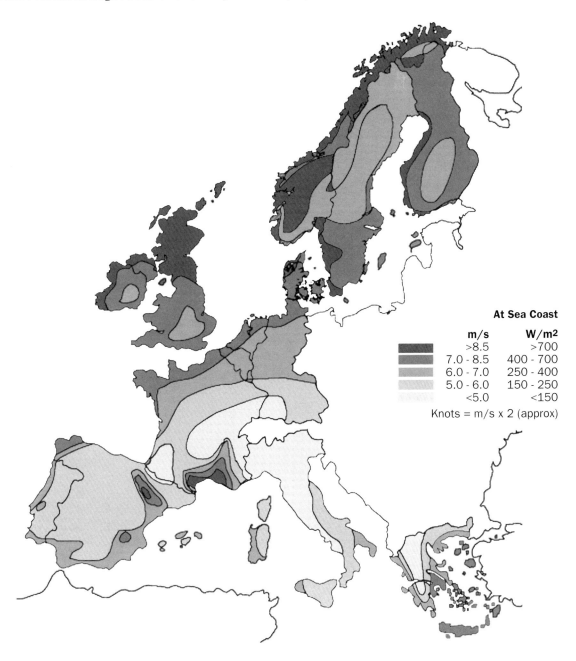

At Sea Coast

m/s	W/m2
>8.5	>700
7.0 - 8.5	400 - 700
6.0 - 7.0	250 - 400
5.0 - 6.0	150 - 250
<5.0	<150

Knots = m/s x 2 (approx)

Estimating Daily Output

Selecting the right size wind machine for your boat is not quite the same as designing a solar system. While you have a variety of solar panel sizes to select from, there are really only two sizes of wind machine: 1 meter, and 5 feet. So selecting a wind machine comes down to deciding whether one of the two available sizes is worth the investment.

Start by determining your average daily load in Ah, just as in Chapter 11. Next, determine the available power in the wind for the areas you plan to cruise, using the annual map (Figure 12.3).

Calculating the expected average electrical power from a wind machine is then a simple matter of multiplying the area swept by the blades by the machine efficiency and the power shown in the map for the area(s) you intend to cruise.

The area of a circle is $\pi \times D^2/4$ (Figure 12.9), so

$$\text{Watts} = \pi \times D^2 \times E \times P/4$$

where:

$\pi = 3.14$
$D =$ blade diameter in meters
$E =$ wind machine efficiency, 0.00 to 1.00
$P =$ annual wind power in W/m^2

Assuming $E = 0.30$ (30%):
$$\text{Watts} = 0.24\, D^2 \times P$$
$$\text{kWh/yr} = 2.10\, D^2 \times P$$
$$\text{Ah/day} = 0.44\, D^2 \times P$$

Example 1: How much power can you expect from a wind machine of 5-foot (1.52 m) blade diameter, 30% efficiency, and 12-foot height in protected harbors in New England in summer and the Florida Keys in winter?

Answer 1: Both locations have average wind power of about 100 W/m^2 at 33-foot height. Assuming harbor locations, at 12-foot height (Figure 12.8) the available power is 60% of the power at 33 feet. Therefore,

$$
\begin{aligned}
\text{Watts} &= 0.24\, D^2 \times P \\
&= 0.24 \times 1.52^2 \times 0.6 \times 100 \\
&= 33 \text{ watts} \\
\text{kWh/yr} &= 2.10\, D^2 \times P \\
&= 2.10 \times 1.52^2 \times 0.6 \times 100 \\
&= 292 \text{ kilowatt-hours} \\
\text{Ah/day} &= 0.44\, D^2 \times P \\
&= 0.44 \times 1.52^2 \times 0.6 \times 100 \\
&= 61 \text{ Ah}
\end{aligned}
$$

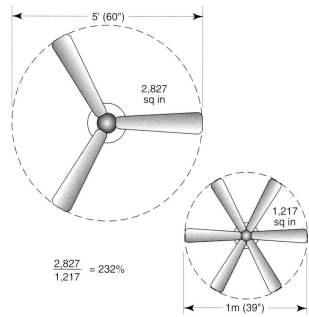

Fig. 12.9 Areas Swept by 5-Foot and 1 m Wind Generator Blades

This wind machine would be well matched to the load of the energy-efficient boat discussed in Chapter 10.

Note that the output of this wind machine could be increased by either of two steps:

1. Changing to a 33-foot mizzen mount would theoretically increase output by a factor of 100%/60% = 1.67.
2. With the 12-foot mount, anchoring in unprotected locations would theoretically increase output by a factor of 75%/60% = 1.25.

Example 2: For the same conditions as in Example 1, how much power would a 1 metre wind machine produce?

Answer 2: The ratio of blade diameter 1 to blade diameter 2 is:

$$
\begin{aligned}
D2/D1 &= 1.00 \text{ m}/1.52 \text{ m} \\
&= 0.66
\end{aligned}
$$

The ratio of outputs is the ratio of diameters, squared:

$$
\begin{aligned}
(D2/D1)^2 &= 0.66^2 \\
&= 0.43
\end{aligned}
$$

The output of a 1 m machine would therefore be: 14 watts, 126 kilowatt-hours per year, and 26 Ah per day.

Table 12.1 Wind Machine Specifications

	Number of Blades	Blade Diameter mm/inches	Weight, pounds	Warranty, years	Amps @10 kn	Amps @15 kn
Aerogen 2 (LVM)	5	585 mm/23"	11	3	0.3	0.9
Aerogen 4 (LVM)	6	190 mm/34"	24	3	1.4	3.5
Aerogen 6 (LVM)	6	1220 mm/48"	28	3	3.0	6.6
Air-X Marine	3	1145 mm/45"	13	3	1.3	5.8
Ferris WP200	2	1500 mm/60"	19	1	4.0	11.2
Fourwinds II	3	1500 mm/60"	22	3	5.6	10.7
Fourwinds III	3	1015 mm/40"	20	3	3.0	6.0
Kiss	3	760 mm/30"	23	3	4.5	10.0
Pacific 100 (Ampair)	6	915 mm/36"	20	3	1.0	2.7
Rutland 503	6	510 mm/20"	8	2	0.3	1.0
Rutland 913	6	915 mm/36"	28	2	1.6	3.8
Windbugger	3	1370 mm/54"	38	1	4.0	10.0

Table 12.1 lists the specifications for the wind machines included in Figure 12.2. As the manufacturers say, "specifications subject to change without notice," so get the latest information before making your purchase.

Number of Blades

Theoretically, the efficiency of a wind machine is unrelated to the number of blades. A two-bladed machine can be as efficient as a six-bladed machine. However, noise level decreases with increased number of blades, and blade diameter. All six-bladed machines are quieter than the two- or three-bladed machines.

Blade Diameter

As already discussed, power output varies with diameter squared, so a large diameter is necessary for large output. On the other hand, weight, noise, and potential danger all increase with diameter as well.

Weight

Weight is a two-edged sword. Light weight makes the machine easier to handle—particularly in the case of a halyard mount—but light weight may equate to a flimsier construction and smaller continuous rated output.

Amps at X Knots

Watch out! This may be the output when the machine is cold, before self-regulation kicks in. Make sure the rating for maximum continuous output is at least as large as the claimed 15-knot output.

Other Specifications

Voltage

Some machines are regulated to produce constant voltage. If so, select a regulator that can be adjusted for your battery type. As pointed out in Chapter 3, gelled-electrolyte batteries can be ruined by long-term charging at over 14.1 volts DC. When a manufacturer claims its machine is "battery regulated," watch out! Such machines cannot be left unattended for long periods.

Brushes

If a machine is used continuously, it may require new brushes every year. If this sort of maintenance doesn't appeal to you, check with the manufacturer, or go with a brushless machine.

Slip Rings

Slip rings pass current from a swiveling wind machine to the power cables leading to the battery. Without slip rings a wind machine cannot make more than a few revolutions before fouling its cable. A ±180° swivel-mount has no slip rings but tracks the wind 99% of the time.

Shutdown

This is the most important safety factor. A machine that must be manually secured in high winds is at best inconvenient and at worst dangerous. Even if the machine has an automatic governor or brake, make sure the braking device is guaranteed to at least 50-knot winds. Otherwise, you are likely to have a broken or burned-out machine within a year.

Electrical Installation

Figure 12.10 shows a wind machine electrical installation. Voltage and current meters are not shown but are often supplied with wind machines. If they are, simply follow the manufacturer's directions for installation.

A solar system is also shown in the figure because wind and solar are often combined. The installation is designed so that the wind and solar systems are completely independent, though complementary. Deleting the solar system has no effect on the wind system hookup.

Elements of the installation include:

1. *Fuses or circuit breakers.* Because a short circuit in one of the battery positive leads could lead to fire or explosion of the battery, all positive battery leads except those from the alternator are required to be overcurrent-protected, as close to the positive battery terminals as possible.
2. *Blocking diodes.* Most wind machines are little more than DC motors. Blocking diodes prevent current from the batteries from spinning the wind machine backward in the absence of wind. They also act as isolation diodes, preventing the battery with greater charge from discharging into the battery with lesser charge when there is

no wind. Note that the blocking diodes are installed downstream (down-current) of the alternator isolation diodes so that the voltage drops are not additive.
3. *Charge controller.* Unless the wind machine contains a voltage regulator, a charge controller should be inserted in the output to prevent overcharging of the batteries. The manual bypass switch shown is provided to allow periodic equalization of the batteries.

Some charge controllers dump excess current into heat-sinked transistors. Others divert current to an external load, such as a 12-volt water heater element. In any case make sure the controller can handle the maximum output current.

All of the DC wiring standards and practices discussed in Chapter 6 apply to wind machine installations as well. Make sure the ampacity of the output conductors exceeds the wind machine's maximum output. Sizing the conductors for a 3% maximum voltage drop is not as important with wind machines as with solar panels, however, since the open-circuit voltage in winds over 10 knots is at least 20 volts and the voltage regulator is clamped at less than 15 volts. I'd use a 10% drop.

Fig. 12.10 Electrical Hookup of Wind Generator (Solar Optional)

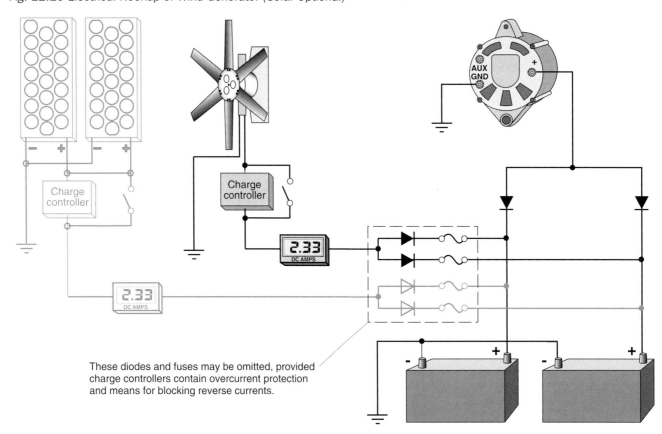

These diodes and fuses may be omitted, provided charge controllers contain overcurrent protection and means for blocking reverse currents.

Figure 12.11 shows a common large wind machine (the 5-foot Fourwinds) mounted in all possible configurations on a 35-foot ketch. Most wind machines can be mounted in several configurations with mounting accessories available from the manufacturer. Check with dealers for the possibilities.

Pole Mount

Of the three mounting options, the stern pole is the most common. The pole type and size is usually specified by the machine supplier. Bracing is provided either by two lengths of rigid stainless tubing to the deck or by one rigid standoff to the backstay plus two guywires to the deck. Pole height should be such that the blade clears the head of the tallest crew, but can be secured without standing on a pulpit rail.

The advantages of the pole mount are that it is accessible from the deck and that it allows use while under sail. Disadvantages include smaller output due to low height, relatively high noise level, and potential danger to unwary crew.

Mizzen Mounts

Mizzen mounts, for boats with a second mast, raise the wind machine for greater output and decreased danger. In spite of the height, if an unbalanced machine is mounted near the midpoint of the mast, noise levels may be even greater than those for the pole mount. Blade distance from the mast is also important in reducing noise levels. Note that Fourwinds offers four different mizzen mounts.

The four types of mizzen mounts differ chiefly in the ability to swivel into the wind: 0° (fixed in forward direction), 180°, and 360° (unlimited). The fixed mount is extremely limiting, being useful only when the boat is anchored or on a mooring. The 180° mount allows operation in all conditions except running downwind. This is a small disadvantage, however, since the apparent wind speed is reduced by the speed of the boat. If a lot of downwind sailing is contemplated, some wind machines (Fourwinds, Ferris, and Ampair) can be adapted to towing behind the boat.

Halyard Mount

While the ability to raise a wind machine to great height would seem to promise the highest output, least noise, and greatest safety, a halyard-mounted machine should not be raised beyond the reach of a person standing on deck. Shutdown or recovery of a halyard-mounted machine in a high wind can be exceedingly dangerous. In addition, the hassle of deployment, recovery, and storage at every anchoring makes them less popular.

In spite of these negatives, some owners swear by the halyard mount, claiming deployment and recovery in less than 3 minutes, as well as lowest initial cost.

Large halyard-mount machines are usually two-bladed because they are most conveniently stored in the V-berth and handled through a forward hatch.

Radar Arch Mount

In line with the modern trend of mounting *everything* on an aft radar arch or on davits, the Fourwinds offers a radar arch mount with 360° freedom. The mount makes logical sense, but many feel it compromises the aesthetics of a sailing vessel.

Noise

After safety, the most common concern about wind machines is the level of noise generated at moderate to high wind speeds. Manufacturers have made some progress in recent years in abating noise.

First, as pointed out earlier, the fewer the blades, the greater the noise. Because of this, only one two-blade machine (the Ferris) remains on the market. The majority now offer either three or six blades.

Second, the more aerodynamic (more like an airfoil) the shape of the blade, the less the noise. The blades of the newest machines closely resemble airplane propellers.

Third, mounting a machine rigidly on a pole or mast directly connected to the deck results in vibration being transmitted to the deck. The deck then acts like a drumhead, amplifying the sound. Some manufacturers now offer rubber shock mounts to decouple the vibrations before reaching deck level.

Fig. 12.11 Wind Generator Mounting Options

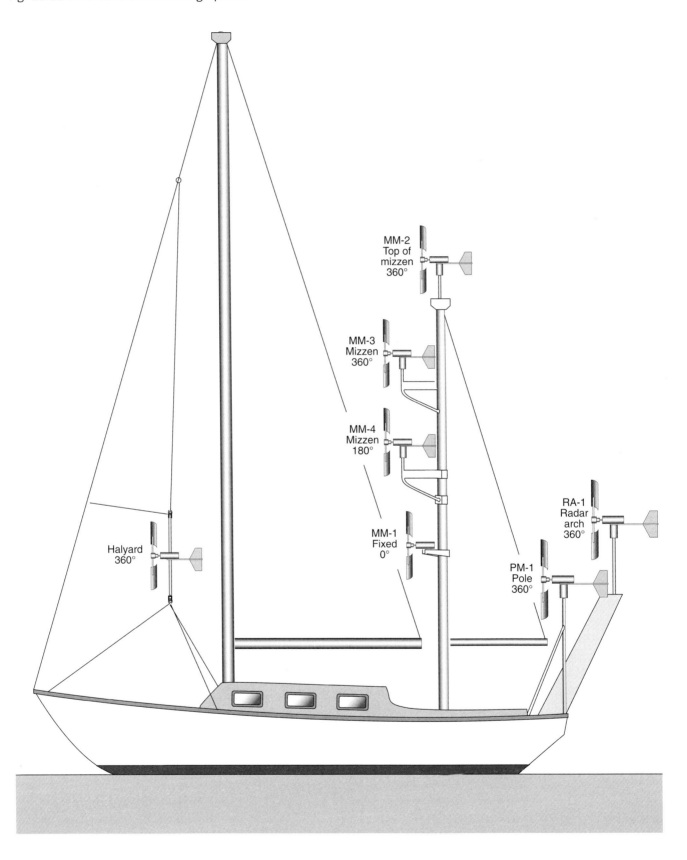

MM-2
Top of
mizzen
360°

MM-3
Mizzen
360°

MM-4
Mizzen
180°

RA-1
Radar
arch
360°

MM-1
Fixed
0°

PM-1
Pole
360°

Halyard
360°

Many wind machines can be converted to water generators. Figure 12.12 shows the outputs of four water generators versus water speed. All are sized to carry the electrical load of a typical cruising boat at less than hull speed. The drag typically slows a boat by a small fraction of a knot, and they are usually deployed only as needed to recharge the batteries.

They are popular with downwind passagemakers who are already equipped with wind machines, since relative airspeed downwind is low, but water speed is high. Most mount the generator on the stern rail and trail the propeller unit with a line sufficiently stiff to transmit the torque to the generating unit (Figure 12.13). Manufacturers generally recommend carrying several spare propeller units on long passages. The reason is obvious: the spinning prop looks suspiciouly like live bait to a large fish!

The electrical installation for dual units is the same for both wind and water operation, and is described in Figure 12.10.

Fig. 12.13 Aquair 100 Mounted on a Stern Rail

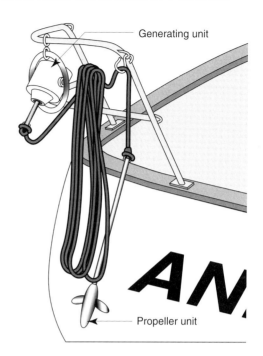

Fig. 12.12 Water Generator Output Curves

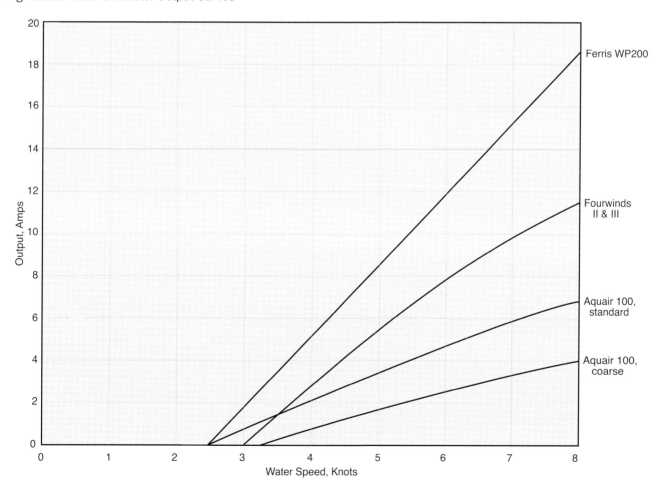

CHAPTER 13

Installing Electronics

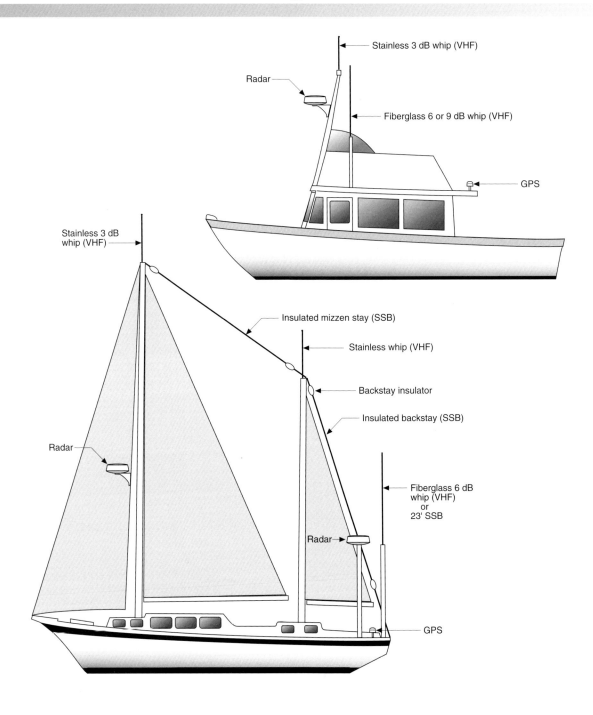

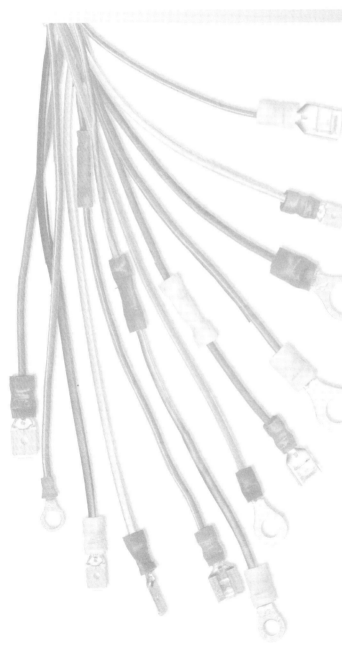

If you can install a towel rail, you can install an electronic cabinet or case. But there is often more to a successful electronic installation than meets the eye.

This chapter focuses on communication and also navigation electronics—that is, electronics that use antennas.

Antennas are intended to receive signals. It is important that the incoming signals not be attenuated, so much attention must be paid to antenna cable and connectors in addition to proper receiver and transmitter installation. Receivers and transmitters include VHF radio, GPS, SSB, and radar.

The problem is they also receive electrical noise, so we give step-by-step procedures for identifying the sources and reducing the level with electrical filters.

Antennas

Few things are as satisfying as installing your own electronics. Repairing digital electronic circuitry is beyond the abilities of most, but installation is not.

Installation requires only an understanding of the DC wiring standards and practices in Chapter 6, wire and connectors available through chandleries and mail-order catalogs, and the principles outlined in this chapter.

With these in hand, you should be able to install any piece of marine electronic equipment over a weekend, and as well as any professional. The obvious benefits are a significant costs saving and satisfaction at accomplishing a professional job. The less obvious benefit occurs when something goes wrong, and you find that you are now able to retrace your steps and often locate the problem.

The equipment covered in this chapter includes VHF and SSB radios, GPS, and radar. From an installation standpoint, all marine electronics are similar. You'll find that the principles and techniques apply to stereos, televisions, depth sounders, and wind indicators, as well.

Antenna Types

You can find books on antenna design and specific antenna designs in electronics and ham radio magazines. My advice, however, is to start with the antenna recommended or supplied by the manufacturer of the equipment. Many antennas are designed to work only with a specific brand and model of equipment. After you have the equipment up and running, you may decide to experiment with a different antenna. The original antenna will then serve as a reference.

Antenna Location

Figures 13.1 and 13.2 show a variety of antennas and locations that will be referenced in the discussions of particular equipment types.

VHF and radar signals travel in straight lines, so their antennas should be mounted high.

GPS signals travel line-of-sight from outer space and, except for the requirement for a relatively clear view of the sky, are independent of height.

SSB and ham signals arrive from space, having bounced one or more times off the ionosphere. While antenna performance is independent of height, their great lengths (23 to 60 feet) require height at one end.

Radar and GPS have wavelengths of the same order,

or smaller than, objects on the boat. Objects with a diameter more than 1 inch (such as a mast) can reflect or block the signal, creating blind zones.

Finally, signals are at least partially absorbed by grounded rigging. Antennas placed too close to metal standing rigging thus suffer loss of signal strength. The exception is the use of an insulated (ungrounded) backstay as a long SSB or ham antenna. To avoid interference, antennas that are used to transmit as well as receive should be spaced from other antennas.

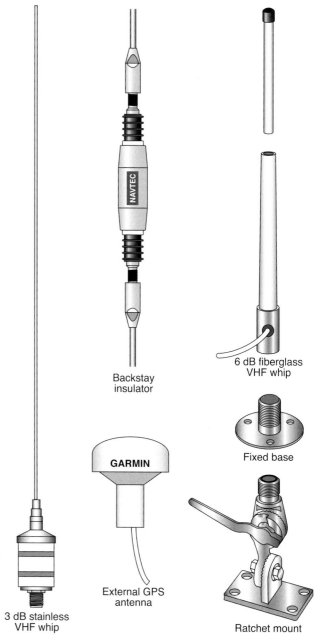

Fig. 13.1 Marine Antennas

Backstay insulator

6 dB fiberglass VHF whip

Fixed base

GARMIN

External GPS antenna

Ratchet mount

3 dB stainless VHF whip

Fig. 13.2 Locating Antennas

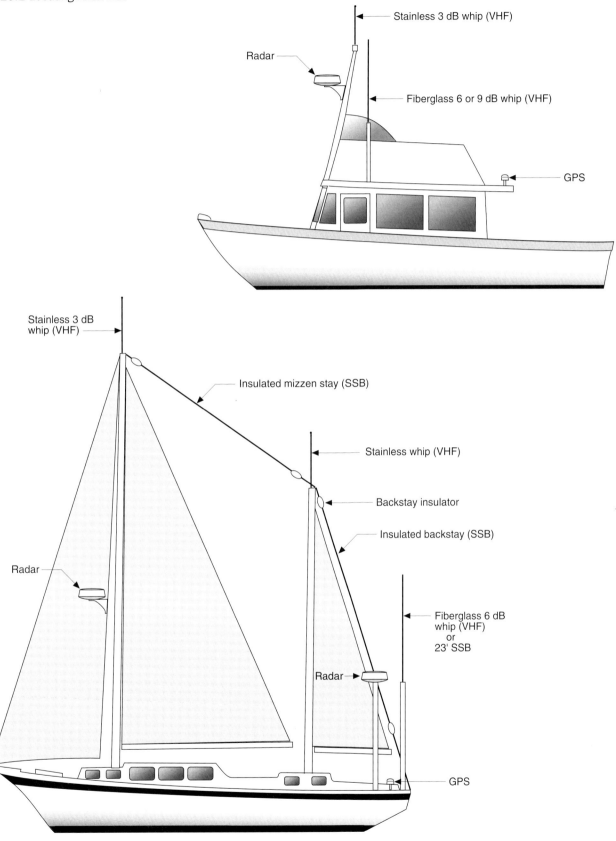

Stainless 3 dB whip (VHF)

Radar

Fiberglass 6 or 9 dB whip (VHF)

GPS

Stainless 3 dB whip (VHF)

Insulated mizzen stay (SSB)

Stainless whip (VHF)

Backstay insulator

Insulated backstay (SSB)

Radar

Fiberglass 6 dB whip (VHF) or 23' SSB

Radar

GPS

Antenna Cable and Connectors

To minimize interference from shipboard electrical noise, all antennas aboard a boat are, or should be, connected to their respective receivers with coaxial cable. Table 13.1 lists the most common coaxial cable types and their specifications.

Table 13.1 Coaxial Cables

Specification	RG-58/U	RG-8X	RG-8/U	RG-213
Nominal O.D. (mm)	4.75	6	10	10
Conductor mm^2	0.75	1.5	3	3
Impedance, ohms	50	50	52	50
Attenuation per 100 Feet				
@ 50 MHz	3.3 dB	2.5 dB	1.3 dB	1.3 dB
@ 100 MHz	4.9 dB	3.7 dB	1.9 dB	1.9 dB
@ 1,000 MHz	21.5 dB	13.5 dB	8.0 dB	8.0 dB

Conductor size is important in transmitters where large currents may result in resistive loss of power in the cable.

Impedance of the antenna cable should match the output impedance of the transmitter in order to maximize signal strengths.

Attenuation is the loss of transmitted power in the cable between transmitter and antenna. Each 3 decibels (dB) of loss is equivalent to a reduction in power at the antenna of 50%.

Coax cables may have identical specifications, yet vary greatly in quality. Cables aboard boats are exposed to salt spray, sunlight, oil, and sometimes battery-acid mist. Use only the highest-quality cable, consisting of tinned center conductor and braid, solid polyethylene dielectric, and UV-resistant, non-contaminating outer jacket.

Figure 13.3 shows the cable adapters and feed-throughs available at most chandleries and electronic component stores.

Figure 13.4 shows the assembly of UHF connectors on both large and small coaxial cables. Figure 13.5 demonstrates the similar assembly of BNC connectors on RG-58/U, RG-59/U, and RG-8X coaxial cables.

Solderless versions are not recommended in marine applications due to the moist environment and the likelihood of corrosion, which solder excludes. After assembly the connector and cable should be sealed with adhesive-lined, heat-shrink tubing, as shown in Figure 13.6, to exclude moisture.

Fig. 13.3 Cable Adapter and Feed-Throughs

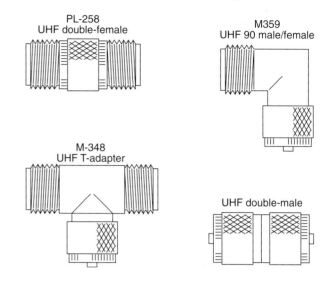

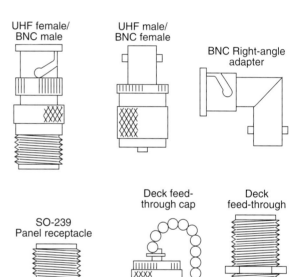

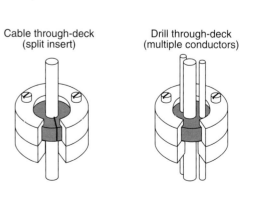

Fig. 13.4 Assembly of PL-259 Connectors

ON RG-58/U, RG-59/U, AND RG-8X CABLES

STEP 1: Slip on shell and adapter;
strip outer jacket back 16mm (5/8")

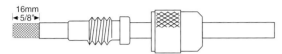

STEP 2: Bend back braided shield

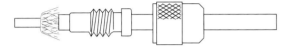

STEP 3: Slip adapter under braided shield

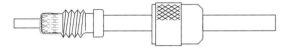

STEP 4: Strip center conductor 12mm (1/2") and tin

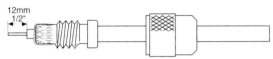

STEP 5: Screw on body and solder tip and braid
through holes in body

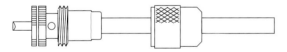

STEP 6: Screw shell onto body

ON RG-8/U AND RG-213 CABLES

STEP 1: Slip on shell and strip to center of conductor
and back 3/4"

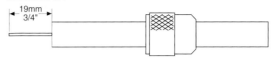

STEP 2: Strip outer jacket additional 8mm (5/16")

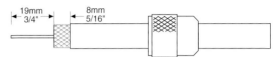

STEP 3: Slip on body, making sure shield does not contact
center conductor, and solder tip and shield through holes

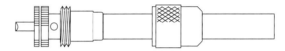

STEP 4: Screw shell onto body

Fig. 13.5 Assembly of BNC Connectors

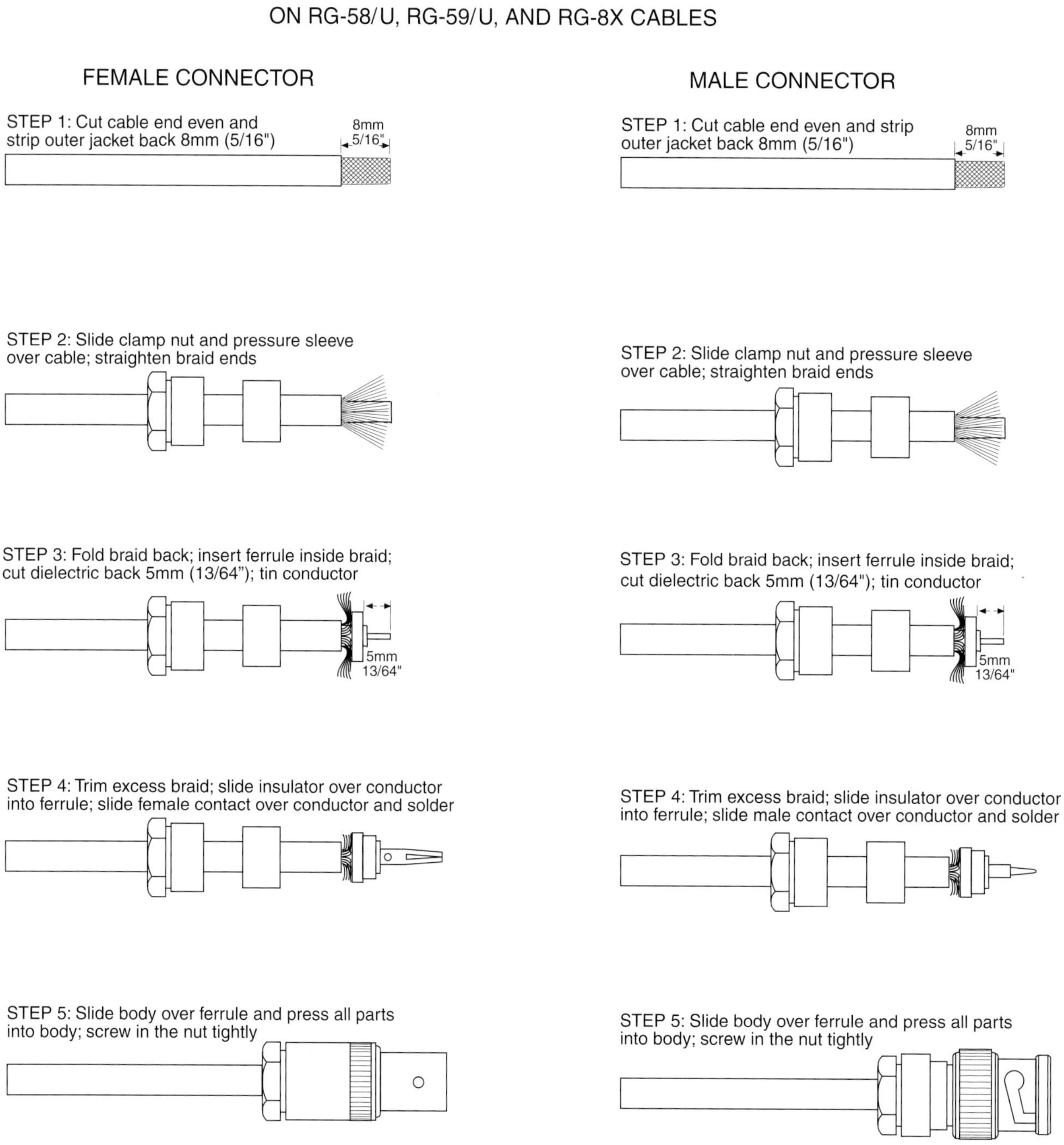

ON RG-58/U, RG-59/U, AND RG-8X CABLES

FEMALE CONNECTOR

STEP 1: Cut cable end even and strip outer jacket back 8mm (5/16")

8mm
5/16"

STEP 2: Slide clamp nut and pressure sleeve over cable; straighten braid ends

STEP 3: Fold braid back; insert ferrule inside braid; cut dielectric back 5mm (13/64"); tin conductor

5mm
13/64"

STEP 4: Trim excess braid; slide insulator over conductor into ferrule; slide female contact over conductor and solder

STEP 5: Slide body over ferrule and press all parts into body; screw in the nut tightly

MALE CONNECTOR

STEP 1: Cut cable end even and strip outer jacket back 8mm (5/16")

8mm
5/16"

STEP 2: Slide clamp nut and pressure sleeve over cable; straighten braid ends

STEP 3: Fold braid back; insert ferrule inside braid; cut dielectric back 5mm (13/64"); tin conductor

5mm
13/64"

STEP 4: Trim excess braid; slide insulator over conductor into ferrule; slide male contact over conductor and solder

STEP 5: Slide body over ferrule and press all parts into body; screw in the nut tightly

Moisture is the enemy of marine connectors. At least 90% of all marine electronics problems are due to corrosion in connectors and conductors. Water that penetrates the connector wicks into the stranded center conductor and shield and travels far into the cable. Corrosion turns copper into powdery copper oxide, thinning the conductors. In addition, the copper oxide is an insulator, so resistance goes up and signal strength goes down.

Figure 13.6 shows three defenses against moisture:

1. Making a nonwaterproof connection inside a waterproof box with the conductors entering the box from beneath.

2. Drip loops near the connector force water running along the conductor to drop off before reaching the conductor. The loops cannot prevent incursion of water falling directly on the connector, but they minimize guttering. A single drip loop at the base of a vertical run diverts water running down the mast.

3. Adhesive-lined, heat-shrink tubing seals the connector to the cable, preventing water leaks. The heated tubing shrinks (up to 85%), and the adhesive flows, sealing the connection.

Fig. 13.6 Protecting Coax Connections Against Moisture

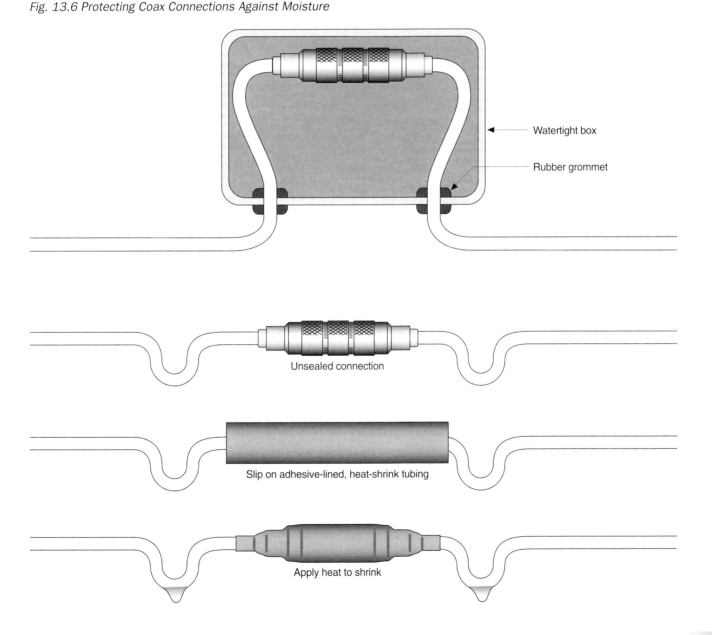

Watertight box

Rubber grommet

Unsealed connection

Slip on adhesive-lined, heat-shrink tubing

Apply heat to shrink

VHF Radio

Three factors affect how far away a properly working VHF radio can be heard:

1. *Cable transmission loss.* As indicated in Table 13.1, power loss increases with frequency and decreases with cable diameter. At the VHF frequency of 157 MHz, the lengths of coaxial cable for a 3 dB (50%) power loss are RG-58—49 feet; RG-8/X—66 feet; and RG-8/U—111 feet. A sailboat with a 15 metre/50-foot mast and a 5 metre/16-foot run will lose half its VHF transmitting power if it uses RG-8X (most boats do). The loss would be reduced by 50% by switching to the larger-diameter RG-8/U or RG-213.

2. *Antenna gain.* As shown in Figure 13.7, antennas can be designed to concentrate the radiation toward the horizon to a greater or lesser degree. The concentration is expressed as gain in dB. Generally, the longer the antenna, the greater the gain. Popular models and their lengths are 3 dB—1 metre/38 inches; 6 dB—2.5 metres/8 feet; and 9 dB—5.75 metres/19 feet. A masthead, 3 dB, 1 metre/38-inch whip antenna is the most appropriate for a sailboat because mast height compensates for low gain, and the less flattened pattern allows for heeling under sail. Bridge-mounted 6 dB and 9 dB antennas are best for powerboats because they do not heel.

Fig. 13.7 VHF Antenna Gain

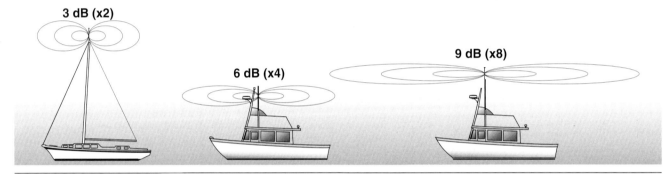

3. *Antenna height.* VHF transmission is line of sight. Transmit/receive distance is the same as the distance two observers at the same heights can see each other. Figure 13.8 demonstrates the principle. Table 13.2 lists the distances, versus the heights, of the two antennas.

The distances in Table 13.2 are based on the formulas:

$$D = 1.17\sqrt{H}$$
$$D_1 + D_2 = 1.17(\sqrt{H_1} + \sqrt{H_2})$$

where D is in nautical miles (nm) and H is in feet.

Actual transmission distances are observed to be about $1.22\sqrt{H}$, about 4% greater than the theoretical values under average conditions. Thus, two sailboats with 60-foot masts can be expected to communicate about 19 nm.

Powerboat antennas should be as vertical as possible. "Raking Reduces Radiation"

Table 13.2 Line-of-Sight Distance, in nautical miles, for VHF Radios

Receiver Height, ft	Transmitter Height, feet								
	5	10	20	40	60	80	100	200	400
5	5	6	8	10	12	13	14	19	26
10	6	7	9	11	13	14	15	20	27
20	8	9	10	13	14	16	17	22	29
40	10	11	13	15	17	18	19	24	31
60	12	13	14	17	18	20	21	26	33
80	13	14	16	18	20	21	22	27	34
100	14	15	17	19	21	22	23	28	35

For metric heights: ft x 0.3048

Fig. 13.8 Line-of-Sight Transmit/Receive Distance for VHF Radio

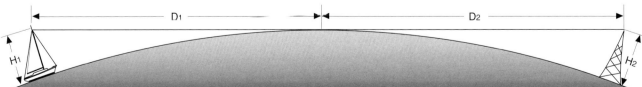

GPS

GPS receivers are supplied with matched antennas. With signal frequencies of about 1.5 gigahertz, the wavelengths are about 8 inches, and the antennas tiny. Location requirements are that the antennas have clear views of the sky and be located outside the radar beam and a few meters away from VHF and SSB antennas. Antenna power is low, so RG-58 cable is acceptable.

SSB or Ham

Both marine single-sideband and ham HF transceivers operate in the same approximate frequency bands. SSB transmissions are restricted to designated SSB frequencies, and ham radio transmissions are restricted to FCC-designated ham bands. The two transceiver types, however, are otherwise functionally identical. Although it is illegal to operate a ham transmitter as an SSB transmitter (except in an emergency), removal of a single diode allows the ham radio to transmit on all frequencies, from 300 kilohertz to 30 megahertz.

There are two types of SSB antennas. A 23-foot whip antenna works well down to 4 megahertz on both power- and sailboats. The antenna should be mounted vertically and located out of easy reach, since touching it may result in radiation burns.

A second option, available on sailboats, is an insulated backstay. The backstay, insulated with special fittings at upper and lower ends, acts as a simple "longwire" antenna. To protect crew from radiation burns, either the bottom insulator and electrical connection should be placed at least 2 metres/7 feet above the deck, or a length of rubber hose should be slid over the exposed lower portion.

Both antennas require tuners to achieve maximum output. The tuners may be built into the radio chassis or a separate unit installed near the antenna. Most ham operators feel the separate units work better in the relatively low-frequency SSB bands.

Both antenna types work well. The advantages of the 23-foot whip include smaller size, lower cost, and a vertical orientation for omnidirectional transmission. The insulated backstay results in a cleaner deck and captures more incoming signals.

Use either RG-8 or RG-213 coax to connect transceiver and tuner. Attenuation is less in the 2- to 12-megahertz SSB bands than in the 157-megahertz VHF band, but output currents are much greater for the 150-watt SSB than the 25-watt VHF, so we need a larger center conductor.

Fig. 13.9 Single-Sideband (SSB) Antenna and Ground Connections

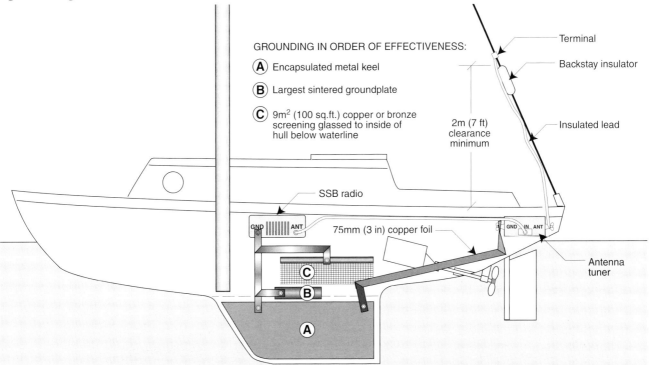

GROUNDING IN ORDER OF EFFECTIVENESS:

(A) Encapsulated metal keel

(B) Largest sintered groundplate

(C) 9m² (100 sq.ft.) copper or bronze screening glassed to inside of hull below waterline

Terminal

Backstay insulator

Insulated lead

2m (7 ft) clearance minimum

SSB radio

GND | | | | | | ANT   75mm (3 in) copper foil   GND IN ANT

Antenna tuner

Radar

As with GPS, radar units include matching antennas. The transmission frequency of around 9,500 megahertz (9.5 gigahertz) corresponds to a wavelength of about 25mm/1 inch. The radar waves are therefore easily blocked by metallic objects, such as masts, greater than 25mm/1 inch in diameter.

A second location requirement is that the antenna—essentially a microwave generator—be located a minimum of 2 feet/600mm from humans. (The first microwave ovens were aptly named *Radar Ranges!*) Just forward of the steering station on a flying bridge is not a good location!

The third location criterion is height. Since radar transmission is line of sight and limited in distance by the curvature of the earth, the higher the antenna, the farther you can see. On the other hand, the radiation has a vertical beam width of about 40°, so objects more than 20° below the horizontal will not be seen either. In choosing an antenna height, you thus need to balance the need to see large, distant targets and small, close objects.

Figure 13.10 shows both far ($D_1 + D_2$) and near (N_1) distances. Table 13.3 lists the far distances (range) for combinations of radar and target heights. Table 13.4 similarly shows the near distances (blind zone) for combinations of radar and target heights.

The near distance can be calculated from:

$$N_1 = H_1/\tangent\ 20°$$
$$= 2.75 \times (H_1 - H_0)$$

For example, a 40-foot-high antenna cannot see surface objects closer than 110 feet. Reducing the antenna height to 20 feet reduces the blind zone radius to 55 feet.

Note that it is the difference in height between the antenna and the target that determines the blind zone. A 40-foot-high antenna can see a 20-foot-high target, such as another boat, at a distance of 55 feet.

The cable between the radar antenna assembly and the display unit typically contains a dozen conductors. Use only the type of cable supplied with the unit.

Assuming you are skilled at soldering multi-pin connectors, you can shorten the supplied cable by any degree. A longer cable can generally be ordered as well. A third option is to purchase an extension cable with matching connectors.

The extension cable is very useful in the case of mast-mounted antennas in sailboats. Provided the original cable and the extension cables join at the mast step, stepping and unstepping the mast requires only connecting and disconnecting the cable. In any case, never locate cable connectors in the bilge, where they may be subject to corrosion.

Table 13.3 Radar Line-of-Sight Range in Nautical Miles

Radar Ht (H_1), ft	Target Height (H_2), feet								
	5	10	20	40	60	80	100	200	400
5	5	6	8	10	12	13	14	19	26
10	6	7	9	11	13	14	15	20	27
15	7	8	10	12	14	15	16	21	28
20	8	9	11	13	14	16	17	22	29
25	9	10	11	13	15	16	18	22	29
30	9	10	12	14	16	17	18	23	30
40	10	11	13	15	17	18	19	24	31
50	11	12	14	16	17	19	20	25	32

For metric heights: ft x 0.3048

Table 13.4 Radar Near Range (Blind Zone), N1, in Feet

Radar Ht (H_1), ft	Target Height (H_0), feet								
	0	1	2	3	5	10	15	20	30
5	14	11	8	5	–	–	–	–	–
10	27	25	22	19	14	–	–	–	–
15	41	38	36	33	27	14	–	–	–
20	55	52	49	47	41	27	14	–	–
25	69	66	63	60	55	41	27	14	–
30	82	80	77	74	69	55	41	27	–
40	110	107	104	102	96	82	69	55	27
50	137	135	132	129	124	110	96	82	55

For metric heights: ft x 0.3048

Fig. 13.10 Radar Range and Blind Zone vs. Heights of Antenna and Target

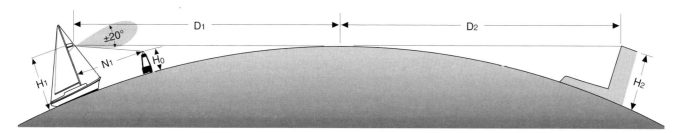

Receiver/Transmitter Installation

Location

1. *Install in a dry location.* As we saw in Chapter 3, moisture serves as an electrolyte and promotes corrosion. Salt spray has a way of infiltrating anything located on deck or in the cockpit. A thin film of salt on a circuit board may have much lower resistance than many of the circuit components, effectively shorting them out and altering, if not disrupting, performance. In my experience a standard enclosure in a dry location causes fewer problems than a "waterproof" enclosure in a wet location.

2. *Prevent overheating.* Electronics are designed to operate in any temperature a person can tolerate. They are designed to dissipate internally generated heat either by conduction through the case, by natural convection through vents, or by fan-forced convection. The most common mistakes are to restrict ventilation and to pile heat-producing electronics on top of each other with insufficient space between.

3. *Do not strain cables.* Install the equipment so that both antenna and power cables are secure but not taut. Excessive tension on the conductors can pull the connectors apart.

4. *Keep away from magnetic compasses.* Direct current produces a magnetic field around a conductor. The fields can be reduced but not eliminated if the power leads are either coaxial or twisted. Even stronger magnetic fields are caused by radio-speaker magnets and ferrite-rod radio antennas.

5. *Secure firmly at a good viewing/listening angle.* Equipment cases are usually supplied with convenient mounting brackets that allow either vertical or horizontal mounting. Secure the mounting bracket to a bulkhead or overhead with panhead self-tapping stainless screws.

12-Volt DC Power Hookup

1. Do not install more than one radio on a single circuit. If you do, VHF and SSB radios may interfere with each other through their power leads.

2. GPS receivers contain memories that retain coordinates and reduce settling time considerably. Turning off the equipment's power switch does not disconnect the power to the memory, but a drop in voltage may erase the memory. Powering navigation electronics from the house battery rather than the engine-starting battery will help prevent memory loss.

Grounding or Earthing

If there is a separate chassis, or case, ground or earth (usually a wing nut labeled "Gnd"), then:

1. Run a 6mm^2 minimum copper grounding wire to ground.
2. Run a separate ground from each chassis.
3. On a steel or aluminum boat, ground to the hull as close as possible to the equipment. On a wood or fiberglass boat, make the common ground point either the engine negative terminal or an external ground plate.
4. SSB/ham transmitters require special attention to ground (see Figure 13.9). Grounding conductors should be of 75mm/3-inch-wide copper foil and connected to a large area of bronze screening epoxied to the inside of the hull, a large sintered copper external ground plate, or an internal metal keel. Provided that all underwater metals are bonded, the boat's ground may prove sufficient. Remember, however, that bonding all underwater metals may increase corrosion.

Harnessing Electrical Noise

Conducting a Noise Audit

If you still have a loran set, don't dump it until you have first conducted a noise audit of your boat's electrical system. Most loran sets will display the signal-to-noise ratio (SNR) of their received 100-kilohertz loran signals. In this mode, they are marvelous tools for detecting radio frequency noise aboard your boat. Here's how:

1. Disconnect shore power.
2. Turn off all electrical equipment, including lights, refrigeration, receivers and transmitters, inverter, generator, and engine.
3. Turn on the loran and let it settle.
4. Call up the SNR display (see your owner's manual). If any of the SNRs (at least one master and three slave stations per master should be available anywhere in the United States for display) is greater than 50, proceed to the next step. If all of the SNRs are less than 50, select another loran chain having greater SNRs.
5. Note on a pad of paper the SNR values of one of the stations for a few minutes, then average the values to obtain the "clean-boat" reference SNR.
6. Start the engine and bring it up to its normal cruising rpm. Compare the SNR now displayed with the engine running to the previous averaged clean-boat reference SNR. If the SNR has dropped by more than 20% (from 50 down to 40, for example), your engine alternator or generator is a source of noise.
7. Repeat Step 6 for each additional piece of equipment, one at a time; i.e., turn off the previous piece of equipment before testing the next item. Any item that causes a greater than 20% drop in SNR is a source of noise that needs to be corrected. Between each of the tests recheck the reference SNR, with all equipment off, to make sure it hasn't changed.

Curing Noise

The first step in curing a noise problem is to recognize how electrical noise is generated and how it penetrates electronic equipment. Figure 13.11 shows that electrical equipment can be divided into *noise generators* (alternators, generators, ignitions, regulators, DC motors, fluorescent fixtures, and some types of digital electronics) and *noise receivers* (radios and electronic navigation devices).

Sometimes a single piece of equipment falls into both categories. I am reminded of my autopilot, whose DC motor caused noise in my radios, but whose electronic control went crazy when I transmitted on a nearby handheld VHF.

Fig. 13.11 Radio Frequency Interference (RFI) Generators and Receivers

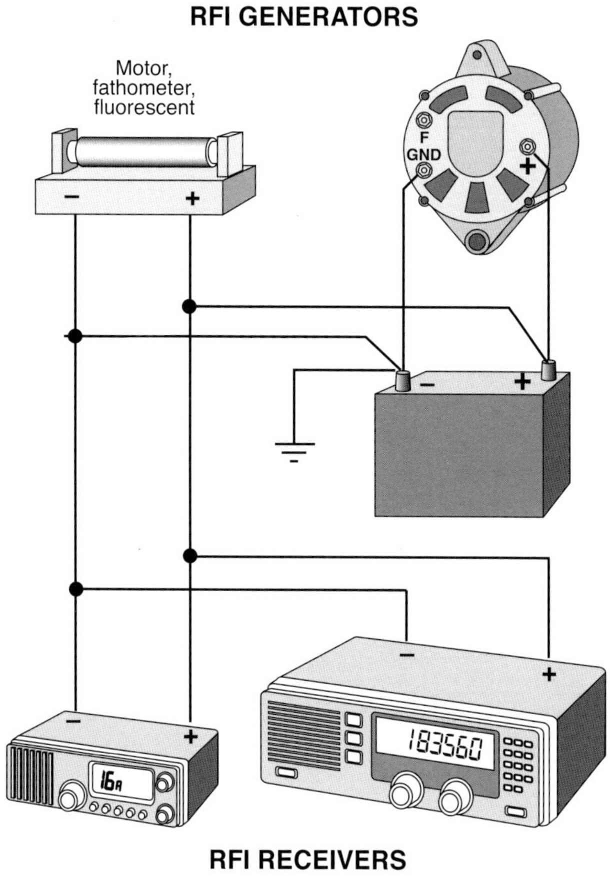

RFI GENERATORS

Motor, fathometer, fluorescent

F GND

RFI RECEIVERS

Cures fall into two categories: shielding and filtering.

Shielding consists of enclosing sensitive electronics in a metal case and connecting the case to ground, thereby shunting radiated noise to ground. By enclosing power and signal leads in shielded cable and connecting the cable shield to the metal case, we shunt noise induced in the leads to ground, as well.

Filtering utilizes capacitors and inductors. Capacitors conduct AC but block DC, while inductors conduct DC but block AC. The ideal 12-volt source is pure DC. Noise, on the other hand, is AC, either generated by the alternator or generator, or picked up by power leads acting like antennas. To reduce the amount of AC in a DC supply, we place capacitors across the + and – leads and inductors in series with the leads.

Capacitors for 12-volt DC applications should be rated at 50 working volts (50 WVDC) minimum. Large capacitors are generally polarized electrolytics, so make sure you observe proper polarity.

Inductors are rated by the maximum continuous DC current they can carry, as well as the value of inductance. For electronic navigation equipment, a 5-amp rating is generally sufficient. For DC motors (pumps and autopilots), a 10-amp rating is common. Alternators and generators require ratings that match or exceed their peak output ratings. Inductors with 50-, 70-, and 100-amp ratings are common.

In the case of noise on power leads, the unprotected length of lead serves as an antenna, picking up the noise. Thus, it is important to install the filter as closely as possible to the noise generator or the receiver.

Sometimes a single capacitor or inductor will reduce the noise to an acceptable level. More powerful solutions are provided by a variety of special commercially available filters, combining capacitors and inductors, as shown in Figure 13.12.

Fig. 13.12 A Typical RFI Filter

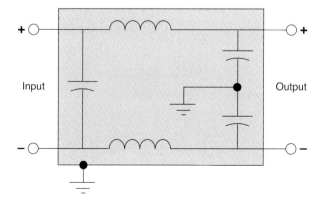

Figure 13.13 lays out a step-by-step attack on electronic noise. The first six steps attack the noise sources, since killing but a single source may reduce the noise to an acceptable level on all receivers. The last four steps treat the receivers individually.

The plan also proceeds roughly in order of increasing cost. It is assumed that, as each step is implemented, all previous cures are left in place.

1. Run separate grounding conductors from the alternator (or generator) case and from the cases of the affected equipment to boat ground.
2. Install a 10,000 µF, 50 VDC electrolytic capacitor across the alternator + output and ground terminals.
3. Install a 1 µF, 50 VDC capacitor from the voltage regulator battery terminal to ground.
4. Install 1 µF, 50 VDC capacitors across the + and – power input leads of all motors, fluorescent fixtures, and the depth sounder.
5. Install an alternator filter across the alternator + output and ground terminals. The filter rating must exceed the output ampere rating of the alternator.
6. Install commercial 10-amp filters across the + and – power input leads of all motors and 10-amp filters across the + and – power input leads of fluorescent fixtures and the depth sounder.
7. Install 1 µF, 50 VDC capacitors across the + and – power input leads of all affected electronics.
8. Install 1 µF, 50 VDC nonpolarized capacitors from the + power lead to chassis ground and the – power lead to chassis ground.
9. Install commercial 5-amp line filters across the + and – power input leads of each piece of affected electronics.
10. Enclose affected electronic equipment in screened-metal enclosures, or wrap in foil tape and connect the enclosure, or tape, to boat ground.

In case all of the above grounding, shielding, and filtering prove insufficient, the only remaining option is relocation of the antenna, cables, or the equipment itself. Remove both antenna and equipment chassis from their mounts and connect temporary power and antenna leads. Experiment with the location of the antenna and chassis and the routing of supply and antenna cables until the best results are obtained.

Electrical Filters

Fig. 13.13 Incremental Attack on Electronic Noise (see text)

STEP 1. Ground All Cases

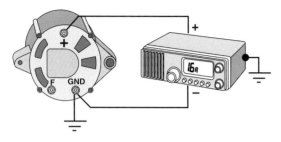

STEP 2. Capacitor across Alternator Output

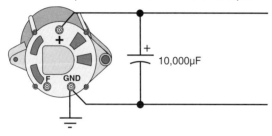

STEP 3. Capacitor on Regulator Input

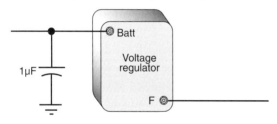

STEP 4. Capacitor on Accessory Supply

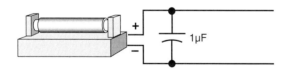

STEP 5. Alternator Filter

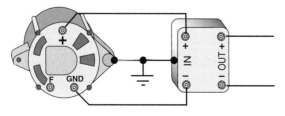

STEP 6. Filter on Accessory Supply

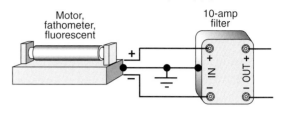

STEP 7. Capacitor on Equipment Supply

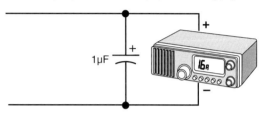

STEP 8. Capacitors from Supply to Gnd

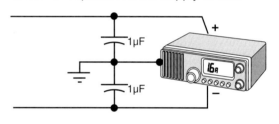

STEP 9. Filter on Equipment Supply

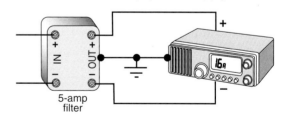

STEP 10. Grounded Equipment Screen

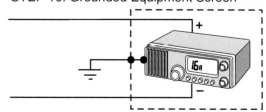

CHAPTER 14

Do-It-Yourself Projects

PROJECT 6: Expanded-Scale Analog Battery Monitor

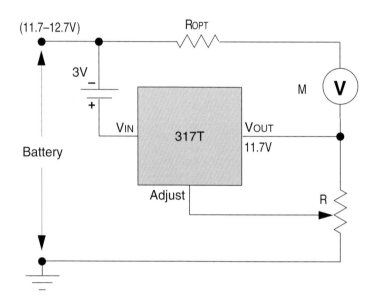

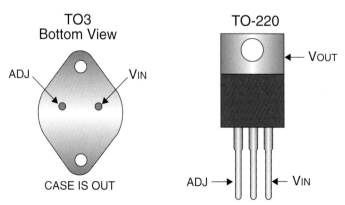

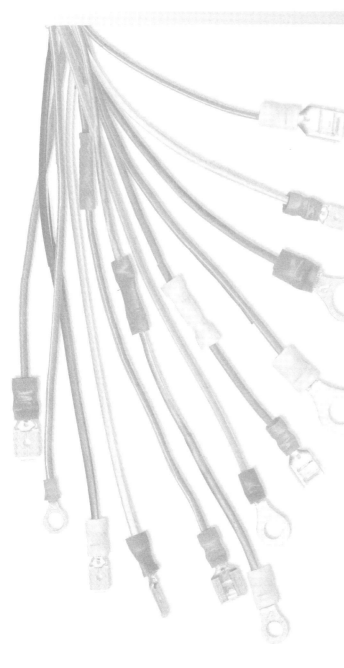

This chapter describes thirteen do-it-yourself projects that are fun and can be completed in an afternoon. By doing these projects, you can increase your understanding of electricity and electronics, upgrade your boat's electrical system, and save money—all at the same time.

Each project can be completed in a Sunday afternoon and typically costs less than a bottle of wine. Most of the components are available at electronic component stores.

The RadioShack part numbers are of little use in Europe, as there are few if any such outlets, but may assist with part identification, or enable purchase by mail order.

There are many suppliers of electronic components in the UK: Maplins and RS Components have a branch in most cities, and there are suppliers on the internet.

Passive Circuit Components

Projects are always more fun and generally more successful when you understand how they work. To understand the behavior of a circuit, you first have to understand how each of its components works. A few of the integrated circuits listed are actually complex circuits containing, in a single small package, hundreds of components. For these we will have to settle for an action/reaction, or input/output understanding. Each of the discrete components is described in a thumbnail sketch below.

Conductors

No connection. A conductor is shown as a solid line. Where conductors simply cross in a circuit diagram, there is no connection.

Connected conductors. When two or more conductors are electrically connected, the connection is indicated by a dot at the intersection. Think of the dot as a small blob of solder on the connection.

Connectors. Connectors are used to mate conductors when assembling or installing equipment. Connectors may mate single conductors, as in AC and DC distribution circuits; a shielded pair, as in coaxial antenna connections; or dozens of conductors, as in computer applications.

Resistors

Fixed resistor. A zigzag symbol indicates a fixed-value resistor. The resistance in ohms is constant regardless of current, temperature, or any other variable. The ability of a resistor to dissipate heat (calculated as $W = I^2 \times R$, where W = watts, I = amps, and R = ohms) is determined mostly by the size of the resistor. The value (ohms and precision) of a resistor is shown by a series of colored bands, as shown on page 267.

Variable resistor. A zigzag with an arrow through it indicates a resistor whose resistance value can be changed. Externally there are three terminals: one at each end of the full resistance, and a third ("wiper") connected to a contact, which slides along the resistance wire or film. The contact is generally moved by turning a screw or knob.

The value of the variable resistor is its maximum value, which can be read with an ohmmeter across the two end terminals. By connecting to the wiper terminal and the appropriate end terminal, we can have a resistance that increases or decreases with clockwise rotation of the screw. Using all three terminals, you have, in effect, two resistors, which form a voltage divider.

Low-power variable resistors are known as trimmers or trimpots; medium-power variable resistors are potentiometers; and high-power variable resistors are rheostats.

Thermistor. In reality a semiconductor, the thermistor (T) is a component whose resistance changes with temperature. Thermistors are specified by their resistance at 25°C, for example 10 kW (10,000 ohms) at 25°C.

If the variation of resistance with temperature were linear, measuring temperature with an ohmmeter would be a simple matter. Thermistors are more often used to control temperature, however, using the deviation in resistance from a set point as an error signal.

Capacitors

Nonpolarized capacitor. If electricity is like water, then capacitors are like pressurized water tanks: the higher the voltage you place across them, the more electric charge they store. Electric charge is measured in coulombs, which equal 6.24×10^{18} electrons. A 1-farad capacitor stores 1 coulomb of charge at a potential of 1 volt, 10 coulombs at 10 volts, etc.

Electronic circuits require much smaller charge storage, however, so the more common units of capacitance are the microfarad, or μF (10^{-6} farad), and the picofarad, or pF (10^{-12} farad).

Most capacitors are made of extremely thin, interleaved or wound, films of insulation (the dielectric) and aluminum. At high potentials the insulation can break down, so capacitors are also rated by their maximum working voltage.

Polarized capacitor. A device that is halfway between a capacitor and a battery is the electrolytic capacitor, which stores charge in a chemical electrolyte. The advantage is large capacitance in a small size. The disadvantage is that, as with a battery, reversing the voltage will damage the capacitor. Such polarized capacitors can be used only where the applied voltage is always of the same sign.

You can identify polarized capacitors by the + and – markings next to their leads.

Batteries

Single cell. A single electrochemical cell is generally used to supply power at low voltage. Nominal voltages for common cells are:

- Alkaline   1.50
- Carbon zinc   1.50
- Lead acid   2.10
- Lithium ion   3.60
- Lithium metal hydride   1.20
- Mercury oxide   1.35
- Nickel cadmium   1.25
- Zinc air   1.45
- Zinc chloride   1.50

Battery. The word *battery* means a group of cells. By packaging cells in series, manufacturers create batteries of nearly any voltage, the most common being 6, 9, and 12 volts. You can create a battery of nearly any voltage yourself by connecting cells in battery holders, which are designed to hold multiples of AAA-, AA-, C-, and D-size cells.

Switches

SPDT switch. The single-pole, double-throw is the simplest form of switch, allowing a single conductor (pole) to be routed to either of two routes (throws).

Think of the SPDT switch as a switch in a railroad track, shunting the track to either of two destinations. Of course, one of the destinations can lead nowhere, in which case the switch acts like a simple On-Off light switch. An SPDT switch used in the simple On-Off mode can be wired to be normally open (NO) or normally closed (NC).

DPDT switch. Going back to the railroad analogy, if you consider the two rails to be two conductors, then the railroad switch is analogous to the double-pole, double-throw switch. Two poles are switched simultaneously to one of two destinations. You can also think of the DPDT switch as being two SPDT switches ganged, or locked together.

Given enough layers and contacts, rotary switches can switch any number of poles to any number of destinations. They are specified as X-pole, Y-position.

Examples include: 1-pole, 12-position; 3-pole, 4-position; 2-pole, 8-position.

PB switch. Push-button switches are of two types: push-on, push-off; and momentary contact. The first is often used to control power On-Off and to activate options. The second is to activate a circuit or function briefly, such as a battery indicator or a microphone transmit switch.

Relay. The relay is an electrically activated switch. Current through its coil pulls on a magnetic slug, which activates a switch. The automotive solenoid is a high-current relay where a few amps from the keyed ignition switch activate the high-current (several hundred amps) switch on the starter motor. Electronic relays are rated by:

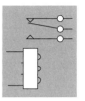

1. Input coil characteristics
2. Output switch maximum voltage and current

Sometimes the input coil voltage and resistance are specified, allowing you to calculate the current using Ohm's Law.

Example:
Coil: 12 VDC, 43 milliamps
Contacts: 2 amps, 120 VDC

Relays can have more than two poles, but they are always either single- or double-throw.

Overcurrent Devices

Fuse. A fuse (fusible link) protects a circuit from excessive current and damage by melting and breaking the circuit. The fuse is obviously a one-shot deal! In spite of the hassle of having to carry replacements, the fuse is still popular, due to low cost and high reliability.

Circuit breaker. You can think of the circuit breaker as a relay whose input current is routed through its output switch. The rated current of the circuit breaker is also the current required to activate the relay. Upon reaching its rated current, the circuit breaker disconnects itself, interrupting current flow to everything downstream of its output. Most circuit breakers operate on the same magnetic principle as coil relays. Some, however, contain a thermally activated bimetallic switch that opens at high temperature and won't close again until the temperature drops. Such thermal breakers are common in motors.

Passive Circuit Components

Lamps

Incandescent. The incandescent lamp is simply a miniature version of the ubiquitous household lightbulb. Its tungsten filament acts like a high-temperature resistor, glowing white-hot at normal operating voltage. Incandescent bulbs are rated by volts, either amps or watts, and type of base. By filling lamps with a halogen gas, which does not react with the filament, lamp manufacturers have been able to increase filament operating temperatures, which results in both greater light output and higher efficiency. The halogen lamps recommended in Chapter 10 are examples.

Neon. Neon bulbs contains no filaments to burn out. Instead, light is emitted by neon gas, which is stimulated by electric current. Neon bulbs require at least 60 volts to operate, and give off little light, but they consume little power and last indefinitely. They are often used as indicator lights in 120 and 240 VAC circuits.

Meters

Ammeter. The principles of both ammeters and voltmeters were discussed in Chapter 2. The ideal ammeter passes current with no voltage drop. In other words, it appears to a circuit as a resistor of near-zero resistance. Real ammeters come very close to the ideal with resistances on the order of 0.001 ohm.

There are two fundamentally different ammeter styles: analog and digital. The difference between analog and digital presentation is best exemplified by analog (sweep hands) and digital (LCD digits) watches. Analog is best for quick recognition; for accuracy you need digital.

Beware of cheap analog meters. They do not stand up well to the marine environment. On the other hand, the differences between high- and low-cost digital meters are often more in styling and name than in performance. The integrated circuitry inside the cases may be identical.

Voltmeter. Voltmeters are just ammeters with a high resistance in series with the input. The ideal voltmeter would appear to a circuit as an infinite resistance. The input resistance of real voltmeters ranges from 5,000 to 50,000 ohms per volt for analog meters and 1 to 10 megohms for digital meters.

Neither ammeters nor voltmeters must always be dedicated. A single panel meter can monitor an unlimited number of voltages or amperages by routing its input through a rotary switch. I use a £5 pocket digital volt-ohm meter Velcroed to my electrical panel, with its leads plugged into test jacks. When I need it for troubleshooting, I simply unstick it and substitute whatever test leads are appropriate to the job.

Motors

Motor. The most common motor on a boat is that driving the bilge pump. All small-boat bilge pump motors run on 12 VDC and consume from 2 to 20 amps. Start-up and locked-rotor currents can be three to four times as great, however, so contact ratings of switches and relays are important.

Fan. Most of the fans in a boat run on 12 VDC. A useful fan for the do-it-yourselfer is a zero-maintenance, brushless, and nearly noiseless fan originally developed for cooling computers. Sizes range from about 2 to 6 inches square. Drawing little current, they are ideal for circulating air through the condenser coils of small marine refrigerators under thermostatic control.

Acoustic Devices

Speaker. Speakers reproduce a range of frequencies, i.e., voice or music. They may also be used to emit very loud fixed-frequency sounds, as in burglar alarms and ship's horns. Speakers are rated by maximum power consumption in watts, frequency range, and input impedance, which is nearly always 8 ohms.

Piezo electric buzzer. A buzzer is an acoustic transducer that produces a single-frequency sound. Its primary use is as an alarm, indicating such things as:
- Too high voltage
- Too low voltage
- Too high temperature
- Too high water in the bilge

They are available in fixed frequencies from about 1 to 5 kHz. Current consumption depends on sound level and ranges from about 10 milliamps, which can be driven directly by integrated circuits, to 100 milliamps, which requires a driver transistor or relay.

Diodes

Rectifier diode. The most common diode passes current in the direction of the arrow but blocks current in the reverse direction. Actually, a minimum voltage of about 0.6 volt must be exceeded in the silicon diode (0.25 volt in a germanium diode) before current begins to flow in the forward direction. In the forward direction the diode looks, to a circuit, like nearly zero resistance and a voltage drop of 0.6 volt. In the reverse direction, it looks like infinite resistance.

With too high a forward current, diodes can overheat and be destroyed; at excessive reverse voltage, they will break down.

Diode specifications, therefore, include maximum forward current and peak reverse voltage. For example, a 1N4001 diode is rated at 1-amp continuous forward current and 50 volts peak reverse voltage.

Rectifier diodes are used in high-current applications, such as power supplies and battery chargers. Signal diodes handle a few milliamps and are used in signal processing. An example is the 1N914, rated at 10-milliamps continuous forward current and 75 volts peak inverse voltage.

Zener diode. All diodes break down and pass current in the reverse direction when the voltage exceeds their rating. Zener diodes are carefully manufactured to break down at precise voltages, ranging from 2 to

200 volts. The characteristic of switching from nonconducting to conducting at a precise voltage is used to regulate voltage in a circuit.

Light-emitting diode (LED). When free electrons flow across a diode junction, some electrons fall back into their normal, lower-energy states, releasing the extra energy in the form of radiation. In the rectifier and zener diodes, the frequency of the radiated energy is outside the range of visible light. In the LED gallium, arsenic, and phosphorus replace silicon, and the released radiation falls within the visible range. LEDs are available in red, green, yellow, and white.

Threshold voltages (voltage at which the LED begins to emit light) are typically 1.5 volts, rather than 0.6 volt. LEDs are rated, in addition to color, by maximum forward current and maximum reverse voltage. In practice, a resistor is placed in series with the LED to limit the forward current to the nominal value. Light output, however, is nearly linear with forward current, so the LED can run usefully at lower current and light levels simply by increasing the series resistance.

Since LEDs can be destroyed by reversing the leads, it is important to distinguish the anode (+ voltage lead) from the cathode (– voltage lead). If a specification sheet with a drawing is not available, polarity can be checked by connecting to a battery of 1.5 volts, which is sufficient to cause light output but generally less than the peak inverse voltage.

Active Circuit Components

NPN transistor. Transistors are usually explained in terms of electrons and holes. I prefer a water analogy, which will serve our purposes well enough.

Figure 14.1 shows the three terminals of the NPN transistor: base, collector, and emitter. The small arrows show the direction of current flow in the leads: I_B, I_C and I_E. Note that the arrow in the emitter lead serves the same purposes and distinguishes the NPN from the PNP transistor.

The transistor is constructed like a pair of diodes connected back-to-back. Current I_B will flow from the base to the emitter, in the direction shown, whenever the base is at a higher voltage than the emitter.

Now the analogy—the base acts like a valve in the collector-to-emitter waterpipe. A small change in I_B results in a large change in I_C and I_E. The ratio of current changes is called the forward current gain:

$$h_{FE} = \Delta I_C / \Delta I_B$$

Typical values of h_{FE} range from 20 to 100.

The most common use of the transistor is to multiply current and, thus, increase the power of a signal.

PNP transistor. The PNP transistor functions in exactly the same way as the NPN transistor, except that its diodes are reversed. Figure 14.2 shows the lead definitions and current directions in the PNP transistor. Due to the reversal of diodes, current I_B will now flow whenever the base is negative relative to the emitter. Current gain is again defined as:

$$h_{FE} = \Delta I_C / \Delta I_B$$

The choice between PNP and NPN transistors depends on the supply voltage configuration of the circuit.

MOSFET. Both the field effect transistor (FET) and the metal-oxide semiconductor field effect transistor (MOSFET) act like transistors, except that the controlling input signal is a voltage rather than a current. Since almost no current flows into the input lead (the gate), the input resistance of the MOSFET is virtually infinite. FETs and MOSFETs are therefore primarily used where high input resistance is required. Applications where this characteristic is especially useful are operational amplifier inputs and digital voltmeters. Figure 14.3 shows the circuit symbol and the pin designations of the IRF510 power MOSFET.

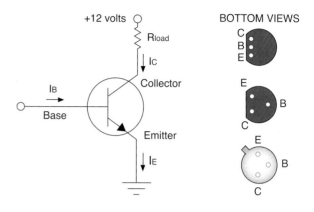

Fig. 14.1 NPN Transistor

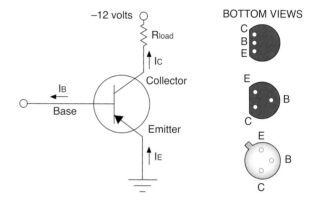

Fig. 14.2 PNP Transistor

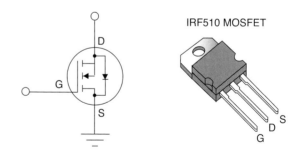

Fig. 14.3 MOSFET (IRF510)

Operational amplifier. If we were to describe a perfect amplifier, its specifications would read:

- Voltage gain = ∞
- Input resistance = ∞ Ω
- Input offset voltage = 0 volts

A real opamp, the LM353, costs less than $1.00 in single quantity and has the following specifications:

- Voltage gain > 10^6
- Input resistance = $10^{12} \Omega$
- Input offset voltage < 0.002 volt

The usefulness of the opamp derives from its essentially infinite voltage gain and input resistance. Figure 14.4A shows the basic opamp. Since the output voltage is limited by the supply voltage (usually ±15 VDC, although single-voltage operation is possible too), infinite voltage gain implies zero volts between the positive (V_{in+}) and negative (V_{in-}) inputs. Further, since the input resistance is infinite, no current flows into either input.

Figure 14.4B shows the opamp as a voltage follower.

Fig. 14.4 A Few Useful Operational Amplifier Circuits

Zero difference voltage means that $Vin_+ = V_{in-}$, and since $V_{out} = V_{in-}$, then $V_{out} = V_{in}$. The voltage follower is used to simply boost current while maintaining voltage.

Figure 14.4C shows an inverting amplifier with voltage gain. Since no current flows into the – input, and since the – input is at the same potential as the + input (ground), then the input current flowing through R_1 must cancel the feedback current through R_2: $I_1 = -I_2$.

Then, using Ohm's Law,

$$I = V/R,$$
$$V_1/R_1 = -V_2/R_2$$
$$V_2 = -V_1(R_2/R_1)$$

Figure 14.4 shows a variety of other useful opamp configurations (D, E, F). To understand how they work, you need remember only that $V_{in+} = V_{in-}$.

The equation relating V_{out} to V_{in} can then be derived from equating the input and (negative) feedback currents flowing into each input.

A. Basic Operational Amplifier

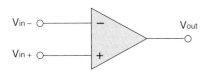

B. Unity-Gain Voltage Follower:
Vout = Vin

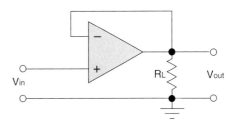

C. Inverting Amplifier
Vout = – Vin

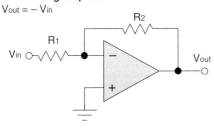

D. Non-Inverting Amplifier
Vout = Vin(R2/R1)

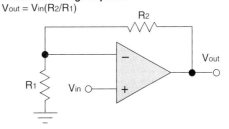

E. Summing Amplifier
Vout = – (Rf/R1 x V1 + Rf/R2 x V2 + ...)

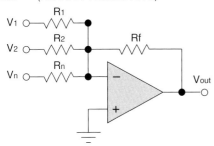

F. Difference Amplifier
Vout = – (V1 – V2)R2/R1

1. AC Polarity Indicator

The ABYC recommends reverse-polarity indicators on all AC main panels. It also suggests that the resistance of such indicators be at least 25,000 ohms in order that they not bypass any isolation transformer or galvanic isolation diodes installed in the shore-power circuit. This two-lamp circuit consists of a green neon lamp across the hot and neutral conductors and a red neon lamp across neutral and ground. Proper polarity is indicated by a green light alone. If the red light comes on, either alone or with the green, something is wrong. To install the lamps, drill $\frac{5}{16}$-inch holes in the distribution panel and press in.

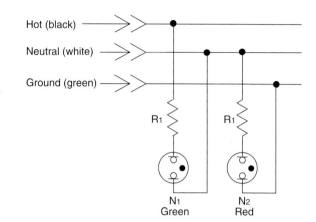

Components

Part	Description	RadioShack #
N1	Green 120-volt neon lamp	272-708
N2	Red 120-volt neon lamp	272-712
R1	33 kΩ, ¼-watt resistor	271-1341

2. LED Panel Indicator

Many DC distribution panels come only with circuit breakers or fuses, so it is difficult to tell at a glance whether a circuit is on or off. Others come with battery-draining incandescent indicator lamps. One of these low-current LED indicators can be installed on the output side of each circuit breaker and fuse to indicate, with a soft glow, when the circuit is on. The LED specified consumes only 0.012 amp. Ten LEDs will consume 3 Ah of battery power per 24 hours. To install, drill press-fit holes in the panel adjacent to each fuse switch or circuit breaker. Press in the LED and solder the 1 kΩ resistor between the LED anode (see specification sheet for lead identification) and the hot terminal. Connect the LED cathode to the panel ground bus.

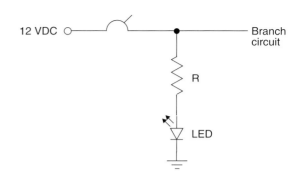

Components

Part	Description	RadioShack #
R	1 kΩ, ¼-watt resistor	271-1321
LED	Red, T1 (3mm), LED	276-026

3. AC Frequency Meter

The ABYC recommends an AC frequency meter on the AC distribution panel fed by any onboard generator. The zener diode in this circuit clips incoming 120-volt AC sine waves to 6.2-volt DC square waves. Capacitor C_1 differentiates the square waves into positive and negative pulses. Diode D_1 shorts the negative pulses to ground, but diode D_2 passes the positive pulses, which are then averaged by the inertia of the ammeter, M.

To calibrate, connect the circuit to shore power (60 Hz), and adjust R_2 until M reads exactly 60 mA.

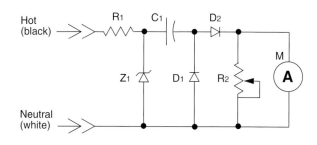

Components

Part	Description	RadioShack #
R1	100 kΩ, ½-watt resistor	271-1131
R2	10 kΩ, 1-turn potentiometer	271-1715
C1	0.22 µF capacitor	272-1070
D1, D2	1N914 signal diode	276-1122
Z1	6.2 V zener diode	276-561
M	0–100 µA panel meter	none

4. Small Battery Eliminator

If you are tired of replacing expensive batteries in your electronics, you can make a "battery" that will supply up to 1.5 amps at any voltage from 1.5 to 10 volts DC, drawing from your ship's battery. The 317T is an adjustable, three-terminal, integrated-circuit voltage regulator in a package smaller than a coin.

To install, solder the circuit as shown, connect V_{in} to 12 VDC and adjust trimpot R until V_{out} reads the desired voltage. Then connect V_{out} and Ground to the battery terminals of the electronic equipment.

You may wish to pack the circuit into a cardboard or plastic cylinder of the same dimensions as the battery you are replacing. An alternative is to wrap the circuit in foam and then stuff it into the battery slot. If the 317T gets too hot to touch, mount it on the optional heat sink.

Components

Part	Description	RadioShack #
317T	Adjustable voltage regulator	276-1778
R	1kΩ trimpot	271-280
*	Optional heat sink (not shown)	276-1368

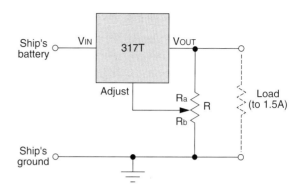

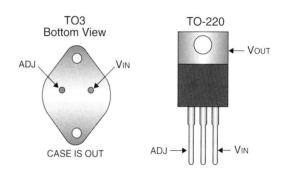

Projects

5. Low-Battery Voltage Alarm

In this circuit a 741 operational amplifier compares the voltage of zener diode, Z, to a voltage determined by the ship's battery and the voltage divider, R_3 and R_2.

When the battery voltage falls below the preset lower-voltage limit, the voltage at the opamp's V_{in-} terminal drops below the zener's 6.2 volts, and the output of the opamp rises to the battery voltage, lighting the LED. A 10-milliamp Piezo buzzer could replace the noiseless LED for an audible alarm.

To set the battery's low-voltage alarm point, monitor the battery voltage with a digital voltmeter. When the voltage reaches 12.00 volts, for example, adjust R_3 until the LED or buzzer just comes on.

A two-stage alarm can easily be constructed, which will give a visual LED warning at 50% discharge, for example, and a more dire audible warning at 75% discharge.

To construct, replace the 741 with a 1458 dual operational amplifier, feed the – input of the second amplifier with a second R_2/R_3 voltage divider, and drive the Piezo buzzer with the output of the second amplifier. Calibrate the two setpoints as before, using a digital voltmeter to monitor battery voltage.

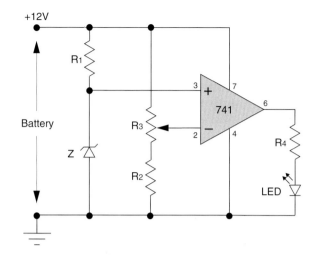

Components

Part	Description	RadioShack #
R_1	10 kΩ, ¼-watt resistor	271-1335
R_2	1 kΩ, ¼-watt resistor	271-1321
R_3	10 kΩ, 15-turn trimpot	271-343
R_4	1 kΩ, ¼-watt resistor	271-1321
Z	1N4735, 6.2 V zener diode	276-561
LED	Red, T1 (3 mm), LED	276-026
741	741 operational amplifier	276-007

6. Expanded-Scale Analog Battery Monitor

The problem with monitoring battery voltage with an analog panel meter is that the normal 5% accuracy of the meter is equivalent to about 50% of the battery's capacity. What is needed is an electronic magnifying glass to focus on the battery's 11.7- to 12.7-volt range.

In this circuit, a 317T adjustable voltage regulator is used to provide a constant 11.70 VDC. The 0- to 1-volt DC voltmeter then reads the difference between the ship's battery voltage and the reference 11.70 volts. Assuming 12.70 and 11.70 volts represent 100% and 0% charge, 0 to 1 volt on the voltmeter represents 0% to 100% charge.

The 3 VDC alkaline battery (can be two AA alkaline cells in a battery holder) boosts the regulator source so that the output can still deliver 11.7 volts, even when the ship's battery drops to 11.7 volts.

The 0- to 1-volt voltmeter can be replaced by R_{opt} and an ammeter, as shown in the component list.

Of course a digital voltmeter may be used, in lieu of the analog meter.

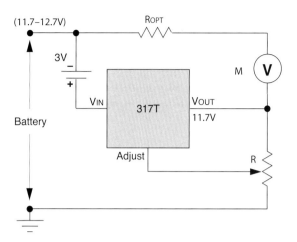

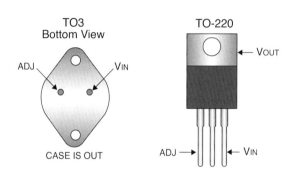

Components

Part	Description	RadioShack #
317T	Adjustable voltage regulator	276-1778
R	1 kΩ, 15-turn trimpot	271-342
M	0–1-volt DC meter	none
R_{opt}	10 kΩ resistor for 100 μA meter	271-1335
R_{opt}	1 kΩ resistor for 1 μA meter	271-1321

Projects

7. Expanded Digital Battery Monitor

This circuit utilizes the incredibly useful, yet inexpensive, LM3914 Dot/Bar Display Driver to display the charge status of a boat's batteries in 0.1-volt increments.

The LEDs can be of different colors, further enhancing the status indication. For instance, if your normal discharge range is 90 to 50%, the top five LEDs could be green (indicating OK) and the bottom five LEDs red (indicating need to charge).

To calibrate the circuit, connect a digital voltmeter to the battery terminals. First charge the battery fully and let it come to its fully charged rest voltage (approximately 12.65 volts). Adjust potentiometer R_3 until LED #10 lights, indicating full charge. To establish the fully discharged state, let the battery discharge until the voltmeter reads 11.65 volts, and adjust potentiometer R_2 until LED #1 lights.

From this point on, the battery voltage will be indicated by which LED is lit, in increments of 0.1 volt.

As an option, and at the cost of slightly higher power consumption, the display can be converted to a bar graph simply by connecting pin 9 to Battery +.

Components

Part	Description	RadioShack #
LM3914	Dot/bar display driver	900-6840
R_1	47 kΩ, ¼-watt resistor	271-1342
R_2	200 kΩ, 15-turn trimpot	none
R_3	100 kΩ, 15-turn trimpot	none
C_1	47 µF electrolytic capacitor	272-1027
C_2	0.1 µF capacitor	272-1069
LEDs	10-segment LED bar graph	276-081
	or individual red	276-026
	or individual green	276-022

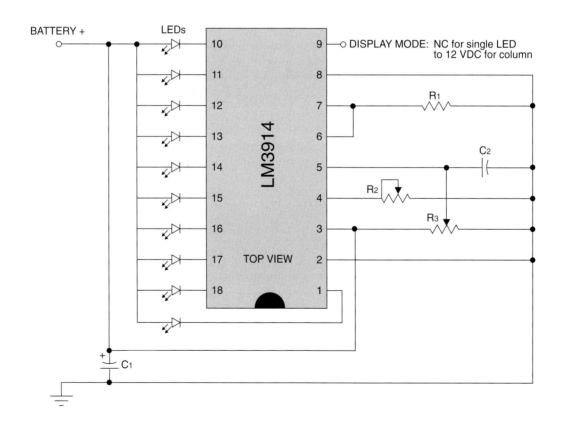

8. Automatic Anchor Light

The typical mast-top anchor light consumes 12 watts. Over a 12-hour period, it will drain 12 Ah from the battery. If you leave the boat unattended and leave the anchor light on (as you must legally), it will draw down the battery at 24 Ah per day!

This circuit saves battery power by automatically switching on at sunset and off at sunrise. At sunset, the resistance of the cadmium sulfide photoresistor increases, increasing the voltage to the NPN transistor, Q. The transistor provides the current to close the coil of the relay and feed 12 VDC to the anchor light.

The red LED indicates when the anchor light is on. A single-pole, three-position rotary switch allows selection between automatic, manual, and off modes.

Note that the cadmium sulfide photoresistor must be placed so that it is not illuminated by the anchor light. Otherwise it will interpret the anchor light as sunlight and cause the light to turn on and off rapidly.

Components

Part	Description	RadioShack #
R_1	1 kΩ, ¼-watt resistor	271-1321
R_2	10 kΩ, 1-turn potentiometer	271-282
R_3	1 kΩ, ¼-watt resistor	271-1321
P	Photoresistor	276-1657
Q	2N2222 NPN transistor	276-2009
Relay	12 V, 400 Ω, 10 A SPDT	275-248
SW	SPDT switch, center Off	275-654
LED	Red, T1 (3 mm), LED	276-026
741	741 operational amplifier	276-007

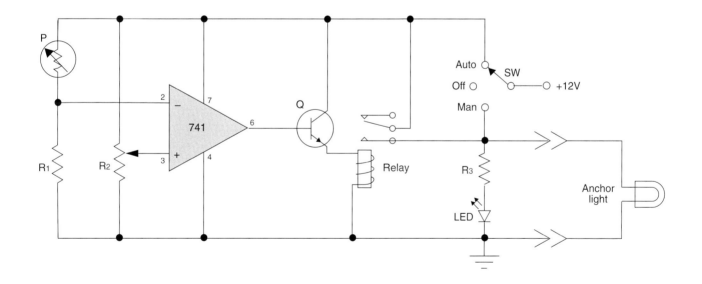

Projects

9. Cabin Light Dimmer

Halogen cabin lamps are great for reading, but not very romantic for dining. Furthermore, dimming your cabin lights will save on battery power.

The heart of this circuit is the integrated circuit 555 timer. The 555 runs as a multivibrator (digital oscillator) with its frequency determined by R_1, R_2, R_3, and C_1. Pin 3 of the 555 controls the gate of the MOSFET, Q, which supplies current to the cabin lamps in the form of square waves of modulated width.

The percentage of normal voltage supplying the lamps is equivalent to the percentage-on time of the pulses, which is controlled by adjusting trimpot R_2. This effective voltage across the lamps can be varied from about 4.5 to 11.0 VDC.

The dimmer circuit is switched in and out of the circuit by switch SW. Individual cabin lights can still be switched on and off with their own switches.

Since the life of the very expensive halogen lamps is extended markedly by reduction in supply voltage, you might consider leaving the dimmer circuit on all the time, set at the minimum power level required for the task at hand.

If the circuit load is more than 5 watts, check the operating temperature of the 555. If too hot to touch, attach a heat sink to the integrated circuit.

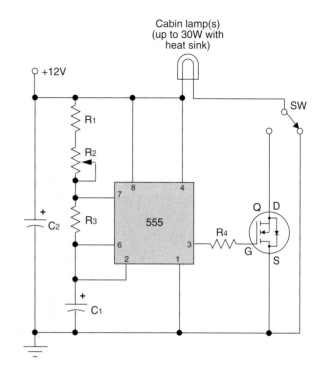

Cabin lamp(s) (up to 30W with heat sink)

Components

Part	Description	RadioShack #
R_1	100 Ω, ¼-watt resistor	271-1311
R_2	5 kΩ potentiometer	271-1714
R_3	1 kΩ, ¼-watt resistor	271-1321
R_4	10 kΩ, ¼-watt resistor	271-1335
C_1	0.047 µF capacitor	272-1068
C_2	22 µF capacitor	272-1026
Q	IRF-510 power MOSFET	276-2072
555	555 timer integrated circuit	276-1723
SW	SPDT switch, center Off	275-654
*	Heat sink for Q (not shown)	276-1368

10. Bilge High-Water Alarm

Automatic bilge pump switches are notorious for failing. Although not usually dangerous, having bilge water rise above the cabin sole is not very good for the rugs or the joinery. This circuit gives an audible warning when the bilge water rises to the level of the normally dry probe.

The 741 opamp acts as a voltage comparator. The − input voltage is set at +6 VDC by the voltage divider formed by R_2 and R_3. With a dry probe, the + input voltage is near 0 VDC, so the output of the 741 is near 0 VDC.

With the probe immersed in water, however, the voltage at the + input rises to over 6 VDC, and the 741 output goes to 12 VDC. Transistor Q boosts the output of the 741 to drive the Piezo transducer. R_4 prevents the + side of the probe from shorting to ground through the bilge water.

An inexpensive and convenient probe can be made from a section of television twin lead with each conductor stripped back about 1 inch and tinned (soldered) to prevent corrosion. The probes should be mounted well above the normal bilge high-water level, so that they remain dry except when the regular bilge switch fails.

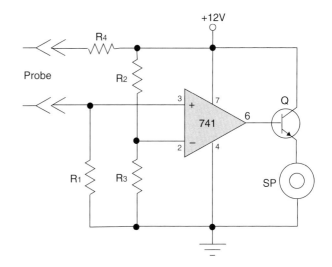

Components

Part	Description	RadioShack #
R_1	100 kΩ, ¼-watt resistor	271-1347
R_2	100 kΩ ¼-watt resistor	271-1347
R_3	100 kΩ, ¼-watt resistor	271-1347
R_4	10 kΩ, ¼-watt resistor	271-1335
Q	2N2222 NPN transistor	276-2009
741	741 operational amplifier	276-007
SP	Piezo transducer	273-075
Probe	TV twin-lead antenna wire	15-0004

Projects

11. Water Tank Monitor

Few things are more annoying than unexpectedly running out of water or having to lift deck hatches and unscrew access plates to check the level of water in your tanks. This circuit gives a visual warning when your water tank reaches a predetermined level.

The 741 operational amplifier acts as a voltage comparator. The + input voltage is set by the voltage divider formed by trimpot R_2.

Run a length of television twin-lead antenna cable into your water tank from above. Strip about 1 inch of insulation from each of the two conductors and solder the exposed wire to prevent corrosion.

With the probe immersed in water, the voltage at the – input is near +12 VDC. As soon as the water level drops below the probe leads, the resistance between the leads increases to near infinity and the – input voltage drops to zero. The amplifier output rises to the supply voltage and lights the LED warning light.

Add a switch to the +12 VDC power lead if you don't wish to monitor the tank continuously.

Components

Part	Description	RadioShack #
R_1	220 kΩ, ¼-watt resistor	271-1350
R_2	100 kΩ trimpot	271-284
R_3	1 kΩ, ¼-watt resistor	271-1321
LED	Red, T1 (3 mm), LED	276-026
741	741 operational amplifier	276-007

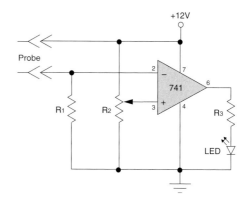

12. Electronic Ship's Horn

The circuit is a multivibrator (Q_1 and Q_2) with a frequency of $2\pi/R_1C_1 = 280$ Hz. Transistor Q_3 boosts the output current to drive the 8 Ω, 25-watt speaker. Pushing the momentary contact switch, SW_1, sounds the horn.

Play with resistors R_1 to achieve the pitch that is most pleasing to you, although 280 Hz is close to the frequency of most commercial horns. A speaker with higher impedance can be used with an impedance-matching transformer.

Using switch SW_2, the speaker can be connected to the hailer output found in the rear of many VHF radios, allowing the speaker to be used as a bullhorn as well.

Components

Part	Description	RadioShack #
R_1(2)	100 kΩ, ¼-watt resistor	271-1347
R_2(2)	1 kΩ, ¼-watt resistor	271-1321
C_1(2)	0.22 µF capacitor	272-1070
Q_1	2N2222 NPN transistor	276-2009
Q_2	2N2222 NPN transistor	276-2009
Q_3	TIP-3055 NPN power transistor	276-2020
SW_1	Momentary contact switch	275-609
SW_2	DPDT switch, 6 A	275-652
SP	Power horn, 8Ω, 25-watt	40-1440

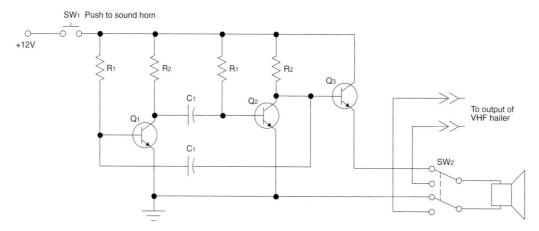

13. Refrigeration Fan Control

The efficiency of a refrigerator is affected greatly by the temperature of its condenser coil. Many small, 12 VDC boat compressors are located in warm or constricted spaces. Such condensers need fans to remove the heat from the coils.

This circuit uses a tiny thermistor, taped to the condenser tubing, to detect the need for air flow. The tape over the thermistor protects it from the direct flow of cool air, so that it measures the temperature of the coil rather than that of the moving air.

The opamp compares the voltages of two voltage dividers formed by R_1/R_T (– input) and trimpot R_2 (+ input). When the temperature of the thermistor rises above the set point, its resistance drops, the voltage at the negative input drops, and the output voltage of the inverting amplifier rises. Transistor Q boosts the opamp output current to close the relay and turn on the fan.

The temperature at which the fan comes on (the set point) is adjusted with trimpot R_2. Trimpot R_3 adjusts the gain of the amplifier and, thus, the hysteresis, or the difference between turn-on and turn-off temperatures.

Components

Part	Description	RadioShack #
R_1	10 kΩ, ¼-watt resistor	271-1335
R_2	20 kΩ, 15-turn trimpot	900-8583
R_3	100 kΩ trimpot	271-284
T	Thermistor, 10 kΩ @ 25°C	271-110
Q	2N2222 NPN transistor	276-2009
K	12 V, 400 Ω, 10 A SPDT relay	275-248
741	741 operational amplifier	276-007
F	Blower fan, 12 VDC	273-243

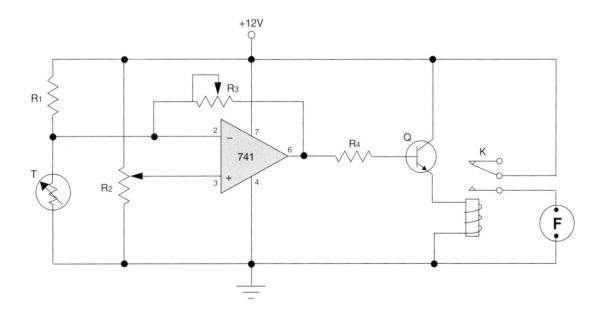

Appendices

This section includes some useful tables, starting with conversions from Imperial to Metric, and vice versa. The formula for converting from Celsius to Fahrenheit degrees is awkward and difficult to compute in your head, so we thought a table of temperature conversions would be useful. Similarly, in wiring there is often a need to perform power conversions from the mechanical horsepower of motors to electrical watts.

Both copper conductors and coaxial cables suffer losses as functions of length, so we have included handy tables of resistance of copper wire and losses in coaxial cables and a cable size conversion table.

Although DC and AC color codes for marine wiring are discussed in the text, other wiring color codes exist, so we have presented them all together.

When performing electronic installation and repair, it is often necessary to identify the characteristics of components. With the trend toward miniaturization, it is increasingly difficult for manufacturers to print, and for us to read, information directly on the component. This is especially true for resistors and capacitors. Thus the manufacturers have resorted to cryptic codes involving colors and single alphanumeric characters as aids in identifying resistors and capacitors.

For the mathematically inclined, we offer all of the useful electrical formulas that you might need in performing electrical calculations.

Finally, three useful schematic diagrams are reproduced (courtesy of BMEA), which can be the basis for Engine and DC Power Control; Engine and DC Power Distribution; and AC Control and Distribution. There is a section on the Recreational Craft Directive (RCD), which enforces the use of ISO Standards, and thus has a bearing on all leisure marine electrical installations.

The original US version of this edition of *The Boatowner's Illustrated Electrical Handbook* was based on the American Boat and Yacht Council (ABYC) *Standards and Recommended Practices for Small Craft*. Although the standards used elsewhere in the world for DC and protection circuitry are broadly similar, there are significant differences in the standards and practices for AC circuits.

This UK and European Edition has been adapted to comply with ISO standards, as promulgated by the British Marine Electronics Association (BMEA) in their *BMEA Code of Practice* (fourth edition). This is available as a PDF file on a CD, which also includes the complete ISO standards, for £75 + VAT (£88.13).

Guidance on the above standards is listed below.

European Union

European Recreational Craft Directive (RCD). RCD standards are mandatory on boats constructed in EU countries, and on vessels built elsewhere and offered for sale in the EU, and include the following International Standards Organization (ISO) standards:

> *ISO10133:2000. Small Craft—Electrical systems—Extra-low-voltage DC installations.*
> *ISO13297:2000. Small Craft—Electrical systems—AC installations.*
> *ISO8846:1990 Small Craft—Electrical devices—Protection against ignition of surrounding flammable gas.*

ISO standards can be purchased online at: *www.iso.org/iso/en/prods-services/ISOstore/store.html.*

Lloyd's Register. *Rules and Regulations for the Classification of Yachts and Small Craft, 1978.* The Rules are used when a boat is to be built to Lloyd's Register (LR) Class rules.

BMEA (British Marine Electronics Association): *Code of Practice for Electrical and Electronic Installations in Small Craft—4th Edition*. This standard is available direct from the British Marine Federation Technical Department; tel: 01784 223634 or email: *technical@ britishmarine.co.uk*.

The Recreational Craft Directive - a Summary

The Recreational Craft Directive (RCD) is applicable throughout the EU and EEA, and is designed to protect the boat-buying and boat-using public, enable freedom of movement of goods, and has applied since June 1998 to all boats offered for sale between 2.5 and 24 metres in length. It covers all the essential aspects of a boat's design and construction, with the emphasis on safety. Electrical installations, which must follow ISO Standards, are an intrinsic part of the Directive.

In January 2007 the last phase of a new Amending Directive came into effect. This extends the scope of the original directive to include limiting boat and engine sound and exhaust emissions, to bring personal water craft within its scope, and to update some of the original regulations. A new relaxation is the facility to import a used boat from outside the EU using the new "Post Construction Assessment" PCA rules.

All new boats on sale in the EU must comply with the RCD and must exhibit the CE mark on the builder's plate to indicate compliance. If you buy a boat that does not comply, then you will have difficulty selling it.

The new engine exhaust emission and noise rules particularly apply to 2-stroke engines. These rules came into effect on January 1st 2007, but only apply to new boats and engines.

The RCD does not apply to brokerage and private sales of second-hand craft which were first sold in the EU, although if that boat was first placed on the EU market after June 1998 it should have been CE marked, and if not, it may have been sold illegally.

Any second-hand commercial craft, or any other exempt craft, being bought with a view to conversion for recreational use will have to comply with RCD, and to do so must undergo a "Post Construction Assessment".

A new or secondhand boat imported from outside the EC, and not CE marked, must be shown to comply with the regulations by undertaking a Post Construc-tion Assessment. This means employing a third party, known as a Notified Body, who will carry out the assessment and deal with the technical and compliance formalities. There are four Notified Bodies in the UK and many others throughout the rest of the EU. You may choose which one to use from the list available through the DTI website below.

Further information on the RCD is available from the Department of Trade and Industry (www.dti.gov.uk/innovation/strd/ecdirect/page12637. html), and from the RYA (www.rya.org.uk/Knowledge-Base/technical/reccraftdir.htm).

RYA and the British Marine Federation together run a RCD document download site should you want to study the regulations in depth (www.rcdweb.com). Hampshire County Council's website has a comprehensive set of plain language information at www.hants.gov.uk (search using "RCD").

United States

The United States Coast Guard: *Title 33, CFR 183*. These contain federal mandatory requirements for electrical systems on boats. Many of the Title 33 regulations are directly referenced in the ABYC standards. In no case do the two conflict. The text is available on the web at: *www.access.gpo.gov/nara/cfr/waisidx_99/ 33cfr183_99.html*.

National Marine Electronics Association (NMEA): *Installation Standards*. This standard is for the installation of marine electronics, primarily on large vessels. It is complementary to the ABYC recommendations, but with an emphasis on electronics. To visit NMEA on the web, go to: *www.nmea.org*.

National Fire Protection Association (NFPA): *National Electrical Code (NEC)*. This single United States national code governs all wiring on land, including marinas. To visit NFPA on the web, go to: *www.nfpa.org*.

Canada

Transport Canada: *TP1332 E—Construction Standards for Small Vessels—Section 8 Electrical Systems*. The single, comprehensive set of standards for pleasure vessels constructed in Canada. Access complete text at: *www.tc.gc.ca/marinesafety/TP/TP1332/menu.htm*.

English/Metric Conversions

Table A1 English to Metric Conversions

	English to Metric			Metric to English	
Multiply	**By**	**To Get**	**Multiply**	**By**	**To Get**
LENGTH					
Inches	25.4	Millimeters	Millimeters	0.0394	Inches
Inches	2.54	Centimeters	Centimeters	0.3937	Inches
Inches	0.0254	Meters	Meters	39.37	Inches
Feet	30.48	Centimeters	Centimeters	0.0328	Feet
Feet	0.3048	Meters	Meters	3.281	Feet
Yards	0.9144	Meters	Meters	1.094	Yards
Miles	1.609	Kilometers	Kilometers	0.6215	Miles
AREA					
Inches^2	645.16	Millimeters^2	Millimeters^2	0.00155	Inches^2
Inches^2	6.4516	Centimeters^2	Centimeters^2	0.155	Inches^2
Feet^2	929.03	Centimeters^2	Centimeters^2	0.00108	Feet^2
Feet^2	0.0929	Meters^2	Meters^2	10.764	Feet^2
Yards^2	8361.3	Centimeters^2	Centimeters^2	0.00012	Yards^2
Yards^2	0.8361	Meters^2	Meters^2	1.196	Yards^2
Miles^2	2.59	Kilometers^2	Kilometers^2	0.3861	Miles^2
VOLUME					
Inches^3	16.387	Millimeters^3	Millimeters^3	6.1×10^{-5}	Inches^3
Inches^3	16.387	Centimeters^3	Centimeters^3	0.061	Inches^3
Feet^3	0.0283	Meters^3	Meters^3	35.33	Feet^3
Yards^3	0.7646	Meters^3	Meters^3	1.308	Yards^3
ENERGY					
Ergs	10^{-7}	Newton-meters	Newton-meters	10^7	Ergs
Joules	1	Newton-meters	Newton-meters	1	Joules
Joules	10^7	Ergs	Ergs	10^{-7}	Joules
Joules	0.2389	Calories	Calories	4.186	Joules
Joules	0.000948	Btu	Btu	1,055	Joules
Joules	0.7376	Foot-pounds	Foot-pounds	1.356	Joules
Calories	0.00397	Btu	Btu	252	Calories
Joules/see	3.41	Btu/hr	Btu/hr	0.293	Joules/see
Btu/hr	252	Calories/hr	Calories/hr	0.00397	Btu/hr
Horsepower	746	Watts	Watts	0.00134	Horsepower
F°	0.556	C°	C°	1.8	F°
°F	0.556 (°F – 32)	°C	°C	1.8 x °C + 32	°F

Table A2 Fahrenheit Degrees to Celsius Degrees Conversion[1]

F°	C°	F°	C°	F°	C°	F°	C°	F°	C°	F°	C°
212	100	170	76.7	128	53.3	86	30.0	44	6.7	2	−16.7
211	99.4	169	76.1	127	52.8	85	29.4	43	6.1	1	−17.2
210	98.9	168	75.6	126	52.2	84	28.9	42	5.6	0	−17.8
209	98.3	167	75.0	125	51.6	83	28.3	41	5.0	−1	−18.3
208	97.8	166	74.4	124	51.1	82	27.8	40	4.4	−2	−18.9
207	97.2	165	73.9	123	50.5	81	27.2	39	3.9	−3	−19.4
206	96.7	164	73.3	122	50.0	80	26.6	38	3.3	−4	−20.0
205	96.1	163	72.8	121	49.4	79	26.1	37	2.8	−5	−20.5
204	95.6	162	72.2	120	48.8	78	25.5	36	2.2	−6	−21.1
203	95.0	161	71.7	119	48.3	77	25.0	35	1.7	−7	−21.6
202	94.4	160	71.1	118	47.7	76	24.4	34	1.1	−8	−22.2
201	93.9	159	70.6	117	47.2	75	23.9	33	0.6	−9	−22.8
200	93.3	158	70.0	116	46.6	74	23.3	32	0.0	−10	−23.3
199	92.8	157	69.4	115	46.1	73	22.8	31	−0.6	−11	−23.9
198	92.2	156	68.9	114	45.5	72	22.2	30	−1.1	−12	−24.4
197	91.7	155	68.3	113	45.0	71	21.6	29	−1.7	−13	−25.0
196	91.1	154	67.8	112	44.4	70	21.1	28	−2.2	−14	−25.5
195	90.6	153	67.2	111	43.8	69	20.5	27	−2.8	−15	−26.1
194	90.0	152	66.7	110	43.3	68	20.0	26	−3.3	−16	−26.6
193	89.4	151	66.1	109	42.7	67	19.4	25	−3.9	−17	−27.2
192	88.9	150	65.6	108	42.2	66	18.9	24	−4.4	−18	−27.8
191	88.3	149	65.0	107	41.6	65	18.3	23	−5.0	−19	−28.3
190	87.8	148	64.4	106	41.1	64	17.8	22	−5.6	−20	−28.9
189	87.2	147	63.9	105	40.5	63	17.2	21	−6.1	−21	−29.4
188	86.7	146	63.3	104	40.0	62	16.7	20	−6.7	−22	−30.0
187	86.1	145	62.8	103	39.4	61	16.1	19	−7.2	−23	−30.5
186	85.6	144	62.2	102	38.9	60	15.5	18	−7.8	−24	−31.1
185	85.0	143	61.7	101	38.3	59	15.0	17	−8.3	−25	−31.6
184	84.4	142	61.1	100	37.7	58	14.4	16	−8.9	−26	−32.2
183	83.9	141	60.6	99	37.2	57	13.9	15	−9.4	−27	−32.7
182	83.3	140	60.0	98	36.6	56	13.3	14	−10.0	−28	−33.3
181	82.8	139	59.4	97	36.1	55	12.8	13	−10.5	−29	−33.9
180	82.2	138	58.9	96	35.5	54	12.2	12	−11.1	−30	−34.4
179	81.7	137	58.3	95	35.0	53	11.7	11	−11.7	−31	−35.0
178	81.1	136	57.8	94	34.4	52	11.1	10	−12.2	−32	−35.5
177	80.6	135	57.2	93	33.9	51	10.5	9	−12.8	−33	−36.1
176	80.0	134	56.7	92	33.3	50	10.0	8	−13.3	−34	−36.6
175	79.4	133	56.1	91	32.7	49	9.4	7	−13.9	−35	−37.2
174	78.9	132	55.6	90	32.2	48	8.9	6	−14.4	−36	−37.7
173	78.3	131	55.0	89	31.6	47	8.3	5	−15.0	−37	−38.3
172	77.8	130	54.4	88	31.1	46	7.8	4	−15.5	−38	−38.9
171	77.2	129	53.9	87	30.5	45	7.2	3	−16.1	−39	−39.4

[1] $°C = (°F − 32)/1.8$

Power Conversions

Table A3 Kilowatts (kW) to Horsepower (hp) Conversion[1]

HP	kW	HP	kW	HP	kW
0.1	0.13	28	37.5	64	85.8
0.2	0.27	29	38.9	65	87.2
0.3	0.40	30	40.2	66	88.5
0.4	0.54	31	41.6	67	89.8
0.5	0.67	32	42.9	68	91.2
0.6	0.80	33	44.3	69	92.5
0.7	0.94	34	45.6	70	93.9
0.8	1.07	35	46.9	71	95.2
0.9	1.21	36	48.3	72	96.6
1	1.34	37	49.6	73	97.9
2	2.68	38	51.0	74	99.2
3	4.02	39	52.3	75	101
4	5.36	40	53.6	76	102
5	6.71	41	55.0	77	103
6	8.05	42	56.3	78	105
7	9.39	43	57.7	79	106
8	10.7	44	59.0	80	107
9	12.1	45	60.3	81	109
10	13.4	46	61.7	82	110
11	14.8	47	63.0	83	111
12	16.1	48	64.4	84	113
13	17.4	49	65.7	85	114
14	18.8	50	67.1	86	115
15	20.1	51	68.4	87	117
16	21.5	52	69.7	88	118
17	22.8	53	71.1	89	119
18	24.1	54	72.4	90	121
19	25.5	55	73.8	91	122
20	26.8	56	75.1	92	123
21	28.2	57	76.4	93	125
22	29.5	58	77.8	94	126
23	30.8	59	79.1	95	127
24	32.2	60	80.5	96	129
25	33.5	61	81.8	97	130
26	34.9	62	83.1	98	131
27	36.2	63	84.5	99	133

[1] 1 kW = 1.341 hp

Table A4 Horsepower (hp) to Kilowatts (kW) Conversion[1]

HP	kW	HP	kW	HP	kW
0.1	0.07	28	20.9	64	47.7
0.2	0.15	29	21.6	65	48.5
0.3	0.22	30	22.4	66	49.2
0.4	0.30	31	23.1	67	50.0
0.5	0.37	32	23.9	68	50.7
0.6	0.45	33	24.6	69	51.5
0.7	0.52	34	25.4	70	52.2
0.8	0.60	35	26.1	71	52.9
0.9	0.67	36	26.8	72	53.7
1	0.75	37	27.6	73	54.4
2	1.49	38	28.3	74	55.2
3	2.24	39	29.1	75	55.9
4	2.98	40	29.8	76	56.7
5	3.73	41	30.6	77	57.4
6	4.47	42	31.3	78	58.2
7	5.22	43	32.1	79	58.9
8	5.97	44	32.8	80	59.7
9	6.71	45	33.6	81	60.4
10	7.46	46	34.3	82	61.1
11	8.20	47	35.0	83	61.9
12	8.95	48	35.8	84	62.6
13	9.69	49	36.5	85	63.4
14	10.4	50	37.3	86	64.1
15	11.2	51	38.0	87	64.9
16	11.9	52	38.8	88	65.6
17	12.7	53	39.5	89	66.4
18	13.4	54	40.3	90	67.1
19	14.2	55	41.0	91	67.9
20	14.9	56	41.8	92	68.6
21	15.7	57	42.5	93	69.4
22	16.4	58	43.3	94	70.1
23	17.2	59	44.0	95	70.8
24	17.9	60	44.7	96	71.6
25	18.6	61	45.5	97	72.3
26	19.4	62	46.2	98	73.1
27	20.1	63	47.0	99	73.8

[1] 1 hp = 0.7457 kW

Resistance of Copper Wire

Table A5 Resistance of Copper Wire at 77°F (25°C)

AWG	Feet/Ohm	Ohms/1,000 Feet
0000	20,000	0.050
000	15,873	0.063
00	12,658	0.079
0	10,000	0.100
1	7,936	0.126
2	6,289	0.159
3	4,975	0.201
4	3,953	0.253
5	3,135	0.319
6	2,481	0.403
7	1,968	0.508
8	1,560	0.641
9	1,238	0.808
10	980.4	1.02
11	781.3	1.28
12	617.3	1.62
13	490.2	2.04
14	387.6	2.58
15	307.7	3.25
16	244.5	4.09
17	193.8	5.16
18	153.6	6.51
19	121.8	8.21
20	96.2	10.4
21	76.3	13.1
22	60.6	16.5
23	48.1	20.8
24	38.2	26.2
25	30.3	33.0
26	24.0	41.6
27	19.0	52.5
28	15.1	66.2
29	12.0	83.4
30	9.5	105

Table A6 Resistance of Copper Wire at 149°F (65°C)

AWG	Feet/Ohm	Ohms/1,000 Feet
0000	17,544	0.057
000	13,699	0.073
00	10,870	0.092
0	8,621	0.116
1	6,849	0.146
2	5,435	0.184
3	4,310	0.232
4	3,425	0.292
5	2,710	0.369
6	2,151	0.465
7	1,706	0.586
8	1,353	0.739
9	1,073	0.932
10	847.5	1.18
11	675.7	1.48
12	534.8	1.87
13	423.7	2.36
14	336.7	2.97
15	266.7	3.75
16	211.4	4.73
17	167.8	5.96
18	133.2	7.51
19	105.5	9.48
20	84.0	11.9
21	66.2	15.1
22	52.6	19.0
23	41.7	24.0
24	33.1	30.2
25	26.2	38.1
26	20.8	48.0
27	16.5	60.6
28	13.1	76.4
29	10.4	96.3
30	8.3	121

Losses in Coaxial Cables

Table A7 Signal Loss (Attenuation) in Decibels (dB) per 100 Feet in Coaxial Cables

Signal Frequency	RG-6	RG-8X	RG-11	Cable Type RG-58	RG-174	RG-213	RF-9913	RF-9914
1 MHz	0.2 dB	0.5 dB	0.2 dB	0.4 dB	1.9 dB	0.2 dB	0.2 dB	0.3 dB
10 MHz	0.6 dB	1.0 dB	0.4 dB	1.4 dB	3.3 dB	0.6 dB	0.4 dB	0.5 dB
50 MHz	1.4 dB	2.5 dB	1.0 dB	3.3 dB	6.6 dB	1.6 dB	0.9 dB	1.1 dB
100 MHz	2.0 dB	3.6 dB	1.6 dB	4.9 dB	8.9 dB	2.2 dB	1.4 dB	1.5 dB
200 MHz	2.8 dB	5.4 dB	2.3 dB	7.3 dB	11.9 dB	3.3 dB	1.8 dB	2.0 dB
400 MHz	4.3 dB	7.9 dB	3.5 dB	11.2 dB	17.3 dB	4.8 dB	2.6 dB	2.9 dB
700 MHz	5.6 dB	11.0 dB	4.7 dB	16.9 dB	26.0 dB	6.6 dB	3.6 dB	3.8 dB
900 MHz	6.0 dB	12.6 dB	5.4 dB	20.1 dB	27.9 dB	7.7 dB	4.2 dB	4.9 dB
1 GHz	6.1 dB	13.5 dB	5.6 dB	21.5 dB	32.0 dB	8.3 dB	4.5 dB	5.3 dB
Impedance	75 ohm	50 ohm	75 ohm	50 ohm	50 ohm	50 ohm	50 ohm	50 ohm

Table A8 Signal Loss in Decibels (dB) in Coaxial Cables

Loss in Decibels (dB)	Power Ratio	Voltage Ratio
0.0	1.000	1.000
0.5	0.891	0.944
1.0	0.794	0.891
1.5	0.708	0.841
2.0	0.631	0.794
2.5	0.562	0.750
3.0	0.501	0.708
3.5	0.447	0.668
4.0	0.398	0.631
4.5	0.355	0.596
5.0	0.316	0.562
6.0	0.251	0.501
7.0	0.200	0.447
8.0	0.158	0.398
9.0	0.126	0.355
10	0.100	0.316
20	0.010	0.100
30	0.001	0.032
40	0.0001	0.010

Table A8a Cable Sizes AWG/Metric Conversion Table

AWG	Metric Equivalent mm²	Metric Cable Size mm²
20	0.52	0.75
18	0.82	1.0
16	1.32	1.5
14	2.1	2.5
12	3.3	4
10	5.32	6
8	8.5	10
6	13.5	15
4	21.3	25
2	33.7	35
1/0 (0)	53	70.0 (50.0 if current capacity not exceeded)
2/0 (00)	67.6	70
3/0 (000)	84.4	95
4/0 (0000)	107	120

*Table A9 Marine Engine DC Wiring Color Code
(Adapted from ABYC Standard E-11, Tables XIV and XV
and applicable to most marine engine installations)*

Color	Conductor Use
Green or green with yellow stripe(s)	General DC grounding
Black or yellow	General DC negative
Red	General DC positive
Yellow with red stripe	Starter switch to solenoid
Brown with yellow stripe, or yellow	Fuse or switch to blower—If DC negative is yellow, positive must be brown with yellow stripe
Dark gray	Fuse or switch to navigation lights Tachometer sender to gauge
Brown	Generator armature to regulator Auxiliary terminal to light and regulator Fuse or switch to pumps
Orange	Ammeter to alternator or generator output and accessory fuses or switches Distribution panel to accessory switch
Purple	Ignition switch to coil and electrical instruments Distribution panel to electrical instruments
Dark blue	Fuse or switch to cabin and instrument lights
Light blue	Oil-pressure sender to gauge
Tan	Water-temperature sender to gauge
Pink	Fuel-gauge sender to gauge
Green/stripe, except G/Y	Tilt and/or trim circuits

Table A10 BMEA and ISO Color Code for 240 VAC Conductors

European and UK Practice		USA Practice	
Conductor	**Colors**	**Conductor**	**Colors**
Live	Brown	Ungrounded (hot)	Black
Neutral	Light Blue	Grounded (neutral)	White
Ground(ing)/Earth	Green/Yellow	Ground(ing)/Earth	Green

Both color groups conform with ISO standards.

*Table A11 Electronic Wiring Color Code
(from the Electronic Industries Association [EIA])*

Color	Conductor Use
Black	Ground, DC negative
Blue	Transistor collector, FET drain
Brown	Filament
Gray	AC main power
Green	Transistor base, diode, FET gate
Orange	Transistor base 2
Red	DC+ power supply
Violet	DC– power supply
White	B-C minus bias supply, AVC-AGC return
Yellow	Transistor emitter, FET source

Table A12 Power Transformer Color Code

Color	Conductor Use
Black	Both leads of an untapped primary
Black	Common lead of tapped primary
Black/Yellow	Tap of tapped primary
Black/Red	End of tapped primary

Table A13 Audio Transformer Color Code

Color	Conductor Use
Black	Ground
Blue	End of primary
Brown	End of primary opposite blue
Green	End of secondary
Red	B+, center tap of push-pull loop
Yellow	Center tap of secondary

Table A14 Stereo Channel Color Code

Color	Conductor Use
White	Left channel high
Blue	Left channel low
Red	Right channel high
Green	Right channel low

Useful Electrical Formulas

Direct Current (DC)

Ohm's Law

where:

V = voltage, volts
I = current, amperes (amps)
R = resistance, ohms
P = power, watts

$$V = I \times R$$
$$= P/I$$
$$= (P \times R)^{1/2}$$

$$I = V/R$$
$$= P/V$$
$$= (P/R)^{1/2}$$

$$R = V/I$$
$$= P/I^2$$

$$P = I^2 \times R$$
$$= V \times I$$
$$= V^2/R$$

Resistors

In Series: $R = R_1 + R_2 + R_3 + \ldots$
In Parallel: $R = 1/(1/R_1 + 1/R_2 + 1/R_3 + \ldots)$

Capacitors

In Parallel: $C = C_1 + C_2 + C_3 + \ldots$
In Series: $C = 1/(1/C_1 + 1/C_2 + 1/C_3 + \ldots)$
Charge (coulombs) = C(farads) $\times V$

Alternating Current (AC)

Ohm's Law

where:

V = voltage, volts
I = current, amperes (amps)
Z = impedance, ohms
P = power, watts
q = phase angle

$$V = I \times Z$$
$$= P/(I \times \cos q)$$
$$= (P \times Z/\cos q)^{1/2}$$

$$I = V/Z$$
$$= P/(V \times \cos q)$$
$$= P/(Z \times \cos q)^{1/2}$$

$$Z = V/I$$
$$= P/(I^2 \times \cos q)$$

$$P = I^2 \times Z \times \cos q$$
$$= V \times I \times \cos q$$
$$= V^2 \times \cos q/Z$$

Reactance

where:

X_L = reactance of an inductor, ohms
X_C = reactance of a capacitor, ohms
H = inductance, henrys
C = capacitance, farads
F = frequency, Hertz
π = 3.14

$$X_L = 2\pi \times F \times H$$
$$X_C = 1/(2\pi \times F \times C)$$

Impedance

In Series: $Z = [R^2 + (XL - XC)^2]^{1/2}$
In Parallel: $Z = R \times X/(R^2 + X^2)^{1/2}$

Power Factor, pf

$$pf = \text{True power/Apparent power}$$
$$= \cos\theta$$
$$= P/(V \times I)$$
$$= R/Z$$

Resistors are generally too small to allow the imprinting of identifying information. For this reason standard resistors are coded with color bands.

Figure A1 and Table A15 demystify the color code. *Example:* What is the resistance of a resistor with brown, red, orange, and silver bands? *Answer:* 12,000 ±10% Ω.

Fig. A1 The Markings on Resistors

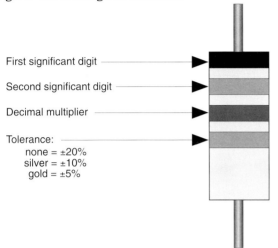

First significant digit

Second significant digit

Decimal multiplier

Tolerance:
   none = ±20%
   silver = ±10%
   gold = ±5%

Table A15 Resistor Color Codes

Band Color	Digit	Power of 10	Decimal Multiplier
Silver		10^{-2}	0.01
Gold		10^{-1}	0.1
Black	0	10^{0}	1
Brown	1	10^{1}	10
Red	2	10^{2}	100
Orange	3	10^{3}	1,000
Yellow	4	10^{4}	10,000
Green	5	10^{5}	100,000
Blue	6	10^{6}	1,000,000
Violet	7	10^{7}	10,000,000
Gray	8	10^{8}	100,000,000
White	9	10^{9}	1,000,000,000

Table A16 Standard Resistance Values in Ohms

Bold values available only in ±10% tolerance. All other values available in ±5% tolerance. Values beginning with 10, 15, 22, 33, 47, and 68 also available in ±20% tolerance.

First Band	Second Band	Gold	Black	Brown	Third Band Red	Orange	Yellow	Green	Blue
Brown	Black	1.0	10	100	1,000	10,000	100,000	1,000,000	10,000,000
Brown	**Brown**	**1.1**	**11**	**110**	**1,100**	**11,000**	**110,000**	**1,100,000**	**11,000,000**
Brown	Red	1.2	12	120	1,200	12,000	120,000	1,200,000	12,000,000
Brown	**Orange**	**1.3**	**13**	**130**	**1,300**	**13,000**	**130,000**	**1,300,000**	**13,000,000**
Brown	Green	1.5	15	150	1,500	15,000	150,000	1,500,000	15,000,000
Brown	**Blue**	**1.6**	**16**	**160**	**1,600**	**16,000**	**160,000**	**1,600,000**	**16,000,000**
Brown	Gray	1.8	18	180	1,800	18,000	180,000	1,800,000	18,000,000
Red	Black	2.0	20	200	2,000	20,000	200,000	2,000,000	20,000,000
Red	Red	2.2	22	220	2,200	22,000	220,000	2,200,000	22,000,000
Red	Yellow	2.4	24	240	2,400	24,000	240,000	2,400,000	
Red	Violet	2.7	27	270	2,700	27,000	270,000	2,700,000	
Orange	Black	3.0	30	300	3,000	30,000	300,000	3,000,000	
Orange	Orange	3.3	33	330	3,300	33,000	330,000	3,000,000	
Orange	**Blue**	**3.6**	**36**	**360**	**3,600**	**36,000**	**360,000**	**3,600,000**	
Orange	White	3.9	39	390	3,900	39,000	390,000	3,900,000	
Yellow	**Orange**	**4.3**	**43**	**430**	**4,300**	**43,000**	**430,000**	**4,300,000**	
Yellow	Violet	4.7	47	470	4,700	47,000	470,000	4,700,000	
Green	**Brown**	**5.1**	**51**	**510**	**5,100**	**51,000**	**510,000**	**5,100,000**	
Green	Blue	5.6	56	560	5,600	56,000	560,000	5,600,000	
Blue	**Red**	**6.2**	**62**	**620**	**6,200**	**62,000**	**620,000**	**6,200,000**	
Blue	Gray	6.8	68	680	6,800	68,000	680,000	6,800,000	
Violet	**Green**	**7.5**	**75**	**750**	**7,500**	**75,000**	**750,000**	**7,500,000**	
Gray	Red	8.2	82	820	8,200	82,000	820,000	8,200,000	
White	**Brown**	**9.1**	**91**	**910**	**9,100**	**91,000**	**910,000**	**9,100,000**	

Identifying Capacitors

Large capacitors, such as electrolytics, have their values printed plainly on them, but small disk and film capacitors usually display just two or three code numbers.

Most will have three characters, where the first two are the first and second significant digits and the third is a multiplier code. Unless a different unit is specified, the units are assumed pico (10^{-12}) farads. Table A17 shows the multipliers.

In addition there may be a fourth character (letter) indicating tolerance (see Table A18).

Finally there may be a number-letter-number code for temperature coefficient (see Table A19).

Table A20, at bottom, shows the capacitance value markings for capacitors manufactured in Europe.

Fig. A2 The Markings on Capacitors

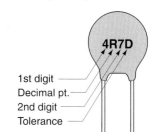

FOR VALUES 10 pF
Example: 0.01µF ±20%

- Tolerance
- Zeroes
- 2nd digit
- 1st digit

FOR VALUES < 10 pF
Example: 4.7 pF ±0.5%

- 1st digit
- Decimal pt.
- 2nd digit
- Tolerance

Table A17
Capacitor Value

Digit 3	Multiplier
0	1
1	10
2	100
3	1,000
4	10,000
5	100,000
6	one
7	none
8	0.01
9	0.1

Table A18
Capacitor Tolerance

Code	Tolerance
B	±0.1 pF
C	±0.25 pF
D	±0.5 pF
E	±0.25%
F	±1%
G	±2%
H	±2.5%
J	±5%
K	±10%
M	±20%

Table A19 Capacitor Temperature Coefficients

First (letter)	Min. °C	Second (number)	Max. °C	Third (letter)	Change w/temp
Z	+10	2	+45	A	+1.0%
Y	−30	4	+65	B	±1.5%
X	−55	5	+85	C	±2.2%
–	–	6	+105	D	±3.3%
–	–	7	+125	E	±4.7%
–	–	–	–	F	±7.5%
–	–	–	–	P	±10.0%
–	–	–	–	R	±15.0%
–	–	–	–	S	±22.0%
–	–	–	–	T	+22%, −33%
–	–	–	–	U	+22%, −56%
–	–	–	–	V	+22%, −82%

Table A20 European Capacitance Value Code

pF	Code	pF	Code	pF	Code	pF	Code	µF	Code	µF	Code	µF	Code
1.0	1p0	10	10p	100	n10	1,000	1n0	0.010	10n	0.10	100n	1.0	1m0
1.2	1p2	12	12p	120	n12	1,200	1n2	0.012	12n	0.12	120n	1.2	1m2
1.5	1p3	15	15p	150	n15	1,500	1n5	0.015	15n	0.15	150n	1.5	1m3
1.8	1p8	18	18p	180	n18	1,800	1n8	0.018	18n	0.18	180n	1.8	1m8
2.2	2p2	22	22p	220	n22	2,200	2n2	0.022	22n	0.22	220n	2.2	2m2
2.7	2p7	27	27p	270	n27	2,700	2n7	0.027	27n	0.27	270n	2.7	2m7
3.3	3p3	33	33p	330	n33	3,300	3n3	0.033	33n	0.33	330n	3.3	3m3
3.9	3p9	39	39p	390	n39	3,900	3n9	0.039	39n	0.39	390n	3.9	3m9
4.7	4p7	47	47p	470	n47	4,700	4n7	0.047	47n	0.47	470n	4.7	4m7
5.6	5p6	56	56p	560	n56	5,600	5n6	0.056	56n	0.56	560n	5.6	5m6
6.8	6p8	68	68p	680	n68	6,800	6n8	0.068	68n	0.68	680n	6.8	6m8
8.2	8p2	82	82p	820	n82	8,200	8n2	0.082	82n	0.82	820n	8.2	8m2

Schematic Distribution Diagrams

Table A21 Engine and DC Power Distribution

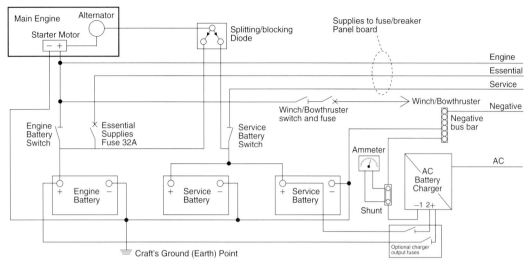

Table A22 DC Power Distribution

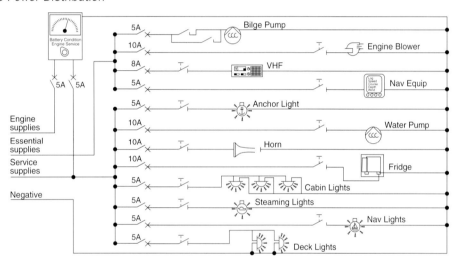

Table A23 AC Power Distribution

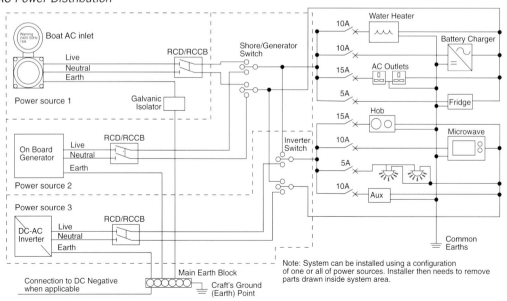

Note: System can be installed using a configuration of one or all of power sources. Installer then needs to remove parts drawn inside system area.

Glossary

Absorbed glass mat (AGM) battery: sealed battery in which the electrolyte is held in a fiberglass felt like a sponge.

AC grounded conductor: a current-carrying conductor that is intentionally maintained at ground potential. This is also known as the neutral conductor.

AC grounding conductor (green or green w/yellow stripe): a protective conductor, which does not normally carry current, used to connect the metallic, non-current-carrying parts of electrical equipment to the AC grounding system and engine negative terminal, or its bus, and to the shore AC grounding conductor through the shore-power cable.

Air terminal: a device at the uppermost point of the lightning protection system to dissipate the charge or start the lightning ground process.

Alternating current (AC): current that periodically reverses direction.

Alternator: a generator that produces an alternating current. In an automotive or marine alternator, the alternating current (AC) is changed to direct current (DC) by internal diodes.

Ammeter: a meter connected in series with a circuit that measures the current flowing through the circuit.

Ampere: the unit of measure for electric current that equals 1 coulomb (6.24×10^{18}) of electrons per second.

Ampere-hour: a current flow of 1 ampere for 1 hour; a measure of the electrical energy stored in a battery.

Amphoteric: capable of reacting chemically with an acid or a base. Aluminum is amphoteric, and highly susceptible to corrosion when overprotected.

Anode (galvanic mode): the electrode of an electrochemical cell with the more negative potential. The less noble metal of an electrolytic cell that tends to corrode.

Antenna: a conductor whose purpose is to transmit and/or receive radio waves.

Antenna gain: the ratio of power radiated in a desired direction to that radiated at right angles to that direction; measured in decibels (dB).

Armature: the windings in a generator that rotate.

Atom: the smallest quantity into which a chemical element can be divided and still maintain all of the qualities of that element.

Battery: a chemical apparatus that maintains a voltage between its terminals.

Battery bank: two or more storage batteries connected in series to provide higher voltage, or in parallel to provide increased capacity.

Battery charger: a device designed primarily to charge and maintain a battery, or batteries, supplying DC loads.

Battery cold cranking performance rating: the discharge load in amperes that a battery at 0°F (−17.8°C) can deliver for 30 seconds and maintain a voltage of 1.2 volts per cell or higher.

Battery isolation switch: a switch in line with the battery whose purpose is to connect or disconnect the battery.

Battery reserve capacity: the number of minutes a new fully charged battery at 80°F (26.7°C) can be continuously discharged at 25 amperes and maintain a voltage of 1.75 volts or higher per cell (10.5 volts for a 12-volt battery or 5.25 volts for a 6-volt battery).

Bleeder resistor: a resistor in the output of a power supply that removes the output voltage after the power supply is turned off.

Blocking diode: a diode that allows the charging of multiple batteries from a single source without allowing current flow between the batteries.

Bonding: the electrical connection of the exposed, metallic, non-current-carrying parts to the ground (negative) side of the direct current system.

Bonding conductor: a normally non-current-carrying conductor used to connect the non-current-carrying metal parts of direct current devices on the boat to the boat's bonding system.

Branch: a current path in a circuit.

Bulk charge: the stage of battery charging usually defined between 50% and 75 to 80% of battery capacity.

Bus bar: a heavy copper bar or strap in circuit panel boxes carrying current to all of the terminals.

Capacitance: the electrical size of a capacitor in farads. Equal to the amount of charge stored divided by the voltage across the capacitor.

Capacitor: a device that stores electrostatic charge when a voltage is applied.

Cathode: the electrode of an electrochemical cell with the more positive potential. The more noble metal of an electrochemical cell that tends not to corrode.

Cathodic bonding: the electrical interconnection of metal objects in common contact with water, to the engine negative terminal, or its bus, and to the source of cathodic protection.

Cathodic disbondment: the destruction of adhesion between a coating and its substrate by products of a cathodic reaction.

Cathodic protection: reduction or prevention of corrosion of a metal by making it cathodic by the use of sacrificial anodes or impressed currents.

Cell: the smallest unit of a battery. Also an electrochemical system consisting of an anode and a cathode immersed in an electrolyte. The anode and cathode may be separate metals or dissimilar areas on the same metal. The cell includes the external circuit that permits the flow of electrons between the anode and the cathode.

Chassis: the metal structure that supports the circuits and components of a piece of electronic equipment.

Choke: an inductor placed in series in a circuit to oppose changes in current.

Circuit: a complete electrical path from one terminal to the other of a voltage source.

Circuit breaker: an automatic switch that opens when current exceeds the specified limit.

Coaxial cable: a two-conductor cable where the center conductor is surrounded by an insulating dielectric layer, a conducting shield, and an outside insulating sheath.

Coil: turns of wire that have inductance.

Cold cranking amps (CCA): the current in amps that a battery can deliver at 0°F for 30 seconds at a voltage of 1.2 volts minimum (7.2 volts for a 12-volt battery).

Common bonding conductor: an electrical conductor, usually running fore and aft, to which all equipment bonding conductors are connected.

Conductance: a measure of the ability to carry current. The inverse of resistance.

Conductor: any material having little electrical resistance.

Conduit: a pipe, either conducting or nonconducting, in which conductors are run.

Continuity: an uninterrupted electrically conducting path.

Corrosion: the deterioration of a metal by chemical and electrochemical reaction with its environment.

Corrosion controller: an automatic or manually operated device, in a controlled or regulated cathodic protection system, to regulate the flow of electric current for corrosion control.

Corrosion monitor: an installed hull potential meter (voltmeter) capable of measuring the voltage difference between a reference electrode and a metal hull, or cathodic bonding system, when they are immersed in the same electrolyte.

Coulomb: the unit of measurement of electrical charge. One coulomb equals 6.24×10^{18} electrons.

Couple: two dissimilar metals or alloys in electrical contact with each other that have different potentials and become anodes or cathodes when in common contact with an electrolyte. A couple may also be formed on the surface of the same metal.

Cranking performance (also referred to as marine cranking amps @ 32°F): the discharge loads, in amperes, that a new, fully charged battery at 32°F (0°C) can continuously deliver for 30 seconds, and maintain a terminal voltage equal to or higher than 1.2 volts per cell.

Current: the flow of electrons through a material.

Current density: for corrosion purposes the current per unit area of the anodes or cathodes expressed in milliamperes per square foot.

Cycle: a complete oscillation of voltage and/or current, from plus to minus and back to plus.

DC grounded conductor: a current-carrying conductor connected to the side of the power source that is intentionally maintained at boat ground potential.

DC grounding conductor: a normally non-current-carrying conductor used to connect metallic non-current-carrying parts of direct current devices to the engine negative terminal, or its bus, for the purpose of minimizing stray-current corrosion.

Deep cycle battery: a lead-acid battery having thicker plates in order to withstand repetitive deep charge/discharge cycles.

Dezincification: a corrosion phenomenon resulting in the selective removal of zinc from copper-zinc alloys.

Dielectric: a material with high electrical resistance.

Dielectric shield: in a cathodic protection system, an electrically nonconductive material, such as a coating, or plastic sheet, that is placed between an anode and an adjacent cathode to avoid current wastage and to improve current distribution to the cathode.

Diode: a semiconductor that allows current flow in one direction but not the opposite direction.

Direct current (DC): current that flows in one direction.

Double-insulation system: an insulation system comprised of basic insulation and supplementary insulation, with the two insulations physically separated and so arranged that they are not simultaneously subjected to the same deteriorating influences (temperature, contaminants, and the like) to the same degree.

Double-pole switch: a switch having two sets of contacts, allowing two conductors to be switched simultaneously.

Drip loop: a dip in a wire or cable to interrupt the flow of water along the run.

Driving potential: voltage difference between the anode and the cathode of a couple.

Earth ground: a point that is at the same potential or voltage as the local earth.

Electrode: a conductive material, in an electrolyte, through which electrical current enters or leaves.

Electrolysis: chemical changes in a solution or electrolyte due to the passage of electric current. This term is also loosely applied to corrosion processes. However, since the term refers to solution phenomena, not to corrosion, its use to indicate corrosion should be discouraged.

Electrolyte: a liquid in which ions are capable of migrating. A liquid capable of conducting a current. Solutions of acids, bases, and salts in water are electrolytes.

Electromagnet: a magnet formed by wrapping wire around an iron core.

Electron: one of the subatomic particles with negative charge that surround the nucleus of an atom and determine its chemical properties.

Energy: the ability to do work. The unit joule equals 1 watt for 1 second.

Engine negative terminal: the point on the engine at which the negative battery cable is connected.

Equalization bus: a metallic strap, which may be installed on the interior of a boat, substantially parallel to the exterior lightning ground plate, and connected to the lightning ground plate at both ends. Secondary lightning conductors can be connected to the equalization bus. The equalization bus provides a low-resistance path to the lightning ground plate.

Glossary

Equalization charge: charging a lead-acid battery at a voltage sufficient to cause rapid gassing, the purpose being the conversion of crystalline lead sulfate on the plates back to lead and sulfuric acid.

Equipment housing: the outside shell of equipment supplied by the manufacturer of the device, or a box, shell, or enclosure provided by the equipment installer. This shell provides personnel protection from electrical hazards, burns, rotating machinery, sharp edges, and provides protection to the device from mechanical damage or weather.

Excitation: a voltage applied to the field winding of a generator in order to initiate charging.

Excitation winding: a separate, small winding in the stator of brushless alternators to initiate charging.

Farad: the unit of capacitance. The size of a capacitor is 1 farad when it stores 1 coulomb of charge with 1 volt across its terminals.

Field winding: a coil of wire used to generate a magnetic field in a generator or alternator.

Filament: the high-resistance wire in a lamp that glows white-hot to produce light.

Filter: an electrical circuit containing reactive elements that passes certain frequencies and blocks others.

Flashing a field: applying an external DC voltage momentarily to a field coil.

Float charge: the voltage that will just maintain a battery at full charge without overcharging.

Fuse: a conductive device that melts and breaks the circuit when current flow exceeds the rated amount.

Galvanic corrosion: the corrosion that occurs at the anode of a galvanic couple caused by the flow of ions (galvanic current) from the anode to the cathode through an electrolyte.

Galvanic couple: two dissimilar metals in electrical contact in an electrolyte.

Galvanic current: the electric current that flows between metals or conductive nonmetals in a galvanic couple.

Galvanic isolator: a device installed in series with the grounding (green or green w/yellow stripe) conductor of the shore-power cable to block low-voltage DC galvanic current flow, but permit the passage of alternating current normally associated with the grounding (green or green w/yellow stripe) conductor.

Galvanic series: a list of metals and alloys arranged in order of their potentials as measured in relation to a reference electrode when immersed in seawater. The table of potentials is arranged with the anodic or least noble metals at one end and the cathodic or most noble metals at the other.

Gassing: the generation of hydrogen and oxygen when a lead-acid battery is overcharged.

Generator: a machine that produces AC electricity when its coils are spun inside a magnetic field.

Giga (G): prefix meaning 10^9 or 1 billion.

Grid: one of the lead-alloy frames that conduct current to and support the active material in a lead-acid battery.

Ground: a surface or mass at the potential of the earth's surface, established at this potential by a conducting connection (intentional or accidental) with the earth, including any metal area that forms part of the wetted surface of the hull.

Grounded conductor: a current-carrying conductor that is connected to the side of the source that is intentionally maintained at ground potential.

Ground fault: an unintended leak of current to ground.

Ground fault circuit interrupter (GFCI): a device intended for the protection of personnel that functions to deenergize a circuit or portion thereof within an established period of time when a current to ground exceeds some predetermined value that is less than that required to operate the overcurrent protective device of the supply circuit. A circuit breaker that acts to interrupt current flow whenever its current limit is exceeded or a ground fault leak is detected.

Ground fault protector (GFP): a device intended to protect equipment by interrupting the electric current to the load when a fault current to ground exceeds some predetermined value that is less than that required to operate the overcurrent protection device of that supply circuit.

Grounding conductor (Earth): a conductor not normally carrying current provided to connect the exposed metal enclosures of electric equipment to ground, the primary function of which is to minimize shock hazard to personnel.

Half cell (reference electrode): one electrode in an electrochemical cell used as a reference for measuring the potentials of other metals.

Heat-shrink tubing: an insulating sleeve that shrinks dramatically when heated.

Henry (H): the unit of inductance. A 1-henry coil produces 1 volt when the rate of change of current through it is 1 ampere per second.

Hertz: frequency unit of 1 cycle per second.

Horsepower: a measure of power equaling 746 watts.

Hot: any wire or point in a circuit that is not at ground voltage. (See live)

Hull potential: the composite potential (voltage) of the hull cathodic surfaces in an electrolyte as measured against a referenced electrode.

Hydrometer: an instrument for determining the specific gravity (density) of liquids—specifically the electrolyte in a lead-acid battery.

Ignition protection: the design and construction of a device such that under design operating conditions:

- it will not ignite a flammable hydrocarbon mixture surrounding the device when an ignition source causes an internal explosion, or

- it is incapable of releasing sufficient electrical or thermal energy to ignite a hydrocarbon mixture, or
- the source of the ignition is hermetically sealed.

Impedance: the resistance to current flow in an AC circuit.

Impressed current system: a cathodic protection system that utilizes a direct current source (usually with battery) to attain the required millivolt shift in the metallic parts to be protected.

Incandescent lamp: a lamp in which the light is produced by current flow through a filament.

Inductance: measure of the back voltage produced in a coil when current is changing. Unit is the henry.

Induction motor: an AC motor where the rotor is driven by the rotating magnetic field in the stator.

Insulator: any material that is used because of its great electrical resistance.

Interference: unwanted electrical signals superimposed on the desired signal.

Inverter: an electrical device that converts DC power to AC power.

Ion: an electrically charged atom or group of atoms. A form of current flow in liquids and wet wood.

Isolation transformer: a transformer in which power is transferred from primary (input) to secondary (output) coils magnetically without any conductive path.

Isolator: a device installed in series with the grounding (green) conductor of the shore-power cable to effectively block galvanic current (direct current [DC]) flow but permit the passage of alternating current (AC) to provide a path for ground fault currents.

Kilo (k): prefix meaning 10^3 or 1,000.

Leakage resistance: the resistance (usually very high) across a device that is ideally a nonconductor.

Life cycles: the number of charge/discharge cycles a battery can withstand before it loses 50% of its capacity.

Lightning bonding conductor: a conductor intended to be used for potential equalization between metal bodies and the lightning protection system to eliminate the potential for side flashes.

Lightning ground plate (or strip): a metallic plate or strip on the hull exterior below the waterline that serves to efficiently transfer the lightning current from the system of down-conductors to the water.

Lightning protective gap (air gap): a form of lightning arrestor wherein a small air space is provided between two metallic plates, with one connected directly to the vessel grounding plate or strip, and the other to an operating electrical system, such as a radio transmitter or receiver.

Lightning protective mast: a conductive structure, or if nonconductive, equipped with a conductive means and an air terminal.

Live: having a non-zero electrical potential. (See hot)

Load: any device in a circuit that dissipates power.

Load test: a battery test wherein a high current is withdrawn for a short period.

Main down-conductor: the primary lightning conductor from the top of the mast to the lightning ground. ABYC Standard E4 calls for a minimum conductivity equal to that of a 4 AWG copper conductor.

Mega (M): prefix meaning 10^6 or 1 million.

Metal oxide varistor (MOV): a semiconductor device that is normally nonconductive, but which shorts to ground when struck by a high voltage such as lightning.

Micro (μ): prefix meaning 10^{-6} or one millionth.

Milli (m): prefix meaning 10^{-3} or one thousandth.

Nano (n): prefix meaning 10^{-9} or one billionth.

Negative ion: an atom with one or more extra electrons.

Noble: the positive direction of electrode electrical potential relative to other material in the galvanic series.

Noise: an unwanted electrical signal; also known as interference.

Ohm: the unit of electrical resistance.

Ohmmeter: a device that measures electrical resistance.

Ohm's Law: the mathematical relationship between current through and voltage across an element of a circuit.

Open circuit: a break in a circuit path that prevents the flow of current.

Open-circuit potential: the potential of an electrode measured with respect to a reference electrode or another electrode when no current flows to or from it.

Overcurrent protection device: a device, such as a fuse or circuit breaker, designed to interrupt the circuit when the current flow exceeds a predetermined value.

Panelboard: an assembly of devices for the purpose of controlling and/or distributing power on a boat. It includes devices such as circuit breakers, fuses, switches, instruments, and indicators. Also known as circuit board or control panel.

Parallel circuit: a circuit in which there is more than one path through which current can flow.

Parallel path: a path to ground that may be followed by a lightning strike. This path is separate from the path formed by the primary lightning conductor.

Passivation: the formation of a protective oxide film, either naturally or by chemical treatment, on certain active-passive metals like stainless steels.

pH: an expression of hydrogen-ion activity, of both acidity and alkalinity, on a scale whose values run from 0 to 14 with 7 representing neutrality.

Pico (p): prefix meaning 10^{-12} or one million millionth.

Glossary

Points: metal contacts designed to make and break electrical circuits.

Polarity: the sign (+ or −) of a voltage.

Polarity indicator: a device (usually a lamp) that indicates whether shore-power leads are connected properly (hot to hot, neutral to neutral) or are reversed.

Polarization: the deviation from the open-circuit potential of an electrode resulting from the passage of current, such as from anodes and impressed current systems.

Polarized system AC: a system in which the grounded and ungrounded conductors are connected in the same relation to terminals or leads on devices in the circuit.

Polarized system DC: a system in which the grounded (negative) and ungrounded (positive) conductors are connected in the same relation to terminals or leads on devices in the circuit.

Positive ion: an atom that has lost one or more electrons.

Potential difference: the force that causes electrons and other charged objects to move. Same as electromotive force and voltage.

Potentiometer: a variable resistor with a sliding contact whereby the output voltage can be varied from zero to full input voltage.

Power: the rate at which energy is used or converted. The unit, watt, equals 1 ampere through times 1 volt across.

Power supply: a voltage source, not a battery, that supplies current at a fixed voltage to a circuit.

Primary lightning conductor: the main vertical electrical path in a lightning protection system formed by a metallic mast, metallic structure, electrical conductors, or other conducting means, to a ground plate, ground strip, or a metallic hull.

Primary winding: the input winding of a transformer.

RCD (Residual Current Device): see Ground fault circuit interrupter.

Readily accessible: capable of being reached quickly and safely for effective use under emergency conditions without the use of tools.

Rectifier diode: a high-current semiconductor device that allows current flow only in one direction.

Reference electrode: a metal and metallic-salt (e.g., a silver-silver chloride half cell) mixture in solution that will develop and maintain an accurate reference potential to which the potential of other metals immersed in the same electrolyte may be compared.

Reference potential: the voltage difference between a reference electrode and a metal when they are immersed in the same electrolyte.

Relay: an electromechanical switch in which a small input current switches a much higher output current.

Reserve capacity: the number of minutes a 12-volt battery at 80°F will deliver 25 amps before its voltage drops below 10.5 volts.

Residual magnetism: the magnetic field remaining in a core after current in the field winding ceases.

Resistance: opposition to electric current. The unit is the ohm, which equates to a voltage drop of 1 volt across a device through which 1 ampere of current is flowing.

Reverse polarity: a situation in which positive and negative conductors or terminals are reversed.

Rheostat: a variable resistor.

Ripple: AC voltage superimposed on a DC voltage.

Sacrificial anode: a less noble metal intentionally connected to form a galvanic cell with a more noble metal for the purpose of protecting the more noble metal from corroding.

Screening: sheet metal or metal screening placed around electronic equipment to shunt electrical noise to ground.

Secondary lightning conductor: a conductor used to connect potential parallel paths, such as the rigging on a sailboat, to the primary lightning conductor, or to the lightning ground plate, strip, or equalization bus.

Secondary winding: an output winding of a transformer.

Self-discharge: the gradual discharge of a battery not connected to a load due to leakage between its terminals.

Self-limiting: a device whose maximum output is restricted to a specified value by its magnetic and electrical characteristics.

Self-limiting battery charger: battery chargers in which the output remains at a value that will not damage the charger after application of a short circuit at the DC output terminals for a period of 15 days.

Separator: nonconductive material that separates the plates of a battery.

Series circuit: a circuit having only one path through which current can flow.

Shaft brush: a carbon or metalized graphite block that makes electrical contact to a rotating, or otherwise moving, shaft in order to improve electrical contact to the cathodic bonding system.

Sheath: a material used as a continuous protective covering, such as overlapping electrical tape, woven sleeving, molded rubber, molded plastic, loom, or flexible tubing, around one or more insulated conductors.

Shielding: an electrically conductive sheath or tube surrounding conductors and connected to ground in order to protect the conductors from noise.

Shore-power inlet: the fitting designed for mounting on the boat, of a reverse-service type, requiring a female connector on the shore-power cable in order to make the electrical connection.

Short circuit: a path, usually accidental, with little or no electrical resistance.

Shunt: a conductor of known resistance placed in series with a circuit to indicate current flow by measurement of the voltage drop across this conductor.

Side flash: an arc-over discharge that occurs from the lightning system to any metallic object.

Signal-to-noise ratio (SNR): the power ratio between a signal (meaningful information) and noise (meaningless).

Sine wave: the shape of a graph of voltage versus time in an AC signal. All rotary generators produce this waveform.

Slip rings: one or more continuous conducting rings that mate to shaft brushes to provide electrical contact to rotating, or otherwise moving, shafts in order to improve electrical contact to the cathodic bonding system.

Slow-blow fuse: a fuse that allows motor start-up currents in excess of its rating for a short time.

Solenoid: a relay used to switch heavy currents such as those in a starter motor.

Specific gravity: the ratio of the density of a material to the density of water. In a lead-acid battery, the specific gravity of the electrolyte is a measure of the battery's state of charge.

Spike: a high voltage peak superimposed on a DC voltage.

Stator: the stationary armature of an alternator inside of which the rotor turns.

Storage battery: a group of cells permanently electrically interconnected, and contained in a case.

Stray-current corrosion: corrosion that results when a current from a battery or other external electrical (DC) source causes a metal in contact with an electrolyte to become anodic with respect to another metal in contact with the same electrolyte.

Sulfation: the crystallization of the lead sulfate of a lead-acid battery plate, which occurs when the battery is left discharged. It hinders the battery reactions and thus reduces battery capacity.

Surge: a voltage and/or current spike.

Surge protector: a solid-state device that shunts (conducts) surges to ground.

Switch: a device used to open and close circuits.

Switchboard: an assembly of devices for the purpose of controlling and/or distributing power on a boat. It may include devices such as circuit breakers, fuses, switches, instruments, and indicators. They are generally accessible from the rear as well as from the front and are not intended to be installed in cabinets.

Tails (or Pigtails): external conductors that originate within an electrical component or appliance installed by their manufacturer.

Terminal: a point of connection to an electrical device.

Thermistor: a solid-state device whose resistance varies strongly with temperature.

Tie-wrap: plastic strap for bundling conductors and cables.

Tinning: coating a wire or terminal with solder in order to prevent corrosion or to facilitate a solder connection.

Transformer, isolation: a transformer meeting the requirements of E-11.9.1 installed in the shore-power supply circuit on a boat to electrically isolate all AC system conductors, including the AC grounding conductor (green) on the boat, from the AC system conductors of the shore-power supply.

Transformer, polarization: an isolated winding transformer, i.e., a "dry type," encapsulated lighting transformer, installed in the shore-power supply circuit on the boat to electrically isolate the normally current-carrying AC system conductors, but not the AC grounding conductor (green) from the normally current-carrying conductors of the shore-power supply.

Transient voltage surge suppressor (TVSS): a semiconductor device designed to provide protection against voltage and current spikes.

Trickle charge: a continuous low-current charge.

Trip-free circuit breaker: a resettable overcurrent protection device designed so that the means of resetting cannot override the current interrupting mechanism.

Ungrounded conductor: a current-carrying conductor that is completely insulated from ground and connects the source of power to the utilization equipment. In direct current systems (DC), this conductor will be connected to the positive terminal of the battery. In alternating current systems (AC), this conductor will be connected to the "live" side of the shore-power system, or to the appropriate terminal of an onboard auxiliary generator.

Volt (V): the unit of voltage or potential difference.

Voltage drop: reduction in voltage along a conductor due to the current carried and the finite resistance of the conductor.

Voltage source: a device that supplies the voltage to a circuit.

Voltmeter: device for measuring voltage or potential difference between two points of a circuit.

Watertight: so constructed that moisture will not enter the enclosure.

Watt (W): unit of measurement of power. One watt is 1 ampere through times 1 volt across.

Wavelength: the distance between identical phases of two successive waves, usually from peak to peak or from zero-crossing to zero-crossing.

Weatherproof: constructed or protected so that exposure to the weather will not interfere with successful operation.

Windings: coils of current-carrying wire in a generator, motor, or transformer.

Zone of protection: an essentially cone-shaped space below a grounded air terminal, mast, or overhead ground wire, wherein the risk of a direct lightning strike is substantially reduced.

Index

A

absorbed-glass mat (AGM) batteries, 40–41
absorption cycle, 36, 37, 59, 60, 138
ABYC. *See* American Boat and Yacht Council (ABYC)
air terminals, 77
alternating current (AC). *See also* circuits, AC
    AC standards, 145–46
    advantages of, 129, 130
    budget, figuring, 131–34
    color codes for conductors, 121, 126, 155, 163
    converting to DC, 123
    equivalent DC voltage, 116–17
    frequency, 116, 118
    frequency meters, 143, 234
    grounding, 120, 121, 148, 164–66
    impedance, 118, 124
    measurement of, 124–25
    Ohm's Law, 116
    phase, 50–51, 115, 116–17, 118
    polarity indicators, 149, 233
    polarity testing, 127
    power factor, 115, 118
    production of, 50–51
    rectification, 52–54
    resistance component of impedance, 124
    safety, 115, 119–20, 145
    short circuits, 120
    sources, 130
    voltage, 116–17, 124
alternators. *See also* voltage regulators
    belts, 63
    charging setups, 61–62
    DC output from, 52–54
    excite circuits, 58, 69
    galley alternator, 50
    installation, 63
    matching to load, 43, 49
    operation of, 49, 50–56
    pulley alignment, 63
    rotors and brushes, 55
    troubleshooting, 64–69
    types of, 57
alternator-type generators, 140
aluminum, 89
American Boat and Yacht Council (ABYC) standards
    batteries, 46
    bonding systems, 86
    cathodic protection, 87, 91
    galvanic isolators, 166

    ignition protection, 110–13
    Standards for Small Craft, 1
    wiring, 93, 145–46
    wiring connections, 107
ammeters, 16, 18, 19, 125, 228
ampacity, 97, 98, 145, 146, 148, 155–61
amperage rating, 97, 99
ampere-hours, 32
amperes, 5, 8–12, 131
amplifiers, 245
analog test instruments, 15, 16–18, 19, 228
anchor lights, 186, 239
antenna cable and connectors, 212–15
antennas
    installation, 209
    lightning protection systems, 77, 78
    location, 210–11
    types of, 210, 216
appliances
    AC versus DC, 130
    conservation conversions, 180
    load calculation, 38–39, 131–34, 150–53
armature-type generators, 140, 141
attenuation, 108, 212

B

backstay insulators, 210, 211, 217
batteries
    ABYC standards, 46
    battery banks, 44
    chemical reactions, 28–30
    composition of, 28–29, 30
    costs of, 42–43
    dimensions, 40
    discharge, depth of, 42–43
    discharging, 7, 27, 29, 30, 34–35
    electrical model, 31
    fully discharged, 29, 33
    galley battery, 28
    installation, 27, 46
    life cycles of, 42
    loads and, 38–39, 44
    monitoring, 27, 32–33, 236–38
    parallel connections, 7, 27, 44
    phases of, 29–30
    self-discharging, 31, 33
    series connections, 7, 27, 44
    shedding, 30, 138
    sizes, 27, 40, 42, 44
    specifications, 35
    sulfation, 30, 42
    temperature and, 31, 33, 34, 36
    troubleshooting, 64–69

    types of, 40–41, 227
    weight of, 44, 45
    winter storage, 33
battery boxes, 45
battery cables, 102
battery chargers, 123
battery charging
    absorption cycle, 36, 37, 59, 60, 138
    bulk cycle, 36, 37, 59, 60, 138
    charge controllers, 59–60, 193
    charge indicators, 19
    charging recommendations, 27, 37
    charging setups, 61–62
    chemical reaction during, 29–30
    equalization, 30, 37, 59, 60, 138
    float cycle, 36, 37, 59, 60, 138
    gassing, 30, 36, 37
    optimally fast charging, 36–37, 138
    overcharging, 30, 36, 37
    parallel connections, 7
battery eliminator, 235
battery isolation diodes, 58, 66, 68
battery selector switch, 7, 44
belts, alternator, 63
bilge, wiring in, 102, 218
bilge high-water alarm, 241
bilge pump motors, 228
blocking diodes, 187, 193
bonding conductors, 72, 73
bonding systems
    bond-and-protect principle, 86
    components of, 72–73
    controversy surrounding, 71
    purpose of, 71, 72
    stray-current corrosion, 71, 84–86
    unbond-and-isolate principle, 86
brass, 89
bronze, 89, 90
brushes, 55, 141, 143
bulk cycle, 36, 37, 59, 60, 138
buzzers, 20, 228

C

cabin light circuits, 21–24, 96
cabin light dimmer, 240
capacitors, 221–22, 226
cathodic protection, 82, 84, 86, 87–88, 91
cavitation erosion, 90
charge controllers, 59–60, 193
charge-indicator lamp, 58
circuit breakers, 193, 227
    AC, 154
    DC, 93, 103–4

Index

generators
    ampacity, 148
    circuit examples, 167–8
    output frequency, 142, 143
    output voltage, 142, 143
    sizes and AC budget, 134
    transfer switches, 139, 148
    troubleshooting, 143
    types of, 140–41
    use, 129, 130, 140
GPS units
    antennas, 210–11, 217
    installation, 233
    signals, 224, 231
green grounding wire, 120, 164–66
grounded conductors, 72
ground fault circuit interrupters, 121, 154, 167, 175, 178
grounding conductors, 72, 73, 77
grounding wire, green, 120, 164–66
ground plates, 77

H

ham radios
    antennas, 224–25, 231
    grounding, 233
    installation, 233
    signals, 224, 231
heat energy, 7
heat guns, 105
heat-shrink tubing, 105, 106, 162
Hertz, 50, 116, 118
homemade testers, 15, 20
horn, ship's, 256
hydrometers, 32

I

ignition protection, 93, 110–13
impedance, 108, 118, 124
inductors, 235–36
insulators, 4
interference, 135, 223, 233, 234–36
inverters
    ampacity, 148
    battery charging, 138
    operation of, 135
    sizes and AC budget, 133–34
    specifications, 136–37
    transfer switches, 139, 148
    types of, 135
    use, 129, 130

isolation diodes, 57, 62
isolation transformers
    circuit examples, 167–8
    overcurrent protection, 154
    purpose of, 122, 149, 166

K

kinetic energy, 7

L

lamps, 242. *See also* lighting
lead-acid batteries, 28–29
light-emitting diodes (LEDs), 174, 175, 229
    panel indicators, 233
light energy, 7
lighting
    cabin light circuits, 21–24, 96
    cabin light dimmer, 254
    conservation conversions, 172, 174–75
    load calculation, 38–39, 150–53
lightning, 74–75
lightning protection systems
    components of, 72, 73, 75, 77
    copper conductors, 75
    protecting people, 78
    surge protection, 78
    zones of protection, 75–76
lightning-protective masts, 75, 77
load calculations
    AC, 131–34, 150–53
    and batteries, 38–39, 44
    DC, 98
loads
    parallel, 6
    series, 6
    solar power, 184
loran sets, 220
lugs, 105

M

masts, lightning-protective, 75, 77
metal-oxide semiconductor field effect transistors (MOSFET), 230
metals, galvanic series of, 80–82
moisture protection, 215
motors
    circuits, 95
    load calculation, 150–53
    locked-rotor currents, 118, 228
    overcurrent protection, 103

start-up currents, 118, 131, 137, 228
types of, 228
multimeters, 19, 21, 24, 124–25

N

National Electric Code, 1
noise, electrical, 135, 209, 219, 220–21
noncathodic corrosion, 89–90
NPN transistors, 56–57, 230

O

Oersted, Hans, 50
Ohm, Georg, 5
ohmmeters, 17
ohms, 5, 8–12
Ohm's Law, 3, 5–6, 8–12, 116
open circuits, 4
operational amplifiers, 231
overcurrent protection, 93, 103–4, 154, 227

P

panelboards, 149
panel meters, 19
parallel loads, 6
parallel voltage sources, 7
photovoltaic panels. *See* solar power
Piezo electric buzzer, 20, 228
PNP transistors, 230
polarity indicators, 149, 232
polarity testing, 127
polarization transformers, 167
polarized receptacles, 121, 163
potential energy, 7
power, 7, 8–12. *See also* electric current
power consumption. *See* loads
power factor, 115, 118
power-generation costs. *See* energy costs
projects, do-it-yourself
    AC frequency meter, 234
    AC polarity indicator, 232
    automatic anchor light, 239
    bilge high-water alarm, 241
    cabin light dimmer, 240
    electronic ship's horn, 242
    expanded digital battery monitor, 238
    expanded-scale analog battery monitor, 237
    LED panel indicator, 233
    low-battery voltage alarm, 236
    refrigeration fan control, 243

small battery eliminator, 235
water tank monitor, 242
projects, parts for, 225
propellers, 77, 90
Prosine inverters, 136

R

RCD radar units
    antennas, 210–11, 218
    installation, 218, 219
    signals, 210, 218
radio frequency interference, 135, 209, 219,
    220–21
RadioShack parts, 225
receptacles
    galley receptacles, 163
    polarized receptacles, 121, 163
    shore power, 146, 147
rectification, 52–54
rectifying diodes, 52–54, 123, 229
refrigerators
    conservation conversions, 173, 176–79
    fan controls, 243
    insulation, 173, 178, 179
    operation of, 176–79
regulators. *See* voltage regulators
relays, 227
resistance, 4–5, 17, 24, 100
resistance component of impedance, 124
resistors, 226
rotors, 55

S

Schottky blocking diode, 187
sealed batteries, 30, 37, 40–41, 138
semiconductors, 226
series loads, 6
series voltage sources, 7
shields, electrical noise, 221
shocks, electrical, 119–20
shore power
    cables, 146–47
    circuit examples, 167–8
    connections, 146–47
    isolation transformers, 122, 149, 154, 166
    overcurrent protection, 154
    phase, 117
    reverse-polarity warning, 127
    transfer switches, 139, 148
    use, 130
short circuits, 120

signal diodes, 52
single-sideband (SSB) radios
    antennas, 210–11, 217
    grounding, 219
    installation, 219
    signals, 210, 217
solar power
    choosing, 184
    collector materials, 185
    energy costs, 43, 172, 184
    installation, 192–4
    operation of, 185
    output estimations, 190–1
    output specifications, 187
    panel costs, 186
    panel location, 194
    panel orientation, 188–89
    rules for, 194
    specifications of panels, 186
    wind power and, 184
soldered connections, 105, 106, 162
soldering irons, 105
solid state voltage regulators, 56–57
speakers, 228
specific gravity, 32–33
stainless steel, 89–90
Standards for Small Craft (ABYC), 1
standby power, 137
starter motors
    circuits, 95
    locked-rotor currents, 118, 228
    overcurrent protection, 103
    start-up currents, 118, 131, 137, 228
starting batteries, 30, 40–41, 46
step-down transformers, 122
stray-current corrosion, 71, 83–86
sulfation, 30, 42
surge protection, 78
switches, 227

T

temperature
    battery charging and, 36
    battery discharge and, 31, 33, 34
    specific gravity and, 32
    wire insulation ratings, 99, 155–61
terminals. *See* connectors
test instruments, types of
    analog test instruments, 15, 16–18, 19,
        228
    digital test instruments, 15, 18, 19, 228
    homemade testers, 15, 20

multimeters, 19, 21, 24, 124–25
thermistors, 240
three-phase AC, 50–51, 117, 118
through-hull fittings, 72, 85
tools, electrical, 105
transfer switches, 139, 148
transformers, 116, 122–23
transistors, 56–57, 230
troubleshooting
    alternators, 64–69
    batteries, 64–69
    circuits, 18, 21–24, 115, 126
    engines, 64
    generators, 143
Type-N alternators, 57, 68
Type-P alternators, 57, 69

U

U.S. Coast Guard ignition protection stan-
    dards, 110–13

V

VHF radios
    antennas, 210–11, 216
    installation, 219
    signals, 210, 216
voltage, 4–5
    AC, 116–17, 124
    monitoring, 236–38
    sources, 7
voltage drop, 100, 116
voltage regulators
    bypass controls, 49, 59
    charge controllers, 59–60
    charging setups, 62
    operation of, 56
    purpose of, 49, 55–56
    types of, 56–57, 59
voltmeters, 17, 19, 228
volt-ohm meters, 18, 228
volts, 5, 8–12

W

water-generated power, 197, 207
waterproof connections, 215
water tank monitor, 242
watts, 131–34
whip antennas, 210, 211, 216, 217
Wind Energy Resource Atlas of Europe, 201
Wind Energy Resource Atlas of the US, 200

Index